THE CONTINUING STORM

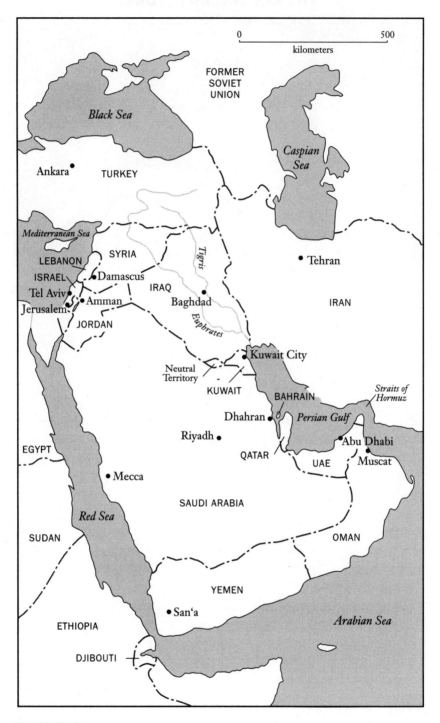

The Middle East

the continuing storm

Iraq, Poisonous Weapons, and Deterrence

Avigdor Haselkorn

Yale University Press · New Haven and London

Designed by Richard Hendel.

Set in Janson type by
Keystone Typesetting, Inc., Orwigsburg, Pennsylvania.

Printed in the United States of America by
R. R. Donnelley & Sons Company, Harrisonburg, Virginia.

Library of Congress Cataloging in Publication Data

Haselkorn, Avigdor.

The continuing storm : Iraq, poisonous weapons and deterrence /
Avigdor Haselkorn.

p.   cm.

Includes bibliographical references and index.

ISBN 0-300-07582-0 (alk. paper)

1. Persian Gulf War, 1991.   2. Weapons of mass destruction — Iraq.
3. United States — Military policy.   I. Title.

DS79.744.C46H37   1998

956.7044′21 — dc21   98-36785

                                                               CIP

A catalogue record for this book is available from the British Library.

The paper in this book meets the guidelines for permanence and durability
of the Committee on Production Guidelines for Book Longevity of the
Council on Library Resources.

10 9 8 7 6 5 4 3 2 1

In loving memory of my parents

Yitzhak and Slava Haselkorn

Contents

Acknowledgments

I wish to acknowledge the crucial support, wise counsel, and continued friendship of Bruce Bueno de Mesquita of the Hoover Institution at Stanford University. My thanks for the support, guidance, and tolerance of A. F. K. Organski of the University of Michigan, who unfortunately passed away before the completion of this book. George N. Lewis of the Defense and Arms Control Studies Program at MIT was kind enough to spend time with me and provide much-needed insight and material. Matthew Meselson of the Department of Biochemistry at Harvard University offered valuable insight and material regarding his investigation into the 1979 anthrax incident in Sverdlovsk.

Richard Graglia offered many helpful comments on the manuscript. Kathy and Michael Pincus of Real World Intelligence and Jeffrey Harrison of Applitech deserve much credit for their patience, help, and incredible computer wizardry.

I am grateful to John S. Covell, senior editor at Yale University Press, who in 1996 saw an early version of the work and boldly threw his hat into the ring. Special thanks to Jenya Weinreb, my manuscript editor, for a superb job. Her help with the manuscript was simply invaluable.

Finally, to my beloved family—my wife, Sarah, and our daughters, Ravid, Tmirah, and Ateret—who stood by me despite having to live, if figuratively, with Saddam for the past few years, sincere apologies. You surely deserve a more civilized housemate.

Main Personalities of the Gulf Crisis

Maj. Gen. Amnon Shahak
*Head of Military Intelligence Branch (AMAN), later Deputy Chief of Staff and,
as of January 1, 1995, Chief of Staff of the IDF*

Itzhak Shamir
Prime Minister

Lt. Gen. Dan Shomron
Chief of Staff of the IDF

SAUDI ARABIA

Gen. Khaled bin Sultan
Commander of Joint Forces

SOVIET UNION

Marshal Sergei Akhromeyev
Military Adviser to President Gorbachev

Aleksander Bessmertnykh
Foreign Minister (as of January 1991)

Maj. Gen. Viktor Filatov
Editor in Chief of Military Historical Journal

Mikhail Gorbachev
President

Gen. Vladimir Lobov
Chief of Staff of the Combined Armed Forces of the Warsaw Pact

Col. Gen. Stanislav Petrov
Chief of USSR Ministry of Defense Chemical Troops

Yevgeny Primakov
Special Envoy to the Middle East

Gen. Leonid V. Sherbashin
Head of First Main Directorate of the KGB (until September 1991)

Eduard Shevardnadze
Foreign Minister (until January 1991)

UNITED NATIONS

Richard Butler
*Executive Chair of the Special Commission for the Disarmament of Iraq
(UNSCOM) (as of July 1997)*

Ambassador Rolf Ekeus
Executive Chair of UNSCOM (until July 1997)

Rep. Les Aspin
Chairman of the House Armed Services Committee, later Secretary of Defense

James A. Baker
Secretary of State

George Bush
President

Richard Cheney
Secretary of Defense

Lawrence Eagleburger
Deputy Secretary of State

Robert Gates
Deputy National Security Adviser

April Glaspie
Ambassador to Iraq

Lt. Gen. Charles Horner
Air Commander of U.S. Central Command (CENTCOM)

Gen. Colin Powell
Chairman of the Joint Chiefs of Staff

Gen. Norman Schwarzkopf
Commander in Chief, CENTCOM

Gen. Brent Scowcroft
National Security Adviser

John Sununu
White House Chief of Staff

William Webster
Director, Central Intelligence Agency (CIA)

Paul Wolfowitz
Undersecretary of Defense for Policy

1990

August 2

Iraq invades Kuwait and occupies the country.

August 6

President Bush orders U.S. military units to Saudi Arabia to ward off a possible Iraqi invasion.

August 8

Iraq proclaims a union with Kuwait and says that it will not attack Saudi Arabia. But in a nationally televised address, President Bush demands the "immediate, unconditional, and complete" withdrawal of Iraqi forces from Kuwait. He announces the dispatch of U.S. forces to the Gulf, saying that their mission is "wholly defensive . . . they will defend themselves, the kingdom of Saudi Arabia, and other friends in the Persian Gulf." Operation Desert Shield is in full swing. Shortly thereafter, according to Iraqi accounts, Iraq begins a crash program to weaponize biological warfare agents.

August 12

Saddam Hussein links the withdrawal of Iraqi forces from Kuwait to Israeli withdrawal from the "occupied territories" (including the Golan Heights) and southern Lebanon.

August 13

Iraqi officials label foreign nationals in Iraq and Kuwait "restrictees," who will not be allowed to leave until the crisis is over.

August 15

Iraq accepts Iran's terms for ending the Iran-Iraq war.

August 18

Iraqi officials announce that foreign nationals held in Iraq and Kuwait will be transferred to military bases and other strategic installations to act as "human shields."

August 28

Saddam Hussein issues a decree proclaiming Kuwait the nineteenth province in Iraq's administrative structure.

September 23

Saddam Hussein threatens to retaliate to the "stifling of the Iraqi people" by destroying the oil fields in the Middle East and by attacking Israel.

September 28

Rep. Les Aspin, chairman of the House Armed Services Committee, reveals that U.S. intelligence believes that Iraq has succeeded in developing biological weapons and will be able to deploy them in early 1991.

October 1

Israel announces that it will begin distribution of gas masks to the civilian population on October 7. The process is expected to take several months.

October 8

During riots on Temple Mount in Jerusalem, Israeli security forces kill 21 Palestinians.

October 23

In appreciation of Soviet and French diplomatic efforts, Iraq announces that it will allow French nationals to leave Iraq and Kuwait.

November 8

President Bush orders a further 150,000 troops to the Gulf. The reinforcement will raise U.S. troop strength in the Gulf to more than 380,000 by early 1991.

November 18

Saddam Hussein says that he will free the hostages starting on Christmas Day, "unless something happens that mars the atmosphere of peace."

November 29

The U.N. Security Council passes Resolution 678, authorizing the member states to "use all necessary means" to eject Iraqi forces from Kuwait by January 15, 1991.

December 1

Saddam Hussein orders the arming of Iraq's biological weapons.

December 2

Iraq test-fires three upgraded Scuds from a site near Basra, in southeastern Iraq. After traveling 400 miles west toward Israel, the missiles land in a remote part of the Iraqi desert.

December 6

Saddam Hussein announces that he will free all hostages "soon." Unlike his statement of November 18, this offer has no conditions attached.

December 9

Gen. Colin Powell and Gen. Norman Schwarzkopf discuss the issue of a declaratory policy concerning retaliation against an Iraqi attack with biological or chemical weapons.

December 10

The U.S. Defense Intelligence Agency and the Central Intelligence Agency establish the Iraqi Interagency Biological Warfare Working Group (IIBWWG) to assess Iraq's biological warfare threat.

December 12

Saddam Hussein nominates Lt. Gen. Saʻdi Tumah Abbas, a seasoned veteran of the Iran-Iraq war, as defense minister.

December 17

Saddam Hussein publicly reiterates Iraq's chemical warfare capability, especially its binary chemical weapons and its ability to reach Israel.

December 23

Iraqi biological aerial bombs are deployed at three air bases. Biological warheads for missiles are hidden at two other sites.

December 27

The Pentagon announces that it will begin vaccinating U.S. troops in Saudi Arabia against biological warfare agents. Britain follows suit.

1991

January 7

The Hammer Rick secure communication link between the U.S. Defense Department and the Israeli Ministry of Defense is inaugurated.

January 9

U.S. Secretary of State James Baker and Iraqi Foreign Minister Tariq Aziz meet in Geneva but fail to reach an agreement.

January 12

Lawrence Eagleburger, deputy secretary of state, and Paul Wolfowitz, undersecretary of defense for policy, arrive in Israel for political and strategic talks.

January 17

Operation Desert Storm begins with a sustained air campaign.

January 18

In the first Scud attack on Israel, six missiles hit the Tel Aviv area and two fall in the Haifa area. All the missiles carry conventional warheads.

January 24

CIA Director William Webster and his deputy, Richard Kerr, brief top U.S. defense and national security officials: "[Iraqi] chemical warheads should be taken seriously."

January 28

Defense Secretary Richard Cheney and Gen. Colin Powell are briefed at the Pentagon by Maj. Gen. Ehud Barak, the IDF's deputy chief of staff, about Israel's plans to counter the Iraqi mass destruction threat.

February 11

Israeli Defense Minister Moshe Arens meets with President Bush at the White House and presents the IDF's plan to launch an operation into western Iraq to clear the Scuds.

February 16

Iraq launches its first missile attack on the Israeli nuclear reactor at Dimona, in the Negev.

February 21–22

Iraq begins to destroy Kuwait's oil wells. The action takes place on the eve of Tariq Aziz's visit to Moscow and coincides with a tough speech by Saddam Hussein, who pledges to continue the fight irrespective of the diplomatic efforts pursued by the Gorbachev regime.

February 24

Desert Storm's ground offensive begins.

February 25

An Iraqi al-Hijarah missile armed with a concrete warhead, apparently aimed at the Dimona nuclear reactor, falls in the Negev.

Baghdad Radio announces that Iraqi forces have been ordered to withdraw from Kuwait to positions held before August 1, 1990. This announcement claims that the order represents compliance with U.N. Security Council's Resolution 660.

February 26

Saddam Hussein announces on Baghdad Radio the withdrawal of Iraqi forces from Kuwait; however, he does not renounce Iraq's claim to Kuwait, and he claims victory for Iraq.

February 27

Kuwait is liberated. American forces fight Iraq's Republican Guard 50 miles west of Basra. Israeli Defense Minister Arens phones U.S. Defense Secretary Cheney to warn of a likely Iraqi mass destruction attack on Israel.

President Bush decides to "suspend hostilities."

March 3

Cease-fire talks take place at Safwan, near the Iraq-Kuwait border.

April 3

The U.N. Security Council passes Resolution 687, requiring Iraq to disclose within 15 days all its nuclear, chemical, and biological weapons and stocks, and all ballistic missiles with a range greater than 150 kilometers. Iraq unconditionally agrees to cooperate in the destruction, removal, or rendering harmless, under international supervision, of these capabilities. A Special Commission (UNSCOM) is set up to monitor the process.

1992

August 2

In response to Iraqi air attacks on Shi'a Muslims in southern Iraq, the United States and its allies impose a "no-fly zone" south of the 32nd parallel.

December 28

U.S. planes shoot down an Iraqi MiG-25 violating the "no-fly zone."

1993

January 7

After Iraq refuses to remove missiles that it introduced into southern Iraq, the United States and some of its Gulf War allies attack missile sites and a nuclear facility near Baghdad.

June 26

U.S. warships fire 24 cruise missiles at the Iraqi intelligence headquarters in Baghdad in retaliation for Iraq's role in a plot to assassinate former President Bush during his visit to Kuwait.

1994

October 7

Following threats of action if U.N.-imposed sanctions are not removed, Iraq moves troops toward Kuwait. The troops are pulled back after the United States dispatches a carrier group and warplanes to the region. Within weeks, the United States withdraws some 54,000 troops.

1995

June 21

President Clinton signs Presidential Decision Directive 39 (PDD-39), which states: "The United States shall give the highest priority to developing effective capabilities to detect, prevent, defeat and manage the consequences of nuclear, biological and chemical materials or weapons used by terrorists."

1996

August 31

Baghdad sends troops into northern Iraq and captures Irbil, a key city inside the Kurdish "safe haven" protected by U.S.-led forces. The United States vows to retaliate.

September 3

U.S. ships and airplanes fire cruise missiles at select air defense targets in Iraq. President Bill Clinton extends the southern "no-fly zone" to the suburbs of Baghdad.

1997

October 29

In response to UNSCOM's demands for access to suspected CB sites, Iraq orders all American inspectors to leave in one week and demands the halt of U-2 reconnaissance flights. The U.N. Security Council warns Iraq of "serious consequences" if it does not reverse its decision.

November 12

The U.N. Security Council unanimously adopts Resolution 1137 (1997), which, among other things, condemns Iraq's continued violations of its obligations and demands that Iraq rescind its decision of October 29 and cooperate "fully" and "immediately" with the Special Commission.

November 13

Iraq expels six American weapons inspectors; in response, the United Nations removes the entire team.

November 14

President Clinton orders the aircraft carrier *George Washington* and four other ships to the Gulf.

November 20

Iraq reverses course and allows the return of UNSCOM inspectors.

December 15

Iraq's Deputy Prime Minister, Tariq Aziz, informs Richard Butler, the head of UNSCOM, that the inspection teams will not be allowed into "presidential sites" despite U.N. demands for unrestricted access throughout Iraq.

The Defense Department announces plans to inoculate all U.S. military personnel (1.4 million troops on active duty and another 1 million reservists) against anthrax.

December 22

The president of the U.N. Security Council makes a statement stressing that failure by Iraq to provide UNSCOM with immediate and unconditional access to any site, or category of sites, is unacceptable and a clear violation of the relevant U.N. Security Council resolutions.

January 26

Richard Butler, executive chair of UNSCOM, confirms reports that his team had evidence that Iraq had loaded biological agents onto missile warheads.

January 29

Israeli officials confirm that they are considering a program of mass inoculation against a biological attack.

January 31

U.S. Secretary of State Madeleine Albright arrives in Israel, where the IDF, in conjunction with the Health Ministry, has been conducting a series of emergency response exercises in case of an attack with unconventional weapons on a population center. Albright reportedly requests that Israel maintain a low profile in the current crisis with Iraq. The United States and Israel are said to have renewed the Hammer Rick secure communication line, which linked their Defense Ministries during the Gulf War.

February 2

The Israeli government begins a campaign to ease public concerns regarding the crisis with Iraq. Lt. Gen. Amnon Shahak, the IDF's chief of staff, declares that Israel's deterrent capabilities should be sufficient to prevent Iraq from attacking. It is revealed that Israel has asked the United States to provide it with large quantities of vaccine against anthrax and the means to identify biological agents.

February 3

A survey published in an Israeli newspaper suggests that half of all Israelis do not feel "protected" in case of a biological or chemical attack.

February 7

U.S. Secretary of Defense William S. Cohen meets with his counterparts from Europe's biggest nations to enlist their support for air strikes.

February 8

U.S. Secretary of Defense William S. Cohen meets with Israeli Defense Minister Itzhak Mordekhai in Munich. Mordekhai confirms that Israel requested "certain items" to bolster its defense against the Iraqi threat. It is reported that in a meeting with German Defense Minister Volker Ruehe, Mordekhai thanked Germany for agreeing to supply Israel with 180,000 gas masks. In Jerusalem, Prime Minister Benjamin Netanyahu emphasizes that Israel reserves the right of self-defense.

February 10

In the House of Commons, British Foreign Secretary Robin Cook repeats the findings of a British intelligence report on Saddam Hussein's leftover chemical and biological cache. The report also states that Iraq may still be hiding missiles or may be able to assemble a small missile force on short notice.

February 15

U.S. Secretary of State Madeleine K. Albright meets "secretly" with U.N. Secretary General Kofi Annan to agree on the terms to be presented to Saddam Hussein in order to resolve the crisis over UNSCOM's inspection.

February 16

U.N. Secretary General Kofi Annan announces that he intends to go to Baghdad in search of a diplomatic solution to the UNSCOM crisis.

February 17

In an address to the Joint Chiefs of Staff and Pentagon staff, President Clinton defines the objective of a possible military action in Iraq: to "seriously reduce his [Saddam Hussein's] capacity to threaten his neighbors."

February 18

In a town meeting at Ohio State University, Secretary of Defense Cohen and Secretary of State Albright declare that the United States is "not seeking to topple Saddam Hussein, nor to destroy his country." Albright says that U.S. policy is "to contain him."

February 22

U.N. Secretary General Kofi Annan reaches an agreement to allow UNSCOM's inspectors to resume their work in Iraq and to inspect eight "presidential sites" for proscribed materials, thus temporarily easing the crisis.

March 9

Iraq notifies the United Nations that it has arrested Nassir al-Hindawi, regarded as the father of Iraq's biological weapons program, on suspicion that he was about to leave the country with confidential documents. The United States believes that the purpose of the arrest was to deny UNSCOM access to Hindawi.

March 23

The British government issues an all-ports terrorist alert after intelligence warns of a plot by Saddam Hussein to smuggle anthrax into the United Kingdom.

May 22

President Clinton orders the stockpiling of vaccines and antibiotics to treat massive numbers of civilians in the event of an attack against the

United States using biological weapons. Reportedly, the move is part of PDD-62 and PDD-63, which are designed to enhance the U.S. ability to prevent chemical, biological, or digital (also known as "cyberwar") attacks and, if deterrence fails, to respond to the consequences. Simultaneously, the Pentagon decides to spend $50 million to create biological response units in the National Guards of 10 of the most populous states.

June 24

In a briefing to the U.N. Security Council, Richard Butler, executive chair of UNSCOM, says that U.N. excavations at a site called al-Nibai, northwest of Baghdad, reveal that Iraq had put VX nerve agents into missile warheads before the Gulf War. The Iraqi News Agency calls the findings "baseless and mere fabrication." Iraq's deputy prime minister, Tariq Aziz, warns in an interview in a Madrid paper, "If the U.S. insists on maintaining sanctions in spite of the progress Iraq has made [in disarming its mass destruction capability], there may well be another crisis."

August 5

Iraq announces that it is ending all cooperation with UNSCOM, and demands its restructuring. Only surveillance cameras set by the commission will be allowed to operate.

August 12

Iraq announces that UNSCOM inspectors will not be allowed to act on any suspected violations that they discover in the future.

August 20

Responding to U.N. pleas for resuming cooperation, Tariq Aziz states: "The [Iraqi] decision is final and will not change. . . . [The Special Commission has] completed its task in the field of disarmament."

Abbreviations

ACDA	Arms Control and Disarmament Agency
AMAN	Agaf Modi'in (Israel Defense Forces' intelligence branch)
ATBM	anti-tactical ballistic missile
AWACS	airborne warning and control system
BW	biological warfare
CB	chemical or biological
CBW	chemical or biological warfare
C&C	command and control
CENTCOM	U.S. Central Command
CIA	Central Intelligence Agency (U.S.)
CW	chemical warfare
DIA	Defense Intelligence Agency (U.S.)
DPRK	Democratic People's Republic of Korea
IAF	Israeli Air Force
IDF	Israel Defense Forces
IFF	identification friend-or-foe
IIBWWG	Iraqi Interagency Biological Warfare Working Group
IRBM	intermediate-range ballistic missile
IRGC	Islamic Revolution Guard Corps
MRBM	medium-range ballistic missile
NATO	North Atlantic Treaty Organization
NBC	nuclear, biological, and chemical
PLO	Palestine Liberation Organization
RCC	Revolutionary Command Council (Iraq)
SRBM	short-range ballistic missile
SSM	surface-to-surface missile
TEL	transporter-erector-launcher
UAV	unmanned aerial vehicle

UNSC	United Nations Security Council
UNSCOM	United Nations Special Commission for the Disarmament of Iraq
USAF	United States Air Force
WMD	Weapons of mass destruction

Rethinking the Gulf War

The crisis in the Persian Gulf, which erupted when Saddam Hussein ordered his troops into Kuwait on August 2, 1990, was, from its outset, a dispute in the shadow of Iraq's weapons of mass destruction. Curiously, this fundamental aspect of the war has not received much attention in the various accounts of the fighting.[1] Iraq's failure to use its deadliest weapons, especially its large stockpile of poison gases, may be partly responsible for this negligence. In any case, information has now become available that can mend this skewed understanding of the conflict.

Iraq has been recognized as a major chemical weapons power at least since its eight-year war with Iran (1980–1988), when it used such weapons. Naturally, there was much talk before and during the Gulf conflict about the prospect that the Iraqis would resort to chemical warfare (CW) against the forces of the anti-Saddam coalition, led by the United States. New information, however, points to Iraq's readiness to use *biological* weapons during the conflict, an aspect heretofore not publicly known. These revelations came in the wake of the defection to Jordan, on August 8, 1995, of Saddam's son-in-law Hussein Kamil Hassan al-Majid. As head of Iraq's Ministry of Industry and Military Industrialization until 1990, Kamil Hassan was also put in charge of the biological warfare (BW) program after it was launched in 1985.[2] After the Gulf War Kamil Hassan—first as defense minister and later as the director of the Ministry of Industry and Minerals and the Organization of Military Industrialization—led Iraq's efforts to conceal its proscribed weapons program from international inspectors. Following his escape, Iraq disclosed to the United Nations Special Commission for the Disarmament of Iraq (UNSCOM) its preparations to launch BW. According to Rolf Ekeus, the Swedish diplomat who until July 1997 was executive chair of UNSCOM, "it is certain that Iraq's biological weapons were fully developed." Moreover, he said, these weapons seem to have been "Baghdad's last trump card and could have been fired immediately—which is really unique. Bombs with biologically effective material were already stationed at military air bases and rocket launching sites. This is an absolute novelty — worldwide."[3]

There was never any doubt that the war to eject Saddam from Kuwait would be a dangerous undertaking, perhaps fought only shortly before the Iraqi dictator would acquire nuclear weapons. But the 1995 disclosures may indicate that the danger was even greater than first realized. As Ekeus has put it: "What shocks me in retrospect is the realization that the world was facing an enormous catastrophe, of which we did not even have a clue. Such a situation must be unique in the history of mankind."[4] If the Western world was truly ignorant, then the intelligence failure in Iraq may be without precedent. But if Western intelligence did accurately assess the threat of Saddam's mass destruction weapons, then how can we explain some of the prewar rhetoric of senior Bush administration officials who seemed to threaten the ouster of Saddam? For example, CIA Director William Webster stated in October 1990: "I find no real confidence that that area will ever be secure again as long as he [Saddam Hussein] is there unless there is some countervailing force in the area . . . or unless he has been disassociated with his instruments of mass destruction in one form or another."[5] Would Webster have called for such drastic measures against Saddam if he knew the horrible price that the Iraqi leader could exact?

Similar questions may be posed to Israeli officials. In 1995 the chief of staff of the Israeli Defense Forces (IDF), Lt. Gen. Amnon Shahak, who at the time of the war served as the head of AMAN (*Agaf Modi'in*, or Intelligence Branch), was asked whether his department had learned anything new from the disclosures in the wake of Kamil Hassan's defection. Shahak answered that AMAN was "working on this" in order to "provide us with lessons to learn." He added: "I believe we will not be surprised when the work is finished. It appears that we had very good information about what was happening in Iraq and, perhaps even more than having solid information, we had a real appreciation of its real ability."[6]

If Shahak's statement is true, then why did Israel decide not "to make any preparations whatsoever toward the possibility of an Iraqi attack with biological weapons," given the havoc an effective BW strike could wreak on a civilian population?[7] Did the country lack vaccines in sufficient quantities? Or had the authorities concluded that Saddam's BW threat was minuscule, especially once a gas mask had been distributed to every Israeli citizen?[8] In that case, how can we explain the intense pressure that Israel put on the United States to let the Israeli military attack Iraq's Scud missiles before the Iraqis launched a mass destruction attack? Did the Israelis invoke Iraq's weapons of mass destruction as a political ploy to force President Bush to intensify the war against the Scuds? Or did the Israeli government fear that such a barrage would cause mass panic and perhaps even anarchy among the population, whatever its actual damage?

In order to answer these questions, it is useful to discuss the nature and effects of biological weapons.

Anthrax, Botulinum Toxin, and Aflatoxin

Biological warfare is the intentional dissemination of disease via living organisms (for example, bacteria or fungi), viruses, or infective material derived from them.[9] According to Iraq's first statements, during the Gulf War Iraq deployed a total of 191 biological munitions, including 113 filled with botulinum toxin, 60 filled with anthrax agents, and 18 filled with aflatoxin.[10]

Anthrax is caused by the bacteria *Bacillus anthracis*, a living organism that must reproduce in the body to cause an effect. Each bacterium produces and releases only a small quantity of anthrax toxin as it grows, but as the bacteria multiply, more toxin is secreted.

Anthrax has three forms, which are characterized by the mode of entry into the body: cutaneous, which is contracted through cuts in the skin; gastrointestinal, which is contracted through ingestion; and pulmonary, which is contracted through inhalation. The principal form exploited for military purposes has been pulmonary anthrax, which mainly affects the lungs and the pleura. A dose of as little as one nine-millionth of one gram of anthrax, or .11 micrograms, is fatal within one to seven days almost 100 percent of the time to those who inhale the minute spores. The higher the dose, the shorter the incubation period.[11] Indeed, inhalation, unlike the other routes, represents a particularly effective path for CBW purposes because the natural process of breathing causes a continuing flux of biological agents to exposed individuals.

Pulmonary anthrax is difficult to diagnose early because the disease is biphasic. Initial symptoms are nonspecific and mimic a severe viral respiratory illness like influenza. These symptoms usually improve two to three days later, but the improvement is followed by the sudden development of respiratory distress (a condition known as hypoxia, in which the body is starved for oxygen, along with a condition known as dyspnea, or labored breathing). Additionally, victims suffer from widening of the mediastinum, the mass of tissues and organs separating the two lungs, which also comprises the heart. They soon become hypotensive (with subnormal blood pressure) and cyanotic (with blue-black skin). About half the victims also develop meningitic signs (inflammation of the membrane covering the brain and the spinal cord). Death usually occurs 24 hours after the onset of the second phase.

Although gastrointestinal anthrax is fatal "only" about 75 percent of the time and cutaneous anthrax less than 10 percent of the time, and although the disease responds well to penicillin (if administered shortly after the onset of symptoms), 12 of the 13 well-documented cases of anthrax in the United States have been fatalities.[12] This is because the disease is fairly rare, and often the diagnosis is made only after death. In addition, penicillin-resistant strains exist naturally, and one such strain has been recovered from a fatal human case.[13]

Because of the bacteria's ability to exist as a spore — with a natural armorlike coat, which develops when growing bacteria are exposed to such adverse conditions as extreme heat or cold — anthrax can remain dormant but effective for years. The spore may remain viable in water and is resistant to chemicals, drying, and sunlight. It is this specialized form of the bacterium that infects humans. As a result, contaminated territory is rendered unusable and uninhabitable for generations.[14] In effect, spores remain inert until an environment conducive to their active stage is found. Once in contact with a warm, moist environment, like the lungs or an open wound, they transform into a vegetative and active stage. Although anthrax is highly infectious, transmission usually occurs when people handle infected animals. The chances of its being transmitted from person to person are virtually nonexistent. This is one of the principal reasons for its adoption as a biological warfare agent, as the risk of the infection spreading to one's own troops is minimal. In addition, effective vaccines do exist, so a country that had developed anthrax as a BW agent could protect its own troops.[15]

Botulinum, unlike anthrax, is a toxin. Toxins are poisons of natural origin. Strictly speaking, they should be discussed separately from biological weapons. They are inanimate and incapable of multiplying, but they are generally more stable and faster-acting than biological weapons, and therefore are more likely to be effective militarily. "Unlike biological weapons, there is no danger of the agent's spreading, reinfecting, mutating, or lying dormant. The toxin disappears with the victim."[16] Historically, toxins have not been used in warfare, and there are many fewer allegations of their use than of the use of biological weapons. One reason is that an "attack with toxins is likely to be quickly perceived as an attack," whereas BW can be mistaken for a natural phenomenon.[17] Because toxins, unlike chemical agents, are not volatile and with rare exceptions do not directly affect the skin, an attack designed to infect large numbers of people over a wide area would most likely deliver toxins to target populations in the form of respirable aerosols. As such, the utility of toxins as effective mass destruction weapons is limited by their toxicity and ease of production.[18]

In some respects, toxins are closer to chemical than biological weapons.[19] Nevertheless, toxins and biological weapons are often lumped together, a relationship that was further ingrained by the 1972 Biological and Toxin Weapons Convention, which outlawed the development, production, and stockpiling of both biological and toxin weapons.[20] Therefore, in this book, unless otherwise mentioned, the terms *biological weapons* and *biological warfare* refer to both biological weapons and toxins.

Botulism is caused by intoxication with any of several distinct neurotoxins produced by the bacillus *Clostridium botulinum*. Unlike most bacteria, which need oxygen to multiply, *Clostridium botulinum* is anaerobic. As it grows, it begins to secrete toxins — proteins of which seven different but related types (designated A through G) have so far been discovered. These different types are produced by different strains of the clostridial bacillus. The toxins cause similar effects when inhaled or ingested, although the timing may vary depending on the nature of the exposure and the dose received.[21] The most studied and characterized of the types is botulinum toxin A, which is produced in especially large quantities by the so-called Hall strain. Its median lethal dose (the dose sufficient to kill 50 percent of a population, known as LD_{50}) is assessed at about 0.001 micrograms (that is, one billionth of a gram) per kilogram of body weight. Although aerosol toxicity is less, it is still exceedingly potent. For example, under ideal meteorological conditions, 8 kilograms of aerosolized botulinum toxin A would be sufficient to kill 50 percent of the population in an area of 100 square kilometers.[22] As Type A toxin is about 15,000 times more toxic than the chemical agent VX and 100,000 more toxic than the nerve gas sarin, it qualifies as the most toxic compound per weight of agent.[23]

Once in the body, the toxin binds to nerve endings (presynaptic nerve terminals) at the point where the nerves join muscles (neuromuscular junctions). It acts to prevent the release of acetylcholine, thus blocking neurotransmissions that normally signal the muscles to contract. The result is weakness that starts in the cranium and descends. Initially, victims also show signs of gastrointestinal distress and impaired vision and speech. Respiratory distress follows in short order, and death comes as a result of paralysis of the respiratory muscles.

Botulinum toxin is especially suited for use in biological warfare. Because the toxin is not living in any sense of the word, its dissemination presents few of the problems associated with true biological material. It can be handled much more harshly without affecting its potency, and there is absolutely no danger of its spreading to the force that disseminated it. The lethal dose is minimal, and the mortality rate is high. Inhalation of a fraction of a microgram — as much as would easily fit on a pinhead — would be fatal in 100 percent of cases. In fact, humans seem to be more susceptible than most other species to botulinum toxin. By the time symptoms develop — from 24 hours to several days after aerosol exposure, depending on the dose — treatment has little chance of success. Virtually all targeted personnel will die if they have not been either vaccinated in advance, a process that usually requires multiple injections over several months, or pretreated with antitoxin before symptoms appear. To complicate matters further, botulism is difficult to detect. Laboratory testing is generally not helpful for diagnosis, and because botulism is not a disease, there is no natural resistance to it.[24]

Botulinum toxin offers most of the characteristics required of an effective biological weapon. Indeed, although protein toxins produced by bacteria are more difficult to manufacture than plant toxins, botulinum toxins are so very toxic that lethal aerosol weapons could be produced in adequate quantities with relatively easily attainable technology. In addition, the toxins are fairly stable for a year when stored at temperatures below 27 degrees Celsius (88 degrees Farenheit).[25] It is the most controllable of the biological arsenal and for years was expected to be "the first to move from the development laboratory to the field of operations" if biological weapons were ever used.[26]

Unlike anthrax agent, whose characteristics of environmental resistance, aerosol infectivity, and lethality make it most suitable for strategic missions against such wide-area targets as civilian population centers, botulinum toxin would likely be used in tactical situations. That is because experimental data suggest that it decays fairly rapidly, generally within an hour in bright sunlight, whereas anthrax agent would cause long-term contamination.

The third biological agent said to have been used to arm Iraq's weapons is aflatoxin. The production of aflatoxin, a naturally occurring toxic metabolite produced by molds, is somewhat puzzling. These poisons are commonly the result of the fungal contamination of food grains, usually while in storage. Iraq researched the production of aflatoxin from the fungi *Aspergillus flavus* and *Aspergillus parasiticus*. This work led to the development of methods for growing aflatoxin-producing organisms on wet rice. But aflatoxin does not make an effective lethal weapon unless victims are exposed to very high doses. Rather, it can cause vomiting, abdominal pain, and gastrointestinal hemorrhage, and epidemiological studies suggest that over prolonged periods it can cause liver cancer in humans. Iraq's presumed intention to use it as a biological weapon is therefore mysterious.[27]

How Effective Are Biological Weapons?

There are contradictory claims regarding the effectiveness of biological weapons. In revealing Iraq's BW readiness during the war, Ekeus said that the use of biological weapons, "which seems to have been possible at any time, would have killed millions of people."[28] The Pentagon estimated that just one Soviet Scud missile warhead filled with botulinum could contaminate more than 3,700 square kilometers given "ideal weather conditions and an effective dispersal mechanism."[29] In general, those raising the alarm over BW argue that strategy has become increasingly dependent upon civil defense and that microbiological weapons are well suited for large-scale civilian targets.[30]

Because the quantities required to infect are much less than those needed to poison, the dosage of typical BW agents needed to kill a person is less by a factor of about one million than the lethal dose of typical CW agents.[31] The greatly enhanced potency of BW agents also means that the downwind distances over which such agents can have an effect are significantly greater than the distances for CW agents. Assuming comparable and favorable meteorological conditions, CW agents are hazardous for about 1 kilometer downwind, whereas for toxins the distance is about 10 kilometers, and for true BW agents it is a few hundred kilometers.[32] Thus, lethal biological weapons could conceivably decimate large populated areas.[33]

In contrast, it has been argued that much of the thinking about BW is based on a myth. The legendary potency of biological weapons, some theorists maintain, is overestimated because of the literal interpretation of toxicities. "The minute amounts of toxin, viral and bacteriological materials required to kill or incapacitate has produced an almost universal belief that they constitute the basis of some of the most efficient weapons science has developed."[34] In fact, numerous governmental studies in the United States and elsewhere have concluded that biological weapons are "an impractical instrument of warfare."[35] Even UNSCOM seems to have been divided in its assessment of the potential impact of an Iraqi BW scenario.[36]

There is no doubt that biological weapons face important hurdles on the way to becoming potent instruments of warfare. The overall effectiveness of such weapons is determined by two important considerations: the efficiency of the agent in causing death or incapacitation, and the efficiency of the delivery system.

The effectiveness of a bacterial agent, such as anthrax, is assessed by several criteria. First is infectivity. This refers to the dose of material required to set up a spreading infection in the host so that the organism can establish itself there and begin to reproduce. The second is virulence. This measures the damaging effects produced when this dose of organisms initiates infection. In other words, it reflects the nature of the disease that is produced. The third important property is stability. A highly virulent and infective organism will clearly be of no use if it is killed rapidly upon exposure to the atmosphere or upon incorporation into a missile or a bomb. There are additional required properties, such as resistance to antibiotics, but they are of secondary importance.[37]

Virtually none of the naturally occurring disease-causing organisms possess a complete spectrum of properties that would make them "perfect" biological agents. In almost every case, at least one of the three main properties must be altered if the organism is to be used as a biological weapon. Such alterations, however, have been problematic. For example, biological warfare researchers have so far failed to develop predictable agents capable of producing epidemics among humans. There is a lack of basic knowledge of the susceptibility of many of the mammals, birds, reptiles, amphibia, and insects that would be exposed during an airborne BW attack. Thus, even the most perfect physical protection of humans could turn out to be useless, as protected humans could later become the victim of newly established disease reservoirs in animals and insects. As a result of this unpredictability, a sort of non-use pact has existed in the BW area among the world's major military blocs.[38]

It may even be argued that because of the uncertainties involved with biological weapons, BW is almost by definition an option of last resort. For example, estimates of lethal doses to humans, which are critical in assessing the potential effectiveness of an agent, assume that the average person weighs 70 kilograms and are normally based on extrapolation from experiments with animals. In the case of botulinum toxin, the lethal dose has been obtained from experiments with mice, and aerosol toxicity is based on a "mathematical model that has been field tested and found to be valid."[39] However, toxicities are likely to vary widely with the kind of animal used, and it is not always certain that a result is valid for humans.[40] The minimum dose also depends on the method by which the agent or toxin is administered.

The failure of several bioterrorist attacks attempted by the Japanese doomsday cult Aum Shinrikiyo highlights additional constraints. In these cases, the flops apparently resulted in large part from problems with the materials themselves. The cult reportedly used botulinum toxin Type A in its April 1990 attacks, and even sprayed the poisonous mists in the streets of central Tokyo, but there were no casualties. It could have been that the strain was weak. Consistency is difficult to achieve even within a strain — some batches of Type A will kill while others will not. Aum's resort to anthrax in 1993 was equally unsuccessful because of deficiencies in the anthrax. The agent was clearly not Vollum 1B — an exceptionally deadly strain that is usually preferred for BW purposes.[41]

In the case of anthrax, the size of the particles is crucial to its infectivity. Unless a relatively uniform cloud of invisible anthrax particles or droplets is dispersed in the optimal size of 1–5 microns in diameter, allowing the particles to remain suspended for extended periods, the attack will be futile.[42] Moreover, although in theory a single microorganism should be able to produce an infection once it has taken hold in the body and begun to reproduce, in practice this is rarely the case. Thus 20,000 inhaled bacilli greater than 2 microns in diameter are needed to cause a pulmonary anthrax infection, with the number growing if the particle size increases.[43] The relatively long incubation period is another impediment, at least insofar as tactical BW is concerned. For example, although pulmonary anthrax may be extremely lethal, its incubation period can last up to seven days. Naturally, the longer the delay, the more impractical use of the weapon on the battlefield. Another drawback of anthrax is its persistence in the soil, which would render its usefulness on the battlefield, and in some cases even its strategic usefulness, questionable.

Other problems with biological weapons relate to constantly changing atmospheric conditions and to the means of dissemination. Both could also render large proportions of the microorganisms ineffective. For example, prediction of atmospheric dispersion of any BW agent is uncertain to a degree. There is the problem of atmospheric turbulence — random air movement that constantly varies in speed and direction. But turbulence could have an important impact on the effectiveness of a BW attack because by churning and mixing the atmosphere, it causes any airborne substance to diffuse. Moreover, atmospheric turbulence near the Earth's surface differs from that at higher levels. The effect of heat from solar radiation that causes warm air to rise and cool dense air to descend, together with disturbances around surface obstacles (such as hills or mountains), makes low-level winds extremely irregular and difficult to predict. In addition, biological agents are sensitive to heat, ultraviolet light, humidity, and blast. In fact, because of the ultraviolet radiation in sunlight, nighttime has traditionally been considered the best time for biological attacks. A nighttime aerosol attack, for instance, would seek to take advantage of the ground losing heat by radiation and of the "lid" of warm air that limits the upward movement of the aerosol. Even then, the half-life of the disseminated cloud of infective particles may be only a few minutes, with the number of viable organisms rapidly declining once released into the air. Although some hazard remains, the chances of causing infection declines quickly in proportion to this "bacteriological decay."[44] Further, BW agents are also subject to "physical decay." There is progressive reduction in the effective particle concentration due to dilution, settling out under gravity, washing out by rainfall, and impact upon surfaces.[45] Some microorganisms react unfavorably to the high acceleration rates that are common to the delivery by a missile. Given these facts, Iraq's reliance on botulinum toxin as the fill for most of its missiles, and its selection of the highly resistant anthrax spores for others, are understandable.[46]

Iraq's Biological Weapons

Iraq initially declared that it produced a total of 11,000 liters of concentrated *Clostridium botulinum*, the bacterium necessary for manufacturing botulinum toxin. Subsequently, it admitted that, using a *Clostridium botulinum* strain imported from the United States, it produced almost 20,000 liters of the solution. Of this, 12,000 liters were used in field testing or to fill warheads; unused toxin was stored at al-Hakam (Iraq's main BW production facility). The strength and type of botulinum toxin contained in the Iraqi solution are still unknown.[47]

Iraq also claimed production of 8,500 liters of concentrated anthrax bacteria. Of this, 6,000 liters were used to fill weapons, and the remainder was stored at al-Hakam. The solution, which was developed from culture collections imported from France and the United States and from local isolates, had an anthrax spore and cell count of 10^9 spores per milliliter.

In addition, the Iraqis said they produced about 2,000 liters of aflatoxin, an unknown quantity of which was used to fill weapons.[48] According to Ekeus, the Iraqis experimented with biological weapons like this — which could seriously wound, rather than kill — because they figured that "it is more expensive for the enemy to have to tend to its wounded than to bury its dead." The production of *Clostridium perfringens*, which Iraq admitted to, could be mentioned in this regard. Infection with this species of the *Clostridia* bacteria causes gas gangrene once vegetative spores penetrate the skin through open wounds. The alpha toxins secreted by the bacteria cause tissue death (necrosis), destruction of blood (hemolysis), and local decrease in blood circulation (vasoconstriction), which often require amputation of limbs. When aerosolized, this agent can cause severe gastric effects. Iraq also said that it produced ricin, a natural derivative of the castor bean *Ricinus communis*, which is grown widely there and has an LD_{50} of 3 micrograms per kilogram ingested. It kills by impeding breathing and blood circulation. Although ricin's aerosol toxicity is higher, it is still marginal, requiring a large quantity to cover a wide area effectively. Thus its weaponization is unlikely. Presumably, neither gas gangrene nor ricin was used by Iraq to fill weapons (see Appendix B, Table 1).[49]

A secret plant at Salman Pak, some 32 kilometers southeast of Baghdad along the Tigris River, served as the center for the Iraqi bacteriological weapons program. In this facility, which covered about 3 square kilometers and contained laboratories constructed by German companies, four anthrax strains were characterized, their media and storage requirements were established, and inhalation studies to determine their pathogenicity were conducted in animal models. Scaled-up production of the anthrax simulant *Bacillus subtilis*, and eventually of anthrax itself, was accomplished. In addition, in 1989 some 190 liters of concentrated ricin solution was produced at Salman Pak. Iraq contends that botulinum production began in early 1988 at a building at the al-Taji military-industrial complex just north of Baghdad, known as the al-Taji Single Cell Protein Plant. In March 1988, al-Hakam was selected as a new site for biological weapons production. Located in the western desert some 55 kilometers southwest of Baghdad, the al-Hakam Single Cell Protein Production Plant, as it was called, was a brand-new facility designed from the outset for the production of BW materials. This 3-by-6-kilometer plant included separate research, development, production, and storage areas. According to Iraq, actual production of anthrax and botulinum toxin began there in spring 1989. Between 1989 and 1990, Iraq manufactured some 500,000 liters of BW agents at this site. As the program expanded, additional facilities were set up. Beginning in early 1990, for example, scientists at the Daura Foot and Mouth Disease Center at al-Manal investigated five viruses for their potential as biological weapons. Aflatoxin was produced at a facility in Fudaliyah known as the Agricultural and Water Research Center, in the northeast outskirts of Baghdad, and wheat cover smut, which generates black growth on cereal grains, rendering them inedible, was produced as an economic weapon at both Salman Pak and Mosul (in northern Iraq). Iraq's main CW facility (and the world's largest CW facility at the time),

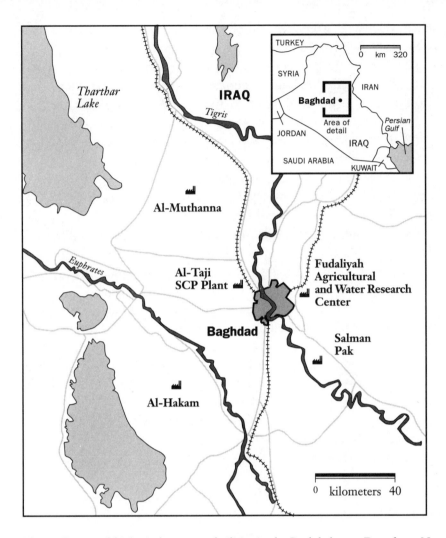

Map 1. Suspected biological weapons facilities in the Baghdad area. Data from *New York Times*, February 26, 1998.

al-Muthanna—which Western intelligence dubbed the Samarra site, after the neighboring city—was also used. In 1985, research on anthrax and botulinum was initiated at this plant, which was officially called the State Establishment for the Production of Pesticides and was located 60 kilometers northwest of Baghdad. Their toxicity, growth characteristics, and survivability were evaluated. But in 1987 Iraq decided to commence full-scale production of BW agents, and the program was transferred to the Salman Pak facility. Al-Muthanna remained the site where the bombs and missile warheads were assembled (see Map 1).[50]

The arming of Baghdad's biological weapons began on December 1, 1990, two days after the United Nations Security Council passed Resolution 678, authorizing the coalition forces to use "all necessary means" to eject Saddam's forces from Kuwait if they failed to withdraw by January 15, 1991. Of the 191 weapons carrying biological agents and toxins that were deployed during the Gulf War, 166 were bombs for airplanes and 25 were warheads for a version of the Soviet surface-to-surface missile known as Scud B. This Iraqi version, dubbed al-Husayn (after the grandson of the Prophet Muhammad), was capable of reaching Saudi Arabia and Israel.[51] On December 23, the weapons were transported to five different locations, all well north of the Kuwait theater of operations. According to Iraqi statements, the aerial bombs filled with biological agents were deployed to three airfields. They were placed in open pits far from the coalition bombing targets, then covered with canvas and buried with dirt. The biological warheads for al-Husayn missiles were hidden, some in a railroad tunnel and some in earth-covered pits near the Tigris canal. None of the Iraqi biological weapons were hit during the subsequent air attacks by the coalition.[52]

Since biological weapons were first conceived, considerable work has been done to overcome their limitations. Experiments during World War II showed that the effectiveness of air-delivered biological weapons was increased by using numerous small bomblets or aerosol-type dispensers rather than a few large devices, which tended to concentrate the agent around the point of dispersal, causing uneven distribution and wasting material. Yet, in spite of some apparent improvements in anthrax's infectivity, estimates of bomblet efficiency actually declined by 1950. In that year an official U.S. report gave the number of improved E-96 cluster 4-pound (1.82-kilogram) anthrax bomblets necessary to cause 50 percent casualties as 11,420 per square mile (2.6 square kilometers). This represented at least a 43.7 percent increase from the number of bomblets that would have supposedly caused 50 percent *fatalities*, according to a British government document from November 1945.[53]

Assuming these data to be correct, Iraq needed to deliver 20,720 kilograms (45,680 pounds) of payload using the E-96 bomblets in order to cause 50 percent casualties in an area of 2.6 square kilometers. This represented a potentially important limitation for the Iraqis given that in order to reach Israel, the Iraqi al-Husayn missile traded payload for greater range. It carried a 300-kilogram warhead instead of the original 985-kilogram warhead mounted on the Soviet R-17 version, known in the West by its NATO code name, SS-1c Scud B.[54] According to the first statement of the Iraqis, they loaded 10 warheads with anthrax. They also loaded 50 anthrax bombs. The bombs were identified as R-400 type, with a gross weight of 400 pounds (182 kilograms) each.[55] Assuming that the relation between the mass of the warhead and its effective payload was similar to that in the VX-filled warhead of the original Soviet SS-1c, where payload amounted to some 60 percent of mass, the Iraqis could have delivered only 3,990 anthrax bomblets of 1.82 kilograms each to the target via their missiles and bombs.[56] However, they could have also delivered some 13,260 kilograms of payload, or some 7,286 bomblets, via the 13 other warheads and 100 bombs filled with botulinum toxin (see Appendix B, Table 2). In theory, the Iraqis could have thus fired a total of 11,276 bomblets filled with BW materials. As estimates of the population density in the metropolitan Tel Aviv area run between 20,000 and 25,000 residents per 2.6 square kilometers, it may be concluded that the Iraqis could have caused massive Israeli casualties. Indeed, the affected area would have increased dramatically, and so would the number of dead and injured, if the calculation assumed that Iraq effectively dispersed the same payload above the target instead of using bomblets in ground bursts.[57]

The previous scenario depended on the assumption that all the Iraqi BW weapons reportedly available at the time were fired at Israel. According to this picture, every weapon was armed with bomblets, reached its intended target, and detonated as planned.[58] Finally, it was also assumed that the targeted population was in the open and unprotected.[59] Clearly, these are best-case assumptions from Iraq's point of view. In contrast, possible hitches must be considered, including the destruction by coalition aircraft of some or all of the missile launchers on their way to the launching areas, technical malfunctions, or attrition of Iraqi planes at the hands of coalition pilots and the Israeli Air Force (IAF). When more realistic operational and technical assumptions are taken into account, it has been argued, "the number of casualties caused directly by [Iraqi] biological weapons probably would have been low."[60]

Yet even if the Iraqis were incapable of executing a highly effective attack with biological weapons, the social, political, and strategic implications of such an assault on a civilian population could have been calamitous. First, crude biological weapons or aerosols would endanger large numbers of lives once they released their lethal agents into the air, even if they did not cause major disasters or epidemics. Second, the various calculations of effectiveness do not give an accurate account of the panic likely to spread in the targeted population. The ensuing chaos could even lead to a total societal breakdown. Military planners have long recognized the so-called anxiety factor as one of the key aspects of strategic BW. Whether these weapons stand out for their insidiousness or not, because of the invisibility of germ warfare, even a small biological attack in a large city would cause the public to fear further assault anywhere, anytime.[61] Third, a biological or chemical attack, even if unsuccessful, would have been viewed as a step across the threshold between conventional and unconventional weapons. The targeted country might be expected to retaliate accordingly. Fourth, as Israeli Defense Minister Moshe Arens said at the time, Israel faced "dangers unprecedented in the history of mankind — an entire civilian population has never before been threatened" with chemical or biological warfare.[62] The deliberate targeting of civilians for an attack with mass destruction weapons would have only reinforced the certainty of a massive retaliation if such a heinous act had been perpetrated.

In light of the revelations concerning Iraq's preparedness for BW, a review of some of the basic thinking about the Gulf crisis may well be in order. For instance, Saddam's decision to invade Kuwait can be viewed as influenced by Saddam's belief that the Iraqi arsenal of chemical and biological weapons would deter any foreign intervention. Further, it is appropriate to inquire whether strategic deterrence was in fact responsible for keeping the Gulf conflict within the confines of a limited war, as has been previously believed. Finally, what role, if any, did Iraq's mass destruction weapons play in President Bush's decision to terminate hostilities abruptly? After all, it had been generally expected that the United States would continue the fight until the Iraqi dictator was removed from power.[63]

This book is an inquiry into the impact of mass destruction weapons on the outbreak, conduct, and termination of the Gulf crisis. In contrast to most works published about the war, it argues that the mere presence of such weapons in the region had a profound impact, in each of these phases, on the thinking of key decision makers in Iraq, Israel, and the United States. Indeed, only by exposing the hidden role of unconventional weapons in each of these phases can a valid explanation be offered to the paradox that has emerged in the aftermath of the conflict: although operation Desert Storm was launched under the banner of the "new world order," and one of its major goals was to disarm a dangerous dictator of his mass destruction weapons, in its wake the proliferation of such weapons received a material boost. Today Iraq is still believed to possess at least the components of chemical and biological weapons and long-range missiles. Worse yet, extremist regimes from North Korea in the east to Libya in the west are energetically developing similar or even more frightening munitions.

In trying to reconstruct the role of mass destruction weapons in the Gulf War, three hurdles must be overcome:

Secrecy. There is still a veil of secretiveness shrouding the thinking and actions of the major players in the Gulf crisis with regard to their nuclear, chemical, and biological weapons. In some respects, there are currently more data available on the Iraqi thinking and capabilities in this area than on that of the key members of the anti-Saddam coalition. Israel, which feels especially vulnerable to the threat of mass destruction from the Arab or Muslim world, is particularly reluctant to reveal its thinking and preparations concerning unconventional warfare. As the research presented here is overwhelmingly based on information gleaned from the open sources, this potential drawback must be kept in mind. Even the recently declassified U.S. intelligence on Iraq's chemical and biological (CB) weapons capabilities during the Gulf War does not entirely alleviate this constraint.

Credibility. If anything was learned from the Gulf crisis, it is the cavalier manner with which Iraqi leaders handle the truth. At times Baghdad seemed to be bent on deluding the entire international community, confident that it could get away with blatant lies and deception. Under these circumstances, accepting Iraqi statements at face value would be exceedingly naive. Despite this caveat, current research has made significant headway in accurately reflecting Iraqi thinking in the Gulf crisis, and especially Saddam's strategy with respect to his mass destruction option.

Bias. This book relies to a degree on the memoirs of some of the key decision makers involved in the Gulf crisis. As is often the case, almost all contain disagreements with other accounts of the period, and some also dispute in part at least the recollection of the other authors. It should be taken for granted that in depicting their role in the conflict, these authors have all sought to claim their place in history. Thus, they have likely accentuated their role while downplaying those of their colleagues. They probably also have attempted to minimize their mistakes.

Since 1996, more than 10,000 pages of intelligence documents have been released by the U.S. government in connection with the controversy over the so-called Gulf War syndrome.[64] This material presents several potential problems. First, it is impossible to determine the authenticity of the documents in terms of their dates and content. For example, intelligence agencies could have taken the opportunity to portray themselves in a favorable light. Second, it is impossible to determine the completeness of the documents. The criteria used in selecting these papers for release are not clear. Apparently for reasons of security and secrecy, many documents contain deletions and omissions. Third, there is the question of context. When, where, or how these documents were used, if at all, remains unclear. In fact, most contain a disclaimer advising the reader that the material is "not finally evaluated intelligence."

Nevertheless, the disclosures provide a unique opportunity to examine some of the data and estimates that must have reached U.S. leaders during the crisis. These documents are presumably intended to convey to Gulf War veterans what the U.S. government knew about Iraq's CBW plans and actions. It would be a cruel hoax indeed to make these papers public if altogether different assessments had in fact been made by the intelligence community. Thus it seems reasonable to conclude that, overall, these documents present a true picture of the information and assessments disseminated at the time by the U.S. intelligence apparatus. The repetitive nature of many of the papers also supports this conclusion. The documents, then, must have had a significant influence on the decision-making process during the crisis.

In selecting the sources for this research, all the previous considerations were taken into account. However, to the extent that bias and deliberate manipulations were able to slip through, this work is flawed.

The Invasion of Kuwait

The immediate pretext for the attack on Kuwait was its "aggression" against Iraq. Baghdad charged, for example, that Kuwait wanted to destroy the Iraqi economy by flooding the oil market and driving prices down. This, according to Saddam Hussein, was part of a conspiracy with the United States and Zionism to undermine Iraq's military program. Addressing the Iraqi nation over Baghdad Radio on July 17, 1990, Saddam said that "certain" Gulf rulers had "thrust a poisoned dagger into our back." Still, many students of the Gulf War expressed astonishment as to the timing of the Iraqi invasion of Kuwait, which took place on August 2, 1990. If Saddam had only waited until the completion of his program to develop nuclear weapons, possibly only a few months away according to some estimates, Iraq would have succeeded in its aggression.[1] The United States would have probably concluded that the risks of dislodging the Iraqi military from Kuwait were simply too great.[2] At least this was the view of Cuban leader Fidel Castro, who asked rhetorically whether "the United Nations would have done the same [against Iraq] if a nuclear power was involved. . . . I wonder if the United Nations would have declared war and in so doing brought the end of the world."[3]

It has been widely argued that Saddam's decision to invade Kuwait was reached after the Iraqi leader had concluded that there would be only token opposition from abroad to his aggression. Several calculations led Saddam to believe that the occupation of Kuwait would in the main be received as a fait accompli by powers both inside and outside the region and, most important, by Washington. The first, more general argument was relayed in 1996 by Staff Maj. Gen. Wafiq al-Samarra'i, who until May 1991 served as Iraq's head of military intelligence (*al-Estikhabarat al-'Askariyya*). According to him, Saddam had thought that U.S. involvement in Vietnam "had badly damaged its willingness to use military power. [He believed] Vietnam had been an outright defeat militarily and politically."[4] In the wake of America's bitter experience in Vietnam, Saddam concluded, Washington would have little inclination for a new confrontation thousands of miles from its shores.

Saddam had two more specific reasons for expecting little international opposition to Iraq's aggression. First and foremost, he recalled Washington's continuous courtship of Baghdad during the war with Iran, and he was confident that the United States was unlikely to stand in his way.[5] The Iraqi leader might have even perceived a green light from Washington concerning the invasion of Kuwait. April Glaspie, the U.S. ambassador to Iraq, informed Saddam on July 25, 1990, that the United States had "no opinion on Arab-Arab conflicts, like your border dispute with Kuwait."[6]

Second, the weapons in Iraq's possession were more than enough to discourage any remaining opposition to the attack on Kuwait, or so Saddam probably thought. The Iraqi leader saw his extensive arsenal of mass destruction weapons, especially Iraq's known CW capacity, as a strategic umbrella to dissuade any foreign interference in his plans.

The Evolution of Iraq's Chemical Warfare

Iraq, by the time it attacked Kuwait, was widely recognized as having sizable stockpiles of chemical arms, and the Iraqi army was even described as "the world's most experienced in the use of chemical weapons on the battlefield."[7] This notoriety came about as a result of Iraq's repeated resort to CW during its war with Iran. Indeed, between 1983 and 1988, Iraq used chemical weapons on a scale not seen since World War I. Special chemical troops — which were responsible for the care, building, and transportation of chemical munitions — were integrated throughout all the branches in the Iraqi armed forces. The task of delivering the weapons themselves was left to Iraqi regular army and air force units. Following the example of their Soviet allies, Iraq's chemical troops had a status approaching that of a separate combat arm. They included units and subunits responsible for chemical defense, radiation and chemical reconnaissance, meteorological analysis, and decontamination. Each corps had a chemical battalion, each independent brigade or division had a chemical company, and regiments were assigned chemical platoons.[8]

Three distinct phases could be discerned in Iraq's CW against Iran. From August 1983 until 1986, CW was employed in a strictly defensive role, to disrupt or halt Iranian offensives. During this period, the Iraqis initially employed mustard gas but later shifted to using both mustard and nerve gases. In a transitional phase lasting from late 1986 to early 1988, Iraq used chemical weapons preemptively against staging areas before Iranian offensives, while continuing to rely on CW to disrupt these offensives.

Finally, and most significantly, Iraq used massed nerve gas strikes as an integral part of its well-orchestrated offensives in the spring and summer of 1988.[9] These three phases are worth examining in more detail.

Mustard gas comes in several varieties, all compounded from carbon, hydrogen, sulfur, and chlorine. The oldest are Levinstein mustard (H) and distilled sulfur mustard (HD). The gas is named after the mustard smell associated with H.[10] Mustard gas, the best-known "blister agent" (the painful sacs produced on affected surfaces may take months to heal), was Iraq's initial choice undoubtedly because it is easier to produce, handle, and deliver than nerve gas. For the Iraqis, mustard gas was also especially attractive because of its persistence — it could be used to deny territory to an enemy force for days.[11] The Iraqis used aerial bombs, among other weapons, to spread the gas. The smallest bomb was the LD-250, a modification of the Spanish 250-pound smoke bomb BR-250-WP. Each LD-250 normally contained 64 liters of mustard gas and was equipped with an air burst fuse (so that the bombs detonate before hitting the ground) to ensure contamination of a wide area.[12]

Even during the first phase of their employment during the Iran-Iraq war, chemical weapons were viewed by Iraq as compensation for Iran's larger forces. That is, for Iraq chemical weapons served as a "force multiplier." As a matter of fact, senior Iraqi generals gradually came to believe that these weapons were instrumental in preventing Iran from massing its forces for the long-awaited final offensive. It was only natural, then, that Iraq soon took the next step in its CW program and developed nerve agents that could rapidly kill large numbers of Iranian troops. Maj. Gen. Maher Abdul Rashid, commander of the Iraqi Third Corps near Basra, commented: "If you gave me a pesticide to throw at these worms of insects [the Iranians] to make them breathe and become exterminated, I'd use it."[13] On March 17, 1984, Iraq unleashed the nerve agent tabun against the Iranians, thus becoming the first nation in history to use nerve gas on the battlefield.

Tabun (known as GA) is about four times as poisonous as mustard gas if inhaled. It was developed — together with another nerve agent, sarin (GB) — by German scientist Gerhard Schrader at the I.G. Farben Leverkusen Laboratories in the 1930s.[14] Tabun's LCt_{50}, the concentration required to kill 50 percent of the population exposed to it for a certain time, is given as 150 mg-min/m^3 — which means that if twenty Iranian soldiers inhaled, for one minute, air that contained 150 milligrams of tabun in every cubic meter, ten of them would die.[15] The Iraqis packed tabun into modified BR-250-WP aerial bombs, among other weapons, and equipped them with impact fuses, in line with the Soviet CW doctrine of arming nonpersistent gas bombs with such devices.[16]

Tabun, however, was evidently insufficiently lethal in Iraqi eyes. Because of its poor quality, the gas was unstable and decomposed quickly. Iraq soon began using sarin, whose LCt_{50} drops as low as 25 mg-min/m^3 when men breathe rapidly owing to activity, excitement, or fear, as soldiers on the battlefield do.[17] Moreover, individuals poisoned by GB display, with minor variations, the same sequence of symptoms regardless of whether the poison enters the body by inhalation, absorption, or ingestion. In addition, sarin, like tabun, is nonpersistent — it stays in the target area for periods of only 10 to 30 minutes (under calm wind conditions and desert temperatures). When forces are advancing rapidly, sarin provides a quick-acting means to kill enemy personnel in the target area without inhibiting the forward maneuver. In short, the introduction of sarin boosted Iraq's offensive potential. It quickly became the chemical agent of choice for delivery by the Iraqi artillery.

Although the agent was not used effectively in 1984, by the beginning of 1988, the Iraqis had developed "effective offensive doctrine for the use of nerve agents, which fully integrated CW into fire support plans."[18] Both nerve agents and blister agents were used successfully in the final offensives that defeated the Iranians in 1988, with chemical weapons targeted specifically against command and control facilities (C&C), artillery positions, and logistics areas.[19]

The Debut of Terrorist Deterrence: Halabja and the "Binary" Chemical Weapon

In March 1988, Iraq's use of chemical weapons against its own Kurdish population became common knowledge when the specter of a major Iranian breakthrough in Kurdistan drove Saddam to use poison gas against the town of Halabja. The Kurds in the area had long sought independence from Iraq and had therefore sided openly with the Iranians. It is unclear what type of chemicals the Iraqis used or how many casualties the town suffered.[20] But survivors and Iranian officials claimed that the gas was dropped from airplanes in 100-liter containers that vaporized on impact.[21] Iranian doctors said that the Kurds may have been hit by cyanide gas either mixed with or dropped along with mustard gas bombs.[22] The severely depressed bone-marrow production reported in surviving victims certainly indicates that other chemical agents with longer-lasting effects had been present along with faster-acting agents. According to Aubin Heyndrickx, head of toxicology at Rijks University in Ghent, Belgium, who had extensive experience with victims of Iraqi CW, the evidence indicated use of cyanogen chloride, a quick-acting blood agent, together with mustard gas and nerve gas.[23]

Julian Perry Robinson, a CW expert at the University of Sussex, pointed out that the odd thing about the Iraqi use of chemical weapons on the Iranians and the Kurds is that casualties achieved with the poison gases could easily have been matched or bettered by bombs or other conventional explosives.[24] The use of CW as the Iraqi weapon of choice can be best understood, therefore, as a deliberate effort to spread fear among the opposition. The medium *was* the message.

This point is critical for understanding Saddam Hussein's political thinking. Saddam holds an unshakable belief in the effectiveness of a strategy that may be labeled terrorist deterrence (see Chapter 3). He deliberately selects means that are likely to cause maximum shock and to intimidate his opponents into submission. Such was the case on March 1, 1988, when he began a sustained bombardment of Tehran with al-Husayn missiles, causing nearly 8,000 casualties (including 2,000 fatalities) and forcing a quarter of the Iranian capital's population to flee for fear of an Iraqi resort to gas.[25] He must have felt further assured of his strategy's success when the Iranians likened the Iraqi use of poison gas against the Kurds to the dropping of the atomic bombs on Hiroshima and Nagasaki by the Americans in 1945.[26] Apparently the expressions of horror from around the world regarding Halabja only served to convince Saddam that he possessed an effective deterrent. The Iraqis soon confirmed the chemical attack on Halabja themselves.[27]

Under "terrorist deterrence," then, Saddam's open — even boastful — adoption of extremist means was designed to convey to his enemies a determination to go to any length to win a battle. Surrender, it was implied, was simply not an option. Several months before the attack on Kuwait, for example, Saddam openly and repeatedly bragged about Iraq's development of a binary chemical weapon. A binary weapon is made of two reagents, themselves nontoxic, which are stored separately in the weapon. The fusion of the two chemicals into a lethal gas is done in the bomb or the missile warhead after it has been launched toward the target. The idea is to create a toxic agent at the point of use rather than manufacture it for long-term storage or for immediate insertion into a delivery vehicle that is then stockpiled until needed.

In April 1990, possibly coinciding with the flight-testing of a missile carrying a binary chemical warhead, Saddam warned Israel of Iraq's new capabilities: "We do not need an atomic bomb. We have the binary chemical. Let them take note of this. We have the binary chemical. According to our information only the United States and the Soviet Union have it. It exists in Iraq."[28]

Undoubtedly, the alarmed reaction by U.S. officials—who expressed "concern" over Iraq's escalating rhetoric—and Washington's intensified efforts to reach an accommodation with Baghdad merely reinforced Saddam's confidence in his strategy of terrorist deterrence. In a meeting with a delegation of U.S. senators headed by Robert Dole (R-Kans.), who rushed to the Middle East, Saddam said: "I have said: If Israel uses atomic bombs [to strike Iraq], we will strike it with the binary chemical weapon. I reiterate that if Israel does this, we will do that."[29] His first deputy prime minister, Taha Yasin Ramadan, explained that when Saddam threatened to use these weapons to "make fire eat half of Israel" if it attacked Iraq, he meant that he would "not stop the fighting before half of Israel is set on fire. . . . This statement reflects an achievable objective, I do not want to divulge the details, however, the required capabilities have been secured for such battles."[30]

It is unclear whether the disclosure of the binary chemical capability was made in preparation for Iraq's invasion of Kuwait or was meant to deter an Israeli attack, as Baghdad had claimed (see Chapter 3). Either way, Saddam obviously saw the new weapon as a major deterrent. However, as soon as Saddam made his announcement, doubts were raised as to whether Iraq had indeed developed a binary chemical weapon. Some Israeli analysts questioned the Iraqi announcement, citing the difficulties the United States had encountered in developing its binary Bigeye VX aerial bomb.[31] Further, even if the Iraqis had developed binary chemical munitions, why would Israel need to take special notice of this alleged Iraqi weapon? It is true that by avoiding the mixing of the chemicals beforehand, the Iraqis could conceivably store large quantities of precursor materials without worrying that their chemical weapons would become inert.[32] Also, as the chemicals used in the binary weapon are not chemical agents and have lower toxicity, they are easier to purify than unitary chemical agents and are safer to handle. But binary weapons deliver relatively less agent per kilogram than unitary munitions.[33] For Israel, the introduction of these weapons into the Iraqi arsenal made little difference. The feeling was that the announcement was merely the latest in a series of publicity stunts on the part of Saddam.

In fact, it seems that Saddam's concept of a "binary" chemical weapon covered a number of approaches that the Iraqis had adopted to increase the effectiveness of their CW. In this he reflected the Iraqi army's close adherence to Soviet military doctrine. The Soviet definition of binary weapons covered a wider spectrum of options than the American definition. The American approach stresses the safety factor in terms of weapon storage and handling, leading to a design in which two "innocent" chemical precursors are stored in the weapon in readiness but in which toxic agent is created only when they are mixed together in or over the target area. In Soviet practice, by contrast, safety was much less of a factor. Their military doctrine advocated use of mixed agents in order to enhance the effectiveness of CW. A possible option mentioned at the time was a weapon containing a main agent mixed with a penetrant or discipline breaker. The main agent was designed to kill or injure, while the "secondary" agent was meant to achieve other objectives — for example, to terrorize or to inhibit military operations.[34]

In the Iraqi case the concept of a binary weapon covered, for one thing, a crude technology for storing alcohol in nerve gas bombs, which Iraq acquired in 1984 or 1985 and used during the second half of the Iran-Iraq war. These were not truly storable binary weapons in the American sense, where precursors are kept in the bomb and automatically mixed. The Iraqis were perfectly content to prefill the bombs with suitable alcohols (such as isopropyl alcohol) and then, just a few days before their use, manually add and stir in another precursor, such as difluoromethylphosphonate (DF). Thus they could produce GB without having to handle the chemically unstable agent itself.[35] The shelf life of DF is much longer than that of GB, and its storage is safer and less complicated.[36] In addition, producing DF is much easier than manufacturing chemical agents because of its lower toxicity. The resulting GB is potentially purer and more stable than the GB produced by other means.[37] The binary approach also allowed the Iraqis to sustain their production level of sarin, as some binary precursors, including isopropyl alcohol, could be purchased commercially. Reportedly, after the Gulf War, UNSCOM discovered 336 R-400 bombs that each contained 102 liters of "binary" GB.[38]

Second, the Iraqis, by applying the binary concept, hit on another way to achieve their as yet unfulfilled goal of inflicting mega-deaths. The "dual chemical" weapon came about as a result of the Iraqi military's experience with CW in the war with Iran. When Iraq first used mustard gas against Iranian troops, "the idea was to break Iranian morale through the sheer horror of a chemical attack. . . . [However], this did not work."[39] Even when Iraq switched to nerve gas, fatalities "barely" reached 20 percent, according to Heyndrickx.[40] In part, the problem stemmed from faulty CW tactics.[41] But it was also the result of the low quality of the Iraqi chemical weapons. For instance, Iraq's unitary nerve gas munitions contained significant impurities and thus underwent rapid hydrolysis. As a result, the shelf life of these weapons was only four to six weeks.[42]

By applying the binary approach, the Iraqis could soon improve the effectiveness of their CW by introducing a weapon armed with a "cocktail" of chemicals. The mixed-agent weapons apparently had two main attractions. First, the visible gases associated with the use of mustard gas were not present, making detection more difficult. Second, treatment to counter the effects of the cocktail was difficult, if not impossible, and any decontamination process would be elaborate and protracted.[43]

The increased lethality of the dual chemical weapon was potentially of great significance, as Iraq would need fewer weapons to inflict a given level of damage. This was particularly important in connection with the Iraqi threats to use CW against far-away targets, like Israel.[44]

The Iraqis experimented with various mixes of chemical agents to find the most lethal compound. By 1985 the Iraqis were using chemical weapons containing a mixture of mustard gas, cyanides, and nerve gases (normally sarin and tabun), packed separately and mixed by the force of the explosion. Fatalities rose to 60 percent.[45] This mixture also made treatment more difficult. Dr. Gernot Pauser, one of the attending physicians at Vienna's Second Surgical University Clinic, where eight Iranian soldiers were brought after an Iraqi gas attack in March 1985, said that their injuries were caused not only by mustard gas but also by other toxic agents. "We don't know yet exactly what else was involved. It is some agent containing cyanides," he said. Dr. Pauser added that these patients, unlike the previous Iranian CW victims he had treated, not only had damage to the lungs, skin, and bone marrow, but in addition their liver was poisoned and their blood oxidation was blocked.[46]

One of the first weapons Iraq modified into carrying a chemical cocktail payload was the munition for the 122-millimeter multiple rocket launcher. The Iraqis devised rockets with an inner metal tube that would accept at least two, and possibly three, plastic canisters containing CW agent. The canisters allowed the Iraqis to mix or match chemical agents. Each rocket was assessed to carry 8–12 kilograms of agent. During the final phase of the war with Iran, the weapon was used widely. In the short al-Faw battle, for example, an estimated 1,500–2,000 122-millimeter rockets were fired during the second day's attack, causing an estimated 5,000 Iranian casualties and mass flight of Iranian troops — a phenomenon that did not occur in earlier battles (see Appendix B, Table 3).[47]

Given the al-Faw experience, allegations that Iraq used some chemical "cocktail" against Halabja gain credence. Christine M. Gosden, a professor of medical genetics at the University of Liverpool who went to the Kurdish town ten years after the bombing, told a U.S. Senate committee that the attack had involved multiple chemical agents. The chemicals included mustard gas and the nerve agents sarin, tabun, and VX. Referring to the reported use of cyanide, she said that it was possible that an impure form of tabun, which has a cyanide residue, released the cyanide compound. She added:

> Saddam Hussein clearly intended to complicate the task of treating the Halabja victims. At a minimum, he was using Halabja as part of the Iraqi CW test program. Handbooks for doctors in the Iraqi military show sophisticated medical knowledge of the effects of CW. The Iraqi military used mustard gas in the "cocktail," for which there is no defense or antidote. And it is also worth noting that Saddam did *not* use the nerve agent soman. . . . This is noteworthy because it shows that Hussein's experts were also well aware that pyridostigmine bromide—one of the chief treatments against nerve agent—is relatively ineffective against tabun, sarin, and VX, but highly effective against soman, the only agent he *did not* use.[48]

The use of Iraq's "dual chemical" weapon against other Kurdish targets is almost certain. The workings of this Iraqi weapon were even described in some detail by Kurdish refugees. Reportedly, this kind of bomb, which was used in May 1988 against the Kurdish village of Guptapa, does not explode with a loud bang. A big explosion would instantly atomize the chemicals, preventing the mixing from taking place, and the weapon would shatter into countless pieces of flying shrapnel. Instead, the dual chemical bomb "makes a sort of a popping sound which allows the two chemicals contained within the tube (separated from one another by an inner casing) to mix. The casing keeps its form, breaking up into large chunks of metal. . . . The inner casing is about one sixteenth of an inch thick; the outer is at least one eighth of an inch thick."[49]

Iraq clearly was prepared to use chemical cocktails during the Gulf War. Following the war, UNSCOM discovered 30 CW Scud warheads. Of these, 14 were of the binary type. They were found with alcohol already in the warheads and with canisters of DF at the site for filling into the warheads just before firing.[50] The 16 remaining warheads were loaded "ready to go" with a mixture of GB and another nerve agent, GF.[51] Two French officers, who participated in UNSCOM inspection missions to Iraq, reported in the *Cahiers de Mars*, a publication of the students of the French Military Academy, the discovery of an entire array of Iraqi weapons, including the Scud warheads, containing a ready-to-use chemical cocktail.[52] In the cocktail, GB—which was discovered in bombs, 122-millimeter rockets, and warheads for Scud B missiles—was mixed with "an agent which is known but apparently was not used until now for military purposes—GF—which is less volatile than sarin and has characteristics close to soman."[53] The choice of the mixture, the officers wrote, "corresponds to the search for greater efficacy, especially at high temperature, but it could also be a way of reducing import problems relating to the raw materials" involved in its production. They also reported that the chemical aerial bombs they inspected, weighing between 250 and 500 kilograms, were filled with between 60 and 150 liters of mustard gas or between 100 and 250 liters of the GB-GF mixture. The Scud B warheads, weighing some 300 kilograms, contained 150 liters of the compound.[54]

In its report on the Gulf War, the Pentagon determined that the production of the semi-persistent nerve agent GF was undertaken by the Iraqi research and development establishment "when Western nations restricted the export of chemical precursors required for Soman [GD]."[55] However, the choice had other equally important motives. Cyclohexylmethylphosphonofluoridate (GF) is a G-series nerve agent whose physiological effects, therapy, and methods of protection and detection are similar to those of sarin. But GF is more persistent and more readily absorbed through the skin. Whereas GF is a liquid agent that will remain in the target area for several hours, sarin will dissipate in a few minutes at the temperatures found in the Middle East. And although GF is not as toxic as sarin by inhalation, it is markedly more toxic by absorption through the skin. Thus in the case of percutaneous exposure, the LCt_{50} of GF is 45–50 mg-min/m^3 (for a 90-kilogram man), while sarin's is $1,700$ to $3,500$ mg-min/m^3. The Pentagon's Defense Intelligence Agency (DIA) estimated that "since the persistence of GF will necessitate that forces remain in personal protection gear for longer periods than for sarin, [U.S.] personnel will experience significant heat stress and degradation of performance."[56]

The confusion regarding Saddam's assertion that he possessed a "binary" chemical weapon was largely put to rest after the Gulf War. The inspectors of UNSCOM sought to clarify with the authorities in Baghdad their understanding of the term "binary sarin," which was also used in Iraqi declarations to the U.N. secretary general. They reported that in the Iraqi terminology, "binary sarin" refers to "a chemical munition containing both GB and [another nerve agent,] GF," which in the West would be classified instead as a "dual chemical weapon.[57] Thus, while some observers questioned the existence of Iraqi cocktail weapons, UNSCOM is on solid ground in asserting that "the Iraqis were capable of employing both binary and mixed agent weapons."[58]

In retrospect, it is clear that Iraq's Scud missiles could have posed a formidable lethal threat to a civilian population. And indeed, when Saddam threatened to use the "binary chemical" against Israel in April 1990, most Western nations expressed concern about his intentions, regardless of whether they thought his weapon was a true binary or a dual chemical one. Saddam, while planning the invasion of Kuwait, must have felt reassured by this international outcry.

In fact, the Iraqis may have even deliberately taken steps to focus world attention on their readiness for CW on the eve of the attack on Kuwait. In a surprising break with their custom of using front companies or third parties to purchase sensitive gear, "Iraqi agents" tried to obtain nerve gas antidotes in Britain "only days before the invasion of Kuwait," as the magazine *Jane's Defence Weekly* reported on August 24, 1990. Allegedly, the Iraqis were searching for nerve agent preparation sets, issued to soldiers as part of their anti-CW defense, which comprise tablets taken before exposure to nerve gas. When the Iraqis were rebuffed in Britain, they moved their operation to Germany, while other Iraqi agents were said to have sought another kind of antidote — injected after a nerve gas attack — in Sweden.

Iraq's Hidden Option: The Biological Weapons

The Iraqi judgment that there would be little, if any, outside resistance to the aggression against Kuwait was also based on a much less advertised capability. By the time Saddam ordered his troops into Kuwait, the Iraqis had already spent some $100 million on their offensive BW program and had a significant stockpile of biological warfare agents.[59] In addition, Ambassador Rolf Ekeus noted: "It is . . . reasonable to assume that, given that biological weapons were considered strategic weapons and were actually deployed, detailed thought must have been given to the doctrine of operational use for these weapons of mass destruction."[60] In fact, UNSCOM was able to uncover evidence that Iraq had developed BW as both a strategic and a tactical option. Paralyzing weapons were mostly meant for tactical use, while lethal weapons were assigned strategic missions.

Ekeus revealed that Iraq tested its biological weapons on big mammals — sheep, monkeys, and donkeys — in both Salman Pak and al-Hakam. Field trials for biological weapons were carried out, according to the Iraqis, as early as March 1988, using aerial bombs filled with anthrax simulant (to avoid the long-term contamination hazard) and botulinum toxin. Effects were observed on test animals. In November 1989, additional weaponization tests were conducted using anthrax simulant, botulinum toxin, and aflatoxin in 122-millimeter rockets and R-400 bombs. Live firings of 122-millimeter rockets filled with agents were conducted in May 1990 to test the weapon under operational conditions. Reportedly, UNSCOM even discovered videos showing the dropping of BW bombs from an airplane in which animals within 250 meters of ground zero were killed.[61] Consequently, it appears that Iraq had mastered at least a crude delivery technique for its BW agents, which had to be aerosolized to become a mass-killing weapon.[62]

At about the same time, the Iraqis approached two European companies about devising a warhead with a restraining parachute for their al-Husayn missile.[63] Such a device would have allowed the warhead to spray its lethal payload while descending to target, assuming that the necessary aerosol technology was somehow also made available to Baghdad.

These preparations, and the various tests they had carried out, suggest that the Iraqis were able to overcome key problems, including that of producing just the right size of anthrax spores, before their attack on Kuwait.[64] Although Iraq's delivery methods were sometimes primitive, the results were nevertheless lethal. The weaponization of agents, including BW bombs and missile warheads, before the Gulf War indicates that Saddam estimated he had an operational capability ready to go. As Ekeus noted: "The simple fact that they [the Iraqis] placed bacteriological agents in missile warheads at least proves that they had confidence in their capacity."[65]

It is even probable that Iraq was in possession of an operational BW capability earlier than it has admitted. Although Iraq contended that it had begun a "crash" program to weaponize BW agents only after its invasion of Kuwait, it also told UNSCOM that part of the impetus for acquiring a BW option was to find inexpensive weapons capable of killing thousands of Iranians and sowing panic in enemy ranks.[66] Indeed, by Iraq's own account it flight-tested an indigenously produced Scud warhead filled with chemical agent simulant as early as 1985.[67]

There is only a short distance between the development of a warhead capable of carrying CW agents and one designed to deliver BW material. However, according to the Iraqi version, the 1985 missile test was meant to determine whether it was possible for another country to threaten Iraq with such means. It claimed to have learned from the test that this was possible, but it asserts that it did no further work in response to this discovery and did not restart its special warhead development until five years later, in 1990. Iraq stated that it then designed, developed, produced, and began to fill warheads in less than three months.[68] Amazingly, by the time the war broke out, Iraq had a full array of bombs and missiles carrying BW material.

There are other reasons to question the Iraqi timeline of its biological program. Note the 19-month gap between Iraq's first and second BW tests. The Iraqis claimed that no further trials were conducted during this period. But in 1988 Saddam apparently was already plotting to attack Tehran with aerial bombs and missiles carrying BW agents (see Chapter 3). Iraq's original goal of acquiring a BW capability was, after all, as a weapon against Iran. In contrast, if the Iraqi story is correct, acquisition of BW weapons was accomplished only two years *after* the Iran-Iraq war ended.

Iraq told UNSCOM that it also looked for a BW option as "a viable deterrent in answer to a possible attack by Israel using nuclear weapons."[69] But if this were true, weaponization of BW agents should have started at least in February 1990, when Baghdad first warned of an impending Israeli military aggression against Iraq. Indeed, whereas Iraq claimed to have produced 1,782 liters of aflatoxin for filling weapons between October 1 and December 31, 1990, UNSCOM has determined that "given the facilities, equipment and personnel available [at the time], such large production would not have been possible."[70] Production must have started much earlier.

A similar conclusion may be reached with regard to other components of the Iraqi BW program, specifically its development of effective dispersal systems. Iraq claims that only in late 1990, after the invasion of Kuwait, did it initiate two parallel programs to use modified drop tanks as biological agent spray tanks. The tanks would be fitted either to a piloted fighter or to a remotely piloted aircraft guided by a piloted aircraft. Each tank was designed to spray up to 2,000 liters of anthrax over the target. Allegedly, field trials for both programs were first conducted in January 1991.[71]

UNSCOM's technical assessment experts have concluded, however, that this Iraqi timeline is suspect. In contrast, they said that the "evidence that Iraq was investigating patents in the area [of the spray tank project] *several years* before the claimed start of weapon development is . . . of concern."[72] Indeed, the investment in the spray tanks indicates that when it attacked Kuwait, Iraq might have already been in possession of dried BW agents. Such agents are more difficult to produce, but would have presented more of an aerosol threat, than a wet suspension of either spores or toxins.[73]

If information released by the Central Intelligence Agency (CIA) is true, then "in the fall 1990, Iraqi President Saddam Hussein ordered that plans be drawn for an airborne delivery of biological warfare agent."[74] It is unlikely that such an order would have been given if the Iraqi leader had not been fairly confident that his military already had the operational capacity to execute such a critical mission. During the war, U.S. intelligence actually photographed an Iraqi SU-22 "Fitter" at an air base 10 kilometers southwest of An Nisiriyah (probably Tallil air base) "with a possible chemical/biological spray tank on the inboard port side pylon." The equipment would support "the hypothesis of a possible C/B spray tank."[75]

The conclusion seems warranted that Iraq's BW program had become operational long before the Gulf crisis. Indeed, it may even be said that Saddam would not have invaded Kuwait had he not secured a BW option beforehand.

Saddam's Erroneous Assessment

Saddam must have been quite surprised when, in spite of Washington's "green light" and Iraq's mass destruction umbrella, not to mention Baghdad's deceitful practices, President Bush announced, on August 8, 1990, his decision to dispatch U.S. troops to the Gulf.[76] Bush also issued a categorical demand for the immediate, unconditional, and complete withdrawal of Iraqi forces from Kuwait.

It appears that in reaching his erroneous assessment about the likelihood of a foreign intervention, Saddam committed two mistakes. First, he overestimated the value of his chemical weapons as a strategic deterrent. In the Iran-Iraq war, poison gas had had a decisive role in forcing the Ayatollah Khomeini to, in his words, "drink poison" and sue for peace. The Iranian Majles (Parliament) Speaker Hashemi Rafsanjani once wept in public while describing the impact of Iraq's CW.[77] Saddam took the experience of the war with Iran, in which gas eventually caused the Iranian military to lose its most potent weapon — its will to fight — to mean that Iraq possessed an absolute weapon capable of stopping modernized armies as well.[78] Saddam surmised that no foreign power would dare think of a military intervention if its troops could be subjected to such a horrible weapon. Fully confident of his deterrent, he declared, one day after the invasion of Kuwait, that Iraq would turn the Gulf into "a graveyard for those who think of committing an aggression."[79]

Second, Saddam evidently assumed that his opponents, particularly the United States, possessed reliable information that revealed how advanced his BW capability was. For example, a document dated August 3, 1986, which was reportedly captured by guerrillas of the Kurdish Democratic Party and later released in London, referred to an inventory of "chemical and biological" materials in the hands of the Iraqi army.[80] Two years later, an outbreak of typhoid fever in the Kurdish camps of Baynjan and Jajnehan in al-Sulaymaniyah Province, which caused 150 deaths, was said to have been caused by a unique bacterium cultured by Iraqi scientists in laboratory conditions. Major outbreaks of typhoid from contaminated water usually involve several different strains of bacteria, and normally include other organisms, such as cholera. But a report in the British magazine *New Scientist* said that all the bacteria isolated in al-Sulaymaniyah were from a single typhoid strain.[81]

Whereas U.S. intelligence and other intelligence services had long suspected that Iraq was actively researching typhoid as a biological weapon, "U.S. officials" were later quoted as claiming that there "appears to be no evidence" that Iraq had deployed germ warfare against the Kurds.[82] But they probably knew better. According to Heyndrickx, Iraq did use typhoid germs against the Kurds in 1988. "We know that from members of [the humanitarian organization] *Médecins du Monde* who worked at the Turkish border. . . . The Turks kept it quiet because they were friends with Saddam Hussein at the time. The victims were cared for secretly in Turkey," he stated, adding that Iraq had blocked all attempts to investigate.[83] A former official of the U.S. State Department and of the Arms Control and Disarmament Agency described the episode as follows: "Hypothetically, a government that wanted to conduct genocide against people in a particular region could do so and claim the outbreak was natural. Iraqi Kurds, an ethnic minority, claimed that a typhoid outbreak among their ranks might have been purposely caused by the Iraqi government."[84]

More important, judged by numerous reports in the Western media at the time, the Iraqi biological weapons program was viewed with grave concern by the major Western powers. The Iraqis could have concluded that their potential enemies were awed by their BW capability.[85]

Saddam might have overestimated the abilities of Western intelligence, as well. Baghdad had high regard for the U.S. intelligence-gathering capability as a result of its own experience. Between 1982 and 1988, the United States had reportedly shared with Baghdad certain intelligence information, including photo-reconnaissance data and some narrative text reports derived from signal intelligence, as part of the Reagan administration's "tilt" toward Iraq to prevent an Iranian victory in the war between the two countries. As a result, the Iraqis had a golden opportunity to learn about U.S. intelligence capabilities. As one U.S. specialist in signal intelligence said, the Iraqis "could see how radio silence and land lines worked. They could see the raw product and how it contrasted with what they received from their own intelligence."[86]

Iraq's long association with the KGB (*Komitet gosudarstvennoy bezopasnosti*, or Committee of state security), as part of its 20-year alliance with the Soviet Union, might have also contributed to its overly high opinion of U.S. intelligence.[87] For example, the Iraqis were interested in finding ways to thwart U.S. espionage collection and even asked the Soviets to help in this matter.[88]

In fact, at the time of the August invasion, Iraq's ability to fashion weapons from biological strains, particularly anthrax bacteria and botulinum toxin, was considered "improbable" by U.S. intelligence.[89] The Americans drew this conclusion despite the relatively large number of Iraqi students who in the early 1980s were immersed in the study of microbiology and toxicology at British universities and at various French technical institutes.[90] Only by late August 1990 did the DIA reverse itself and conclude that Iraq had an active anthrax program; a few days later it expanded the assessment to include botulin toxin.[91] Notwithstanding, even as late as December 1990, the DIA had to report that "considerable uncertainty continues to exist on the Iraqi BW program in general, to include the amount of agent available, the degree to which it has been weaponized, the complete spectrum of agents and types available, and the exact role of suspect facilities."[92] As Robert M. Gates had testified during his nomination for director of the CIA, after the Iran-Iraq war ended in July 1988, "our intelligence assets were shifted away."[93]

Whatever U.S. intelligence knew about Iraq's gas and germ weapons, in Saddam's mind his attack on Kuwait was all but risk-free. The international circumstances were favorable to begin with. And Iraq's overt mass destruction capability was more than enough to dissuade any residual opposition to the invasion. Further, the still-covert BW option provided the Iraqi leader with destructive powers akin to that of a superpower, or so Saddam probably believed. In hindsight, mass destruction weapons in the hands of Saddam made the invasion into Kuwait inevitable.

Prewar Strategic Deterrence

Deterring war with the United States was, in Saddam's mind, preferable to fighting. If Iraq could have avoided war, there would have been no challenge to the annexation of Kuwait.[1] With Kuwait under its wing, Iraq's oil reserves would have almost doubled from 100 to 195 billion barrels, some 20 percent of the world's known deposits. Iraq would have acquired effective control over more than 20 percent of the world's oil output (as of 1989) and about 56 percent of OPEC's production, thus dominating the cartel's price-setting power.[2] Most important, Iraq's nuclear, chemical, and biological weapons installations, which Saddam knew would be targeted the moment fighting erupted, could have been preserved. The nuclear armament program would have received a substantial boost with the infusions of new oil revenues. Essentially, Saddam's vision of Iraq's role in the region and beyond would have come closer to reality. Further, even though he thought that Iraq would prevail in a war, there was always a chance that his assessment would turn out to be wrong.

There is little question that Saddam was surprised by the introduction of U.S. troops into Saudi Arabia in early August. On August 15, 1990, the Iraqi leader hastily offered Iran a permanent settlement to their dispute that represented virtually a complete capitulation to Tehran's demands and in essence annulled the eight years that Iraq had spent fighting the Iranians. Under the proposal Iraq accepted the 1975 Algiers treaty, which Saddam had abrogated in 1980 and which gave both countries sovereignty over the Shatt al-Arab waterway. Saddam also agreed to the withdrawal of Iraqi troops from as much as 2,600 square kilometers of Iranian territory that they still occupied. In large measure, Baghdad's initiative was aimed to free Iraqi forces stationed on the eastern frontier with Iran so that they could join the confrontation with the U.S.-led forces to the south.[3]

Saddam was uncertain of the intentions of the ostensibly defensive U.S. forces dispatched to the Gulf. Although on several occasions he played up the "aggressive" designs of the arriving Americans, there is good reason to believe that this was done for political reasons, namely, to galvanize Arab and Muslim support. Initially, Saddam considered the U.S. deployment an opportunity to divert attention from the attack on Kuwait and to portray the crisis as a conflict for the sake of Arabism and Islam.[4] However, as he was unsure of Washington's motives, Saddam adopted a posture of signaling his desire for peace while pledging that if war came Iraq would vanquish its opponents. "We are in a position to destroy any aggression," he said. "We do not want war to come about despite the fact that we can smash any aggression."[5]

Iraq's option of mass destruction naturally figured in this strategy. By alluding to this capability, Saddam sought to dissuade anyone in Washington who might have been itching for a fight. Using language familiar from Iraq's CW against Iran, he stated, for example, "This is not a threat, but this is a fact — whoever attacks Iraq will find in front of him columns of dead bodies which may have a beginning but may not have an end."[6] This apocalyptic rhetoric was also meant to strengthen the hands of the "peace camp" in the West and to support Moscow in its efforts to avert a catastrophic war.

Saddam sought to dispel the notion that his inability to threaten American territory would work to the advantage of the United States.[7] He pointed out that Iraq's vulnerability was offset by that of U.S. interests in the region. As he put it: "The weaponry owned by Iraq might not be capable of reaching the United States, but it can reach its allies."[8]

Yet it appears that during the early days of the crisis Saddam felt the need to compensate for what he evidently saw as his conventional military weakness. Thus, sometime in August, while Iraq was rushing reinforcements to the south, Saddam took steps to convince his enemies that he was preparing for CW. That month the Iraqis loaded several aircraft with chemical bombs, then unloaded the planes in a move that some intelligence analysts believed was "intended as a warning to the U.S."[9] Further, in a press conference on August 9, Baghdad's ambassador to Athens announced that Iraq would use chemical weapons if it was attacked by the United States or Israel.

Although the Iraqi threats were probably issued as a defensive measure, they were viewed credibly because, as Gen. Khaled bin Sultan, the Saudi commander of the Joint Forces, has written, the United States feared that Saddam would take the offensive and attack the lightly armed 82d Airborne Division with chemical weapons as it arrived in Saudi Arabia.[10]

It remains unclear why Saddam also chose, at the same time, to take Western hostages. On August 13, Iraqi officials indicated for the first time that foreigners who happened to be in Iraq or occupied Kuwait were "re-strictees" who would not be allowed to leave until the crisis was over. On August 17, the speaker of the Iraqi parliament, Sa'di Mehdi Saleh, announced that some of the restrictees would be given "appropriate accommodations" at factories and military industrial installations, and at army and air bases, around the country. Two days later Saddam announced that he would free the foreign nationals if the United States withdrew its forces from Saudi Arabia and promised not to attack, and if the worldwide trade boycott on Iraq were lifted.[11]

On the face of it, Iraq's hostage taking indicates that Saddam was fearful of an allied attack, possibly a punitive air strike, immediately after the U.S. forces had been deployed to Saudi Arabia. Yet it can also be seen as attesting to continued uncertainty in Baghdad about U.S. motives. Iraq's deputy prime minister, Taha Yasin Ramadan, referred to the holding of foreign nationals as a "deterrent for war" until diplomacy could find a peaceful solution to the crisis.[12] The Iraqis might have viewed the hostage taking simply as an insurance policy, in case the United States was bent on aggression. But such a policy could have backfired, enraging the United States further and cementing the coalition against Iraq, rather than dissuading an attack. Moreover, it could be argued, the taking of hostages and their deployment as human shields in effect undermined the credibility of Saddam's mass destruction threat. Why would Baghdad add fuel to the fire by seizing hostages even as it was threatening mass destruction attacks, Western analysts were liable to wonder, unless Saddam did not expect to unleash CW or mistrusted its effectiveness?

The Strategy of Terrorist Deterrence

The affair highlights Saddam's view of deterrence in general, and especially deterrence vis-à-vis a superior enemy. According to this view, in order to deter an enemy like the United States, one must use terrorist deterrence — a strategy in which the efficacy of any act undertaken against the enemy is determined by the terror that this action causes in the opponent. That is, one must show willingness to engage in acts that are patently abhorrent to Western thinking. Deterrence à la Saddam is the cumulative effect of such acts. It is a systematic effort to instill maximum fear in the heart of the enemy. The more shock and aversion are caused by a specific declaration or action, the more effective it is deemed to be. The impact of each act is added to the one caused by its predecessor, and the sum total is the deterrent effect. Unlike the Western "delicate balance of deterrence," the arithmetic of terrorist deterrence is striking in its gory simplicity. It was amply demonstrated by Saddam when he warned against the folly of attacking Iraq: "When [in response] Iraq attacks installations and factories in cities, it is expected that children, women, men, and civilians inside the installations will also die, in addition to the soldiers who will die on the front in Iraq. This is of course in addition to the destruction in all aspects of life."[13]

Terrorist deterrence did not come about as a result of some carefully crafted doctrine. Rather, it was the natural extension of Saddam's fundamental approach to political life. For "Saddamism," one keen observer has pointed out, is "a true regime of terror"; it "is a phenomenon rooted in violence, in the manipulation of the tools and means of violence to achieve expressly political ends."[14]

With this mindset, threatening to use chemical weapons against civilian population centers — or, as Saddam had put it on April 2, to "have fire eat half of Israel" — is not just permissible, but the horrified reactions to such threats in the West and elsewhere are seen as proof of the effectiveness of the deterrent. Similarly, the revulsion and anger expressed in the West over Iraq's hostage taking could only make any future hideous threat, such as the use of chemical or biological weapons, more credible. In turn, in Saddam's eyes there was no contradiction between threatening to resort to mass destruction weapons and deploying human shields against a potential U.S. air attack.

Judging by the reaction of U.S. commanders to Saddam's mass destruction threats, he might have been right. Throughout the conflict, Saddam's strategy of terrorist deterrence was the main reason his enemies adopted a worst-case approach in projecting his intentions and future actions. For example, he deliberately took steps to whip up fears that Iraq might resort to CW. In September, Iraq inaugurated its "missile diplomacy," which was to become a key element of its strategy for "crisis management" throughout the conflict, by reportedly test-launching an al-Husayn missile armed with a chemical warhead. The idea was undoubtedly to demonstrate Iraq's ability to hit distant targets.[15] Simultaneously, the Iraqis established at least six chemical decontamination sites in southern Iraq in apparent preparation for use of poison gas. The sites, capable of handling a large number of Iraqi forces, were located just across from the Kuwaiti border. Iraq was also believed to have established chemical weapons storage sites south of Basra.[16] By late October, CIA Director William Webster could report that Iraq "was preparing its troops for chemical warfare."[17]

In fact, the less was Saddam seen as able to preempt the arriving troops conventionally (as a result of the steady buildup of U.S. forces), the greater was the credibility with which his CW threats were perceived. As General

Khaled put it, "After the first few weeks, it seemed highly improbable that Saddam would dare launch a conventional attack: The Coalition was far too strong. But the possibility of his using nonconventional weapons remained a persistent worry right to the end."[18] Khaled even contended that Saddam's CW threat had a profound psychological impact on the coalition commanders, causing them to perceive the Iraqi military as a "formidably dangerous enemy" and eventually leading Gen. Norman Schwarzkopf, the U.S. commander, to overarm for Desert Storm.[19]

If Khaled is correct, then Iraq's CW option, and especially its role in Saddam's strategy of terrorist deterrence, might have had a dual effect. On the one hand, it prolonged the occupation of Kuwait, as the United States needed more time to prepare for the war. On the other, it assured such imbalance between Iraq's conventional forces and those that the United States would want to assemble, that a decisive Iraqi defeat was inevitable unless Saddam was ready to escalate to mass destruction weapons. In this context, Saddam's mass destruction weapons could be viewed as strategically counterproductive.

Saddam cared little about the potential downside of his strategy, however. He was preoccupied with building an unquestionable record of credibility to assure the effectiveness of his maximalist threats. This effort was not without risk. Terrorist deterrence, as a rule, connotes a willingness to "go all the way." But the more Saddam applied this approach, and the greater the perceived credibility of his threats, the easier it became to convince the world that he was a dangerous lunatic who must be stopped. It was this fast-growing consensus that formed the basis for Bush's successful coalition-building effort, including the unprecedented participation of several Arab countries. Furthermore, Saddam's strategy was also risky in another way. If terrorist deterrence failed and war came, the enemy could feel compelled to wage an all-out battle.

Throughout this period Iraq's BW option stayed virtually in the background, with only oblique references, if any, made by the Iraqis to this capability. There were several reasons why Saddam chose to limit himself almost exclusively to the threat of CW to deter the United States from launching a war.

First and foremost, Saddam was apparently unconvinced that war was in the offing. The Iraqi leader invaded Kuwait probably after concluding that Washington was still well disposed toward him. If anything, it was the various manifestations of the Bush administration's favorable attitude toward Baghdad that had likely encouraged Saddam to invade.[20] Saddam also believed that the United States had learned a lesson from its experience in Vietnam (see Chapter 2).

Second, Saddam ostensibly felt that Iraq's chemical arsenal was sufficient to deter any residual inclination of the United States to oppose him, especially given his record of terrorist deterrence in the Iran-Iraq war and against the Kurds. Even if the dispatch of U.S. troops suggested otherwise, there was a substantial difference between deploying forces to defend American interests in Saudi Arabia and committing them to war against an enemy heavily armed with mass destruction weapons. As Saddam told U.S. Ambassador April Glaspie, while alluding to Iraq's experience in its war with Iran, "yours is a society which cannot accept 10,000 dead in one battle."[21] It was natural for the Iraqis to assume that Washington, knowing full well that Iraq would not hesitate to employ its CW armaments, would not risk an attack. Moreover, until November, U.S. deployments in Saudi Arabia were publicly advertised by Bush administration officials as solely defensive in nature, with the aim of protecting Saudi Arabia from possible Iraqi aggression.[22]

Such was Iraq's confidence in the effectiveness of its CW deterrent that it apparently used the disclosure of its binary chemical weapon as a way to shield the existence of its BW capability. Iraqi Foreign Minister and Deputy Prime Minister Tariq Aziz (falsely) asserted that Iraq had a policy of announcing all weapons in its possession in order to prevent any aggression. "When it acquires any military capability, Iraq announces it honestly to deter adventures," he declared.[23] The fact that the Iraqis began assembling their biological weapons only on December 1, 1990, fully four months *after* the onset of the Gulf crisis, indicates that Saddam did not initially expect the United States to go to war over Kuwait. Ironically, Bush and his lieutenants might have reinforced this conviction when they repeatedly warned of the existence of unconventional arms in the hands of Iraq in the months preceding the war.[24]

Third, if Iraq announced its BW capability, it risked provoking an American preemptive strike while its biological weapons were still unassembled. In this respect, Baghdad likely took into consideration the September 28 disclosure of Rep. Les Aspin (D.-Wis.), then chairman of the House Armed Services Committee, that the U.S. intelligence community believed that Iraq had succeeded in developing biological weapons and would be able to deploy them in early 1991. Aspin's revelations came only days after CIA Director Webster had publicly acknowledged for the first time that Iraq had a "sizable stockpile" of biological weapons. But Aspin added that the information about Iraq's BW capability "would be a factor" in the Bush administration's decision on when to commence military action against Iraq, thus leaving the impression that the United States might seek to preempt the operational deployment of the weapons.[25]

Preparations for War

As the Gulf crisis escalated, especially after President Bush announced, on November 8, the doubling of U.S. forces in the Gulf "to insure the coalition has an adequate offensive military option," Saddam realized that there was a real danger of war breaking out. But on December 6, Saddam suddenly announced that he would free all hostages "soon." There were no conditions attached to the offer, and Saddam explained the move as a "humanitarian gesture" to help spur a diplomatic solution to the crisis.[26]

On the face of it, Saddam's decision implied the abandonment, at least temporarily, of terrorist deterrence. Was Saddam so frightened by the U.S. buildup that, in a stark departure from his long-standing convictions, he was ready to cave in?

Two factors suggest otherwise. First, Saddam and his lieutenants repeatedly asserted that Iraq would win a war against the United States.[27] Such statements have been commonly viewed as mere posturing. But there is substantial evidence to the contrary. It is impossible to ascertain precisely when Saddam became convinced that Iraq would win a conventional engagement against the United States, but he firmly believed such would be the case (see Chapter 4).[28] His Revolutionary Command Council told the Iraqi citizens to prepare for the "mother of all battles" as early as late September, vowing that there was "not a single chance of retreat" on Kuwait.[29] And in his videotaped address to the American people the next day, Saddam said that the war with Iraq would be like "repeating the Vietnam experience, only this time . . . more violent and more casualties."[30]

Further, the announced release of the hostages in itself indicates Saddam's confidence that Iraq would be victorious. Saddam said at the time that the gesture was made possible because Iraq had built up its defenses to the point where it no longer needed human shields. Iraq's enhanced military posture would either provide effective deterrence or assure victory if deterrence failed. In any case, the deterrent "services" of the hostages were no longer required.[31] Besides, the political costs of continuing to detain innocent civilians were no longer justified, whereas their release could yield political dividends.

Second, the release of the hostages coincided with other moves indicating that Saddam was now bracing for war. Freeing the hostages was part of an Iraqi dual-track policy, in fact. On the one hand, Saddam intensified the efforts to prevent war, as this was Iraq's preferred outcome. On the other, he accelerated the preparations for a conventional fight he intended to win. Either way, Saddam evidently thought, Iraq would emerge the winner. If a settlement was reached, Iraq would retain some of the captured Kuwaiti rich oil fields, at least. Iraq's key strategic and economic facilities would emerge from the crisis unscathed, and its status in the region would receive a substantial boost. But if war broke out after all, Iraq would be ready and its enemy — the United States — would be defeated. Although Saddam would have preferred not to fight a war, in his mind, Iraq was in a win-win situation regardless.

Both courses of action — new attempts to prevent war and intensified efforts to prepare for it — reveal that the Iraqi leader now believed that war was a real possibility. For example, the release of the hostages was meant to thwart Bush's otherwise certain aggression, or so Saddam contended.[32] Just a few days later, on December 12, 1990, Saddam replaced his defense minister, Gen. Abd al-Jabbar Khalil Shanshal, with Lt. Gen. Sa'di Tumah Abbas, a seasoned veteran of the Iran-Iraq war. The arming of the biological weapons so soon after the U.N. Security Council issued its ultimatum of November 29 (ordering Iraq to withdraw from Kuwait by January 15) also suggests that Saddam must have thought war was approaching. The Iraqis must have concluded that unless they assembled their weapons before fighting began, there was a good chance that this option would be neutralized. "If war erupts," Saddam said, "these [scientific and economic] installations will be the target of this war as clearly stated by some Western officials and by Western media."[33]

Germs in the Basement: The U.S. Factor

The question arises, if Baghdad was so certain about the prospects of war that it rushed to assemble its BW option, why did it not publicize Iraq's ultimate weapon once it became operational, in a last-ditch effort to deter the Americans? At this point, the reasons for secrecy seemed no longer valid: the United States seemed likely to go to war despite Iraq's CW threat, and now that Saddam had assembled his biological weapons, the risk of a preemptive strike was minimal. Would not terrorist deterrence call for Saddam to advertise his capacity for BW?

The answer is that the decision to keep the BW option hidden reveals Saddam's confidence in his victory. He was sure that Iraq would win the war by inflicting massive casualties on U.S. troops using *conventional* weapons only. To block the Americans from using unconventional weapons, he relied on open threats to employ CW. Concomitantly, he could afford to keep Iraq's BW capability in reserve as a last resort.

Given Saddam's plan, the disclosure would have been clearly uncalled-for. But Iraq kept its BW capability hidden also because of the potential costs of such an unveiling. In his meeting with Senator Dole's delegation in April 1990, Saddam indicated that he perceived a distinction between chemical and biological weapons. When asked by Senator Dole about reports that Iraq was developing "a virus to destroy whole cities," Saddam responded: "We are aware of what the biological weapons mean. We are aware if such a method were used, the situation would become uncontrollable. Therefore rest assured about this point. . . . Thus, we have no biological weapons, but we do have chemical weapons."[34]

Although this statement was made months before the threat of war had appeared and was clearly aimed to shield Iraq's evolving BW program, it may contain some insights into Saddam's thinking. First, the statement is remarkable in that it contains an implicit admission that Iraqi officials had considered the pros and cons of biological warfare. Second, Saddam seemed to be saying that BW was by definition a last-resort option because biological weapons were uncontrollable. For example, if they were used against U.S. forces in and around the Arabian Peninsula, biological agents could spread over the territories of some Arab regimes friendly to Baghdad. Under some worst-case scenarios, even areas in the southern Soviet Union could be contaminated. Certainly much of Iraq, including Baghdad itself, would be in danger.[35] Third, under these circumstances, an Iraqi threat to resort to BW for anything short of a last resort could be simply dismissed by the enemy as a bluff. Fourth, conversely, if the Iraqi warning was believed, it would likely facilitate Bush's coalition-building efforts and even provide a strong rationale for launching an aggression against Iraq: such a declaration would in fact prove Bush's thesis about the need to confront the danger from Baghdad. Fifth, Saddam himself could be declared a war criminal for brandishing biological weapons. Thus, should war break out, Iraq would be legitimizing the formal expansion of U.S. goals to include the installation of a new leadership in Baghdad.

Although it could be argued that the aforementioned constraints reflect Western thinking and that Saddam typically embraces such potentially reckless behavior to frighten his enemies, a distinction has to be made. It is true that as an avid practitioner of terrorist deterrence, Saddam often resorts to acts that seem irrational from a Western perspective. However, he is certainly *not* crazy. In this case, he had hardly any incentive to take such risks, as Iraq could issue credible CW threats if it sought to deter war.

Another reason for hiding the arming of the biological weapons was that U.S. intelligence, had it discovered the operation, could have interpreted it as preparation for an attack. Although Baghdad did not expect to have to resort to BW, its continuing silence regarding its capability was probably also aimed to prevent the inoculation of U.S. troops. The Iraqis may have figured that if war broke out after all and the circumstances warranted, they would thus be in a position to surprise the Americans. As Taha Yasin Ramadan has stated, "No state would reveal its possession of a weapon before it was used."[36]

This view may sound improbable because it clearly fails to distinguish between conventional weapons and weapons of mass destruction. Mass destruction weapons have primarily been instruments of deterrence in the context of the Cold War. But the fact that Iraq chose not to publicize its new capability yet opted to arm and move the biological weapons out of danger, not to mention deploy them in readiness, may be viewed as evidence that Saddam was looking to administer a strategic surprise when the time finally came.[37] During the war with Iran, Iraq had consistently denied that it was developing chemical weapons and even stated that it would not use them unless Iran did so first. But Iraq did indeed develop and use chemical weapons before Iran did.[38] Further, in 1981 Israel suspected that Saddam's search for nuclear weapons was driven by other than simply deterrent motives. This suspicion led Israel to destroy Iraq's Osiraq reactor preemptively.

In spite of all Iraq's secrecy, on December 27, four days after the Iraqis had reportedly deployed their combat-ready biological weapons at various sites, the Pentagon announced that it would begin vaccinating U.S. troops in Saudi Arabia. One day later, Britain said that it would follow suit.[39] It is not known what effect, if any, these announcements had on Baghdad. Saddam could have suspected that the United States had discovered his secret. If so, he might have concluded from the U.S defensive response that his enhanced mass destruction posture had effectively deterred a preemptive attack. More likely, however, the Iraqis probably figured that the United States undertook the inoculations as a precautionary move given that war was now imminent, not because of some specific information.

The U.S. and British announcements should have told Saddam that despite his weapons of terror, the United States and Britain were ready to go to war. The vaccinations were an indication that the United States was already assessing Iraq's BW capability as operational. The Iraqis could also have believed that the inoculations had diminished the effectiveness of their BW threat against the U.S. forces. In any case, the inoculation had called into question the benefits of an Iraqi disclosure of the new BW posture as a deterrent to the United States.

Germs in the Basement: The Israeli Factor

The possible role of Israel must also be considered. Reportedly, back in 1989, Israel had asked the United States to pass a warning on to Iraq that if it continued the biological weapons program, Israel would act to destroy it.[40] Moreover, the Iraqi leader involved Israel in the Gulf conflict early on, and later in the crisis threatened it directly on numerous occasions.[41] Consequently, Israel could have had a pretext to act against the Iraqi strategic threat. Inadvertently, the U.S. decision to inoculate its troops against some biological warfare agents also meant that Israeli and Saudi cities had become Saddam's priority targets for BW, even if they had been spared until then. This decision by the United States thus provided a powerful new incentive for Israel to try and eliminate the Iraqi threat in advance. Could it be that Iraq kept quiet about its BW possibility because it assumed that Israel would react forcefully if the assembling of the weapons became known in Jerusalem? The historical record clearly suggested to Saddam the reality of a preemptive Israeli strike. He had not forgotten the destruction of the Osiraq nuclear reactor by the Israelis in 1981. By the time of the invasion into Kuwait, his concern over the possibility of a new Israeli strike against Iraq's evolving mass destruction programs was so great that U.S. Secretary of State James A. Baker has described it as paranoia.[42]

During the January 1990 celebrations marking the 69th anniversary of the founding of the Iraqi Army, Saddam vented his fears in public: "We want to assert and warn that any attempt by the Zionist entity to strike against our scientific or military installations will be confronted with a precise reaction, using the means available to us according to legitimate right to self defense."[43]

The Iraqis even claimed that the disclosure in April 1990 of their binary chemical weapon was triggered by information that a "far bigger" Israeli attack than the one in 1981 was "imminent."[44] However, the truth might have been different: Iraq's mass destruction program had expanded so dramatically that it was simply unimaginable to Saddam that Israel would not challenge his attempt to reshape the strategic balance in the Middle East. Thus, even when Egyptian President Hosni Mubarak persuaded Israeli Prime Minister Yitzhak Shamir to pledge that Israel would not attack, Saddam remained suspicious.[45]

In a bid to enhance Iraq's deterrence of the alleged Israeli strike, Saddam resorted to the well-known tactic of voluntarily and publicly cutting off his own escape route. He told delegates of the International Confederation of Arab Trade Unions, gathered in Baghdad, that he "would like to explain the characteristics of the [chemical] weapons [and missiles] we have so you will not see any Iraqi excuses. Our missiles can reach Israel, and our planes can also reach Israel. . . . I have explained to you the capabilities Iraq possesses so you will find no Iraqi excuses when they fail to reply forcefully to the aggressors."[46]

Moreover, it was Saddam's contention that Israel was in cahoots with "Western imperialism," and first and foremost, the United States. Three days after he had first aired his allegations about Israel's planned attack, official reports stated that Baghdad had asked the U.S. government to explain why one of its AWACS planes was flying near the Turkey-Iraq border on April 5, 1990.[47]

It is possible to argue that Saddam's fuss over Israel's alleged plans to attack Iraq's strategic targets was a political coverup designed to portray his enormous military buildup defensively. Perhaps he played the Israeli card to facilitate Iraq's planned aggression against Kuwait. The issuing of a warning to Israel, for example, might have been a convenient excuse for Iraq to disclose its binary chemical weapon, which Saddam may have publicized to deter any interference in his designs on Kuwait. Or Saddam could have issued his threats in order to extract assurances from Israel, so that Iraq could invade Kuwait without fearing that the Israelis would seize the opportunity to attack.

Nevertheless, strong evidence indicates that Saddam took the threat from Israel seriously. He invested huge sums in hardening, concealing, and dispersing his entire mass destruction program.[48] In fact, the Iraqis used duplication to such an extent that UNSCOM inspectors later used the discovery of one element of the Iraqi nuclear program as an indication that a similar one probably existed somewhere else in Iraq.[49] Iraq's extensive efforts to shield its strategic assets plainly indicates the extent of its concern over another Israeli preemptive strike.

It is, therefore, reasonable to assume that the Iraqi decision to secretly arm its BW option was in part motivated by fear that in case of war, Israel, not just the United States, would launch another Osiraq-type preemptive strike. The Iraqis may have kept quiet about their new posture also in hopes of deceiving Israel and the United States into preemptively attacking vacant strategic installations instead of the combat-ready BW force they had assembled. This, too, would have supported the goal of surprising Iraq's enemies.

Germs in the Basement: The Soviet Connection

Finally, it is possible that Saddam thought he could afford to deemphasize the BW option because the Soviets were, in a way, doing his job for him (see Chapter 7). Key figures in the Gorbachev regime repeatedly warned of the disaster that would befall the world if war broke out. For example, Soviet envoy Yevgeny Primakov, who was dispatched by Soviet President Mikhail Gorbachev to mediate the conflict, often spoke of the "catastrophe" that a military solution was likely to trigger.[50] This message, whatever its motives, indirectly benefited Saddam's deterrent gambit, or so the Iraqi leader must have surmised.

The Strategic Deterrent and the Last-Resort Option

Once Iraq had armed its biological weapons, Saddam felt confident that if Iraq could not deter war, its strategic arms would survive an attack. Consequently, he could now rely on these arms to fulfill their original mission as last-resort weapons. But because he downplayed Iraq's BW capability, he inevitably had to highlight its readiness for CW in order to deter the United States. In the meantime, the trumpeting of Iraq's CW capability was also meant to shield Iraq's last-resort option against an attack during the sensitive time when the BW munitions were being readied. Saddam took new steps to remind his enemies of Iraq's capabilities — Scud missiles armed with binary chemical warheads and capable of reaching Israeli and Saudi cities. Accordingly, there was an immediate noticeable escalation in Iraq's "missile diplomacy." On December 2, 1990, the Iraqis test-fired three medium-range missiles, identified as "upgraded Scud missiles." They were launched from a site near Basra, in southeastern Iraq, and traveled more than 600 kilometers west toward Israel to land in a remote part of the Iraqi desert.[51] Moreover, Iraq had openly warned commercial airliners to keep out of its airspace after midnight the night before the test, but it gave no reason for the caution. As a result, Israeli pilots were reportedly ordered to their planes, and U.S. aircraft were apparently ready to retaliate if the missiles turned out to be directed at targets in Saudi Arabia. "A lot of people were in their cockpits ready to go," one U.S. official was quoted as saying.[52] On December 27, another Iraqi missile test reportedly took place, with allied forces again scrambling to their positions.[53] These effects must have been greeted with satisfaction in Baghdad.

Simultaneously, Saddam issued verbal reminders to Israel and the rest of his enemies concerning Iraq's CW capability. He declared: "You recall when they were making preparations for Israel to attack us. Then we clearly said that if Israel were to attack, we would strike it, and if it were to attempt or believe that it would be sufficient for it to possess a nuclear bomb, we were capable of burning half of Israel. We said this in April [1990], *before* the current event."[54] Shortly afterward, the warning turned even more specific: "We did not say that if Israel attacked us with a nuclear bomb we would attack it with a nuclear bomb. We said we will attack it with the binary weapon."[55] In addition to the deterrent motives of these declarations, it is likely that the emphasis on CW was meant to divert attention from Iraq's BW preparations.

The threat of an Israeli preemptive strike against the newly constituted Iraqi BW force was certainly considered in Baghdad; however, the fact that Iraq avoided publicizing its new capability suggests that Saddam may have convinced himself that his new missiles, armed with "binary" chemical warheads, provided Iraq with an effective strategic deterrent. Even if Israel did attack, he may have reassured himself, his BW force was capable of withstanding even a nuclear strike now that it was concealed in several well-dispersed sites. So the Israeli factor probably played an important role in inducing the Iraqi shift from a BW option to a secret BW *force*. But it is unlikely that Baghdad's decision to continue keeping its BW force secret was dictated by fears of an Israeli preemption.

At any rate, compared with the defiant waving of his CW "sword," Saddam seemed satisfied with the ambiguity that he himself helped foster over the BW option early in the crisis. For example, despite having denied that Iraq had biological weapons, Saddam told Senator Dole: "If there is anyone in the world, if he is our enemy and fears biological weapons, let him come, and together we will scrap biological weapons."[56] He also told the senator: "As to whether scientists have done research on this or that germ, I do not give a guarantee and I do not deny it."[57] Ironically, the Iraqi leader in effect adopted a version of Israel's "bomb-in-the-basement" posture, namely, a policy of keeping a secret strategic force as a last resort, while using the ambiguity over this capability to deter potential enemies.[58] By secretly preparing his biological weapons for action, Saddam likewise was looking to establish a last-resort deterrent.

After the war the Iraqis essentially admitted that their BW preparations had been linked to a possible last-resort scenario. Tariq Aziz described the plan as follows: "We explained to the United Nations the circumstances [under which] we could have used them [biological weapons] during the Gulf war. The unit commanders on the ground were authorized to use them if Baghdad had been attacked with nuclear weapons and if they were unable to communicate."[59]

Aziz's explanation sought to portray the Iraqi BW capability as a defensive option that would be activated only if Iraq itself was attacked with mass destruction weapons. If Aziz was to be believed, Iraq's BW option was purely a second-strike weapon. But this explanation must be viewed circumspectly from both the political-strategic and the operational points of view. With reference to the political-strategic perspective, it is vitally important to understand what in Saddam's eyes constitutes last-resort circumstances. In democratic countries such emergencies would normally be associated with some national calamity, but in the case of Saddam Hussein such a scenario would likely involve a threat to either his personal survival or his ability to control the country. As General al-Samarra'i noted: "The anthrax bombs were regarded, just as they are today, as a weapon of last resort, to be used only if Saddam's regime collapsed around him."[60] A nuclear attack on Baghdad could indeed belong in this category, but other scenarios involving exclusively conventional weapons could not be ruled out. For example, a U.S. advance on Baghdad would certainly be viewed by Saddam as spelling last-resort circumstances for him and his regime. "When Saddam Hussein tells the world that if it were within his power he would start World War III before ever relinquishing office voluntarily," wrote noted Iraqi political commentator Samir al-Khalil, "he means exactly that."[61] General al-Samarra'i reported that in 1988, during the Iran-Iraq war, Saddam had plans to attack Tehran with "biological as well as chemical weapons," using aerial attacks and missile strikes, but he changed his decision after Iraq scored victories on the battlefield.[62] Not surprisingly, at that time Ramadan asserted: "We have missiles and other weapons that can annihilate huge numbers of people. We take into account the population factor in Iran, and we do our best to avoid human losses. Therefore, we have weapons that can annihilate large numbers of enemy troops."[63]

Thus, if Saddam intended to use strategic mass destruction attacks only in last-resort circumstances, this does not necessarily mean that he would have launched such weapons only in response to his enemies' use of unconventional munitions. Clearly, the coalition leaders did not think so. As soon as hostilities commenced, they launched preemptive attacks against Iraq's mass destruction capabilities, thus indicating that they believed that Saddam might view chemical or biological weapons as first-strike weapons.

From the operational perspective, there are also good grounds to challenge Aziz's implication that Iraq's biological weapons constituted a second-strike force meant exclusively for defensive purposes. For instance, why would Saddam order the assembly and transportation of Iraq's biological arms to their launching sites, despite the obvious risk of being discovered by his enemies, unless he planned to resort to these weapons in the future and was worried that the coalition air attacks would deny him this option? Throughout the Gulf crisis, Saddam's threats of causing a global disaster, presumably an indirect reference to his BW capability, were never tied to a nuclear scenario. These threats were often addressed to "whoever attacks Iraq." Only after the war, when the Iraqis were looking for an alibi to explain their newly discovered readiness to resort to BW, did the link to a nuclear strike emerge. Even the fact that Saddam kept his BW capability secret, partly as a means to surprise his enemies, strongly implies that he was set on using mass destruction weapons first. Not surprisingly, a document that UNSCOM unearthed after the war confirms that the Iraqis held discussions about attacking Israel with biological weapons. In a secret working paper submitted to the top echelon of the Iraqi defense establishment and to President Saddam Hussein, on the eve of the Gulf War a proposal was made that Iraq launch an attack with biological weapons on Israel "on its own initiative, rather than as retaliation for any attack by Israel."[64]

Nevertheless, the formula that Aziz offered deserves a closer examination. In essence, it is a rehash of an older version used by Saddam in a bid to deter Israel, except that the first version mentioned only chemical weapons in describing the Iraqi strategic response, whereas Aziz included the BW option as well. On that earlier occasion Saddam said:

> We have given instructions to the commanders of the air bases and the missile formations that once they hear Israel has hit any place in Iraq with the atomic bomb, they will load the [binary] chemical weapon with as much as will reach Israel and direct it at its territory. For we might be in Baghdad holding a meeting with the command when the atomic bomb falls on us. So, to make the military order clear to the air and missile bases' commanders, we have told them if they do not receive an order from higher authority and a city is struck by an atomic bomb, they will point toward Israel any weapons capable of reaching it.[65]

Saddam's statement goes to the heart of the Iraqi concept of terrorist deterrence. Unlike Western strategies, terrorist deterrence recognizes no tension between the size of the threat and its credibility. Frequently, the bigger and more indiscriminate the threat, the less believable it is in the eyes of the target audience. Terrorist deterrence recognizes no such gap, not because it was able to bridge it through some doctrinal innovation but, conversely, because it is seemingly so primitive. Terrorist deterrence is an approach that seeks to make the unbelievable credible. Saddam, then, meant to assure Israel of the certainty of Iraq's mass destruction response. He was promising an Iraqi version of a doomsday machine, where retaliation is automatic and thus inevitable. It was left to the Israelis and the rest of the world to ascertain whether Saddam had taken leave of his senses. Would he allow that much latitude to his base commanders? If they wanted to impress him, or if they feared the consequences of inaction, they could plunge Iraq into a destructive war with Israel on the pretext of some rumors of an attack, combined with difficulties in communicating with Baghdad. Worse yet, they could use the threat of CW or BW to attempt political blackmail against Saddam, or even to stage a military coup under the protective umbrella of these weapons.

Nor was there much thought given in Baghdad to the potentially counterproductive nature of this retaliatory posture. Yet, if the Israelis had believed that Saddam had accurately described Iraq's C&C arrangements, they could have become more nervous. To the extent that they believed Saddam had the wherewithal to launch a surprise mass destruction attack on Israel, they might have concluded that it was essential to eliminate Iraq's capability for mass destruction before it was used against Israeli cities through some accident or miscalculation.

Normally, such considerations would have undermined the credibility of the threat. But Saddam undoubtedly expected that his unblemished reputation for executing terrorist deterrent threats would nullify such doubts and buttress his deterrent posture vis-à-vis Israel and his other enemies.[66]

On both the political-strategic and operational grounds, the inescapable conclusion is that the Iraqi leader would have been the first to employ strategic — that is, countercity — mass destruction strikes if he believed that last-resort circumstances were threatening him. And although it could be argued that by opting for a covert BW posture Saddam had given up a potentially crucial element in his efforts to deter the U.S. from going to war, Baghdad was not so convinced. First, Iraq used its known CW capability as an effective substitute. More important, Saddam was not too worried about the loss of the BW *deterrent*, because he expected to win the war conventionally.

Wartime Strategic Deterrence

Although Washington failed in its effort to compel Iraq out of Kuwait peacefully, and although Saddam Hussein could not deter the United States from launching operation Desert Storm, efforts at deterrence continued throughout the Gulf War, which began on January 17, 1991. Even earlier, as soon as Saddam realized that war was inevitable, he sought to use his mass destruction option to ensure a conventional engagement and a victory over the United States.

It is possible to argue that Saddam's strategy came about as a result of U.S. strategic deterrence. Saddam must have realized that Iraq could not resort to weapons of mass destruction for fear of a nuclear response from the United States, and he was thus forced to adopt an alternative plan. By all indications, the American nuclear option played a prominent role in Baghdad's calculations. But this does not mean that the Iraqi leader and his military cohorts were dubious about winning the war conventionally. In this sense, fighting a conventional war was from the outset Saddam's preferred strategy. In the months before the war he and his lieutenants cited a variety of reasons why Iraq would prevail in a conventional war with the United States. For example, they questioned the motivation of American soldiers.[1] Saddam continually referred to the American experiences in Vietnam and Lebanon as proof that the United States had no staying power.[2] He alleged that the U.S. approach to war was hopelessly dependent on advances in military technology, and therefore totally inadequate. "The United States depends on the Air Force," he said on one occasion, "[but] the Air Force has never decided a war in the history of wars."[3] While touting the weaknesses of the United States, Saddam also often mentioned the military advantages of Iraq. He suggested, for example, that as a result of the Iran-Iraq war his troops were battle hardened and ready for the modern battlefield. After all, this was the "most recent war in the world."[4] He warned Bush that the United States "will not be able to define the battlefield, arms and time [of the fighting]. . . . The battle will be prolonged and heavy blood will be shed."[5]

Saddam was hoping for a political, not military, victory in the Gulf War. He believed that he would triumph if, in the course of the ground war, Iraq inflicted substantial casualties on the Americans. On one occasion he even mentioned a casualty figure that he believed would break America's will to fight: "We are sure that if President Bush pushes things toward war and wages war against us — his war of aggression which he is planning — once five thousand of his troops die, he will not be able to continue the war."[6] Shortly after the war started, Saddam explicitly put forward his vision of victory: "When the war is fought in a comprehensive manner . . . the scale of death and the number of dead will, God willing, rise among the ranks of atheism, injustice and tyranny. When they begin to die and when the message of the Iraqi soldiers reaches the farthest corner of the world, the unjust will die and the banner of God is great will flutter with great victory in the mother of all battles."[7] Accordingly, before the war began, Iraq's senior generals were ordered to have their troops inflict "maximum casualties" on U.S. soldiers when the fighting started.[8] Saddam expected that once American casualties began to mount, opposition to the war in the United States would intensify and Bush would be forced to negotiate his way out of the quagmire. As he noted: "Peoples in the West have no interest in a war. . . . Evidence of this is that war has not erupted yet but anti-war demonstrations are staged. What would happen if war erupts?"[9]

Saddam's anticipation of victory cannot be viewed as some wild fantasy. In hindsight, perhaps, it may seem unrealistic. But before the war itself, the perceptions among U.S. civilian and military leaders did not necessarily contradict Saddam's impression. President Bush himself expressed fear that a prolonged conflict would erode U.S. public support, "as it did in the Vietnam . . . conflict."[10] To win the war, Saddam was ready to sacrifice hordes of Iraqi soldiers in order to exact the much smaller toll of American troops that he believed was necessary to defeat the U.S. politically. According to one analyst, he was "a great believer in the eventual victory of the side willing to suffer most."[11] Undoubtedly, Saddam was also intoxicated by what he saw as the prospect of victory and the worldwide implications of such a coup.[12]

The Doctrine of Strategic Reciprocity

Saddam, then, was willing to pay the price of causing a political earthquake of such magnitude, but he envisioned a constraint of a different nature. Iraq had to assure that once the American ground offensive bogged down, the United States would not try to break the deadlock by resorting to unconventional arms. Originally, Saddam looked to his mass destruction weapons to deter the United States from such a move. Therefore, he announced a doctrine of strategic reciprocity. While stressing that the Scuds in Iraq's possession could "carry nuclear, chemical and biological warheads," Saddam stated repeatedly that "we will use weapons that match those used by our enemy against us." So that there would be no doubt about the credibility of this deterrent, Saddam said, "I believe that you have now found out that we have done everything we have said."[13] Undoubtedly he was referring to his statement from early January 1991, in which he promised, "If we must suffer the first blow, whether at the front or here in Baghdad, and whether or not Israel participates directly in the aggression, they will suffer the second [blow] in Tel Aviv."[14] And in fact, the day after the coalition launched its air campaign, the first Iraqi Scud missiles landed in Israel.

At any rate, as late as mid-February 1991, Iraqi leaders, such as Deputy Prime Minister Sa'dun Hammadi, continued to publicize their doctrine of strategic reciprocity.[15] And in 1995, Tariq Aziz affirmed that strategic reciprocity was the basis for Iraq's war plan: "Even before the Gulf war our leadership decided: As long as the enemy uses conventional weapons, we will stick to them, too. However, if nuclear weapons had been used against Iraq, our military had the order: Use any weapons you have got, including chemical and biological combat agents."[16] The doctrine was adopted because Iraq believed it could win the war conventionally. As one observer put it, Iraq tried "to threaten using unconventional weapons in order to allow a conventional war it hoped to be able to win or to prevail in long enough."[17]

Once Saddam realized, by the second week of the war, that the United States was delaying its ground war, Iraq tried to force the United States to hasten the attack by turning to its favorite strategy of terrorist deterrence and threatening to resort to unconventional arms. "If the high-altitude bombings against Iraq are not stopped," warned Abd al-Amir al-Anbari, Iraqi ambassador to the United Nations, "we would have no choice but to resort to weapons of mass destruction."[18] This threat, however, came only after the attempt to draw Israel into the war, via the firing of conventionally tipped Scuds there, had failed. The Iraqis then thought their solid terrorist deterrent image would infuse credibility into the threat and force Bush's hand. Even if the contradiction between the two positions — the reciprocity doctrine and the threat to use mass destruction weapons first — was recognized in Baghdad, it was ostensibly viewed as nonproblematic given that the net result of this contradiction would be greater ambiguity over Iraq's true intentions. Undoubtedly the Iraqis hoped that the uncertainty about their plans would benefit their dual goal of deterring the United States from using unconventional munitions and compelling Washington to stop the strategic bombing campaign and begin the ground offensive.

Saddam probably never meant to carry out the threat of using mass destruction weapons if the United States did not cease its aerial assault, presumably because he was convinced that this would play into American hands. The threat was, therefore, nothing but a bluff. It was issued by a relatively low-level representative of the Iraqi government and never repeated, ostensibly out of concern that it might have jeopardized the unbroken credibility of Saddam's terrorist deterrence. Equally important, Saddam was positive that he had devised the optimal strategy to win the engagement conventionally. As a measure of his confidence, it may be recalled that Saddam never wavered from his maximalist position on Kuwait, even though he was offered numerous political payoffs. The United States expected that even a cosmetic gesture from the Iraqis would have triggered a "nightmare scenario" — splintering Bush's painstakingly built coalition.[19] Saddam, however, did not budge. He simply refused to negotiate any surrender of Iraq's sovereignty over all of Kuwait; to him, Kuwait had ceased to exist on August 2, 1990. Only if the bombings had undercut Iraq's ability to inflict deaths on the Americans would he have changed his mind. If anything, the U.S. conduct of the war must have only served to solidify his belief in Iraq's eventual success: "O brothers, O people: Note how those who feared a ground battle have now avoided the showdown for over a month. . . . They are doing this . . . to cover up their inability to confront our land forces in southern Iraq."[20]

For Saddam, the real test of his strategy would come only when the two armies slugged it out with conventional weapons, as in some of the big ground battles of the Iran-Iraq war. As the ground offensive approached, the Iraqis used deception to convince the United States of their readiness for CW, in order to force the coalition to wage a *conventional* "mother of all battles." In late February "allied officials" could report that "in recent days" Iraq had moved large quantities of 130-millimeter chemical shells to the front.[21] U.S. intelligence also detected possible Iraqi chemical preparations, including the movement of 11 trucks from the Samarra chemical weapons plant, located 60 kilometers northwest of Baghdad.[22] On February 22, General Norman Schwarzkopf received a report indicating that "Iraq's leaders were telling their troops to prepare for chemical warfare because the Americans are going to use chemicals against them. This is the same technique they used in the Iran war when they used chemicals."[23] Another report said that Iraqi troops were authorized to use chemical weapons at their discretion.[24]

The Absence of Chemical and Biological Warfare

The question remains as to why Saddam did not resort to mass destruction weapons even during the last stages of the war. When the ground war finally began on February 24, Iraq's defenses quickly crumbled, and the road to Baghdad was cleared. Saddam must have realized that his strategy to win the conflict had failed and that instead of a political victory the conventional war would result in a decisive Iraqi military defeat. Even if the BW option was reserved exclusively for last-resort circumstances, like a U.S. push toward Baghdad, why did Saddam not employ mustard gas, for instance, to block the advancing allied columns? There is certainly no question that at the time of the Gulf War, Iraq possessed a large cache of readily deployable chemical weapons. Aside from the Scud warheads and aerial bombs mentioned in Chapter 2, in the years since the war the United Nations has supervised the destruction of more than 38,000 munitions capable of carrying, or actually filled with, chemical agents.[25] Were the original orders — to maintain strategic reciprocity — upheld even though this strategy proved disastrous? Or had new orders been issued but for some reason not carried out?

A variety of theories have been offered as to why Iraq refrained from using chemical weapons tactically. One possible explanation is that Saddam was constantly fed misinformation about the war by at least some of his top generals. Such practices had been used previously by some Arab commanders, most prominently during past Arab-Israeli wars, and it is not inconceivable that they were repeated in Iraq.[26] More important, during the Iran-Iraq war, Iraqi commanders had been reluctant to question Saddam's authority despite his lack of a military background.[27] Saddam was known to have executed senior Iraqi army officers who, in his words, "did not undertake their responsibilities" during the Iran-Iraq war.[28] By the time operation Desert Storm was launched, it was widely reported that Lt. Gen. Nizar Khazraji, chief of staff of the Iraqi army, had been removed because Saddam was angry that key aspects of the invasion into Kuwait had gone awry.[29] Such an environment was hardly conducive to reporting bad news. It would not be surprising, then, if the Iraqi leader had been provided with rosy reports about Iraqi progress until late in the war.[30]

Others have pointed out a variety of operational constraints that, they allege, could have prevented Iraq from using CW on the battlefield. U.S.

military experts, for example, cited the deterioration of the chemical munitions during the months of the prewar embargo. It was said that most of the nerve gas Iraq possessed deteriorates markedly after 30 to 45 days. Therefore, Iraq probably waited as long as possible before filling chemical munitions.

Other operational arguments centered on the destruction by allied bombers of hundreds of artillery pieces, which was the main way to fire chemical weapons once Iraq's air force had been neutralized. Further, even if poison gas had reached Iraqi troops at or near the front, it was said, many battalion or battery commanders might never have received the orders to use these weapons because communications with headquarters were so disrupted by the relentless air attacks.[31] Captured Iraqi prisoners of war said that most of the units had inadequate protection against chemical weapons — in some cases not even gas masks — and thus could not engage in CW.[32] There were also suggestions that the fast-paced U.S. advance, along with unfavorable wind conditions, may have prevented the Iraqis from resorting to CW. It was said, for example, that on February 24, during a decisive phase in the battle, a sudden shift in winds rendered Iraq's use of CW improbable. Had the Iraqis proceeded to use chemical munitions, they would have simply ended up contaminating themselves.[33]

Gen. Maurice Schmitt, chief of staff of the French Armed Forces, even asserted that Iraq failed to use chemical weapons probably because "his generals refused to carry out Saddam Hussein's orders." According to Schmitt, the generals knew that they would be "violating international commitments" made by their country and that they would therefore be running "some risks." He maintained that the Iraqi generals were also reluctant to endanger their troops, "given the certain reactions which would come" if they resorted to CW.[34]

In reality, the reason for Iraq's failure to use chemical weapons might have been altogether different. Lt. Gen. Thomas Kelly, chief of operations for the U.S. Joint Chiefs of Staff, confirmed that U.S. forces had not found any stockpiles of chemical weapons behind Iraqi lines in Kuwait or southern Iraq.[35] The Saudi commander, General Khaled, asserted flatly that "no stock of chemical weapons were issued to Iraqi forces in the field."[36] During the cease-fire talks held at Safwan, Iraq, on March 3, 1991, Lt. Gen. Sultan Hashim Ahmad, the Iraqi deputy chief of staff, told General Schwarzkopf that Iraq never deployed any chemical weapons or other weapons of mass destruction in Kuwait.[37] Indeed, the Pentagon has stated that "the reason chemical weapons were not used during the war was that they were not made available to the Iraqi troops."[38]

This would tend to indicate that Saddam had been so certain of his conventional war strategy that he made sure none of his commanders could possibly interfere with it by deciding to use mass destruction weapons on his own.[39] The Iraqi leader was sure that the United States, not wishing to repeat its fatal mistake of Vietnam, would seek to use unconventional arms to avoid a humiliating political defeat. In Vietnam, the United States had probably been dissuaded from doing so by the specter of a Soviet, and possibly Chinese, response. But in the Gulf, Saddam stood alone. He estimated that the United States had deployed unconventional munitions to the conflict zone. As Tariq Aziz told Secretary Baker during their meeting in Geneva on January 9, "I assure you we know exactly what [weapons] you've moved to the area."[40]

On the one hand, Saddam had to deter Washington from turning to these weapons, so he threatened to use his own mass destruction arsenal. Former British Prime Minister Edward Heath, in testimony to the U.S. Congress on December 20, 1990, quoted statements made to him by Saddam at a meeting in October. According to Heath, Saddam said: "If the going gets hard then the British and the Americans will use atomic weapons against me, and chances are that Israel will as well, and the only thing I've got are chemical and biological weapons, and I shall have to use them. I have no alternative."[41] He announced his doctrine of strategic reciprocity and took steps to convince the United States of Iraq's readiness for CBW.

On the other hand, he also had to assure that Washington would be given no pretext to use unconventional weapons. Therefore, his troops were not to be issued any chemical munitions. If the battle turned against him, he figured, he still had the option of launching strategic mass destruction strikes against Israeli or Saudi cities. In short, in Saddam's mind the probability that the United States would have to turn to mass destruction weapons in order to avoid defeat was greater than the likelihood that Iraq would be so required. By the time Saddam had realized his mistake, it was simply too late. The allied air campaign made it difficult to issue chemical munitions to the troops. Furthermore, the fast-paced advance of the U.S. ground forces quickly rendered impractical any effort to reequip the front-line Iraqi units for CW. Besides, Saddam knew he still had the option of using mass destruction weapons strategically to stop the war.

If this scenario is true, however, then what prevented Saddam from resorting to *strategic* CW attacks? Why did he not dispatch Iraqi planes to drop chemical bombs on Saudi or Israeli cities, or order the launching of chemically tipped Scuds aimed at those targets? In the case of Israel it may be possible to speculate, as some Israeli officials have done, that Saddam was fearful of a possible Israeli nuclear response. Even if we accept this argument for the moment, it remains a puzzle why Saddam avoided hitting Saudi cities with chemical weapons.

At first glance, two other theories may seem more helpful in explaining Saddam's restraint. First, it has been argued that operational difficulties may have also hindered Iraq with regard to strategic CW. For example, the two French officers who were part of the U.N. mission to monitor Iraq's chemical capability wrote that Iraq's preferred delivery vehicle, in view of the volume of available agent, was obviously the airplane. This, they argued, could explain why chemical weapons were not used by the Iraqis during the Gulf operations, given that the Iraqi planes were grounded from the start by allied air operations. Other Iraqi planes—like the Su-24 *Fencer*, a highly capable all-weather low-flying fighter-bomber capable of delivering a 3-ton bombload a distance of 1,300 kilometers using external fuel tanks, which could have reached Israel without refueling—were transferred to Iran during the early stages of the war (and as of 1998 had not been returned).[42]

Moreover, they observed, the Scud's chemical warhead, because of its design, did not seem capable of withstanding the rise in temperature linked to the missile's reentry into the atmosphere.[43] Other experts, however, reached the opposite conclusion. John Gee, the head of one of the U.N. inspection teams sent to Iraq, reported that the Iraqis were "perfectly capable of launching" 30 Scud missiles fitted with chemical warheads filled with nerve agent, and these weapons were "technically capable of exploding on impact."[44] He speculated that one reason why Iraq did not launch its chemically tipped Scud missiles during the war might have been difficulty in moving the warheads from their storage sites, due to the allied air campaign. Among other targets, the allied planes attacked highways, bridges, and railways, which could have prevented Iraq from transporting any of its chemical stock.[45]

A second, widely accepted theory has downplayed the role of operational constraints in Iraq's decision making. Instead, it asserts, Saddam did not execute his strategic chemical, or for that matter biological, threat because of stern U.S. warnings. The CIA, in its "Report on Intelligence Related to Gulf War Illnesses," has stated: "We assess that Iraq probably did not use these [CB] weapons because of a perceived threat of overwhelming Coalition retaliation." President Bush, for example, had informed Saddam in a letter dated January 5, 1991, that if Iraq resorted to mass destruction weapons, the consequences for Iraq would be frightful.[46] The warnings could have been viewed as an implicit threat that the United States would respond with weapons of mass destruction, possibly nuclear ones.

This hypothesis has recently been confirmed by the Iraqis themselves. According to Rolf Ekeus, Iraq's failure to use biological weapons was directly linked to Washington's deterrent messages: "We [UNSCOM] are told [by the Iraqis] that they were afraid of a nuclear riposte by the Americans," he said.[47] Aziz may have indirectly verified this interpretation in a 1995 interview. Asked whether Iraq expected the United States to use nuclear weapons during the war, Aziz responded by saying: "This was part of our strategic calculations. That is why we had given special instructions" to Iraqi forces to respond with mass destruction weapons.[48] He was even more explicit subsequently, strongly implying that the U.S. deterrent had been effective: "We did not think it was wise to use them [chemical weapons]. . . . To use such kinds of weapons in such kind of war with such kind of an enemy."[49]

The notion that Iraq was deterred from strategic use of chemical or biological weapons because of U.S. warnings may be comforting. Nevertheless, there are five weighty reasons to doubt its veracity.

1. *The difficulty of deterring last-resort use.* Deterring a desperate enemy armed with mass destruction weapons is akin to stopping a determined suicide bomber. Why would Saddam care about the nature or severity of the promised punishment if he was convinced that his end was looming anyhow? Because of the near-total identification between the Iraqi regime and the person of Saddam Hussein, there was little doubt in the Iraqi leader's mind that his ouster was key to the U.S. plans to contain Baghdad. This is why he prepared last-resort weapons ahead of time. Moreover, both U.S. and Israeli intelligence assessed that CB attacks were all but assured if Iraq was defeated and Saddam believed that his rule was on the brink of collapse. It is simply illogical to predict, on the one hand, that Saddam would use mass destruction weapons as a *last resort*, while asserting, on the other hand, that his refraining from CBW indicates that Iraq was deterred. It is more likely that the war ended before Saddam felt that he was backed against a wall.

2. *The nature of the U.S. warning.* Officially Washington never issued a clear-cut nuclear warning to Baghdad. Further, the explanations provided by former Bush administration officials, which may be taken as implicitly supporting Baghdad's claim, were not unconnected to political agendas. These officials would probably maintain that the ambiguity Washington wrapped around the issue actually worked to deter Saddam. But precisely

what kind of ambiguity was Saddam noticing—the calculated vagueness, or the inadvertent ambiguity caused by infighting in the Bush administration? And did the inadvertent ambiguity act to buttress the official ambiguity, or did it detract from it?

In his memoirs, General Schwarzkopf writes that he and Gen. Colin Powell, then chair of the Joint Chiefs of Staff, held a telephone conversation on December 9, 1990, in which the two discussed the issue of a declaratory policy with regard to retaliation against biological or chemical attack: "The chairman said he was pressing the White House to inform Tariq Aziz that we would use our unconventional weapons if the Iraqis use chemicals on us. The chairman believed that Secretary of State Baker would deliver this message to the Iraqi foreign minister."[50]

Yet the question of proper U.S. response to Iraq's use of mass destruction weapons remained unresolved through the end of the war. For example, General Powell's account of the warning to Saddam is at variance with that of General Schwarzkopf. Powell makes it clear that when he spoke of "unconventional" response by the United States to an Iraqi mass destruction attack, he meant hitting exceptional targets, not using unconventional munitions. Still, the United States had to be prepared for Saddam's worst impulses. On January 15, the day that the U.N. Security Council had set as the deadline for Saddam to withdraw from Kuwait, Powell began drafting a warning to Saddam, which said: "Only conventional weapons will be used in strict accordance with the Geneva Convention and commonly accepted rules of warfare." If, however, Iraq used mass destruction weapons, the United States would "destroy your merchant fleet, destroy your railroad infrastructure, destroy your port facilities, destroy your highway system, destroy your oil facilities, destroy your airline infrastructure." Moreover, Powell recounts, he kept the worst threat to the end—one that he admits was a pure bluff: "If driven to it . . . we would destroy the dams on the Tigris and Euphrates rivers and flood Baghdad, with horrendous consequences."[51] Although the message was not cleared in time to be delivered to Aziz, Powell writes, it was circulated, and its meaning "was not lost on our side."[52]

Secretary of State Baker was not among those who adhered to General Powell's approach. Baker reports that although Powell asked him to deliver a warning "in the bluntest possible terms," he preferred a policy of "calculated ambiguity" over the matter. Accordingly, Baker recounts telling Aziz: "If the conflict involves your use of chemical or biological weapons against our forces, the American people will demand vengeance. We have the means to exact it. If there is any use of weapons like that, our objective won't just be the liberation of Kuwait, but the elimination of the current regime in Baghdad, and anyone responsible for using those weapons would be held accountable." Baker adds that he "purposely left the impression that use of chemical or biological agents by Iraq would invite tactical nuclear retaliation," but he does not elaborate on how he thinks he conveyed this notion.[53]

The message eventually transmitted to the Iraqis was therefore a watered-down version of what Schwarzkopf, or even Powell, had in mind, and one that deliberately avoided mention of any use of unconventional weapons as an American response to Iraq's use of mass destruction arms. Indeed, Baker's warning that the U.S. war objectives would expand if Iraq resorted to CBW could not have deterred Saddam, for the Iraqi leader was already sure that the moment war started, the United States would launch attacks on strategic targets inside Iraqi territory, including in Baghdad itself (see Chapter 3). Saddam could have even suspected that the United States was laying a trap. The Americans might have been trying to assure that Iraq would not use mass destruction weapons by pretending that the United States intended to conduct a limited war.

The ambiguity of the U.S. position on the proper response to Iraq's use of mass destruction weapons was as much a result of the conflicting stands within the Bush administration as it was part of a calculated policy. Press reports, for example, stated that U.S. military leaders had decided not to resort to unconventional weapons even in retaliation against an Iraqi use of chemical or biological weapons.[54] CIA Director William Webster even told the *Washington Post* in December that the United States was confident in its massive conventional capability in the region and that the use of unconventional munitions would introduce a new dimension that might carry heavy costs in future relationships with countries in the region. White House Chief of Staff John Sununu found it prudent at one point to give assurance that there was no likelihood that the United States would resort to tactical nuclear weapons.[55]

Some Israeli observers suspected that this ambiguity was evidence of Washington's indecisiveness and reluctance to use unconventional weapons against Iraq even if the need arose. When Secretary of Defense Richard Cheney seemingly endorsed an Israeli nuclear retaliation to an Iraqi mass destruction attack, these Israeli observers asked whether "the United States expected Israel to do the dirty work in the Gulf war. . . . If the United States wishes to make threats about employing nuclear means in reaction, it should speak in first person singular."[56] Could Saddam have reached a similar skeptical assessment?

If he did, then how is it possible to explain General al-Samarra'i's assertion that Saddam took the U.S. warnings to mean that the "allies would nuke him" if Iraq employed mass destruction weapons?[57] From the outset, Saddam's approach to the war, especially his threats to use mass destruction weapons in order to deter the United States from using unconventional arms, implied that he believed that the United States was well disposed toward using such weapons in certain circumstances. He could not conceive of a country's waging war without employing all the means at its disposal to secure a victory or deny one to the enemy. The American use of atomic bombs on Hiroshima and Nagasaki during World War II made a lasting impression in this respect. Although Baghdad publicly condemned the bombings, it is safe to assume that Saddam admired the action. On June 26, 1990, he told Karen Elliott House of the *Wall Street Journal* that the killing of "civilian men, women and children" in the Iran-Iraq war was no different than the bombings of Hiroshima and Nagaski, where "whole cities were wiped out." In fact, in response to the U.S. condemnation of Iraq's use of poison gas in the war with Iran, the Iraqi foreign ministry was openly indignant: "The United States may be the last country with the right to speak about morals. It is the only country that used atomic weapons, destroying Hiroshima and Nagasaki during World War II with the pretext of reducing the war's duration and the number of victims."[58] Of all countries, the United States should have been the staunchest supporter for the Iraqi action, Baghdad protested.

Naturally, Saddam assumed, well before Washington delivered its ultimatum, that he needed to deter the United States from using nuclear weapons in the coming war. In this respect, the U.S. warnings were, at best, irrelevant. At worst, Saddam could have noticed the bickering within the administration and begun to question his own notion of the American disposition toward nuclear attack.

But even if Saddam's perception — that the Americans were inclined to resort to nuclear weapons — was based on the Hiroshima and Nagasaki bombings and not on the U.S. warnings, couldn't this American inclination still have helped dissuade Saddam from using CBW? If this is true, it could be argued that the use of atomic weapons in Japan not only saved American lives there but also might have spared the lives of countless inhabitants of the Middle East, and possibly those of U.S. soldiers, by deterring Iraq from employing mass destruction weapons during the Gulf War. Owing to the next three reasons, however, this scenario is not very likely.

3. *The failure of similar U.S. warnings.* If the U.S. nuclear threat was

effective in deterring Iraq from resorting to mass destruction weapons, how can it be explained that equally harsh warnings failed demonstrably? In his letter to Saddam, for example, President Bush warned not just against Iraq's use of CBW. He wrote: "Let me state, too, that the United States will not tolerate the use of chemical or biological weapons or the destruction of Kuwait's oil fields and installations. . . . The American people would demand the strongest possible response. You and your country will pay a terrible price if you order unconscionable acts of this sort."[59] Bush did not distinguish between the offenses, threatening the same "terrible" consequences for all of them. Baker used similarly strong language during his meeting with Aziz in Geneva. And yet Saddam proceeded to demolish most of Kuwait's oil wells, beginning on February 21, 1991.

Saddam also attacked Israeli population centers, despite the stern warning of both the United States and Israel. Israel had even promised overwhelming retaliation if attacked. Nevertheless, beginning on January 18, 1991, Iraq launched a systematic campaign of missile attacks on Israel, which lasted virtually until the end of the war and, with a few exceptions, deliberately targeted Israeli cities (Map 2). In fact, Saddam must have known that he would be taking an extraordinary risk in attacking cities, as the targeting of civilians was considered an especially grievous offense in both Washington and Jerusalem. Yet not only did the Iraqi propaganda machine highlight the attacks, but it practicably suggested that poison gas might be used against Israeli civilians as well.[60]

4. *Iraq's preparations for nuclear war.* Saddam's preoccupation with the threat of a nuclear attack grew along with his determination to acquire nuclear weapons. Early on, he inferred that the acquisition of nuclear weapons was a sine qua non for realizing his political vision.[61] Whether he intended to launch a nuclear attack or deter one, by the time Iraq invaded Kuwait, Saddam had spent ten years planning for nuclear war.

As early as 1979, two years before the Osiraq attack, Iraq had begun construction of numerous tunnels capable of concealing Scud missiles and their launchers.[62] Iraq also purchased mobile launchers for its Scud missile force in an effort to increase its survivability. During the Iran-Iraq war, the Iraqis took full advantage of the U.S. "tilt" toward them to advance their scheme. In 1982, an Iraqi military delegation visited one Belgian air base and one NATO air base in the Federal Republic of Germany.[63] That June, Iraq awarded the Belgian company Six Construct International (Sixco) a $380 million contract to supervise the construction of eight hardened air bases "to stricter standards than those demanded by NATO."[64] According to one source, the "aim of this extravagant program, code-named Project

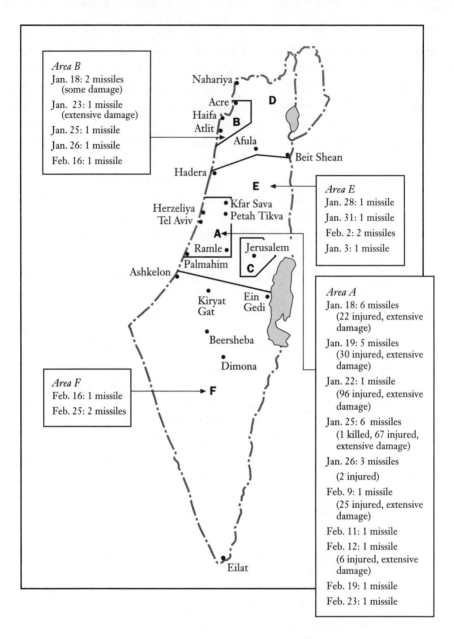

Area B
Jan. 18: 2 missiles
    (some damage)
Jan. 23: 1 missile
    (extensive damage)
Jan. 25: 1 missile
Jan. 26: 1 missile
Feb. 16: 1 missile

Nahariya
Acre
Haifa
Atlit
B
D
Afula
Beit Shean
Hadera
E

Area E
Jan. 28: 1 missile
Jan. 31: 1 missile
Feb. 2: 2 missiles
Jan. 3: 1 missile

Herzeliya
Tel Aviv
Kfar Sava
Petah Tikva
A
Ramle
Jerusalem
Palmahim
C
Ashkelon
Ein Gedi
Kiryat Gat
Beersheba
Dimona

Area F
Feb. 16: 1 missile
Feb. 25: 2 missiles
F

Area A
Jan. 18: 6 missiles
    (22 injured, extensive damage)
Jan. 19: 5 missiles
    (30 injured, extensive damage)
Jan. 22: 1 missile
    (96 injured, extensive damage)
Jan. 25: 6 missiles
    (1 killed, 67 injured, extensive damage)
Jan. 26: 3 missiles
    (2 injured)
Feb. 9: 1 missile
    (25 injured, extensive damage)
Feb. 11: 1 missile
Feb. 12: 1 missile
    (6 injured, extensive damage)
Feb. 19: 1 missile
Feb. 23: 1 missile

Eilat

Map 2. A summary of Iraq's Scud attacks on Israel. Data from *Jerusalem Post International Edition*, March 9, 1991.

505, was to bury Iraq's advanced warplanes in . . . hardened anti-nuclear bases 50 meters below ground."[65] Five of the bases were located east of Baghdad, four on the Iranian border and the fifth on the Syrian border. The other three were facing Saudi Arabia. In all, some 300 aircraft shelters were constructed under those air bases.[66] The Zurich-based company Luwa AG installed filters against chemical attack and nuclear fallout in these installations.[67]

Over the next four years, Sixco built a total of 17 air bases in Iraq. Military sources in Baghdad said that these facilities, along with vital industrial plants, were also protected against electromagnetic pulses (EMP).[68] But there was more. Every government building in Baghdad was to be equipped with an underground bunker. The Iraqi Air Force Headquarters in Baghdad, for example, reportedly had a bunker designed to protect against the effects of an air burst of a 250-kiloton nuclear weapon, and against chemical and bacteriological weapons.[69] British companies submitted designs for enough underground bunkers to shelter 48,000 soldiers. These bunkers included facilities for a "long stay," including decontamination rooms.[70]

It was estimated that during its eight-year war with Iran, Iraq spent more than $2.5 billion on its strategic shelter program, "despite the lack of any clear threat from the Iranian air force."[71] Clearly, Saddam was making preparations to fight in an NBC environment long before Washington issued any warnings toward Baghdad. And these preparations were made before he had come to believe that Iraq could deter an Israeli nuclear attack through the introduction of binary chemical weapons and long-range delivery systems.

The publicity given by Iraq to its readiness against a nuclear attack prior to the onset of the Gulf War is also indicative of Saddam's mindset. In mid-December 1990, for example, Iraq's head of public security announced that the citizens of Baghdad and other major Iraqi cities would be evacuated in case of a nuclear, chemical, or bacterial attack launched by the United States or Israel.[72] The Iraqi press even published instructions to citizens in case of a nuclear attack.[73] On the eve of the war, Saddam claimed that he had issued instructions for any evacuation of Baghdad to be completed within 48 hours.[74] Even if these pronouncements were part of a propaganda campaign, they indicate the persistent preoccupation of Saddam with the nuclear scenario. His message to Washington was that the use of nuclear weapons would be futile, as Iraq had already prepared for such an eventuality.

5. *Iraq's terrorist deterrence.* The final reason to downplay the effect of the

U.S. nuclear warnings has to do with Saddam's belief in the effectiveness of his terrorist deterrence. Saddam was certain that the United States would not resort to nuclear weapons because Washington was perfectly aware that such a step entailed disastrous consequences.

In principle, the adoption of terrorist deterrence as a basic doctrine is a risky undertaking because it forbids, almost by definition, backing down in the face of a formidable foe. Such a retreat would call into question the central idea of this strategy, which is designed to defeat a superior enemy through projecting what the West would call an irrational readiness for a "fight to the death." Terrorist deterrence is a gamble that what the enemy is willing to pay for its victory is less than the cost that the "terrorist deterrer" would exact before being destroyed.

Given this strategy, recoiling in the face of a threat would have a heavy price. It could suggest that the posture of terrorist deterrence was just a facade. It could even entail a heavy political cost domestically because, in the case of Iraq, the legitimacy of the regime rested on the intimidation of its own subjects.[75]

In fact, although the world's attention was mostly focused on Iraq's military buildup on the Kuwaiti front, it was the deterrence of a U.S. resort to unconventional weapons that was viewed in Baghdad as an absolute must for a political victory over America. It is improbable that Saddam would have gone to war unless he thought he could deter the U.S. nuclear option. To think otherwise is to risk misunderstanding all of Saddam's strategy in the Gulf crisis as well as his general political vision. The fact that he never retrenched on Kuwait, and finally took on the United States alone, certainly indicates that he felt assured of neutralizing the U.S. nuclear option.

Such an assertion might sound odd. Can it be seriously suggested that Saddam, the leader of a developing nation of 17 million people, thought that he could deter the premier superpower of the world from resorting to nuclear weapons? Or, for that matter, how can it be said that Saddam predicated his strategy on forcing Washington to engage in a conventional battle, even if the tide went against the United States?

There is no question that Saddam could not compete with the United States in weaponry and destructive power. The United States might have solved the problem of an Iraqi chemical attack on its troops through protective suits and antidotes to poison gas. Saddam might have even believed that vaccinations had eliminated the threat of BW to the American soldiers. But his judgment that he could deter the United States from nuclear weapons had another basis. He knew that the United States did not have a solution for his tactic of holding Israeli and Saudi population centers at the mercy of mass destruction attacks. This was his original message to Ambassador Glaspie even before he went into Kuwait. On that occasion he ominously spoke of being able to offset Iraq's inability to threaten the United States directly, by holding hostage its regional interests. And every Scud that fell inside Israel or Saudi Arabia fueled the ominous notion of a CB attack on the civilian population centers there.

Moreover, the Iraqis took care to spread rumors that they might use chemical or bacteriological weapons in terrorist attacks around the world. Saddam also threatened terrorism during the meeting with Glaspie: "We know that you can harm us. But we too can harm you. Everyone can cause harm according to their ability and their size. We cannot come all the way to you in the United States, but individual Arabs can reach you."[76]

Clearly, the Iraqis estimated that the U.S. military lacked a solution to this covert threat of terrorism. When asked, a month into the crisis, whether Iraq rejected terrorism, Tariq Aziz replied: "That depends on the Western world's attitude. If it declares war on us, our obligations toward it end." If the West were to threaten the "Arab people with genocide," Aziz continued, "I am free of any moral obligations toward the French, American, or British governments." He wondered: "Why should I worry about France's stability, if it sends its warships to bomb Iraq and kill Iraqis?"[77] As the war drew nearer, the threats became more explicit. On January 7, in a speech carried over Baghdad Radio, Saddam warned that Iraq's battle would extend over the "whole world," involving "every struggler and fighter whose hand can reach out to harm . . . [the] aggressors."

Soon after the war broke out, Iraqi officials began talking of a "secret weapon," which they might unleash. The Arab press reported that this was a reference to a "network of secret agents in Europe" prepared to use chemical and biological weapons in attacks across the continent. "Their targets have been defined: airports and airline offices, plants, schools, trains and railroad lines, oil refineries and even hospitals in which the wounded [from the Gulf] will be undergoing treatment."[78] To make sure this message was widely disseminated, terrorist threats were made against several European mass media organizations, like the BBC.

Ample evidence indicates that the Iraqi terrorist threat of mass destruction was regarded as highly credible. Even before the war, for example, "security experts" from West Germany were quoted in the press as doubting that Iraq had sufficient facilities to mass-produce biological weapons. Instead, they said, there is "the fear that the worldwide terrorist attacks announced by Saddam might not only be bomb attacks. One or two liters of anthrax spores, sprinkled in the subway networks of the big cities of New York, Paris, Berlin, or Frankfurt-am-Main, could infect millions of people."[79] Indeed, in 1989 U.S. intelligence had estimated that the chances were 50–50 that international terrorists would escalate to the use of poison gas against mass targets "within the next two years." L. Paul Bremmer, then director of the U.S. State Department's office of counterterrorism, noted that terrorists could fill a five-gallon jerry can with nerve or mustard gas, wrap it with detonator cord, and "set it off at an airport, seaport or hotel lobby."[80] Although this assessment did not specifically refer to Iraq or to the United States, the terrorist threats from Baghdad must have been viewed in Washington as confirmation of its dire prophecy.

Once the crisis in the Gulf had erupted, the CIA warned: "We cannot rule out that Iraq may have contingency plans to use biological agents covertly."[81] According to the CIA,

> Iraq could attack targets out of range of even its missiles by using special forces, civilian government agents, or foreign terrorists to hand-deliver biological or chemical agents clandestinely. Even in regions within range of Iraq's bombers and missiles that might be the most effective way to attack specific sites with such weapons. . . . Even before it invaded Kuwait, Baghdad had been cultivating a number of Palestinian terrorist groups, including several — such as the Abu Nidal Organization and the PFLP–General Command — with operational capabilities in numerous countries especially in Europe. Already some of these terrorist groups have publicly volunteered to attack U.S. targets on behalf of Iraq.[82]

It was repeatedly pointed out that such BW agents as botulinum toxin and, to a lesser degree, anthrax bacteria, "lend themselves to covert dissemination" because even small amounts placed in water or food supplies are "sufficient to kill large numbers of people." The difficulty in distinguishing between a naturally occurring epidemic and covert dissemination "could provide sufficient cover for Iraq to use BW without suffering retaliation."[83] Whereas botulinum toxin was especially suitable to "terrorize large population centers," anthrax spores could be used "to considerable advantage for covertly attacking air fields and aircraft carriers either preemptively or during hostilities."[84] The easy transportability of these agents "also offers Saddam the prospect of covertly delivering — through terrorist or special forces personnel — biological weapons on targets in almost any country."[85]

These two elements, then — Iraq's ability to target Israeli and Saudi population centers, and the specter of Iraqi-sponsored mass destruction terrorist attacks across Europe and the United States — were the two halves of a strategy of terrorist deterrence designed to keep the United States from using unconventional weapons. By relying on his overt capability for CW via SSMs, Saddam could try and stop the U.S. military from advancing on Baghdad by threatening Israel strategically, knowing that the Iraqi covert CB option would dissuade a U.S. nuclear punishment. Indeed, because Iraqi-sponsored worldwide CB terrorism could be unleashed even after Saddam's regime had been obliterated, a U.S. nuclear riposte for an Iraqi CB attack on Israel would be a senseless act.

Alternatively, if the United States planned on using tactical nuclear weapons to extricate itself from a conventional quagmire, it would find itself facing similar dilemmas. Washington could not be sure that Israel would not suffer an Iraqi CB retaliation, or that its European allies would be spared the nightmare of covert mass destruction attacks. Such covert attacks could even be directed against U.S. territory per se, precisely as Saddam had warned.

Saddam could see the seriousness with which his mass destruction threats were taken. Israeli citizens and U.S. soldiers were all carrying gas masks. Every Scud attack on Israel was checked for CB agents before the all clear was sounded. Even in the United States, many civilians felt that the Iraqi threats of CB terrorism were serious enough to warrant the purchase of gas masks. "After seeing others in the Middle East prepare for chemical warfare, [many Americans] too felt they needed to be ready. Saddam Hussein was thus able to generate a level of fear and anxiety over terrorism that had been unmatched in the history of this nation."[86] Indeed, it has been reported that the day the war began, President Bush was "accompanied by a secret service agent who held a gas mask in a green military bag. . . . [It was] the day's most ominous image."[87] Under these circumstances, and given Iraq's prime interest in forcing a conventional fight, there was little incentive for Iraq to actually resort to CB terrorism. Indeed, it appears that the Iraqi threat of launching mass destruction terrorism was a successful ruse.[88]

As a measure of his confidence in terrorist deterrence, Saddam rarely stayed at any of his five nuclear-resistant bunkers during the war.[89] Obviously, he did not expect a nuclear attack. Instead, Saddam's command centers were to be found in small houses in residential areas. As General al-Samarra'i observed, "He reckoned the allies would never deliberately attack civilian districts. He was using his own people as human shields."[90] It was precisely on the basis of such insight into the Western notions of morally repugnant actions that Saddam could be so sure about the effectiveness of his terrorist deterrence. He could even take on the vastly superior

United States by challenging the foundation of its global power—its nuclear might. As Aziz told Baker in Geneva: "You are an advanced country, and have moved tremendous weapons to our region. . . . We know the efficiency and the destructive power of each weapon [you moved to the area]. . . . I say this without arrogance . . . The present leadership will continue to lead Iraq now and in the future. Those who will disappear are not in Iraq, but some of your friends in the region."[91]

Iraq's claim that it was deterred from CBW by an American nuclear threat, then, cannot be taken at face value. Initially, Iraqi officials said that they viewed Bush's letter as a threat to overthrow Saddam's regime, not as a nuclear warning.[92] When asked about Iraq's reason for not using chemical weapons, captured Iraqi commanders gave an altogether different explanation. They contended that allied troops were better protected than their own, and thus the Iraqis would have suffered many more casualties in an exchange.[93] Incredibly, Brig. Gen. Richard Neil of the U.S. Marines said that prisoner debriefings had "yielded the impression that the Iraqis were not comfortable operating in a chemical environment." Lt. Gen. Thomas Kelly stated in a press briefing that "the Iraqi Army was very uncomfortable, we are finding out from POWs, about the use of chemical weapons because they are not familiar with it."[94]

Whatever the case, there are sufficient grounds to conclude that Iraq's new claim about the effectiveness of the U.S. nuclear threat is politically motivated. Baghdad is seeking to portray itself as a defensive power whose possession of mass destruction munitions is no cause for alarm, despite its record of having used such weapons. It maintains now that Iraq would have used mass destruction weapons only if the United States had used nuclear arms. With this claim Baghdad implies that it can be trusted with CB weapons. As Aziz told Secretary of State Baker, "We are a diligent, active government. We work hard, read, analyze and follow up."[95] Baghdad would have us believe that the people who rule Iraq fully comprehend the awesome power of mass destruction weapons, abide by the tenets of the Western deterrence doctrine, and are seeking simply to establish regional strategic stability. Iraq's retention of its BW cache even today serves this purpose of safeguarding the balance of powers in a volatile area. In turn, the U.S. insistence on Baghdad's revealing its mass destruction capability is also motivated by political considerations, not strategic need. Washington is carrying out a political vendetta against the Saddam Hussein regime for daring to stand up to the United States. It seeks to prevent the emergence of a new power pole in the Gulf region. As Aziz has put it: "Everything has been scrutinized by the inspectors [of UNSCOM] with a zeal that sometimes borders on the hysterical. In any event, we have opted for openness. And what have we got in return?"[96] By projecting an image of strategic responsibility, the Iraqis may be seeking to secure their remaining biological weapons, especially after UNSCOM had purportedly disarmed the bulk of Iraq's CW capability.[97] Under these circumstances, an impetuous embrace of the notion of a deterrable Iraq is likely to lead to a surprise the next time Saddam decides to redraw the Middle East map.

Missile Diplomacy Transformed

In Saddam's mind, threatening to strike cities in Saudi Arabia or Israel with mass destruction weapons was from the outset a last-resort option. It was part of a terrorist deterrence strategy to convince his opponents that an attempt to rid the world of the Saddam Hussein regime would carry a prohibitively high price and so should not be tried. In this sense, as long as the fighting did not threaten Saddam's political survival, the U.S. nuclear threat was superfluous. The chemical weaponry Saddam assembled to reach Israeli or Saudi cities, along with the biological weapons he readied for countercity strikes, was purposely kept in reserve. This strategic arsenal was meant to prevent only one scenario—a U.S. attempt to oust the Iraqi dictator. Only under such circumstances can an argument supporting the putative role of American deterrence be evaluated. Intelligence analysts, however, were in agreement that, if pressed to the wall, Saddam would resort to CBW regardless of the U.S. deterrent warnings.

Although much about Saddam's intentions is still unknown, the following picture can be pieced together from the publicly available sources. Once the war erupted, Saddam's missile diplomacy shifted from a means of deterrence to an instrument of compellence. He began firing Scud missiles at Israel in order to force the Israelis to enter the war. There should be no question that the Israeli card was carefully played to nullify America's strategy in the war, which, Saddam knew, would involve a sustained air campaign. This air assault could hamper Iraq's goal of achieving a political victory over the United States through the fighting of a protracted conventional ground war. Saddam calculated that once Israel joined the battle, the anti-Iraq coalition would disintegrate and the political legitimacy of the war would vanish. As a result, the United States would be forced to stop the war. Alternatively, the United States would be compelled to hasten its ground attack and suffer the high casualties and domestic political dissent that were envisaged in Baghdad. Either way, a stalemate would be forced on the United States through Iraq's firepower and brilliant leadership. The scenario, involving Israel, then, was conceived as an added assurance that Iraq would prevail in the conflict.

As embroiling Israel in the war was of considerable import, Baghdad acted promptly to magnify the provocation of its sneak attack through psychological warfare. After the first salvo of eight Scuds landed in Israel, Baghdad Radio declared: "These missiles poured out of the sky, making Tel Aviv and other targets a crematorium last night, the night of 18 January."[98] By obliquely referring to the Nazi extermination of Europe's Jews, the Iraqis were deliberately stirring fears of an imminent gas attack to force the Israelis into action.

Yet the Iraqis used only conventionally tipped Scuds in their attacks, even though two days earlier a spokesman for the IDF had stated that "an Iraqi chemical attack is more probable than a conventional one and it's in that vein that we've prepared our rearguard."[99] When asked why Iraq had withheld its chemical munitions against Israel, General al-Samarra'i admitted: "Some of the Scud missiles were loaded with chemical warheads. They were kept hidden throughout the war. We didn't use them because the other side [Israel] had a deterrent force."[100] This statement could be viewed as confirmation that Iraq was deterred by the threat of an Israeli resort to nuclear weapons. Such a conclusion would be premature, however. When Iraq fired the Scuds into Israel, its aim was to entangle Israel in the war conventionally, not to have the Israelis retaliate with mass destruction weapons. The Iraqi incentive to use CW against Israel at this stage of the war was simply nonexistent. Therefore, it is wrong to state categorically that the Israeli nuclear deterrent was effective. Rather, the chemically mounted Scuds that General al-Samarra'i describes were probably kept in reserve as part of Iraq's last-resort deterrent. After all, Saddam did attack Israel despite Prime Minister Yitzhak Shamir's warning that Iraq "will pay a terrible and a horrible price" for so doing — a formula that was viewed as an indirect reference to an Israeli nuclear retaliation.[101] Ironically, it was the Israeli warnings themselves, combined with the IDF's solid reputation for meting out the promised punishment, that probably served as an incentive for Saddam to attack. He was sure that Israel would respond to his aggression expeditiously and be drawn into the war.

The Iraqi effort to embroil Israel in the war peaked on February 16, at 2005 hours local time, when two Scuds landed in Israel. One of the missiles was evidently aimed at the Israeli nuclear plant in Dimona. Although the Scud carried a conventional warhead and the missile missed its target, the attack was carefully aimed at exerting maximum pressure on Israel and the United States. By threatening Israel's prime nuclear installation, Saddam was signaling that the war was about to escalate dramatically. He evidently sought to force Washington to advance its timetable for the ground war. But the attack also intensified the pressure on Israel to join the battle. Further, the targeting of Dimona was clearly meant to avenge the Israeli attack on the Osiraq reactor and to solidify Saddam's position of leadership in the Arab world. By striking at the symbol of Israel's technological and strategic superiority, Saddam was trying to prove that Iraq had reached strategic parity with the Israelis and that, as he had pledged several months earlier, the Arabs could not be "stepped upon" any longer.[102]

Baghdad Radio openly advertised the attack, and the excited Arab press immediately followed with accounts about the "severe damage" inflicted on Dimona.[103] Remarkably, Israel, in a break with its practice of identifying by code the areas where Scuds landed, openly admitted that an Iraqi Scud attack had been aimed at Dimona. Israel was apparently signaling to Washington that the conflict was about to take an ominous turn, which meant that the United States had to clean up the Scuds promptly or let the IDF do the job itself.[104] The bottom line is that both Iraq and Israel were engaged in some sort of "nuclear brinkmanship" vis-à-vis Washington.

On February 25, one day after the ground war had begun and as the extent of the rout became clearer in Baghdad, the role of the Scuds in Saddam's war strategy underwent a transformation yet again.[105] On that day, Iraq fired the last two Scuds on Israel. The first one hit at 0337 hours and the second at 0536 hours local time. Both missiles landed harmlessly in what was described as "an unpopulated area in the south of Israel."[106]

One of these Scuds — the second — attracted special attention. In a 1995 interview Israel's chief of staff, Lt. Gen. Amnon Shahak (who at the time of the Gulf War was chief of the IDF's Intelligence Branch), was asked his reaction to this missile, which had landed in Israel with "a warhead different from everything we had known: It was full of concrete and metal, and we can assume it was a primitive model of a biological warhead." General Shahak responded: "It is possible. I cannot be certain, but I believe that no one builds a warhead made of concrete just for fun. Concrete could contain several things, including biological matter."[107] Concrete, AMAN (Israeli military intelligence) thought, could be used to "protect the bugs inside."[108] That is, it could shield the warhead against the friction and heat generated during the missile's reentry into the atmosphere, which would otherwise destroy its BW payload well before it reached the target. Yet, because there have been no reports of Iraq's firing Scud missiles armed with mass destruction warheads against Israel, it can be safely assumed the warhead in question did not carry a payload. What, then, could be the rationale for the firing of this missile?

If this was indeed a model, or a simulant, of an Iraqi BW warhead, it may suggest that Saddam might have embarked on a last-ditch effort to draw Israel into the war, hoping that this would stop the fighting. It has been said that the concrete Scud was aimed at the Dimona nuclear reactor.[109] If so, Saddam could have calculated that if the conventional attacks on the reactor had failed to force Israel's hand, perhaps the threat of an Iraqi mass destruction strike on Dimona would do the trick. Under such circumstances, Saddam might have thought, Israel would have no choice but to go after the Scuds with or without U.S. approval. In fact, the Israeli press published a letter from Prime Minister Shamir to President Bush that had essentially committed Israel to such a course of action.[110]

Israeli analysts did indeed consider the possibility that Saddam was seeking to force Israel's hand. Accordingly, he could have calculated that an Israeli intervention would lead to a conflagration between Israel and Jordan, because the Israelis would probably have to cross Jordan's skies to get to western Iraq. Under such circumstances, they figured, Saddam could claim that he had to shift his military to the west to aid his sister country, and he could thus rescue his army from the Kuwaiti trap while avoiding the humiliation of ordering a retreat.[111]

There are, however, several problems with the view that the concrete-armed missile was aimed to force an Israeli intervention. First, Saddam had to believe that Israel would consider the warhead a harbinger of a biological attack. Israel would thus intervene in the war, but for Saddam's plan to work, Israel would have to use only its conventional forces, and the IDF would have to limit its operation to western Iraq. Second, Dimona would have been a dubious choice of target to provoke Israel into action. Assuming that Saddam sought to exert maximum pressure on Israel to intervene, he would have likely fired his missile at an urban target most vulnerable to CBW rather than a hardened strategic installation. Finally, if Saddam miscalculated and the Jordanians did not challenge the IDF, or if the coalition survived, the war could go on even after the Israeli army had deployed in western Iraq. The exercise would have produced a two-front situation, in which a new western front against Iraq would open just as its military was facing defeat in the east.

Therefore, another possibility is that the firing of this particular Scud at Israel was meant as a warning shot. Saddam knew that he was facing a decisive defeat on the battlefield, and the possibility that U.S. forces would advance on Baghdad must have suddenly looked quite real. As General al-Samarra'i recalled, Saddam "thought that his downfall was imminent. He asked me straight out 'Do you think that the allies will come as far as Baghdad.' He was quite desperate and frightened."[112] Indeed, by firing the Scud into Israel's sparsely populated Negev desert, the Iraqis could have tried to avoid the Patriot anti-missile defenses, which were deployed in Israel to cover chiefly its population centers in the north and center of the country.[113] It is as if Baghdad wanted to make sure its message got through. If this scenario is true, then the role of the Scud had been abruptly transformed from an instrument of positive compellence (aimed at forcing the opponent to undertake an undesirable action) to one of deterrence and negative compellence (aimed at forcing the opponent to cease an action already under way).

Saddam was apparently hoping to convince his enemies that if they were thinking about toppling him, he was ready and able to bring down Israel and perhaps the entire Middle East with him. But why did he select Israel as the channel for conveying this message if the United States was meant to be the target audience?

Throughout the Gulf crisis, Iraq made it abundantly clear that it saw oil wells and Israel as America's prime interests in the region.[114] The destruction of Kuwait's oil fields started some time on February 21 or 22, with the detonation of some 150 wells.[115] The action coincided with a tough speech by Saddam, who pledged, on the eve of Tariq Aziz's visit to Moscow, to continue the struggle irrespective of the diplomatic efforts pursued by the Gorbachev regime. But by then Saddam was surely aware of how precarious his military position was.[116] The devastation of the Kuwaiti oil wells was thus vintage terrorist deterrence, aimed at forcing the United States to stop the war.[117] Because this calculated atrocity failed in its mission, however, Saddam had to search for more dramatic means to bring the message home to Washington. Threatening America's other interest — Israel — with mass destruction weapons was his last chance to stop the war.

There are other possible reasons why Saddam may have selected Israel as his target for the mass destruction threat.

First, he may have wanted to let the United States know that even if its troops were well protected against CBW, he could cause severe harm to other U.S. interests.

Second, at this stage of the war Saddam's primary goal was to stop the fighting before U.S. troops arrived in Baghdad. If he hoped to deliver a deterrent message aimed at ending the conflict, he would want to minimize the risk that this message would end up escalating the fighting. Because

Israel had absorbed repeated Scud attacks without retribution, Saddam might have assessed that his warning shot would be less likely to cause escalation if it were fired at Israel rather than at U.S. troops. In this, he might have sought to take advantage of the U.S. efforts to keep Israel out of the conflict.

Third, Iraq, by highlighting its ability to reach Israel, was hinting that it could hit the kind of target most vulnerable to a biological or chemical attack — the civilian population.[118] In line with terrorist deterrence, Iraq may have sent a message indicating its *maximum* potential to cause damage.

Conversely, Saddam may have opted for a strategic threat against Israel because he was ill prepared for tactical mass destruction attacks against U.S. troops. After all, he planned to win the war conventionally. Even if Iraq had inoculated its soldiers in advance, of which there is no evidence, Saddam knew that germ warfare — whose success depends on a variety of external factors and whose effects take time to develop — would be a treacherous undertaking. Tactical BW strikes could have been ineffective, if not counterproductive. The Iraqi Air Force had been knocked out of the skies since early in the war, and the Scuds lacked an inertial guidance system, which made them inaccurate and incapable of hitting point targets. By intimating that Israel was the intended target for his biological weapons, Saddam could have indicated that these potential constraints were not relevant, indirectly enhancing the credibility of his BW threat.[119]

Fifth, threatening BW against Israel had greater credibility compared with delivering such a warning to fellow Arabs located where U.S. troops were stationed.[120] And finally, the Iraqis were undoubtedly aware that communication between Israel and the United States was instantaneous. In fact, U.S. satellites acted as early warning stations for Israel throughout the war, and on January 22, Israeli Foreign Minister David Levy even announced that the United States would provide Israel with real-time satellite reconnaissance data coordinated by a "joint apparatus."[121] During the war, the IDF's headquarters in Tel Aviv were known to have a direct communication link with the Pentagon — a secure satellite telephone line known as Hammer Rick.[122] The Iraqis could have estimated that their warning shot would be reported to the United States forthwith.

Either way — whether Iraq sought to force an Israeli intervention or to warn off its enemies — the concrete-armed Scud could have been useful. As long as the missile was seen as a prelude to an Iraqi mass destruction attack on Israel, Saddam could have achieved his goal. If Israel joined the fray against U.S. wishes, there was a good chance that the United States would stop the war. Alternatively, if the Scud was seen as a warning, the United States would likely conclude that there was a risk of a mass destruction scenario if the U.S. advance continued. It was, therefore, reasonable for Saddam to expect that the United States would end the war in this case, too. In other words, Saddam had little to lose. In the wake of his signal he hoped that the fighting would end either because Israel intervened militarily in the war or the United States heeded his warning.

Deterring Last-Resort Circumstances

On February 25, the same day as the firing of the concrete-armed missile, it was announced that Iraqi forces had been ordered to withdraw from Kuwait. And on February 27, President Bush decided to stop the war. Although it is impossible to pinpoint Saddam's motives for firing the Scud in question, the evidence is clear that the Iraqi mass destruction threat was directly responsible for President Bush's decision. For instance, Moshe Arens, Israeli defense minister at the time, disclosed that Israel was on the verge of entering the conflict when the fighting was abruptly "suspended": "Our objective was to help eliminate the Iraqi missiles. The threat continued to the last day. If the war had lasted one week longer, you would have seen Israeli army action against the Iraqi missiles."[123]

Arens could have been seeking to shore up Israel's deterrent image in view of criticism about the IDF's passivity in the war. He himself admitted that by putting into motion the preparations for intervention, Israel hoped to exert pressure on Washington to assign more resources to Scud hunting in western Iraq.[124] But there is little reason to doubt the veracity of his account. The Israeli defense establishment was worried that the need to support the ground campaign would not leave the coalition sufficient air resources to tackle the Scud threat in western Iraq. It estimated that, at the same time, Saddam's incentives to resort to CBW would mount. The Israelis argued that if Saddam used mass destruction weapons, Israel might be forced to respond with unconventional means. Thus, it would be better for both countries if Washington allowed the IDF to enter the war in order to preempt Saddam's ability to fire Scud missiles tipped with chemical or biological warheads at Israel's population centers.

Subsequently, it was disclosed that when the war ended, the IDF was training for a combined air-ground operation against the Scud missile sites in western Iraq. As Arens put it: "We were very close to setting the Israeli operation in Iraq into motion after we concluded that the anti-Iraq coalition was steadfast, that Iraq would be defeated in the war, and in light of our assessment that Jordan would not start a war against Israel in the wake of Israeli overflights of its territory. We thought the IDF could make a contribution to eliminating the missile threat against Israel."[125]

The Israeli defense establishment ostensibly thought that it had a proposition the United States could not refuse. America would be given a chance to pursue the war to its final victory while Israel would take care of the threat of Saddam's resort to the mass destruction option. In effect, the Israelis offered Bush a political carte blanche: the United States would not be held accountable for the possible consequences of pursuing the war, provided that Israel was allowed to switch from a passive to an active defense. Implicitly, the Israeli plan also offered to substitute conventional intervention for possible retaliation with unconventional weapons. So profound was the miscalculation of the Israeli defense officials that, in all likelihood, they promptly reported the firing of the Iraqi concrete warhead to the United States.[126] They were hoping that the news would persuade Washington to finally give the IDF the green light for a military intervention. By all indications, however, the Israeli effort backfired. Israeli leaders must have been stunned when Bush found a way out of his dilemma by hastily stopping the war. The sense of betrayal was readily noticeable in Arens's comments: "We planned and trained on an action, not only as retaliation, but an attack which would have harmed Iraq's capability to threaten us. I do not believe we can say it would have destroyed the threat, but it would have certainly reduced it. To conclude, I say that had the war continued another few days, then the IDF would have operated in western Iraq. . . . If you ask me whether I regret that the war ended a week too early, then I say yes, I regret it, from all points of view."[127]

By ending the war, Bush calculated, he would avoid the threat of a mass destruction scenario altogether, while preventing Israel from joining the fray and possibly complicating his Gulf strategy. Regarding the Israeli factor, Washington must have recalled the announcement earlier that month by Israel's deputy chief of staff, Maj. Gen. Ehud Barak, who said that the IDF had "very good operational plans" to deal with the Scuds and that the Israeli military's "fingers itched" to implement them. Worse yet, Barak added that Israel preferred to coordinate its actions with the United States but that "in some situations" it might be forced to move unilaterally and merely notify the Americans.[128]

There is no question that the United States had become aware of Israeli thinking during the war. Postwar accounts provide a solid base for deciphering what likely transpired as a consequence. According to General Powell, at a meeting on January 28 in the office of Defense Secretary

Richard Cheney, Israel presented its plan to launch a combined air-ground assault into western Iraq to destroy Iraqi Scud launchers. Powell writes that General Barak stated at the meeting: "If we don't go in and clear out the Scuds, Saddam may use them to deliver chemical warheads when you [the United States] launch your ground offensive. They may fire nerve gas or a biological warhead at our cities. If that happens, you know what we must do."[129] General Powell continues: "I had a pretty good idea what he meant. Israeli missile crews were reportedly on full alert. And who knew what they would be firing."[130]

It is not clear whether Powell was already aware of the conversation between Arens and Cheney, held over the secure phone on January 26. According to Arens's account, the talk touched on the specter of an Iraqi mass destruction attack:

ARENS: We are concerned over the possibility that they [the Iraqis] would start using chemical warheads. We ought to coordinate what will be the response; it [the chemical attack] could happen any day.

CHENEY: We must assume that he [Saddam] has chemical warheads. We do not discuss publicly what will be our response in case he unleashes chemical weapons. Have you any ideas in this regard?

ARENS: We cannot discuss it over the phone. We ought to meet face to face to discuss this. It [the chemical attack] could happen suddenly and require an immediate response.[131]

Even if Powell was unaware of this conversation, within a week the Israeli estimate was repeated — this time publicly. The IDF's chief of staff, Lt. Gen. Dan Shomron, said on February 5: "We understand that it is quite possible that the Iraqis have developed the necessary technology to mount chemical and biological weapons on missiles. Also I would like to stress the fact that there is a great possibility of Iraq practicing such technology; that is to say, the day Iraq will use it is imminent. If and when the Iraqis use chemical warheads, however imperfect and low in technological level they may be, they will threaten us gravely."[132]

Whether Israel alerted its nuclear forces or not is of little consequence to the scenario that unfolded. What counted was the fact that Israel's leaders gave Powell ample reason to believe that if Iraq launched a mass destruction attack on Israel, the Israelis would retaliate with nuclear weapons.

Even before the war, Israeli Prime Minister Shamir's warning — that Iraq would pay a "terrible and a horrible price" if it attacked Israel in order to drag it into the whirlpool — had been unanimously interpreted in the Israeli print media as the first open Israeli nuclear threat.[133] And if anybody took Israel's restraint in the war as suggesting continued passivity on its part, the prime minister soon dispelled that misperception by undertaking his own version of cutting off his own escape route. His "personal message" to President Bush, sent on February 4, 1991, was promptly leaked to the Israeli press. In it Shamir wrote: "I am sure you understand that if an attack on us causes a significant loss of life or if an unconventional warhead is used, such a situation would become intolerable and would call for an immediate response by us."[134]

Undoubtedly the leaking of the letter to the press was meant to signal to the Iraqis as well as to the United States the certainty of the Israeli retaliation if CB weapons were used. By publicizing the letter, Shamir in effect tied his own hands. The implication was that he could not go back on a public pledge. Ze'ev Schiff, Israel's leading military commentator, advised Saddam and the rest of the Arab world to heed the Israeli warnings:

> Neither Shamir's government nor any other Israeli government can avoid taking severe action if many of its citizens are hurt. The pressure for it will come from the masses. . . . It is obvious that Israel will in no way tolerate a chemical attack that could cause enormous fatalities to its civilian population. The use of gas against Israel also carries symbolism, a reminder of the Holocaust. This is why such a painful attack could make Israel lose its inhibitions and restraints. Whoever expects a routine Israeli reaction to such a situation will find himself wrong. It is worth mentioning the claim the Arabs made in the past, that chemical weapons are meant to counterbalance nuclear weapons. They were warned that the situation could be different: the use of chemical weapons could amplify a terrible reaction, not neutralize it. . . .
>
> There is another issue to which Israel has always been particularly sensitive — its deterrent capability. Military circles have always maintained that if the Arabs cross a certain barrier of fear, nothing would stop them from heavier attacks on Israel. . . . This means that an Iraqi attack on Israel will not only be considered from the aspect of the damage it causes, but also with regard to the level of deterrence Israel's reaction would yield. . . . This means that a serious blow to Israel would require a much more massive and drastic reaction to deter the other side. A country that has to plan its strategy this way will find it hard to consider moral and international constraints very much.[135]

To make things worse from General Powell's point of view, some vague remarks by Secretary of Defense Cheney, made on the eve of the Shamir letter, were widely interpreted in Israel as endorsing its use of nuclear weapons in response to an Iraqi mass destruction attack. Cheney was asked in a television interview whether Saddam was refraining from using chemical weapons against Israel because he feared that Israel would use "tactical nuclear weapons" in response. Cheney replied that Saddam should indeed be "worried."[136] Cheney apparently sought to counter the impression, created by the remarks of John Sununu, that the United States would not use nuclear weapons in the Gulf. It was known that Sununu's statement had caused consternation in Israel. For example, Saddam could have understood that Iraq would be taking no great risk in employing chemical weapons.[137] Or he could have thought that the presence of U.S. troops in the Gulf acted as a constraint on Israel's ability to use nuclear weapons. Thus, Defense Minister Arens repeated Cheney's formulation almost verbatim in both the U.S. and the Israeli media.[138]

In fairness, it must be said that in general the Shamir government shied away from open warnings of nuclear retaliation against Iraq. To avoid possible escalation, deterrent statements were initially made against an Iraqi attack generally.[139] The question of Israel's possible reaction to Baghdad's use of mass destruction weapons was hardly addressed. Clearly, the idea was to avoid public discussion of a scenario that would have required the issuing of a markedly different warning, presumably one alluding to nuclear weapons. This practice was kept even though the credibility of the warnings was likely called into question by promising the same "horrible" punishment for both an Iraqi conventional attack *and* a CB attack. Moreover, Israeli civilian and military leaders continued to speak ambiguously of "grave" consequences even after similar language had already failed to deter the conventional Iraqi missile attacks.

When, toward the war's end, officials were pressed on the question of an Iraqi CB attack, there was still no direct reference to retaliation with nuclear weapons. Arens, for instance, would only hint of a possible shift to nuclear strategy as the cornerstone of Israel's deterrence posture. In denying that Israel's conventional deterrence had been eroded as a result of its inaction in the face of the Scud attacks, he nevertheless said: "I believe that our deterrent capability is first and foremost based on our military might, which is immense. I believe that it is not a secret; it is known to the entire world, including the Arab world."[140]

Still, there were ample reasons for Powell to view General Barak's message in the gravest light (see Chapter 6). Consequently, he was the first to push for an end to the war. According to his memoirs, Powell first discussed stopping the war with General Schwarzkopf on the morning of February 27, 1991, Washington time.[141] Deputy National Security Adviser

Robert Gates recalled, however, that during the daily briefing at the White House on February 26, General Powell had already argued for ending the fighting.[142] Yet even this was not soon enough for some Bush administration officials, and perhaps not even for Powell himself. General Khaled has reported: "As early as the morning of February 25, Schwarzkopf had informed me, to my great surprise, that he might soon receive an order from President Bush to stop the war."[143]

It would be sheer naiveté to assume that only by sheer coincidence was Schwarzkopf's surprising statement made on the same morning that Iraq's concrete-and-iron Scud warhead landed in Israel. After all, when the Bush administration alerted Schwarzkopf about the impending order, even the city of Kuwait — the prime objective of the war — was still in Iraqi hands. By contrast, if we assume that the war's end was indeed linked to the perception of a growing Iraqi CBW threat, then Saddam's mass destruction card must have failed to deter Israel. There is no evidence in the public sources that Israel had ever approached the United States with a demand to stop the war. On the contrary, if Arens and the IDF had their way, the Iraqi warning might have provoked an Israeli preemption if not for Bush's decision to "suspend hostilities."

Apparently, at this stage of the war, the IDF estimated that it had a good chance of minimizing Iraq's CBW threat, for several reasons. First, it was probably assessed that owing to the allied air campaign, only a limited number of CB warheads remained in Saddam's hands.

Second, the IDF believed that the threat of a mass destruction attack by the Iraqi Air Force was also all but eliminated. Iraq's most capable aircraft either had fled to Iran, had been destroyed by the coalition war planes, or simply did not dare to take off.[144] Even if an Iraqi plane took the risk to attack, the Israeli Air Force was more than capable of intercepting it.

Third, because Iraq's aerial capability was essentially negated, the operational problems confronting the IDF's plan for an incursion into western Iraq were also eased.[145] Therefore, the Israelis apparently calculated that the prospects of neutralizing most of the remaining Scuds in western Iraq via the IDF's joint air-ground operation had significantly improved.[146]

Fourth, there was hope in the Israeli defense establishment that the civil defense measures enacted to protect the population would prove effective, especially against a degraded Iraqi CB threat. As General Shomron said: "The damage that could be inflicted by such missiles is very small when the home front is as prepared as it is today."[147] The optimism was based on an assessment that the first two factors, individually and jointly, had a positive impact on the effectiveness of Israel's civil defense effort, and the campaign planned by the IDF would further enhance Israel's passive defenses.

Fifth, and most important, the Israelis were convinced that they did not have much choice. Evidently, unaware of President Bush's readiness to stop the fighting suddenly, Israeli leaders had braced themselves for the inevitable Iraqi mass destruction attack which would come once U.S. troops began advancing on Baghdad. In their minds, this scenario made an IDF preemptive strike an absolute must. For all these reasons, the Israeli defense establishment had concluded that acting promptly to contain the Iraqi CBW threat was a risk worth taking. If it facilitated the U.S. effort to eliminate the problem of Saddam Hussein, the endeavor was especially worthwhile.

As for the United States, it is impossible to ascertain which consideration was more important to Bush and Powell. Was it the fear of a mass destruction attack on Israel and that nation's likely response, or was it the political risks of an Israeli intervention?

Based on an assessment of the likely costs, the U.S. president would have wanted to prevent Iraq's resort to mass destruction weapons more than he would have feared the consequences of an Israeli entry into the war. Bush apparently calculated that if Saddam attacked Israel with chemical or biological weapons, Israel would respond with unconventional means, possibly even with nuclear weapons. He was apparently advised that even if Israel was given the green light for a military intervention, the operation could not be viewed as a foolproof solution to the Iraqi mass destruction threat. An Iraqi chemical or biological warhead could still hit Israel.[148] But, according to Secretary of State Baker's account, sometime in December 1990 Bush privately decided not to respond with mass destruction weapons even if Iraq employed chemical weapons against U.S. troops.[149] Bush, then, wanted to keep the war conventional *at all cost*. Evidently, Kuwait's oil fields were not worth a full-blown Iraqi-Israeli exchange of mass destruction weapons. To prevent the war from spilling into uncharted territory, the only option was to stop the fighting once Saddam was seen as possibly signaling his intention to escalate to mass destruction weapons.

Bush also had to worry about the worst-case possibility that an effective Iraqi CB warhead would cause heavy casualties in Israel. The president had apparently already been told that "only one Anthrax warhead on target, even using the al-Husayn missile, would be required. Anthrax can contaminate an area for years."[150] In fact, by that time, U.S. intelligence was on record as warning that "effective dissemination [of the agent] was not even necessary if a BW warhead were to be used as a terror weapon against civilian populations."[151] Furthermore, an authoritative U.S. government panel, assembled during the crisis to assess the Iraqi BW threat specifically, was emphatic: "Civilian population would be at risk to attacks by whatever means the Iraqis chose to disseminate the anthrax spores."[152] Under these circumstances, Iraq's use of BW against Israel would have surely led to a dangerous escalation, or so Bush must have thought.

Alternatively, it has been argued that in a White House meeting between Bush and Arens on February 11, 1991, General Barak (who accompanied the Israeli defense minister) was able to inform the U.S. president directly about the IDF's plan to deal with the Scuds. The Israeli representatives used the opportunity to explain that because of the growing threat of an Iraqi CB attack on Israel, it was essential that the IDF be given the go-ahead to act. Arens told the president that Israel was "fast approaching" the point where it would have "no choice" but to act against the Scuds.[153] Bush, however, remained unmoved. He argued that "the coalition was destroying Iraq's military potential, and Israel's entry into the war would drastically alter the situation." Israel's intervention "would pose a threat to the very existence of the coalition," even at this advanced stage of the war, he said. That is, it could split the coalition on the eve of the ground war. "As he [Bush] is responsible for the lives of U.S. soldiers, he was unwilling to consider favorably anything which could aggravate the danger they faced."[154]

Saddam's mass destruction threat, then, was either directly or indirectly responsible for Bush's "premature" decision. If the war was halted because Iraq's concrete warhead was seen as signaling its readiness to escalate to unconventional weapons and attack Israel, then Saddam was able to use strategic blackmail to deter the United States from pursuing the war further.

Even if Bush was more worried about the political consequences of Israel's entering the fray than about a CBW scenario, Saddam's mass destruction option proved its strategic worth. With Saddam in an increasingly precarious military situation, Washington must have realized, especially in the wake of Iraq's concrete warhead, that its ability to restrain the IDF from attacking the Scuds was fast eroding. Accordingly, the Iraqi CB option indirectly forced the cessation of hostilities. It is possible to state, then, that the *credibility* of Saddam Hussein's mass destruction threat was either directly or indirectly responsible for saving the regime of the Iraqi dictator.

Either way, what clinched the American decision to stop the war was undoubtedly a call made by Arens to Cheney in the afternoon of February 27 (it was still morning in Washington) over the Hammer Rick link. Ostensibly to congratulate the U.S. defense secretary on the American successes in the ground war, Arens voiced grave concern that Saddam would resort to CW against Israel "precisely now." Arens continued: "Israel must take action to neutralize this threat."[155]

Little wonder that later the same day Bush announced a cease-fire. Clearly, the president had more pressing reasons for his decision than those he cited, namely, the accomplishment of the liberation of Kuwait and the defeat of the Iraqi Army. It may be even argued that although Saddam displayed profound unfamiliarity with the modern conventional battlefield, he exercised Iraq's unconventional option masterfully. As a result, the United States was prevented from pursuing the war further and Saddam survived in power. Even if the war was stopped to prevent an Iraqi last-resort move generally, not because of a specific Iraqi warning shot, it cannot be said that U.S. deterrence worked. Indeed, the opposite may be true. The fighting ended before U.S. (or, for that matter, Israeli) deterrence could be put to the test. Washington was so convinced that it could not deter or neutralize Saddam's CB threat that it opted to stop the war rather than risk a cataclysmic conflagration.

In this line of thinking, Israel's passivity was instrumental in rescuing Saddam. Its inaction could have invited the Iraqi leader to send a deterrent signal there. Yet if so, Israel's wartime acquiescence also made it possible for Bush to end the war just as Armageddon was approaching. At any rate, the fact that the mass destruction option saved Saddam's life and regime probably means that it is naive to expect the Iraqi dictator to give up these weapons or the ability to reconstitute them quickly.[156]

Ending the War

Why did Saddam Hussein's deterrent prove effective in dissuading the United States from continuing the war? The answer is that the United States and Israel judged him to be both able and ready to follow through with his threat of mass destruction.

Estimating Iraq's Capability

There are several reasons why Saddam was considered able to carry out his threat. First, despite American efforts to locate and destroy Iraqi Scud launchers, by the war's end it was estimated that Iraq could still fire such missiles into Israel.[1] Moreover, the Patriot anti-missile defenses deployed in Israel since the first week of the war had proved a meager protection against the Scuds.[2] Ironically, even if the Patriot had been effective, the interception of a Scud carrying a CB warhead in the skies over Israel would not have necessarily removed the threat of contamination from its cities.[3]

True, it has been argued that the coalition air campaign forced the Iraqis to move their Scuds out of their "launch boxes," a development that supposedly curbed their ability to hit the main population centers in Israel or, for that matter, Saudi Arabia.[4] This assertion, however, is not entirely correct. As late as February 23, two days before the concrete warhead fell in the Negev, an Iraqi Scud landed in the center of Israel, some 10 to 15 kilometers southeast of Tel Aviv. Specifically, the missile fell east of the strategically sensitive Israeli Aircraft Industry complex, not far from the Ben Gurion Airport, the country's main terminal.[5] As one U.S. Air Force study has put it: "At best, it can be said that counter-Scud efforts only maintained 'pressure' on Iraqi missile operations and that Scud CAP [combat air patrols] operations apparently were successful at harassing but never halting Iraqi launch operations. The harsh reality is that air power did not stop Scud employment."[6]

Throughout the conflict, Iraq repeatedly demonstrated its ability to reach Israel. Even one missile armed with a CB warhead could have transformed the war if it hit an Israeli city. Given that Iraq launched as many missiles in the last eight days of the war as it did during the first seven, that was a realistic possibility, which both Jerusalem and Washington must have recognized.[7] Indeed, the IDF's preparations for a military intervention, with the purpose of silencing the Scuds, certainly indicates Israel's belief in the credibility of the Iraqi missile threat even at the close of the war.

Second, Saddam was able to exercise effective command and control over key elements of his mass destruction option throughout the war. Although Ambassador Rolf Ekeus was reportedly shocked by the lax controls over the BW weapons, the fact remains that Saddam was able to use this strategic option precisely as he planned.[8] Following the war, it has been confirmed that the orders for launching Scuds tended to come from a "very high level."[9] Thus, none of the CB weapons were released as long as Baghdad did not perceive last-resort circumstances. Once Saddam became convinced that the ground war might spill into Baghdad, however, a single shot comprising an unarmed missile with a starkly different warhead was launched, or so it would appear. Without question, the continued resilience of the Iraqi Scud forces' C&C links, the result of their heavy reliance on fiber-optic and coaxial land lines and on couriers, allowed it to continuously pose a realistic threat of chemical or biological SSM attack on Israel.[10] As a DIA document stated: "The coalition's inability to permanently degrade SRBM [short-range ballistic missile] command and control is also significant. . . . Even in the last days of the war Baghdad retained a sufficient capability to initiate firings from new launch areas and to retarget SRBMs from urban to military and high-value targets, such as the Dimona nuclear reactor."[11]

Assessing Saddam's Intentions

Even if Iraq had proved its capacity to fire Scuds into Israel and to preserve its C&C capability, Saddam's deterrent gambit would have failed if his threat to resort to mass destruction weapons had not also been perceived as a credible one. But attaining such credibility was not a simple task. Essentially, Saddam was threatening to launch strategic mass destruction attacks even though such recourse could bring a nuclear response, and thus the destruction of Iraq, from either Israel or the United States. The question is, then, why was Saddam's mass destruction option in general, and in particular his supposed warning, taken so seriously even though it was in effect a suicidal threat? Several reasons can be suggested.

1. *The debut of al-Hijarah.* AMAN certainly had several less dire explanations for Iraq's Scud warhead of concrete and steel rods. Some analysts likely saw it purely as a political message. They noticed that although the

warhead was delivered by another variant of the Scud B, the Iraqis portrayed the delivery vehicle as a brand-new missile called *hijarat ababeel,* or "flying stones," better known as al-Hijarah.[12] In October 1990, Saddam had already claimed that Iraq was in possession of a new long-range missile by that name, in connection with a deadly clash between Israeli security forces and Palestinian rioters in Jerusalem.[13] Throughout the Gulf imbroglio, he tried to link a resolution of the crisis over Kuwait to the settlement of the Palestinian problem. And it was assumed that the missile was named for the Palestinian uprising, or *intifada,* because the youth of the Palestinian revolt were commonly known in the Arabic press as the "children of the stones."[14] In addition, AMAN analysts must have pointed out that by naming the concrete-armed missile of February 25 for the preferred weapon of the intifada, Saddam attempted to repay the Palestine Liberation Organization (PLO) for its staunch support of Iraq during the crisis.[15]

In the same vein, it could have been argued that Saddam's urge to demonstrate his defiance of U.S. power was such that he resorted to virtually any means available to make his point. To prove the continued viability of his stand, despite his increasingly precarious position, even an untested, unarmed prototype of a missile was hastily pressed into action. Saddam apparently counted on creating uncertainty in the minds of his enemies, although they could have read such a missile as evidence of his desperation.

Others in AMAN probably pointed out that by unveiling a new missile called al-Hijarah, Saddam sought to deliver on repeated Iraqi promises to "surprise" the allies with new sophisticated weapons while still not resorting to unconventional weapons.[16] In this view, it would be a mistake to read too much into the affair, as the Iraqis often resorted to such practices for either political or deceptive reasons. For example, the Iraqi Military Communiqué No. 52, released on February 17, 1991, asserted that four new missiles identified as being of al-Hijarah type had been involved in attacks on Israeli targets the night before. This claim was made even though, just a few hours before the debut of al-Hijarah was announced, Baghdad issued a bulletin that identified the missiles as the standard al-Husayn type. It said that three of the missiles had been fired at the Dimona reactor and the fourth at Haifa harbor in northern Israel.[17]

With regard to the concrete warhead, it could be taken as evidence that some of the Iraqi Scud units had run out of armed missiles after direct hits to their missile storage shelters.[18] Compared with the salvos of Scuds fired at Israel in the first two weeks of the war, the landing of a single concrete-armed missile at this late stage could have indicated that such a shortage had developed. Assuming that AMAN believed the missile was aimed at Dimona, this explanation would have looked especially apt given that the latest event came in the wake of one and possibly two other attacks with conventional warheads against the same facility. Perhaps the Iraqi missile crews fired a training warhead because they were scraping around for weapons yet could not be seen as disobeying Saddam's orders. After all, a missile must be fitted with some warhead as a ballast in order to be able to fly to its target.[19]

Others probably argued that arming the Hijarah with a concrete warhead was a natural course given the extent of modifications incorporated in the missile.[20] The Iraqis could have needed a practice run before the introduction of a new weapons system. Presumably, the new weapon was rushed into service owing to the dwindling stock of al-Husayns or the increasing difficulties of operating from western Iraq under the coalition air threat, or both. After all, it was probably pointed out, the Hijarah had undergone only rudimentary testing before the war.[21] Saddam could have even been bluffing. He may have launched his missile in an attempt to exploit Israeli and American fears of a possible act of desperation on his part. Saddam wanted to be seen as ready to go all the way — that, after all, was the core motivation of his strategy of terrorist deterrence.

Against these relatively benign interpretations, however, stood more chilling ones. The concrete in the warhead could have been a shield for a BW payload, and both Israel and the United States anticipated that, at this stage of the war, Saddam would resort to mass destruction weapons. To the extent that al-Hijarah was seen as a longer version of al-Husayn launched from farther inside Iraqi territory, the concrete-armed missile was a signal that Iraq could reach Israel with mass destruction weapons despite President Bush's boasting of the "darndest search-and-destroy effort that's ever been undertaken" against the Scuds in western Iraq.[22] Some analysts may have noted that firing a missile dubbed hijarat ababeel against Israel at this late stage transcended the Palestinian connection. There was a broader religious context to the name, which had to be taken into account, because in the Middle East the past shapes the motivation for and the legitimization of the present.

In sura 105 of the Qur'an, *tyaran ababeel*, or flying birds, are mentioned as having gathered over the holy mosque of Mecca. The Qur'an relates that these black birds saved Mecca from certain destruction at the hands of

Habashi (ancient Ethiopian) hordes who came riding in on a herd of elephants. The birds used their strong beaks to hurl "stones of baked clay" at them.[23] Saddam Hussein undoubtedly had this imagery in mind when he called his missile *hijarat ababeel*—"flying stones." The implication was that Saddam was warning his enemies that, just as in the case of Mecca, Iraq was ready to resort to its miracle weapons and use the modern version of baked clay stones—concrete warheads "baked" by atmospheric heat while delivering their deadly biological cargo—to save Baghdad from the approaching hordes of the Western infidels.

Perhaps some analysts even recalled the meeting Saddam held with his army commanders in December 1990 in preparation for the "mother of all battles." "May God be my witness," he said, "that it was God who wanted that which occurred [the occupation of Kuwait], and not us. I mean our role has been zero." As proof, Saddam went on to tell his generals that he had recently learned "that the symbol of Mr. Bush's party is the elephant." While referring to the rescue of Mecca by the tyaran ababeel, he went on to cite from the Qur'an as follows: "Hast thou not seen what thy Lord did with the Men of the Elephant?" and added: "I mean, when I heard this . . ." According to one account, "Saddam's voice [then] slowly fades into silence as if astounded at the wondrous implications of the Qur'anic verse he has just quoted. There follows a fifteen second silence and one of Iraq's top military commanders takes to mumbling barely audible verses from the Qur'an in the background. 'It is the will of God,' says another commander loudly. . . . George Bush and his army of 500,000 Americans were going to meet the same fate [as the elephant-riding Habashis], Saddam was telling his army commanders in December 1990."[24]

If they put the two events together—the meeting on December 1990 and the firing of al-Hijarah on February 25, 1991—these analysts must have asked themselves the following questions:

- At the meeting, was Saddam already preparing the grounds for the possible use of mass destruction weapons? Was he in effect telling his commanders that they should obey an order to use CB weapons, if one were issued, because it was by divine sanction that the American elephant had to be stopped from invading Baghdad?
- Was the firing of a concrete-armed missile dubbed al-Hijarah indicative of Saddam's state of mind toward the war's end? Did he perceive himself to be in the midst of the Qur'anic battle against the Elephant Men, an engagement over which human beings have little control? Was he involved in a reenactment of the ancient script,

which would inevitably culminate in the use of Iraq's modern "stones of baked clay" to save Baghdad?

- Was the Iraqi leader searching for an alibi, so that if catastrophe were to strike the Iraqi people, he could maintain that he had just carried out God's will?
- Was the invoking of al-Hijarah's Qur'anic roots just part of a calculated exercise in psychological warfare — the strategy of terrorist deterrence — aimed to unnerve the United States and Israel? Saddam was never a pious man, and even if he truly believed that the almighty was behind the invasion of Kuwait, how could he explain why God would engineer such a humiliating ejection of "his" Iraqi forces from its land?
- Finally, could Saddam's myth-building effort in December 1990 have had little to do with mass destruction weapons? Was he simply trying to assure his army commanders of the coming victory by implying that supernatural forces were on their side? At the time, Palestinians in the West Bank and many Arabs elsewhere took Saddam's Qur'anic imagery to mean just that.[25] As Saddam was telling his generals of their certain victory, what would be the Iraqi rationale for resorting to mass destruction weapons anyway? The subsequent landing of the "stone-age" Scud in the Negev could then be taken figuratively. It was aimed to shore up the morale of the Iraqi troops by rekindling their memories of a wondrous Qur'anic victory in the face of adverse odds.

It is not known what role the missile's destination played in the debate within AMAN. Opponents of the worst-case interpretation of al-Hijarah probably argued that if it had been a CB warning shot, Saddam would have aimed the missile at an urban center, to communicate the maximum potential threat, rather than at an isolated strategic site, like the Dimona reactor.

Proponents of the worst-case approach, however, believed that the targeting of the nuclear facility must have been deliberate and thus significant in gauging Saddam's intentions. The Iraqi leader had frequently made the connection between the Israeli nuclear threat and Iraq's mass destruction weapons. Anthrax, for instance, because of its ability to render an area inaccessible for long periods of time, would make an excellent weapon against a strategic target like Dimona, which Saddam had had in his sights at least since the 1981 Israeli attack on Osiraq. Some in the IDF have long argued that the Arabs would not dare attack Jewish population centers with CB weapons. Rather, they would use them against strategic and military sites, like the nuclear facility at Dimona. They could then threaten to escalate to countercity attacks, hoping to prevent an Israeli nuclear retaliation and force a cease-fire on their terms.

Besides, if this was a warning shot, Dimona was a means to deliver the message, not necessarily the target of the actual CB attack. To communicate his intentions to the Israelis, Saddam selected the reactor because of the link he often made publicly between the Israeli nuclear threat and Iraq's mass destruction weapons. He might have thought that, under the circumstances, there was a better chance that Israel would decipher his warning if Dimona were the medium. The follow-up CB missile strike would have been aimed at an Israeli population center.

Israel and the United States, then, faced daunting uncertainty about Saddam's intentions. Despite all the innocuous possible explanations, it could not be ruled out that the concrete and metal warhead was an ominous sign. Even if some thought the *probability* of a mass destruction scenario was minimal, the *possibility* was sufficient to wield critical influence on the prosecution of the war. Taking a chance on Saddam seemed too risky a proposition, as an error could have had disastrous consequences. If Iraq possessed an advanced biological warhead with an aerosol capability, the actual target it selected could be only marginally significant, given Israel's size and population geography. An effective attack using anthrax agents could cause large-scale contamination of Israeli territory long after Saddam himself had departed from the scene. Would not such a scenario fit in with the "Samson strategy" the Iraqis (as we shall see) had warned about? Besides, some of the benign theories were surely unconvincing. As is now known, Iraq never did exhaust its stock of armed Scuds. But the IDF's continued insistence on preempting the Scuds, especially toward the war's end, indicates that even then it had rejected the notion that the concrete warhead signified Iraq's running out of ammunition. Perhaps Baghdad realized that no meaningful military result would be achieved by firing salvos of missiles. It may have decided to conserve its firepower for the final showdown. Beyond this, the goal of the Scud missile was from the start political, not military. Throughout the war it gave Iraq the capacity to transform the conflict in an instant.

2. *The intelligence conception.* The effectiveness of Saddam's mass destruction deterrent was directly linked to three factors. First, there was a general view in Israel and elsewhere that Saddam could not be counted upon to act in an altogether rational manner, at least not in Western terms. This perception was the direct result of Saddam's strategy of terrorist deterrence. Consequently, some observers stressed that Iraq did not fear large num-

bers of dead.[26] President Bush noted on one occasion that Saddam "has never possessed a weapon that he didn't use."[27] During the war this view became even more pronounced. Israeli Defense Minister Moshe Arens, for example, observed that "in certain respects, [Saddam] proved a man whom the Americans, for one, have failed to deter."[28] Gen. Dan Shomron concurred: "Saddam Hussein is ready to pay any price, which is why as far as he is concerned deterrence does not exist, not even where the United States is involved."[29]

This position seemed to be a remarkable turnaround. In public Israeli leaders had confidently predicted before the war that Israel's deterrent power would dissuade Saddam from attack. Shomron, for instance, questioned whether the Iraqi leader would be so foolish as to open another front against Israel, "which is a very strong country and which Saddam Hussein acknowledges or at least can estimate its striking capability against him should he dare to strike [it]. . . . He would very much like to avoid war with Israel."[30]

Once the Israeli deterrent failed and conventionally armed Scuds began falling on Israel, the public assessment was reversed. Before the all-clear sign was given, for example, Israeli civil defense teams checked every Scud warhead for possible chemical agents, although this was in direct contradiction to the official line, which decried the chances of an Iraqi CW strike. A few hours before Washington made its decision to stop the war, Shomron reiterated: "Saddam Hussein is not deterred, not only by Israel but by a superpower such as the United States."[31]

It could also be argued, however, that from the outset uncertainty prevailed in Israel as to whether Saddam would carry out his threats to attack. For example, early on in the crisis Shomron stated: "I believe there is a very high probability [Israel] will not be involved [in the conflict]. At the same time, we are not excluding such a possibility, and we are getting ready."[32] The distribution of gas masks to Israeli citizens before the war, the raising of the Israeli Air Force's alert level (including a sharp increase in the number of sorties flown), and the partial mobilization of IDF's reservists also indicate suspicions about Saddam's intentions.[33] But publicly, the emphasis was on calming the population and averting panic, and on signaling Iraq that Israel wished to stay out of the fray. Although the extent of such private fears among the Israeli leadership cannot be known, they were grave enough for Israel to undertake costly precautionary measures. Thus the seeds of the doomsday scenario, which Israeli officials felt faced them toward the end of the war, were planted long before any Scud had landed, by Saddam's record of terrorist deterrence.[34]

Second, on top of this assessment, there was a growing consensus in Israel and the United States that Saddam was feeling cornered. Even before the war, some "high-placed Iraqi sources" were quoted in an Israeli newspaper as promising that Saddam, like his biblical predecessor in the case of the Philistines, would adopt a "Samson strategy" when necessary and would "take Israel with him, and the oil wells."[35] By the time Saddam's warning shot landed in Israel, 517 of Kuwait's 950 oil wells were ablaze, and some had already been burning for three days.[36] The landing of the concrete Scud in the Negev was tantamount to the dropping of the other shoe of this strategy. Saddam, after all, had pointed out: "We have done everything we have said."

Third, above all, the role of the conception that prevailed among both the American and Israeli intelligence communities cannot be overemphasized. There was an overall consensus that when the chips were down Saddam would turn to his mass destruction option without hesitation. Based on documents released in connection with the investigation of the "Gulf War syndrome," it appears that even before the war started, CIA analysts estimated as follows:

> We judge that Saddam would refrain from using biological weapons until he perceived his situation to be desperate — such as if he were being severely pressed by allied military advances. . . . *Saddam would probably precede any use of biological weapons with more or less explicit threats* to try to achieve his goals short of actual use and the attendant risk of retaliation. If his threats were not heeded, however, we believe Saddam might order a biological warfare attack. . . . Saddam might order BW missile strikes whether he hoped they would reverse his fortunes or had already concluded his cause was hopeless. In the latter case, he would want to take as many of his enemies as he could.[37]

Chief of Staff Shomron delivered an almost identical appraisal:

> It was our assessment even before the outbreak of the war that when it breaks out, Saddam Hussein might well launch missiles against Israel. We said then that when he is distressed and pushed to the wall, that would be the stage when he might deploy chemical weapons as the last resort to extort a heavy price and perhaps even halt the war at a stage in which he will not have been completely defeated.[38]

At the root of this assessment were "official Iraqi statements that justify the use of any weapon to defend its territory." Moreover, "Iraq's use of chemical weapons in its war with Iran shows that Iraq is prepared to back rhetoric with action." On the basis of the Iran-Iraq war, U.S. intelligence analysts further stated: "We believe Iraq views its use of chemical weapons against Iran as a decisive factor in the outcome of the war."[39] The resort to CW "in both tactical and operational situations could suggest that given the alternative of defeat, and the fall of his regime, he [Saddam] would employ BW weapons, the desperation scenario."[40] Iraq's lack of experience in using biological weapons would "probably not prevent a decision to use them," given that Iraq was the "first nation to use nerve agents on the battlefield."[41] As a matter of record, the DIA pointed out, Saddam's "history shows a demonstrated willingness to use weapons that are deemed unsuitable or banned by treaty."[42] Nor did the Iraqi dictator show any hesitation in ordering attacks on purely civilian targets, as demonstrated in 1988 during the Iran-Iraq "War of the Cities" and subsequently by the chemical attacks on the Kurds.

Aside from his compelling record, U.S. intelligence also saw Saddam's personality traits as potentially conducive to the initiation of BW. Although most Iraqi officials "probably" have no religious or personal compunction about using any weapons of mass destruction in defense of their country, "Saddam Hussein would be especially unfaltering in considering resort to biological weapons. Saddam is cold-blooded, ruthless, and extremely persistent in pursuing his long-term goals, in our judgement."[43]

On the Israeli side there was no dispute of this view. As early as September 13, 1990, Defense Minister Arens told his American counterpart in their meeting in Washington: "It is likely [Israel] will be attacked by missiles, possibly of the kind which carry chemical warheads."[44] During the war, the concern among the Israeli defense establishment heightened after Iraq threatened in mid-January to resort to "weapons which we have so far refrained from using." In Arens's mind it was clear that the Iraqis "were hinting of their readiness to resort to chemical weapons. As they have made good on their threats in the past, we [Israel] had to take this possibility into account, especially as their desperation was intensifying with the persistence of the coalition's attacks. So far it seemed as if nothing could deter Saddam Hussein. Although he probably assumed that Israel possessed atomic weapons, he was not deterred from firing the Scuds. It was only scant consolation that even the military might of the United States was not enough to deter him from going to war against the United States and its allies."[45]

Notably, the controversy over the significance of al-Hijarah did not impair the prevalence of the intelligence doctrine on the last-ditch Iraqi use of CB weapons. Naturally, proponents of the worst-case interpretation saw al-Hijarah as validating this assessment ex post facto. But even those who apparently objected to viewing al-Hijarah as a prelude to a BW attack continued to subscribe to the conception that Iraq would turn to mass destruction weapons as a last resort. Arens, for example, apparently considered alternatives other than the worst-case scenario: "We were amazed to find out that one of the missiles they fired [on February 25] carried a block of reinforced concrete, instead of [an operational] warhead. They might have launched one of their test missiles by mistake, or have run out of 'live' missiles in the sector that night, yet insisted on fulfilling their allotted 'quota.' "[46] Nevertheless, it was Arens who, two days later, called Secretary of Defense Cheney to warn dramatically of the coming last-resort Iraqi CW attack and to demand that Israel be allowed to act. In fact, Arens might have even hinted that Israel was about to launch a preemptive strike.

Even those who had earlier fought against the distribution of gas masks to Israeli citizens, considering it a premature act that could encourage an otherwise improbable Iraqi chemical attack, agreed that Saddam would use unconventional weapons as a last resort. Their point was that, based on the experience of the Iran-Iraq war, Saddam resorted to CW only in extreme situations of national distress.[47] An Iraqi debacle in the ongoing ground war coupled with the specter of a U.S. advance on Baghdad clearly belonged in this category.

The bottom line was that the "Israeli military strongly believed that Saddam would authorize chemical warfare in desperation as the allied ground attack neared. Arens feared the odds of parrying such an attack were slim."[48] In fact, although U.S.-Israeli intelligence cooperation reached its lowest ebb in the months before the war, the two countries' estimates of Saddam's last-resort strategy were strikingly similar.

In addition, at least one of the U.S. decision makers saw eye to eye with Arens. General Powell was troubled by the likelihood of an Iraqi last-resort strategy based on mass destruction weapons. From the outset he estimated that the "wild card in this conflict was whether or not the Iraqis might resort to germ warfare."[49] As soon as the order to dispatch U.S. troops to Saudi Arabia was issued, Powell was thinking about Iraq's mass destruction option: "We knew from CIA estimates that the Iraqis had at least a thousand tons of chemical agents. . . . We briefly considered and then rejected sending over U.S. chemical weapons. The Iraqi chemical threat was manageable. Our troops had protective suits and detection and alarm systems. In battle we would be fast-moving and in the open desert, not trapped as civilians might be. A chemical attack would be a public relations crisis, but not a battlefield disaster. What to do about Iraq's biological capability, however, remained a more troubling question."[50]

For General Powell, the Iraqi biological arsenal was "hanging like a specter over the desert."[51] Already in October 1990, the DIA had warned that "U.S. and allied forces are assessed to be at significant risk if BW operations are undertaken by Iraq. This assessment is based on: 1. Our belief that Iraq has the capability to tactically and strategically deploy biological weapons. 2. The presence of significant intelligence gaps including — a. Lack of knowledge of Iraqi BW release and use doctrine. b. Absence of details on specific agents. c. Probable existence of unidentified agents. d. Minimal information which specific BW delivery systems would be used. 3. (Portion classified). 4. And the expected mass allied casualties resulting from a successful BW attack."[52]

Shortly after, Powell undoubtedly became aware of the report of the Iraq Interagency Biological Warfare Working Group, which estimated that the Iraqi BW stockpile "consists of at least one (1) metric ton of dried anthrax and up to 15 kgs of botulinum toxin."[53] He quickly assigned Brig. Gen. John Jumper to oversee U.S. defenses against chemical and biological weapons. In particular, he later wrote, there was a need to prepare against "one of the biological agents we believed the Iraqis possessed . . . botulinum toxin, one of the deadliest known to man."[54] Even on the eve of the war, Powell recalls, he remained less concerned over the possible Iraqi use of chemical weapons. "But the biologicals worried me, and the impact on the public the first time the first casualty keeled over to germ warfare would be terrifying."[55]

Based on the assessments of the CIA, the DIA, and the IDF, however, one could well argue that the United States and Israel were setting themselves up for a mass destruction scare. The IDF intelligence, just as it had misread Syrian and Egyptian intentions before the Yom Kippur War in 1973, became imprisoned within its own dominant conception of the unfolding events in 1991.[56] This time, that conception pertained to Saddam's likely last-resort moves. It is possible that AMAN even used new information — the landing of the concrete warhead — to reconfirm ex post facto an a priori hypothesis about Saddam's likely act of desperation. Indeed, it may be said that, having been stung by its best-case estimate in 1973, which enabled the Arabs to launch a devastating surprise attack on Israel, AMAN now took the opposite approach and adopted a worst-case scenario so as to avoid another intelligence failure. For its part, U.S. intelligence was similarly adhering to a conception about Saddam's last-resort strategy that was implicitly based on the notion that Saddam was undeterrable. Did the U.S. and Israeli intelligence overreact, thus leading to a premature end to the war? This question shall be addressed in detail in Chapter 8.

3. The impact of uncertainty. Whether Saddam indeed fired a warning shot or not, in the final analysis what mattered was the way his enemies thought he would act if backed into a corner. In the wake of al-Hijarah the suspicion must have emerged that the anticipated Iraqi mass destruction scenario was in the offing. Or, put differently, in light of Iraq's latest missile, dismissing the possibility of such a cataclysmic event became harder.

Saddam's terrorist deterrence strategy had a role in forming this conception. But the view that Saddam could be planning a mass destruction surprise gained prominence because of the absence of information to the contrary in both Israel and the United States. AMAN apparently estimated that in August 1990, when Kuwait was invaded, Iraq still lacked the technology to manufacture an effective dispersal system for the chemical warheads of its al-Husayn missiles. AMAN analysts also assessed, however, that it would require some three months for the development of such a system, assuming that Iraq launched a crash program following the attack on Kuwait. In the meantime, Western technicians who had been helping Saddam decided to hurry home before the bombs began to fall. And AMAN could not determine definitively whether the Iraqis had actually developed such a warhead even without their help.[57]

To compensate for its intelligence shortcomings, Israel adopted a worst-case approach specifically with regard to Iraq's warhead technology. For example, when General Shomron was asked about Saddam's ability to fit chemical warheads to his missiles, he replied:

> It is hard to tell. . . . We have known for some time now that Iraq was developing chemical warheads for its different Scud missiles. It is undergoing an accelerated process. Furthermore, it is also experimenting. It is very hard to tell precisely at what development stage they are now. Hence the constant doubts as to whether or not these warheads are operational. They can no doubt manufacture primitive warheads and have already experimented with them. Whether they have stockpiled operational chemical warheads, that is hard for us to tell. Still, our operational assumption is that they can fire them, even if they are primitive, and even if they wreak lighter damage than a regular warhead carrying the load it is capable of, they are still capable of causing real damage.[58]

Shomron openly asserted that Israel was not alone in its quandary. When asked whether Israeli intelligence could have known "about these means [the chemical warheads] ahead of time," the chief of staff broadly hinted that U.S. intelligence was facing a similar dilemma: "Look, in this area our intelligence does not work alone but in coordination with large and highly funded intelligence bodies. They trade information. What we know is what all the countries — apart from Iraq, naturally — that deal in searching and locating what there is, know. Thus, that intelligence is the combination of a comprehensive intelligence effort. We do not have an unambiguous answer. We know a lot, but we do not know what development level he has achieved precisely now."[59]

The gap in Israel's intelligence regarding Iraq's missile capability was a prolonged one. In April 1990, Deputy Chief of Staff Ehud Barak said that Saddam "may have an operational SSM warhead which could be equipped with gas."[60] Brigadier General "Y," head of the Israeli Air Force intelligence, pointed out soon after the onset of the Gulf crisis that Israel was aware that Syria had developed an ability to manufacture chemical warheads for its Scud missiles. In turn, there was "no reason to assume that the Iraqis do not have the same capability."[61] But months later, Yossi Sarid, member of the Foreign Affairs and Defense Committee of the Knesset (Israeli parliament), wrote: "Seven months after the [Kuwait] crisis erupted and two months after the outbreak of the war, we cannot yet give credible answers to [numerous questions like]: . . . Does Iraq have the ability to launch a chemical warhead-missile? . . . Does Iraq have biological-weapon warheads and the capability of firing them?"[62]

Instead of hard data, then, the United States and Israel were confronted with uncertainty. They decided it was better to err on the side of safety. Henceforth, Israel was to adopt a worst-case approach, as a substitute for verifiable information, regarding Saddam's ability to fire Scuds with mass destruction warheads. For example, Maj. Gen. Avihu Bin-Nun, commander of the Israeli Air Force, said that although Saddam was not believed to have operational chemical warheads, "just to be prepared, we [the IDF] assume they have less than 20 nonconventional warheads."[63] Indeed, AMAN's head at the time, Maj. Gen. Amnon Shahak, purportedly admitted that in 1991 the intelligence community made a mistake in its information gathering, but not in evaluating the significance and weight of the data collected. In a briefing to the Knesset's Foreign Affairs and Defense Committee, Shahak was cited as saying: "Concerning the biological and chemical weapons [in Iraq's possession,] there was a need to prepare for the worst, because we did not have exact and verified information on whether Iraq has chemical warheads."[64]

The results of this worst-case approach had been evident throughout the war, when Israelis were told to stay in sealed rooms in their apartments rather than rush to air-raid shelters. The idea was to provide better protection against an attack with poison gas or germ weapons, substances that would tend to concentrate near the ground because of physical decay of aerosolized agents, or because of Iraq's so-called primitive warhead technology. Given that Saddam fired only conventionally tipped missiles, however, a paradoxical situation developed where Israeli citizens were left vulnerable to air attack in their apartments, while the military insisted on keeping the original orders just in case an Iraqi mass destruction attack was launched. As Arens said: "In recent weeks we operated on the assumption that they have the capability of attaching chemical warheads to missiles. I believe we had to act on that assumption."[65] General Bin-Nun, who insisted that Iraq "does not have the technology to employ special detonators required for the missiles to explode at the altitude necessary to effectively disperse the chemicals," likewise justified the orders to stay in sealed rooms by citing "the possibility, although very slight, that he [Saddam] might nevertheless have an effective chemical warhead with a capability of causing heavy damage."[66]

If such a warhead existed in the Iraqi arsenal, casualties in Israel could have indeed been heavy. A single chemical warhead that efficiently dispersed 70 kilograms of sarin nerve agent over Tel Aviv would have created, under average weather conditions, an area of about 0.01 to 0.03 square kilometers in which unprotected people would have died. Under worse weather conditions from the point of view of the defender—like calm, clear nights—the lethal area would have increased to 0.2 to 0.3 square kilometers. Given the population density of the metropolitan Tel Aviv area, a single air burst of a sarin-filled al-Husayn warhead would have had the potential to kill hundreds, perhaps thousands, of unprotected people.[67]

Although the availability of gas masks and sealed rooms would have substantially reduced casualties, damage would still have been considerable. "It is commonly assumed that sealed rooms greatly reduce the dose received, but in fact a chemical agent will still leak in. Even tightly sealed rooms will not afford much protection unless they are thoroughly ventilated as soon as the [poison] cloud passes, for otherwise the occupants will receive about the same dose as individuals remaining outdoors, but at a slower rate. . . . [Moreover] if Iraq had used chemicals, the ensuing panic, which creates symptoms that can be mistaken for nerve agent poisoning, undoubtedly would have led to far more casualties from heart attacks, atropine injections and anxiety."[68]

A similar BW warhead filled with anthrax agent or botulinum toxin would have caused far greater losses in either case. The CIA calculated that an al-Husayn missile carrying an aerosol warhead containing some 100 kilograms of dried anthrax spores would theoretically produce a maximum area of lethal contamination of 1,600 square kilometers. That would correspond to a dispersion area about 90 kilometers long and 15 kilometers wide at the widest point. A similar payload of botulinum toxin would produce a maximum area of lethal contamination of 21 square kilometers. Anthrax spores in solution would produce a lethal contamination area of about 110 kilometers. Iraq only needed a few effective BW-tipped missiles in its stockpile to cause significant casualties. In fact, the CIA analysts wrote, "it probably would take only one BW warhead to neutralize any one given target."[69]

4. Timing. The effectiveness of Saddam's perceived suicidal threat was enhanced by its timing. When the Iraqi leader apparently signaled his self-destructive intentions, Iraq had already been defeated militarily. Thus, the incentive to pay the much higher price that Saddam had suddenly threatened to exact for continuing the war, was quickly diminishing.

Whatever the exact impact of al-Hijarah on the thinking in the United States and Israel, the threat of the war escalating to unconventional weapons, as forecasted by the intelligence in both countries, must have been decisive. Recall that to General Powell, for one, it simply made no sense to risk a doomsday scenario when a victory declaration could be issued in a few short hours, ending the war (see Chapter 4).

Even if Saddam's mass destruction capability had been severely eroded by the relentless U.S. bombing, Washington had to assume that a surviving chemical or biological warhead could hit Israel and would be likely to cause a dramatic escalation. Moreover, the United States estimated that it had little chance of stopping Israel in such a case. Washington had been successful in physically preventing the Israeli Air Force from entering the war against the Scuds, by not releasing the IFF (identification friend-or-foe) electronic codes to Israeli pilots; these electronic devices would have enabled coalition pilots to distinguish friendly aircraft from enemy planes and thus prevent clashes with the Israelis.[70] In the minds of U.S. leaders, however, such barriers did not exist when it came to an Israeli retaliation with mass destruction weapons. In response to an Iraqi CB attack, Washington, rightly or wrongly, expected Israel to resort to its nuclear *missiles*. It was only prudent for Washington to assume the worst, and it quickly determined that in view of its battlefield successes the risk was simply unacceptable. Thus, if there was a warning, it was timed impeccably, owing partly to the changing circumstances of the war and partly to Saddam's undiminished ability to control his CBW option despite Iraq's worsening military situation.

Saddam Hussein's suicidal threat would not have been taken credibly but for his enemies' worst-case approach regarding Iraq's CB missile capabilities. The timing also worked in Saddam's favor. These factors, while necessary, would not have been sufficient unless two other elements had been present: Saddam's record of making good on his threats, and the widely shared perception that he was an undeterrable lunatic. President Bush even referred to him in his Gulf War diary as "the madman."[71] For the presence of these two final conditions, Saddam can thank his strategy of terrorist deterrence.

Cease-Fire "Negotiations"

It has been the view that the Gulf War cease-fire came about as a result of a one-sided U.S. initiative, and that its terms were imposed unilaterally by President Bush. On closer examination, however, it is evident that the cease-fire was the result of U.S.-Iraqi "negotiations" held in the shadow of Saddam's mass destruction weapons. Saddam was apparently so confident that his mass destruction threat was effective that instead of using his warning just to block the feared U.S. advance toward Baghdad, he quickly tried to apply it to a wholesale rewriting of the war's outcome. Ostensibly, he thought that the United States would be so interested in ending the fighting after he displayed his threat, that he could dictate the terms of the cease-fire. If his terms were accepted, Saddam figured, his chances of political survival would be much improved.

Around midnight on February 25, 1991, Saddam had Baghdad Radio announce that "orders have been issued to our armed forces to withdraw in an organized manner to positions they held prior to August 1, 1990. This is regarded as practical compliance with Resolution 660" of the U.N. Security Council (UNSC).[72] Saddam offered this olive branch within a few hours of his warning shot, apparently in the belief that his demonstrated readiness to engage in a radically different type of warfare should stop in its tracks any possible advance into Iraq. As reportedly stated by Lt. Gen. Sultan Hashim Ahmad, one of the Iraqi representatives to the March 3, 1991, cease-fire talks at Safwan, Baghdad "had not expected the Coalition troops to enter Iraqi territory once Iraq had announced its withdrawal from Kuwait."[73] Undoubtedly, Saddam also hoped that the warning would yield him better cease-fire terms.

Even after being forced to personally announce over Baghdad Radio, in the early morning hours of February 26, the withdrawal of Iraqi troops from Kuwait, Saddam was far from sounding like a defeated leader at the mercy of his enemies. He depicted the war as an Iraqi victory achieved in the face of all adversity. More important, he did not even renounce Iraq's claim to Kuwait but, rather, reminded his listeners that the "gates to Constantinople were not opened before the Muslims in their first struggling attempt." In fact, he declared, "the Iraqis will remember and will not forget that on August 8, 1990, Kuwait became part of Iraq legally, constitutionally and actually."[74]

President Bush naturally saw Saddam's speech as proof that he was interested not in peace but in regrouping to fight another day. In response, Bush stated that nothing would satisfy him short of Iraq's unconditionally accepting all relevant UNSC resolutions. Although Tariq Aziz soon informed the Security Council that Iraq was ready to rescind its official annexation of Kuwait, to release all POWs, and to pay reparations, the Iraqis continued to bargain. In return for their concessions, they demanded an immediate cease-fire and an end to the U.N.-imposed sanctions.[75] The Iraqis also failed to mention acceptance of the rest of the UNSC resolutions. Only after the UNSC had rejected these terms did Iraq inform the United Nations that it was willing to abide by the remaining Security Council resolutions.

It can be argued that Saddam's terrorist deterrence was clearly unsuccessful in mitigating the UNSC resolutions. Conversely, it was Bush who on every occasion was able to force the Iraqi leader to abide by U.S. will. At times this enforcement required that Saddam publicly humiliate himself, a move that Baghdad undoubtedly took as a deliberate attempt by Washington to undermine the Iraqi dictator's regime.[76] And yet Saddam complied. How, then, can the argument that Saddam was able to deter the United States through his mass destruction threat be sustained? If Washington was so intimidated, how can Bush's unwavering stand on enforcing the UNSC terms be explained?

In fact, Saddam's attempt to rewrite the war's outcome was only a partial failure. His emergence from a crushing military defeat with much of his instruments of power intact, and his reign unperturbed, cannot be overlooked. As one account stated: "For a military operation that had been born of such extraordinarily deft and successful diplomacy and prosecuted with such skill and vision, it was a tragic conclusion, one that no amount of postwar celebration could disguise. There could be no doubt that America and its allies had triumphed over Iraq's army on the battlefield. But inasmuch as victory suggests a decisive defeat of an opponent, there was none. This triumph without victory was perhaps the most striking irony of the entire conflict."[77]

By repeatedly comparing Saddam to Hitler, Bush had strongly implied that, just as in World War II, in the Gulf America's goal would be an unconditional surrender, this time by the Iraqis.[78] On several occasions Bush and his lieutenants called either on Saddam to step aside or on the Iraqi people to take matters into their own hands.[79] In the eyes of many, these statements revealed the administration's "true agenda."[80] Yet, unlike the Nazi ruler, Saddam was allowed to stay in power and to a large extent even control the sequence and pace of his country's compliance with the UNSC resolutions. This is a rather surprising outcome and one that could be directly tied to Saddam's credible threat of resorting to mass destruction weapons.

After all, had President Bush actually wished to pursue his "agenda," the political and diplomatic grounds for going after the Iraqi leader were readily available. Recall that in the letter that Secretary of State Baker showed Tariq Aziz before the war, Bush had warned that he would hold Saddam personally responsible if the Kuwaiti oil fields were torched, which, of course, they were. Instead, in May 1991 the administration announced that "all possible UN sanctions will be maintained until he [Saddam] is gone. Any easing of sanctions will be considered only when there is a new government [in Iraq]."[81] Clearly, Washington made the removal of the Iraqi leader an explicit goal of its policy, but "not until its [Washington's] military forces were being withdrawn."[82]

From this perspective, Bush's toughness during the final days of the war was mostly grandstanding. General Khaled, the senior Saudi participant in the Safwan cease-fire talks, notes that the United States brushed aside his suggestion that the discussions be conducted with an Iraqi member of the Revolutionary Command Council, rather than with some generals: "I found this [Iraqi representation] very unsatisfactory. I told Schwarzkopf we should insist that the Iraqis send to the talks a member of the RCC . . . so as to project the right political symbolism and underline the reality of Saddam's defeat. We had won the war, so it seemed right to me that we should meet Iraqis of a higher, rather than lower, rank than ourselves, if for no other reason than to deflate Saddam's ego and help bring him down."[83]

In hindsight, General Khaled writes, if the allies had insisted on the presence in Safwan of an RCC member, "and had the pressure on Saddam been kept up for a little longer," then the "face of Iraq and the Gulf might well have been changed for the better."[84] These observations, whatever they are worth, should at least help put to rest the contention that in deciding to stop the war, President Bush was responding to strong pressures from Riyadh.[85] In Khaled's mind it was the United States that "was evidently not prepared to press the point."[86] Likewise, the commander of the British forces in Desert Storm, General de la Billière, tried to argue against stopping the war, even summoning help from Downing Street, but to no avail.[87] The U.S. forces in the field were also taken by complete surprise.[88]

About the talks in Safwan, Khaled writes:

> I had the strong feeling that . . . the meeting at Safwan was planned as an exercise in propaganda, a media event of little political, or even military, substance. Rather than a formal surrender, or any sort of public recognition that Saddam had lost the war, it was proposed that we "discuss" with the Iraqis a number of technical problems [for example, the release of POWs], all of which could, in my opinion, have been handled more effectively by our staff.
>
> I was left with the feeling that the U.S. was not seeking a formal Iraqi surrender, or did not think one appropriate.[89]

The inescapable conclusion is that despite his military defeat, Saddam was able to reach an unwritten understanding with the Bush administration. He was ready to pay lip service to UNSC demands provided that key elements of his mass destruction option, his political insurance policy, remained intact. From Saddam's perspective the United States was unquestionably looking for a face-saving formula. If Washington were truly determined to disarm Iraq's mass destruction option, he figured, the United States would not have stopped the war. The U.S. decision to "suspend" hostilities so soon after Iraq issued its strategic threat could only mean that the Iraqi deterrent signal had been effective. In that case, why would the Americans believe that Iraq would give up in peace what the United States did not dare seize by war?

The essentials of this "deal" have been in evidence long after the war. As long as Saddam's CB weapons remained a last-resort option, Washington was satisfied solely with preserving the U.N.-imposed sanctions. Despite Saddam's flagrant violation of Resolution 687, which called for Iraq to dismantle its mass destruction capability, the United States had in effect reconciled itself to exerting only passive pressure on Baghdad. In turn, the Iraqi leader was reassured that no forceful effort would be made to terminate his political insurance policy — the CB arms. To mollify his "doomsday" threat, compliance had become Saddam's choice, not his obligation. Only when the Iraqi leader attempted to rewrite these "rules" and apply his deadly cache politically, in a bid to remove the sanctions altogether, was Washington forced to rethink its stand (see Chapter 9).

It cannot be claimed that the prolonged stalemate was the result of an information gap — that is, that only recently had the United States become aware of Saddam's leftover BW capabilities. On February 24, 1993, CIA Director James Woolsey told a Senate committee: "Iraq's biological weapons capability is perhaps of greatest immediate concern. Baghdad had an advanced program before Desert Storm, and neither war nor inspection has seriously degraded this capability."[90]

The telltale signs of a U.S.-Iraqi "understanding" had surfaced even earlier. Under Resolution 687 of April 3, 1991, Iraq was to submit, within 15 days, a declaration of the locations, amounts, and types of all chemical and biological weapons, as well as all missile systems. Also to be declared were all stocks of agents, and all facilities for research, development, support, and manufacturing. Iraq failed to comply with these provisions. Instead, Baghdad claimed that it had destroyed most of its mass destruction weapons and delivery systems unilaterally and without international supervision, although such action was in direct contravention of Resolution 687. Worse yet, Iraq's work on proscribed weapons systems continued even after the adoption of the resolution.

The American response was strangely scant. Although the pattern of Iraqi violations had become evident while the U.S. Desert Storm forces were still very much present on the scene, their withdrawal from the Gulf area continued uninterrupted. No wonder that the exasperated Ambassador Ekeus was ready to declare his mission over in January 1995, seven months before the new information on Iraq's BW capability came to light.[91]

President Bush, it would appear, was offered the semblance of a victory so that the United States would stop the war. In return, Saddam was allowed to continue in power. Both sides were satisfied because the price of deviation from this deal was simply judged by both to be too high. For Saddam, failure to abide by the U.S. demands could have forced the United States to take the war into Baghdad. This would have led Saddam to resort to CBW against Israel. Given Israel's likely unconventional response, that would have surely meant committing suicide. At the same time, for Bush to reject the limited victory agreed to by Baghdad would have meant stepping into the abyss. And if there were any doubts left in Washington as to the gravity of this danger, the Israelis reportedly tested a "nuclear-capable" missile shortly before the war ended. Although it is safe to assume that the launch, if it took place, was primarily meant for the benefit of Soviet spy satellites and thus for Baghdad, it can be also said that

Jerusalem was "hinting to the Bush administration that Israel would be ready to use nuclear weapons to stop the Scud offensive."[92] Naturally, there was little taste for this, especially as Bush and his aides were happy to assume that a sound military defeat would lead to the Iraqi leader's downfall anyway.[93] Was this what General Powell had in mind when he warned Bush against the danger of fighting past the "rational calculation"?[94] It must have been. Even two years after the war, it was easy to trace Gen. Powell's perception of the threat he thought he was facing. In 1993 he was quoted as stating: "The one that scares me to death, perhaps even more so than tactical nuclear weapons, and the one we have the least capability against is biological weapons."[95] In fact, of all the top U.S. decision makers, General Powell stands out as the most open in expressing his fears over an Iraqi BW scenario in the Gulf.

Saddam Claims Victory

But if Saddam was really able to use a suicidal threat to deter the United States from pursuing the war deep into Iraq, why would he not promptly trumpet his victory over Bush? Is it reasonable to assume that a leader uncertain of his political survival would forfeit such an opportunity to solidify his hold on power? Perhaps Iraq's silence about its mass destruction threat should be taken as proof that the landing of the concrete warhead was indeed a benign event, and that it was the American and Israeli conception of Saddam's last-resort strategy, rather than Saddam himself, that forced an end to the fighting. That is, it was the perception of threat, rather than one actually made, that hindered the United States. In that case, to the extent that the concrete warhead did play a role in the decision to terminate the war, it was merely a self-fulfilling prophecy.

As plausible as this explanation may sound, the record is rather different. A careful reading of the events since the end of the Gulf War reveals how Saddam finally claimed victory over the United States or, more precisely, how Iraq disclosed the role of its mass destruction option in thwarting its enemies.

It must be remembered that the war had weakened Saddam and his military machine. Consequently, in the months immediately after the war, Saddam's first priority was to shield his leftover CB capabilities from the prying eyes of the UNSCOM inspectors. As Ekeus has noted: "It appears from documentation and other information that the Iraqi leadership has been trying to retain strategic capabilities relative to all the proscribed weapons categories."[96] Over time, the aim was to rebuild and even improve Iraq's capabilities in these areas, despite Resolution 687. Saddam expected that once UNSCOM completed its mission, the sanctions would be lifted and the business of rearming Iraq could begin in earnest. He thought that the UNSCOM inspectors would be out of Iraq in no time. As he reportedly told his lieutenants at a meeting in the Presidential Palace soon after the war: "The Special Commission is a temporary measure and we will fool them and we will bribe them and the matter will be over in a few months."[97] In the meantime, Iraq would lie low so as not to jeopardize their departure.

Had Saddam suddenly claimed that his readiness to resort to CB weapons during the war had blocked Iraq's opponents, his own scenario would have been undermined. In the wake of Resolution 687, Saddam could not advertise his strategic deterrent without playing into the hands of UNSCOM. Instead, until summer 1995, Iraq consistently denied that it had ever engaged in the development of *offensive* biological weapons. Moreover, it claimed, the program was destroyed long before the Gulf War to prevent it from contaminating the Iraqi countryside if it became a target of an Israeli air strike. The Iraqi Foreign Ministry stated officially that "Iraq completely halted [military] biological research work in the spring of 1990 when it anticipated the possibility of an aggression on it. It also affirmed [to UNSCOM inspectors] the nonexistence of any biological activity for military purposes, or any biological weapons or instruments at all."[98] If Baghdad had declared that in February 1991 its BW threat forced Bush to stop fighting, it would have automatically admitted that its previous claims were bogus. Such an assertion would have likely reinvigorated the hunt for Iraq's leftover mass destruction weapons. Obviously, Saddam could not afford such an outcome.

In his mind, the strategic rationale for keeping his last-resort option a secret did not diminish with the end of the war. On the contrary, in the aftermath of the conflict, keeping mum became mandatory given the presence of the UNSCOM inspectors in his country. In fact, Iraq not only tried to keep its BW option secret but also endeavored to use the alleged dismantling of the program for its political purposes: it sought to capitalize on the misgivings of some neighboring countries, which during the war had warned that the allied bombing of Iraqi CB sites would produce a fallout hazard to their territories. The idea was to help Iraq portray itself as a responsible member of the world community, which even in the face of adversity took steps to assure international security. Further, by denying the existence of its BW option, Iraq was aiming not only to alleviate the pressures to disclose its mass destruction arms but also to have the U.N. sanctions lifted altogether. All these objectives would have been jeopardized if Saddam had gone public with his BW deterrent.

What is more, there was no real need for Saddam to point to the role of CB weapons in achieving victory. Following the war, Iraq issued numerous "conventional" victory claims, boasting of the Iraqi soldiers' successes vis-à-vis the "30-nation aggression." For instance, in an address celebrating the 73d anniversary of the founding of the Iraqi army, Saddam claimed that "the United States announced a unilateral cease-fire . . . they said we should confirm the cease-fire which they announced unconditionally and unilaterally." He said that he promptly sent a message to Staff Lt. Gen. Sultan Hashim Ahmad, the army chief of staff (who was to represent Iraq at the upcoming cease-fire talks), stating: "You are the victors."[99] Vice President Ramadan said: "The battle was at its height, Bush did not achieve his objective, that is why he accepted the cease-fire. He knew what the reaction in the United States would be if U.S. losses mounted."[100] For his part, Tariq Aziz asserted that Bush's original objective was to reach Baghdad. Owing to the valiant resistance of Iraq's ground units, however, the United States realized that such an advance would be very costly. "This forced Bush to withdraw."[101]

Accordingly, what followed the war were years of denial, deceit, and concealment of the Iraqi mass destruction capability. Even when Iraq ostensibly decided to "cooperate" with UNSCOM (from 1993 to fall 1994), the cooperation did not extend to disclosures of the true state of the CBW program, which was kept secret.[102] And between September 1994 and June 1995, Baghdad reverted to its previous stance. On July 1, 1995, in the wake of new discoveries by UNSCOM, Iraq at last acknowledged having had an offensive BW program but still denied the weaponization of agents. It admitted the production of a solution containing botulinum toxin, and an anthrax solution. Yet, it claimed to have destroyed the material and abandoned the program in October 1990, as the Gulf War approached.[103] Iraq maintained that it had lived up to its obligations under the Biological Weapons Convention, which prohibits the development, production, and stockpiling of bacteriological and toxin weapons.

Then, in August 1995, in the wake of Hussein Kamil Hassan's defection earlier that month, Iraq presented "dramatically new information on its past biological warfare program, including details concerning weaponization, and additional agents and sites."[104] But even after these new revelations, Iraq continued to lie about its mass destruction program and keep it from UNSCOM's reach.

Naturally, the question arises, why did Saddam bother to come clean after Kamil Hassan's defection? In view of the subsequent continuation of the policy of denial, deceit, and concealment, what motivated Saddam to provide Ekeus with "a gigantic collection of documents" about Iraq's BW program?[105] What could explain the sudden, and short-lived, attack of "candor" which afflicted Baghdad in August 1995?

Ekeus reported that the Iraqis had told him that the decision to release the information was aimed to minimize the importance of Kamil Hassan and his information.[106] Other observers speculated that Saddam understood that he could not keep his son-in-law quiet and therefore decided to preempt his disclosures and gain political points with the United Nations by "producing a flood of information on the weapons program."[107] According to U.N. officials, the Iraqis had concluded that they had only until the end of that year to push for sanctions relief. After that would come the U.S. presidential election season, during which President Clinton would never lift the embargo for fear of appearing soft. "So the regime was promising '100%' cooperation with the U.N., according to Ekeus."[108]

There is probably some truth in these explanations. In hindsight, the disclosure had the familiar markings of a deceitful scheme that Baghdad had practiced with regularity ever since the cease-fire went into effect in 1991. Evidently, Saddam thought that he would finally convince the United States that Iraq had provided a "full, final and complete disclosure" of its deadly arsenal, as required by U.N. resolutions. The crippling sanctions would thus be lifted. But if this was Saddam's aim, it is puzzling that Ekeus could have stated in October 1995, only two months after the new disclosures: "Iraq is not cooperating with us as it should be. . . . They are misleading us now. . . . Even after the information they submitted in August after Kamil Hassan's defection, they have still submitted erroneous information to us."[109] "Somewhere [during this time period]," Ekeus said, "a decision was taken to stop the process of cooperation and we [UNSCOM] ran into the usual policy of blockage."[110]

The key to this series of events is that Saddam had been itching to disclose his true capability ever since the Gulf War ended. He had become increasingly frustrated with the new team in the White House, who showed no sign of flexibility on lifting the sanctions. Perhaps a reminder of Iraq's capacity for exacting a frightful punishment was required to convince President Clinton to emulate his predecessor. After all, Bush himself had regained his senses only at the last minute.

For months Saddam actively prepared the grounds for his dramatic unveiling. Thus, Baghdad's dramatic change of tone in the fall of 1994 occurred because Saddam realized that despite Iraq's "cooperation" the sanctions were not about to be removed and that UNSCOM's snooping was about to become a permanent fixture of the Iraqi scene. In late September 1994, Saddam suddenly reinvoked the theme of Iraq's capacity for disrupting the world order, which had been characteristic of his dire warnings during the Gulf crisis itself. While blasting the continued embargo on Iraq, Saddam said, "When the patience of the Iraqis, as a bloc, nears the phase of restlessness or when we feel that the Iraqis will be starved, then we will, by God, open for them all the storehouses of the universe."[111] And in case anyone missed the significance of this message, the Iraqi press explained: "America should not imagine that the destruction of Iraqi missiles, etc., has deprived the Iraqi people of its ability to influence and change the course of history. . . . Does America realize the meaning of opening the storehouses of the world through the Iraqi people's will? . . . Does it realize the meaning of each Iraqi being a missile crossing countries and cities?"[112] It was pointedly stated that "when man is convinced that death is his inevitable fate, there remains no deterrence to stop him from taking the most dangerous steps" to alter the course of events.[113] One newspaper, addressing Ekeus directly, asked rhetorically whether he did not know "that history says: When peoples reach the brink of collective death they are able to universalize death so that all are included!"[114]

These apocalyptic prophecies were not only meant to intimidate the United States and its allies in the UNSC into submitting to Baghdad's demands. They were equally aimed to create the last-resort atmosphere suitable for lending credence to the introduction of Iraq's ultimate threat. In January 1995 Saddam reintroduced his fatalistic line, the one he first promulgated before the Gulf War. "Iraq's basic power lay in its belief that almighty God will protect Iraq," he announced on the fourth anniversary of the Gulf War. And as if his Qur'anic prophecy had come true, he went on to say: "After a long duel, in which all weapons of destruction, devastation and killing were used . . . Iraq and its army emerged alive and capable, in the name of God. . . . This drove the aggressors crazy. They realized they had failed utterly."[115] He seemed to be saying that no matter what was in store for Iraq, God would again help it foil the evil plans of the modern Habashis.

The defection of Kamil Hassan, though certainly not engineered by Iraq, provided him with a golden opportunity to reveal Iraq's true potential for causing mayhem. Given that he must have known the kind of privileged information Kamil Hassan had access to, Saddam undoubtedly concluded that the secrets of Iraq's mass destruction weapons were about to be compromised.[116] But true to terrorist deterrence, instead of admitting a setback, he sought to use the breach to advance his political goals. By allowing the United Nations a short glimpse into Iraq's mass destruction capabilities, Saddam had multiple objectives in mind, beyond Iraq's familiar deceitful motives. First, he was sending a message to his Iraqi enemies and their potential supporters that the defection of a pillar of the regime should not be taken as evidence that its power had somehow diminished. Anyone who might contemplate extending support to a plot against his regime should know what kind of danger he could put his country into.[117]

Second, Saddam was likewise seeking to intimidate the United Nations, and especially the United States, into removing the economic embargo. He was divulging not only Iraq's deadly BW arsenal but, more important, his readiness to resort to it. He sought to send a credible warning that there was a limit to his patience regarding the sanctions. Iraq still had the capacity to "turn the tables on its enemies."[118] Moreover, he apparently insinuated, pushing Iraq to disarm its CBW capabilities and leaving Saddam at the mercy of his enemies would force him to undertake actions of historical and global implications. As the United States had now been made aware of his preparations for BW during the war, its leaders should not doubt his will to use these horrific weapons in extremis. In short, just as with the termination of the Gulf War itself, Saddam was trying to blackmail the United States into accepting his terms: "Satisfy yourself with my disclosures or else," was the message. In this sense Ekeus did not disappoint Saddam: his genuine expressions of shock over the revelations, especially Iraq's intrawar readiness for BW, were undoubtedly welcomed by the practitioners of terrorist deterrence in Baghdad.

Third, Saddam could finally prove that the Gulf War was not a defeat but a tie, as he had long claimed. Indeed, Baghdad's determination to behave as an equal negotiating partner with the United Nations, arguing every point, was at the root of its standoff with UNSCOM. This attitude contrasted starkly with the Western view of Iraq as a defeated aggressor on which unconditional demands — expressed in U.N. resolutions — could legitimately be made. As Usama al-Hitti, Iraq's oil minister, once asked: "Did the Gulf War end in a cease-fire or a defeat?"[119] According to Saddam, the American acceptance of the cease-fire was proof that Iraq could not be defeated. The United States thereby signaled its recognition of the potential cost of a fight to a final victory. As Saddam was surely aware of his deadly stash, it is all but inconceivable that he saw the U.S. acceptance of the cease-fire as decoupled from Iraq's last-resort option. To him, the decision to halt the fighting implied U.S. awareness of Iraq's strategic potential. The cease-fire, then, codified Iraq's ability to exercise terrorist deterrence effectively against the United States. As Saddam has said: "Had it not been for Iraq's steadfastness, the United States' appetite for aggression would have spread in many parts of the world."[120]

For all these reasons, Saddam sought to seize the opportunity and reveal at least something of his true capacity for BW. Thus, only one day after Kamil Hassan defected, Ekeus received an urgent letter from Tariq Aziz summoning him to Baghdad for "new and important revelations."[121] On August 20, 1995, after meeting with Aziz, Ekeus headed to the Habbaniyah military air base, intent on departing Iraq. A "high-ranking Iraqi officer," he recalled, "asked me to postpone my departure for a couple of hours. I was taken to a farm that belonged to General Hussein Kamil [Hassan], 50 minutes' drive south from Baghdad. There the military showed me eight containers, each the size of a room, and 148 metal boxes full of documents which were stored in two locked poultry brooding buildings."[122] The official Iraqi story was that Kamil had hidden the evidence from the government in his farm, known as the Haidar Chicken Farm. However, Ekeus observed, the steel cases "had not a speck of dust on them," a clear clue that they had been quickly planted.[123]

Moreover, U.N. officials said that Iraq must have "carefully screened" the documents before turning them over, because photos of the farm taken by a reconnaissance aircraft showed many containers that "were later removed from the site."[124] As relayed by Ekeus's successor, Richard Butler:

> The Farm was seized by [Iraq's] Special Security on August 9, and that material was brought to the site at that time. The Farm had been used to store material [related to Iraq's proscribed weapons programs] earlier. This material was probably contained in the containers observed [in aerial photography] in July 1995. . . . However, this material was not at the Haidar Farm on August 8, 1995. High-level defectors have informed the Commission that this material was, on August 8, stored at a number of locations throughout the Baghdad area to include residences associated with several high-ranking Iraqi Government officials. The Special Security Organization might have quickly acted to consolidate those caches, and from August 9 until August 18, worked to sort the material into two categories: what was to be turned over to the Commission, and what was to be retained.[125]

Of all the boxes delivered to Ekeus at the Haidar farm, "there was a single, small, wooden box of documents about the biological weapons program."[126] Iraq claimed that all the other documents with regard to its BW program had been destroyed in 1991 on orders of Kamil. However,

UNSCOM noted, "This event could not be confirmed."[127] The Iraqis maintained that the box contained whatever had been preserved or collected after the destruction, but "the source of these documents [could] not be established."[128] To top it all off, the 700,000 pages of documents related to Iraq's NBC programs contained "sparse" relevant information, which had been "buried within a massive volume of extraneous data." It was "intended to create the appearance of candor and overwhelm UNSCOM's analytic resources."[129] Upon examination of the documentary material, UNSCOM and the International Atomic Energy Agency concluded that "despite advertisements to the contrary, Iraq did not release its most important weapons of mass destruction–related documents."[130] Instead of a hurried disclosure forced on a "panicked" regime, the handover bore all the markings of a carefully planned operation aimed to advance specific political objectives.[131] Saddam let UNSCOM and the world see what he wanted them to see.

Following this revelation, Baghdad modified its position. It maintained that it destroyed the biological agents *after* the war, not in 1990 as it had previously pretended.[132] Saddam could now point to his successful mass destruction threat during the war. On January 17, 1996, the fifth anniversary of the Gulf War, he announced over Baghdad Radio, "The Iraqis defeated the enemy by preventing [him] from throttling the base of the capability of the faithful [Arab] nation and centre of its radiation [Iraq]."[133] As if to support this astonishing claim, the mouthpiece of the Iraqi Defense Ministry soon asserted: "A short time after the cease-fire which was unilaterally called by the Americans, information started to emerge in the world press and publications about the fighting capabilities of the Iraqi Armed Forces and the resilience they have shown."[134] On the same day INA, the Iraqi news agency, relayed this message in its English broadcast. Thus Saddam found a way to claim his mass destruction prowess during the Gulf War after all. The idea was to unveil the Iraqi threat without providing further ammunition to the U.N. arms inspectors and their supporters. After all, the weapons were officially no longer in existence. Saddam, it must be assumed, even meant to help his friends at the UNSC as they sought to phase out the sanctions. Concurrently, however, his blackmail powers were enhanced, as new uncertainties about the fate of the Iraqi CB arsenal were inevitably created. This way, Saddam surmised, the exercise would end up expanding rather than narrowing Iraq's room to maneuver vis-à-vis the United States and the United Nations. Yet, he calculated, even if the disclosure of his capacity for annihilation failed to achieve the lifting of the sanctions and to deter further inspections, as long as his leftover CB cache remained hidden, the bet was worthwhile.

Saddam might well think that Iraq today is more susceptible to attack given that his regime faces enemies on all sides, Iraq's military capabilities comprise a fraction of its prewar arsenal, and he cannot publicize a strategic deterrent because of UNSC Resolution 687. Paradoxically, the erosion in Iraq's leftover conventional capabilities brought about largely by years of sanctions has meant that its dependence on the mass destruction option has increased.[135] At present, Iraq's sole strategic deterrent is the uncertainty surrounding the existence of its CB cache. In turn, the case for maintaining a secret last-resort deterrent is presently more compelling than when Iraq invaded Kuwait.

By insisting on keeping a secret deterrent at all costs, Saddam indicates that in his mind the conflict is not over, and that he sees the CB option as his political insurance policy. The last thing the Iraqi leader would want, under the circumstances, is to announce formally that his gas and germ weapons enabled Iraq to triumph over America. He knows full well that such bragging would energize the international efforts to disarm him of this option and undermine those who are pressing the UNSC to lift the sanctions. Therefore, unless Saddam is ready for another confrontation, open proclamation of Iraq's glorious defeat of the United States via its mass destruction threat will have to be deferred.

Simply put, as long as UNSCOM does not provide Iraq with a clean bill of health regarding its CB capabilities, any attempt to use these capabilities to openly claim victory in the Gulf War would be counterproductive. Under such circumstances, the announcement would be liable to be perceived as a dangerous provocation, regardless of when Iraq claims it destroyed its cache.

Besides, it is not entirely clear that such a victory declaration by Saddam would necessarily endear him to his Iraqi audience. Some are likely to wonder why, if Iraq's mass destruction threat indeed deterred the United States, was this warning not issued earlier in the war, thus saving thousands of Iraqi lives and avoiding the ruin of the Iraqi economy. Others might wonder why Saddam gave these weapons up without getting the sanctions lifted. Still others may conclude that, given the likely Israeli response, Saddam in effect was ready to commit national suicide rather than surrender. Moreover, on previous occasions Saddam spoke of resort to CBW in response to an Israeli surprise nuclear attack on Baghdad. In this scenario he unquestionably emerged as the defender of the nation. Saddam was the leader who in his foresight undertook to protect Iraq's greatness against the inevitable "Zionist aggression." In the Gulf War, however, the Israeli card could not be played so well. If a calamity had befallen the Iraqi people, it would have been because of Saddam's ill-fated decision to invade Kuwait, coupled by his readiness to take on the United States single-handedly. Furthermore, boasting of one's readiness to confront a theoretical nuclear threat is rather different from informing the residents of Baghdad that their personal survival had recently been put in grave jeopardy. At least some among the military ranks were likely to conclude that their leader was a madman who must be removed.

A mass grave in al-Sulaymaniyah Province, in northeast Iraq near the border with Iran, where Iraqis buried entire families of Kurds. Kurdish leaders say that their villages were typically bombed, beginning in 1987, with a combination of mustard gas and nerve gases. Afterward, villages were razed by Iraqis wearing chemical protection suits and gas masks. This early evidence shows that Iraq was willing to use poison weapons against a civilian population.
Françoise de Muder — SIPA

American soldiers training in Saudi Arabia in preparation for Iraqi use of poison gases during the Gulf War.
Official U.S. Air Force Photo/Staff Sergeant F. Lee Corkran

A Patriot missile launches toward an incoming Scud missile to protect Riyadh, the Saudi Arabian capital. The Patriot anti-missile defenses provided only scant protection against Scud attacks on Saudi Arabia during the Gulf War and were even less effective in shielding Israel.

Gary Kieffer/ZUMA

The remains of a Scud being collected near Riyadh. The Scud, a missile of
Soviet origin, was considered by some as a "stone-age clunker," a cheap
weapon for low-tech war, with limited range and poor accuracy. Nevertheless, Iraq's Scuds were capable of creating terror among a civilian
population, and just one Scud — if loaded with a chemical or biological
agent — could have transformed the war in an instant.

Official U.S. Navy Photo/PH2 Susan Carl

Starting on February 21, 1991, Iraq's forces unleashed environmental terror by setting ablaze more than half of Kuwait's thousand oil wells. This action provides an example of Saddam Hussein's "terrorist deterrence," which is aimed to shock and intimidate his enemies.
Gary Kieffer/ZUMA

The third UNSCOM inspection in Iraq, August 31–September 9, 1991: an Iraqi worker in protective gear climbs into a chemical-agent missile warhead to open it for sample taking. Iraq was to account for all nuclear, biological, chemical, and long-range missile systems before U.N. sanctions imposed in 1991 could be lifted. But by 1998, this still had not been done, yet U.N. solidarity on the issue appeared to be eroding.

U.N. Photo 158637/Shankar Kunhambu

The sixth UNSCOM inspection in Iraq, October 22–November 2, 1991: a member of the UNSCOM team from the United States inspects a 500-kilogram mustard-filled aerial bomb with a sonar-resonance system. In this inspection, the 26-member team counted thousands of bombs, shells, and warheads filled with lethal chemical agents, many of them damaged and leaking in the storage areas.

U.N. Photo 158684/H. Arvidsson

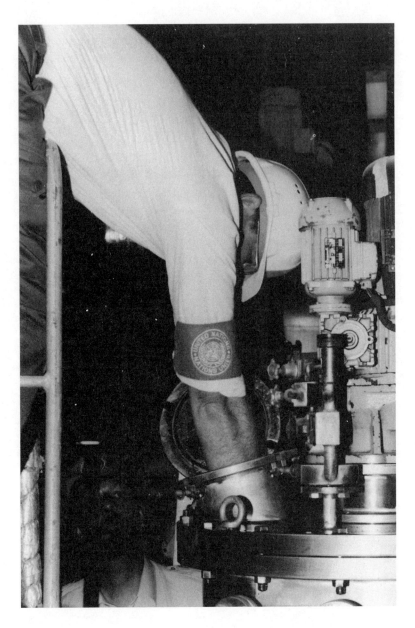

U.N. biological weapons inspectors taking samples from fermenters at al-
Hakam Single Cell Protein Production Plant, 55 kilometers southwest of
Baghdad, which was used to produce anthrax and botulinum toxin for
biological warfare. This was one of five sites around Baghdad suspected of
being involved in the production of BW materials. The main facility of al-
Hakam was destroyed in June 1996.

U.N. Photo 158667/H. Arvidsson

The Israeli Nuclear Shadow

The Israeli nuclear alert, which General Powell alleges took place, had a minor impact, if any, on Washington's perception of the events in the Middle East in late February 1991. Similarly, the role of the Soviet Union (discussed in Chapter 7) also had only an indirect influence on U.S. decisions during this period. The key elements that propelled the thinking in Washington were that Saddam Hussein could resort to weapons of mass destruction in a last-ditch effort, that he could have the wherewithal to carry out such an attack, and that an Iraqi CB strike on Israel could lead to heavy civilian casualties. Even if Israel had no nuclear weapons, the third consideration alone would likely have led President Bush to stop the war. But the United States also believed that if such a scenario were to unfold, Israel would probably retaliate with nuclear weapons regardless of whether its forces were already on alert. To the extent that U.S. intelligence did suspect an Israeli nuclear alert, or to the extent that Soviet concerns found a sympathetic ear in Washington, the pressures to end the war only mounted that much further.

In spite of Israel's best efforts to keep its nuclear force in the shadow, the mere presence of this capability in the conflict area cast a long shadow on the decision-making process in Washington. What is more, many Israelis also believed that it played an important role in assuring their defense. A poll conducted in Israel toward the end of the Gulf War even found an "astonishing rise" in the number of people condoning the use of nuclear arms. Some 88 percent of participants replied that they "could live with" the use of nuclear weapons, compared with a mere 53 percent who said so in 1987 and 36 percent in 1986.[1]

Even so, the questions remain: Why did the United States conclude that Israel was likely to respond with nuclear weapons to an Iraqi CB strike? Was this view in error? And did Israel in fact put its nuclear force on alert, as General Powell implied?[2]

An Israeli Nuclear Response?

It has been flatly asserted that Israel had no intention of using its nuclear force during the Gulf War.[3] How could Powell seriously believe that Israel would resort to nuclear weapons given the presence of U.S. troops in the theater? In any case, the argument goes, it would be simply inconceivable for Israel to employ nuclear weapons without prior consultations with the United States. Rather, allegations about Israel's nuclear intentions could be a cover-up for Washington's efforts to block the IDF from entering the war. Washington was perhaps concerned that Israeli participation would jeopardize the cohesion of the coalition and endanger America's position in the Arab world in general. U.S. leaders presumably recognized, however, that if Saddam fired CB weapons into Israel, the United States would be unable to prevent Israel from sending its military into Iraq. Therefore, Bush had to stop the war when Saddam's presumed warning shot landed in the Negev.

Although this line may appeal to some analysts, there were in fact solid grounds for the United States to conclude that Israel would indeed retaliate with nuclear weapons to an Iraqi CB strike on its cities. Two years before the Gulf crisis, for example, Itzhak Rabin, then Israeli defense minister, reacted to the indiscriminate firing of Scud missiles against cities during the Iran-Iraq war as follows: "The Arab states must reckon that Israel is ready to protect her rear, both defensively and offensively, and I suggest to [their] leaders [that] if any one of them is contemplating using chemical weapons, [they must] realize that Israel has the means to inflict ten-times-larger punishment on the populations of the belligerent Arab countries."[4] Based on this declaration, Washington undoubtedly concluded that Israel had publicly adopted a nuclear countercity strategy to deter an Arab mass destruction attack on its major population centers.[5]

During the Gulf crisis itself, U.S. convictions that an Iraqi mass destruction attack would lead to an Israeli nuclear response must have solidified. In their bid to deter Saddam from using chemical or biological weapons against their cities, Israeli leaders issued stern warnings, which were widely interpreted as alluding to nuclear weapons. Prime Minister Shamir, for example, said that Saddam would "put himself and his country at a very, very grave risk" if he attacked Israel with chemical weapons.[6] Secretary of Defense Cheney even implied that the United States did indeed believe that Israel would resort to nuclear weapons if hit by chemical weapons (see Chapter 4).

Yet Rabin, who served as Israel's defense minister until nine months before the war, thought that the Shamir government's warnings to Iraq were too vague, especially once Israeli cities had already been attacked. Worse yet, the adoption by the government of passive defensive measures, like the distribution of gas masks to Israeli citizens, could be misinterpreted in Baghdad as implying readiness to absorb a chemical attack. In an interview published two days before the ground war was to begin — the phase during which AMAN estimated that Iraq was most likely to resort to CB weapons, and three days before the concrete warhead fell in the Negev — Rabin stated: "We have made it clear, using clandestine but also open channels, that our response to enemy strikes on Israel's home front will be the destruction of Arab capitals."[7]

At the minimum Rabin was seeking to create uncertainty in the minds of Arab leaders regarding the possible resort to nuclear means, in order to enhance Israel's deterrence posture. More likely, however, he was aiming to clarify that even though the government in Israel had changed, its nuclear countercity doctrine had not.[8] Realizing that Israel's effort to deter an Iraqi attack had failed, and fearing a similar outcome with regard to Saddam's CB option, he was convinced that ambiguity about Israel's "horrible" retaliation should be exchanged for certainty. Before the war, Rabin had contended that "nuclear weapons do not have any role in the crisis," so his shift must have reflected a sense of growing alarm.[9] Between him and Shamir, Washington must have concluded that an Iraqi resort to CBW would surely trigger an Israeli nuclear retaliation. In fact, when General Barak reminded General Powell of what Israel "must do" under such circumstances, Powell likely understood this to be a reference to Rabin's nuclear countercity doctrine.

During the conflict, if not before, the United States became less confident that its troop presence in the area would dissuade Israel from using nuclear weapons. In 1986, renegade Israeli nuclear technician Mordekhai Vanunu had revealed that such raw materials as lithium 6, tritium, and deuterium were being produced in Dimona, and ever since, speculation had been rife that Israel could produce enhanced radiation weapons, better known as neutron bombs.[10] Such weapons are aimed to destroy living organisms while producing minimal physical destruction. In this sense they resemble the effect of chemical weapons. Unlike chemical agents, however, a neutron bomb would not be influenced by the weather and its lethality would diminish rapidly beyond the target area itself.[11] Now, on the eve of the ground war, speculation appeared in the local press that since the 1960s Israel had concentrated on developing "clean" nuclear munitions aimed to minimize radioactive fallout.[12] This was after Maj. Gen. (Res.) Avigdor Ben Gal, a Knesset member of the Labor party, called on the United States to use "non-contaminating" tactical nuclear weapons to destroy Iraq's strategic infrastructure.[13] The statement could have been read as implying that Israel had developed nuclear weapons that could be used against Iraq with minimum risk to U.S. troops in the area.

Of course, the United States had expected to be consulted before an Israeli attack with nuclear weapons. No doubt it would have vehemently opposed the move. But, in the final analysis, if an Iraqi CB strike caused heavy losses in Israel, Jerusalem could have simply notified Washington of its decision.[14] As long as U.S. intelligence believed that Israel had the ability to reach Baghdad via nuclear-armed missiles, there was little Washington could do to prevent the attack.

Indeed, it appears that instead of trying to block Israel, the United States tried to assure that the IDF's response would be limited to conventional munitions. Deputy Secretary of State Lawrence Eagleburger, who arrived in Israel for consultations on January 12, 1991, strongly opposed an Israeli military intervention in the imminent war. He granted the Israelis one exception, however. "We all understood," he was cited as saying, "that if they got hit by chemical weapons not only would they respond but they should."[15] Eagleburger did not specify what kind of an Israeli retaliation the United States had in mind, but it is safe to assume that Washington sought to limit the attack (or attacks) to conventional weapons. It is unclear whether the United States understood that a great deal depended on the toll of dead and wounded among Israeli civilians. In any case, Barak's message to Powell on January 28, and Powell's anxious reaction (see Chapter 4), make it clear that Israel never committed itself to retaliating with conventional weapons only.

It is likely that the Shamir government had decided that Israel could downplay its nuclear option. Yet Washington had no reason to believe that Israel would not resort to such weapons if Iraq attacked it with chemical weapons. On the contrary, in retrospect there are ample grounds to question whether Israel would have opted for a conventional response to an Iraqi CB attack.

First, Israel would have likely decided on a horrible punishment in order to restore its deterrent capability vis-à-vis the Arabs, considering that the unconventional threshold had been crossed. As Ze'ev Schiff argued, the mere fact that an Arab country had dared to fire mass destruction weapons at Israel would have been viewed as an extremely dangerous precedent. Second, whatever the actual toll, if Israeli civilian population centers had been hit rather than military targets, the offense would have been considered especially grievous.

Third, Israeli leaders had pledged to respond to any Iraqi attack. For example, before the war Defense Minister Arens warned: "Israel will stay out of a war if it is not attacked by Iraq. We hope that this will be the case, but if we are attacked — and we have heard threats from Baghdad — we will immediately retaliate. And I can tell you that our response will not be a 'low profile' response!"[16] Following the first Iraqi missile attack on Tel Aviv and Haifa, he said: "We have said publicly and to the Americans that if we were attacked we would react; we were attacked, we will react, certainly. We have to defend ourselves."[17] Yet Israel remained passive. It would have been inconceivable for Israel to fail, yet again, to carry out its threat of a horrible punishment if it wished to preserve any shred of credibility in the eyes of its Arab enemies.

Fourth, the possibility of mass casualties due to Iraqi CBW must be taken into account. Although Prime Minister Shamir had said publicly that Iraq's resort to CW "could not threaten our very existence," implying that a nuclear response was out of the question, he reportedly admitted that "if, God forbid, there [had] been a hit causing the deaths of dozens of civilians, he would not have been able to keep his cool."[18] And this was in reference to attacks with Iraq's conventionally armed Scuds. Even these attacks created a mini-revolt in the Israeli cabinet. On January 19, after the third Scud attack on Israel, a small group of Israeli ministers and army officers demanded immediate retaliation. They argued that the grave warnings Israel had issued before the war to deter Iraq had failed. "Now these ministers believed a nuclear strike should be considered so that the whole world would understand the message: No one can get away with attacking Israeli cities!"[19] One can only imagine what would have happened if an Iraqi CB attack had caused heavy losses of civilian lives in Israel.

There was one more reason why nuclear retaliation would have been high on the Israeli agenda under such circumstances. Two years after the war, Ze'ev Schiff wrote: "Looking back, it seems that during the war it was learned that even Israel's offensive capability was deficient. . . . It is impossible to divulge any details here, but the significance is that between a routine military response — dropping ordinary bombs [in response to an Iraqi missile attack] — and the most drastic one lay very few possibilities, and not all would have been sufficiently effective. I hesitate to use the term blunder [*mekhdal*], but there was definitely negligence. Since then, efforts have been made to rectify the situation, but that requires a great deal of time and money."[20] From this statement, it is possible to infer that the only alternative Israel had in case of an Iraqi CB attack was the use of nuclear arms.

It is not clear to what extent the United States was privy to this information, or whether Powell suspected that Barak had overstepped his mandate. Nonetheless, fear was rampant in Washington that an Iraqi CB attack on an Israeli city would trigger a retaliation with unconventional weapons. In fact, following the first Scud attack on Tel Aviv, Israeli civil defense teams had erroneously detected sarin nerve gas in one of the Iraqi warheads. Soon another report reached Washington indicating that an "unusual number of ambulances" were racing through the city.[21] Reportedly, Eagleburger then told his colleagues at the White House that Israel would retaliate by firing Jericho surface-to-surface missiles.[22] Because Washington firmly believed that the Jericho's primary mission was as Israel's strategic deterrent, the implication was that an Israeli nuclear retort was imminent. Indeed, in view of Rabin's strategic retaliation doctrine, any other prediction by the officials at the White House would have qualified as wishful thinking.

Ironically, by blocking the Israeli plan for conventional preemption against the Scuds, Washington may have made such an Israeli response almost inevitable. And the belief in an Israeli unconventional response was certainly reinforced by the pronouncements of various Israeli civilian and military leaders before and during the Gulf War. But Israel could not have avoided issuing such public warnings. It faced a difficult dilemma. To deter Iraq, it had to issue strong warnings promising resort to terrible weapons, given that its entire civilian population was faced with a credible threat of mass destruction attacks. Yet Israel also needed to signal Washington that nuclear weapons were not under consideration. The results of such acrobatics could have been counterproductive in both respects.

A Nuclear Alert?

Given the preceding analysis, Israel's strategic posture during Desert Storm could be summarized as one of nuclear ambiguity on the declaratory level coupled with nuclear delay in practice: Prime Minister Shamir would have dearly liked to avoid the use of nuclear weapons. For political, strategic, and operational reasons, he thought that there was nothing to be gained but much to be lost if Israel overplayed its nuclear hand, let alone alerted its nuclear forces in advance. Israel, he thought, could afford to keep its bomb in the basement, literally.

At one point in the crisis it even appeared as if Israel were signaling its intention to absorb an Iraqi CB attack, by pointing to its second-strike capability. It was made known that the IAF had undergone extensive training and upgrading to face an NBC threat. These preparations apparently started well before the war, after the IAF commander predicted that Iraq would develop chemical warheads for its Scuds and that such missiles could land on Israeli air bases. The Iraqis, he stated, would "not dare" to attack Israeli civilian targets.[23] Consequently, new Israeli-made NBC sensors were deployed in its air bases, and pilots were given new flight jackets specifically designed for operating in an NBC environment. The IAF's headquarters and its main C&C centers were equipped with central protective systems, making personal NBC protection unnecessary. These centers were "hardened, and impenetrable to BC agents as well as to the effects of nuclear radiation." Moreover, a "large simulation exercise" indicated that IAF personnel could operate unhindered under such conditions. "The planes continued to take off as normal, although they underwent a decontamination phase which lasted a few minutes. The ability to withstand an NBC environment was plainly demonstrated."[24]

To deter Iraq, Israel could have fielded its nuclear force.[25] It could then have relied on Soviet reconnaissance satellites and Jordanian air patrols to convey its deterrent message to Baghdad.[26] Such a display of Israel's nuclear readiness would have surely been detected by U.S. intelligence as well and would have signaled to Washington the seriousness of the Israeli dilemma. The pressure on the United States to hunt down the Scuds would have mounted, in line with Israeli interests. Jerusalem might have also viewed Washington as an indirect channel to Saddam, hoping that the U.S. relationship with his Soviet allies would facilitate the transmission of Israel's deterrent message to Baghdad.

Instead, Israel issued vague warnings but at the same time opted for a nuclear stand-down. In Jerusalem it was felt that such a posture had both political and strategic merits. Israel was not interested in incurring Washington's wrath unnecessarily.[27] Its chosen posture would facilitate the U.S. prosecution of the war. And Israel also sought to avoid any provocative moves, which might have forced Saddam to use CB weapons for fear that his destruction was imminent. Yet if Saddam attacked with mass destruction weapons anyway, Israel would have both the capability and the legitimacy to respond in kind.

Contrary to General Powell's claim, Israel did not put its nuclear force on "special alert."[28] Pentagon officials who feared an Israeli nuclear retaliation to an Iraqi CW attack were said to have been reassured after "U.S. intelligence picked up no evidence that Israel had moved nukes into position to launch against Iraq."[29] Why, then, did Washington not only estimate that an Iraqi mass destruction attack would trigger an Israeli nuclear retaliation, but also suspect, based on Powell's account, that Israel had alerted its nuclear missile force already? One possibility is that Powell's claim amounted to a political dirty trick. As the general must have known the state of the Israeli nuclear force, the implication is that he was simply trying to invent an alibi for his efforts to stop the war. Powell's obscure reference to "reports" of the Israeli alert may indicate that he could not really point to any hard information on the subject. This would tend to substantiate the theory that for Powell, the alleged Israeli nuclear alert was just an excuse to stop the war.

The reality, however, was different. Powell was most concerned with the readiness of the Israeli nuclear missile force. He was not so worried about an alert of the Israeli Air Force because the United States, by withholding the IFF codes, had a quasi veto power on the IAF's nuclear mission. Not so with regard to Israel's surface-to-surface missiles known as Jericho. There was little the United States could do if Israel decided to fire them at Iraq, or so Powell evidently thought.

In fact, this view was erroneous and resulted from a failure in U.S. intelligence collection. The United States "did not seem to know that the new Jericho [a missile dubbed the Jericho IIB] was not yet fully operational and thus Israel did not have a ready option for an unmanned strike on Baghdad, the only target that might satisfy a quest for vengeance."[30] After the Gulf War, some ministers of the Likud party reportedly pointed to Labor's Rabin — in his capacity as defense minister from 1984 until shortly before the war — as responsible for the failure. They charged that he had not invested sufficient funds in upgrading the Jericho.[31]

Another possible reason for the delay in the deployment of the improved Jericho was Moscow's loud objections. The weapon was of such concern to the Soviet Union that it publicly exposed an Israeli test of the improved missile. Moscow demanded that Israel stop the development of its intermediate-range ballistic missile (IRBM), pointing out that with a range of 1,500 kilometers the missile could reach targets in the southern USSR, and that its relatively low accuracy indicated that it was meant to carry a nuclear warhead.[32] As a result, the issue was "raised in bilateral meetings at the highest level, with Israel consistently trying to reassure the Kremlin on this point."[33]

U.S. intelligence mistakenly believed that the new Jericho was operational largely because in the previous 30 months Israel had launched two experimental satellites into orbit using the IIB version of the Jericho.[34] The United States apparently concluded that development of the new version meant that its Jericho II surface-to-surface variant, in testing since mid-1987, had become operational. Israel, it was estimated, now possessed a homemade missile with an extended range of more than 1,400 kilometers, nearly twice the distance to the Iraqi capital. One report, apparently citing data of the DIA, said that Israel was believed to have about 100 of the Jericho II missiles.[35] Indeed, it would appear that even if Washington had had valid information about the status of the Jericho "follow-ons," it would not have necessarily made a different assessment. A report by the Washington-based Wisconsin Project on Nuclear Arms Control said that the Pentagon estimated that even the Jericho I was capable of reaching Tehran, and thus certainly Baghdad, provided that "aeronautical adjustments" were made.[36] Moreover, only a minimal number of such missiles would have been required to inflict enormous damage, assuming that Israel had armed them with nuclear warheads.

It is possible that Powell's concern over the Jericho was heightened because of Israeli actions at the time. On December 21, 1990, Israel conducted a missile test into the eastern Mediterranean, which caused U.S. forces in the Gulf to go on alert.[37] It is not clear whether Israel was scrambling to put together a missile capable of reaching Baghdad or employing a deliberate ruse for the benefit of Iraq or the United States, or both.

On January 18, following the first Scud attacks on Tel Aviv and Haifa, Arens contacted Washington to demand that Israel be allowed to retaliate. President Bush's advisers staunchly opposed such a step. An aerial or ground operation aimed at the Scuds in western Iraq was seen as politically risky because it entailed flying over Arab countries, like Jordan, in order to reach Iraq. But later that night, National Security Adviser Brent Scowcroft "called Cheney at the Pentagon with new guidance from the White House: we'll try very hard to restrain the Israelis . . . but if they insist on retaliating, the Jericho might be preferable to a full-scale attack with air or ground troops."[38]

There is no contradiction between this proposal and Eagleburger's earlier grim forecast of a nuclear response via Jericho. Eagleburger was speaking of a unilateral Israeli reaction to a presumed nerve gas attack on Tel Aviv that caused heavy civilian casualties. He and his colleagues felt justified in their view that Israel would respond with nuclear weapons. By contrast, Scowcroft's idea was to exert a measure of control over the Israeli response, as he assumed that Israel would react anyway. Under this plan Israel undoubtedly was to arm its Jerichos with conventional warheads so as to retaliate in kind for the conventional Scud attacks on its cities. In Washington it was felt that this response, if there had to be one, would be militarily appropriate and politically expedient.

Two important conclusions could be derived from this episode. First, the conduct of both Scowcroft and Cheney, and the earlier commentary by

Eagleburger, indirectly confirm that the United States was in the dark with regard to Israel's SSM capability. U.S. intelligence grossly overestimated Israel's ability to hit Baghdad via Jericho missiles.

Second, the episode is indicative of the gap that developed between Israel's thinking and that of the United States. This divergence was largely caused by Washington's studiously avoiding any contact with Israel before the war, despite Israel's incessant requests. The Bush administration thought that such contact could interfere with its efforts to erect an anti-Saddam coalition including some Arab countries.[39] In this case, Arens turned down the U.S. suggestion to fire the Jericho on Baghdad, arguing, according to one account, that it " 'would accomplish nothing, and it might make matters even worse' by provoking the Iraqis to resort to chemical weapons."[40] He undoubtedly did not reveal that Israel could not reach Baghdad via the Jericho. Equally important, although the U.S. proposal was meant to satisfy Israel's desire for vengeance, it did not address the real Israeli problem of suppressing the Scuds in western Iraq.[41]

The U.S. "solution" demonstrates that Washington still did not grasp the acuteness of the Iraqi strategic threat as seen in Israel. On the contrary, it implies that at least during the early stages of the war, Saddam's ability to fire CB-mounted Scuds into Israel was viewed skeptically at the White House. But these failures of estimation guaranteed that, in short order, the Iraqi threat to Israel would become Washington's main headache throughout the campaign.[42] Incredibly, the American misconception of Israel's strategic dilemma persisted even when the United States — or, for that matter, Israel — had failed to deter Saddam and Scuds had begun falling on Israeli cities.

If these conclusions are correct and Israel truly lacked missiles capable of reaching Baghdad, the United States, by denying the IAF access to its IFF codes, unknowingly made an Israeli aerial nuclear attack an extremely dangerous and thus much less likely mission. Washington, it transpires, could have relieved its anxiety over the specter of an Israeli nuclear response but for its overestimation of the IDF's missile arsenal. Had the IDF also been allowed to mount a conventional attack on the Scuds in western Iraq, these worries could have been further allayed. It turns out, insofar as the Israeli nuclear factor was concerned, that the United States could have prosecuted the war until the final collapse of Saddam's regime.

But this does not mean that the war was stopped "prematurely." Iraq could still have resorted to CBW against Israeli civilians if Saddam thought that the United States was moving on Baghdad. In the final analysis, whether Israel could have resorted to nuclear weapons or not, this Iraqi threat would have still hung over the White House, forcing Bush to make the same fateful decision.

A Shadow of Dimona?

The shadow that nuclear weapons had cast over Washington's Gulf War strategy was not only the result of Israeli actions or inaction. It was also the product of Saddam's moves. Specifically, the Iraqi leader's efforts to target the Israeli nuclear reactor at Dimona were closely monitored by the United States. The potential vulnerability of Dimona to Arab attack was recognized from the inception of the project. The burying of key production facilities underground was only partly motivated by Israel's quest for secrecy. In addition, in every Arab-Israeli war Israel had taken special steps to protect the installation.

Could it be said that what counted in Washington was the possibility that Saddam had begun to zero in on the Dimona reactor in the final days of the war? Perhaps, although the doomsday scenario of an Iraqi-Israeli exchange with mass destruction weapons was merely a theoretical possibility, a realistic nuclear peril of a different nature did indeed compel Bush and Powell to stop the war. For instance, the Pentagon could have been concerned that a hit on the Dimona reactor with a conventional weapon could result in the release of dangerous nuclear fallout over the surrounding countries.

Nevertheless, there is good reason to believe that such a scenario was not among Washington's chief concerns. This was especially true during the last days of Desert Storm. Before the war, the Israeli military reportedly assessed that Iraq could have launched attacks against their country with about 100 aircraft that had been deployed in two air bases, known as H-2 and H-3, in western Iraq, about 600 kilometers away from Israel. But AMAN was confident that the IAF and air defenses would destroy 90, and probably up to 96, of the Iraqi aircraft.[43] The chances of an Iraqi aircraft penetrating into Israel were considered small also because of the long distances, which meant that most of the Iraqi planes would have required in-flight refueling, and because the Iraqi Air Force would be fighting the U.S. Air Force.[44]

Even four Iraqi aircraft laden with conventional weapons could have presented a formidable danger to Dimona. However, this threat subsided quickly following the destruction of many of Iraq's planes by the coalition air forces and the abrupt relocation of many other planes to Iran. Moreover, the fewer Iraqi aircraft there were, the more likely Baghdad would want to use them against the Israeli population centers rather than its strategic targets. Saddam would have simply opted for the biggest punishment he could inflict with what was left. As General Bin-Nun had said: "A single kamikaze plane coming here with a load of chemical bombs could cause damage equal to a torrent of Scuds. That is why despite the decline in the [air] threat, we operate on the basis of the worst-case scenario and continue to invest a lot in defending Israel's skies. We have deployed many anti-aircraft missiles and our planes are in the air around the clock. Ever since the beginning of the war we have spent thousands of expensive air hours to avoid being surprised."[45] Although Saddam's motivation to launch a "kamikaze" aerial attack on Israel must have grown late in the conflict, the threat to the Dimona nuclear facility from Iraqi aircraft actually diminished. Therefore, the vulnerability of Dimona to Iraqi aircraft would not have played a role in President Bush's decision to stop the war.

This left the possibility that one of the conventionally armed Scuds would hit the reactor building, causing nuclear contamination over a large area. But the CEP, or accuracy, of the basic Soviet SS-1c Scud B model is such that at its maximum range of 300 kilometers half the impacts would be more than one kilometer from the target.[46] Moreover, the modifications made to the missiles by Iraq decreased its accuracy even further. Because the range of the missile was roughly doubled and because the CEP is roughly proportional to the range, the operational accuracy of al-Husayn would be halved simply owing to range extension. Further, toward the end of the war the accuracy of the Scuds declined greatly, possibly because of the campaign carried out by the coalition aircraft. Thus, based on its Gulf War performance, the al-Husayn missile might have a CEP of about 4 kilometers. But if the missiles fired late in the war are included, the data suggest an even larger CEP — but no greater than about 7 kilometers.[47]

Even if it is assumed that the Iraqi al-Hijarah had a CEP of 2 kilometers, the probability that a single shot of such a missile would have hit the reactor dome was 17 in 1 million, or virtually negligible.[48] The odds of hitting the reactor would not improve much even if 100 al-Hijarahs were fired.[49]

Still, Powell could have been worried about the worst-case possibility that an Iraqi lucky shot would hit the reactor building by chance. Yet it is not clear that such a hit would have caused significant damage. A conventional Scud warhead that hit the American barracks in Saudi Arabia on February 26 impacted on a reinforced concrete floor and created a crater 1 meter deep by 3 meters wide.[50] It is reasonable to assume that the reactor dome in Dimona would have withstood the impact of such a blast. In fact, Israel did not even bother to deploy a Patriot unit to protect Dimona, opting instead to position the seventh battery, staffed by Dutch soldiers, near Jerusalem.[51]

A conventional hit on the Dimona complex, however, would have been a politically significant event and could have forced Israel to intervene in the war. Thus, to the extent that such a scenario was of concern, it must be concluded that it was the U.S. opposition to an Israeli intervention that decided the issue for Powell and Bush, not the Iraqi threat to the Dimona reactor per se. By the same token, it must be said that under such circumstances Saddam's threat to Dimona turned Israel's nuclear strategy on its head. Not only did Israel's vague nuclear threats not deter Iraq from attacking its population centers, but Saddam was able to hold its prime nuclear facility hostage and use it to politically blackmail the United States.

The Soviet Factor

The Soviet Union was deeply apprehensive about the Gulf crisis. The standard reason given by the Soviets for their staunch opposition to a military solution to the Kuwait crisis was that the Persian Gulf was "literally next to our southern borders."[1] But there were other reasons as well. In the Kremlin, concerns ranged from fear that an Iraqi defeat would undermine Moscow's standing in the Middle East to worries over the impact of such an outcome on the Muslim populations of the USSR.[2] Above all, Moscow had an interest in denying the United States a victory that would boost America's stature in the world at a time when the Soviet position was crumbling.[3] Yevgeny Primakov, a veteran of the Cold War and President Gorbachev's personal emissary, was open on this point. He noted, "The question remains: will the other side [the United States] try to take advantage of the situation [in the Soviet Union] in its own interests?"[4] The Soviets had little problem with Saddam Hussein's political goal of containing the United States. As noted by Primakov, some circles in the United States wanted not only withdrawal from Kuwait but also the destruction of Iraq's capability. Primakov affirmed, "Moscow opposes the destruction of Iraq's military power."[5] While President Bush sought to defeat Saddam, Moscow worked hard to salvage him from his predicament.

The Soviets had no illusions about Saddam's chances. They knew he would be soundly beaten. Soviet Foreign Minister Eduard Shevardnadze, on a visit to Ankara before the war, even said so privately to his Turkish hosts. He noted that the Soviet Union, as the supplier of most of Iraq's arms, was familiar with the various weapon systems of the Iraqi military. "When the power and structure of these weapons are compared to those of the other side, a great discrepancy can be perceived. It is impossible for Saddam to resist his opponents with this force and these weapons. He will be defeated."[6] Moreover, Shevardnadze delivered a similar message to Tariq Aziz himself. "I openly said that the Iraqi leadership was acting in a suicidal manner," he recounted.[7]

Nevertheless, publicly the Soviets tried to deny the allies the victory by promising a tough and bloody battle. The idea ostensibly was to dissuade the United States and its allies from going to war, and subsequently to stop the conflict before an Iraqi military collapse. Even on the eve of the coalition's ground offensive, Moscow kept warning of the dire consequences likely to follow if the attack was launched. Albert Chernishev, the Soviet ambassador to Turkey, pointed out that the Iraqi troops "have been at war for eight years. Bombs and missiles do not overly bother them. They are also used to a great deal of bloodshed." In contrast, the American units were "made mostly of reservists," he said, "and they have none of this experience." This was essentially Saddam's line, too, before the war. Moreover, Chernishev warned, "You need two or even three times more troop strength for a successful attack. However, there is no question of such superiority now."[8]

The existence of munitions of mass destruction in the region no doubt was partly responsible for the Soviet line. Soviet President Mikhail Gorbachev even brought along his chief military adviser, Marshal Sergei Akhromeyev, to the U.S.-Soviet summit meeting in Helsinki on September 9, 1990. The marshal delivered a grave assessment about Iraq's military capabilities in general, and specifically with regard to its mass destruction arsenal. He warned that war would bring tremendous devastation.[9] As if this were not enough, Primakov—who, as Secretary of State Baker noted, "had known Saddam for more than two decades"—warned the Bush administration that the Iraqi leader had a "real Masada complex" and thus would prefer to commit suicide rather than surrender.[10] Thus, soon after the crisis in the Gulf erupted, the Soviets were already hard at work to fashion the U.S. intelligence conception of Saddam's last-resort strategy in a bid to save his regime from collapse.

Political Maneuvering

Additionally, ample evidence suggests that the Soviets tried to use the presence of CB weapons in Iraq to their political advantage. They concentrated on the regional mass destruction threat to discourage the United States from launching Desert Storm. Gen. Leonid Sherbashin, the head of Soviet espionage, strongly implied that the KGB used the warming relationships between the superpowers, and Moscow's apparent willingness to share information about the Iraqi military with the United States, to spread a deterrent message among the American military planners. He said: "The Americans knew nothing about chemical weapons [in Iraq]. All the information we offered was objective and its purpose was to avert what actually happened."[11] By advertising Iraq's chemical and biological capabilities, Moscow sought to galvanize world opinion against the war. It even publicized reports of unrest among the citizens of its southern republics, allegedly caused by fears of chemical and germ warfare in the Gulf, in a bid to convince Washington of the earnestness of its concern.[12]

But the emphasis on the mass destruction threat was meant to furnish Moscow with other political dividends as well. For instance, Moscow furnished Saudi Arabia with gas masks and Soviet Antonov transports ferried to Riyadh some 100,000 such masks, which the Saudis contracted from civilian depots in Hungary and Czechoslovakia.[13] By stressing the threat of CBW, Moscow tried not only to help its allies in Baghdad but also to establish inroads into other Gulf states and generally to appear as a responsible power bent on safeguarding global security. Although the strategy was clearly aimed to keep one leg in each camp, it was at least partially successful. Soviet diplomacy during the crisis paved the way for the restoration of relations between Moscow and Riyadh and the establishment of diplomatic relations with Bahrain.

Once the war began, the Soviets tried their best to bring it to a swift end. In numerous interviews, high-ranking Soviet commanders, stressing that the Soviet Ministry of Defense "has not exchanged information on such questions with Iraq and has not conducted cooperation in this field," recited in detail what the "open sources" revealed about Saddam's chemical and biological weapons capabilities.[14] For example, Col. Gen. Stanislav Petrov, chief of the Soviet Ministry of Defense Chemical Troops, reported that Iraq could produce some 1,000 tons of "poisonous materials" a year, kept a stock of 2,000–4,000 tons of war gases (mostly mustard gas, tabun, and sarin), and stored as much as 500,000 different types of chemical artillery shells. Although Baghdad claims to have in its possession binary chemical weapons, Petrov went on, "nobody knows what type they are or what their components are." The Iraqis, according to the general, also had at their disposal BW agents of typhus, cholera, anthrax, and tularemia, along with stocks of agents for "extremely rare" African and Asian diseases that are "usually untreatable and lead to death."[15]

Soviet commanders also warned about the possible regional consequences of Iraq's use of chemical and biological weapons. Gen. Vladimir Lobov, chief of staff of the Combined Armed Forces of the Warsaw Pact, stated: "There is the threat of [such] mass destruction weapons as chemical agents and also germ warfare. We are aware of their effects should they be used. For instance, bacteriological weapons transcend frontiers. This may be dangerous for the USSR. In particular its southern parts."[16] And ranking Soviet military officials also complained about the potential hazards involved in the strategic bombing campaign against Saddam's chemical, biological, and nuclear facilities. General Petrov, for example, said that Iraq's possession of toxic weapons in the form of botulinum toxin could not be ruled out. "One hundred grams of this substance could kill hundreds of millions of people," he warned. And "if a strike is carried out against the sites where these weapons are stockpiled, the consequences could be entirely unpredictable."[17]

As if to prove this point, the Soviets quickly reproduced information which alleged that the coalition's bombings had caused BW casualties among the Iraqis. The Soviet news agency TASS, for instance, circulated a story in English, first reported in an Egyptian newspaper, which said that after an air raid by coalition forces on a biological weapons production facility not far from Baghdad, "50 guards at the plant died of an unknown and rapidly progressing disease." The casualties were described as having suffered from "injuries of the lungs, the circulatory and intestinal systems." A physician in a Baghdad hospital was cited as saying that "the infection was spreading" in the Iraqi capital. Moreover, similar outbreaks were said to have begun in Basra, Mosul, and Tikrit in the wake of the allied bombing of nearby CB facilities. The disease "was assuming a massive character and there was a point to speak of an epidemic," TASS reported.[18]

Undoubtedly, the aim was to stop the war before Saddam was defeated. Despite the poor showing of the Iraqi military, Marshal Akhromeyev sought to dissuade the United States from pursuing the battle by warning of the tenacity of the Iraqi army. General Lobov declared that "what is happening at the moment goes far beyond what was decided by the United Nations. The war in the Gulf has become a means of destroying Iraq's civilian population and the economic potential."[19] Such was the determination of the Soviet high command to end the fighting that clashes with some senior members of the Gorbachev regime, who lent political support to the goal of ejecting Iraq from Kuwait, became commonplace.[20]

At one point, Moscow's television even carried an undocumented report which said that "in our opinion" it remained uncertain whether Iraq had suitable warheads to deliver chemical weapons. "We do know," it went on to state, "that not all that long ago Baghdad tried to buy these warheads from us, but it was met with refusal."[21] Although Moscow aimed primarily at calming its citizens' fears over a possible CW scenario in the Gulf (fears that were possibly stirred by its own reporting and misinformation), the USSR also sought to respond to both domestic and foreign criticism, which blamed the current crisis on years of lavish supplies of advanced

Soviet weaponry to Iraq. Indirectly, the Soviets were denying that the USSR was facing a problem of its own making.

Genuine Soviet Concerns

Still, it is impossible to dismiss the Soviet protestations regarding the threat of CBW in the Gulf as merely part of a cynical political ploy. With its Caucasus republics situated only 200 kilometers from Iraq, Moscow was understandably watchful, especially with regard to the biological weapons threat. Some actions undertaken by the Soviets at the time imply their genuine concern. As Soviet Foreign Minister Aleksander Bessmertnykh revealed in an address to the USSR Supreme Soviet: "From the onset of hostilities in the Persian Gulf zone, permanent monitoring of the atmosphere, with the object of establishing the presence of poisonous substances and morbific microbes, has been carried out along the southern borders of the Soviet Union. So, in this sphere, the necessary measures have been taken."[22]

It appears that this Soviet anxiety emanated in part from historical reasons but was also due to the specific nature of its alliance with Iraq. With regard to history, there is little question that the Soviet Union had an enduring preoccupation with weapons of mass destruction, or *oruzhiye massovogo porazheniya*. In World War I the Imperial Russian Army sustained some 475,000 casualties from gas, of whom approximately 56,000 died. In 1918, the Red Army formed its own chemical defense service, and in the 1920s chemical warfare continued to be given high priority, as one of the principal concerns in the secret collaboration with the German *Reichswehr*. Throughout World War II, the Soviet high command continued to take the threat of chemical attack very seriously. In 1943, for example, 40,000 men on the Kalinin Front were exposed to mustard gas in an exercise practicing decontamination procedure.[23]

Following World War II, the Soviets continued to accord high priority to defense against chemical and biological attacks.[24] For example, in the Soviet ground forces, the Military Chemical Forces (*Voenno Khimicheskaya Voiska*, or VKhV) formed a separate arm consisting of at least 60,000 men in peacetime, with some estimates putting the figure closer to 100,000. According to U.S. Defense Department estimates, this number would have risen to 138,000 during wartime. VKhV troops were equipped almost entirely for chemical defense, had no access to delivery systems, and were supported in their operations by troops from other military branches, yet they constituted the world's largest corps of NBC personnel.[25]

Following the installation of the Gorbachev regime on March 10, 1985,

Moscow's opposition to the spread of mass destruction weapons, especially in the Middle East, mounted. Gorbachev's loyalists were worried that a regional flare-up would aggravate the nascent superpower relations and possibly interfere with the effort to slow down the strategic arms race.[26] They were particularly unnerved by Syrian efforts to develop chemical weapons and long-range delivery systems, fearing that the buildup would lead to an Israeli preemptive strike.[27] In Moscow, many had begun to feel that future hostilities in the Middle East could well involve unconventional weapons. In March 1988, in the wake of repeated Syrian requests to acquire the Soviet SS-23 IRBM, Col. Gen. Vladimir K. Pikalov, then chief of the USSR Chemical Defense Troops, arrived in Damascus. The general wanted to clarify Syria's intentions in the CW field, but the Syrians stonewalled and managed to keep him well away from their sensitive CW plants.[28] In response, not only did Moscow reject the Syrian request for the SS-23, but Pikalov, who returned to Damascus that June, informed his hosts that the USSR was adamantly opposed to the spread of chemical weapons.[29] At the International Conference on Halting the Dissemination of Chemical Weapons, held in Paris in late 1988, Moscow rejected Arab efforts to focus attention on Israel's nuclear program. The Soviets felt "the danger arising from the spread of chemical weapons was the most pressing issue, and they insisted upon facing up to it immediately."[30] Naturally, the Gulf War must have been regarded by the Gorbachev regime as the realization of its long-held fears.

The general Soviet preoccupation with NBC weapons was also influenced by two other considerations, specifically related to Moscow's alliance with Baghdad. First, as a result of their long-standing relations with the Iraqi military, the Soviets were in a good position to assess Iraq's NBC capabilities accurately. For example, in February 1991 the Soviets mentioned the possibility that Saddam had manufactured a "radiological bomb."[31] At the time, some experts saw these revelations as a scare tactic aimed at intimidating the coalition into an early cease-fire. The timing of these Soviet revelations, on the eve of the ground war, was deemed suspect. UNSCOM later reported, however, that in the late 1980s Iraq had indeed experimented with radioactive bombs, and that 75 of the bomb casings were unaccounted for. Three bombs were tested before the Iraqis decided that the radioactive material — irradiated zirconium oxide — did not travel far enough from the bomb crater to be a significant impediment to enemy troops.[32]

Second, the Soviets were especially uneasy over the prospect of an Iraqi resort to CBW against the coalition, especially U.S. forces. Reports have alleged that Iraqi chemical personnel, including the commander of the

Iraqi Chemical Warfare Corps, Brig. Mustafa Kamal Abd-al-Jabir, were trained in the USSR.[33] Suspicions were also raised that Iraq had gained access to the Soviet binary *novichock* ("new guy") series of chemical warfare agents, whose introduction into military service in the USSR was rumored, or information relevant to the development of these compounds.[34] If Iraq had obtained samples of them, it could have analyzed and produced them with readily available materials. At the minimum, the Soviets must have been deeply troubled by some of the delivery systems available to the Iraqis. Moscow was apparently anxious that Iraqi CBW would involve delivery systems of Soviet origin, like the Scud B and Su-24 fighter-bomber, or perhaps a modified version of them.[35]

Already during the Iran-Iraq war, speculation had been rife among U.S. analysts regarding the origin of some of the chemical munitions used by the Iraqis.[36] But now the situation was much more worrisome. In 1989, Vladimir Pasechnik, a Soviet microbiologist, defected to England. He was the first high official of the Soviet BW program known as Biopreparat to escape to the West. In fact, Pasechnik had been the director of the Institute of Ultrapure Biopreparations in Leningrad. His defection revealed that the Soviets were very much involved in the development of offensive BW agents, in gross violation of their commitments under the Biological Weapons Convention.[37] It would have been natural for the United States to ask whether Iraq's secret BW program was all due to independent initiative or whether, in contrast, their Soviet patrons had a role in it. In short, given Pasechnik's defection, Moscow's fears of the adverse consequences that an Iraqi resort to BW would have for the USSR must have been heightened. Even in the absence of the new information, there could have been severe repercussions in terms of relations with America if U.S. troops were attacked with CB arms carried by or inside Soviet weapons. At the minimum, an Iraqi resort to mass destruction weapons would provide ample ammunition to some "propagandists" in Washington who could see an opportunity to scuttle the recent warming in U.S.-Soviet relations.

The Gorbachev regime was aware that some American politicians had already wondered aloud about the precise role the Soviets had played in Iraq's invasion of Kuwait. Worse, some in Moscow appeared to be bent on aiding the incipient anti-Soviet "campaign" in the United States. For example, veteran Middle East analyst Igor Belayev quoted "reliable sources" as confirming that both the KGB and the GRU (*Glavnoye razvedyvatelnoye upravleniye*, or Chief intelligence directorate of the Soviet General Staff) knew about the impending invasion. However, "on the question of the date, and even more the hour, of the invasion, opinions differ."[38]

As the ground war drew closer, Moscow's anxieties mounted. The Soviets undoubtedly assessed that Saddam was facing a humiliating defeat. When Yevgeny Primakov arrived in Baghdad on February 12, 1991, he told Saddam point blank: "Your troops in Kuwait are going to be wiped out in a ground war."[39] Yet despite Saddam's professed readiness to pull out of Kuwait, he continued to prevaricate. Thus, when Tariq Aziz arrived in Moscow on February 21, 1991, the Soviets strongly reiterated their warning. But, based on Primakov's sorry results and on an unyielding speech by Saddam hours before Aziz arrived, Moscow could find little assurance that Saddam was getting the message.[40] As Secretary of State Baker has put it: "To the end the Iraqis were just as inflexible with the Soviets as they have been with us in Geneva. Whenever the Arabists [in the Kremlin] appeared to regroup and persuade Gorbachev to authorize a new dialogue [to end the war], the Iraqis thwarted their traditional benefactors. Consistently, the Iraqis were their own worst enemy."[41]

The Soviets had evidently concluded that they had only marginal influence in Baghdad, and when the time came, they would not be able to prevent Saddam from resorting to mass destruction weapons. Ambassador Chernishev could only hope that "common sense exists in Baghdad and that chemical weapons will not be used."[42] Moscow may have even estimated that Saddam could become more desperate and thus dangerous the longer the fighting went on. As Primakov stated, alluding to the possibility that Iraq's worsening military situation could force Saddam to use CB weapons, "If some kind of large-scale war begins, with the use of weapons of mass destruction, then of course, that might also directly affect our interests."[43] In this they shared the Israeli and U.S. assessments that the more precarious Saddam's military situation became, the greater were the chances that he would use chemical or biological weapons. It is reasonable to assume that Moscow was genuinely worried that even if the United States did not respond with nuclear arms, Israel would.[44] The Soviet Union's concerns about the Israeli nuclear option were long-standing.[45] Moscow might have become alarmed by some of the deterrent statements made by Israeli leaders before and during the conflict. The Soviets likely intensified their monitoring of the status of Israeli nuclear forces throughout the war.

The Soviet Role in the Gulf War

The Soviets saw their only hope to be the arrangement of an immediate cease-fire to stem what Gorbachev had called "increasingly alarming and dramatic" developments in the Gulf.[46] This solution was meant to serve Soviet interests vis-à-vis both the United States and Iraq. On the one hand,

Moscow was still hoping that a cease-fire would block a ground war and prevent a smashing U.S. victory. They would thus have spared an ally heavily armed with Soviet weaponry from a humiliating defeat. On the other hand, the cease-fire was also meant to block Saddam. The Soviets feared that an Iraqi military collapse, or the threat of it, would lead Saddam to use mass destruction weapons. In this sense, Gorbachev could have genuinely believed that he was helping Bush.

Although none of the Bush administration officials have commented on the subject, the Soviets no doubt made their concerns known to the United States. They even implied as much publicly:

> We are worried by statements that have been made recently at the political level, and in reports in the influential mass media about the possibility of the use of mass-destruction weapons during the course of hostilities. We consider absolutely impermissible the use of chemical, bacteriological and nuclear weapons. We have made this firm position known to everyone. As USSR President M. S. Gorbachev warned in his statement of February 9, if this occurs, then all world politics and the whole world community would be shaken to its foundations. There can be no doubt about this. We have also made the appropriate contacts through diplomatic channels.[47]

But there are some disturbing, albeit shadowy, signs that Moscow might have gone beyond verbal protestations. It is possible that some high-ranking Soviet generals took it upon themselves to force a cease-fire. Presumably they could not accept that the Soviet Union would indirectly help the United States subdue a long-time partner in the fight against American imperialism. On February 19, 1991, it was reported that "a senior Soviet military delegation [representing] the general command of the Soviet army" had arrived in Baghdad to meet "a number of Iraqi military commanders."[48] Among the Soviet visitors was Maj. Gen. Viktor Filatov, the hard-line editor-in-chief of the Soviet magazine *Voyenno-istoricheskiy zhurnal* (Military historical journal). Over the next few days, Filatov repeatedly predicted an Iraqi victory in the war.[49] Curiously, in a report filed by Filatov from Iraq for one of the Soviet Union's most conservative newspapers just days before the war was stopped, he recalled how U.S. B-52 bombers, "with their chemical and bacteriological weapons," once operated in Korea and Vietnam. On the basis of his experience in Baghdad, Filatov declared, "Nothing has changed in the U.S. . . . The only difference being that now they [the B-52's] are loaded not with bombs but with cruise missiles which are smarter than bombs. Primarily they kill people."[50]

This ominous reference could be viewed as indirectly preparing the grounds for an Iraqi resort to CB weapons in retaliation to their alleged use by the United States. What is more, the article appeared days after a Soviet CW expert, Maj. Gen. Igor B. Yevstafyev, had charged that the allied destruction by conventional munitions of chemical bomb stores containing 200–500 tons of sarin and tabun "would result in casualties among the population at a distance of several tens [of] kilometers." Therefore, the general proclaimed, "In my view, the destruction of such facilities [by the coalition air forces] could be equated with chemical warfare."[51]

This position was echoed by General Petrov, who said in an interview with the Soviet Defense Ministry's newspaper *Krasnaya zvezda* (Red star) on February 23, 1991: "Chemical weapons in the broadest sense have already been used on the territory of Iraq as a result of the strikes by aircraft and missiles against facilities for the production and storage of munitions containing chemical agents." Petrov went on to say: "Personally, I believe that the Americans should not have hit chemical weapons storage facilities. This provokes Iraq into using these weapons. . . . One must assume that [Saddam] Hussein has kept such an important argument in war as chemical weapons well hidden."[52] The implication of these statements was that an Iraqi resort to poison gas would be an act of self-defense, given that chemical warfare had already been unleashed against the Iraqi population by the coalition forces, and that in fact the United States had left Iraq no choice but to resort to chemical weapons. For Saddam it was a "use it or lose it" proposition.

General Yevstafyev went even further. A few days after his initial remarks, he wrote that chemical weapons can produce "a military effect" only if they are used on a massive scale. "Iraq does not have the resources necessary for that." Moreover, given that U.S. troops were protected against CW, American casualties would amount to no more than 10–15 percent among the troops. Therefore, he concluded: "Iraq's only alternative [is] a missile chemical strike on cities."[53]

Even officials of the Gorbachev government thought that this declaration was provocative.[54] But the question arises of whether Saddam's flawless exercise of his mass destruction option owes its brilliance to Soviet guidance. Alternatively, did some hard-line Soviet generals play an indirect role? Was Saddam encouraged to fire his warning shot by the expressions of support and implicit understanding that came from "renegade" Soviet generals?

There is no overt evidence that such was the case. But the scenario that unfolded toward the close of the Gulf War has a historical precedent of sorts. During the 1973 Yom Kippur War, Egyptian forces fired one or more Scud missiles, for the first time in the history of warfare, at the Deversoir area, west of the Suez canal, where Israeli forces were assembled. The details of the incident are still uncertain. But it appears that the firing took place five minutes before a cease-fire was to go into effect on October 22, 1973. The missile attack could be viewed as a warning to Israel to abide by the terms of the truce and stop the IDF's advance into Egypt, or it would face a dramatic escalation in the fighting.[55]

Although Egypt had chemical weapons in its possession at the time of the war, and even made extensive use of mustard gas and an asphyxiating agent (possibly phosgene) in its war in Yemen in the 1960s, it certainly did not have chemical warheads for its Scuds.[56] Not surprisingly, Cairo's missile threat failed to deter the Israelis, who proceeded to encircle the Egyptian 3d Army. The Soviets then alerted seven airborne divisions for possible intervention in support of Egypt. Moreover, U.S. intelligence picked up signs of nuclear material, possibly warheads for Scud missiles, on board a Soviet ship heading from the Black Sea to Egypt. The United States responded to these developments by declaring DefCon 3, a global strategic alert. The ship, after docking in Alexandria, Egypt, returned to the USSR, having never unloaded its suspicious cargo.[57] Nonetheless, a second cease-fire promptly went into effect and remained intact until a disengagement of forces could be arranged between the Egyptian army and the IDF.

There is no question that at the close of the Yom Kippur War consultations and coordination between Cairo and Moscow were frequent. President Sadat agreed to the terms of the first cease-fire only after receiving personal assurances from Soviet leader Leonid Brezhnev that the USSR would intervene militarily in support of Egypt if the fighting resumed.[58] Therefore, based on the 1973 scenario, it would appear that in the context of the Middle East, the Soviets viewed the Scud as a strategic weapon capable of transmitting an effective deterrent message. Soviet commanders might have believed, or could have concluded from the crisis, that this capability would have a decisive influence on the enemy once the risk of a strategic missile strike was augmented via a credible threat of escalation to unconventional munitions.

Another intriguing question has been raised by comments made by Gen. Sherbashin. While flatly asserting that the KGB "did not contribute any support for Iraq," he nevertheless revealed that the KGB had passed a warning to "our Iraqi counterparts [in intelligence]" about U.S. intentions to go to war. "We warned them honestly," he said.[59] With regard to the war's end, the general's comments are even more fascinating: "I, as an intelligence official, did not believe that the Americans would stop at the Iraqi border but that they would carry on. All the signs indicated that they would carry on until Saddam Hussein was removed. I do not know why they did not."[60]

Was this the kind of advice that the KGB passed along to its "counterparts" in the Iraqi Mukhabarat? If so, did this message have any role in shaping Saddam's belief that "he might be charged with war crimes and hunted down by their [the coalition armies'] special forces?"[61] Clearly, if such a warning had been delivered to Baghdad, it could have figured in Saddam's decision to transmit his last-resort signal. The Iraqi leader could have certainly reached a similar conclusion independently. But if a KGB message predicting his ouster reached Saddam during the last days of the war, he was likely to take it as a final confirmation of his worst fears, as he would naturally have assumed that Soviet intelligence had access to U.S. war plans.

At present, however, it is impossible to point out with confidence any concrete Soviet role in the firing of the Iraqi warning shot against Israel. At this stage, such a proposition remains in the realm of speculation. Therefore, the conclusion must be that Moscow, whether because of its political interests or genuine concerns, or both, acted throughout the Gulf crisis as an amplifier for Saddam's interests. But compared with the specter of an Iraqi-Israeli exchange of strategic blows with mass destruction weapons, which some in Washington envisioned in late February 1991, the Soviet factor exerted only an indirect influence on the decision to end the war.

During the war itself, Moscow's diplomatic maneuvering vis-à-vis the Bush administration was rather futile.[62] Nevertheless, the Soviets were apparently at least partly responsible for the revision of the U.S. intelligence assessment of Iraq's CBW threat. They were also able to communicate to President Bush directly their grim view of the consequences of war with Iraq. Even if the message was suspect, it would have been imprudent for the president simply to brush off what Secretary of State Baker called Primakov's "apocalyptic view" of Saddam, especially in light of Marshal Akhromeyev's appraisal of Iraq's mass destruction potential.[63] In this respect, the Soviets probably contributed to the makeup of the U.S. conception of Saddam's last-resort strategy.

The Hidden Role of Mass Destruction Weapons

What kind of strategic insights can be derived from the encounter with CB weapons during the Gulf War? After all, it is ironic that the one aspect that most observers all but ignored in analyzing the conflict has now become the main preoccupation of military planners and strategic thinkers everywhere. Based on the preceding analysis, it is apparent that throughout the Gulf crisis, Iraq, the United States, and Israel attempted to exercise effective strategic deterrence. In fact, it appears that Saddam Hussein reached his decision to invade Kuwait at least partly because of his confidence that his weapons of mass destruction provided a credible deterrent against any external intervention. Although the United States and Iraq adopted drastically different battle tactics, they both expected to win the war conventionally. More important, each suspected that the other would turn to unconventional weapons if the war seemed to be going badly, and both sought to deter such a recourse. Deterrence in both cases was to be achieved by threats, open or ambiguous, of resorting to unconventional weapons.

The United States, Iraq, and Israel all used ambiguity to enhance their strategic deterrence. In the case of the United States, the ambiguity masked a decision not to resort to nuclear weapons even if Saddam used mass destruction weapons. In the case of both Iraq and Israel, however, ambiguity was very nearly replaced with certainty.

Iraq

Saddam Hussein, perhaps more than any other contemporary leader, views mass destruction weapons as a cornerstone of his strategy. How, then, can we explain his remarkable restraint in the Gulf War? The fact that Saddam did not employ CB weapons in the Gulf War, even when faced with the certainty of a military defeat, could be considered proof that nuclear deterrence (in this case, on the part of Israel) can create strategic stability even in a region as volatile as the Middle East. But such a conclusion would be premature. Saddam did not face last-resort circumstances. The war was stopped to prevent such a scenario and the probable resort to CB weapons by Iraq. Thus a paradox emerges: for nuclear deterrence to have worked, one has to assume rationality on the part of Saddam. Yet at the same time, Saddam was perceived as a madman posing a credible threat of an Iraqi Samson strategy.

Even the Iraqi decision to keep covert its BW capability after it had been armed cannot be linked directly to Saddam's fear of an Israeli or American preemptive strike. Instead, Iraq's biological weapons, and a portion of its chemical weapons, were set aside exclusively for last-resort circumstances. Baghdad's choice of biological weapons for this mission was apparently linked to its realization of the uncontrollable nature of germ warfare. Yet the mission itself, rather than the threat of preemption, prescribed a clandestine posture. By the same token, there are good grounds to believe that if last-resort circumstances had materialized, Iraq would have resorted to a first-strike countercity strategy using mass destruction weapons against Israel — and, less likely, against Saudi Arabia (see Chapter 3). The suicidal attack could have been foreshadowed by the demonstration shot of an Iraqi Scud armed with a chemical warhead landing in the sparsely populated Israeli Negev.[1]

But why would Saddam fire a warning shot instead of a real CB-armed missile when he suspected that last-resort circumstances were fast approaching? Is it not possible to view this action as evidence that Saddam had in fact been deterred? After all, the terrorist deterrence strategy involves using all one's might to win a war. The Iraqis were also keen on surprising their enemies strategically, and they would not ordinarily warn the opponent about the imminent introduction of a new weapon. Perhaps the Iraqis were telling the truth when they asserted that the U.S. nuclear "threat" had deterred them from resorting to mass destruction weapons. Could President Bush and General Powell have overestimated the reality of the Iraqi mass destruction threat? Was their ending the war a case of self-deterrence?

Naturally, there is no clear-cut answer to this critical question. We can only speculate as to whether Saddam would have indeed used strategic CBW if the United States had not heeded his warning and publicly called off the march on Baghdad. But it cannot be ignored that, from an operational point of view, Iraq's warning shot was simultaneously a dry run for the real thing. The Iraqi warning was effective because its promise of a Samson-type punishment was viewed as credible. After all, why would Saddam exercise restraint if he were convinced that his time had come? It would be illogical to assume that the very elements that made Saddam's threat believable enough to stop the war would have rendered it unbelievable if the war had continued. As General al-Samarraʻi has observed with regard to Iraq's Scud missiles and biological weapons: "He [Saddam] wouldn't have gotten them if he didn't intend to use them."[2]

If this analysis is correct, however, why would Iraq's ultimate weapons remain inactive even as the United States was trying to circumvent the need to march on Baghdad by killing Saddam himself?[3] Could the Iraqi "restraint" be taken as evidence that Saddam was bluffing? The answer is in the negative. In fact, it is not clear that Saddam even knew of the attempts on his life, given the disruption in the Iraqi communications caused by the coalition bombings. On the contrary, Saddam probably saw no point in executing his threat just when a cease-fire was about to go into effect. To do this would have been to sign his death warrant just when he was about to be resurrected.

Even if Saddam did not know of specific attempts to kill him, the fact that the United States wished him dead was no news in Baghdad. The analogy to Hitler was certainly not promising, and some even clearer pronouncements from Washington must have reached Saddam's ear. The question is, did Saddam believe that the United States could in fact harm him? Did he really feel threatened by U.S. efforts to kill him?

During the war, the Iraqi leader hid among the civilian residents of Baghdad, figuring that the United States would not commit a massacre to finish him off even if his whereabouts became known. If he learned about the U.S. attacks on Iraq's C&C bunkers, they must have vindicated his thinking. As far as Saddam was concerned, it was a possible U.S. advance on the Iraqi capital, doubtless entailing the destruction of the Baʻath regime's elements of political control — like the remaining Republican Guards divisions — that presented the main threat to his survival. Paradoxically, the U.S. attempts at decapitation from the air could have even served to reassure Saddam. For instance, he could have surmised that the aerial hunt meant that the United States did not plan to attack Baghdad on the ground. In short, Saddam must have thought that as long as the United States was searching for him in vain, there was a good chance that he and his regime would survive. But if he overreacted and responded to Washington's "shots in the dark" by unleashing BW against Israel, he would surely seal his fate. Even if he personally survived, Israeli or American reaction could transform Iraq into an unviable and thus ungovernable entity. And indeed, Iraq's answer to the U.S. targeting of Saddam — the masterminding of a plot to assassinate Bush — indirectly confirms that this was the thinking in Baghdad (see Chapter 9).

Had Saddam thought that Iraq's biological weapons were ineffective, he would not have relied on them as a last-resort option to save his regime. In fact, Saddam would probably have stayed out of Kuwait altogether and would certainly not have confronted the United States single-handedly, if he had thought that his BW option was a mere bluff. Saddam presumably fired a warning shot, and not the real thing, because he did not wish to commit national suicide, but he would have if there had been no other choice. "I pray to God I will not be forced to use these [NBC] weapons," he told Peter Arnett of CNN on January 28, "but I will not hesitate to do so should the need arise."[4]

A warning shot was the natural extension of this logic. It was also an optimal solution to Saddam's predicament. On one hand, it was certainly preferable to doing nothing, which, in Saddam's mind, was tantamount to allowing the United States to continue to Baghdad. On the other hand, if Iraq fired a mass destruction shot, one involving a real CB warhead even if it were targeted to cause no casualties, Israel could still respond with its promised "terrible, horrible" reaction. By firing a warning shot, Saddam found a middle ground that avoided the pitfalls of the other two courses of action. He evidently assumed that his warning shot would be effective, as even the threat of national suicide had been rendered believable by his continued practice of terrorist deterrence.

It is critical to understand that for Saddam, potential power is useless; power is what one is willing to use. There is not even the slightest compunction in wielding the most extreme measures against the enemy because it is taken as a given that the enemy would act likewise if given the chance. Political agreements are only means to gather additional strength and stymie powerful rivals until such time as they can be safely eliminated. Deception, then, is a way of life.

Although the United States could in theory be the most powerful nation on earth, in practice its power is severely constrained by strict norms of conduct, and therefore it could be defeated by lesser nations. Thus, although Saddam's practices may be justifiably repulsive to the West, they are not crazy. They are logical within their own terms of reference. After all they kept him in power whereas President Bush, his supposed vanquisher, is long gone.

Mass destruction weapons were a natural complement to Saddam's terrorist deterrence strategy. In fact, these weapons, aimed at instilling maximum fear in his enemies, were a sine qua non for Saddam's political grand design.[5] However, the utilization of the Iraqi mass destruction option in the Gulf crisis cannot be viewed as an unmitigated success. Partly this was because of Saddam's unrealistic view of the significance of CW on the battlefield. The Iraqi leader erroneously thought that his CW record regarding Iran and his own Kurdish opponents would act as a surefire deterrent. In addition, the keeping of Iraq's biological weapons secret throughout the crisis, to be used exclusively as a last-resort deterrent, was also problematic.

Saddam looked to his mass destruction option to accomplish several missions. First, his chemical weapons, and the ambiguity over his biological weapons, were intended to shield his invasion of Kuwait from foreign interference. It was thought that regional and even global powers would think twice before they even reacted to the Iraqi aggression. The Iraqi leader trusted his mass destruction deterrent because he was confident that his terrorist deterrence credentials had enhanced its credibility in the eyes of Iraq's enemies. From the strategic point of view, Saddam thus thought that Iraq's development of CB weapons would give him more room to maneuver. The acquisition of such arms meant a new license to launch aggressions against his neighbors. In turn, the weapons were applicable even if not used on the battlefield. It is unclear whether Saddam thinks that his mass destruction shield will be sufficiently effective for him to attack countries that themselves have mass destruction weapons. His previous victims — Iran, the Kurds, and Kuwait — certainly lacked such weapons. Would Saddam attack Iran again, now that it also possesses chemical, and possibly biological, weapons?

Much could depend on the kind of weapons in Iraq's hands. For example, the acquisition of nuclear weapons could renew Saddam's quest for rearranging the map of the Middle East. It is impossible to say whether the United States would have sent its forces to the Gulf if the full extent of Iraq's BW option had been known at the time. But Saddam must have concluded that his current CB arsenal had failed in accomplishing its mission as a strategic umbrella. His interest in developing longer-range missiles and nuclear weapons even today is thus understandable.

Second, Iraq's mass destruction weapons were meant to deter the United States from going to war over Kuwait. It could be said that Saddam failed in this mission as well, but such a conclusion would be premature. There should be little doubt that from a certain undeterminable point on, he earnestly believed that Iraq would win a conventional war *politically* against the United States. Therefore, many of his prewar allusions to Iraq's CW potential were issued in support of the third mission of his mass destruction option — to force the United States to wage a conventional "mother of all battles." He must have figured that he could not lose: if the mass destruction threats deterred war, Iraq would score an impressive military and political victory. But if war did erupt, an equal strategic achievement — if not indeed a greater coup — was likely, provided that the threat of Iraq's mass destruction weapons forced the United States to conduct a conventional campaign. In fact, Saddam was so confident in this strategy and his coming victory that he avoided distributing chemical munitions to his front-line units, thus foreclosing the option of resorting to CW when the battle turned into a rout.

The final mission of Iraq's mass destruction option was as a weapon of last resort. Saddam knew that he could afford to go to war because he possessed the ultimate insurance policy against U.S. attempts to oust him. A portion of his chemical weapons and all of his biological munitions were assigned to this mission. As a result, Iraq could pose a credible mass destruction threat to the civilian populations of Israel and Saudi Arabia, to which neither the United States nor these two of its allies had an effective answer. Moreover, his lieutenants had repeatedly hinted that Iraq would resort to terrorism across Europe and America if forced to. It was left to Iraq's enemies to surmise whether such terrorist attacks would involve CB weapons. In this, Saddam was fully successful because he was judged to have the capability to execute his "doomsday" threat. Equally important, owing to terrorist deterrence methods, Saddam was commonly viewed as a madman ready to carry out his suicidal threat. In all these respects, the Gulf War demonstrates the subordination of Iraq's military strategy to the ultimate goal of protecting the regime of Saddam Hussein. Iraq "fought a political war, with an eye set on Saddam's postwar survival."[6]

The synchronicity between Baghdad's announcement of its willingness to withdraw from Kuwait and the landing of al-Hijarah in the Israeli Negev, earlier that day, cannot be ignored. It was as if Saddam were testing U.S. intentions. His message was as follows: "Because Iraq is pulling out of Kuwait, there are no more grounds to continue the war. But if you reject this deal and continue the offensive, I shall conclude that your aim is not only the liberation of Kuwait but the destruction of my regime. In that case, I am prepared to use mass destruction weapons against Israel." Saddam even believed that once he had played his mass destruction card and Washington had signaled its interest in ending the war, he could sweeten the humiliating demands imposed by President Bush as a precondition to a truce. Although this attempt failed, Saddam succeeded in reopening the bazaar, and the haggling was now over the price of the cease-fire deal, not over whether one would be struck. The fact that Saddam thought he could afford to bargain, even though his army was on the run, indicates that he was reassured that the United States no longer posed a threat to his regime.

Even today Iraq's incredible, at times openly contemptuous, explanations of the whereabouts of its missing mass destruction weapons convey its confidence in its deterrence. In the wake of the Gulf War, Baghdad is in effect telling the world: "We know that you know that we are lying. But we all know that you are not going to do anything about it."

The role of Scud missiles in Saddam's strategic deterrence is worth special mention. Because Saddam was assumed to have mass destruction warheads, Iraq could attempt to use the Scuds as a political weapon during the crisis. Before the war, the Scud took part in an Iraqi "missile diplomacy," aimed to convey deterrent messages to the United States and Israel. During the war, they were aimed to bring Israel into the conflict and thus torpedo Washington's game plan. The attacks on Israel and Saudi Arabia were also meant to elevate Saddam's stature in the Middle East and beyond. Finally, the Scud proved instrumental in stopping the war and rescuing the regime of Saddam Hussein. Given how little Saddam invested in this "piece of junk," as some American generals have called the Scud, Saddam sure got his money's worth. In addition, Saddam has managed to reveal the true strategic import of such missiles even though they have never yet actually flown toward their targets armed with CB warheads. Make no mistake: the proliferation of missile technology to rogue countries around the world is heralding a strategic transformation of the first order.

Israel

It may be said that in the Gulf War Israel inadvertently helped Saddam twice: first, by remaining militarily inactive throughout the conflict, which not only helped Saddam directly but may have invited Saddam's warning shot; and second, by entirely miscalculating U.S. strategy and presenting Washington with an either-or scenario. Israel's ultimatum helped Bush reach the decision to end the war "prematurely," from Israel's point of view. As Shamir has asserted: "When we heard about the U.S. President's decision to stop the war and to leave Saddam in his seat, it will be no exaggeration to say we almost fell off our seats. No one expected it; it was a big surprise."[7] Instead of facilitating the war, Israel thus contributed to Saddam's survival. And because of its miscalculation, Israel played no role in the conduct of the war itself (except perhaps by influencing the campaign against the Scuds) but assumed a decisive role in ending the conflict.

Yet, in the Gulf conflict Israel had few options. Its passivity in the final days of the war was forced on it because of the strong objections of the United States to Israeli action. Its assessment of Saddam's likely next desperate move, which appears in retrospect to have played an important role in the U.S. decision to stop the war, reflected the consensus of its analysts. There is no basis to assume that AMAN doctored its estimate to impress the Bush administration into letting the IDF operate against the Scuds. In fact, there were strong Israeli interests militating against intervention. At any rate, if no key officials in Washington had shared the assessment of Israeli intelligence, its warnings would have fallen on deaf ears. It may even be argued that although Saddam used Israel's passivity to his advantage, his warning shot served its interest, as well as those of the United States and Iraq, in keeping the conflict within the confines of a conventional war. At the time, however, this outcome was certainly not a part of the Israeli incentives to hold back.

As it perceived a growing threat of a strategic attack with mass destruction weapons, the IDF offered what it saw as an entirely valid military solution. In hindsight, however, it is obvious that the IDF's plan would have fallen short of neutralizing the Iraqi strategic threat to Israel. Thus, to the extent that Bush's move to stop the war was motivated by his doubts over the effectiveness of the IDF's proposed solution, and especially by the potential consequences of a failed Israeli attempt to eliminate the Iraqi CB threat, this decision was correct. In this sense the Gulf War demonstrates the interaction between leaders who were convinced that they had no choice:

- Saddam likely suspected he was faced with an assault on Baghdad and thus had "no choice" but to threaten a suicidal mass destruction attack.
- Key Israeli leaders were convinced that they faced an attack with mass destruction weapons and thus had "no choice" but to act. They figured that launching a preemptive strike into western Iraq to destroy the Scuds was by far preferable to retaliating with nuclear weapons. Curtailing the threat was undoubtedly more rational than exacting a horrible punishment. Moreover, retaliation with nuclear weapons would have entailed political and other costs and would possibly have endangered U.S. troops in the Gulf.
- President Bush thought that he had "no choice" but to stop the war, given the predominant conception of Saddam's last-resort strategy and Israel's preparations to enter the war. At the same time, he was aware that the military objectives of Desert Storm had been largely accomplished. The U.S.-Israeli clash was unavoidable given that the United States was pursuing its global interests and Israel was tending to its regional security concerns.

The Israeli assessment of the Iraqi mass destruction threat as credible was based on a combination of enduring perceptions and key assumptions deliberately adopted during the crisis. Because of his terrorist deterrence methods, Saddam was seen as undeterrable, especially toward the close of the war. Israel's unsuccessful attempt to warn Saddam against an attack was an important element in shaping this view. But Washington's failure to discourage the Scud bombardment even after it had publicly warned that such an attack would set off a "vigorous American response" undoubtedly also left a deep impression on Arens and Shomron.[8] The failures of both these warnings should put into question the thesis, happily endorsed by the Iraqis, that the U.S. nuclear "threats" had a deterrent impact on Baghdad.[9]

Israel also opted for a worst-case approach, which assumed that Iraq had the operational capability to deliver mass destruction weapons via its Scud missiles. This approach was necessary owing to the gap in the intelligence information. The Israeli case thus demonstrates that the presence of mass destruction weapons dramatically narrows the margins of error for intelligence assessments, a predicament that could benefit aggressors like Saddam. Further, the Gulf War establishes that when NBC weapons are involved, even a technical uncertainty can have far-reaching, possibly historical, implications.

On the face of it, AMAN failed on at least two counts. First, there is no evidence that the Iraqis were planning to use concrete warheads to deliver BW payloads. Even though there was never a consensus among AMAN's analysts concerning a possible link between al-Hijarah and a mass destruction threat, the debate would not have taken place but for a failure in the collection aspect of the intelligence work. Had reliable and timely information been acquired, AMAN analysts could have known whether concrete warheads were being employed by the Iraqis for BW purposes, and would not have been limited to mere speculation.

Yet this failure must be put in perspective. Even if al-Hijarah turns out to be merely a "missile with a kinetic warhead," as one UNSCOM inspector has put it, the question remains whether the concrete-armed missile had special significance under the circumstances.[10] In order to decide for sure, we would have to know whether Saddam indeed intended his concrete warhead as a warning shot. But it was perfectly valid for AMAN's analysts to deduce, based on the concrete-armed al-Hijarah and Saddam's dire circumstances, that the Iraqis were preparing to introduce a new weapon system into the war and, furthermore, that the new missile might be equipped with a different type of warhead. Indeed, after the war UNSCOM uncovered an Iraqi document that linked an unspecified surface-to-surface missile with the Iraqi nuclear program. It contained a memo from the Ministry of Defense to the Iraqi Atomic Energy Commission, which spoke of "using a concrete warhead device to test the missile."[11] Besides, in October 1990, information had reached the DIA that Iraq was producing al-Hijarah missiles for use against oil wells and people, through the "release [of] poison clouds."[12] Whether AMAN also had this information is not known. Unfortunately, UNSCOM still lacks solid information about Iraq's BW warheads.[13] Nor is it clear how many al-Hijarah missiles were in Iraq's inventory to begin with.

In hindsight, there are solid grounds to believe that Saddam did intend al-Hijarah as a warning shot. The fact that he prepared a last-resort option before the war shows that he was suspicious of U.S. intentions from the outset. He also was not planning to surrender. Why, then, would Saddam Hussein forsake a readily available bargaining chip and go, seemingly empty handed, to cease-fire negotiations with an enemy he believed was planning to kill him? Did he think that throwing himself at the mercy of an implacable foe was preferable to playing the card that he had deliberately readied to ward off such a situation? Not only would Saddam have had to abandon the strategic bargaining tools in his reserve and instead trust the United States to have renounced its dark aims, but this astonishing transformation in Saddam's thinking would have had to occur when he was most vulnerable — after Iraq's military defenses had crumbled. If al-Hijarah had merely carried some kinetic warhead, Saddam would have even telegraphed to his enemies that his ability to hold Israel hostage, his main defense, was nearly exhausted. But Saddam never expected his rivals to exercise restraint under such circumstances. His own record would attest to this even if his vanquished opponents could no longer do so.

Moreover, in view of Saddam's attempts, since the Gulf War, to exercise extortion under the shadow of his poison weapons, it is inconceivable that he had readied a last-resort option yet failed to apply it *politically* even when faced with circumstances by far more ominous than at any time since the war. Furthermore, terrorist deterrence would have also ruled out taking part in negotiations without first intimidating his interlocutors. On the contrary, it may be said, Saddam would not have gone to cease-fire negotiations unless he had fired his warning shot. After all, he had blown up Kuwait's oil fields although the United States had warned the such an act would make him directly culpable. The shot was aimed to assure that he could wrest a deal he could live with (literally), and to make sure that the Americans kept up their side of the bargain.

Finally, unwillingness to consider that Saddam resorted to strategic blackmail amounts to an abandonment, without good cause, of the very thinking that was adhered to almost universally during the crisis and that eventually led to the decision to suspend hostilities. To dismiss Iraq's warning shot is implicitly to embrace Iraq's claim that it was deterred by the U.S. warnings. Such countenance not only defies logic, considering that Iraq has lied about virtually every other aspect of its policy on mass destruction weapons, but is tantamount to ignoring Saddam's record during the war. In particular, his entrenchment in Kuwait, the missile attacks on Israel, the blowing up of the Kuwaiti oil fields, and his readiness to launch BW at an instant—actions taken in the face of grave warnings—all point to Saddam's resistance to being deterred.

In contrast, it must be recognized that Iraq's mass destruction weapons were a precondition for the invasion of Kuwait. They were also the reason that Saddam took on America single-handedly. It is unlikely that Saddam would not turn to these arms to extricate himself from the quagmire once his plan had failed. Even today, with the Iraqi leader preferring to risk confrontation with the United States and lose billions in unearned oil revenues rather than surrender his CB weapons, it is clear that Saddam still regards this option as his ace in the hole. Is it reasonable to assume that when his fate was hanging in the balance, he failed to play this card even politically?

The second failure of AMAN involves its worst-case approach with regard to the existence of an "effective" or "operational" CB warhead in Iraqi hands. In fact, such a warhead, which could disseminate its payload as an inhalable aerosol at some prescribed altitude, was reportedly unavailable to the Iraqis. Instead, according to one source, "Iraqi biological warfare munitions depended on impact detonation for primary dispersal of agents."[14] As such a method is exceedingly inefficient, it has been said, the effect of Iraq's BW weapons "would have been limited to contaminating a relatively small area of ground surrounding the point of impact and exposing nearby individuals to aerosolized pathogens or toxins."[15] If impact detonation was indeed Iraq's only option, then the information gap that AMAN (and U.S. intelligence) had to contend with regarding Iraq's warhead technology may have cost Bush his total victory.

Yet strong suspicions remain that at least some of Iraq's BW munitions could have dispersed their payloads in the air prior to impact.[16] Even if these doubts eventually turn out to be unwarranted, it is important to understand that the minimalist interpretation of the threat is based on the BW munitions that Baghdad declared as having been deployed before the war—that is, bombs and warheads. It does not take into account Iraq's potentially most important BW delivery system—the remotely piloted airborne platform. However, an Iraqi general has told UNSCOM that just before the Gulf War, Iraq began a crash program designed to give it the capability to "wipe out Israel's population with germ weapons."[17] The plan would have used MiG fighters, each carrying some 1,135 liters of anthrax solution. They were to be flown by remote control and to release the agent over Israel from specially modified fuel tanks using a sprayer of Iraqi design. "Baghdad's ambition was to command the plane to fly over Israeli territory, begin releasing the germs once it crossed the border, and eventually crash land it."[18] One pilotless plane was flight-tested before the war began, but according to the Iraqis, the attack was never attempted.

Although the capacity of the spray tank mentioned in this report is about half that of the one mentioned earlier, it appears that the two relate to the same project.[19] According to UNSCOM, the plane in question was a MiG-21 equipped with a 2,200-liter belly tank taken from a Mirage-F1 fighter plane. During the test, which was conducted in January 1991, the remotely piloted plane sprayed a solution laden with biological simulant over a practice-range target using a technique known as line-source laydown. It flew low at a constant rate of speed and headed on a straight line parallel to the target. This way an even spread was achieved and the prevailing winds and other meteorological conditions were utilized to disperse the agent efficiently.[20] The Iraqis claimed that the test was a failure. Yet three additional drop tanks "were modified and stored, ready for use."[21] Little wonder that the UNSCOM technical assessment team has concluded that "the significance [of the drop tank project] is greatly underplayed [by Baghdad,] considering that this weapon appears to be the most efficient produced by Iraq."[22]

Even if only one of these Iraqi MiGs had been able to deliver its deadly cargo to target, the BW threat to Israel would have undergone a qualitative transformation. Consequently, anything short of a worst-case approach in the intelligence estimates would have been utterly irresponsible. Furthermore, as would come to light later, on the eve of the war Israel was made aware of the Iraqi test.[23]

Moreover, even if Saddam had only BW weapons that were relatively primitive, in their delivery and in other respects, there is no dispute that the "targeted population's terrified reaction to such an attack would have caused more harm than the weapons themselves."[24] Nor has the "optimistic" toll count taken into consideration the possibility that, owing to its inferior standard, a "primitive" Iraqi BW warhead could have disintegrated and released its BW payload in mid-air. Although such unplanned dissemination could have occurred at an altitude so high that the payload would have been largely diluted by the atmosphere, lower-level disintegration could have been problematic.[25] The area of contamination would have been a fraction of that produced by an aerosolized ejection of the payload at an ideal height, but the level of contamination could possibly have been higher.[26] Even if particles of all sizes were scattered, instead of a uniform cloud of 1–5 microns, it may be worth recalling that as little as 1 gram of aerosolized botulinum toxin can in theory kill some 1.5 million people.[27] The simple fact remains that when it comes to BW, estimates of casualties (or, for that matter, the effectiveness of civil defense measures) remain speculative.

Given these kinds of uncertainties, the possession of solid intelligence about Iraq's warhead technology would not necessarily have removed the need to adopt a worst-case approach with regard to the Iraqi BW threat. Finally, it is doubtful that the course of the conflict would have been altered even if AMAN had been dead certain that Iraq possessed only "primitive" CB warheads. Any resort to CBW by Iraq would have dramatically increased the likelihood of an Israeli nuclear retaliation. It was this scenario that President Bush wished to avoid at all cost.

The bottom line is that AMAN and U.S. intelligence did err on the side of safety but that both were correct in adopting this approach. Moreover, as the fundamental worst-case forecast—that Saddam would resort to CBW in extremis—seems to have been borne out by the new revelations, the cost of the (mistaken) worst-case estimate regarding Iraq's warhead technology was immaterial. For General Shahak, the fundamental validity of the approach was obviously enough to claim its success. The general implied that the later findings about Iraq's BW capabilities provide proof that AMAN's forecast of a mass destruction scenario in the closing days of Desert Storm was right on target.[28] Shahak, possibly in order to silence some critics, seemed to be saying that in view of Saddam's proven readiness for CBW, whether an intelligence conception forced an end to the war is no longer a pertinent question. Indeed, Ambassador Ekeus himself would have likely endorsed the general's claim that the worst-case approach was a success. He has reported that at the time of the Gulf War there existed Scud missiles with biological and chemical warheads deployed in western areas for "exclusive use" against Israel.[29]

When AMAN learned about Iraq's ability to affix CB warheads to its Scud missiles is still a matter of conjecture. If Iraq's assertion that it first tested a chemically mounted Scud in 1985 is true, then AMAN's information on the eve of the Gulf War was dangerously outdated. When it finally caught up, its estimate of the number of Iraqi CB warheads possibly available was at least four times less than what Iraq had apparently produced before the war.

But in view of Shahak's self-congratulatory comments, it is impossible to escape the impression that AMAN knew more than it let on publicly. It appears that privately Israeli intelligence was convinced of Iraq's ability to deliver a "primitive" mass destruction warhead against an Israeli city. General Bin-Nun spoke of "less than 20" such warheads, which would have exploded on impact, as possibly in Iraqi hands. As noted, the intelligence dilemma was whether Iraq also had an "operational" or "effective" warhead.

The IDF may have preferred to lump the two warheads together because then it could present the issue as a "theoretical" mass destruction threat, which required some precautionary measures against a "hypothetical" worst-case possibility. The approach could have been politically motivated and aimed to prevent panic. Also, it could act to defuse public pressure to take action against the Scuds irrespective of U.S. objections. Such a public outcry could have been expected if the IDF's message had been that Iraq was certainly capable of hitting Israel with some 20 primitive CW warheads. Further, by focusing on the worst-case theoretical threat instead of the likely primitive CW attack on Israeli cities, the IDF did not appear to have neglected the security of Israel in the case of Iraq.

By focusing on the genuine ambiguity about the existence of an advanced Iraqi warhead, the Israeli government could issue civil defense orders against CW as if these were only precautionary measures dictated by a remote worst-case possibility rather than by the certainty that Iraq could fire primitive CB warheads against Israel. After all, from the defensive point of view the different types of warheads would have mattered little. Either way, Israelis would have been instructed to stay in their sealed rooms and don protective gas masks whenever the warning sounded. But the difference would have been in the number of likely Israeli casualties.

Finally, although Israeli leaders focused almost exclusively on the Iraqi chemical threat, they must have known better. In fact, as a result of the poor accuracy of the al-Husayn missiles, agents with a greater theoretical area of lethal contamination would have provided a greater cost-benefit ratio to the Iraqis. In this respect, biological and toxin agents have a significant advantage over chemical agents. A modified Scud filled with approximately 200 kilograms of VX nerve agent could theoretically produce an area of lethal contamination of one square kilometer. By contrast, under optimal conditions the same amount of fill with anthrax could lethally contaminate an area of several thousand kilometers. Thus, the worse off

Saddam's position became — that is, the fewer the number of modified Scuds left in his arsenal, and the greater the difficulties of aiming them at Israel — the stronger was his rationale for firing al-Husayns armed with biological weapons, assuming that aerosol warhead technology was available to Baghdad.

A sophisticated chemical or biological attack on Israel that caused many casualties would have certainly led to an Israeli nuclear retaliation. But even a primitive one, if it had been aimed at an Israeli population center, would have significantly increased the probability of such an Israeli punishment. McGeorge Bundy was thus correct when he observed: "The Gulf War will command a durable place in the history of nuclear danger."[30] Still, this perceived danger was in part the result of U.S. intelligence's overestimating the Israeli nuclear missile capability.

There is no evidence that Israel went on nuclear alert during the conflict. In fact, the available information points in the opposite direction. In retrospect, it is doubtful that the more visible nuclear strategy would have had a greater deterrent impact on Iraq. Saddam would still have had to fire his warning shot, even if Israel openly displayed its nuclear readiness, because the alternative in his mind was to allow the allies to march to Baghdad unhindered. Nevertheless, in view of the worst-case approach adopted by the Israeli defense establishment at the time, the Israeli nuclear stand-down is surprising.

Undoubtedly, the posture was politically motivated. Yet there were other reasons as well. Shamir's decision to downplay Israel's nuclear option was apparently linked to his view that, even if displayed, it would be ineffective in deterring the "madman of Baghdad," as he dubbed Saddam.[31] In addition, Shamir was almost exclusively preoccupied with the specter of a chemical, rather than biological, attack on Israel. The presence of U.S. troops on the scene was regarded as a hindrance, as well as a substitute, to an Israeli nuclear strategy. The lack of a suitable delivery system presented severe operational constraints for an Israeli resort to the nuclear option. Finally, the deemphasis on its nuclear capability reflected an anomaly in Israel's security thinking. Although the war proved that the Israeli nuclear option was conceived of as a weapon of last resort, the definition of such circumstances was called into question. On the eve of Desert Storm, some Israeli leaders were still clinging to the traditional view that "last resort" meant exclusively the imminent destruction of the country. Arab acquisition of long-range missiles and CB weapons had implications for Israeli nuclear strategy that were not well understood. For example, by opposing an IDF military operation on the one hand, while keeping Israel's bomb in the basement on the other, Shamir indicated his willingness to absorb an Iraqi CB attack.[32]

Nevertheless, the daily contact with the U.S. Defense Department was left in the hands of Arens via the Hammer Rick, and he perceived the situation quite differently. Arens was a vocal adherent of the concept of Saddam's last-resort strategy, and the need to preempt it. His argument, it appears, was that barring an IDF preemptive action, Israel would be forced to resort to unconventional weapons, as this would be the only proper response to an all-but-certain Iraqi CB strike on Israeli cities. Therefore, the Israeli defense minister presumably bears the main responsibility for Israel's inadvertent contribution to Bush's decision to end the war. Saddam's CBW preparations certainly back Arens's contention about Iraq's undeterrable last-resort strategy, but ironically, he now maintains that the Iraqi dictator did not resort to such weapons because of Israel's strategic warnings. Ostensibly, in his zeal to question Bush's decision to suspend the war, Arens also undermined his own previous argument in favor of an IDF intervention.

Be that as it may, the conclusion seems justified that Israeli security doctrine has lagged behind the techno-strategic changes in the region. The tension finally became public during the war, when Rabin pressed the Shamir government to announce that a CB attack on Israeli civilians would trigger a countercity nuclear response even if the downfall of the state was not imminent.[33] The Gulf War, then, may have contributed to a subtle transformation in the mission of the Israeli nuclear arsenal. Originally, Israel's nuclear option was conceived to deter the Arabs from overrunning the country via a conventional invasion. In the wake of the Gulf conflict, however, it can be posited that its primary mission has become the deterrence of an Arab or Muslim mass destruction attack.

Throughout the war, the Israeli predicament was that steps taken to buttress its nuclear deterrence also unnerved Washington. This was the case even though Israel opted to speak vaguely and carry a small stick. By limiting itself to general warnings, Jerusalem sought to send Baghdad a deterrent message yet imply that Israel had no interest in escalating the conflict. The aim was to deter, not provoke, Saddam. Even if Israel was aware of the negative consequences that some of its warnings had on key people in Washington, it had little choice, given that it opted for a nuclear stand-down while the United States vetoed a conventional military action by the IDF against the Scuds.

Israel's wartime *actions* were similarly problematic. For example, Israel conducted missile tests during the war, possibly because it was scrambling to put together some delivery vehicle capable of reaching Baghdad. Still, there is little doubt that the firings were also meant to deter Iraq and signal Washington of the Israeli distress. In this respect, the missile tests were a bluff that could have backfired from an Israeli point of view. Although it is unclear what effect, if any, the tests had on Saddam, they probably reinforced Washington's conviction that the war must be stopped forthwith.

Israel apparently believed, erroneously, that enhancing its strategic deterrence was a mutual U.S.-Israeli interest. The allusion to the Israeli nuclear deterrent was intended to support the U.S. conventional war strategy and allow the battle to continue to a decisive victory over Iraq. Thus, in sum, the Israeli nuclear strategy during the Gulf War was misconceived in terms of Israel's security needs, ineffective as far as Saddam was concerned, and ultimately counterproductive regarding its relations to the United States.

The United States

In theory, the United States should have welcomed the IDF's plan to preempt an Iraqi CB attack. The specter of Iraqi gas or germ warfare against Israeli cities was, after all, the main threat that the United States could not defend against. Moreover, when Iraq launched Scud missiles into Israel "during the first 48 hours of the war," as the CIA had predicted, the White House must have suspected that the intelligence warnings of an Iraqi last-resort strategy based on CB weapons would also prove right.[34]

Washington, however, was worried about the IDF's chances of success. The consequences for the United States of adopting the Israeli plan could have been dire if the IDF's operation did not totally eradicate the Iraqi strategic threat. In this context, Iraq's firing of al-Hijarah was probably viewed in Washington as evidence that Baghdad was in the possession of operational missiles with ranges in excess of al-Husayn. Therefore, the IDF's hunt for launchers would have to be hugely expanded.[35] And consequently, an Iraqi-Israeli mass destruction scenario could still ensue even after the IDF was deployed in western Iraq. The only sure way to prevent such a dreadful outcome was to stop the war. By all indications, the U.S. calculation was correct. A year after the war Arens himself had to admit that "nobody in the IDF expected the [proposed] operation to eliminate the missile attacks altogether."[36] Besides, U.S. leaders could have thought that even if the Israeli intervention in western Iraq was effective, it would not make much difference. In desperation, Saddam could still fire CB-tipped Scuds from sites in the south against Saudi population centers.

Washington was also motivated by political considerations, however.

Bush was concerned that if Israel joined the fight, the Arab members would withdraw from the coalition and thus strip it of its political legitimacy. To this extent, America's political interests stood in the way of its final victory, not to mention its stake in establishing strategic stability in an extremely dangerous region. So long as Saddam remained in power and was armed with mass destruction weapons, such stability would be difficult, if not impossible, to achieve.

In Bush's own statements explaining the decision, and in all the memoirs published thus far by the key U.S. decision makers involved in the Gulf War, the following reasons have been given for the president's order to suspend the fighting:[37]

- The president wanted to stay within the confines of the U.N. mandate, which authorized only the liberation of Kuwait.
- For a variety of geopolitical reasons, the United States was not interested in the "Lebanonization" (where infighting between warlords devastated the country) or disintegration of Iraq. Washington was also aware of the objections of its Arab coalition partners to such an outcome.
- Pursuing the war deep into Iraq would have cost more American lives but would not have substantially changed the outcome of the war.
- Even if Saddam was captured and his regime toppled, the U.S. forces would still be confronted with a prolonged occupation of the country.
- Marching into Baghdad could have brought the collapse of the coalition and made Saddam a nationalist hero. In addition, the odds of finding Saddam were quite improbable.
- The Iraqi army was largely defeated, and U.S. commanders did not want to appear as vengeful butchers in front of the world media.
- President Bush had promised the American people to bring the troops home by July 4 and was not looking for a long entanglement.[38]

Rather than weigh the merits of each of these arguments, I shall note that not one of the accounts mentions the increasing threat of an Iraqi resort to mass destruction weapons, or Israel's preparations to enter the war, as having any bearing on Bush's decision.[39] Even some vague formulation, simply stating that "Saddam could have done something desperate" if the war continued into Baghdad, is not offered as a factor. Were the U.S. policy makers oblivious to these possible developments? Was there such an intelligence failure that the decision makers in Washington were simply unperturbed by the growing talk in the Middle East of a likely mass destruction scenario? Or did the United States actually believe that the air campaign had destroyed all of Saddam's mass destruction stocks, despite the Iraqi leader's warning shot?

Even before the war there was solid evidence that the United States was concerned about the Iraqi mass destruction threat in general, and specifically with regard to an attack on Israel with CB weapons. The CIA even observed that "in retrospect, CIA assessments that Iraq would use chemical weapons may have influenced President Bush's decision to warn President Saddam Hussein of grave consequences for such use."[40] Concerning the Israeli scenario, Secretary of Defense Cheney, on January 16, 1991, used the Hammer Rick to alert Arens that fresh information indicated that the Iraqis were developing a remotely piloted MiG-21, designed to carry chemical bombs. "He [Cheney] said the information seemed to him very credible."[41] The notion that the United States neglected the Iraqi mass destruction threat toward the war's end — when it appeared to be peaking — is therefore ludicrous.

Nor can it be said that American leaders were worry-free because they were certain that the Iraqi CB threat had been removed by the coalition's attacks. Secretary of State Baker has admitted that "during the war, we had learned that Saddam Hussein's program to develop weapons of mass destruction was both more substantial and better concealed than we had believed at the outset."[42] Moreover, General Schwarzkopf, in his first meeting with Iraqi commanders to spell out the permanent cease-fire conditions on March 3, 1991, demanded that the Iraqis "indicate any storage sites they'd established for chemical, biological, and nuclear weapons. The last thing we needed was for our troops to stumble onto such sites unaware."[43] How can we reconcile the rampant talk among U.S. officials of a mass destruction threat before and during the Gulf War with the silence about the subject regarding the war's end?[44]

In fact, the U.S. decision to halt the war must have been the outcome of a widely shared perception that Saddam was undeterrable, and an intelligence conception that predicted he would resort to CBW in extremis. Ending the war was also aimed to block the Israeli preparations to enter the conflict, which were intended to prevent this very scenario from unfolding. Undoubtedly some intelligence analysts saw the concrete warhead that landed in the Negev on February 25 as validating ex post facto the conception about Saddam's last-resort strategy. But others felt that assigning a mass destruction role to al-Hijarah was tantamount to a self-fulfilling prophecy. Nevertheless, the disagreement did not impair the overall consensus: intelligence in the United States (and Israel) continued to assess that Saddam would resort to CB weapons if he thought that Baghdad would fall. To the end, U.S. intelligence also estimated that despite the coalition's efforts, Iraq could still carry out such an attack against Israel. The grim forecast left Bush with few choices but to halt the fighting.

The Gulf crisis demonstrates, then, that conferring on an enemy, let alone a leader of a country in the possession of CB weapons, the image of a lunatic grants that leader tremendous bargaining powers. Although the idea might have had a sound political rationale — it drove home the urgency of dealing with the Iraqi Hitler and galvanized world opinion — from the strategic point of view the campaign backfired. It accorded Saddam's suicidal threat believability that ordinarily would have been difficult to attain.

Would the war have been stopped even if al-Hijarah had not been fired? Probably, as the intelligence concept remained unchanged throughout the conflict, and the United States had no effective solution to Saddam's continued ability to keep Israel hostage. But the more important question is whether the theory of Saddam's last-resort stand proved accurate or whether, in contrast, intelligence "stole" Bush's victory. Although whether Saddam would have eventually ordered a mass destruction attack on Israel is a matter of conjecture, the revelations about his CBW preparations strongly point to the accuracy of the intelligence estimate. Indeed, as the conception was in all probability correct, the possibility that al-Hijarah was no ordinary missile is enhanced.

Although experts have now begun debating whether Saddam's BW program amounted to a diabolical plot of global implications or was evidence of amateurism and substandard technology, during the war itself the calculations were quite different.[45] Uncertainty dictated adoption of a worst-case approach insofar as Iraq's CBW capabilities were concerned. Moreover, Washington dreaded the crossing of the threshold into unconventional warfare, which even an ineffective Iraqi CB attack would have heralded.

It is safe to state that the U.S. decision to end the war had a hidden motive. It allowed Bush a way out of a difficult dilemma: risk a potential catastrophe or let Israel enter the conflict. Indeed, even if Israel had been allowed into the war, a mass destruction warhead could have still landed in Israel. Saddam might have even viewed the Israeli intervention as proof that the United States had decided to go all the way.

It may not be an exaggeration, then, to say that the official reasons for ending the Gulf War, a conflict that from its start was fought in the shadow of a "madman" in possession of mass destruction weapons, bear little relation to the actual decision making. There is in fact no need to refute every reason that the Bush administration cited for ending the war in order to establish the validity of the argument presented in this book. The hypothesis about the role of the Iraqi mass destruction threat in the decision to stop the war stands alone and should be judged on the basis of the evidence presented to support it. The main test should be, Is the evidence offered here of such standard as to prove the theory? For if it is, its consequence is of such a qualitatively different nature that all other reasons simply pale in comparison. That is, of course, assuming that the U.S. "war cabinet" was made of rational people, as this book has argued.

At the same time, it is astounding that despite its natural suspicions of Washington, the usually intrusive Western press has accepted the Bush administration's explanations for ending the war essentially at face value. This was done in spite of the open worries of both U.S. and Israeli leaders about the Iraqi mass destruction option during the conflict itself, and the successive revelations about Saddam's CB arsenal since.

Ironically, it would have been vastly more reassuring to know that Bush had halted the war because he was horrified by the consequences of pursuing his "real agenda" in Iraq, than to conclude that he led a group of reckless fanatics who were either ignorant of, or indifferent to, the reality of the mass destruction threat late in the war. And yet, by keeping silent over the mass destruction factor in their calculations, it appears that the president and his aides have implicitly supported the second notion. They could have felt that disclosing the role of Iraq's CB weapons in its calculations would have unnerved Israel. That nation could have switched to an open nuclear deterrent or even launched a preemptive attack on Iraq if it could have traced Iraq's hidden CB stocks. A U.S. admission that the Iraqi strategic option had acted as an effective deterrent could have further boosted the proliferation of mass destruction weapons. It could have also elevated Saddam's political stature in the region. But such rationales, if they were even considered, were less than decisive.

Israel did not come out of the war reassured by U.S. conduct. The long-range missiles and CB warheads left in Iraq's hands in the aftermath of Desert Storm certainly would have had a greater influence on Israel's strategic thinking than the factors Washington cited as reasons for ending the war. As Lt. Gen. Ehud Barak, by then chief of staff, has said: "I would not like to try and guess or predict [whether Saddam will attack Israel again in case of another confrontation with the United States], but there are hundreds of Scud missiles in Iraq. I do not know how many of them are of the al-Husayn type [and are capable of reaching Israel]. Our working assumption is that they have missiles, and we know that they also have both mobile and stationary launchers. As for Saddam Hussein's considerations about whether to use them or not: These are not easy considerations, and I hope he is well aware of the difference between the present situation and the situation during the Gulf War."[46] Shortly after the Gulf War, the IDF launched one of its rare major organizational reforms and established the Home Front Command. It is specifically designed to cope with the threat of ballistic missile and mass destruction attacks on Israel's population centers.

Similarly, radical regimes like those of North Korea, Syria, Iran, and Libya have drawn their own conclusions from the Gulf War (see Chapter 9). The conflict demonstrated the strategic value of low-tech and low-cost weapons vis-à-vis the United States and its allies in the Middle East. Not surprisingly, in its aftermath, extremist governments in the Middle East and beyond rushed to expand their CB and long-range missile arsenals dramatically, in the process extinguishing any anti-proliferation hopes that the Bush administration might have had. Worse yet, Washington's silence about the mass destruction threat at the end of the Gulf War impeded U.S. attempts to galvanize world opinion in favor of its efforts to stop the spread of poison gas and germ warfare capabilities.

As for Saddam's stature, the fact that he was left to rule Baghdad still in the possession of untold quantities of CB weapons speaks volumes in the Middle East and beyond, even if officially he was defeated. Many have certainly asked themselves why Saddam is so keen to hang on to his CB weapons if they were actually useless during the war and utterly irrelevant to the outcome of the conflict.

These adverse outcomes have even been recognized by Secretary of State Baker. He wrote: "Much of our planning in this regard [Bush's post-war agenda for the Middle East] was predicated on the assumption that Saddam would not survive in power. When he consolidated his authority in the months after the end of hostilities, much of the agenda's rationale was undermined."[47] Baker's statement could be viewed as indirectly admitting that the inconclusive end to the war triggered negative strategic consequences in the region. In fact, during a subsequent confrontation with Saddam, he confirmed this inference by writing: "Rogue regimes around the world are watching closely. If Saddam fails to comply [and disclose his mass destruction arsenal] and we allow him to escape yet again by simply making more promises, these regimes will conclude, probably correctly, that proliferation has won. And they will be emboldened."[48] Baker all but admits that there was a link between America's inaction and Saddam's CB deterrent, at least as far as the perceptions of radical regimes were concerned.

The silence about the issue can be traced to political considerations.

Washington was undoubtedly worried that admitting the truth would have exposed the United States to criticism that its "tilt" toward Baghdad during the Iran-Iraq war allowed Saddam to develop, and even use, a strategic arsenal that he predictably turned against his American sponsors once they stopped acquiescing to his grand political scheme. Yet such criticism was leveled regardless, and stopping the war was itself politically costly.[49]

Therefore, the political rationale must have been different. The common denominator of all of the explanations provided by President Bush and members of his administration for the decision to stop the war is that they imply a unilateral U.S. initiative. It was entirely up to the U.S. president to stop or continue the fighting. In this way, the impression is created that the Gulf War was an unmitigated success for the Bush administration. Bush and his colleagues would dearly like to avoid admitting that in ending the Gulf War they had to submit to Iraqi blackmail. In 1994, shortly before Ekeus made his startling revelations, the U.S. Department of Defense was even said to "maintain that the Iraqi military did not weaponize its biological warfare program."[50]

At the time, an acknowledgment of Iraq's powers of extortion would have likely doomed President Bush's chances for reelection. Today an admission of that nature is liable to cast that administration's place in history in an unfavorable light. So long as the "suspension" of Desert Storm is seen as a unilateral American act, Bush's decision to go to war is validated in hindsight.

In view of the evidence presented in this book, however, the question of why the Gulf War ended "prematurely" has been settled. Instead, the question now should be, why was it started? This is not an attempt to question the justness of the war or the strategic need to disarm a dangerous dictator of his mass destruction weapons. Instead, we should question the soundness of the decision-making process and the strategic planning. After all, in retrospect it is clear that President Bush took a huge gamble when he ordered the attack. In retaliation for the bombing of his capital, Saddam could have responded immediately with a barrage of chemical weapons against Israel. Such an attack would have probably led to an Israeli nuclear retaliation. Instead of a conventional conflict, the region would have been plunged into a horrific total war with untold consequences. Indeed, when seen in this context, Saddam's decision to invade Kuwait looks almost understandable. He must have reasoned that the risk of such a scenario would deter the United States from coming to Kuwait's aid.

Although the Iraqi mass destruction threat figured prominently in the minds of U.S. leaders, it appears that President Bush was able to reach his decision to go to war based on four assumptions. First, he apparently hoped that U.S. warnings would be effective in deterring Saddam from using CB weapons. This hope, however, was not shared even by the coalition commanders. Many of them strongly suspected that Saddam would resort to chemical weapons. General de la Billière, the commander of the British forces, wrote in his memoirs: "We fully expected that he [Saddam] would use them [chemical weapons] against us."[51] As a result, the general reportedly commissioned "urgent studies" to determine whether bodies tainted with chemical or biological agents could be decontaminated or would require immediate cremation.[52] De la Billière relates: "At first we thought it highly probable that the Scuds would carry gas and every raid had to be followed by a tiresomely long twenty-minute wait before chemical checks of the environment could be carried out."[53] Even more significantly, the general noted: "I had little doubt that Riad would come under a missile attack, possibly with chemical warheads."[54]

As for the American perspective, the U.S. Army's official history of the war states: "Underlying much of the training [of U.S. troops] was the concern that the Iraqis might use chemical weapons. . . . Outwardly, American military spokesmen minimized the threat, calling chemical weapons indecisive and relatively harmless with proper countermeasures. But the Army's logistical agencies rushed to meet the demand for protective gear and antidotes. The specter of American troops, unable to breach Iraqi lines and caught in a rain of chemical-laced artillery shells, haunted American generals."[55] A DIA assessment made one week into the war could not have been more specific: "Saddam evidently believes the U.S. has both a chemical and a nuclear potential in the theater, but DIA assesses that this would not deter him from employing chemical weapons against coalition forces."[56] In fact, some intelligence estimates had even envisaged an Iraqi preemptive use of mass destruction weapons against coalition forces in case war was imminent. "Iraq would use CW in preemptive or integral operations. It would certainly use CW in any defensive situation to prevent its forces from being defeated or pushed back in Kuwait or Iraq. . . . BW would most probably be used prior to the initiation of hostilities against large concentrations of personnel, such as troop areas in the rear and cities."[57] Of course, the prewar inoculation of thousands of U.S. and British troops against some types of BW attacks also imparted a rather low opinion of the effectiveness of U.S. strategic deterrence of Iraq.

As Desert Storm military commanders and planners were doubtful that the U.S. warnings would deter CB attacks on their own troops, America's ability to dissuade Iraq from attacking Israel with such weapons should have been viewed with even greater circumspection. Indeed, the notion that the United States could deter Iraq must have been severely shaken once Iraqi Scuds began falling on Israel. One can only imagine the crisis that must have erupted in the White House before it became clear that the Iraqi missiles were conventionally armed.

Although President Bush could have determined that even if Iraq used CW against his troops, the United States would not retaliate in kind, Israel was an entirely different matter. Its response to an Iraqi mass destruction attack could have torpedoed the American plan in an instant, thereby altering the course of history. Instead of a "brilliant triumph," Bush would have stood accused of responsibility for a holocaust. After all, it does not seem likely that Washington had received assurances from Israel that it would not resort to unconventional means in case of an Iraqi CB attack. If anything, General Barak's message to General Powell (and possibly Bush himself), and Prime Minister Shamir's letter, suggested the opposite.

Suddenly, it was all in the hands of coalition pilots and British commandos, along with hurriedly dispatched U.S. commandos, to ensure that Bush's plan succeeded by preventing Iraq from launching CB weapons against Israel.[58] Secretly, Washington, once it realized the dimensions of the strategic dangers ahead, also pursued the effort to end the war by "decapitation" — it made Saddam Hussein a top-priority target despite the obvious risk that the Iraqi leader would respond by resorting to CB weapons.[59]

The second assumption that Bush made when considering whether to go to war was to trust the U.S. intelligence capability. He figured that even if deterrence failed, intelligence would successfully locate the vast majority of Iraq's mass destruction capabilities and long-range missiles. He believed that U.S. intelligence could identify the relevant production, assembly, and storage facilities of Iraq's NBC programs. In fact, although U.S. intelligence had six months to pull together its resources, it failed almost catastrophically in assessing Iraq's strategic weapons capabilities. Intelligence underestimated the amount of botulinum Iraq had made by at least a thousandfold and the amount of anthrax Iraq had produced by at least a factor of eight.[60] During the crisis, intelligence largely missed Iraq's BW preparations. On the eve of the war, the DIA reported that it "still [did] not know the types of biological weapons [in the Iraqi order of battle] with definition except for the forty [ground-based] aerosol generators acquired in the spring 1990." The agency also said that it had "no information on how Iraq might use biological weapons."[61] Two weeks into the war, the DIA reported that it was "possible that anthrax and botulinum toxin [had] been weaponized in aerial bombs. We have no positive information, however, to indicate that the Iraqis have done so." Weeks after Iraqi BW weapons had been armed and deployed, the DIA could only report that it believed that "Iraq has the technical capability to have produced BWA [biological warfare] warheads for their SSMs but have no information to indicate that this has been done. We operate under the assumption that such warheads are available."[62]

Intelligence also failed to locate key chemical and biological munitions sites. Military planners were assured before the war that the location of 90 percent of Iraq's chemical and biological weapons — and the aircraft and missiles to deliver them — were known, according to Lt. Gen. (Ret.) Buster Glosson, the director of targeting for the coalition's air campaign. But postwar inspections, he said, showed that intelligence knew about only 30 percent of the locations.[63] Each of the three facilities where Iraq admittedly manufactured biological and toxin weapons escaped notice before the war and survived intact, making it possible for Iraq to continue work on germ weapons well after its military defeat. Instead, U.S. and allied bombers attacked two facilities from which Iraq had already withdrawn all its BW-related equipment, and some refrigerated bunkers where BW munitions "may have never been stored."[64]

Not only was U.S. and British intelligence uncertain as to the number of Iraqi CW warheads, but it was also unable to determine the whereabouts of the Iraqi chemical inventory well into the war. It even located chemical munitions where they were not — in Kuwait![65] Iraq had more Scuds than intelligence estimated, including those of the longer-range variants. In addition, Iraq may have had more launchers than the United States estimated.[66] Finally, intelligence mostly failed to detect Iraq's dispersion of Scud missiles and mobile launchers and support equipment between the end of August 1990 and the end of Desert Storm.[67] In underestimating Iraq's strategic capabilities, intelligence severely jeopardized U.S. plans for a conventional war as envisaged by President Bush. (Nor did it help matters that U.S. intelligence *overestimated* Israel's nuclear delivery capability.)

Bush's third assumption was to rely on the assurances of U.S. military planners, especially those in charge of the planned strategic air campaign, that as soon as hostilities commenced they could neutralize the Iraqi threat of mass destruction attacks and SSMs.[68] During his mission to Israel, on January 13, 1991, Deputy Secretary of State Eagleburger stressed that the armed forces of the United States were "absolutely confident" in their ability to neutralize the missile threat to Israel. According to Arens's account,

Eagleburger said: "Naturally, if hostilities were already in progress, we would strike at all remaining Iraqi threats to Israel. I emphasize the word 'remaining' since according to our plan, once hostilities have commenced, our best judgment is that there will be little left [for the Iraqis] with which to hit you. However, if anything is left, we'll hit it." Eagleburger went as far as to state: "The President would not have asked you to consider giving up retaliation [for an Iraqi attack], unless he was confident that we are capable of—and this we'll do—carrying out this mission [of negating the Iraqi threat] faster and better than the Israeli Air Force could. . . . Our massive punishment of Iraq will dwarf anything the IDF can do. This is no exaggeration."[69]

Even with regard to Iraq's missiles, the U.S. Air Force was confident. As early as December 1990, Gen. Charles Horner, air commander of U.S. Central Command (CENTCOM), predicted to Secretary of Defense Cheney that the air campaign would "preclude" Iraqi missile attacks.[70] Later, the Israelis were told that the missile threat to Israel would be finished off within 24 hours.[71] Little wonder that the White House had satisfied itself that it need not worry too much about Iraq's resorting to poison gas or germ warfare against Israel. As the threat of an Iraqi CB attack had been addressed, Bush must have also figured that the problem of a possible Israeli response had been resolved.

Unfortunately, Bush's confidence in the ability of the U.S. military to neutralize the Iraqi strategic CB threat was largely misplaced. The U.S. Army's history of the war asserts: "The Coalition effort frustrated Iraqi attempts to inflict large numbers of casualties on the opposing forces, as well as on Saudi Arabian and Israeli civilians, and thwarted Iraqi efforts to draw Israel into the war."[72] But the truth is decidedly different. As General Horner admitted after the war: "In Desert Storm Saddam Hussein had more chemical weapons than I could bomb. We had to make a decision to go after the production areas and those storage sites that were in the immediate area of the battlefield. I could not have even begun to take out all of his chemical storage—there are just not enough sorties in the day."[73]

Most glaring was the failure of the coalition air attacks to destroy even one of the chemical or biological warheads that Iraq possessed. In addition, the U.S. Central Command, which was operationally responsible for the war, initially rejected the Scud-hunting mission as having low priority. The Scud threat was viewed as a distraction, and no targeting strategies were developed for attacking Scud facilities. Even when planners did consider the Iraqi missile threat, the focus was on neutralizing fixed sites because it was assumed that "Iraq could significantly threaten Israel only from fixed sites."[74] Yet in fact, the Iraqis relied exclusively on mobile launchers to launch attacks on Israel and Saudi Arabia. And there is no evidence that a single one of these transporter-erector-launchers (TELs) was actually destroyed during the war, despite claims of some 100 "kills," or 300 percent of the total Iraqi force, by air crews and special forces.[75]

General Horner admitted, "We did not do a very good job at finding and destroying Iraq's missiles in Desert Storm because we really had not thought sufficiently about the problems beforehand."[76] This statement speaks volumes about the flawed planning of the war. In fact, the assertions by Desert Storm commanders that the Scud was a "pissant weapon that isn't doing a goddam thing," as General Schwarzkopf put it, indicate at best a profound misunderstanding of the strategic dimension of the conflict.[77] Moreover, in view of the analysis in this book, opposition by planners of the strategic air campaign to the diversion of planes to Scud-hunting missions indicates that this ignorance persisted even during the conflict. As one study found: "Reflecting the views of Generals Schwarzkopf and Horner, planners regarded Iraqi Scuds as 'nuisance weapons.' They believed the best strategy was for the coalition and Israel to absorb these attacks. In their view, to attempt to locate and destroy mobile TELs was sortie-intensive and counterproductive."[78]

This is especially difficult to fathom considering that General Horner himself has written: "I believe Saddam Hussein in many ways was indifferent to nuclear weapons. In fact, sometimes I wonder if he really was not looking for Israel to throw a nuclear weapon at him."[79] Not only is Horner's statement reflective of the effectiveness of Saddam's terrorist deterrence, it is in total variance with the assumptions that Bush had to make to reach a decision to go to war. The general was forced to admit: "The military missed the whole point in Desert Storm. . . . We missed the real impact of the ballistic missile. . . . The ballistic missile had a profound impact on the Coalition nations in Desert Storm, on our forces, and on our understanding of the ballistic missile's own utility. The ballistic missile was the only advantage that Saddam Hussein had in the war."[80]

Even though the U.S. planners strongly argued for focusing on Iraq's strategic targets instead of on the Scuds, U.N. inspectors later concluded that the bombing of Iraq's key chemical and biological facilities did far less damage than initially estimated.[81] The description provided by the head of the Pentagon team assigned to attacking the suspected Iraqi BW storage and production facilities is revealing:

The real challenge was destroying the viability of the biological weapons without spreading the agents and causing massive collateral damage in terms of human lives. The military was simply not prepared for this eventuality.

Several tests were conducted over a very short time to try and find the right kind of enhanced munitions or bomb that would render the biological agent unusable to the Iraqis and not release lethal agents into the atmosphere. The crash program was not fruitful. However, in the effort, computer modeling showed that the design of the suspected biological weapons storage bunkers offered a bombing approach that might inhibit the release of the agents. In the eleventh hour, this concept detailing specific fusing, type of bomb, and angle of attack was telephoned to the CENTCOM planners in Riyadh.[82]

The U.S. practice borders on the unbelievable, given some of the intelligence warnings apparently provided to its military planners at the time. For example, before the war 17 bunkers, some refrigerated, had been identified as possibly storing BW agents (2 more were added to the list during the war). It was calculated that each bunker had a capacity of approximately 440,000 kilograms (7.5 million kilograms collectively for the 17 bunkers), assuming that all the agents were stored in bulk containers. Even if only 0.25 percent of storage capacity had been used, 1,000 kilograms of dried anthrax spores would have been stockpiled in the bunkers. This amount of dried anthrax would represent about one million trillion anthrax spores. Even if 99.99 percent of these spores were killed or somehow contained in the bunker by the bombing, 0.01 percent, or about 100,000 billion spores, would have been left for release into the air. "This translates into 5–10 billion human lethal doses. Alternatively, if only 100 kilograms of dried anthrax spores were stored and 0.01% released, this would translate into 0.5–1.0 billion human lethal doses."[83]

Naturally, the U.S. Armed Forces Medical Intelligence Center warned:

Unless the total and complete destruction of all agent located at the site is an absolute certainty a planner must presume that release of, at least some, deadly concentrated BW agent into the atmosphere in the form of a plume would likely occur following explosive destruction and subsequent overpressure. Depending on the concentration of agent, the elevation of agent plume and environmental factors such as wind speed and inversion conditions, as little as 100 kilograms of anthrax bacteria (representing less than 20 percent of the amount of agent carried in a single Scud B warhead) could travel several hundred miles. Considering the above factors and wind direction many thousand of fatal casualties could be realized in neighboring countries such as Syria, Saudi Arabia, Jordan, Lebanon, Turkey, Israel, Iran, and the Soviet Union.[84]

Nevertheless, U.S. planners felt confident enough to proceed with their attack on the suspected Iraqi BW sites based on a computer model! Was this the basis for assuring President Bush with "absolute certainty" that more than 99.99 percent of the anthrax agents possibly stored at these sites would be destroyed? Or did the U.S. president order the attack on the basis of much lower odds?[85] Even if the "collateral damage" was limited to Iraq itself, such an outcome could have had a major strategic impact. It could have made an Iraqi use of BW, possibly against Saudi or Israeli cities, seem legitimate. In fact, in the aftermath of the attacks on four suspected bunkers at Salman Pak on January 17 and 19, 1990, the DIA was worried about just such a scenario. It warned that 100–500 grams of anthrax spores present at the site could have been released into the air, calculating that the venting of 100 grams of spores under the environmental conditions of the time could have resulted in "less than 5,000 casualties" among the residents of the Iraqi capital.[86] Consequently, the agency warned, "Baghdad has already shown a propensity for using U.S. air strikes for propaganda purposes. With disruption of water and food supplies, and normal hygiene, some diseases become more prevalent. Saddam may take such disease outbreak to accuse the U.S. of waging BW or as a result of attacks on Iraqi BW facilities."[87]

Ironically, the disastrous consequences that the inept U.S. air attack could have wrought were avoided because of the U.S. intelligence failure. The United States was simply unaware that some of its targets had never been used for storing BW-related materials. With regard to the rest, unbeknown to the Americans, any BW-associated equipment or material that might have been stored there had long been relocated. The CIA has concluded: "We assess no biological weapons or agents were destroyed by Coalition forces during the war."[88]

Nevertheless, there was a price to pay for this incompetence. One DIA report, while noting that before the war "a debate [was] apparently underway as to the wisdom of targeting BW/CW facilities," predicted that "leaving the weapons in the hands of Hussein through a period of conflict leaves him the option of invoking BW blackmail at any time he decides to do so."[89]

Bush and Powell had little choice. The growing scent of an Iraqi defeat made them increasingly nervous about the likelihood of a mass destruction scenario exploding in the Middle East, and they did not wish to test their luck any further. Little wonder that the war was stopped not as a result of the field commanders' recommendation but by the orders of the authorities in Washington. By one account, Powell "did not wait until the ground war commanders had their objectives in hand before calling it quits. The decision to end the war was determined more by political than military considerations."[90] This peculiar way of terminating the war — by orders from Washington and not by the recommendation of the field commanders — in itself supports the account of the Gulf conflict presented in this book. It was in Washington that the worries of a mass destruction scenario dominated the thinking, after all.

Critics of Powell's move reveal their fragmentary grasp of the true nature of the war. In general, Desert Storm proves anew that modern warfare is too serious a business to be left for the generals alone. Considering the continued proliferation of mass destruction weapons around the world, this dictum could become nearly universally valid in the foreseeable future. By the same measure, however, the war also indicates that civilian control is by no means a guarantee for superior decision making. For example, Powell deserves much praise for cautioning Bush against relying on air power to carry the day and for fighting Cheney's idea of the "Western Excursion" — a plan to launch from the outset a massive military operation in the far western reaches of Iraq to neutralize the Scuds, threaten Baghdad, and turn the tables on Saddam. In hindsight, the result of such a maneuver would have surely been catastrophic. A panicked Saddam would have likely resorted to his strategic CBW option in response.[91]

As for Bush's final assumption, the president must have been told that even if Saddam resorted to CW against U.S. troops, casualties would be minimal given the protection accorded the soldiers and the fast-moving campaign that was planned.[92] This fourth consideration is still a matter of debate but seems to have been overly optimistic.[93] For example, it has come to light that U.S. troops in the Gulf lacked reliable means to detect quickly either chemical or biological agents at a distance.[94] The Presidential Commission on Gulf War Veterans' Illnesses, as late as 1997, termed the lack of real-time detection capability a "serious deficiency" in the U.S. chemical and biological defense posture.[95] At any rate, given that the first three assumptions have been proved wrong, Bush's decision to go to war must be called into question. In hindsight, it stands as a potentially catastrophic gamble.

On the basis of all of these considerations, President Bush, and more important, multitudes of U.S. troops along with the inhabitants of Israel and the rest of the Middle East, can consider themselves exceedingly lucky. It is uncertain whether Bush would have gone to war if he had formed a correct assessment of the risks involved. Likewise, it seems inconceivable that Israel would have been such a staunch supporter of the war, insisting on Saddam's removal to the end, if it had anticipated the kinds of dangers to which the U.S. strategic, intelligence, and military failures exposed it. Considering these lapses, President Bush's decision to stop the war was the wisest injunction he had issued during the conflict. It was far more reasonable than the decision he made to launch Desert Storm.[96] Many Israeli civilians, whose lives would have been put in grave danger had the IDF's own plan been adopted, were spared because of the suspension of hostilities. In fact, given Saddam's clandestine preparations for BW, the decision to stop the war would have been correct even if the concrete warhead had never landed inside Israel. Nevertheless, one can understand why Saddam thought he could try and rewrite the terms of the cease-fire. He surely believed that Bush would jump at the opportunity to stop the fighting once Iraq made its initial offer. But Bush's response must have so disappointed him that by the time the war was finally halted, Saddam was probably convinced that he was dealing with a lunatic.

The Age of Blackmail and the Crisis of Deterrence

In the wake of the Gulf War, two contradictory trends have been noticeable in the region. First, frantic, even panicky efforts have been made to invent a so-called New Middle East, as Shimon Peres has labeled it.[1] It has been argued that Israel's postwar peace overtures were meant to capitalize on the favorable geopolitical circumstances brought about by the war. The shattering of the "eastern front" — a potentially powerful anti-Israeli coalition composed of Syria, Iraq, Jordan, and Saudi Arabia — and Washington's new preeminent position in the region, presented an important window of opportunity. The total isolation of the PLO after the war, as a result of its strong backing of Saddam Hussein, was also a factor. On top of this, the coincidental collapse of the Soviet Union, the patron of Israel's main Arab enemies, provided an important incentive for Washington and Jerusalem to launch a diplomatic initiative. Some months after the war, however, Peres, Israel's former prime minister, laid the grounds for the coming peace offensive as follows:

> To defend our skies and cities in this era of non-conventional missiles, we need a new security doctrine and defense system. We need a security doctrine responding to dangers from across the border and traversing countries with which we have a border.
>
> In fact, we need not only defensible borders but also a defensible surrounding zone. In order to create such a zone, it is not enough to defend the frontiers encompassing the state, but relations must be established which will contribute to maximum security.[2]

Thus, while many still view the Middle East peace diplomacy in its Palestinian context, the Israeli initiative was unquestionably linked to new strategic thinking spurred on by the Gulf War's mass destruction scare. In the wake of the conflict, key Israeli politicians warned that "the next war will not be conventional."[3] Prime Minister Itzhak Rabin even told Israeli television on September 4, 1992, that in the wake of the Gulf War and the collapse of the Soviet Union, the country had a "window of two to five years" before the threat to its existence mounted. "Therefore," he said, "we have a window of opportunity, and we need to find a way to use it [to reach a settlement]—but not at just any price." As such a position implicitly mistrusts the effectiveness of nuclear deterrence, the Rabin government's urgent efforts to find a political solution to the Arab-Israeli conflict were not surprising. But the mass destruction scenario of 1991 had a similar impact on Washington as well. Soon after the war ended, the Bush administration rushed to convene the Madrid Peace Conference on the Middle East.

It is possible to argue that U.S. interest in the Madrid conference was due to its assessment that the war brought "new opportunities and attitudes" into the Middle East, as Secretary of State Baker put it. For example, he said, the moderate Arab countries who joined the anti-Saddam coalition had "demonstrated their worth as partners." At the same time, the radicals in the region were clearly on the defensive. Furthermore, there were also global favorable conditions. As Baker remarked: "Our status as the last remaining superpower had been enhanced by the war. We have tremendous strength and credibility around the world, and stood at the zenith of our influence in the Middle East. I believed it was time to seize the moment."[4]

Such a view, however, would be only partially correct. As Baker himself admitted, the Madrid Peace Conference was only "the fourth pillar in a five-part agenda" that constituted Bush's "vision" of the postwar Gulf.[5] The agenda's first priorities were new regional security arrangements (including an expanded U.S. naval presence in the area) and regional arms control agreements "to halt the proliferation of conventional weapons and prevent Iraq from rebuilding its weapons of mass destruction program."[6] The convening of the Madrid conference was unequivocally an integral part of a new American strategy to "stabilize the balance of power in the region, prevent Iraqi expansionism and . . . secure the peace."[7]

Indeed, the subsequent collapse of the other four pillars of the American plan, in part because of what Baker calls "our underestimating [of] Saddam Hussein's durability," invariably made the Madrid Conference into the sole U.S. means to achieve these goals.[8] The Arab-Israeli peace diplomacy became synonymous with preventing another mass destruction scenario in the region.

These efforts to establish a new political order in the Middle East must be viewed as additional proof that in 1991 the region came to the brink of chaos. In the aftermath of the war, the notion that strategic deterrence could be relied upon to dissuade even rogue nations from launching an attack was viewed as a piped dream by many in Jerusalem and Washington. Indeed, although Saddam was supposedly deterred from resorting to CBW by the U.S. or Israeli nuclear threat, Secretary of Defense Les Aspin announced soon after the war the "most sweeping" review of U.S. nuclear strategy in 45 years. According to the *Christian Science Monitor*, on September 11, 1993, the "most important problem" to be addressed was the "ominous" issue of the "undeterrables." Prominent among the list of such potential adversaries was Iraq.

With the decline of strategic deterrence, new adherents have emerged for the argument that the only way left to prevent a destructive war in the Middle East is through a regional political agreement. In truth, the Arab-Israeli peace negotiations are linked in more than one way to the conflict. Throughout the Gulf crisis, Saddam had schemed to establish a link between his aggression against Kuwait and the Arab-Israeli conflict. By conditioning a withdrawal from Kuwait on the resolution of the Israeli-Palestinian dispute, he sought to prolong and legitimize the Iraqi occupation. Although Washington blasted the ploy as an attempt at blackmail, it was under American aegis that stepped-up Arab-Israeli peace negotiations commenced soon after the war. From this perspective, Saddam, via his doomsday threat, had the final say.

Whereas the threat of calamity pushed some countries to launch urgent efforts toward a political settlement, radical countries in the Middle East and elsewhere have drawn their own conclusions. Indeed, the diplomatic efforts to find political solutions to long-simmering conflicts have been more than matched by the hectic efforts of radical regimes to arm themselves in line with the lesson of the Gulf War. In the wake of the smashing U.S. military campaign, they concluded that they would not stand a chance in a conventional war against the United States and its allies. Weapons of mass destruction were the only means to prevent the United States from encroaching on their turf.

Thus, the second trend in the Middle East pertains to the accelerated efforts by countries like Syria and Iran to acquire long-range missiles topped with mass destruction warheads. Indeed, the determined efforts to establish the infrastructure for indigenous production of such weapons indicate that Damascus and Tehran have placed a high priority on the acquisition of credible mass destruction capabilities in the wake of the Gulf War. Naturally, this trend has had a major bearing on the first political tendency — the efforts toward peace in the region.

For the Syrian Army, which underwent perhaps four of its worst years in

1987–91 because of the country's economic decline, the Gulf War meant redemption. The guns of Desert Storm had barely fallen silent when it became known that Syria had signed a large arms deal with North Korea, using $500 million of the $2 billion subsidy it had received from Saudi Arabia for its participation in the anti-Saddam coalition. The deal included 60 Scud C missiles and 12 mobile launchers and, for the first time, the construction by North Korea of two factories for the manufacturing of Scud missiles on Syrian soil. One underground facility, near Aleppo, was built for the assembly of the missiles themselves. It reportedly began production in April 1993. Another underground plant, dedicated to the development and production of solid-propellant rocket motors for missiles, was built near Hama. Combined, "Syria is laying the groundwork for a future option to develop a modern, solid propellant SRBM."[9] The Scud C already in its possession has a range of 500 kilometers, making it capable of targeting all of Israel and most of Turkey, and can carry a conventional or NBC warhead weighing 700–800 kilograms — that is, more than twice what the Iraqi al-Husayn can carry.[10] Unconfirmed reports suggest that its warhead design would allow it to carry bomblets or provide aerosol capacity.

A detailed analysis of the Syrian buildup has recently observed:

> Even before the Gulf War, Syria tried to procure surface-to-surface missiles from North Korea and China, but after the war, building Syria's long arm became the top priority national objective. Damascus is now devoting lots of effort and money into what it calls a strategic cover.
>
> The Syrians did not make do with procurement. Due to their bitter experience with the closing of the Soviet tap, they included in the Scud C deal they signed with North Korea in 1992, know-how and technologies to permit them to construct these missiles in North Korea in the first stage, and to do it themselves at a later stage. Iran is helping Syria in this effort.[11]

The Iranians themselves began assembling Scud Bs using North Korean components in 1994, and a year later they started production of a significant number of Scud parts. Reports allege that Iran is looking to extend the range of the Scud B without reducing the size of its warhead, perhaps by switching from liquid to solid fuel. Apparently these efforts are concentrated at the Chinese-built plant near Semnan — where construction of the Oghab artillery rocket began in 1987, followed by assembly of the Mushak 120 SRBM — and at larger plants built by North Korea at Esfahan and Sirjan, which can produce liquid fuels and certain structural components.[12] In May 1992 Iran received the first of 150 Scud C missiles from North Korea. Earlier Iran had placed an order for the North Korean No Dong-1 missile, with a range of approximately 1,300 kilometers and the ability to reach all of Israel (with the exception of Eilat, in the far south). Reports stated that in 1993 North Korea provided Iran with blueprints, and possibly even a single copy, of the No Dong-1.[13] On July 22, 1998, Iran successfully test-fired a Shihab-3 missile, which flew some 800 kilometers from a launch site 150 kilometers south of Tehran. Iranian Defense Minister Ali Shamkhani said that the missile had a range of 1,300 kilometers and was produced "entirely by Iran, without assistance," but most other sources agreed that it was a No Dong-1, or an Iranian derivative produced with the help of Russian technicians. Gen. Mohammad Bager Qalibaf, commander of Iran's Islamic Revolution Guards' Air Force, said that the missile could carry a one-ton warhead and was equipped with an Iranian-produced guidance system, which made it a "very accurate weapon" given its warhead and size. However, most other reports said that the low accuracy of the Shihab-3 meant that it was designed to carry an NBC warhead. As if to emphasize that the Iranian weapon posed a credible threat and that no regional or extra-regional power should delude itself into thinking it could defend against it, Gen. Qalibaf went on to describe the missile in detail. It was 17 meters long, weighed 16 tons, and could travel at a speed of more than 6,900 kilometers per hour at a cruising altitude of 250 kilometers. Thus, according to the general, it was "the least vulnerable to missile defense systems."[14]

Israeli intelligence officials were quoted in the newspaper *Ha'aretz* on July 24 as predicting that the missile would be "fully operational" in "a year or even less." Pentagon Spokesman Kenneth Bacon observed: "Given that Iran has had a lengthy war with Iraq, one of its primary concerns is Iraq, but obviously they don't need an MRBM to deal with Iraq. They have shorter range ballistic missiles they could use if they were worried about Iraq. So they clearly, for whatever reason, have longer range aspirations, and that is worrisome to us, but I believe it should also be worrisome to Russia and it should be worrisome to Saudi Arabia; it should be worrisome to Turkey, and it definitely is very worrisome to Israel."[15]

Importantly, the test occurred although Western intelligence deemed the No Dong project to be plagued by technical or financial difficulties, or both. Even after intelligence revised its estimate, realizing that the No Dong-1 had been operationally deployed by the Korean People's Army for some time, even though it may have been tested only once before, the Iranian test took place ahead of schedule. Indeed, the *Jerusalem Post*, on July 31, 1998, quoted Israeli military sources as saying: "They [the Iranians] are so eager to complete this missile [Shihab-3] that they are shortening [its] stages of development."[16] Incidentally, it was suggested that Libyan money may have been secretly funneled to the development of a North Korean missile with a range of about 1,000 kilometers, but it was not known if the missile in question was the No Dong-1.[17]

The Birth of Club MAD

In fact, a "Club MAD" (that is, mass destruction) has emerged, in which oil revenues from Iran, Libya, and Syria have allowed the Democratic People's Republic of Korea (DPRK, or North Korea) to develop its missile industry, in turn enabling all four countries to pose an increasing strategic threat to their enemies. As a result of the collaboration, the DPRK has reached a production capacity of four to eight Scuds monthly, some for export and some for its own armed forces.[18]

The major role played by Tehran in financing the North Korean missile development program has in turn enabled Iran to pose a direct threat to Baghdad via the Scud C, while Syria could likewise target all of Israel.[19] The Iranians are clearly interested in enhancing the strategic threat to Israel and have actively helped the Syrian missile buildup financially. Judged by the comments made by Iranian Deputy President Seyyed 'Atollah Mohajerani, in the wake of the Gulf War Saddam's terrorist deterrence has found new eager practitioners in Tehran: "The Israelis have a saying which they repeat frequently: 'One hundred years of talk are better than one day of war.' Naturally, the Israelis are sensitive on the issue of war and wish to stay as far away from it as possible. They have a reason. If we take all the aid being given to Israel, not one of the Jews would be prepared to die for Israel; they lack the faith. This is why when some missiles hit Tel Aviv [during the Gulf War], a lot of Jews abandoned their homes. This proves that they merely seek a comfortable life and are not inclined to fighting."[20] The Syrian general staff was similarly impressed by the nightly exodus of residents of the metropolitan Tel Aviv area due to the Iraqi Scud attacks. The Syrians also saw that the Americans were incapable of destroying the Iraqi missiles and their launchers even though they expended great efforts.[21] In short, in the aftermath of the Gulf War Syria and Iran reached the conclusion that low-cost, low-tech mass destruction weapons and SSMs were an effective and relatively invulnerable deterrent against the United States and Israel.

Without a doubt, these observations were important in the decision by Damascus to place new orders for North Korean Scud Cs. As for Iran, the lessons of the war had also assured Tehran that the growing Syrian arsenal of strategic missiles would enable Syria to adopt an "extended deterrence" relationship in support of Iran. With its missiles as a backup, a Syrian warning to Israel not to act against Iran would have to be taken seriously. Generally, the curtailment of Israel's freedom of action as a result of the Syrian missile buildup was certainly in Iran's interest. Conversely, were Israel to defeat Syria in a war, the strategic position of Iran would be adversely affected with respect to both Israel and Iraq.

The cooperation between the four countries has also allowed Pyongyang to pose an SSM threat to all of South Korea. Moreover, without such collaboration, it is doubtful that Pyongyang could have proceeded with the development of the No Dong-1, with which Iran could soon threaten Israel, and the two new missiles, Taepo Dong I and II, believed to have ranges of 2,000 and 6,000 kilometers, respectively. On August 31, 1998, North Korea attempted its first satellite launch, using a three-stage rocket, possibly a variant of the Taepo Dong II. Reportedly, the rocket's final stage was propelled by a solid-fuel engine. The second stage of the rocket passed over Japan's main island of Honshu before plunging into the Pacific, 580 kilometers northeast of the American military base in Misawa.[22] In fact, even the deployment of the No Dong-1 allows Pyongyang to threaten Japan and Taiwan.[23] Moreover, the DPRK is evidently working hard on fitting the No Dong and Taepo Dong missiles with CB warheads.[24]

If the No Dong-1 is eventually deployed in Libya, its leader, Mu'ammar al-Qaddafi, will be able to threaten not only Israel but also Athens, Rome, and southwestern Turkey. In this connection it may be recalled that in 1986 Libya fired Scud B missiles against the Italian island of Lampedusa, possibly targeting a NATO base there, in retaliation for the U.S. air raid against suspected terrorist targets on Libyan territory. In fact, when asked soon after the Gulf War whether there was any truth to reports of a missile deal between Libya and North Korea, Qaddafi declared: "We wish we had missiles with a 1,000 kilometer range, because the presence of these missiles would have prevented the aggression against [Libya], and if America knew that we had such missiles, it would not have hit our children while they were asleep."[25]

All four countries are known to possess extensive stockpiles of chemical weapons. In fact, soon after the Gulf War, the DPRK launched an effort to strengthen its CBW capability.[26] It was reported that Pyongyang had formed chemical platoons within the regimental level.[27] It also launched "full-dress" CW training exercises as part of its tactical unit training. In addition to constructing a chemical weapons testing ground and an "offensive tactical training ground," North Korea was said to hold decontamination exercises. "Over 30 kg of chemicals are supplied to every division every year for training," a South Korean military source reported.[28] The DPRK is currently estimated to have stockpiled between 300 and 1,000 tons of nerve, blood, choking, and blister agents, in at least six depots "distributed like a bar between Pyongyang and the demarcation line [with the Republic of Korea] at the 38 parallel."[29] Eight chemical factories are considered likely production sites, with a total annual production capacity of 4,500 tons of CW agents.[30]

As a result of the post–Gulf War buildup, "chemical weapons may have become an integral part of North Korea's war fighting strategy." The country's huge military, and its civilian population, are "prepared for operations in a contaminated environment."[31] William Cohen, U.S. secretary of defense, has even suggested that the United States has "underestimated the capacity for the launching of a chemical weapons attack by the North."[32]

Syria, according to a November 1983 report of Amnesty International, made extensive use of cyanide gas to put down a rebellion by members of its Sunni minority in the city of Hama. The attack, which took place in February 1982, resulted in the killing of some 18,000 people. But a major turning point in the Syrian CW buildup came in the wake of the Lebanese War. In June 1982 the Israeli Air Force was able to neutralize the Syrian surface-to-air missile network and to down 90 Syrian planes without suffering a single loss. The Syrians promptly reacted by deciding to upgrade their arsenal of mass destruction weapons and long-range missiles, to counter Israel's strategic advantage in the air. After the Gulf War, the Syrian strategic buildup expanded even more dramatically.

Damascus has been especially secretive about its CW program. Nevertheless, recent assessments have dubbed it the most advanced and extensive chemical arms program in the Arab world, now that the Iraqi one has been substantially curtailed. The production of chemical weapons is taking place at three sites: one near Damascus, the second near Hama (where production of VX nerve gas is reportedly under way), and the third is near Safira village in the Aleppo area.[33] The Syrians have invested considerable efforts in the development of chemical fills for the Soviet cluster bomb PTAB-500, which contains bomblets. Having produced thousands of chemical aerial bombs for their Sukhoi-22/20, MiG-23, and Sukhoi-24 aircraft, the Syrians have been hard at work to develop missile warheads capable of delivering sarin and VX nerve gases effectively.[34] According to the newspaper *Ha'aretz* on May 19, 1998, Israel's defense minister, Itzhak Mordekhai, told the Knesset's Foreign Affairs and Security Committee that Syria's military echelon "is primarily engaged in the development of long range SSMs." The missiles, including Scud C, have been equipped with VX nerve gas, which has "changed the strategic balance between Israel and Syria." A high-ranking AMAN officer told the committee that the Syrians were building the missiles with North Korean know-how and Russian materials. The work was made easier because Syria — unlike Iraq, which had to trade payload for range in the case of its al-Husayn missiles — employed the original Soviet-designed Scud warhead (with its mass of 985 kilograms) in its CW preparations against Israel. Syria is also believed to have developed and manufactured binary chemical warheads for its missiles and artillery rockets, as well as binary chemical aerial bombs.[35]

Iran's offensive chemical warfare program began in 1983 in response to Iraq's use of mustard gas against its troops. By 1987 Iran was able to deliver limited quantities of blister (mustard) and blood (cyanide) agents against Iraqi troops using artillery shells. Since 1984, Iran has been producing chemical agents at a steadily increasing rate. In fact, since the signing in 1993 of the Chemical Weapons Convention, Iran has continued to upgrade and expand its chemical production infrastructure and chemical munitions arsenal. Estimates of its current stock range from a minimum of "several hundred tons" of blister, blood, and choking agents to as much as 2,000 tons of these gases.[36] Moreover, there have been reports that Tehran has begun to explore the production of nerve gases, including VX, whose low volatility makes it quite suitable for use in the hot climate of the Middle East.[37] Iran also increased defensive and offensive CW training for its ground forces in 1996 and 1997. In exercises during the summer of 1995, Iranian forces used helicopters to spray their own ships with aerosol liquids, suggesting that Iran is investigating the use of CW (or BW, or both) against ships in the strategically vital Persian Gulf.[38]

Libya is one of the few nations to have used CW since the mid-1980s, having dropped chemical agents from a transport plane against Chadian troops in 1987. Iran supplied the agents in exchange for naval mines.[39] Although the Libyan CW plant in Rabta (which previously produced up to 100 tons of CW agent, mostly consisting of sarin, mustard gas, and phosgene) was closed in 1990 following intense media focus on the facility, it remains capable of renewing production; in fact, the Libyans announced its reopening in September 1995 as a pharmaceutical plant. In 1991 the Libyans, mindful of the Gulf War experience, took steps to disperse and conceal their CW stocks.[40] That year, they began construction of a second CW agent production facility underground in a mountainous area near Tarhunah, 65 kilometers southeast of Tripoli. CIA Director John Deutch has described it as "the world's largest underground chemical weapons plant."[41] The facility covers more than 15 square kilometers and already stores much of Libya's stockpile of chemical weapons. It is thought that it could have already started CW agent production as early as 1996, and some reports have suggested that biological weapons might also be produced there.[42]

The Club MAD countries are also concerned with the development of biological weapons. According to the Russian External Intelligence report, North Korea is conducting experiments with such BW agents as anthrax, cholera, bubonic plague, and smallpox at a number of universities, medical colleges, and research institutes. It said that the tests are being conducted on offshore islands.[43] By contrast, the South Korean Defense Ministry, in its "1991–92 National Defense White Paper," said that North Korea has deployed such bacteriological weapons as cholera and pest after completing "live experiments."[44] The ROK's Agency for National Security Planning subsequently said, in its report to the National Assembly, that Pyongyang's BW program had gone into actual production. According to this report, 13 types of biological agents, including pest and typhus, have already been weaponized and stored in six base locations in the DPRK. North Korea can launch these weapons via Scud missiles, aircraft, helicopters, and even field artillery, the report maintained.[45] A defector who served in a Chemical, Biological, and Radiological Warfare unit of the Korean People's Army has claimed that the DPRK "mass-produced" biochemical weapons developed by the medical school of Kim Il-Sung University and the People's Army Medical College. He also alleged that experiments with biochemical weapons on "living bodies" of political prisoners have taken place in North Korea.[46]

Syria is also "pursuing the development" of biological weapons. The country has an "adequate biotechnical infrastructure to support a small biological warfare program." The Syrians, however, are not believed to have begun any "major weaponization or testing related to biological warfare."[47] The U.S. Defense Department has said that without "significant foreign assistance," Syria is "unlikely to advance to the manufacture of significant amounts of [biological weapons] for several years."[48] This forecast, however, seems to overlook the lesson of the Iraqi BW program.

The Iranian BW program, which commenced in the early 1980s, is hidden within the country's extensive biotechnology and pharmaceutical industries so as to obscure its activities. The Iranian military has used medical, educational, and scientific research organizations for many aspects of BW agent procurement, research, and production. For example, soon after the Gulf War new orders for bioprocessing equipment were placed with European companies. The Federal Prosecutor's Office in Bern, Switzerland, even suspects that the Israeli intelligence agency Mossad was behind the bombing of the Bioengineering Company in Wald, near Zurich, in 1992 and 1993. The machine-building company planned to supply fermenters to Midpsig Company, the Iranian procurement organization that is believed to be a front for the Iranian military. On June 14, 1992, "biological machinery" destined for Iran was blown up on the premises of the Deugro shipping company in Munich. The shipment was also destined for Iran at the order of Bioengineering.[49] By now, Iran has evolved from piecemeal acquisition of bioprocessing equipment and is establishing complete biological production plants that could be converted to producing BW agents.[50] According to the Arms Control and Disarmament Agency, "Iran probably has produced biological warfare agents and apparently has weaponized a small quantity of those agents."[51] By contrast, according to "Israeli intelligence sources" cited by the *Sunday Times* on August 11, 1996, the Iranian program is much further along. Iran, they said, already keeps stocks of anthrax and botulinum in Tabriz, northwest of Tehran, and can produce more BW agents "quickly." The sources alleged that the Iranians can deliver biological payloads via Scud missiles and that "they have a system for dropping them [BW agents] from Soviet-era Sukhoi aircraft."

Finally, Libya is seeking to acquire the capability to develop and produce BW agents. Its BW program has been described as in the "research and development phase," but Libya is not believed to have produced any biological weapons yet.[52] Reportedly, the Libyans have the expertise to produce small quantities of biological equipment for their BW program. They are currently seeking to move to the stage of weaponizing BW agents, perhaps by recruiting foreign scientists to the program.[53]

Mutual Support among Club MAD Countries

Cooperation between the countries of Club MAD is not new and is invariably based on a common ideological hostility toward the United States. These countries also share long-standing concerns about Washington's intentions toward their regimes. In November 1982, for example, North Korea and Libya concluded a long-term friendship treaty, which committed the sides to "exchange military data and specialists" and to "strive to supply the other [party with] weapons not possessed by it" (Article 4). Article 5 of the pact said that "if any of the contracting parties is subject to a threat or an aggression by imperialists and their minions, the other party shall in every way render military and material support and aid to it, regarding it as a threat of an aggression against itself. In that case, the contracting parties shall provide all conveniences for the military support of the other country."[54]

Likewise, a joint communiqué released by the Korean Central News Agency on May 17, 1989, during a visit to Pyongyang by Iranian President Seyyed Ali Khamenei, stated: "The two presidents [Ali Khamenei and Kim Il-Sung] underlined the resolute determination of their respective governments and people to decisively foil the U.S. imperialist aggressions and interventions, especially against the DPRK and the Islamic Republic of Iran." In December 1989, a delegation of the Islamic Revolution Guard Corps (IRGC), headed by its commander, Maj. Gen. Mohsen Reza'i, visited North Korea. Gen. O Chin-U, the DPRK defense minister at the time, promised that his country would "also strengthen anti-imperialist and anti-U.S. joint activities with the Iranian people in the future."[55] Accordingly, a military agreement was concluded, which dealt also with "the exchange of technology and armaments."[56] Reza'i predicted that the pact would "produce results in the long run."[57]

One year later, during the Gulf crisis, a North Korean military delegation with O Chin-U at its head arrived in Tehran. On that occasion the IRGC commander said that military cooperation between the two countries had "become all the more necessary, because the world and regional situation has reached a grave stage and the U.S. imperialists' aggressive moves in our region have become undisguised."[58] Reza'i and his guests were surely referring to the decline of the Soviet Union and to the U.S. muscle-flexing in the Gulf. The deterioration in Soviet power was viewed in Pyongyang as an unmitigated disaster. Although the Iranians anticipated that the collapse of Communism would clear the way for the rise of Islam and the elimination of a potential threat on Iran's northern frontiers, Tehran, too, was disturbed that the prime counter to U.S. "imperialism" had been substantially nullified. Iran was also an indirect beneficiary of the subsequent Iraqi defeat in the Gulf War, but here, too, it shared the DPRK's fears that the American victory would provide an opportunity for Washington to increase pressure on the remaining radical regimes. Iran and North Korea both surmised that the United States would surely not miss the opportunity to establish a Pax Americana now that it had reached the zenith of its power.

This assessment was shared by Syria and Libya as they sought to cement their ties with Pyongyang. Syrian President Hafiz al-Assad described the relations between Syria and the DPRK as "an indomitable friendship capable of overcoming any outside pressure." On the same occasion, he told the visiting Vice Marshal Choe Kwang, chief of the General Staff of the Korean People's Army, that he hoped the "friendship, unity and cooperation between the two armies of Syria and the DPRK will be continuously strengthened and developed."[59] Indeed, the rationale for strategic cooperation with the DPRK must have become compelling in the aftermath of the U.S. victory in the Gulf. All four countries sought to enhance their deterrent postures vis-à-vis the United States via new missiles capable of delivering CB weapons. First came the 1991 DPRK-Syria missile deal. Then, in the twelve-month span beginning in March 1992, five Iranian military delegations, comprising largely missile personnel, were sent to North Korea.[60] In exchange for renewing the exportation of 1 million tons of crude oil per year for five years, Iran was promised new weapons. By September 1996, the ROK Ministry of National Unification estimated, North Korea had exported some 400 Scud B and Scud C missiles to Iran and Syria.[61]

Moreover, the war added new incentives for strategic cooperation between Syria, Libya, and Iran — on the basis of their implacable enmity toward Israel. As Libya's Qaddafi has put it: "The result [of the Gulf War] is that despite everything, Iraq — Israel's only major military rival in the Near East — was crushed without any Tzahal [Hebrew for IDF] soldier being involved. The balance of power has been broken."[62] The Syrian defense minister, Mustafa Tlass, even accused Saddam of "rendering a valuable service to the U.S. during the Gulf War."[63] Not only did the war serve Israel's strategic interests, but it also allowed the United States to expand its military presence in the region. Tlass vowed to establish a "total Arab balance-of-power with Israel and achieve a buildup of a regional deterrent force to American-Western deployment in the Middle East."[64] Thus, two years after Assad had announced that he was ceasing his efforts to reach "strategic parity" with Israel, owing to the economic crisis in his country and Soviet advice, the plan was revived with a vengeance and Saudi money.[65]

The Middle Eastern countries of Club MAD also relied on one another to resist "foreign interference" — a euphemism for the United States — in the region. Immediately after the Gulf War, President Assad and Iranian President Hashemi Rafsanjani held a summit meeting in Damascus to announce that they had decided to promote Syrian-Iranian relations to a "distinguished level." The two countries had long cooperated against their common enemy in Baghdad, especially during the eight-year Iran-Iraq war.[66] Damascus had a keen interest in preventing an Iraqi victory in that war, figuring that such an outcome would elevate Saddam's position in the region at Syria's expense and could also spell danger to the Assad regime directly. On the face of it, the U.S. defeat of Saddam should have meant that Damascus or Tehran would put less stress on bilateral ties. Iran's need for Syria had been weakened given that Iraq could now pose only a limited threat to Tehran's rulers. For its part, Syria was a member of the U.S.-led anti-Saddam coalition and had little reason to antagonize Washington by cementing its ties to the virulent anti-American regime in Iran. The fever-ish efforts by the two countries to strengthen their alliance soon after the Gulf War, despite any possible reservations, reflect the thinking of Club MAD leaders and the new strategic trend in the region. During their summit meeting, Assad and Rafsanjani reiterated their strong opposition to "any interference by foreign countries and forces" in the Middle East. The two presidents were in agreement that the "dangers surrounding the region require the broadest kind of political, security, economic and cul-tural cooperation." They declared that "close cooperation" between their countries was a "basic factor in enhancing . . . the region's security and independence away from any foreign interference."[67]

The anti-imperialist ideology of the DPRK was clearly compatible with that of its Middle Eastern counterparts. The leader of the Iranian delega-tion to North Korea, Majles Speaker Mehdi Karrubi, later recounted that in his meeting with DPRK leader Kim Il-Sung he quoted the late Ayatol-lah Khomeini's statement: "We will die but we will not surrender to the United States," at which point the Korean leader "rose to his feet and fervently applauded."[68]

Indeed, Libyan leader Mu'ammar al-Qaddafi was so distraught over the death of Kim in 1995 that he compared it to the (apparently untimely) pass-ing of Hitler. He said: "At one time Germany relied on Hitler, and when Hitler committed suicide Germany also committed suicide. Yesterday North Korea was an adamant adversary to America. It continued its pro-gram of producing its deterrent weapons against America. . . . Now, since Kim Il-Sung died, American penetration of Korea has begun and North Korea has stopped being a confrontation state against imperialism."[69]

Qaddafi's reaction was predictable. While seeking to cement ties with the other Club MAD countries, he all but openly called for the acquisition of an independent strategic deterrent: "Why do [the Americans] not ban the atomic bomb? Which is the more dangerous, the atomic bomb or the chemical bomb? The atomic bomb is more dangerous. But they would not ban it, because they are an atomic power and can possess it, while the others cannot. The important thing is that the chemical bomb belongs to the poor [countries], which can make it. They [want] to disarm the poor of the weapons to defend themselves."[70]

It appears, however, that the Libyan leader was unduly alarmed. The agreements signed so far between Pyongyang and Washington, aimed to freeze and eventually dismantle the nascent North Korean nuclear program, have had little effect on the continued production and exportation of DPRK missiles to the Middle East. But even if the scenario he envisioned came to pass, Qaddafi could rely on the missile infrastructure already built by the North Koreans in Syria and Iran.

In any case, Qaddafi's statement suggests that for the countries of Club MAD, the Gulf War provided incontrovertible proof of the virtues of an independent strategic deterrent. Their leaders discovered that radical regimes that can field the modern Praetorian Guard — mass destruction weapons and long-range delivery vehicles — survive even if they challenge the world's premier power. Such weapons could overcome the defensive edge that the West relied on through its air supremacy. They could also effectively counter its offensive capabilities. A low-tech solution in the form of inaccurate missiles (sometimes of questionable reliability) and low-cost CB warheads would frustrate the U.S. high-tech dominance of the modern battlefield as evidenced in the Gulf War. Even when CB arms are not used, the combination of SSMs and CB weapons attracts much international attention. Thus the rationale for an even closer political and military cooperation between these militant countries, especially in the field of strategic missiles, received a strong boost from the war.

Club MAD at Work

The workings of Club MAD could be readily observed in the months after the Gulf War. In September 1991, a North Korean ship named *Mupo*, loaded with eight Scud Cs and their associated TELs destined for Syria, was prevented from delivering its cargo after leaks in the press indicated that Israeli gun boats were ready to intercept it in the eastern Mediterranean. The ship was diverted to the Iranian port in Bandar Abbas, just inside the Persian Gulf. Later, it was able to make its way in secret to the Syrian port of Tartus, where it arrived on the eve of the Madrid Peace Conference, scheduled for October 30–November 1, 1991.[71]

In February 1992, the North Korean ship *Dae Hung Ho*, laden with Scud Cs, TELs, and related equipment to the tune of $100 million, left the DPRK on its way to Syria. It was discovered by U.S. ships patrolling the Indian Ocean, and it, too, found shelter in Bandar Abbas after the U.S. Navy was ordered by the White House to stand aside. In May 1992 the operation was completed when Iran secretly airlifted the missile parts to

Syria.[72] A week after the North Korean ship had docked in Iran, another ship, *Iran Salam*, arrived in the Iranian port of Chah Bahar with a cargo of Scud C missiles and production equipment for the Syrian missile factories. It has been said that the factories were meant for both countries, and that there is a reasonable possibility that Syria had already delivered chemical warheads to Iran.[73]

Two months later, Syria test-launched several Scud missiles, including a Scud C, in a move that, the Israeli foreign minister pointed out, "took place when Syria is taking a part in peace negotiations with Israel."[74] Damascus undoubtedly was signaling to Israel that territorial depth — like that provided by the strategic area known as the Golan Heights, which Israel had captured from Syria in the 1967 war — had lost its military value now that Syrian missiles armed with chemical warheads could reach even the remotest points in the country.[75]

Israeli leaders, Syria was intimating, should return the land to Syrian control. Otherwise, the systematic buildup of a full array of chemical agents and delivery systems pursued by Syria, especially since the Gulf War, could enable it to adopt an offensive strategy toward Israel.[76] The Syrians today can use such long-range delivery vehicles as the Su-24 attack aircraft and Scud B and Scud C missiles, and such persistent agents as VX, to try and neutralize Israeli air bases, C&C and radar sites, reserve mobilization centers, and equipment locations. Short-range systems, like rocket artillery and Su-20/22 ground attack aircraft, could deliver nonpersistent agents like sarin against front-line positions to facilitate breakthroughs by Syrian ground forces. The IAF's deep penetration raids, directed at targets in Syria, would be deterred by a threat to deliver CB agents against Israeli cities via strikes by Scud Bs and Cs.

If successful, this strategy would enable Syria to retake the Golan Heights before the IDF could complete mobilization and to present the international community with a fait accompli. Further, rapid Syrian penetration into the heavily populated Heights might discourage the IDF from using air and artillery strikes against Syrian forces.

In view of this analysis, reports that Syrian army brigades have been using CW agents during exercises in the desert, near the Golan Heights, sound ominous.[77] They cast doubt on the assertion that "in the future, Syria will not likely use chemical weapons or ballistic missiles . . . against Israel, or another enemy, unless the regime's survival is at stake."[78]

Already in mid-1992, the Syrian missile tests had demonstrated that the setbacks suffered by the radical camp in the wake of the Soviet demise and the U.S. victory in the Gulf War had been overcome. The Syrians felt confident enough to start exercising their new strategic muscle politically, and to signal to Israel and presumably the United States their readiness for CW.

Numerous other instances of strategic cooperation between the members of Club MAD have taken place over the years. For example, the head of the German BND (Federal Intelligence Service), Konrad Porzner, disclosed that Libya had provided Iran with the construction plans for its chemical weapons production plant in Rabta. Consequently, Iran was "apparently trying to buy the required plant parts."[79] Subsequently, it was reported that Libya had passed the plans for the al-Fatah missile — a 1,000-kilometer MRBM, which Qaddafi tried to develop with the help of German companies — to Iran.[80] Moreover, according to the BND, on at least one occasion Libya served as a transshipment point for 80 tons of missile propellant, which had originated in Russia.[81]

It has been claimed that the Syrian BW program has received "professional assistance" from North Korea.[82] In addition, there is little doubt that Damascus sought and acquired extensive access to information about Iran's CW experiences in its war with Iraq. In return, the Syrians acted as intermediaries between Iran and five West German companies, thus enabling Tehran to take its first steps in the CW field.[83] Soon after the Gulf War, it became known that a large Syrian military delegation had gone to train the Iranians in the operation of the scores of Iraqi aircraft that had been flown to Iran during the war. Undoubtedly, the training included the Su-24 *Fencer*, in Syrian service since 1989.[84] Given that the *Fencer* could reach Israeli territory from Iran, the cooperation between Damascus and Tehran could be viewed as a stopgap measure until Iran could field missiles capable of hitting Israeli targets. In the meantime, Syrian technicians began working in Iran to extend the range of the Scud B missiles that Tehran had acquired from North Korea. On May 12, 1991, Iran test-fired such a modified Scud, which flew eastward a distance of some 500 kilometers.[85] Such a missile, if armed with a CB warhead, could pose a significant threat to U.S. warships patrolling the waters of the Persian Gulf and Indian Ocean. Reports state that Iranian and Syrian engineers and technicians are cooperating on the development of CB warheads for the Scud C. The work is done in the Syrian missile factories built by North Korea.[86]

It may be noted that the original range of the North Korean No Dong-1 missile, which Iran has ordered, was 1,000 kilometers. CIA Director James Woolsey even testified to such a range during congressional hearings in July 1993.[87] However, North Korea sought to extend its range at the request of Iran, which wanted a missile specifically capable of reaching

Israel.[88] If combined with an NBC warhead, the missile could allow Iran to provide Syria with a strategic umbrella of sorts in case of a conflict with Israel. Tehran would simply have no excuse to withhold its support of Damascus — in the same way that, precisely as Saddam had once explained, the missiles in Iraq's possession would compel it to come to the aid of fellow Arabs if they were attacked by Israel.

Already Tehran has made its intentions clear. Although in 1998 it still lacks the ability to reach Israel from Iranian territory by missiles, its leaders hastened to copy almost exactly some of Saddam's favorite terrorist deterrence tactics. The *Tehran Times* newspaper, which ordinarily reflects the views of the Iranian foreign ministry, said in an editorial on October 4, 1995: "Iran is not only capable of destroying any target deep inside Israel, but it can also endanger Israeli interests in any part of the world if the Israelis commit a blunder by attacking Iran." Under the cover of the No Dong-1, or an indigenously produced offspring, Iran will be able to engage openly in saber-rattling against Israeli cities. Moreover, the CB arsenal is apparently also aimed at enabling Tehran to issue, with impunity, threats of resorting to international terrorism.

The Age of Blackmail

The cumulative impact of the collaboration in acquiring long-range missiles and mass destruction weapons, a drive clearly accelerated by the Gulf War, has been to create a de facto strategic parity between, for instance, Israel and Syria, or the United States and the DPRK. Although Israel can still inflict a much greater damage on Syria or Iran than those countries can on Israel, and although the United States can certainly decimate both countries as well as North Korea, the risks from such potential conflicts have risen dramatically. The war established that even if radicals lack weapons capable of reaching American soil directly, they can hold the entire civilian population of regional U.S. allies hostage. This capability will only expand as the range and quantity of missiles in the hands of militant regimes grow, and even remote countries allied with the United States can be effectively threatened. Under these circumstances, proliferation of the "hostage country" strategy, practiced first under Saddam's terrorist deterrence, could simply turn America's regional alliances on their heads. U.S. allies in the region would become leverage against America, rather than assets that serve its strategic and political interests.

More important, the war demonstrated anew the deliberate targeting of civilians for conventional missile attacks. Naturally, the ensuing buildup of CB and SSM capabilities in the Club MAD countries has caused many to fear the worst. And the subsequent news about Saddam's preparations for BW have plainly served to buttress the logic of this worst-case approach. Thus, in the wake of the war, CB threats issued by extremist regimes against enemy cities are liable to be considered more credible than heretofore.

The war demonstrated the immediacy of the threat in another respect as well. In any future conflict, radicals can again be expected to seek to overcome geographical barriers by threatening CBW via terrorism, and thus to imperil directly U.S. military forces and America proper. The confirmation by Louis J. Freeh, director of the Federal Bureau of Investigation, of the existence of terrorist infrastructures of Middle Eastern groups inside the United States, along with similar reports from Europe, may indicate a strategy for radical regimes to project power on the cheap. Such networks provide Syria and Iran, for instance, with the potential to threaten a CB response until such time as they can develop missiles capable of reaching European and U.S. targets directly.

The combined impact of these developments has been to compound the number of "marginal" issues that Israel, the United States, and the West in general would rather not contest with radical countries armed with mass destruction weapons. Chemical and biological arms are tailor-made for dictators who rule by terrorizing their internal and external enemies. Even if Israel is militarily superior to Syria and Damascus is wary of a direct confrontation, Syria can wave its CB weapons with little fear of an escalation. A CB war of nerves is likely to incite panic among Israeli citizens whatever the military balance. Damascus figures that a democratic government will be susceptible to a public outcry against a horrendous war and will favor concessions, regardless of its military might. Moreover, the question of who would win the engagement becomes moot when the victory is bought at an extremely high cost. The highest priority is given to avoiding war, not to winning it. In such an environment, strategic and political blackmail is easily conducted.

In addition, in the wake of the Gulf War, U.S. and Israeli policies imply a much lower confidence in the viability of strategic deterrence as a means of assuring national security. At times it even appeared as if the Israeli government was so alarmed by the new dangers that it took to deliberately advertising the new mass destruction threats, hoping to press the Israeli public indirectly into making difficult concessions. A few days after a Syrian Scud test, the late Itzhak Rabin said: "Syria has ground-to-ground missiles in such quantities and such quality that what we suffered at the hands of Iraq will be child's play in comparison."[89]

The bottom line is that the security of countries like Israel, Japan, Turkey, and Saudi Arabia has diminished, while the security of radical regimes has increased. Such regimes are thus freer to conduct policies utterly inimical to U.S. interests, not to mention that of their neighbors. In this sense, the strategic initiative in the Middle East and on the Korean Peninsula has shifted in favor of radical powers.

Already America's allies feel more exposed. For example, the Persian Gulf states, which had been asked by the United States to supply oil to North Korea as part of the October 21, 1994, deal for ending the DPRK's development of nuclear weapons, informed Washington that if Pyongyang was continuing to supply missiles to Iran, not one drop of oil would reach the North. Robert Galucci, chief of the American delegation to the talks with the DPRK, was dispatched to the Persian Gulf in February 1995. According to a lengthy account in the Israeli paper *Ma'ariv* on April 14, 1995, "he found that the Kuwaitis, Saudis and Omanis were more hysterical than the Israelis about the danger posed by long-range missiles falling into Iranian hands." Then CENTCOM's commander in chief, Gen. Binford Peay, noticed similar apprehensions. While describing Iran's efforts to acquire long-range missiles, including with the help of Russian engineers, in *Jane's Defence Weekly* of May 22, 1996, he was quoted as saying: "Clearly, every senior leader — civilian or military — emir, king, or chief of service that I talk to in the Gulf today describes Iran as the long-term threat."

Further, as a result of the strategic transformation, after a hiatus of some two and a half decades Israel again faces potential threats to its existence. Consequently, Jerusalem has been forced to confront difficult security dilemmas: "The response proposed by the Rabin government [to the Syrian mass destruction threat] is the peace process, even at the price of painful concessions, on the assumption that there is no significance to territorial depth [in the wake of the introduction of long-range missiles into the region]. The response of the opposition [the Likud party] is to move the Syrian point of attack back, as much as possible, in the event of war. In practice, this is the essence of the debate over the future of the Golan."[90]

If, however, Washington believes that a comprehensive settlement is a viable substitute for an unstable regional "balance of terror," it is bound to be disappointed. Club MAD leaders are unlikely to give up their mass destruction weapons because, as Saddam has demonstrated, these arms are the ultimate insurance policy of these regimes. Furthermore, in exchange for such a concession, Syria would likely demand the disarming of Israel's nuclear option. This would leave Israel extremely exposed in its new borders, if a settlement were reached on the basis of trading territory for peace. It would be impossible for any responsible Israeli leadership to discount the danger on the pretext that the risk of an Arab attack had been simply eliminated by the new peace agreement. In fact, from the strategic point of view, the opposite may be true. An agreement that resulted in Israel's giving up both the territories and the nuclear option would likely increase the Arab incentive to attack rather than decrease it. Thus the greater the Israeli territorial concessions, the more would be its reliance on nuclear strategy, and the lesser the likelihood that it would give up this option. Accordingly, if a Syrian-Israeli peace finally came about, mass destruction weapons would be likely to be kept to "guarantee" it. A Syrian-Israeli peace, in turn, would increase the isolation of Iran, and thus its incentive to cultivate its mass destruction option further. Contrary to the prevailing propaganda, then, peace is unlikely to yield more security.

Apparently in a bid to break this cycle, the idea of a U.S.-Israeli defense pact was entertained by Prime Minister Peres.[91] Although the timing of the proposal was made to look as if it was designed to compensate for a possible Israeli withdrawal from the Golan Heights, there is little question that its aim was to prepare the ground for Israel to give up its nuclear option. Israel would be unlikely to seek a U.S. strategic umbrella if it planned to maintain an independent deterrent.

This U.S.-Israeli search for new security solutions was itself indirectly compelled by the radical camp. It is vivid testimony to the gradual shift in the balance of strategic initiative in favor of the Club MAD countries. By now, Assad and Kim Chong-Il, not to mention Saddam, must know that Israel and the United States would like to avoid a confrontation with those countries, and specifically their CB and SSM arsenals, almost at all cost. Thus, the decision to launch a new aggression is exclusively in their court. As long as they refrain from actually going to war, there is little danger to their regimes. At the same time, their mere possession of the new mass destruction capabilities raises the danger of a catastrophe, which is enough to extract political concessions from their "sane" democratic enemies. For radicals, acquisition of mass destruction weapons is a low-cost and low-risk strategy with a potential for a high political payoff. It is likely to be adhered to for the foreseeable future. Indeed, Peres's doctrine only bolsters the rationale for acquiring and maintaining such arms.

Extremists will continue to look to mass destruction weapons to help them indirectly in vanquishing their enemies. They clearly do not see their CBW capabilities as a means to reach some political modus vivandi with their neighbors aimed at guaranteeing greater security for all concerned. To assume that this was the goal would imply that their radical agendas, their political raisons d'être, camouflaged orientations favoring the status quo, while their daily tirades against the international order in general and their neighbors in particular were just a facade. But, as Saddam Hussein has demonstrated, acquisition of CB weapons and long-range missiles by radicals is rarely meant solely as a strategic deterrent. Baghdad viewed these weapons as a shield against foreign interference in the attack on Kuwait. Likewise, there is little question that the continued sponsorship by Damascus of terrorism against Israel and Turkey reflects its assessment that these countries would dearly like to avoid a direct confrontation with a CB-armed Syria.[92]

Mass destruction weapons have already allowed militant leaders to intensify their efforts to redraw the regional geopolitical maps via subversion, terrorism, and intimidation. Such attempts to dismantle the Pax Americana are likely to expand as these regimes' confidence in their strategic deterrents grow. As General Reza'i, the Iranian IRGC commander, said in a 1995 speech: "Are the Americans brave enough to come forward themselves? Would they come face to face with Islam? Several years ago a few Americans were taken hostage in Lebanon by the Hizballah forces there — and it had nothing to do with Iran — and the Americans ran away. They pulled out all their forces from Lebanon. Americans do not have the power of confrontation."[93] And Major General Shahbazi, Iran's chief of the Joint Army Staff, has pointed out, ominously, that the United States may be able to begin a military conflict but will not be strong enough to end it: "This is because only Muslims believe that 'Whether we kill or are killed, we are victors.' Others do not think this way."[94]

Saddam's terrorist deterrence strategy is alive and well, it appears. As such methods proliferate, many in the Middle East and beyond are already worried that some terrorist organization, such as Hamas, Islamic Jihad, or Hizballah, might eventually use mass destruction weapons to blackmail its enemies or to attempt to wipe them off the face of the earth.[95] So-called human bomb exercises conducted by North Korean airborne commandos raise the specter of such a scenario in the East Asian context as well.[96] In fact, such a tactic could be viewed as a primitive but effective solution to the dispersal of CB agents in the air, possibly saving the North Koreans the extra expense and complexity of developing advanced warheads for their missile force.

Further, as Club MAD countries are mostly ruled by dictatorial regimes prone to violence, their possession of mass destruction capabilities acquires a special disturbing feature. Domestic instability leading to civil war or the collapse of any one of these regimes could now spell especially grave regional dangers. For example, reports of a severe economic crisis in North Korea, possibly bordering on a collapse, have evoked the threat of some act of desperation on the part of the DPRK toward South Korea, or a coup attempt in Pyongyang followed by a civil war. Both scenarios could involve the resort to mass destruction weapons.[97] The same may be true with regard to the possibility of a power struggle in Syria once Assad passes from the scene. Already there have been reports that in the aftermath of the Gulf War and the ensuing attempt to topple Saddam, Baghdad either threatened or used chemical weapons against the Shi'a rebels in southern Iraq.[98]

Even if they are not always conspicuous, mass destruction weapons have a distinct political presence during peacetime. The 1995 shipment of 650,000 tons of rice from South Korea and Japan to the DPRK, which was strongly backed by Washington, was motivated by more than humanitarian considerations. It was equally aimed to forestall the resort to the military option by Pyongyang, possibly involving mass destruction weapons, and a dangerous political crisis in the North. The United States and its allies in the region were concerned that North Korea would launch "a desperate and final attack on the South before its food supplies run out."[99] Even if the North Korean military moves along the demilitarized zone at that time were a bluff stemming from fears in Pyongyang that South Korea would exploit the unrest to launch an attack, the miscalculation might have led to an explosion. Either way, the fact that pro-Western regimes are compelled, ostensibly for their own good, to extend support to their enemies suggests a relationship akin to blackmail. Presumably, Washington, Tokyo, and Seoul have concluded that "paying up" is less risky than having to contend with a regime armed with mass destruction weapons that believes it has nothing to lose.[100] In this sense the acquisition of mass destruction weapons, though often meant to deter foreign intervention, has invariably led to externalization of the internal political problems of the regimes so armed.

On February 2, 1996, the United States announced that it would provide an additional $2 million in food aid to the DPRK, in spite of South Korean objections. The ROK had urged Washington to condition any further aid on the North's adopting a more conciliatory stance toward the South and easing military tensions. Seoul was especially alarmed by talk in the United States of lifting additional economic sanctions and removing North Korea from the State Department's list of "terrorist nations." But James Laney, the U.S. ambassador to South Korea, explained the U.S. decision as aimed at safeguarding stability. Apparently, alluding to the DPRK military buildup along the border between North and South Korea, he stressed that "unrest on the Korean peninsula should not be touched off by North Korea's food shortages."[101] Later he rationalized the continued U.S. economic aid to the DPRK as follows: "Military deterrents worked when the North Koreans had something to lose [that is, a working economy]. . . . [The aid] is a self-interested policy to reduce the risks of irrationality."[102] But South Korean officials concluded that "the United States is vulnerable to North Korean pressure."[103] The ROK media was more blunt. It openly called the U.S. policy toward the North "appeasement" brought about by fears that pressuring the DPRK to amend its policy could lead to a military confrontation.[104] After all, Gen. Gary Luck, commander of the U.S. Armed Forces in Korea, has predicted in a report to President Clinton that a war on the peninsula would cause some 1 million casualties, including at least 80,000–100,000 U.S. troops, along with huge economic losses to the U.S., the ROK, Japan, and China.[105]

Seoul's case has a good basis in fact. It was revealed that Japanese police have begun an investigation of a trading company run by a member of the General Association of Korean Residents in Japan (Chongnyon). The man is suspected of smuggling 100 kilograms of sodium fluoride and hydrofluoric acid, which could be used to produce sarin nerve gas or to refine uranium, on board DPRK ships that arrived in Kobe Port to pick up the free rice allocated for North Korea.[106] South Korean President Kim Yong-Sam also disclosed that "most of the 150,000 tons of rice we gave [to North Korea] went to soldiers."[107] In an ironic twist, the upside-down logic of blackmail has led some in the West to argue that the diversion of food supplies to the North Korean military is in the interests of the United States and South Korea, as it will help prevent unrest on the peninsula.

On April 4, 1996, Pyongyang undertook the next step in this game of political extortion by declaring that it would no longer respect the demilitarized zone between the DPRK and the ROK. Many observers interpreted the North's move as an attempt to force the United States into negotiating a separate peace with Pyongyang and bypassing Seoul.[108] In fact, as the DPRK's economy continued to slide, the North's attempts at blackmail became increasingly public. For example, on June 16, 1998, the official Korean Central News Agency declared: "We will continue developing, testing and deploying missiles. If the United States really wants to prevent our missile export, it should lift the economic embargo as early as possible and make a compensation for the losses to be caused by discontinued missile export."[109]

Even when the United States has tried to act tough, the reception has often been less than enthusiastic. Efforts by Washington to tighten the economic noose around Iran, and increase its political isolation, have been criticized for allegedly forcing Tehran to become more extreme and desperate.[110] The U.S. dilemma is typical of other instances of blackmail. Giving in could only encourage greater crimes, while refusing to compromise is condemned as intransigence that will surely force the blackmailers to execute their threats. The spread of mass destruction weapons has assured that this debate will become a permanent feature of the emerging international system. If anything, the policy disagreements are likely to become more urgent, frequent, divisive, and potentially exploitable by political extortionists.

An Iraqi Revanche?

And what about Saddam? It is safe to assume that his mind is preoccupied with one thought — revenge. As soon as the war was over, he set out to punish his main enemies. Egypt's interior minister, Maj. Gen. Muhammad Abd al-Halim Musa, for example, disclosed that Egyptian authorities had arrested an Iraqi "intelligence officer with the rank of a captain" on his arrival at the Cairo airport on March 20, 1991. The Iraqi officer, named Abbas Abbuz Mul, "arrived in Egypt on the orders of the Iraqi President to join a terrorist group to assassinate officials, including the Interior Minister, and blow up a number of vital installations," General Musa said.[111] In 1993, the Iraqi leader even masterminded an attempt on the life of President Bush. Undoubtedly the plot amounted to tit-for-tat, given U.S. efforts to eliminate him during Desert Storm. But the Iraqi-sponsored assassination attempt provides additional insight into Saddam's escalation ladder. During the war he did not need to invoke his last-resort option, as long as the United States was searching for him in the dark. But as a veteran practitioner of terrorist deterrence, there was no question of his tolerating even failed attempts to remove him from power. Invariably, the message was, whoever dares to confront Saddam will end up dead. In fact, Saddam probably concluded from the war experience that he could go after Bush. He might have reasoned that even if the Iraqi role in the assassination was uncovered, the United States would not risk an all-out conflagration to avenge the death of a former president, because the same risky scenario could still unfold.

Under these circumstances, it is important to define the capacity for blackmail that Saddam may still possess. In spite of the adoption of Resolution 687, Iraq adopted "a policy of either total concealment or significant underrepresentation of its proscribed weapons and missile activities, [a policy] Iraq has admitted [to subsequently]." Thus, Iraq had retained two-thirds of its operational missile force, more than half its chemical weapons, and all its biological weapons. It claimed, however, that it destroyed these weapons secretly in the summer of 1991.[112] Still, a recent UNSCOM assessment has said that 817 out of 819 "long-range operational missiles" that Iraq imported from the Soviet Union in the period ending in 1988 have been accounted for. Some were used either in the Iran-Iraq war or the Gulf War. The rest were destroyed by Iraq unilaterally or under UNSCOM's supervision. The commission has said, however, that it has "evidence of the probable existence of a number of additional special [that is, CBW] warheads."[113] It would be unreasonable to assume that Iraq has retained CB warheads yet completely destroyed the means to deliver them. Therefore, the U.S. intelligence estimate that Iraq still possesses up to 25 Scud missiles seems sensible.[114] Iraq may also possess some mobile missile launchers. In this connection it may be noted that Iraq indirectly illustrated its ability to conceal major elements of missile systems from UNSCOM inspectors when, in November 1995, it turned over a previously undeclared SS-21 short-range ballistic missile launcher that it had acquired from Yemen before the Gulf War.[115] In addition, the inventory of proscribed missile propellants has not yet been completed. Iraq is known to have conducted proscribed modification, testing, and acquisition of missiles after the adoption of Resolution 687. Yet equipment to manufacture missile airframes and warheads is still unaccounted for, while "no verifiable material balance from many critical missile components and materials from Iraq's indigenous missile production program can be established."[116]

Earlier, Ambassador Ekeus had also indicated that Iraq was continuing to conceal missiles, although he could not say how many of the leftover Iraqi Scuds were of the extended-range variety.[117] UNSCOM believes that these medium-range ballistic missiles probably are being stored on Iraqi trucks and shuttled between military installations under the control of the Special Republican Guard, one of several Iraqi security organizations involved in protecting Saddam's strategic arsenal.[118] It is difficult to say in what state of readiness the missiles are. In what he himself described as "a very important statement, obviously," Ekeus used the term *force* to describe the remaining arsenal: "I said missile force, which is a change of language from what I had [said] last time. I said missiles [then]. What I mean with missile force is that . . . they have all the elements—I mean transporter-launchers, of course, rocket fuel. . . . Every piece of what is necessary to constitute an operational [missile] force is available in Iraq" (see Appendix B, Table 4).[119] As a U.S. Government White Paper has noted: "Even a small residual force of operational missiles armed with biological or chemical warheads would pose a serious threat to neighboring countries and U.S. military forces in the region."[120]

Still, in terms of its missile potential, Iraq is not viewed by UNSCOM as an immediate threat. First, it is felt that the system established after the war to monitor the Iraqi industry, especially its chemical and biological activities, will not allow Iraq to restore its weapons programs without being detected. Second, the continued U.N. presence in Iraq precludes launch practice for the Scud missile crews. Third, UNSCOM believes that the Iraqi Army would have to retake possession of the missiles from the Special Republican Guard before the force could be put into an operational posture.[121] Presumably, such a shift would be detected in time.

With respect to the agents that the missiles might carry, the United Nations is not yet closing the books on the Iraqi CW effort (see Appendix B, Tables 5 and 6). Contrary to Iraq's claim that its VX project had failed and that no large-scale production had ever been carried out, UNSCOM has said that Iraq produced VX for five years before the Gulf War. In contrast to Baghdad's contention that the program spanned only the period from April 1987 to September 1988, the Iraqi program to develop VX evidently began as early as May 1985 and continued until December 1990 without interruption. Accordingly, the Iraqis produced at least 55 tons of chlorine and had procured some 750 tons of the precursor chemicals phosphorous pentasulfide and diisopropylamine. The Iraqis have maintained that 460 tons of these VX precursors were destroyed by the coalition bombing and that a further 212 tons were unilaterally destroyed without international supervision. Yet UNSCOM has been able to verify the destruction of only 155 tons of these latter 212 tons of precursor chemicals. A further 36 tons were destroyed under supervision by the commission. That leaves more than 600 tons of precursor chemicals unaccounted for — a quantity sufficient for the production of at least 200 tons of VX. In fact, Iraq has not even accounted for its acknowledged production of several metric tons of the VX nerve agent.[122] Although Iraq has consistently claimed that it was unsuccessful in weaponizing VX, because it decomposed within 24 hours, the UNSCOM technical evaluation team has concluded that Iraq was able to produce VX in quantity and had obtained the requisite VX production technology to enable the manufacturing of a VX precursor that is well suited for long-term storage.[123] Indeed, UNSCOM has found evidence that Iraq had put VX into its missile warheads before the Gulf War. According to UNSCOM's head, Richard Butler, the evidence "is utterly unambiguous. These degradation products [VX disulfide and stabilizer] could be from no other substance. These are unique. These were VX. They were found in ammunition, namely a missile warhead. That is weaponization."[124] He said that he "made it clear to [members of the UNSC that] there is no doubt VX was present in some warhead remnants."[125] If true, this finding would make the missing VX precursors that much more critical.

Estimates of Iraq's current biological program are even more problematic. In its report of October 1997, UNSCOM accused Iraq of repeatedly trying to "trivialize" its BW program. It said that Iraq's latest purported "full, final and complete" account of the program, submitted on September 11, 1997, was studied by 15 experts from 13 countries. They concluded that it was "incomplete and contains significant inaccuracies."[126] Bulk warfare agent production appears to be "vastly understated by Iraq."[127] For example, growth media — a laboratory nutrient used in ordinary medical tests but which could also be used in the development of BW agents — is unaccounted for in quantities sufficient for the production of "over three times more" anthrax than Iraq contends that it produced.[128] Actual production of botulinum toxin, too, may have been two or three times the amount declared by Iraq.[129] The chief biological inspector of UNSCOM said: "At the present time, the Commission cannot account with any degree of reliability for Iraq's prohibited biological warfare program."[130] If the elements of material balance of a BW program consist of (1) growth media; (2) microorganisms; (3) production of bulk agents (microorganisms or toxins); (4) production of munitions; (5) the union of bulk biological or toxin agents with munitions to make BW weapons; (6) the destruction of unused bulk agents and munitions; and (7) ultimately the use or destruction of the weapons, then UNSCOM is on record as "unable to verify Iraq's [full, final and complete] declaration in all of these areas."[131] For example, Iraq has not provided any evidence to support its accounts of the kinds of agents that were filled into munitions, the quantity of agents consumed in the filling process, and the quantity and type of munitions filled with each agent. And officials from UNSCOM suspect that Iraq also made more than the 182 BW munitions it claimed in its latest "full, final and complete" disclosure.[132]

The conclusion is that the Iraqi postwar effort to conceal its BW program has been largely successful. Although UNSCOM's chief biological inspector has stated that Iraq retains no weapons filled with botulinum toxin, as this substance in liquid state loses its potency over time, anthrax agent is quite another matter.[133] Indeed, even if Iraq lacked the ability to produce dried BW agents before the Gulf War, at present UNSCOM estimates that such capability is in its hands.[134] Baghdad's capacity for long-term storage of BW agents must be viewed as much enhanced. Correspondingly, Iraq's ability to disseminate agents in aerosolized form has been given a boost. Because a BW program is easier to conceal than a CW one and even a modest capability could have a significant strategic payoff, the closer UNSCOM comes to eradicating Iraq's gas weapons, the more determined Saddam may be to hold on to his biological weapons.

This conclusion seemingly contradicts the latest news from Iraq. According to what were termed "initial results from preliminary excavations," Iraq may have destroyed 45 chemical and biological missile warheads at al-Nibai, 25 miles northwest of Baghdad.[135] If this is true, it would match previous Iraqi statements to UNSCOM and thus enhance the credibility of other still unverifiable Iraqi claims concerning the unilateral destruction of its CB weapons. But if this is the case, why would Iraq opt to suffer seven years of crippling economic sanctions if it could prove in July 1991 that it had destroyed such key aspects of its mass destruction program as its BW warheads?[136]

The answer is that Iraq's unilateral destruction process, carried out in contravention of its cease-fire obligations, was paradoxically meant to allow the speedy resurrection of its NBC programs. First, by using partial unilateral destruction, the Iraqis were able to disguise the diversion of proscribed materials for possible future use. Many critical components, tools, and documents were thus diverted from the unilateral destruction and retained. Second, this route was chosen in order to hide the existence of these weapons and to conceal the level of Iraq's achievement of its weapons development. "Iraq stated [to UNSCOM] that it chose the method of unilateral destruction to conceal specifically both the acquisition or manufacture of certain components and successes that the program had achieved."[137] Such was its determination to hide the level of progress of its mass destruction effort that Iraq has stated that additional steps were taken, after its declaration of the unilateral destruction in March 1992, to secretly excavate and further destroy components in order to assure the concealment of these programs. In short, Iraq used unilateral destruction as an integral part of its plans for future production of mass destruction weapons.

Saddam's ability to quickly restart his CW, BW, and SSM programs has not been significantly hampered by seven years of UNSCOM's work. This capacity is, and will continue to be, the crux of the problem, at least as long as Saddam is in power. Indeed, from a strategic perspective the rationale for keeping a CB option today may look to Saddam more compelling than on the day he invaded Kuwait. Ekeus has revealed that UNSCOM has "documentary evidence about orders from the [Iraqi] leadership to pre-serve a strategic capability. That means to keep the production equipment ready to produce at any given moment."[138] Moreover, it is impossible to overlook the continued existence in Iraq of the key ingredient of his strate-gic reserve: the expertise needed to re-manufacture these weapons at short notice.[139]

Thus, Baghdad has not given up its plans to build larger, longer-range missiles. Numerous Iraqi design drawings, including multistage systems and clustered engine designs, were uncovered by UNSCOM. "If sanctions were lifted, Iraq could probably acquire enough material to return to full-scale production of Scud-type missiles, perhaps within one year."[140]

Baghdad also retains the expertise to quickly resume CW production. "In the absence of UNSCOM inspectors, Iraq could restart limited mus-tard agent production within a few weeks, full-scale production of sarin within a few months, and pre-Gulf War production levels—including VX—within two or three years." Indeed, since the 1991 war, Iraq has rebuilt two factories that it once used to produce chemical agents and has the "capability to shift smaller civilian facilities to CW production."[141]

It has even become evident that some of the extant CW munitions that Iraq insisted have now degraded to inert state and should be removed from UNSCOM's "to do" list have actually retained their effectiveness. Four intact 155-millimeter CW shells were found to be filled with mustard gas of the "highest quality" (purity of 94 to 97 percent), even after seven years of exposure to extreme climatic conditions. "Clearly, these Iraqi munitions could be stored for decades without any loss of quality."[142]

With regard to Iraq's BW program, a former UNSCOM observer noted, "Iraq's former ballistic and cruise missiles and biological warfare components would be easiest and quickest to reassemble."[143] Already Iraq's main missile research facility, Sa'ad 16, which was demolished during the coalition air campaign, has been "completely rebuilt."[144] Additionally:

> The workforce of more than 200 persons who staffed Iraq's BW pro-gram is intact. Iraq's civilian biotechnological infrastructure, compris-ing more than 80 research, development, and production facilities, is whole and well equipped. Since most biotechnological equipment is dual use, some of the currently operative facilities could be rapidly con-verted to biological warfare work. It is prudent to assume that the Iraqis retain hidden stores of freeze-dried organisms from its former bio-logical warfare program. Because Iraq maintains these human, biolog-ical and industrial resources, it could constitute a biological warfare

program rapidly and be able to manufacture militarily significant quantities of BW agents within 6 months. Further, the armorers who adapted chemical munitions to hold biological agents before the Persian Gulf War are still available. With their assistance stockpiled conventional munitions could be modified within the 6-month time frame and loaded with biological warfare agents.[145]

In this overall context, it is important to note that in March 1998, UNSCOM discovered in Iraq a document dated 1994, which indicated the existence, at a site monitored by the commission's missile-monitoring team, of a program for the manufacture of spray dryers to be delivered to al-Hakam, Iraq's principal biological weapons production facility.[146] In September 1997, UNSCOM discovered in Iraq a set of documents related to discussions held by Iraq and a "potential supplier" for the possible importation of a single-cell protein facility. The potential dual-use character of such a plant is "beyond question."[147]

Even though significant elements of the Iraqi mass destruction program have now become public knowledge, the outcome may benefit Saddam — at least in the short run. In Saddam's mind keeping a covert last-resort strategic option has new imperatives. In the aftermath of the Gulf War, he must have concluded that Iraq is surrounded by a host of regional and extra-regional enemies who constantly plot his demise. The only thing that stands between them and their objective is the uncertainty about Iraq's mass destruction weapons. The BW option, therefore, continues to serve as Saddam's trump card in case a threat develops to him or his regime. And, although this capability is hardly secret, it is well concealed so as to prevent UNSCOM from seizing it or any of Iraq's enemies from preempting it. In fact, the Israeli threat must be seen in Baghdad as even more worrisome now, given the Scud attacks during the war and the fact that Iraq has been weakened by the fighting and the subsequent sanctions. Similarly, Baghdad must consider Iran's growing mass destruction program as an added incentive for holding on to its CB cache. Finally, the expansion of Syria's CW arsenal is not without implications to Iraq. Paradoxically, then, for Saddam to disarm his CB weapons in earnest, he must have the reassurance that he can rearm quickly.

In the meantime, UNSCOM's periodic warnings about the mass destruction capabilities remaining in Iraq might have emboldened Saddam inadvertently. Exactly four years to the day after Iraq invaded Kuwait, Baghdad Radio publicized a purported cable from the "fighter commander" of the Iraqi "Surface-to-Surface Missile Corps," pledging to Saddam "that our destructive missiles will be sharp swords against anyone who let himself be seduced into harming the soil of dear Iraq."[148] Some two months later, in the fall of 1994, Iraq massed conventional forces near Kuwait, as the government's controlled press hinted at a possible biological attack if the U.N. sanctions on Iraq were not lifted. The most dramatic threat came on October 12, 1994, in *al-Quds al-Arabi*, a Palestinian paper in London funded by Iraq: "If the Iraqi regime realizes that the United States is after its head, there is nothing strange about its using all the weapons in its possession — banned or unbanned — to defend itself and inflict the heaviest losses on its enemy. One chemical weapon fired in a moment of despair could cause the death of hundreds of thousands. And we are not talking here about the germ and other bombs."[149]

These threats were issued even though Baghdad had already asserted that it had "completely" destroyed its BW program years ago. Thus there is good reason to believe that the BW propaganda was linked to the surprise discovery by UNSCOM in 1994 that in 1988–89 Iraq had acquired 39 tons of growth media packed in barrel containers of 25–100 kilograms, rather than in the usual 5-kilogram pouches. The imports were 200 times more than could possibly be used by all of Iraq's hospitals in legitimate medical care.[150] Its only conceivable purpose, UNSCOM concluded, would have been to mass-produce a large quantity of bacteria.[151]

Indeed, a somewhat similar scenario developed the following year. In March 1995, UNSCOM reported that some 17 tons of the 37 tons of biological growth media acquired by Iraq had not been accounted for. The next month Iraq again tried to apply BW-stimulated political blackmail, as it had done during the Gulf War, to the issue of lifting the U.N. sanctions. Writing in the Baghdad paper *al-Iraq* on April 11, 1995, Nuri Najm al-Marsumi, the second-in-command in Iraq's Information Ministry, warned that Iraq's loss of its missiles and chemical weapons "does not mean it has lost everything."

Whatever Iraq's capability for mass destruction may be, a serious question remains: Why would Saddam even dare to threaten Kuwait again unless he was convinced that the United States would not try to topple him via a Desert Storm 2?[152] Even one of President Bush's own advisers has come to accept this explanation. Writing in the *New York Times* on November 14, 1997, Robert M. Gates, the deputy National Security Adviser during the war, blamed America's "failure to respond forcefully to his [Saddam's] maneuverings in the past" for Iraq's continued challenges to the United States. Most telling was his admission that Saddam's question about U.S. resolve "perhaps began to form when the war ended with him in power." Indeed, Gates pointed out, in 1994 "when the Iraqi forces were pulled back [from the Kuwaiti border], our own were quietly withdrawn, and Mr. Hussein paid no price for his bluff."

On the contrary, as long as UNSCOM is unable to unearth Iraq's remaining CB stocks, the disclosures about its BW option may have infused credibility into a future threat by Saddam of resorting to mass destruction weapons in desperation. The same disclosures certainly increased the uncertainty and risks confronting his rivals. In this sense, even if Iraq's biological weapons are still to be used only in last-resort circumstances, the ambiguity over their continued existence has allowed Iraq to apply them politically. The case can even be made that Iraq's continued hampering of UNSCOM's work, for example by the issuance of numerous "full, final and complete" disclosures regarding its biological weapons program, is deliberately aimed to create the impression that Iraq maintains a hidden BW capability. The frequent blocking of access of the arms inspectors to suspected CB weapons sites, including the staging of public confrontations with some UNSCOM teams, may also be intended to enhance ambiguity. In other words, Baghdad seeks to use UNSCOM's work to support its political agenda.

For example, although Saddam's personal survival is in no immediate danger and his control over the country is as firm as ever, one would hardly know this from the language Baghdad has been using to describe the consequences of the U.N. sanctions. In November 1995, soon after Kamil Hassan's defection, the Iraqi U.N. mission warned that continued sanctions were "tantamount to a war of genocide." The statement was deliberately aimed to cause fears that Iraq could be forced to contemplate a desperate act unless the U.N. embargo were lifted. Indeed, some U.S. analysts have concluded that the Iraqi warnings could justify quite a dramatic action, and they have even issued warnings of a possible resort by Iraq to terrorism with mass destruction weapons, precisely as Saddam would have hoped.[153]

It may be argued that Iraq's policy has been singularly unsuccessful, if not counterproductive, so far. The sanctions are still in place, the Iraqi economy and military are in shambles, and the dangers of a new confrontation with the United States cannot be overlooked. Still, Saddam's calculations are different. His deliberate efforts to rub the American nose in his CB option indicate his unshaken belief in the effectiveness of terrorist deterrence. He expects his rivals to conclude that challenging him is simply too risky. Even if Washington eventually decides to resort to force instead of sanctions, as long the United States is unable to remove him or Iraq's mass destruction weapons, the price of any future conflict will be worth-while politically. Confrontation with the United States in the shadow of Iraqi doomsday weapons may even be useful. It helps Saddam convince his people that America is the cause of their economic misery. Externally, clashing with the United States often galvanizes Arab support for Iraq and is thus politically costly to the U.S. position in the region. Finally, the confrontations demonstrate anew the American inability to remove Saddam from power. In turn, they support the original contention that the Gulf War ended in a tie.

Saddam may even be bent on extending the availability of his mass destruction option to more than last-resort circumstances. In the wake of the Gulf War, Saddam seems to have determined that Iraq needs longer-range weapons to keep hostage additional countries, possibly in Europe, as a precondition to any future attempts to redraw the Middle Eastern map. In his mind, Iraq's recent experiences reconfirm the validity of his basic political doctrine; terrorist deterrence is the surest means of encountering the least resistance even in the face of far stronger opponents. But terrorist deterrence is rooted in simple math; to be effective, it requires that Iraqi CB weapons reach farther and more populous targets, and credibly threaten indiscriminate carnage on an ever increasing scale.

It is in this regard that the cadre of Iraqi scientists, engineers, and technicians that helped develop the country's strategic weapons before Desert Storm, and which has been retained even five years after the Gulf War, acquires its significance.[154] In November 1995, for example, a large consignment of Russian-made equipment to extend the range of missiles was intercepted in Jordan. According to Ekeus, the equipment seemed too advanced to be used by Iraq.[155] The same month, Jordan intercepted a shipment of enough Soviet-made gyroscopes to equip 100 missiles.[156] Simultaneously, during a visit to the region, Ekeus disclosed that UNSCOM suspected Iraq to have secretly produced "missile engines similar to those of the Russian Scud missiles."[157] The total number of al-Husayns built by Iraq could have thus been considerably higher than first thought.[158] In addition, UNSCOM discovered that Iraq was modifying some of its surface-to-air missiles into surface-to-surface long-range missiles. The commission was forced to start a "very ambitious program" of identifying every surface-to-air missile in Iraq's possession and tagging them all, to prevent such a development. Reportedly two-thirds of a "huge number" of such missiles had been tagged by the summer of 1996.[159] According to Ambassador Ekeus, the bottom line is that Baghdad has been able to continue efforts to develop ballistic missiles with ranges of 3,000 kilometers, "capable of reaching all of the Middle East and Western Europe."[160] As if this were not bad enough, Jordanian authorities subsequently announced that they had seized an "extremely dangerous" material destined for Iraq and capable of being used to produce chemical weapons.[161]

Baghdad has certainly concluded by now that getting the sanctions lifted would make its task of reconstituting its strategic forces much easier. But it is caught in a vicious cycle: as long as it keeps its mass destruction reserve hidden, the UN embargo will stay. But the sanctions must be removed if the business of rearming Iraq is to commence in earnest. A possible nightmare scenario could thus present itself. "If the embargo is lifted and sanctions in general are lifted," Ambassador Ekeus has warned, "[Iraq] could [re]start its weapons program, and push our [UNSCOM] inspectors aside." Under these circumstances, he predicted, "there will be a veto against reenforcing the embargo, because of the enormous economic interests involved in keeping the embargo off" and reestablishing trade relations with Iraq.[162]

There is no reason to assume that over time Saddam's scientists and engineers will be unable to perfect their techniques for drying BW agents, and improve aerosol-forming and aerosol-dispersing equipment for aircraft and cruise missiles, if they have not done so already. If this happens, there should be little doubt that Saddam's grand plan is still valid. Three years after the Gulf War he was still asking "What should the Arabs do?" after the "balance [that] was achieved with the support of the former Soviet Union in confronting some plans by the United States, its aides, and its pampered ally—the Zionist entity"—had collapsed.[163] He used this formula back in February 1990 during the Arab summit meeting in Amman to explain why Iraq needed strategic weapons.

Saddam views mass destruction weapons as a sine qua non for survival and as the cornerstone of his master strategy. His ability to exercise strategic blackmail, while diminished, remains substantial. Moreover, the fact that he has lost untold billions in unearned oil revenues, rather than come clean on his CBW cache, suggests that Saddam has confidence in the military worthiness of the remaining arsenal. Consequently, it can be expected that he will again resort to political extortion whenever he perceives a real threat to his political survival. Saddam can still hold his neighbors, including Israeli cities, hostage to CB weapons via overt or covert means if ever he perceives such last-resort circumstances. In this sense the Gulf War failed in assuring the "security and stability of Saudi Arabia and the Persian Gulf," which Bush defined as one of the U.S. national security objectives in the Kuwait crisis.[164] The continued existence of mass destruction weapons in Saddam's hands provides permanent incentive for the Iraqi leader to apply this option politically and to challenge America's power. His attack in 1996 on Arab accommodation with Israel, as "a stand of weakness and humiliation toward the Zionist entity and the United States," is thus truly worrisome.[165] He frequently used such oratory before the war to promote Iraq's mission of acquiring mass destruction weapons.

Israel's Strategic Predicament

The war, the subsequent emergence of a new CBW landscape in the Middle East, and Iraq's continued potential for strategic blackmail have all had profound implications for Israel's security doctrine. In the wake of Desert Storm, the IDF's planners have assumed that the use of CW against the citizens of Israel was no longer a taboo.[166] But conflicting approaches have emerged to the new threat, owing to starkly different assessments of the Israeli deterrence during the war. At one extreme Arens, in a remarkable turnaround, suggested that "in hindsight" the fact that Saddam had chemical warheads but did not fire them at Israel "was one of our successes. We acted the way we deemed appropriate to deter him. . . . If you revert to this period, you will find a number of declarations by the Prime Minister and myself concerning our possible response. And I think that if we are asking ourselves why did Saddam not fire missiles armed with chemical warheads, which he had, it is reasonable that the answer is to be found also in the statements made by us at the time."[167] In Arens's view the venerable Israeli bomb-in-the-basement posture, although somewhat augmented by passive defenses, was an effective deterrent to an Iraqi CBW attack.

At the other extreme, Peres saw the war as proof that in the long run, Israel must relinquish strategic deterrence in favor of a political settlement with the Arab countries, and regional security arrangements. While he was prime minister, the mouthpiece of the ruling Labor party editorialized that "the main reason Saddam did not risk using nonconventional weapons — neither biological or chemical, and definitely not nuclear — was the U.S. sword hanging over his head," rather than the fear of an Israeli devastating retaliation "promised by the Shamir government with public nod from Secretary of Defense Richard Cheney."[168] This line implicitly endorsed Peres's idea of giving up the nuclear option in favor of a defense pact with the United States, as a way of curbing the strategic arms race in the Middle East and facilitating a political solution.

Throughout his career Peres has repeatedly indicated that he views nuclear weapons as a political instrument. When the main threat to Israel's survival was the specter of an Arab conventional attack, the nuclear option was the ultimate deterrent. But with the spread of mass destruction weapons and long-range missiles, these weapons "forced nations to find a political substitute, such as disarmament . . . even in the face of severe hatred."[169] In fact, Peres's New Middle East is an elaborate construct put forward under the lasting impression of the Gulf War and is designed to "overcome the nuclear threat." He wrote: "We in the Middle East must imitate the sane approach of the superpowers: at the height of the cold war, not satisfied by their 'balance of fear,' they realized that cooperation was essential and arms control and arms reduction became the call of the day."[170]

In other words, even if the probability of conflict is low, it still makes perfect sense to look for a political settlement given that the eruption of war would unquestionably have a horrifying impact. What is more, Peres, like some of his Washington counterparts, simply does not believe that a stable "balance of terror" could be attained in a Middle East awash with mass destruction weapons: "Our greatest danger today is from the combination of nuclear weapons and extremist ideology. . . . The concept of deterrence that would be relevant to this type of ideologist deviates so sharply from what would be tolerable to the rest of humanity that the outcome is hard to imagine."[171]

Instead, Peres offered "a gradual long-term process of reciprocal disarmament."[172] And if any doubt remained that the pact with the United States was offered in the context of forsaking the nuclear option, Peres dispelled such uncertainty: "Give me peace and we will give up the atom. That's the whole story. If we achieve regional peace, I think we can make the Middle East free of any nuclear threat."[173]

Evidently, based on the Gulf War experience, Peres has concluded that the Israeli nuclear posture not only failed to deter its enemy but might also have stymied its chief ally, the United States. The political arrangement he advocates is meant to overcome the hazard of relying on strategic deterrence to contain extremist regimes armed with mass destruction weapons. The new reality requires that the region be disarmed from NBC weapons and that a regional security system be set up instead. Moreover, Peres's plan seeks to rectify the dangerous imbalance in the vulnerabilities that has emerged since the war. Peres seems to be saying that Israel, with its small size and high concentration of urban population, is unsuitable for a regional balance of terror based on mass destruction weapons. The Arab or Muslim mass destruction threat would likely intimidate tiny Israel far more than Israel's nuclear deterrent could frighten its enemies. Thus, strategic deterrence — which protected the country as long as it monopolized the mass destruction option — might not be a rational choice in a Middle East filled with CB weapons.

Peres's bold plans for the Middle East may be challenged, however. First, it is highly questionable that his regional collective security solution is politically feasible. Second, with regard to deterrence, the Gulf War experience raises a cardinal problem for the Peres doctrine. Namely, what will convince undeterrable leaders to abide by a political agreement if they wish to violate it? Would not such a scenario prove more threatening to Israel if it gives up its nuclear option? Third, although Israel's extreme vulnerability to NBC weapons cannot be denied, reports about its nuclear arsenal suggest that the country possesses enormous destructive powers.[174] Under these circumstances, the argument about the imbalance of vulnerabilities confronting Israel tacitly assumes a worst-case situation of a unified Arab-Muslim mass destruction front against Israel. Fourth, without examining the merits of the proposed U.S.-Israeli defense pact, it must be recognized that from the point of view of Iraq, Syria, and Iran, such a policy smacks of weakness and fear on Israel's part. What Peres saw as a sane solution is viewed in Tehran and Damascus as the fruit of a successful strategic blackmail. The notion that the new CB arms in their possession will eventually force Israel to remove its ultimate shield — its nuclear option — must have been strengthened as a result.

Rabin's view — that the Israeli deterrent in the Gulf War was insufficient and must be augmented — could be placed squarely between these two poles. Indeed, once he became prime minister, he openly broadcast that the doctrine of massive countercity retaliation was now in place. To dispel any ambiguity that might have emerged in the wake of the Shamir government's nuclear stand-down during the Gulf War, Rabin told the Israeli paper *Ha'aretz* on August 28, 1992, "In case Israeli population centers come under attack with unconventional weapons, Israel will respond massively against the population centers of the attacking country."

Although Rabin avoided any specific reference to nonconventional weapons in describing his massive retaliation doctrine, in effect he took an important step toward abandoning the bomb-in-the-basement posture, or its variant that Arens had defended. Further, the prime minister disclosed on the same occasion that Israel was developing the capability to hit the major cities of fairly distant countries. Undoubtedly he meant to buttress Israel's strategic deterrence by revealing that the deficiencies in Israel's long-range capabilities, which were exposed by the war, were being rectified. In short, the message was, no enemy of Israel should misconstrue the experience of the Gulf War. And to Washington, Rabin was saying, do not count on an Israeli restraint under such circumstances.

Whatever the lessons of the war, it can be concluded that in its aftermath Israel's national security has been linked more closely to its nuclear capability than before. In part, this seemingly paradoxical result stems from the dramatic escalation in the perceived threat to Israel's population centers. It may have come about also because of the paucity of political or strategic alternatives. But, aside from renewed emphasis on the doctrine of massive retaliation as a deterrent, the IDF could be expected to emphasize preemption. Even the development of Israel's sophisticated and expensive anti-tactical ballistic missile (ATBM) system, the Arrow, is unlikely to change this forecast. As long as a single effective BW warhead can cause huge numbers of casualties and prolonged contamination of large areas, the burden on such a system would be insupportable, and reliance on a defensive posture alone would be a risky proposition at best. Accordingly, the Israeli experience with the Scud attacks during the Gulf War "would place heavy pressure on Jerusalem to give high priority to the location and destruction of any weapons capable of reaching Israeli soil in a future conflict. The pressure might be so high that any extraordinary preparations detected around potential launching sites or missile storage facilities could precipitate preemptive counterforce strikes by the IAF."[175]

However, even such an approach could not guarantee against an Arab sneak attack. A surprise missile strike against Israel could be, according to David Ivri, then director general of the Israeli Defense Ministry, "very simple." It could be "relatively easy for a country with which we do not share a common border to launch a sudden war without mobilizing troops or penetrating our territory. It could make all the preparations for the launch in secret and fire missiles at us whenever it sees fit." The best response against such a scenario is to develop a "second-strike capability," Ivri argued. Accordingly, "the goal today is to build the possibility to destroy the missile launchers [preemptively] on the one hand, and create the initial operational capacity to deal an effective counterattack on the other. . . . That is where the answer lies, not in the defense."[176]

The Crisis of Deterrence

The dangers ahead are clear and present. Some have already been recognized and even publicized, whereas others may be felt only indirectly. The hearings held in the U.S. Senate in 1995 regarding the U.S. vulnerability to CBW addressed some of the dangers in the first category.[177] But the impact that the proliferation of mass destruction weapons has had on defense strategy in general, and military doctrine in particular, is not as well understood yet. In Europe, for example, "few people are concerned. Yet it is Europe, not America, which faces the more immediate threat from [Third World] missiles."[178] Even in Israel there have been charges of stagnation in defense thinking, in light of the transformations in the country's political and strategic environments. Urgent calls have been issued for a sweeping revision of the country's concept of national security, especially the IDF's military doctrine.[179]

Washington should be concerned that the expectation for the next war in the Middle East to be fought with unconventional weapons could lessen the chance of a political arrangement in the Middle East. This would be the case especially if Israeli territorial concessions hinged on an American strategic guarantee. The credibility and practical value of a U.S. defense commitment to Israel would necessarily be put into question if Israel perceived the main threat to its security to be an unconventional attack. After all, the United States could not deter Saddam from firing Scuds into Israel or from threatening it with CBW.[180]

Indeed, in the Gulf War, it was the other way around: the Iraqi CB threat to Israel was so real that Washington preferred to stop the war rather than test the resolve of Saddam Hussein. Moreover, this was not even a conflict where Israel was directly involved. In this respect, it is worth wondering whether Iran, given its efforts to acquire missiles capable of reaching Israel, would hold Israeli cities hostage if there were ever a confrontation between the Ayatollahs and the United States. And what would be the U.S. response if Syria fired Scuds armed with chemical warheads into Israel? Would not a U.S. defense pact prove to be more of a constraint on Israel than a deterrent vis-à-vis Damascus? These and other such questions have already been raised in Israel.[181] In addition, it is not at all clear that the American public would want to support such a U.S. defense guarantee in the first place, if the costs of keeping the commitment, in terms of American lives, could be prohibitive.

The dilemma concerning the value of a U.S. defense guarantee is likely to grow, given that the spread of CB weapons and long-range missiles to rogue regimes around the world could force the United States to rethink its commitments. By the year 2000, it is estimated, some 20 nations should be able to build their own ballistic missiles. These missiles could be capable of hitting targets with a margin of error of 300 meters, thanks to modern inertial guidance systems.[182] An intelligence assessment published in the United States in 1995 expressed concern that even antiquated Scud-type theater ballistic missiles could lift and disperse up to 100 submunitions, each between 1 and 5 pounds, of CB agents.[183] The combination of the two technologies suggests that the consequences of even a single accurately targeted weapon could be devastating. In fact, in its effort to develop an effective BW dispersal system, before the Gulf War Iraq had experimented with methods far more efficient at delivering biological or chemical agents than its ballistic missiles were. By all accounts these efforts are continuing. Iraq has been experimenting with several airborne platforms as possible candidates for performing aerobiology missions. As these systems are not expressly prohibited by Resolution 687, which concerned itself with missiles, Iraq is not formally violating the terms of the cease-fire. One of the systems it is reportedly testing is the Czech L-29 trainer, which has been adapted as a remotely piloted vehicle with a 500-kilometer range. During a recent test flight, one such RPV evidently crashed.[184] In addition to the remotely piloted vehicles, UNSCOM has discovered evidence that an Iraqi cruise missile project had been launched before the Gulf War.[185] Currently, Syria is working to develop a cruise missile with a range of "several hundred kilometers," to be armed with a chemical warhead.[186]

The bottom line is that the spread of technologies associated with weapons of mass destruction would require American leaders to exercise extreme caution in deploying forces against any future opponent who possessed such weapons. Even when a decision to dispatch U.S. forces had been made, assembling them in the theater would be a dangerous undertaking. The ability to preempt these forces via accurate missile strikes would be much enhanced. Unlike Desert Storm, the time to gather the forces could be much shorter, with U.S. air contingents possibly having to be ready for an air-to-ground attack in six to eight days rather than a month.[187] In the meantime, the arriving ground forces would have to be kept dispersed until air power and missiles could deal crippling blows to the enemy's ability to deliver mass destruction weapons.[188] These requirements suggest not only a high premium on accurate intelligence but a strategic air campaign of much higher intensity than in Desert Storm.

The old notion that without air superiority "victory" is not possible has again been disproved. Although Iraq lost control of the air early on, it maintained the ability to transform the conflict throughout the war by firing a single CB-armed missile into Israel. The Gulf War demonstrated that the concept of air superiority must be widened to include neutralization of the enemy's remotely piloted vehicles and ballistic missiles. This is in contrast to the Western air combat doctrines, which continue to focus on countering enemy air forces as the primary method of achieving aerospace control.[189]

In some respects, Desert Storm is the model of future wars in the Middle East and East Asia. The military would have to be prepared, from initial conceptual planning through equipping, training, operational planning, and final execution of orders, to operate in and cope with a CB-contaminated environment. Soldiers would need to be inoculated before the war, and during the fighting they would spend much of their time donning protective suits.[190] The threat of attacks with chemical cocktails or a variety of BW agents will have to be addressed in terms of both protection and medical aid. The need for added logistical support—protective equipment, decontamination facilities, and additional medical burdens—would also have a negative impact on planners and deployed forces.[191]

Although such conflicts would likely involve conventional U.S. or Israeli preemptive strikes against the enemy's strategic forces and C&C facilities, an effort would be made to limit the fighting in both the type of weapons used and the targets selected for attack. The targeting of the enemy's capital or its leadership could be a risky proposition, as some of its CB weapons could be left intact. Even the destruction of the enemy's C&C facilities could be counterproductive. Strategy would be dictated by the regional "balance of terror": while Israel and the United States still maintain escalation dominance in terms of the weapons they can use, Syria, Iraq, and North Korea could achieve escalation dominance in terms of the targets they might attack. Cornering the enemy would thus be highly dangerous. Further, even a defeat on the battlefield would provide the enemy with a strong incentive to resort to CW, for instance, to reverse the tide.

Furthermore, even a limited campaign could be quite risky because Club MAD countries may seek to help each other during future crises. Indeed, such assistance has already been rendered in the past. But now these countries may feel more secure and thus more prone to extend such support, given that they are shielded by extensive arsenals of CB weapons and long-range missiles. Thus, in the case of a possible confrontation between the U.S. and North Korea, Iran might seek to stretch U.S. forces thin by simultaneously heating up the Gulf, or even sponsoring terrorist attacks against U.S. targets worldwide. Iran's President Rafsanjani may have hinted at such collaboration when he told the visiting North Korean Foreign Minister Kim Yong-Nam: "Because of U.S. hostile policies toward Iran and North Korea, the two nations are linked together by a shared interest, that is, confronting the bullying and greed of the U.S. government, and they support and back one another in difficult and sensitive times."[192]

Likewise, after warnings to Libya by the United States concerning the

CW plant at Tarhunah, Kim Yong-Nam turned up in Tripoli to "discuss prospects for cooperation between the two friendly countries and ways of strengthening and developing it in all spheres."[193] The DPRK media sought to highlight the potential strategic implications of the visit, given that it took place when tensions on the Korean Peninsulas were mounting as well. It cited Colonel Qaddafi as saying that "Libya pays deep attention to the military provocations committed by the United States against Korea." Accordingly, Qaddafi went on to say: "I hope that the respected leader Gen. Kim Chong-Il . . . will continue to display unrivaled courage in the struggle against imperialism."[194]

Under their CBW shields, radicals seem more confident than ever in plotting to target U.S. forces directly if war comes. Col. Choe Chu-Hwal, the highest ranking North Korean military officer ever to defect to the ROK, has revealed that the DPRK plans to strike U.S. forces stationed in South Korea as its first target if war breaks out on the peninsula. The idea is to inflict massive U.S. casualties in the initial stage of the conflict. The colonel said that DPRK military leaders believe that if attacks are first focused on the U.S. soldiers and "several thousand" American troops are killed or wounded, "it would lead to antiwar sentiments among U.S. citizens and then to the withdrawal of U.S. troops from South Korea."[195] This war script might just as well have been written in Baghdad.

It may even be said that Desert Storm must have been *originally* planned as a limited operation because of the fears that Iraq would escalate to unconventional arms. Washington, having estimated that Saddam was likely to turn to CB weapons when backed into a corner, purportedly decided not to risk a total victory. Moreover, once the U.S. had allowed Iraq to arm and deploy its BW weapons, there was no other way but to suspend hostilities even though victory had not yet been achieved. Thus the indecisive end of Desert Storm was clearly predictable from the outset. Even before the first shot had been fired, President Bush must have known that his Hitler analogy would be in vain.

Although this theory is based on rather shaky assumptions, it is useful in demonstrating that the "solution" of fighting a limited war to cope with the threat of a CB scenario has assured that a dangerous enemy be left to fight another day.[196] In turn, the utility of the military option for Israel, the United States, and its allies has diminished, in itself furnishing the likes of Saddam with a political bonanza.

The Gulf War was a smashing military success, but strategically it backfired. As a result of its inconclusive end, the war

1. encouraged the proliferation of mass destruction weapons and long-range missiles;
2. cemented the strategic ties between the countries of Club MAD; and
3. gave the green light to the growing practice of political blackmail of the world's democracies.

For the future, the net result is that Western security will increasingly be at the mercy of these three interacting perils. Diplomatic efforts to draw extremist regimes into the "new world order" are not only exceedingly difficult but likely to encourage attempts at political extortion. Yet, relying on deterrence as the cornerstone of national security is increasingly perceived as impractical. Strategic deterrence, as has been exercised since World War II, is at a crisis point now that "undeterrable" regimes and possibly terrorists are seen as ready to attack the population centers of their enemies with weapons of mass destruction.[197] Worse yet, active defenses cannot be relied upon to provide foolproof protection for a nation's cities against such threats. Even if such a system could be erected, it could not cope with a ship-borne cruise missile carrying a BW warhead or guerrillas bent on wreaking maximum havoc. In essence, the political utility of CB arms and SSMs has been boosted. Thus, regimes bent on redrawing regional maps and challenging the world order have increasing incentive to acquire, or expand, such armories. Arms control may be on the verge of becoming a pathetic slogan.

Seven years after the Gulf War, international security and world peace are hanging in the balance again. The attempt to secure the new world order through the forceful disarming of a dangerous dictator has failed. On the contrary, in the aftermath of the Gulf War a sea change has been evident in the way that future wars and even domestic terrorism are perceived, both in the United States and elsewhere. In large part this trend is the result of Saddam's ability to focus world attention on the one aspect that implicitly backs his claim that the Gulf War was a tie—Iraq's CB weapons. Moreover, a number of highly militant states now see the ability to threaten the killing of untold numbers of civilians as the crux of a strategy that they should adopt. Although civilian populations were regularly kept hostage during the Cold War period, the possibility of replicating the U.S.-Soviet balance of terror (which kept the peace in Europe for 40 years) in other areas seems a chancy proposition. In the Middle East and on the Korean Peninsula, at least some of the protagonists believe that their enemies are reckless, if not outright irrational. They will not hesitate to unleash poison weapons indiscriminately whatever the punishment, or so they are perceived. Even if mass destruction weapons are not themselves employed, the fear is that they will enable extremists to advance their aggressive designs. Unfortunately, the diplomatic formulas crafted so far to escape this grim future have been akin to paying ransom to blackmailers. The efforts to fashion a "saner" world begun by a few far-sighted leaders must be commended for drawing the correct lessons from the Gulf War and appreciating the gravest challenge to world peace on the eve of the twenty-first century. But these diplomatic efforts will not bring peace. The answers offered so far may indeed lead to a more chaotic, if not anarchic, international system.

Appendix A: Examining Alternative Arguments

This much is certain. During the Gulf crisis, the U.S. decision makers were made aware, by their own sources as well as foreign ones, of the prospect of an Iraqi CB attack on Israel. At home, U.S. intelligence was on record as anticipating such a desperation scenario. Abroad, key Israeli leaders were constantly warning their American counterparts of Saddam's last-resort gamble. To pretend that these warnings went unheeded, as the official reasoning for stopping the war has attempted to do, is simply implausible. In turn, the official line should be set aside. Or, to put it differently, there is hardly a need to prove that the publicized case is wrong, only that the mass destruction argument is valid. Nevertheless, in this appendix I shall demonstrate that many of the reasons the Bush administration cited for ending the Gulf War are less than convincing. First, I shall address the reasons listed in Chapter 8 of this book. Subsequently, I shall deal specifically with new arguments made by President George Bush and National Security Adviser Brent Scowcroft to explain why they did not remove Saddam Hussein.

The claim that Bush was constrained by the U.N. mandate, for example, is not entirely accurate. When UNSC Resolution 678 was adopted in late November 1990, attention was mostly focused on the part that authorized the use of "all necessary means" to eject Saddam from Kuwait. Although the demise of the Saddam regime was not specifically mentioned as a goal, the authority for working toward it lay in an expansive view of the resolution. It authorized the use of force to implement *all* U.N. resolutions — not just the one calling for an Iraqi withdrawal from Kuwait — and also called for the restoration of "international peace and security in the area." As one coalition diplomat has said, "Everyone knew what we were talking about. We put in a sentence that could cover a wide range of things. . . . When we adopted 678, we were thinking then that once we engaged with this man we were going to win clear-cut — it had to end in his total defeat."[1]

With regard to geopolitical constraints, it has been argued that the war was stopped to maintain "a favorable balance of power in the region — that is, keeping neighboring Iran in check — [which] required a reasonably strong Iraq. [Generals Powell and Scowcroft believed that] without Saddam [Iraq] might collapse into civil war, with the Kurds snatching away parts of the north and the Shi'ites doing the same in the south. So, playing a dangerous game of geopolitics, they weakened Saddam on the assumption that they could then control him."[2] This argument, however, is at total variance with the U.S. attempts to kill Saddam during the war, as well as Bush's open call on February 15, 1991, for the Iraqi people to "take matters into their own hands, to force Saddam Hussein the dictator to step aside."[3] Rather, if any balance was responsible for the "suspension" of the Gulf War, it was a local version of the "balance of terror," which the graduates of the Cold War in the Bush administration had little trouble recognizing.

Another version of this argument holds that Bush ended the war because the continued destruction of Saddam's forces would have provided the Islamic Republic of Iran with complete hegemony in the Gulf. This also is a fallacious claim. It suggests that the United States could have removed just enough of Saddam's military power to prevent him from being a menace to his neighbors, yet not so much as to make Iran the regional superpower. The military instrument simply lacks this surgical precision. And no realistic military planning would seriously contemplate such acrobatics as a worthwhile objective. More important, the argument ignores the facts. The military machine left in Saddam's hands after the Gulf War was not the result of an American strategic plan but the consequence of snafus in the areas of both intelligence and operations. First, the U.S. estimate of the destruction of the Iraqi military equipment was inflated. A 1993 CIA study concluded, "Almost 50 percent of the Republican Guard's major combat equipment escaped destruction and remained under Iraqi control."[4] In addition, U.S. commanders erroneously believed that their westward flanking maneuver had cut off the retreat of the Republican Guards. In reality, the "devastation on the battlefield was considerable, but the gate had never been closed and a lot of horses got out."[5] The CENTCOM commanders had fully intended to destroy Saddam's "center of gravity," as it was known, rather than let the leftover Guard divisions slip into Baghdad.[6] Their failure to do this was not for lack of trying, and in fact they believed that they had succeeded. Therefore, in agreeing to Washington's pressure to end the war, they clearly were not concerned with the Iran-Iraq postwar balance of power.

The argument that President Bush feared that going to Baghdad would lead to heavy U.S. casualties is also problematic. It stands in direct contradiction to General Schwarzkopf's description of the circumstances. In his "mother of all briefings" on February 27, 1991, the general noted "how easy it would have been to get to Baghdad. There were only 150 miles distance and no opposition. 'If it had been our intention to overrun the country, we could have done it unopposed, for all intents and purposes,'" he declared.[7] Schwarzkopf, it must be remembered, was speaking on the basis of faulty intelligence; he did not know about the survival of some of Iraq's Republican Guard units. Thus, there is no reason to believe that his assessment was intentionally misleading. Moreover, when the coalition discovered that the Republican Guard had escaped from its trap, Schwarz-kopf's advice to Bush was equally robust: "Frankly my recommendation had been to continue the march . . . and make it a battle of annihilation. And the president made the decision that we should stop the war at a given time and a given place that did leave some escape route open for them to get back, and I think it was a very humane decision."[8]

Furthermore, there was no military or strategic need to capture Saddam himself, which could have bogged down the United States in a futile search. Instead, the goal of pushing to Baghdad would have been the de-struction of the remaining Republican Guard divisions. Such an operation would have been relatively easy to accomplish, considering that the Iraqi forces were on the run and had no air cover whatsoever. In the absence of these units, Saddam, whether he survived or not, would have become largely irrelevant politically. In fact, this was a major rationale for targeting the guards in the first place.[9]

During his final briefing Schwarzkopf was asked if the advance to within 100 miles of Baghdad might have encouraged Saddam to think that the coalition was going all the way. "I wouldn't have minded at all," the general replied.[10] In Washington these words must have been viewed with deep consternation. They were proof that the decision to stop the war had come none too soon. In fact, it may be argued that although the White House cited the likelihood of sustaining heavy casualties as a constraint, the Bush administration was probably more concerned that Baghdad was defense-less. If Schwarzkopf was right that the Iraqi capital was his for the taking, the Bush team must have reasoned, then Saddam had little choice but to resort to CB weapons if the war continued.

Nevertheless, the official line of reasoning for ending the Gulf War was reiterated as late as 1998 in an article by Bush and Scowcroft themselves.[11] Apparently, the order to advance on Baghdad was not issued because the two thought that Saddam would be ousted anyhow: "We were disap-pointed that Saddam's defeat did not break his hold on power, as many of our Arab allies had predicted and we had come to expect." Given that some of the same Arab leaders had previously assured Bush that Saddam would not invade Kuwait, the White House's continued reliance on their advice seems highly questionable. In itself, however, this point cannot be taken as refuting the claim that the Bush team did not see the need to continue the war because, in their minds, Saddam's fate had already been sealed. In other words, attending to an unreliable source could be viewed as evidence of foolishness, but not necessarily of implausibility.

There are, however, more profound reasons to question the veracity of the official version of why the war was halted. For instance, Bush and Scowcroft write that they "hoped" that Saddam would be toppled, possibly by a "popular revolt." Could it be that, given all the intelligence warnings at their disposal, the Bush team honestly believed that Saddam would let himself be displaced without first using CB weapons against his domestic enemies and even their foreign backers? Did they forget the lesson of Halabja—that is, that Saddam was willing to use such weapons against his own people? On the contrary, in Washington it was taken for granted that if Saddam's rule was on the verge of collapse, whether because of U.S. actions or those of his own people, he would not hesitate to resort to CBW. In turn, the tale that Saddam's likely ouster obviated the need to continue the war must be a smoke screen. Both scenarios—a U.S. march to Baghdad or a popular revolt—would still have had to contend with Iraqi CB weapons. In stark contrast, the Bush-Scowcroft line pretends that both routes to remove Saddam were available and that the United States could have chosen freely between them. But the revolt story was never a serious option to remove Saddam, and it cannot be taken as an alibi for why the United States did not march to Baghdad.[12]

The suspect nature of this argument is evident in other respects as well. Bush and Scowcroft argue that "had we gone the invasion route, the U.S. could conceivably still be an occupying power in a bitterly hostile land." But how can we reconcile this forecast with the administration's apparent hope that Saddam's defeat would lead to a rebellion of Iraq's Shi'as and Kurds against him? These ethnic groups together represent the majority of the Iraqi population. If these same forces were, according to U.S. decision makers, capable of ousting Saddam, why would they not welcome an American military push aimed to accomplish this goal? In fact, the postwar revolt by the Kurds and Shi'as against Saddam (in March–April 1991) began on the false assumption that the United States would come to its aid. The rebels repeatedly called on the United States to assist them with air power. It was actually America's passivity that doomed their attempt to unseat Saddam.

Bush and Scowcroft echoed the earlier geopolitical argument, stating that they were "concerned about the long-term balance of power at the head of the Gulf." But this factor could not easily coexist with their hope for a popular uprising. If the balance of power was a real concern, why encourage the Kurds and Shi'as to rise up against Saddam? Could it be that Bush was not aware that such an uprising could threaten Iraq's territorial integrity? Did Washington seriously expect these ethnic minorities, whose dreams of sovereignty were well known, to simply disband and disarm once the main obstacle to the realization of their political ambitions was gone?[13]

Moreover, if the United States was indeed aiming to maintain the regional geopolitical balance once the rebellion fizzled, it should have secretly endorsed Saddam's efforts to preserve his leftover CB cache. Given the destruction of much of Iraq's conventional military capabilities, these leftover gas and germ weapons would have been the only check on a resurgent Iran. And yet Washington continued to point to these weapons as a potential source of regional instability.

Bush and Scowcroft also explain that if they had continued the U.S. advance, "the Coalition would instantly have collapsed, the Arabs deserting it in anger and other allies pulling out as well." How ironic it is, then, to hear some of Bush's own colleagues explain that Arab hesitancy to support the United States during subsequent confrontations with Saddam emanated from doubts about U.S. credibility. Some even ridiculed the U.S. military responses during 1993–1996 as evincing weakness and indecisiveness.[14] It appears, however, that keeping the geopolitical balance has become less of a concern now that Bush's political rivals have taken over the White House.

The true significance of the Bush-Scowcroft account emerges in several places. First, the article refers to the "fog of war" as a factor that influenced the timing of the decision to stop the fighting. Presumably this is an indirect admission that intelligence and operational mistakes led to the escape of several of Iraq's Republican Guard divisions from General Schwarzkopf's trap.

Second, Bush and Scowcroft speak of "eroding" Saddam's threat to the region as one of "our strategic objectives" (the other being ejecting Iraqi forces from Kuwait). This is a much fuzzier term than the ones that guided operation Desert Storm. In order to achieve the U.S. national policy goals that Bush framed in August 1990 in the wake of the Kuwait crisis, General Schwarzkopf, in concert with Secretary of Defense Cheney, listed five operational objectives. Among them were "Destroy the Republican Guards" and "Destroy Iraqi ballistic missile and nuclear, biological and chemical (NBC) capability."[15] The Bush-Scowcroft formula is, therefore, an attempt to adjust the goals of Desert Storm ex post facto. What the U.S. military could not accomplish because of its operational and intelligence shortcomings has now become not a failure but a part of America's original strategic objectives. This way, the legend of the Gulf War as an unmitigated military success is maintained.

Third and most important, Bush and Scowcroft state:

> [At the end of the war] we discussed at length forcing Saddam himself to accept the terms of the Iraqi defeat at Safwan . . . and thus the responsibility and political consequences for the humiliation of such a devastating defeat. In the end, we asked ourselves what would we do if he refused. We concluded that we would be left with two options: continue the conflict until he backed down, or retreat from our demands. The latter would have sent a disastrous signal. The former would have split our Arab colleagues from the coalition and, de facto, forced us to change our objectives. Given these unpalatable choices, we allowed Saddam to avoid personal surrender and permitted him to send one of his generals [to the Safwan cease-fire talks].

It is remarkable that Bush and Scowcroft offered their explanation in March 1998, on the occasion of another tense confrontation with Iraq, which was exclusively focused on Saddam's determination to retain his cache of mass destruction weapons. The Clinton administration even took pains to explain publicly the potentially catastrophic consequences of letting Saddam keep his stash of anthrax and VX agents. Yet these were the same weapons that Saddam had when Bush and Scowcroft were thinking hard about whether to force him to surrender in person. Although the article by Bush and Scowcroft is excerpted from their forthcoming book, the timing of its publication is not without import. Certainly, it was meant to put the best face on the decision that left Saddam in the possession of such horrific weapons. But to judge from their account, Bush and Scowcroft were unconcerned by Saddam's arsenal of death. Their argumentation lacks even the slightest reference to Saddam's NBC programs. How could a president who thought Saddam "never possessed a weapon he did not use" manage to present every reason for stopping the war except this one? Were all these other reasons so vastly more compelling?

The most important aspect of the article by Bush and Scowcroft is, therefore, what it neglects to say rather than what it says. As long as we accept the arguments of Bush and his colleagues as they struggle to explain their stated reasons for ending the war, it will be impossible not to conclude that the president was either dangerously out of touch with the events at the close of the war or was simply acting irrationally. It is far better to believe that he and his cohorts are simply less than truthful.

Notes

1. Cited in Elizabeth Drew, "Letter from Washington," *New Yorker,* March 11, 1983, 83.

2. Ronald Steel, "Unbalanced," *New Republic,* December 8, 1997, 19.

3. For confirmation of U.S. attempts to kill Saddam during the war, see interview of Gen.(Ret.) Brent Scowcroft, in Peter Jennings Reporting, "Unfinished Business: The CIA and Saddam Hussein," ABC Television, June 26, 1997.

4. "Operation Desert Storm: A Snapshot of the Battlefield," cited in John Donnelly, "Hot under the Epaulets," *Salon Magazine,* June 1997 (http://www.salonmagazine.com/june97/clancy970604.html).

5. Michael R. Gordon and Gen. Bernard Trainor, *The Generals' War: The Inside Story of the Conflict in the Gulf* (Boston: Little, Brown, 1995), 429.

6. Ibid, 400–32. On the debate within CENTCOM regarding the targeting of the Iraqi regime's "centers of gravity," see Lawrence Freedman and Efraim Karsh, *The Gulf Conflict, 1990–1991: Diplomacy and War in the New World Order* (Princeton: Princeton University Press, 1994), 316–17.

7. Freedman and Karsh, *The Gulf Conflict* (Princeton: Princeton University Press, 1994), 404.

8. Excerpts of Schwarzkopf's interview with David Frost, aired March 27, 1991, in *USA Today* (http://www.usatoday.com/news/index/iraq/nirq053/htm).

9. Even Saddam understood this reality. He was "noticeably careful" in deploying the Republican Guards. They straddled the border with Kuwait, operating, "at best, as a strategic armoured reserve." Obviously, "Saddam was anxious not to hazard the Praetorian protectors of his rule" (Freedman and Karsh, *The Gulf Conflict,* 280). Astonishingly, General Powell wrote, "We could have killed, wounded, or captured every single soldier in the Republican Guard in that trap. But it would not have made a bit of difference in Saddam's future conduct" (Gen. Colin Powell, *My American Journey* [New York: Random House, 1995], 526).

10. Cited in *Newsweek,* March 11, 1991, 34.

11. Unless otherwise indicated, the following citations are from George Bush and Brent Scowcroft, "Why We Didn't Remove Saddam," *Time Magazine,* March 2, 1998, 31.

12. In fact, Secretary of State Baker downplayed this scenario, indicating, "There wasn't even an organized opposition to Saddam." James A. Baker III, *The Politics of Diplomacy* (New York: J. P. Putnam's Sons, 1995), 437.

13. Powell even wrote: "It would not contribute to the stability we want in the Middle East to have Iraq fragmented into separate Sunni, Shi'a, and Kurd political

entities. The only way to have avoided this outcome was to have undertaken a largely U.S. conquest and occupation of a remote nation of twenty million people." Powell, *My American Journey*, 527.

14. For example, in response to the assassination plot on President Bush in 1993, the United States apparently fired a few cruise missiles at an empty building in Baghdad. And in 1996, when Saddam moved on Kurdish areas in northern Iraq, the U.S. attacked a few radar stations in southern Iraq.

15. *Conduct of the Persian Gulf War: Final Report* (Washington, D.C.: GPO, 1992), 73.

TABLE I *BW agents produced by Iraq*

BW agent (organism)	Declared concentrated amounts (liters)[a]	Declared total amounts (liters)[a]	Comments
Anthrax (*Bacillus anthracis*)	8,500	85,000	UNSCOM estimates that production amounts were actually three to four times more than declared amounts, but is unable to confirm.
Botulinum toxin (*Clostridium botulinum*)	19,400[b]	380,000	UNSCOM estimates that production amounts were actually two times more than declared amounts, but is unable to confirm.
Gas gangrene (*Clostridium perfringens*)	340	3,400	Production amounts could be higher, but UNSCOM is unable to confirm.
Aflatoxin (*Aspergillus flavus* and *Aspergillus parasiticus*)	—	2,200	Production amounts and time frame of production claimed by Iraq do not correlate.
Ricin (*Ricinus communis*)	—	10	Production amounts could be higher, but UNSCOM is unable to confirm.

Source: Data from U.S. Government White Paper, "Iraqi Weapons of Mass Destruction Programs," Washington, D.C., February 13, 1998, appendix A.

a. In this table, "total" refers to the amount of material obtained from the production process, whereas "concentrated" refers to the amount of concentrated agent obtained after final filtration and purification. The concentrated amount is the amount used to fill munitions.

b. Concentrations of 10× and 20×. The higher the concentration, the greater the chance of exposure to a *lethal* dose. Alternatively, the amount of agent required to effectively cover a *given* area varies inversely with its concentration level.

TABLE 2 *BW delivery systems filled and deployed by Iraq: Iraq's versions of 1995 versus 1997*

Agent	Missile warheads (al-Husayn modified Scud B)		R-400 aerial bombs		Total	
	1995	1997	1995	1997	1995	1997
Anthrax	10	5[a]	50	50	60	55
Botulinum toxin	13	16[a]	100	100	113	116
Aflatoxin	2	4	16	7	18	11
Total	25	25	166	157	191	182

Sources: Data for 1995: "Report Submitted by the Executive Chairman of the Special Commission Established by the Secretary-General Pursuant to Para 9 (b) (i) of Security Council Resolution 687 (1991), October 11, 1995," para 75 (w) (www.un.org/Depts/unscom/s95-864.htm). Data for 1997: U.S. Government White Paper, "Iraqi Weapons of Mass Destruction Programs," Washington, D.C., February 13, 1998, appendix A.

[a] Recent excavations of warhead remnants found more traces of anthrax. When pressed, the Iraqis revised earlier "final" figures to say that they had actually filled three times as many warheads with anthrax (16) as with botulinum (5). The admission led UNSCOM inspectors to speculate that Iraq had produced not only more anthrax, but also two kinds of the agent — dried and in solution. *New York Times*, August 7, 1998.

TABLE 3 *Iraqi use of chemical weapons*

Date	Offensive's code name[a]	Location	Type of agent	Approximate casualties[b]	Target population
August 1983	Wa al-Fajr II (IN)	Hajj Umran	mustard	>100	Iranians, Kurds
October–November 1983	Wa al-Fajr IV (IN)	Panjwin	mustard	3,000	Iranians, Kurds
February–March 1984	Khaibar (IN)	Majnoon Island	mustard	2,500	Iranians[c]
March 1984	—	Basra	tabun	50–100	Iranians[d]
March 1985	Badr (IN)	Hawizah Marsh	mustard, tabun	3,000	Iranians[e]
February 1986	Wa al-Fajr VIII (IN)	al-Faw	mustard, tabun	8,000–10,000	Iranians[f]
December 1986	Karbala IV (IN)	Umm al-Rasas	mustard	reportedly in the thousands	Iranians
April 1987	Karbala VIII (IN)	Basra	mustard, tabun	5,000	Iranians
October 1987	—	Sumar, Mehran	mustard, nerve agents	3,000	Iranians
March 1988	Wa al-Fajr X	Halabja	mustard, nerve agents	reportedly in the hundreds[g]	Iranians, Kurds
April 1988[h]	Tawakalna 'alla-Allah (IQ)	al-Faw	mustard, nerve agents	5,000	Iranians
May 1988[i]	—	Shalamche	mustard, nerve agents	N/A[j]	Iranians
June 1988[i]	—	Mehran	mustard, nerve agents	N/A	Iranians
June 1988[i]	—	Majnoon Island	mustard, nerve agents	N/A	Iranians[k]

continued

TABLE 3 *Notes continued*

Source: Data from U.S. Government White Paper, "Iraqi Weapons of Mass Destruction Programs," Washington, D.C., February 13, 1998), 6, unless otherwise noted.

[a]IN (for Iran) and IQ (for Iraq) indicate the party undertaking the offensive. Data are from sources cited in notes c–k below.

[b]The estimates of the total number of casualties may be conservative, if it is true that "20,000 Iranian soldiers were *killed* in Iraqi chemical attacks from 1983–1988." Press statement, "Anniversary of the Halabja Massacre" (Washington, D.C.: U.S. Department of State, March 16, 1988) (http://secretary.state.gov/www/briefings/statements/1998/ps980316a.html); emphasis added.

[c]A U.N. report captured in clinical detail the fate of one Iranian soldier: "Sourab Norooz, age 24, exposed in [March 1984] at Majnoon . . . crepitation [a grating, crackling sound] due to gas in the chest wall, probably resulting from gas gangrene. . . . The patient died that night." Cited in *Christian Science Monitor*, December 13, 1988.

[d]By mid-March 1984, Iran claimed that 1,200 of its soldiers had been killed and 5,000 injured by Iraqi chemical attacks. Dilip Hiro, *The Longest War: The Iran-Iraq Military Conflict* (New York: Routledge, 1991), 105.

[e]Iran alleged that Iraq launched as many as 35 strikes by chemical weapons, causing 4,600 casualties. *Washington Times*, March 23, 1988.

[f]"[Iraqi] chemical weapons caused 20 to 30 percent of Iranian casualties during Iran's February 1986 Al Faw campaign" ("Review of NESA files" [Arlington, Va.: CIA, February 21, 1986] [Gulflink]). Symptoms of the victims indicated simultaneous exposure to two or more different agents. A U.N. investigating team "confirmed that mustard agent (shown by chemical analysis to be 95 percent pure) and tabun were used" in the Wa al-Fajr VIII offensive ("Iran-Iraq: Chemical Warfare Continues" [Arlington, Va.: CIA, November 1986] [Gulflink]).

[g]Iranian sources and some Western observers have claimed a much highter toll, running into the thousands. Iran also used chemicals at Halabja that may have caused some of the casualties.

[h]Data from "AFMIC Special Weekly Wire 32–90 (c)(U)" (Washington, D.C.: DIA, August 1990) (Filename 80638041).

[i]Data on Iraqi CW during the period May–June 1988 are from Hiro, *The Longest War,* 206–7, 209–10.

[j]"Large scale use of nerve agents in 1988 inflicted significant Iranian casualties and greatly supported Iraqi offensive operations." "Iraq's CW Program: More Self-Reliant, More Deadly" (Arlington, Va.: CIA, August 1990)(Gulflink).

[k]In addition, the United States has said that, while "precise" information was lacking, there were "plausible" accounts from Kurdish villagers of numerous Iraqi chemical attacks against civilian villages in 1987 and 1988 — with some attacks as late as October 1988 — in areas close to both the Iranian and Turkish borders (U.S. Government White Paper, 6). A CIA report, however, said that "Iraq used both lethal and nonlethal chemical agents against Kurdish insurgents in late August 1988" ("Iraq's CW Program"). Separately, a U.N. report confirmed that Iraq had dropped mustard gas bombs during an air raid on the Iranian city of Oshnaviyah, a few miles from the northeast corner of Iraq. Iran charged that the attack, which took place on August 2, 1988, injured 2,680 people (*Washington Times*, August 29, 1988). Thus, by the end of the Iran-Iraq war, the Iraqis were experimenting with using mass destruction weapons strategically.

TABLE 4 *Iraqi ballistic missile program*

Item	Initial inventory	Comments
Soviet-supplied Scud missiles (includes Iraqi modifications of the Scud, such as al-Husayn)	819	UNSCOM accepts Iraqi accounting for all but two of the original 819 Scud missiles acquired from the Soviet Union. Iraq has not explained the disposition of major components that it may have stripped from operational missiles before their destruction, and some Iraqi claims — such as the use of 14 Scuds in ATBM tests — are not believable. Gaps in Iraqi declarations and Baghdad's failure to fully account for indigenous missile programs strongly suggest that Iraq retains a small missile force.
Iraqi-produced Scud missiles	unknown	Iraq denied producing a complete Scud missile, but it produced or procured and tested all major subcomponents. UNSCOM has established that by late 1990 Iraq had the capability to indigenously manufacture a limited number of proscribed missiles. One Iraqi document records that the army had possessed 7 Iraqi-manufactured al-Husayn missiles.[a]
Iraqi-produced Scud warheads	120	Iraq claims that all 120 were used or destroyed. UNSCOM supervised the destruction of 18. Recent UNSCOM inspections found additional CB/BW warheads beyond those currently admitted.
Iraqi-produced Scud airframes	2	Iraq claims testing 2 indigenous airframes in 1990. It is unlikely that Iraq produced only 2 Scud airframes.
Iraqi-produced Scud engines	80	Iraq's claim that it melted 63 engines following acceptance tests — and that 53 of them failed quality controls — is unverifiable and not believable. UNSCOM is holding this as an open issue.
Soviet-supplied missile launchers	106	The Soviet Union may have sold more than the declared 10 launchers.[b]
Iraqi-produced missile launchers	4[b]	Iraq has the capacity to produce additional launchers.

Source: Data from U.S. Government White Paper, "Iraqi Weapons of Mass Destruction Programs," Washington, D.C., February 13, 1998, app. C, unless otherwise noted.
[a]"Amb. Richard Butler's Presentation," unofficial text of briefing by Richard Butler to the U.N. Security Council, June 3, 1998, excerpted by Laurie Mylroie (http://www.fas.org/news/un/iraq/s/index.html/980603_unscom.htm).
[b]Numerical data from UNSCOM 1997, 8.

TABLE 5 *Iraqi CW agent stockpiles*

CW agent	Amount declared by Iraq (metric tons)	Potential amount based on unaccounted precursors (metric tons)[a]	Comments
VX	at least 4	200	Iraq denied producing VX until Hussein Kamil Hassan's defection in 1995.
G-type agents (sarin)	100–150	200	Figures include both weaponized and bulk agents.
Mustard	500–600	200	Figures include both weaponized and bulk agents.

Source: Data from U.S. Government White Paper, "Iraqi Weapons of Mass Destruction Programs," Washington, D.C., February 13, 1998, app. B.

[a]These estimates are very rough. They are derived from reports provided by UNSCOM to the UNSC and to UNSCOM plenary meetings. Gaps in Iraqi disclosures strongly suggest that Baghdad is concealing chemical munitions and precursors. Iraq may also retain a small stockpile of filled munitions. Baghdad has the capability to quickly resume CW production at known dual-use facilities that currently produce legitimate items, such as pharmaceuticals and pesticides. UNSCOM has supervised the destruction of some 45 different types of CW precursors (1.8 million liters of liquid and 1 million kilograms of solid).

TABLE 6 *Iraqi CW delivery systems*

Delivery system	Estimated numbers before the Gulf War[a]	Munitions unaccounted for[a]	Comments
Special warheads — al-Husayn (modified Scud B)	75–100[b]	45–70	UNSCOM supervised the destruction of 30 warheads.
Rockets	100,000	15,000– 25,000	UNSCOM supervised the destruction of nearly 40,000 chemical munitions (including rockets, artillery, and aerial bombs), 28,000 of which were filled.
Aerial bombs	16,000	2,000[c]	
Artillery shells	30,000	15,000	
Aerial spray tanks	unknown	unknown	

Source: Data from U.S. Government White Paper, "Iraqi Weapons of Mass Destruction Programs," Washington, D.C., February 13, 1998, app. B.

[a]All these munitions could be used to deliver CW or BW agents.

[b]This number includes 25 special warheads that Iraq claims to have unilaterally destroyed after having filled them with biological agents during the Gulf War (see Table 2). Traces of VX found on missile warheads raise questions about the total number of special missile warheads Iraq says it manufactured for delivering other chemical and biological agents.

[c]A document examined briefly by an UNSCOM inspector at the Iraqi Air Force Headquarters on July 1, 1998, showed that Iraq used far fewer chemical weapons than it claimed in the Iran-Iraq war. The discrepancy suggests that Iraq may still be hiding 6,300 chemical aerial bombs and 730 tons of chemical agents. *Washington Post*, August 17, 1998.

Notes

CHAPTER 1: RETHINKING THE GULF WAR

1. A notable exception is Shlomo Aronson, *The Politics and Strategy of Nuclear Weapons in the Middle East* (Albany: State University of New York Press, 1992), 231–58 and 271–96.

2. In its "full, final and complete" report on the BW program, dated September 1997, Iraq admitted that by early 1974 it had "adopted a policy to acquire biological weapons," notwithstanding its having signed the 1972 treaty banning such weapons. U.N. officials, however, have maintained that the program began even earlier. According to the Iraqi version, only sporadic research into bacteriological weapons was carried out, initially at the al-Hazen Ibn al-Haitham Institute on the Salman Pak peninsula, which closed in 1978. The center was headed by a chemical corps officer who reported directly to then Iraqi president Ahmad Hassan al-Bakr. Iraq claims that the work was poorly directed and that the institute achieved little by its closing in 1978. But U.N. and U.S. officials believe that its aim was to develop poisons for covert use to eliminate the regime's opponents. (Allegedly, Iraq also sought the poisons to destabilize Iran economically — a good five years before open warfare broke out between the two countries.) After all, al-Hazen Institute was a BW and CW research facility sponsored by an agency of Iraqi intelligence. The Iraqis allege that they did not conduct any activities related to biological weapons during 1978–85. But a wider military application for biological weapons was sketched in 1983 by one of the country's preeminent microbiologists, Abdul Nassir al-Hindawi, a graduate of Mississippi State University, who in a secret paper for top Ba'ath officials recommended reestablishing the biological weapons program. According to his own account, Hindawi outlined how the large-scale production of biological weapons could become a major military asset. By 1985 the regime ordered the director of Iraq's CW program to establish a separate complex for making biological weapons at a site known as al-Muthanna. The project was designated a "presidential priority" and exempted from usual constraints on spending and personnel. Initial work focused on the relevant literature, until bacteria strains were acquired from overseas in April 1986. See Arms Control and Disarmament Agency, "Threat Control Through Arms Control: Annual Report to Congress, 1995" (Washington, D.C.: ACDA, July 1996), 67. See also the interview with Rolf Ekeus in *Libération* (Paris), August 29, 1995; and the detailed account in *Washington Post*, November 21, 1997; also Al J. Venter, "Iraq: UNSCOM Odyssey — The Search for Saddam's Biological Arsenal," *Jane's Intelligence Review*, March 1998, 16–20.

3. Interview in *Der Spiegel* (Hamburg), in Foreign Broadcast Information Service (Near East and South Asia), hereafter FBIS (NES), September 5, 1995, 39.

4. Ibid.

5. *Wall Street Journal*, October 26, 1990.

6. Interview in *Davar* (Rosh Hashana Supplement), Tel Aviv, September 24, 1995, 6, author's translation. Hereafter, translations not otherwise noted were provided by the author.

7. Brig. Gen. Uri Manos, civil defense commander, cited in Jerusalem Domestic Service in English, FBIS (NES), January 14, 1991, 63. On the same occasion the general declared that "Israel has an answer to every possible threat, including a biological one." He might have alluded to the stockpiling of antibiotics in some major Israeli hospitals in preparation for a possible anthrax attack. Other than that, Israeli citizens were given personal civil defense kits against chemical warfare, including a personal gas mask and atropine injections, and were ordered to stay in sealed rooms during Iraqi missile attacks.

8. For example, the IDF's surgeon general at the time, Brig. Yehuda Danon, claimed in an interview with Israel Radio: "If we're speaking about chemical warfare, launched by missiles, we are speaking about 100, 120 casualties, most of them lightly wounded" (cited in *Christian Science Monitor*, January 15, 1991). It is possible to argue that Israel avoided taking defensive preparations against germ warfare because the government feared that such action would have legitimized an Iraqi BW attack or created panic among the populace. Similar arguments were made with respect to the distribution of personal anti-CW kits. Yet, in spite of these objections and regardless of the "light" casualties projected, the kits were handed out.

9. Kathleen C. Bailey, *Doomsday Weapons in the Hands of Many: The Arms Control Challenge of the '90s* (Urbana: University of Illinois Press, 1991), 82.

10. See interviews with Ekeus in *Stern* (Hamburg), October 12, 1995, 230–32; *Libération*, August 29, 1995. See also *Independent*, September 5, 1995. In the most recent account provided by Iraq, in September 1997, Iraq claimed that it armed and deployed 182, rather than 191, biological weapons in all. Of these, 157 were supposedly BW bombs (100 filled with botulinum toxin, 50 with anthrax, and 7 with aflatoxin). Of the 25 warheads, 16 were filled with botulinum toxin, 4 with aflatoxin, and 5 with anthrax (U.S. Government White Paper, "Iraqi Weapons of Mass Destruction Programs," Washington, D.C., February 13, 1998, app. A). U.N. officials still suspect, however, that "Iraq made more than the 182 munitions" (*Washington Post*, November 21, 1997).

11. U.S. Secretary of Defense William S. Cohen, paraphrased in *Newsweek*, November 24, 1997, 33. In 1979 an accidental release of anthrax spores occurred within the Microbiology and Virology Institute No. 19 in Sverdlovsk (later renamed Ekaterinburg), a city about 1,500 kilometers east of Moscow in the Ural mountains. The cause of the leak is unclear. Independent measurements following a visit to the site have shown that no more than a gram of anthrax spores, and perhaps only a few thousandths of a gram, escaped from the plant. This minute quantity resulted in the killing of 66 people as far as 4 kilometers downwind of the release (Matthew S. Meselson et al., "The Sverdlovsk Anthrax Outbreak of 1979," *Science*, November 18, 1994, 1202–8; for a discussion of the model employed and calculations performed to estimate the concentration of spores, see Matthew S. Meselson, "Note Regarding Source Strength,"

ASA Newsletter, June 8, 1995, 1 and 20–21). Based on an analysis of some of the tissues of victims, it has been said that the "victims were apparently infected by a mixture of [four] different" strains of anthrax bacilli. Apparently the Soviets were seeking a weapon that could defeat a vaccine (Paul J. Jackson et al., "PCR Analysis of Tissue Samples from the 1979 Sverdlovsk Anthrax Victims: The Presence of Multiple *Bacillus Anthracis* Strains in Different Victims," *Proceedings of the National Academy of Sciences of the USA,* February 1998, 1224–1229; *New York Times, February 3, 1998).* The following picture emerges from the account of the Pentagon's Defense Intelligence Agency (DIA) and from the testimonies of émigrés (*Miami Herald,* March 25, 1987; Nadav Ze'evi, "The Anthrax Was Not Secured," *Ma'ariv* [Weekend Supplement] January 19, 1998, 38–43). The incident occurred on April 2, 1979. The first victim, in critical condition, was rushed to Municipal Hospital No. 40 on April 8. He died the same day. Over the next few days, seven or eight persons from the institute or the nearby Military Compound No. 32 in the Chakalov district were admitted to the hospital. Their symptoms were fever ranging to 104 degrees Farenheit, bluish ears and lips, choking, and difficulty breathing. They died within six or seven hours, and autopsies revealed severe pulmonary edema in addition to symptoms of serious toxemia. Over the next few days the number of fatalities rose to about 40. The first casualties were a fairly large number of male reservists at the military installation, who had been the first to come in contact with the anthrax spores. More casualties occurred among workers in a ceramics factory 2 kilometers from the institute, even though they had been working indoors. Presumably, ventilators had sucked the anthrax agent into the building, which was downwind of the explosion. At least 2 percent of the factory's workforce of 1,500 became contaminated. Eventually, all persons in the affected district were ordered to report for immunization with a Russian-developed vaccine dubbed STI. (Reportedly, out of 59,000 residents who were found suitable for inoculation, 80 percent were vaccinated at least once.) The dead were placed in zinc coffins and covered with chloramine, a decontaminating and disinfecting compound. A special section in the local cemetery, where the graves were dug deeper into the ground, was allocated to the victims. The ceramics factory was sprayed inside and out with the disinfectant, and a large area around the military installation was graded and covered with asphalt. Wild animals in the nearby forest were killed, and dogs in the district were picked up and destroyed. All carcasses were burned. Disinfectant was sprayed from the air over an area of about 5 by 7 kilometers. In all, the DIA said, an area of 50 square kilometers was contaminated. Meselson reported that sheep grazing 50 kilometers away were killed as a result of the release. His account tallies with the émigré reports, which maintain that anthrax cases were discovered in animals in six villages 50 kilometers southeast of the accident. The anthrax epidemic lasted for six weeks, ending in mid-May 1979. Most victims inhaled the spores on the day of the accident. But the longest incubation period resulting in a fatality was 43 days. The average incubation period in Sverdlovsk was 9 to 10 days. (See also *The Sverdlovsk Incident: Soviet Compliance with the Biological Weapons Convention?* Hearing before the Subcommittee on Oversight of the Permanent Select Committee on Intelligence, House of Representatives, 96th Cong., 2d sess., May 29, 1980; *Wall Street Journal*, May 3, 1984, citing "a secret 1980 U.S. intelligence report," and September 15, 1989; Lt. Col. David T. Twining, USA, "Sverdlovsk Anthrax Outbreak," *Air Force Magazine*, March 1981, 124–28.) It was only after the collapse of the Soviet Union that medical confirmation was obtained that the victims died of inhalation anthrax (see Faina A. Abramova, Lev M. Grinberg, and David H. Walker, "Pathology of Inhalation Anthrax in 42 Cases from the Sverdlovsk Anthrax Outbreak," *Proceedings of the National Academy of Sciences of the USA*, March 15, 1993, 2291–94). However, in a rare interview in *Izvestiia* in December 1991, KGB Gen. Andrei Mironiyok, commander of the Sverdlovsk region at the time of the accident, had already revealed that the epidemic was caused by an "accidental release" of anthrax from Biological Institute No. 19. Around the same time, Russian President Boris Yeltsin, who in 1979 served as Communist Party Secretary in Sverdlovsk, ordered an official investigation into the case. In May 1992, he stated that the KGB had admitted that the anthrax outbreak in Sverdlovsk was caused by "a military project" (Ze'evi, "The Anthrax was Not Secured," 43; also *Wall Street Journal*, March 15, 1993). Had the wind blown north toward the city's center instead of southeast, the catastrophe would have been much greater. As it was, the Soviets had made plans for the evacuation of the city's 1.2 million residents.

12. F. Marc LaForce, "Bacillus Anthracis (Anthrax)," in *Principles and Practice of Infectious Diseases*, 3d ed., ed. Gerald L. Mandell, R. Gordon Douglas, Jr., and John E. Bennet (New York: Churchill Livingstone, 1990), 1594; "Iraq's Biological Warfare Program: Saddam's Ace in the Hole," (Arlington, Va.: CIA, circa August 1990) (http://www.dtic.mil/gulflink [hereafter Gulflink]).

13. U.S. Army Medical Research Institute of Infectious Diseases, *Medical Management of Biological Casualties: Handbook*, 2d ed. (Frederick, Md.: Fort Detrick, August 1996), chap. 1 (http://www.usamriid.army.mil/content/FMs/medman/chap1.htm).

14. A spore has been described as a "highly effective survival pack, because it is as much as 10,000 times as resistant to heat as the vegetative cell, and up to 100 times more resistant to ultraviolet radiation. It can survive for years, possibly centuries, in the absence of nutrients" (Arthur H. Rose, *Chemical Microbiology*, 3d ed. [New York: Plenum, 1976], 403). The island of Gruinard, off northwest Scotland, provides an example. Between 1941 and 1943 Gruinard was the site of British experiments with biological weapons, including anthrax. Tests conducted in 1981 showed that anthrax spores were still present in 20 out of 153 soil samples, most of them embedded three inches underground (Venter, "Iraq: UNSCOM Odyssey," 18). In 1990, the British government announced that it had finally cleaned the island, using a mixture of sea water and diluted formaldehyde to wash the land and kill the spores (Seymour M. Hersh, *Chemical and Biological Warfare: The Hidden Arsenal* [London: Panther Books, 1970], 96–97; Leonard A. Cole, *Clouds of Secrecy: The Army's Germ Warfare Tests over Populated Areas* [Totowa, N.J.: Rowman and Littlefield, 1988], 23–31; Bailey, *Doomsday Weapons*, 88). There is some debate about the danger of long-term contamination of anthrax. Some have argued that in the case of Gruinard Island, the anthrax spores, though present, were probably not particularly deadly unless disturbed from the soil. A

territory might be contaminated with anthrax but still be habitable, with some risk that living spores could still persist on the surface (*New York Times*, November 21, 1997). One source indicated that a "secondary" respiratory hazard with infectious agents, such as anthrax spores disturbed from the ground, is likely only in the case of "very heavy contamination" of the soil (Col. David R. Franz, "Defense Against Toxin Weapons" [Fort Detrick, Frederick, Md.: U.S. Army Medical Research Institute for Infectious Diseases, 1997] [http://www.nbc-med.org/FMs/datw/chap1.htm]). Some anthrax spores contained in a German-manufactured germ warfare capsule from Wold War I were revived "from the brink of extinction after they had been stored, without any special precautions, for 80 years." They would likely have caused "lethal infection" if used against horses and reindeer, as the Germans had apparently intended (Scientific Correspondence: Caroline Redmond et al., "Deadly Relic of the Great War," *Nature*, June 25, 1998, 747–48.

15. Brian Beckett, *Weapons for Tomorrow* (New York: Plenum, 1983), 120. As with all vaccines, the degree of protection depends on the magnitude of the exposure. During a biological aerosol attack, the number of infectious or toxic units to which an individual is exposed may be greater than in a natural exposure. In addition, exposure by inhalation may represent an unnatural route of infection with many agents. The efficiency of protection afforded by most vaccines is based on normal (that is, natural) inoculum size and exposure. Consequently, vaccines that are considered effective under natural circumstances may not provide a similar degree of protection to biological aerosols (*Handbook on the Medical Aspects of NBC Defensive Operations [FM 8–9]* [Washington, D.C.: HQ Department of the Army, February 1, 1996], pt. 2: Biological [chap. 3, sec. 4] [http://www.nbc-med.org/amedp6/PART_II/chapter3.htm]). Indeed, in the case of anthrax, vaccine-induced protection is undoubtedly overwhelmed by extremely high spore challenge. Moreover, with regard to therapy, it should be noted that the practice of inducing resistance to penicillin, tetracyclines, erythromycin, and many other antibiotics through laboratory manipulation of organisms is considered quite feasible. See, for example, Lt. Gen. Ronald R. Blanck, army surgeon general, "DoD News Briefing," March 3, 1998 (www.defenselink.mil/news/Mar1998/t03031998_t0303asd.html).

16. Bailey, *Doomsday Weapons*, 91.

17. Ibid., 92.

18. Franz, "Toxin Weapons." Botulinum toxin is naturally inactivated in fresh water in three to six days; chlorinated water supplies inactivate toxin within 20 minutes. Because food-borne and water-borne poisoning avoid the need for technically sophisticated explosive devices or aerial spraying, however, these routes are considered possible avenues for BW terrorist attack. Roger L. Shapiro et al., "Botulism Surveillance and Emergency Response: A Public Health Strategy for a Global Challenge," *Journal of the American Medical Association* (hereafter *JAMA*), August 6, 1997, 434.

19. Toxins are, however, different from chemical weapons in important ways. Because toxins are not volatile, they are no longer a threat even to unprotected humans once they reach the ground. Secondary aerosol formation, which could be caused by vehicular or troop movement over ground previously exposed to certain chemical

agents, or anthrax in some instances, is "unlikely" to pose a "significant threat" in the case of a toxin aerosol. Also, whereas chemical agents may directly affect the skin, toxins are almost always dermally inactive. Franz, "Toxin Weapons."

20. The apparent reason for inclusion of toxin weapons in the convention was that they required facilities similar to those needed for biological weapons. See Bailey, *Doomsday Weapons*, 91.

21. Primate studies indicate that the signs and symptoms may in fact not appear for several days when a low dose of the toxin is inhaled. Signs or symptoms are noticed within a shorter time period following ingestion of toxin or inhalation of higher doses. *Medical Management*, chap. 3 (http://www.usamriid.army.mil/content/FMs/medman/chap3.htm).

22. Franz, "Toxin Weapons," fig. 1. This source gives the aerosol toxicity of botulinum toxin A as an LD_{50} of 0.0025 micrograms per kilogram.

23. Col. David R. Franz et al., "Clinical Recognition and Management of Patients Exposed to Biological Warfare Agents," *JAMA*, August 6, 1997, 407. Methylphosphonothioic acid, or VX, is a "persistent" nerve agent, whereas sarin is considered a "nonpersistent" nerve agent.

24. U.S. Congress, Office of Technology Assessment, *Proliferation of Weapons of Mass Destruction: Assessing the Risks*, OTA-ISC-559 (Washington, D.C.: GPO, August 1993), 54. However, in the years since the Gulf War, a botulinum antitoxin (of equine origin) has been used as an investigational new drug and is thought to be helpful. Animal experiments show that botulinum antitoxin can be very effective *after* aerosol exposure, if given before onset of clinical signs. In fact, administration of the antitoxin is now deemed reasonable even after victims show symptoms of intoxication, provided that the poisoning has not progressed to a stable state. (Once the toxin has reached the nerve fibers, there is little an antitoxin can do to dislodge it.) *Handbook on Medical Aspects*, "Appendix B — Clinical Data Sheets for Selected Biological Agents" (http://www.nbc-med.org/amedp6/PART_II/annexb.htm); *Medical Management*, chap. 3.

25. Franz, "Toxin Weapons"; John Cookson and Judith Nottingham, *A Survey of Chemical and Biological Warfare* (New York: Monthly Review, 1969), 264–65; U.S. Congress, Office of Technology Assessment, *Technologies Underlying Weapons of Mass Destruction*, OTA-BP-ISC-115 (Washington, D.C.: GPO, December 1993), 73. It may be noted that in 1980 French police discovered that the West German terrorist group *Röte Armee Fraktion* (Red Army Faction or RAF) had tried to produce botulinum in a bathtub. It meant to disperse the toxin around the French capital and in the Paris subway system (Joseph D. Douglas, Jr., and Neil Livingstone, *America the Vulnerable: The Threat of Chemical and Biological Warfare* [Lexington, Mass.: D.C. Heath, 1987], 185; Harvey J. McGeorge, "Chemical Addiction," *Defense and Foreign Affairs*, April 1989, 20). Reportedly, the Japanese terrorist group Aum Shinrikiyo attempted to "weaponize" biological warfare agents — i.e., formulate them so that they could be dispersed effectively in aerosol form — as early as April 1990 (*New York Times*, May 26, 1998).

26. Robin Clarke, *We All Fall Down: The Prospects for Chemical and Biological Warfare* (Harmondsworth: Pelican, 1969), 87.

27. "Presidential Advisory Committee on Gulf War Veterans' Illnesses: Final Report," Washington, D.C., December 31, 1996 (http://www.gwvi.gov/ch4.html#4n); Raymond A. Zilinskas, "Iraq's Biological Weapons: The Past as Future?" *JAMA*, August 6, 1997, 419. One theory about Iraq's production of aflatoxin was broached by UNSCOM Commissioner Koos Ooms. He said that because aflatoxin causes fatal liver cancer only after "five to six years," the agent "has no military significance whatsoever. Therefore the only possible conclusion is that the Iraqis have developed aflatoxin as a weapon of genocide against the Kurds" (interview in *De Volkskrankt* [Amsterdam], cited in *CBW Conventions Bulletin*, September 1997, 16). The Iraqis experimented with mixing aflatoxin with chemical agents widely used for riot control. UNSCOM officials have speculated that Baghdad plotted to spray the mix on Kurds or other ethnic minorities, perhaps as part of crowd control, producing an untraceable epidemic of cancer in these groups years later (*Washington Post*, November 21, 1997). This theory, however, does not explain why the Iraqis would arm Scud missiles and aerial bombs with aflatoxin for use in the Gulf War. As an international group of BW experts concluded as late as March 1998, "Iraq was unable to justify the weaponization of aflatoxin" ("Report of the United Nation's Special Commission's Team to the Technical Evaluation Meeting on the Proscribed Biological Warfare Programme," United Nations Security Council [New York: U. N. Headquarters, April 8, 1998], S/1998/308, p. 7 [hereafter UNSCOM/TECH]).

28. Interview in *Der Spiegel*, in FBIS (NES), September 5, 1995, 39.

29. Department of Defense, *Conduct of the Persian Gulf War: Final Report to Congress* (Washington, D.C.: GPO, April 1992), 15. For comparison, with a Hiroshima-type A-bomb, the "primary lethal area" (caused by the blast itself) is 10 square kilometers. Reuven Pedatzur, *The Arrow System and the Active Defense Against Ballistic Missiles* (Hebrew), Memorandum series (Tel Aviv: Joffe Center of Strategic Studies, Tel Aviv University, October 1993), 25.

30. Carl-Goran Heden, "The Infectious Dustcloud," in *Unless Peace Comes: A Scientific Forecast of New Weapons*, ed. Nigel Calder (Harmondsworth: Pelican, 1970), 161–76.

31. Graham S. Pearson, "Prospects for Chemical and Biological Arms Control: The Web of Deterrence," in *U.S. Security in an Uncertain Era*, ed. Brad Roberts (Cambridge, Mass.: MIT Press, 1993), 304 (Pearson was then director general of the United Kingdom's Chemical and Biological Defence Establishment at Proton Down).

32. Ibid.

33. Matthew S. Meselson, "Chemical and Biological Weapons," in *Arms Control: Readings from Scientific American* (San Francisco: W. H. Freeman, 1973), 305.

34. Beckett, *Weapons for Tomorrow*, 119.

35. Admiral Thomas Davies, assistant director of the U.S. Arms Control and Disarmament Agency, cited in ibid., 120. The controversy, it has been pointed out, is well represented in the strikingly different approaches taken by the United States and the

Soviet Union toward developing biological weapons. Although the United States renounced biological weapons as impractical, the Soviet Union concluded that biological agents might have a central military role. See John D. Steinbruner, "Biological Weapons: A Plague upon All Houses," *Foreign Policy*, Winter 1997–98, 89–90; Richard Preston, "The Bioweaponeers," *New Yorker*, March 9, 1998, 52–65.

36. Zilinskas, "Iraq's Biological Weapons," 418–24.

37. For a general discussion of these and other aspects of effectiveness of biological weapons, see Clarke, *We All Fall Down*, 73–79.

38. Heden, "Infectious Dustcloud," 164–65. For example, Japan's use of biological weapons during World War II was halted when Japanese soldiers in Manchuria became sick with the diseases first unleashed on Chinese civilians (Barend ter Haar, "The Future of Biological Weapons," *Washington Papers*, no. 151 [Washington, D.C.: Center for Strategic and International Studies, Georgetown University, 1991], 5; LTC George W. Christopher, USAF, et al., "Biological Warfare: A Historical Perspective," *JAMA*, August 6, 1997, 413). Some scholars have argued, in contrast, that moral inhibitions have acted as the barrier to BW. See Leonard A. Cole, "The Specter of Biological Weapons," *Scientific American*, December 1996, 64–65.

39. Franz, "Toxin Weapons"; *Medical Management*, chap. 3.

40. Beckett, *Weapons for Tomorrow*, 112 and 157 n. 14.

41. *New York Times*, May 26, 1998.

42. A large percentage of aerosol particles larger than 15–20 microns simply drop harmlessly to the ground. Droplets of 5–15 microns can infect the upper respiratory tract; however, these relatively large particles generally are filtered by natural anatomical and physiological processes. Typically, they lodge in the nasal passages or trachea and do not reach the lungs. Only much smaller particles (0.5–5 microns) efficiently reach the alveoli (the small air spaces in the lungs where carbon dioxide is removed from the blood and oxygen is added). Still smaller droplets are inhaled, but most are exhaled and not efficiently retained in humans. See *Handbook on Medical Aspects*, pt. 2 (chap. 1, sec. 3); Franz, "Toxic Weapons."

43. Clarke, *We All Fall Down*, appendix 2; Beckett, *Weapons for Tomorrow*, 112. The relation between the number of viable spores inhaled and the probability of contracting pulmonary anthrax continues to be a matter of uncertainty. The statistical measure of lethality is usually the LD_{50}, or the amount of toxic agent expected to kill 50 percent of an exposed population, and estimates of anthrax LD_{50} range from 8,000 to 50,000 spores. Franz, "Clinical Recognition," 400 (table); Meselson, "Note," 21.

44. Beckett, *Weapons for Tomorrow*, 111.

45. Heden, "Infectious Dustcloud," 166. For a discussion of other variables affecting the effectiveness of BW, see Meselson, "Chemical and Biological Weapons," 305.

46. For example, an aerosol cloud containing the organisms that cause Q fever would decay at the rate of 10 percent per minute. By comparison, the decay rate for anthrax is a mere 0.1 percent per minute. World Health Organization, *Health Aspects of Chemical and Biological Weapons* (Geneva: World Health Organization, 1970), 24.

47. Michael Meagher of the University of Nebraska at Lincoln, who has been leading a team of scientists in trying to develop a new botulinum toxin vaccine for the Pentagon, was quoted as saying: "From what we understand, A is the primary strain that Saddam has." Cited in *Los Angeles Times*, January 29, 1998.

48. Statement by Acting Director of the CIA, George J. Tenet, before the Senate Select Committee on Intelligence, *Hearing on Current and Projected National Security Threats to the United States*, May 2, 1997, 14; Zilinskas, "Iraq's Biological Weapons," 419; *Le figaro* (Paris), February 26, 1998. A somewhat different breakdown was provided by the CIA earlier. It reported, apparently based on Iraqi declarations to the United Nations, that Iraq produced 11,800 liters of concentrated botulinum toxin. Of this total, 6,000 liters were produced at al-Hakam in 1990. An additional 5,400 liters were produced at the Daura Foot and Mouth Disease Center between November 1990 and January 15, 1991. Finally, the remaining 400 liters of concentrated botulinum toxin were produced at al-Taji. These CIA reports were provided 1–2 years *after* Ekeus had cited a figure of 19,000 liters with regard to Iraq's production of the bacterium *Clostridium botulinum* (briefing by Ekeus cited in *Ha'aretz* [Tel Aviv], November 24, 1995). As for concentrated anthrax, the CIA reported that 8,425 liters were produced at al-Hakam in 1990, and 150 liters at Salman Pak (Statement for the Record by Dr. Gordon C. Oehler, Director, Non-Proliferation Center of the CIA, *The Continuing Threat From Weapons of Mass Destruction*, Hearing, U.S. Senate, Armed Services Committee, March 27, 1996 [http://www.odci.gov/cia/public_affairs/speeches/ archives/go_toc_03279 6.html]). But Ambassador Ekeus later indicated that UNSCOM's analysis detected that Iraq has "produced even more [anthrax] than admitted" ("Ekeus: Important Work Ahead for U.N. Commission on Iraqi Weapons," U.S. Information Agency, May 2, 1997). Inspectors from UNSCOM could not establish whether anthrax spores recovered from Iraq contained one or several strains of the bacillus. Some observers have speculated that the Iraqis could have developed spores containing several strains. They cited the close Soviet-Iraqi relations at the time, and evidence from the Sverdlovsk release, as pointing to such a possibility (*New York Times*, February 3, 1998). It should be noted that the average concentrations of weaponized anthrax developed for the U.S. offensive BW program, which was disestablished in 1969, were 60 trillion anthrax spores, or 8 billion human lethal doses, per 3.78 liters (or 1 gallon). The concentration of botulinum toxin produced during the tenure of the U.S. program was roughly 1 billion lethal doses per 450 grams (or 1 pound) ("Iraq Biological Warfare Threat," Filename:0408pgf.90 [Washington, D.C.: DIA, October 22, 1990] [Gulflink]).

49. Interview in *Le Monde* (Paris), September 11, 1995. Thus, the Iraqis conducted research on hemorrhagic conjunctivitis, which results in extreme pain and temporary blindness, at the Daura Foot and Mouth Disease Institute. Production of *Clostridium perfringens* began in August 1990, five years after acquiring a reference strain from the United States, (Zilinskas, "Iraq's Biological Weapons," 419). In strategic terms, these BW agents acted as "force multipliers" in Iraqi eyes.

50. This history is based on ACDA, "Threat Control," 67; Zilinskas, "Iraq's Biolog-

ical Weapons," 418–20; U.S. Government White Paper, "Iraqi Weapons of Mass Destruction Programs," Washington, D.C., February 13, 1998, 5.

51. Data based on interviews with Ekeus in *Stern*, October 12, 1995, 230–32; and in *Libération*, August 29, 1995. See also *Independent* (London), September 5, 1995. However, Iraq's declarations concerning the types and quantities of both chemical and biological warheads in its possession during the war have changed several times since 1991 (see n. 10 above and Appendix B, Table 2). On the development of al-Husayn and key foreign involvement in the project, see Kenneth R. Timmerman, *The Death Lobby: How the West Armed Iraq* (Boston: Houghton Mifflin, 1991), 142–60 and 247–74. For reports about the involvement of West German companies in the al-Husayn project, see *Der Spiegel*, January 28, 1991, 24–27; February 8, 1991, 10–12; February 25, 1991, 112–15; November 18, 1991, 41–52; *Die Welt* (Hamburg), February 11, 1991; *Stern*, February 28, 1991, 31–34. On the role played by Brazilian companies, see *Financial Times* (London), September 18, 1990; *Folha de Sao Paulo*, in Foreign Broadcasting Information Service (Latin America), hereafter FBIS (LAT), February 8, 1991, 16–17, and March 27, 1991, 29. On Egypt's key role, see *Independent*, September 6, 1989; Daniel Leshem, "Surface-to-Surface Missiles in Iraq," *Memorandum* (Hebrew) (Tel Aviv: Joffe Center for Strategic Studies, Tel Aviv University, November 1993), 1–5, 16–19, 23–24, and 33; Adel Darwish and Gregory Alexander, *Unholy Babylon: The Secret History of Saddam's War* (New York: St. Martin's Press, 1991), 85–89 and 170–71. For the role of Austrian firms, see *Profile* (Vienna), March 6, 1989, 42–44, and April 24, 1989, 38–42. For a report of East German help in extending the range of Iraq's Scud B to reach Tehran, see *Independent*, March 22, 1988. On French help, see *L'express* (Paris), February 9, 1991, 10–12. See also Steven Zaloga, "Ballistic Missiles in the Third World: Scud and Beyond," *International Defense Review*, November 1988, 1423–27; James Bruce, "Assessing Iraq's Missile Technology," *Jane's Defence Weekly*, December 23, 1989, 1371 and 1374; Martin Navias, "Ballistic Missile Proliferation in the Third World," *Adelphi Papers* 225 (London: Intentional Institute for Strategic Studies, Summer 1990), 20–21; W. Seth Carus and Joseph S. Bermudez, Jr., "Iraq's al-Husayn Missile Programme," *Jane's Soviet Intelligence Review*, June 1990, 242–48.

52. Office of Weapons, Technology, and Proliferation, "CIA Report on Intelligence Related to Gulf War Illnesses" (Arlington, Va.: CIA, August 2, 1996) (Gulflink); interviews with Rolf Ekeus in *Libération*, August 29, 1995; *al-Sharq al-Awsat* (London), August 31, 1995; *Der Spiegel*, in FBIS (NES), September 5, 1995, 39–40. See also Laurie Mylroie and James Ring Adams, "Saddam's Germs," *American Spectator*, November 1995, 60. One source has claimed the bombs were deployed at two sites, not three. According to this source, 10 of the missiles were hidden in the railway tunnel, and 15 in the holes dug along the Tigris River (Zilinskas, "Iraq's Biological Weapons, 420). The Kuwaiti theater of operations was generally defined as all of Kuwait plus Iraq below 31 degrees north latitude.

53. Beckett, *Weapons for Tomorrow*, 121–22.

54. Information based on Soviet-released data, "Chemical Weapons: New Information Analysed," *Jane's Defence Weekly*, February 27, 1988, 371. However, some sources

indicate that the SS-1c carried only a 965-kilogram warhead. See Leshem, "Surface-to-Surface Missiles," 4; Pedatzur, *The Arrow System*, drawing 1 and p. 61 n. 4.

55. Based on their effectiveness in the CW against Iran, the Iraqis adapted some LD-250 (250-pound) and R-400 (400-pound) aerial bombs to their BW program. They could hold 60 liters and 85 liters of biological solution, respectively. When necessary, the walls of the chambers containing the payload were coated with an inert epoxy paint to protect the biological agents from the toxic effects of contact with metal. Following testing, the Iraqis determined that the R-400 was the more suitable munition for BW, and in 1990, 200 R-400 bombs were produced. Zilinskas, "Iraq's Biological Weapons," 420; ACDA, "Threat Control," 67.

56. The Soviet SS-1c Scud B carried an 884-millimeter warhead containing 555 kilograms viscous VX CW agent. "Chemical Weapons," 371.

57. Reportedly, UNSCOM officials have indicated that the "40 or so gallons" of anthrax and botulinum toxin that in 1997 Iraq said were stored in 21 of the Scud warheads before the war "could kill from 100,000 to a million people" (*Washington Post*, November 21, 1997). However, it seems appropriate to question the great variance in the projection of fatalities. For example, does the topmost figure (one million) assume release of aerosolized biological agents and toxins over the target? Is the potential use of submunitions reflected in the estimated number of fatalities? Also what, if any, targets did this casualty forecast specifically take into account?

58. Although there is no evidence that any of Iraq's chemical weapons had carried bomblets, such technology was within the reach of Baghdad. For example, the Egyptian surface-to-surface rocket Saker-80, produced indigenously and capable of a maximum range of 80 kilometers, is reportedly equipped with a warhead containing 1,000 bomblets (*al-Jumhuriyah* [Cairo], November 8, 1987). Given that Egypt supplied such rockets to the Iraqis, and given the tight military links between Cairo and Baghdad at least until the Gulf War, it could be assumed that the technology had arrived in Iraq (Navias, "Ballistic Missile Proliferation," 228). In addition, Hussein Kamil Hassan had stated that "Iraq manufactures cluster bombs of various forms, sizes and uses" (*al-Thawrah* [Baghdad], April 28, 1989). This claim was later confirmed by U.S. intelligence. The DIA reported that the Baghdad office of the Chilean arms manufacturer Carlos R. Cardoen had discussed "parameters for aerosol testing of botulinum toxin with the home office. Cardoen and Iraq are known to be co-producing 250 and 500 kg cluster bombs [which] are particularly well suited for disseminating BW agents" ("Iraq Biological Warfare Threat," Filename:0408pgf.9 [Washington, D.C.: DIA, October 22, 1990] [Gulflink]; "Bugs and Things," Filename:omeoo4.90d [Washington, D.C.: DIA, December 3, 1990] [Gulflink]). Another paper said: "Iraq has the [BW] agents, the missiles and the submunition production technology to produce these BW weapons" ("Iraqi Biological Warfare [BW] Capabilities," Filename:0503br.90 [Washington, D.C.: DIA, n.d.] [Gulflink]). Thus, though "not available in the Iran/Iraq war," Iraq's "CW/BIO cluster munitions" were "assessed available now," and their use was expected to "greatly increase dispersal on target" ("Iraqi Chemical Warfare Data," File 970613_092596_ui_txt_0001.txt [Washington D.C.: DIA, n.d.] [Gulflink]). The Car-

doen CBU-500 used by Iraq released 240 bomblets that covered an elliptical surface area of up to 45,000 square meters, depending on operational employment ("Iraq BW Capabilities," Filename:0628.rpt.91 [Washington, D.C.: DIA, undated] [Gulflink]).

59. In this regard the mass exodus of residents of the metropolitan Tel Aviv area owing to the Iraqi Scud attacks (*Jerusalem Post,* January 25 and 28, 1991), which was denounced by some Israeli politicians at the time, could be viewed as an effective anti-BW measure even if it was unplanned.

60. Zilinskas, "Iraq's Biological Weapons," 422.

61. On the "insidiousness" of BW, see the debate between Nicholas A. Sims, ("Morality and Biological Warfare," *Arms Control,* October 1, 1987, 11–12), and John J. Haldane ("Ethics and Biological Warfare," *Arms Control,* October 1, 1987, 30–31).

62. Interview on Jerusalem Domestic Service, FBIS (NES), March 1, 1991, 26. See also his interview on Israeli Television Network, FBIS (NES), January 22, 1991, 74; Israeli Chief of Staff, Lt. Gen. Dan Shomron, also emphasized the targeting of civilians as a central consideration. Interview, Israel Television Network, FBIS (NES), January 18, 1991, 37.

63. Many observers have criticized President Bush's decision to "suspend" the war as "premature." For the ensuing debate see, for example, Elizabeth Drew, "Letter From Washington," *New Yorker,* March 6, 1991, 97–103.

64. The documents are posted on the Internet. They can be accessed through http://www.dtic.mil/gulflink/ or directly through http://www.gulflink.osd.mil/. In this book, the indication "Gulflink" relates to all the documents found on this site.

CHAPTER 2: THE INVASION OF KUWAIT

1. Following his defection, Hussein Kamil Hassan claimed that in January 1991, "at the beginning of the war," Iraq was "not far from carrying out its first [nuclear] test, using uranium from our two research Russian and French reactors." He said that the bombing of Iraq's "nuclear facilities" by the coalition "put an end to this attempt" (interview in *Le vif/L'express* [Brussels], October 6, 1995, 69 and 70). On the continuing debate regarding how close Iraq was to obtaining a nuclear bomb, see Anthony H. Cordesman and Abraham R. Wagner, *The Lessons of Modern War,* vol. 4: *The Gulf War* (Boulder, Colo.: Westview, 1996), 901–11; David Albright and Mark Hibbs, "Iraq and the Bomb: Were They Even Close?" *Bulletin of the Atomic Scientists,* March 1991, 16–25; *New York Times,* August 30, 1995.

2. See, for example, McGeorge Bundy, "Nuclear Weapons and the Gulf," *Foreign Affairs,* Fall 1991, 90–91; Barry Rubin, *Cauldron of Turmoil: America in the Middle East* (New York: Harcourt Brace Jovanovich, 1992), 156–57; Jeffrey Record, *Hollow Victory: A Contrary View of the Gulf War* (New York: Brassey's [U.S.], 1993), 101.

3. Havana Tele Rebelde Network, Foreign Broadcast Information Service, Latin America, hereafter FBIS (LAT), February 19, 1991, 5.

4. Interview, "The Gulf War," *Frontline,* PBS, KQED-San Francisco, January 9, 1996. In November 1994, General al-Samarra'i, a member of a prominent Iraqi clan close to Saddam, defected to Syria via the independent Kurdish enclave of northern Iraq.

5. On U.S. policy toward Iraq during this period, see Bruce W. Jentleson, *With Friends Like These: Reagan, Bush and Saddam, 1982–1990* (New York: Norton, 1994), 105–38.

6. See excerpts from a transcript of this meeting as provided by the Iraqis, *New York Times*, September 23, 1990. For an analysis, see Avigdor Haselkorn, "Underestimating Saddam: Why Were the U.S. and Israel Surprised?" *Global Affairs*, special issue 1990, 1–25. The background of the Saddam-Glaspie meeting is discussed in Robert D. Kaplan, *The Arabists: The Romance of an American Elite* (New York: Free Press, 1995), 281–302.

7. *Wall Street Journal*, February 26, 1991. See also the testimony of CIA Director William H. Webster before the Senate Committee on Government Operations, in Colin Norman, "CIA Details Chemical Weapons Spread," *Science*, February 17, 1989, 888.

8. Cordesman and Wagner, *Lessons of Modern War*, 883.

9. "Iraq's CW Program" (Arlington, Va.: CIA, circa August 1990) (Gulflink). Earlier, during the summer of 1982, Iraq had already used the riot control agent CS (orthochlorobenzylidine malononitrile, commonly known as tear gas) when Iraqi troops came in close proximity to Iranian soldiers. The aim was to force enemy soldiers to don protective gear, thus hampering operations (Director of Central Intelligence, "Impact and Implications of Chemical Weapons Use in the Iran-Iraq War" [Arlington, Va.: CIA, circa October 1987] [Gulflink]; "Issues [U]" [Washington, D.C.: DIA, March 15, 1990] [Gulflink]). Credible accounts of *lethal* CW use by Iraq had emerged already in December 1982. According to these accounts, Iraq was using limited amounts of "crude sulfur mustard" to repel night attacks and help break up Iranian human-wave formations (*Los Angeles Times*, January 26, 1984). In the battles of al-Faw, Fish Lake, and Majnoon Islands during the final months of the war, Iraq made heavy use of chemical weapons. For example, in the April 1988 battle to recapture al-Faw Peninsula, the CIA estimated that the Iraqis used well over 100 tons of CW agent. The suddenness and severity of this attack caused havoc among the Iranian defenders. The resulting victory took only 30 hours, which surprised even the Iraqi military planners. Subsequent offensives were preceded by massed chemical attacks, and they met with similar success.

10. Mustard gas can be delivered in either liquid or vapor form and can take four to six hours to corrupt tissue, unless droplets are inhaled. The first symptoms are the reddening of the skin, particularly around the eyes, followed by the formation of large water blisters on all exposed skin. The lungs and throat can become very irritated if the blister agent is inhaled. Damage to eyes and blood cells can be permanent, sometimes leading to blindness, and the blisters take a long time to heal and are vulnerable to infection (William Fowler, "The Veiled Threat: NBC Warfare," *Defence*, January 1, 1988, 36). It should be noted that not all individuals of a species react in the same way to a given dose of chemical agent, some being more or less sensitive as a result of numerous factors, such as genetic background, race, and age (*Handbook on the Medical Aspects of NBC Defensive Operations* [Washington, D.C.: HQ Department of the Army, February 1, 1996], pt. 3, chap. 1 [http://www.nbc-med.org/amedp6/PART_III/chapter1.htm]).

11. The persistence of chemical agents is dependent on such weather conditions as wind, humidity, and temperature. It also depends on whether the agents are dispersed as liquids or aerosols. Gases tend to disperse quickly in hot weather and to persist far longer in cold weather (see *Health Services Support in Nuclear, Biological and Chemical Environment: FM 8–10–7* [Washington, D.C.: Headquarters Department of the Army, n.d.], table 2–10 [http:/www.nbc-med.org/FMs/fm8_107/chapter2.htm]). Often, thickeners are added to modify the persistence of the H and HD gases. The thickened agent is the preferred method for making an area impenetrable. The Iraqis also delivered the gas via solid particulates, usually finely ground silica 0.1 to 10.0 microns in size, impregnated with a mustard agent known as dusty mustard ("Chemical and Biological Warfare in the Kuwait Theater of Operations: Iraq's Capability and Posturing [U]," Filename:0147pgv.ood [Washington, D.C.: DIA, n.d.] [Gulflink]; DCI, "Impact and Implications"). With this method, a fine powdery substance acts as a carrier for the toxic material. The persistence of dusty mustard depends on the carrier's physical characteristics, and its toxicity is the result of the purity of the mustard agent on the dust. The dusty mustard method is reported to be very suitable for the creation of swaths of contaminated territory that act as barriers to an advancing enemy. Another reported advantage of this method is that it is less susceptible to changes in air temperature. Moreover, when disseminated as dry aerosol, the gas is harder to detect. Most important, the methods of dispersal differ with respect to the nature of skin injury, the intensity of lung injuries, and the latent period, with the dusty form being more effective. The latent period can be militarily significant because it affects the time a soldier can continue to fight before the effect of the agent becomes debilitating. The minute particles of dusty mustard are easily inhaled and can corrupt lung tissue in 10–15 minutes. By comparison, the liquid or vapor mustard may not have an effect for 4–6 hours. Under certain conditions, dusty mustard can penetrate semi-permeable protective suits and can also be activated via sweat. The drawback is that the gas tends to adhere to larger particles once settled and is thus less likely to become airborne a second time for inhalation.

12. U.N. investigators who went to the Iran-Iraq border found "partially damaged aerial bombs" and one still unexploded. Samples of "dark brown, oily liquid," which were found in some of the bombs, proved to be nearly pure mustard gas (bis[2-chlorotethyl]sulfide), with only a trace of sulfur. In contrast, the unexploded bomb, which bore the markings "BR-250-WP," contained the nerve agent tabun (ethyl N-dimethyl-phosphoramidocyanidate). See "Report of the Specialists Appointed by the Secretary-General to Investigate Allegations by the Islamic Republic of Iran Concerning the Use of Chemical Weapons" (New York: United Nations Security Council, S/16433, March 26, 1984); Eliot Marshall, "Iraq's Chemical Warfare: Case Proved," *Science*, April 13, 1984, 130–32. See also Judith Perera, "Iraq's Chemical Warfare," *Middle East*, May 1985, 16–17; Peter Dunn, "The Chemical War: Journey to Iran," *Nuclear, Biological, and Chemical Defense and Technology International*, April 1986, 28–35; and "The Chemical War: Iran Revisited — 1986," *Nuclear, Biological, and Chemical Defense and Technology International*, June 1986, 32–37. For general discussions of Iraq's CW in the war with

Iran, see W. Andrew Terrill, Jr., "Chemical Weapons in the Gulf War," *Strategic Review*, Spring 1986, 51–58; Lee Waters, "Chemical Weapons in the Iran-Iraq War," *Military Review*, October 1990, 54–60. On the use of aerial bombs in Iraqi CW, see Cordesman and Wagner, *Lessons of Modern War*, 885 and 929 n. 172. On Iraqi-Spanish negotiations for aerial bombs, see *Ha'aretz*, May 23, 1993.

13. Cited in *Newsweek*, March 19, 1984, 40. See also *Washington Post*, March 7, 1984. Apparently, some of these chemical munitions came from Egypt. Some years later, it was revealed that Egypt had provided Iraq with chemical weapons, and that in tests on Iranian POWs the Egyptian agents proved deadly (*Mayo* [Cairo], September 24, 1990). On Egypt's CW assistance to Iraq, see *New York Times*, March 11, 1989; and *Guardian* (London), September 21, 1993.

14. Nerve agents are divided into G agents, which are nonpersistent, and V agents, which are thickened and persistent. All these agents enter the body through inhalation and also through the skin, and are chemically related to such organophosphate insecticides as malathion and parathion. Like these insecticides, nerve gases inhibit the normal function of the vital enzyme acetylchloinesterase, which normally breaks down acetylcholine, a chemical responsible for causing muscular contraction. Thus, upon exposure to nerve gas, all the muscles — even those pulling in opposite directions — try to contract. The result is that all coordination is lost and the muscles go into a state of fibrillation or vibration. Nerve agent vapor causes symptoms within seconds or a minute of exposure, and death by asphyxia can follow between a few minutes and two hours later, depending on the dosage. Not all symptoms appear in every casualty. For example, miosis (reduction in pupil size) is uncommon in victims exposed to a liquid droplet of nerve agent on the skin unless the droplet is large enough to cause severe effects. The size of the droplet also determines the rapidity of penetration. The larger it is, the sooner the onset of symptoms and the more severe the effects. Frederick R. Sidell, M.D., "Chemical Agent Terrorism," U.S. Army Medical Department, Medical NBC Information Server, n.d. (http://www.nbc-med.org/chapter.html). For a general discussion of nerve gases, see Julian Perry Robinson, "Chemical Warfare," *Science Journal*, April 1967, 33–40.

15. Robin Clarke, *We All Fall Down: The Prospects for Chemical and Biological Warfare* (Harmondsworth: Pelican, 1969), app. 1. These figures apply to men of 70 kilograms engaged in mild activity.

16. The Iraqis were trained in CW by a variety of Warsaw Pact countries. For the role of East Germany, see DPA (Hamburg), Foreign Broadcast Information Service, Eastern Europe, hereafter FBIS (EEU), April 27, 1990, 18; and ADN International Service, East Berlin, FBIS (EEU), August 20, 1990, 22–23; *Independent*, January 30, 1991. Czechoslovakia continued to train Iraqi CW personnel even after the onset of the Gulf crisis; see *Lidove Noviny* (Prague), FBIS (EEU), August 20, 1990, 16. See also Kenneth R. Timmerman, *The Death Lobby: How the West Armed Iraq* (Boston: Houghton Mifflin, 1991), 49–50 and 134–35. On the role of the Iraqi air force in CW during the war with Iran, see "Iraqi Air Force Capability to Deliver Chemical Weapons," Filename:0422pgf.90 (Washington, D.C.: DIA, December 1, 1990) (Gulflink).

17. Brig. Gen. (ret.) J. H. Rothschild, *Tomorrow's Weapons* (New York: McGraw Hill, 1964), 196. The author was U.S. army director of chemical warfare research.

18. Department of Defense, *Conduct of the Persian Gulf War: Final Report to Congress* (Washington, D.C.: GPO, April 1992), 15.

19. Typically, the Iraqis would deposit persistent mustard agent in an Iranian force's rear area and then bombard the front with the nonpersistent nerve agent sarin. Troops fleeing the sarin-contaminated area would then be exposed to mustard as well ("Iraq: Potential for Chemical Weapons Use," Filename:71726882 [Washington, D.C.: DIA, February 1991] [Gulflink]). The use of mustard gas in rear areas also frustrated Iranian plans to launch immediate counterattacks (Dilip Hiro, *The Longest War: The Iran-Iraq Military Conflict* [New York: Routledge, 1991], 206–7).

20. Estimates of fatalities range from "hundreds" to as high as 5,000. For the lower figure, see U.S. Government White Paper, "Iraqi Weapons of Mass Destruction Programs," Washington, D.C., February 13, 1998, 6. For the higher figure, see Christine Gosden, "Why I Went, What I Saw," *Washington Post*, March 11, 1998. Iranian soldiers said that a house-to-house search produced a count of 4,000 civilians killed. *Toronto Globe and Mail*, March 24, 1988; also *Washington Post*, March 24, 1988.

21. See *Washington Times*, March 23, 1988. On December 13, 1988, the *Christian Science Monitor* reported that the Iraqi aerial chemical attack began the night of March 17, 1988. General al-Samarra'i claimed that Saddam had ordered 50 airplanes, each armed with four chemical bombs, to attack the village in revenge for its collaboration with Iran. Interview, CBS-TV, *60 Minutes*, November 23, 1997.

22. *Toronto Globe and Mail*, March 24, 1988.

23. Cited in Jonathan Braude, "CW to be 'Standard Military Practice,'" *Jane's Defence Weekly*, August 27, 1988, 357. On Iraqi experiments with cyanogen chloride, see "U.S. Chemical and Biological Warfare-Related Dual Use Exports to Iraq and their Possible Impact on the Health Consequences of the Gulf War," Report of Chmn. Donald W. Riegle, Jr., and Ranking Member Alfonse D'Amato of the Committee on Banking, Housing and Urban Affairs with respect to Export Administration, U.S. Senate, 103rd Cong., 2d sess., May 25, 1994, chap. 1 (pts. 1 and 2) (http://www.gulfwar.org/reprt/r_1_1.html and/r_1_2.html), hereafter Riegle Report.

24. Cited in *Washington Post* (Health Section), March 29, 1988. A similar argument is made in Andrew Rathmell, "Chemical Weapons in the Middle East: Syria, Iraq, Iran, and Libya," *Marine Corps Gazette*, July 1990, 59. It was noted, based on the experience of the Iran-Iraq war, that "Iraqi MOD [Ministry of Defense] doctrine for use of chemical weapons is based upon the principle that chemical weapons can demoralize and provoke fear in the enemy and this ability is as important as the chemical weapons, capacity to inflict battlefield casualties." "Desert Shield — Iraqi Command & Control Sequence for Chemical Ammunitions Attack," Filename: 27640078_91r.txt (Washington, D.C.: DIA, December 1990) (Gulflink).

25. In August 1987 Saddam Hussein announced that Iraq had successfully tested a new, longer-range Scud dubbed al-Husayn over a distance of more than 500 kilometers. Because Iraq launched no long-range missile attacks on Iran between August 1987

and February 1988, Saddam's claims were viewed with skepticism by Western observers. But following Iran's attack on Baghdad with three of the Scud B missiles it had imported from North Korea on February 29, 1988, it rapidly became apparent that Saddam had spent the intervening months quietly building up a sufficient stockpile of al-Husayns to make a "major strategic impact on the course of the Iran-Iraq War." Rather than adopt the Iranian tactic of firing small numbers of missiles, Iraq fired 189 al-Husayns at Tehran, Qom, and Esfahan over the following three weeks in another chapter of what became known as the "War of the Cities." The attacks had a significant psychological impact and were "one of the factors contributing to Iran's decision to sue for peace" in July 1988. "Patterns of Proliferation — National Briefings: Iraq" (Lancaster: Center for Defence and International Security Studies, Lancaster University, 1996) (http://www.cdiss.org/country4.htm).

26. *Washington Times*, April 1, 1988.

27. For Iraq's admission of CW use in Halabja, see Vice President Taha Muhyi al-Din Ma'ruf, in *Le monde*, November 10, 1988. In retrospect, there is no question that Saddam's calculation was correct. During the Gulf crisis the chemical attacks on the Kurds were cited by U.S. intelligence as among the reasons for taking seriously the Iraqi threats of mass destruction against Israel and Saudi Arabia: "Saddam has demonstrated his willingness to employ chemical weapons against civilians. Iraq conducted chemical attacks beginning in March 1987 against Kurds in northern Iraq in retaliation for Kurdish support of Iran during the war" ("Iraqi Air Force Capability to Deliver Chemical Weapons," Filename:0422pgf.90 [Washington, D.C.: DIA, December 1, 1990] [Gulflink]). Undoubtedly, Saddam would have preferred to publicize his new terror weapon as soon it had been introduced into battle. However, political considerations prevented such a declaration. The initial Iraqi denials of its resort to CW were aimed to stave off antagonizing Iraq's Western arms suppliers (Terrill, "Chemical Weapons," 54–55). Moreover, Iraq's declaratory policy was a function of its evolving CW capability. The larger its chemical arsenal became, and the greater the effectiveness of its CW on the battlefield, the more noticeable were Baghdad's displays of terrorist deterrence.

28. Baghdad Domestic Service, FBIS (NES), April 13, 1990, 34. Subsequently, the Baghdad paper *al-Thawrah*, mouthpiece of the Ba'ath party, reported on April 12, 1990, that in the wake of Iraq's acquisition of the binary chemical weapon "what Washington or others say no longer counts." For the successful testing in April 1990 of an Iraqi SSM fitted with "a binary chemical warhead," see "The Iraq Chemical Warfare Plan" (Arlington, Va.: CIA, August 1990) (Gulflink); "Scud Chemical Agent Coverage Patterns," Filename:0508rept.ood (Washington, D.C.: DIA, August 1990) (Gulflink). See also *New York Times*, March 21, 1996.

29. Baghdad Domestic Service, FBIS (NES), April 17, 1990, 7.

30. Interview in *al-Ahali* (Cairo), May 16, 1990.

31. Daniel Leshem, "Surface-to-Surface Missiles in Iraq" (Hebrew), *Memorandum* (Tel Aviv: Joffe Center for Strategic Studies, Tel Aviv University, November 1993), 29; *Yedi'ot Aharonot* (Tel Aviv), April 3, 1990. Binary chemical bombs cannot make use of

inertia and spin in the same efficient manner as artillery shells, and consequently they require a fairly complicated set of internal gadgetry to bring about the final reaction. Whereas nerve gas bombs, for instance, are little more than exploding tanks of lethal liquids, binaries contain a number of essential mechanical elements that increase the chances of malfunction and therefore the unreliability of the weapon. It could thus be argued that "binary chemical munitions are probably the only example of the military deliberately opting to replace an efficient system with one that will be less reliable and more restricted in application" (Brian Beckett, *Weapons for Tomorrow* [New York: Plenum, 1983], 134). On the debate regarding binary chemical weapons in the United States, see Joseph Palca, "Binary Weapons in Trouble," *Nature*, June 19, 1986, 717; Lois R. Ember, "Battle Looms over Funding of Binary Chemical Weapons," *Chemical and Engineering News*, August 11, 1986, 17; Stephen Budiansky, "Qualified Approval for Binary Chemical Weapons," *Science*, November 21, 1986, 930–32; Manfred R. Hamm, "World Watch: Will Binaries Founder on Allied Rocks," *Nuclear, Biological, and Chemical Defense and Technology International*, 1987 Yearbook, 8. On the Soviet perspective, see John Sartorious, "Viewing Bigeye: Through the Soviet Looking Glass," *Nuclear, Biological, and Chemical Defense and Technology International*, 1987 Yearbook, 10.

32. *Yedi'ot Aharonot*, April 3, 1990.

33. Leshem, "Surface-to-Surface Missiles," 29; Beckett, *Weapons for Tomorrow*, 131 and 134. In contrast, some experts at the Stockholm Institute for Peace Research International have claimed that binaries in fact provide greater efficacy because the agent is formed in the target area itself and is thus released into the air over a longer time. However, a large part of the binary's interior is filled with nonlethal components that help mix the chemicals when the weapon is delivered. Other components also help keep the chemicals separated prior to use. Finally, because the reaction must take place while the weapon is en route to the target, not all the precursor is converted to a chemical agent by the time the round hits the target. As for safety, in theory binary chemical weapons rule out serious accidents because the lethal product simply does not exist until the final seconds before detonation. However, even the precursor chemicals may not be harmless. The sarin precursor DF, for example, can be poisonous in its own right. In low-tech "binary" chemical weapons like the one developed by Iraq, the mixture becomes quite hot because the reaction that forms sarin from the DF and isopropyl is exothermic (emits heat). There is a significant amount of free hydrofluoric acid (HF), a component of DF, in the low-tech munitions as well. It is corrosive to most metals and glasses. The combination of nerve agent, free acid, and heat is particularly deadly. "Estimated Collateral Damage from Attacks on Iraqi Biological, Chemical and Nuclear Facilities," Filename:0502bkg.ood (Washington, D.C.: DIA, December 14, 1990) (Gulflink). See also Beckett, *Weapons for Tomorrow*, 130–37, for a general discussion of binary chemical weapons.

34. Brig. John Hemsely, "The Soviet Bio-Chemical Threat: The Real Issue," *Royal United Service Institute Journal*, no. 3 (1988), 18–19. See also Riegle Report, chap. 1 (pts. 1 and 3).

35. Cordesman and Wagner, *Lessons of Modern War*, 885. Both the GB and GF nerve

agents are made by the reaction of an alcohol with DF, which is also known as difluor. GB is produced by the reaction of isopropyl alcohol (isopropanol) with DF; GF is produced by the reaction of cyclohexyl alcohol (cyclohexanol) with DF. The Iraqis chose GB undoubtedly because GF production is more difficult in the binary configuration, as cyclohexanol is less reactive than isopropanol. The reaction takes longer and may need to be heated.

36. DF can be stored in plastic containers, which would be resistant to fluoride attack, thus extending storage life. "Study on IZ abilities to Conduct Chemical Warfare," Filename:0150pgv.91d (Washington, D.C.: DIA, February 8, 1991) (Gulflink).

37. Unfortunately for the Iraqis, the same chemical engineering problems that had limited the purity of their unitary nerve agents hindered the quality of their DF. DF is made from an organophosphorus chemical and HF. Removing the HF is not a simple task. But DF that contains HF could catalyze decomposition. As a result of the low-quality DF, Iraqi "binary" weapons were judged to be only 50–65 percent effective. See "Inspection of Chemical Warfare."

38. Cordesman and Wagner, Lessons of Modern War, 886.

39. Timmerman, The Death Lobby, 145. Although mustard gases are primarily used to inflict damage rather than kill, they may lead to death if the inflammation of the respiratory tract caused by the agent develops eventually into bronchial pneumonia. Fetizon and Magat, "The Toxic Arsenal," 147.

40. Cited in Timmerman, The Death Lobby, 145.

41. From 1983 through early 1986, the Iraqis frequently used agents under unsuitable weather conditions, when wind carried the agent toward their own troops ("Iraq Chemical Weapons" [Arlington, Va.: CIA, February 20, 1991] [Gulflink]). The Iraqi Air Force's early use of chemical weapons also proved ineffective because of poor employment techniques. Iraq initially applied the same tactics it used for delivering conventional munitions and did not factor in terrain and meteorological conditions, such as wind speed and direction, humidity, and temperature. In addition, Iraqi pilots delivered chemical ordnance at altitudes too high to be effective or too low for bomb fuses to function properly, preventing bombs from detonating ("Iraqi Air Force Capability to Deliver Chemical Weapons," Filename:72928819 [Washington, D.C.: DIA, January 13, 1991] [Gulflink]). The Iraqis later corrected these problems by improving delivery techniques and by using impact fuses. They also learned to disseminate chemical agents in the morning rather than later in the day, when high temperatures would accelerate evaporation. These tactical modifications helped Iraq maximize the effectiveness of its CW.

42. "Briefing Input for HLDG meeting: The Threat," Filename:0601rpt.90d (Washington, D.C.: DIA, December 3, 1990) (Gulflink); "Iraqi Chemical Capabilities," Filename:0156pgv.91d (Washington, D.C.: DIA, February 1991) (Gulflink).

43. "Views on Iraqi Chemical Warfare Capability—Part 2," Filename: 68320872.90r (Washington, D.C.: DIA, September 1990) (Gulflink).

44. For example, it was estimated that in order to inflict 50 percent casualties in an area of 1 square kilometer, the Iraqis needed 4 tons of mustard gas, 2 tons of tabun, or

half a ton of sarin, assuming an air burst and an unprotected population (W. Seth Carus, "Chemical Weapons in the Middle East," *Policy Focus*, no. 9 [Washington, D.C.: Washington Institute for Near East Policy, December 1988], 7). Assuming a 300-kilogram warhead for al-Husayn, Iraq would have to launch at least 14 missiles carrying mustard gas, or 7 carrying tabun, but only 2 missiles loaded with sarin to inflict the same level of damage. If "cocktail weapons" were used, the number of warheads would depend on the specific mix.

45. See "Letter" by Aubin Heyndrickx in *Windhoek Advertiser*, June 16, 1989. See also "Report of the Mission Dispatched by the Secretary-General to Investigate Allegations of the Use of Chemical Weapons in the Conflict Between the Islamic Republic of Iran and Iraq," S/20060 (New York: UN Security Council, July 20, 1988), 13.

46. Cited in *Die Presse* (Vienna), March 24, 1985. Heyndrickx further claimed that in 1984 the Iraqis had used a compound that comprised a mix of "yellow rain" mycotoxin, mustard gas, and a neurotoxin. He said that his laboratory isolated at least two, sometimes three, mycotoxins in each of the urine and stool samples taken from nine Iranian soldiers who had been injured on February 27, 1984, and were sent for treatment to the University of Vienna Hospital. Heyndrickx identified the mycotoxins as Nivalenol, T-2, HT-2, and Verrucarol. "The combined synergistic effects of the two poisons [mustard gas and 'yellow rain'] were absolutely lethal," he said (*Wall Street Journal*, March 13, 1984). "Yellow rain" is made of trichothecene toxins, which are produced by species of the fungal genus *Fusarium*, found in moldy grains and infected crops. This is the only class of easily produced toxins that are dermally active. One billionth of a gram (or nanogram) per square centimeter of skin will cause irritation, and quantities as large as a microgram will cause necrosis, or destruction of skin cells. (For a general discussion of mycotoxins, see Col. David R. Franz, "Defense Against Toxin Weapons" [Fort Detrick, Frederick, Md.: U.S. Army Medical Research Institute for Infectious Diseases, 1997], http://www.nbc-med.org/FMs/datw/chap1.htm"; Alex Ciegler, "Mycotoxins: A New Class of Chemical Weapons," *Nuclear, Biological and Chemical Defense and Technology International*, April 1986, 52–57.) The Iraqis were not believed to be able to produce these substances independently; there was speculation in the Western press that the Soviet Union might have been the source of the Iraqi mycotoxins (*Frankfurter Allgemeine Zeitung*, July 7, 1982; *Ha'aretz*, March 19, 1984). However, Heyndrickx's allegations were strongly disputed by other toxicologists (see *New York Times*, March 19, 1984; Marshall, "Iraq's Chemical Warfare," 132). In fact, based on the 1985 findings, he himself said that Iraq subsequently replaced its chemical "cocktail" with a cyanide-based gas because it killed more quickly (Braude, "CW," 357; Agence France Presse [hereafter AFP] in Foreign Broadcast Information Service, West Europe, hereafter FBIS [WEU], January 30, 1991, 4). Although Heyndrickx's claims might have been premature, in 1987 the Iraqis reportedly were able to purchase, through intermediaries, 100 milligrams of the mycotoxins HT-2 and T-2 (one of the more stable toxins, retaining its bioactivity even when heated to high temperatures) from the West German company Sigma Chemie GmbH, Oberhaching, near Munich (see *Der Spiegel*, January 30, 1989, 16–18). In 1990, the ability of *Fusarium oxysporium*

and *Fusarium granarim* to produce mycotoxins was investigated by Iraqi scientists. Evidently, the fungi were grown on damp, supplemented rice, and toxins were extracted by organic solvents and dried in a rotary evaporator. The Iraqis claim to have produced 20 milliliters of trichothecene-containing solution, some of which was tested on animals. The fate of the remainder is unknown (Raymond A. Zilinskas, "Iraq's Biological Weapons: The Past as Future?" *JAMA*, August 6, 1997, 420). Reportedly, the West German BND (*Bundesnachrichtendienst*, or Federal Intelligence Service) subsequently learned that "the poison from the FRG had a lethal effect during tests on animals" (*Der Spiegel*, August 13, 1990, 82–83).

47. "AFMIC Special Weekly Wire 32–90(c)(u)," Filename:80638041 (Washington, D.C.: DIA, August 1990) (Gulflink); "Iraqi Chemical Munition Characteristics Baseline, Corrected," Filename:73455727 (Washington, D.C.: DIA, September 1990) (Gulflink); "CW/BW Threat Weapon Effectiveness Assessment," Filename: 0500 memo.90 (Washington, D.C.: DIA, December 31, 1990) (Gulflink); "Scud Chemical Agent Coverage Patterns."

48. Prepared Statement of Dr. Christine M. Gosden, Professor of Medical Genetics in the University of Liverpool in the United Kingdom Before the Senate Judiciary Committee, Subcommittee on Terrorism, Technology and Government Information, and the Senate Intelligence Committee, Washington, D.C., April 22, 1998 (http://www.cmep.com). The nerve agent soman (GD) was first synthesized in 1994 and is considered the most toxic of the G-type nerve agents. Gosden has written that the finding of serious congenital malformations with genetic causes occurring in Halabja children born years after the chemical attack suggest that the "effects of these chemical warfare agents are transmitted to succeeding generations." Gosden, "Why I Went."

49. Kanan Makiya (Samir al-Khalil), *Cruelty and Silence: War, Tyranny, Uprising and the Arab World* (New York: Norton, 1993), 138–39. One source speculated the Kurds were attacked with "blue acid"—a mixture of mustard gas and hydrogen cyanide or of mustard gas, hydrogen cyanide, and a G-type nerve agent. Presumably the blue acid was responsible for the unique signature of the Kurdish casualties—bloody vomit with blackened skin. "New Mixture of Chemical Warfare" (Washington, D.C.: DIA, December 1991) (Gulflink); see also *Christian Science Monitor*, September 15, 1988, and March 12, 1992.

50. "Inspection of Chemical Warfare." The warheads were found in the Dujayl area, about 30 kilometers from where Iraq had said they were located (*Christian Science Monitor*, January 23, 1992). UNSCOM was "able to verify" that Iraq had produced at least 50 CW warheads. Of these, 16 warheads were filled with sarin and 34 with binary chemical components ("Report of the Secretary-General on the activities of the Special Commission established by the Secretary General pursuant to paragraph 9 [b] [i] of resolution 687 [1991]," S/1997/774 [New York: United Nations Security Council, October 6, 1997], 17, hereafter UNSCOM 1997). One source said that of the 50 warheads, 9 were destroyed in static testing and 11 had been used in training (Cordesman and Wagner, *Lessons of Modern War*, 886). Iraq itself subsequently claimed that only 5 warheads, not 20, were for CW trials, however.

51. "Inspection of Chemical Warfare."

52. Cited in *Le monde* (Paris), FBIS (NES), September 25, 1992, 12.

53. The persistence of soman (GD) is about the same as GF's. In retrospect, the officers' findings seems to give credence to unconfirmed reports that the Iraqis used 122-millimeter rockets loaded with GB-GF mix in the battle of al-Faw. See also "UNSCOM 20 (CW 6) Inspection Results of Kamisiyah Storage Facility," File 970613_60210020_922_txt_0001.txt (Washington, D.C.: DIA, October 27, 1991) (Gulflink).

54. *Le monde* (Paris), FBIS (NES), September 25, 1992, 12. It could be that the bombs in question were LD-250 and R-400 bombs, weighing 250 and 400 pounds, respectively.

55. Department of Defense, *Conduct of the Persian Gulf War*, 15.

56. "IZ Chemical and Biological Warhead Threat." The Iraqis intentionally produced a 60–40 GB-GF mix in an effort to lower the agent's volatility and increase its persistence in the Middle East climate. UNSCOM estimated the stability of the compound at three months but assessed that once its purity fell under 50 percent, it would become relatively ineffective. "Inspection of Chemical Warfare."

57. U.N. Press Release on Muthanna Inspection, June 9–14, 1991 (New York, United Nations Headquarters, June 24, 1991).

58. Cited in Riegle Report, chap. 1 (pt. 1). For a skeptical view of Iraq's chemical "cocktail" weapons, see Cordesman and Wagner, *Lessons of Modern War*, 883.

59. Jonathan B. Tucker, "Lessons of Iraq's Biological Warfare Programme," *Arms Control*, December 1993, 240. Iraq was estimated to have acquired sufficient microbial media for 74 billion human-lethal doses of botulinum toxin ("Iraq Chemical Warfare Data," 970110_092596_UI_0001.txt [Washington, D.C.: DIA (?), n.d.] [Gulflink]). Following the Gulf War, the Iraqi program was described as a "multi-facility R&D and production system with redundancy and back-up facilities" ("(No Subject Line Found)," Filename:081bda.91p [Washington, D.C.: DIA, March 22, 1991] [Gulflink]; "Nuclear, Missile, Chemical and Biological Warfare Capabilities of Iraq before, during and after DESERT STORM," Filename:003bk.00d [Washington, D.C.: DIA, n.d.] [Gulflink]).

60. Report to U.N. Security Council, cited in "UN: Iraqi Biological Weapons and Ballistic Missile Development Programs Continue," *Near East Report*, December 4, 1995 (http://www.aipac.org/hot/MiddleEast/neriraq.html). After the war, reliable information reached U.S. intelligence that Iraq had stockpiled "extensive quantities" of *Clostridium botulinum* and *Baccilus anthracis* vaccines, "indicating a preparedness to protect its military from the effect of these diseases should the country engage in biological warfare" ("Intelligence Information Report Possible Biological Warfare Capability," 123096_04191200_91_001.txt [Washington, D.C.: DIA (?), April 18, 1991] [Gulflink]). Iraq continues to deny any such planning, but UNSCOM has stated that "military objectives, concepts of use and mechanisms for releasing the weapons would have been defined" (UNSCOM/TECH, 10).

61. Ekeus, interview in *Stern*, February 28, 1991, 31–34; Laurie Mylroie and James Ring Adams, "Saddam's Germs," *American Spectator*, November 1995, 60. On the Iraqi

BW testing program, see Counterproliferation Program Review Committee, "CPRC Report on Activity and Programs for Countering Proliferation," Annual Report to Congress (Washington, D.C.: Department of Defense, May 1996) (http://www.acq.osd.mil/cp/cprc96/ch2.htm); "Report Submitted by the Executive Chairman of the Commission Established by the Secretary General Pursuant to Para 9 (b)(i) of Security Council Resolution 687 (1991)," October 11, 1995, para 75 (s) + (t) (www.un.org./Depts/unscom/s95-864.htm). Hereafter UNSCOM 1995. On the supply by a German company of gas chambers to Iraq, which evidently used them for conducting static BW tests, see *Stern*, February 7, 1991, 31. Contrary to its previous declarations, Iraq, in its September 1997 "full, final and complete disclosure," denied that a field trial took place with six R-400 aerial bombs filled with botulinum toxin, anthrax simulant B, or aflatoxin (UNSCOM 1997, 20–21). Husayn al-Shahrestani, a pioneer of Iraq's atomic energy program who was jailed from December 1979 to 1991 for refusing to help convert the program to the production of nuclear weapons, has claimed that Iraq also carried out CBW tests on humans: "The idea of chemical and biological weapons tempted Saddam. I remember that when I was in prison they took prisoners so that they could experiment with these weapons on their bodies while they were alive.... Saddam tried his biological weapons on the Iraqi people [such as the Kurds?] and did not hesitate to use biological weapons against Iraqi prisoners" (interview in *al-Majallah* (London), FBIS (NES), February 1, 1996, 23). Al-Shahrestani's account seems to support Iranian accusations that Iraq had used Iranian POWs as guinea pigs in BW tests, but which could not be verified (see *Ha'aretz*, July 29, 1996). The U.S. government also stated that it was "possible that Kamil [Hassan] directed Iraq's testing of its chemical and biological weapons on Iranian prisoners of war" (U.S. Government White Paper, 2).

62. Ambassador Ekeus has stated: "[Regarding] bombs for biological [warfare] . . . there we are in disagreement; we feel that they have more sophisticated bombs than they have declared to us" (Address to the Washington Institute for Near East Policy, Washington, D.C., January 29, 1997 [http://www.cdiss.org/ekeus.txt], hereafter Ekeus, "Address"). Indeed, an Israeli newspaper has reported that the R-400 bombs were restrained by parachutes and were capable of spraying their payload while descending to target (*Ma'ariv* [Weekend Supplement], Tel Aviv, January 9, 1998, 43).

63. *New York Times*, August 23, 1995. Supposedly, the appeal aroused suspicions about Iraq's biological research activities.

64. Aerosolized particles of the optimal size (1–5 microns) enable deposition of infectious or toxic particles within alveoli, which provides a direct pathway to the systemic circulation. Moreover, infection by the respiratory route may induce disease at doses lower than those generally associated with naturally acquired infections by the oral route. The subsequent illness may differ from the natural pattern, and the incubation period may be much shorter. *Handbook on the Medical Aspects*, pt. 2, chap. 1, sec. 3 (http://www.nbc-med.org/amedp6/PART_II/chapter 1.htm); Franz, "Toxin Weapons."

65. Interview in *Libération*, August 29, 1995.

66. *Washington Post*, November 21, 1997.

67. UNSCOM 1997, 16.

68. Ibid.

69. Iraq's "full, final and complete disclosure" on its BW program, September 1997, cited in *Washington Post*, November 21, 1997.

70. UNSCOM 1997, 20.

71. Statement for the Record by Dr. Gordon C. Oehler, Director, Non-Proliferation Center of the CIA, *The Continuing Threat from Weapons of Mass Destruction*, Hearing, U.S. Senate, Armed Services Committee, March 27, 1996, http://www.odci.gov/cia/public affairs/speeches/archives/go toc 032796.html); ACDA, "Threat Control," 67; Zilinskas, "Iraq's Biological Weapons," 420. During the war, U.S. intelligence learned that the tanks would have taken approximately two minutes to empty and in this time would have sprayed a path approximately 20 miles long. "Iraqi Biological Weapon Delivery System," CIA 204025 (Arlington, Va.: CIA, January 1992) (Gulflink).

72. UNSCOM/TECH, 9. Emphasis added. UNSCOM is said to be searching for "a dozen special nozzles that Iraq fashioned in the 1980s to spray germs from helicopters and aircraft." *New York Times*, February 26, 1998.

73. In the dry form, more anthrax spores would be aerosolized in the optimal particle size, 1–5 microns, for weaponization ("Collateral Risk Due to Allied Air Strikes on Iraqi Biological Warfare [BW] Facilities," Filename:003pgv.00p [Washington, D.C.: DIA, n.d.] [Gulflink]). Because dry agents float in the atmosphere longer than liquids, anthrax spores in a dry form also represent a greater risk of wide dissemination than a liquid suspension of anthrax. The longer persistence in the atmosphere also means that powders, which are easily mixed with fillers, pose a considerably greater threat through inhalation. Combined, the use of dried agents increases the chances of exposure to a fatal dose. Also, they are better able to withstand the shear forces experienced when disseminated through nozzles with a relatively small orifice (see "Q&A's," Filename:0106pgv.91p [Washington, D.C.: DIA, January 31, 1991] [Gulflink]; "Iraqi Biological Warfare [BW] Developments," Filename:011045di.90 [Washington, D.C.: DIA, October 1990] [Gulflink]). Dried bacteria are more easily stored, while liquid agents lose their virulence relatively quickly. However, whereas liquid agents can be produced in simple facilities, freeze-dried agents must be manufactured in maximum biological containment facilities (known as BL4 and BL3 for the highest and next-highest containment levels). These have airlocks and other devices to prevent accidental contamination. Thus, the production of liquid agents is cheaper and much easier to conceal (Zachary Selden, "Assessing the Biological Weapons Threat" [Washington, D.C.: Business Executives for National Security, February 14, 1997], http://www.bens.org/pubs/bwc.html). It is debatable whether Iraq was able to produce dried agents and to "which degree they have succeeded in making the right size" of anthrax spores (Ekeus, "Address"). Anthrax can be disseminated by aerosol generators either as a freeze-dried powder or as a liquid suspension (see "Hypothetical Biological Warfare Attack with Anthrax," Filename:024pgv.00p (Washington, D.C.: DIA, n.d.) (Gulflink)]. Theoretically, botulinum toxin can be dispensed as either a freeze-dried powder, probably in combination with a filler, or as a liquid. However, Iraq's

experimentation with aerial spray tanks suggests an interest in wide-area contamination, for which aerosolized dried agents are best suited. The acquisition of several hundred modern Italian-made pesticide dispersal systems that were fitted with sprayer nozzles capable of generating aerosols of the optimal size for BW also indicates that the Iraqis had planned to use dried agents and were at least working on producing spores of the correct size. Indeed, U.S. intelligence reported the presence of a "dedicated spore drier at Taji for the 450 liter fermentor [which] strongly indicates that some of the [anthrax] spores were dried" ("Iraqi Chemical Warheads," Filename:035pgv.91d [Washington, D.C.: DIA, n.d.] [Gulflink]). Iraq has even admitted to having bought from the Danish Niro Atomizer Company two spray dryers, which it airlifted into the country in 1989. While confirming that one was installed at al-Hakam, Iraq said it was for a benign use. It further maintained that installation took place only in 1992. In 1997 UNSCOM located the other dryer at a warehouse in a northern Iraqi town, but it was disassembled and cleaned before inspectors could take any samples (*Washington Post*, November 21, 1997). Still, a onetime UNSCOM observer has reported that although Iraq possessed dryers and grinders that could have been used to produce dry anthrax, "all of its deployed biological warfare munitions were filled with wet anthrax. The Iraqis may have been unable to overcome either the technical difficulties or the safety problems inherent in dry anthrax production" (Zilinskas, "Iraq's Biological Weapons," 421). However, there are reasons to doubt the accuracy of this account. For example, although UNSCOM first visited al-Hakam in August 1991, the facility was allowed to continue operating until 1996. The plant went on to produce metric tons of the dry form of the biopesticide *Bacillus thuringiensis*. In December 1994 and June 1995, sampling and analysis of spray driers at the facility showed that the *B. thuringiensis* produced there was in a small particle size (less than 10 microns). This small size was inconsistent with biopesticide applications but well suited for aerosolized biological weapons. The fermentation process used at this facility also lent itself to rapid conversion from production of *B. thuringiensis* to *Bacillus anthracis*. As a result of this technical analysis and Kamil Hassan's revelations, UNSCOM razed the al-Hakam facility in the summer of 1996 (Robert P. Kadlec et al., "Biological Weapons Control: Prospects and Implications for the Future," *JAMA*, August 6, 1997, 352). Little wonder that Ekeus said his inspectors have concluded that Iraq "has the capability to dry . . . anthrax for use as a biological warfare agent" ("Ekeus: Important Work Ahead for U.N. Commission on Iraqi Weapons," U.S. Information Agency, May 2, 1997). In this respect, Iraq's claim that it cannot find the sprayers it had acquired and modified to disseminate BW aerosols must be viewed with grave concern.

74. "Iraqi BW Mission Planning," File:062596_cia_74624_74624 01.txt (Arlington, Va.: CIA, 1992).

75. "Possible Chemical/Biological Warfare," File:950719_22010067_92a.txt (Washington, D.C.: DIA, October 11, 1991). A blown-up vehicle to the left of the aircraft contained hoses and tubing and was possibly a "non-standard decon[tamination] vehicle for C/B munitions."

76. Immediately after capturing Kuwait, Saddam announced that his forces would

withdraw "as soon as the situation settles down and the evil grip is loosened on Arab Kuwait." On August 5, in the face of the growing international outcry, Iraq even staged a hastily arranged mock withdrawal in a bid to convince the world that the invasion was over (see Efraim Karsh and Inari Rautsi, *Saddam Hussein: A Political Biography* [New York: Free Press, 1991], 219–20). President Bush ordered the U.S. military to the Gulf on the evening of August 6, and the first American forces took off for Saudi Arabia on the morning of August 7, although official announcement of the deployment came only on August 8.

77. Robin Wright, *In the Name of God: The Khomeini Decade* (New York: Simon and Schuster, 1989), 182. Ironically, shortly before Iraq's CW had altered the course of the Iran-Iraq war, CIA analysts had stated: "We doubt that their [chemical weapons'] use will be a major factor in deciding the outcome of the war" ("Iran-Iraq: Chemical Warfare Continues—An Intelligence Assessment," [Arlington, Va.: CIA, November 1986] [Gulflink]; "Impact and Implications"). George Shultz, the U.S. secretary of state at the time, even recalled that "U.S intelligence analysts tried to reassure me [about persistent reports of Iraqi CW], asserting that the safety standards the Iraqis were employing were so bad that they would gas themselves before they got to gas anybody else" (George P. Shultz, *Turmoil and Triumph: My Years as Secretary of State* [New York: Charles Scribner's Sons, 1993], 241).

78. The central role played by its strategic weapons in overpowering Iran has had a profound effect on Iraq. The extent of the impact could be gleaned from Iraq's propaganda and contemporary statements of its political and military leaders. As a result, Iraq reasserted its claim for leadership of the Arab world (Amatzia Baram, *Culture, History and Ideology in the Formation of Ba'thist Iraq, 1968–89* [New York: St. Martin's Press, 1991], 109). On the impact of Iraq's CW on the Iranian war effort, see Wright, *In the Name of God*, 174–75 and 184–85. Wright reports that Iran's Islamic Revolution Guards were particularly ill equipped to defend against poison gas; many had beards that did not fit under gas masks.

79. Cited in Karsh and Rautsi, *Saddam Hussein*, 219.

80. *Time Magazine*, January 30, 1989, 45.

81. *Sunday Telegraph* (London), September 25, 1988; Iranian News Agency (hereafter IRNA), Tehran, FBIS (NES), September 26, 1988, 62; *Frankfurter Rundschau* (Frankfurt-am-Main), January 12, 1991.

82. Cited in *Time Magazine*, January 30, 1989, 45. For reports of Iraq's interest in typhoid for BW, see *New York Times*, January 18, 1989; *Washington Times*, January 19, 1989; Adel Darwish and Gregory Alexander, *Unholy Babylon: The Secret History of Saddam's War* (New York: St. Martin's Press, 1991), 110.

83. AFP, FBIS (WEU), January 30, 1991, 4. Heyndrickx maintained that the Iraqis also used cholera bacteria to target the Kurds, evidently implying that the Iraqis used biological weapons on other occasions as well. See also Riegle Report, chap. 1 (pt. 3).

84. Kathleen C. Bailey, *Doomsday Weapons in the Hands of Many: The Arms Control Challenge of the '90s* (Urbana: University of Illinois Press, 1991), 84.

85. For example, in a paper issued in October 1988, Senator John S. McCain III (R-

Ariz.) said that it "seems" Iraq has a research center for chemical and biological weapons at Salman Pak. He stated, "This center includes underground and heavily sheltered facilities and is known to work on nerve gas research. It is unclear whether it is to be the center of Iraq's biotoxin effort." Subsequently, in a speech on the Senate floor, the senator charged that the United States had sent Iraq tularemia bacteria, which was used in the 1960s to develop U.S. biological weapons. The bacteria produces an illness commonly known as rabbit fever, and McCain said that Iraq was employing it for similar military purposes (*Washington Post*, January 19, 1989; for other such reports, see *New York Times*, January 18, 1989, citing U.S. "government officials"; *Washington Times*, January 19, 1989, citing "a State Department official"). The senator's charge obviously was duly noted in Baghdad, as Iraq's ambassador to the United Nations, Abd al-Amir al-Anbari, promptly denied it (*Washington Post*, January 26, 1989). But, in a widely circulated report, Reuters quoted an unnamed Israeli official as saying: "We know they [the Iraqis] have developed a military biological capacity. They have completed the research and development phase for this type of warfare. They may have samples but have not started to manufacture actual biological weapons nor, more importantly, have they yet acquired any airborne weapons, such as sophisticated missiles, to deliver the bacteria they worked on" (cited in *Washington Times*, January 19, 1989; *Washington Post*, January 19, 1989). By contrast, *ABC World News Tonight*, on January 17, 1989, reported that "U.S. and Israeli intelligence sources" believe that Saddam Hussein could have referred to a "missile capable of carrying biological weapons to cities in Iran and Israel" when he spoke of Iraq's developing a "super weapon." For its part, the West German government confirmed that it had information indicating that "research activities" were being carried out in Iraq in the sphere of "bacteriological weapons." It said there were also "isolated indications" that production may have started (DPA, in FBIS [WEU], January 23, 1989, 11; see also *Der Spiegel*, January 30, 1989, 16–18, citing BND reports).

86. *Washington Post*, November 3, 1991.

87. In 1973, Yuri Andropov, then head of the KGB, secretly agreed to oversee the reorganization of Iraq's intelligence services along Soviet lines. Among other things, the deal involved the training of Iraqi personnel in Soviet intelligence schools and the sharing of intelligence on other nations. See Samir al-Khalil, *Republic of Fear: The Inside Story of Saddam's Iraq* (New York: Pantheon, 1990), 12–13; Christopher Andrew and Oleg Gordievsky, *KGB: The Inside Story* (New York: Harper Perennial, 1990), 549–52; Brian Freemantle, *KGB: Inside the World's Largest Intelligence Network* (New York: Holt, Reinhart and Winston, 1984), 12–13.

88. *Washington Post*, November 3, 1991, citing "two former U.S. intelligence officials." The newspaper reported that on one occasion Saddam had personally shown one Soviet "defense official" a U.S. satellite image and asked for help in concealing objects from the U.S. spy orbiters. "The Soviets responded with training in military deception tactics and communications security."

89. Rick Atkinson, *Crusade: The Untold Story of the Persian Gulf War* (Boston: Houghton Mifflin, 1993), 87–88.

90. The BW program, according to the Iraqis, was under the direction of two British-trained scientists: Gen. Amer Sa'adi, who obtained a master's degree in chemistry from Oxford University, and Rihab Rashid Taha al-Azawi, who received her doctorate in biology from the University of East Anglia in Norwich in 1984. Overall supervision was conducted by Hussein Kamil Hassan, as head of Iraq's Organization of Military Industrialization, and Ahmed Murthada, a British-trained engineer in charge of procurement (*Washington Post*, November 21, 1997; *Sunday Times* [London], February 19, 1995). Reportedly, al-Azawi, whose Ph.D. dissertation dealt with a toxin produced by a pathogen that affects the tobacco plant, was the director of the al-Hakam facility (*al-Sharq al-Awsat*, January 29, 1995). After the war, British authorities reportedly decided to monitor students from the Middle East who were studying biology or chemistry in British institutions. This decision was made after it had become apparent that Iraqi second- and third-degree students who attended British universities held important positions in Saddam's nuclear, biological, and chemical programs upon their return (*Independent*, March 16, 1993). UNSCOM allegedly even obtained a list of 150 scientists and technicians who worked in the BW area in Iraq. "All those who have doctorates in their area of specialization admitted to the UN team that they received their training at British universities" (*al-Sharq al-Awsat*, September 15, 1995). Ironically, one month before the invasion of Kuwait, the Foreign Office in London had issued a letter to British universities and biotechnology companies. It warned that Arab, especially Iraqi, spies were heading to the United Kingdom masked as students to "study the latest developments in the fields of bacteriology, virology and human engineering" (cited in *Yedi'ot Aharonot*, July 9, 1990). On the presence of Iraqi students at French technical institutions, including for the purpose of studying "microbe biochemistry," see *Le canard enchaîné* (Paris), February 20, 1991.

91. Atkinson, *Crusade*, 88.

92. "Critical Node Iraq BW Facility," Filename:003me.90d (Washington, D.C.: DIA, December 7, 1990) (Gulflink).

93. Cited in *Washington Post*, November 3, 1991. Gen. Leonard Peroots, director of the DIA until 1989, acknowledged that in 1990 too many American eyes and ears were still directed at the USSR and not enough at the Gulf. Cited in John K. Cooley, *Payback: America's Long War in the Middle East* (New York: Brassey's [US], 1991), 222. See also Record, *Hollow Victory*, 65.

CHAPTER 3: PREWAR STRATEGIC DETERRENCE

1. Ambassador Glaspie has said that the United States never expected that "the Iraqis were going to take all of Kuwait" (interview, *New York Times*, September 11, 1990). Her statement seemed to imply that if the Iraqi troops had seized only the border strip — rather than occupying all of Kuwait and ousting its government — then the Bush administration would not have reacted as forcefully as it did. For a similar report, see Judith Miller and Laurie Mylroie, *Saddam Hussein and the Crisis in the Gulf* (New York: Times Books, 1990), 21.

2. Haim Barkai, "The Persian Gulf War and the U.S. (Non) Energy Policy," *Middle*

East Focus, Summer–Fall 1992, 2. Barely a month after the invasion, Baghdad unveiled a detailed economic development plan for Iraq based on the exploitation of both Iraqi and Kuwaiti oil resources. See interview with Saʻdun Hammadi, Iraq's deputy prime minister, Baghdad Domestic Service, FBIS (NES), September 11, 1990, 33–35.

3. The hasty military preparations (see Michael R. Gordon and Gen. Bernard Trainor, *The Generals' War: The Inside Story of the Conflict in the Gulf* [Boston: Little, Brown, 1995], 185), and the offer to Iran, fly in the face of Saddam's claim that "we did anticipate the possibility of fighting with the U.S. armies during the 72 hours that followed [the invasion of] 2 August" (Iraqi News Agency [hereafter INA], FBIS [NES], January 14, 1991, 41). Tariq Aziz, the Iraqi foreign minister and later deputy prime minister, also claimed that Iraq foresaw the events that followed its attack on Kuwait (interview in *Milliyet*, Istanbul, FBIS [NES], June 4, 1991, 14). Nevertheless, there are reasons to doubt the veracity of these accounts. Saddam apparently hoped to counter widespread criticism in the Arab world, accusing him of mishandling the crisis, by alleging that he had accurately anticipated the events that followed the invasion. Privately, however, he admitted in a meeting with Soviet envoy Yevgeny Primakov that "on 15 August 15, [1990,] I gave up all the fruits of the eight-year war against Iran and returned to the previous situation" (Primakov's account, in *Pravda* [Moscow], March 2, 1991). Moreover, if the Iraqi claims about Saddam's perfect foresight are true, they would tend to put his decision-making abilities in an even worse light. If he guessed what would happen, why did he not decide to continue the attack into Saudi Arabia or to preempt the vulnerable coalition forces that arrived there in the first weeks after the invasion? Incidentally, Saddam's fateful mistake in halting the attack on the Saudi border resembles his blunder during the Iran-Iraq war. At that time, instead of allowing his forces to advance after the initial attack, he ordered them to halt as early as a week after the outbreak of hostilities. This decision not to follow up Iraq's military successes allowed Iran to regroup and counterattack, leading to a "reversal of the course of the war" (Efraim Karsh, "The Iran-Iraq War: A Military Analysis," *Adelphi Papers* 220 [London: International Institute for Strategic Studies, Spring 1987], 34–35).

4. See Saddam's "call" to the Arab masses and all Muslims, entitled "Save Mecca and the Tomb of the Prophet from Occupation," Baghdad Domestic Service, FBIS (NES), August 13, 1990, 45–47; "Open letter" to Egyptian President Husni Mubarak, Baghdad Domestic Service, FBIS (NES), August 24, 1990, 28 and 30. For a general discussion of Saddam's attempts to play the Islamic card, see James Piscatori, "Religion and Realpolitik: Islamic Responses to the Gulf War," in *Islamic Fundamentalisms and the Gulf Crisis*, ed. James Piscatori (Chicago: Fundamentalism Project, American Academy of Arts and Sciences, 1991), 3–11; John L. Esposito, *The Islamic Threat: Myth or Reality?* (New York: Oxford University Press, 1992), 103–4.

5. "Open letter," August 24, 1990, 26. On Saddam's early overtures of peace toward Washington, see also Efraim Karsh and Inari Rautsi, *Saddam Hussein: A Political Biography* (New York: Free Press, 1991), 220. In contrast, Saddam warned President Bush: "In all circumstances, whether you chose war or boycott, you will lose and be defeated. And we will achieve victory, with God's help." "Text of open letter," Baghdad Domestic

Service, FBIS (NES), August 22, 1990, 27. See also news conference with Austrian President Kurt Waldheim, Baghdad Domestic Radio, FBIS (NES), August 27, 1990, 29–30.

6. News conference with Austrian President Kurt Waldheim, 27.

7. This geostrategic imbalance was a thorn in Saddam's side from the outset. He told Ambassador Glaspie during their July 25 meeting: "We cannot come all the way to you in the United States, but individual Arabs may reach you" (transcript of meeting, *New York Times*, September 23, 1990). In Saddam's mind, terrorism was evidently a sort of geostrategic equalizer vis-à-vis the United States.

8. INA, FBIS (NES), August 30, 1990, 29.

9. *New York Times*, September 25, 1990.

10. Gen. Khaled bin Sultan (hereafter "bin Sultan"), *Desert Warrior: A Personal View of the Gulf War by the Joint Forces Commander* (New York: Harper Collins, 1995), 184. The piecemeal projection of U.S. forces into the region contributed to the problem. The scenario envisioned by Defense Department planners provided three weeks for the arrival of the initial heavy combat forces and eight weeks for five divisions to be in place with their equipment. But owing to insufficient sealift capabilities, after the first month only the marines and the army's lightly armed 82d Airborne Division had taken up positions. Fortunately for the United States, Saddam opted for a defensive posture aimed to deter war. See Andrew E. Gibson and Commander Jacob L. Shuford, USN, "Desert Shield and Strategic Sealift," *Naval Ware College Review*, Spring 1991, 6–19.

11. *Facts on File*, August 24, 1990, 613–14. By October, well over 600 foreigners were being held at strategic sites.

12. Cited in *Los Angeles Times*, October 5, 1990.

13. Baghdad Domestic Service, FBIS (NES), August 29, 1990, 24. Curiously, Saddam attempted to paint this countercity strategy as aimed at militarily significant targets. Such a concession to Western norms would not naturally belong in a policy of terrorist deterrence. In this case, Saddam could afford to create this impression because it did not detract from the message that Iraq would kill children, women, and civilian men if war erupted.

14. Samir al-Khalil, *Republic of Fear: The Inside Story of Saddam's Iraq* (New York: Pantheon, 1990), 274 and 276.

15. *Los Angeles Times*, September 14, 1990, quoting "U.S. and Arab officials." In contrast, after the war it was reported that "al-Husayn chemical warheads have never been flight tested. Three chemical warheads were tested using a hydrocarbon simulant (NFI)." "Statements on the Iraqi Chemical Warfare (CW) Program (U)" (Washington, D.C.: DIA, September 1991) (Gulflink). But see UNSCOM 1995, para 42.

16. On the discovery of the sites, see "Iraq-Kuwait Border Dispute," cia_93666_72540_07.txt (Arlington, Va.: CIA, September 1990) (Gulflink); "Summary of Iraqi CW Activity," cia_93671_72545_19.txt (Arlington, Va.: CIA, September 1990) (Gulflink); "Possible CW Munitions Storage," cia_93680_93680_01.txt (Arlington, Va.: CIA, December 1990) (Gulflink); *New York Times*, September 25, 1990.

17. *Wall Street Journal*, October 26, 1990.

18. Bin Sultan, *Desert Warrior*, 258–59. Apparently, Saddam gave no serious thought to preempting the coalition forces in Saudi Arabia because his first priority was to deter war. He was convinced that he could do so via terrorist deterrence: "It was an almost fatalistic approach, wholly dependent upon political calculations in Washington which he could influence only by making any war seem as terrible as possible." Lawrence Freedman and Efraim Karsh, *The Gulf Conflict, 1990–1991: Diplomacy and War in the New World Order* (Princeton: Princeton University Press, 1994), 276.

19. Bin Sultan, *Desert Warrior*, 311–12.

20. See Bruce W. Jentleson, *With Friends Like These: Reagan, Bush and Saddam, 1982–1990* (New York: Norton, 1994), 139–78. Even after the invasion there were voices in Washington that opposed taking a strong stand against Saddam. Secretary of State James Baker reportedly expressed reservations about the forceful tone of Bush's remarks, which committed the United States to reverse Iraq's conquest of Kuwait (*New York Times*, September 23, 1990). On Bush's early disinclination to confront Saddam militarily, see Margaret Thatcher, *The Downing Street Years* (New York: HarperCollins, 1993), 816–28; John Newhouse, "Misreadings," *New Yorker*, February 18, 1991, 72.

21. See transcript of meeting, *New York Times*, September 23, 1990.

22. One observer wrote that Saddam believed that Desert Shield, as the prewar U.S. deployment into Saudi Arabia was called, "was a gigantic bluff aimed at scaring him out of Kuwait." Jeffrey Record, *Hollow Victory: A Contrary View of the Gulf War* (New York: Brassey's [U.S.], 1993), 36–37 and 95.

23. Interview with CNN relayed by INA, Baghdad, FBIS (NES), December 11, 1990, 17.

24. For example, at a White House news conference, President Bush said: "We're dealing with a dangerous dictator all too willing to use force who has weapons of mass destruction and is seeking new ones." Later, in response to a reporter's question, the president said: "I am concerned — from the very first time I spoke on this subject — I think in August, I mentioned [Iraq's] weapons of mass destruction, I believe — certainly early on — and I am concerned about it" (transcript of press conference [Washington, D.C.: White House, Office of the Press Secretary, November 30, 1990], 1 and 5). General Khaled maintains (perhaps in contradiction to an earlier assertion made in his book) that the alarm expressed by various coalition officials about Saddam's military capabilities was part of a deliberate ruse. The idea was to "lull [Saddam] into a sense of false security" (Bin Sultan, *Desert Warrior*, 187). Either way, Saddam was apparently reassured by the anxieties that the Americans had openly expressed.

25. *Facts on File*, October 3, 1990, 738.

26. Ibid., December 7, 1990, 902.

27. For example, as early as August 1990, Tariq Aziz predicted that if war broke out, "it will be a bloody conflict and America will lose and be humiliated" (ibid., August 24, 1990, 614). On November 3, Saddam said: "We have plenty of breath for fighting, and we will eventually kick out the occupiers. What should we fear? The Americans will be defeated, no matter how many they are" (ibid., November 23, 1990, 865).

28. The shift in Saddam's thinking could be gleaned indirectly from the correspond-

ing changes in Iraq's military posture in Kuwait. As the U.S. force continued to build, especially with the arrival of heavy tanks beginning in late August, Iraq began to replace its offensive-oriented tank divisions in Kuwait with infantry units best suited for defense. Gen. Carl E. Vuono, USA, "Desert Storm and the Future of Conventional Forces," *Foreign Affairs*, Spring 1991, 66.

29. *Facts on File*, September 28, 1990, 719.

30. *New York Times*, September 26, 1990.

31. In their meeting in Baghdad on January 13, 1990, Saddam told U.N. Secretary-General Javier Pérez de Cuéllar: "The Iraqis are certain as if they had seen the results beforehand that they will defeat the aggressor." "Full Text" of minutes of the meeting, *al-Dustur* (Amman), February 9, 1991.

32. Saddam apparently saw the release of the hostages as a means to block Bush's war plans. He said that the hostages should be freed because of "a change in the American public opinion which will impose restrictions on the decisions and intentions of the evil ones, led by Bush, the enemy of God." INA, Baghdad, December 6, 1990.

33. Baghdad Domestic Service, FBIS (NES), August 29, 1990, 24; INA, FBIS (NES), August 30, 1990, 29. Before the coalition's air campaign began, the Iraqis relocated virtually all their biological agent production equipment to al-Hakam and other facilities. This move also implies that Saddam expected his biological weapons to be a high-priority target if war broke out.

34. Baghdad Domestic Service, FBIS (NES), April 17, 1990, 9.

35. For example, modeling done by the CIA to trace the effects of attacks on Iraq's CW munitions by coalition air forces has discovered that during much of the period in question winds rarely blew in a southerly direction. See Statement of George J. Tenet, Acting Director, CIA, before the Committee on Veterans' Affairs, Hearings on Persian Gulf War Illnesses, U.S. Senate, January 9, 1997 (http://www.senate.gov/~veterans/tenet.htm).

36. Interview in *al-Tadamun* (London), FBIS (NES), May 2, 1990, 14. The notion that Baghdad kept quiet about its BW preparations in order to achieve surprise assumes that the Iraqis estimated they would be incapable of defeating the vaccines if administered.

37. In an editorial written on the eve of the war, one of Baghdad's newspapers stated: "There will be no restrictions on the Iraqi fighter in terms of the type of weapons he uses or the way he uses them, whether these Iraqi weapons are known or unknown. In the mother of all battles there will be surprises that will please the faithful people and will break the backbone of the aggressors" (*al-Jumhuriyah* [Baghdad], January 14, 1991). Staff Maj. Gen. Bariq 'Abdallah, commander of Khadimah forces, also promised that "big surprises" were awaiting the forces of the "American-Zionist-Atlantic aggression" (INA, FBIS [NES], February 15, 1991, 23).

38. In contrast, it has been argued that Iraq resorted to CW in "desperation," and only after its efforts to warn Iran against launching further human-wave attacks had failed. Indeed, it is said, Iraq first used tear gas in the war in a bid to gauge the world's reaction. It was the lack of an international outcry that finally persuaded Saddam to

switch from a purely defensive application of CW to an offensive strategy (see Richard M. Price, *The Chemical Weapons Taboo* [Ithaca: Cornell University Press, 1997], 137–38). Price argues counterintuitively that Iraq's conduct reveals that the chemical taboo was not breached during the Iran-Iraq war. The same "normative constraint" may have also played a role in the non-use of chemical munitions during the Gulf War (see pp. 134–52). This argument, however, overplays the influence of a putative universal code of warfare and ignores the role of specific strategic and political considerations. The result runs counter to the Iraqi experience, for instance. Iraq's flagrant violations of *signed* international treaties (e.g., the 1968 Non-Proliferation Treaty and the 1972 Biological Weapons Convention) suggest at best a rather cavalier attitude toward an unwritten universal norm of conduct. Indeed, Taha Yasin Ramadan, while pledging to use "all types of weapons" in defending "our territories," specifically ruled out any Iraqi restraint for the sake of the "international community" (interview, *al-Musawwar* [Cairo], May 20, 1988). Saddam's favorite terrorist deterrence approach, which regards breaking Western-imposed taboos as an effective means of enhancing the regime's reputation as undeterrable, is also overlooked. Indeed, what is viewed as adherence to the chemical weapons taboo could be easily traced to Iraqi expediency. Its initial "restraint" regarding resort to CW could be explained as intended to facilitate Iraq's links to its Western arms supplier, and as a result of concern that the U.S. could shift its support to Iran in response (W. Andrew Terrill, Jr., "Chemical Weapons in the Gulf War," *Strategic Review*, Spring 1986, 54–55). Iraq's early resort to tear gas, then, was meant primarily to test what impact the introduction of gas warfare would have on the battlefield. (The initial success achieved with the use of a simple riot-control agent certainly encouraged Iraq to switch to lethal agents.) Further, Price's argument ignores the possible role that the 1981 Israeli preemptive attack on Iraq's nuclear reactor played in Saddam's initial hesitancy regarding CW (after all, numerous Iraqi representatives had charged that there was a "secret alliance" between Iran and Israel at the time). Price's thesis also disregards any technical or logistic hurdles that Iraq had to overcome, and which undoubtedly influenced the timing, scope, and orientation of its CW operations. In general, the vastness of Iraq's investment in mass destruction weapons does not lend itself to an argument about Iraq's abidance by the chemical taboo.

39. *Facts on File*, December 31, 1990, 959. The announcements were made despite fears that the news would cause panic among Saudi citizens. There was also concern over how the decision would be viewed by the other coalition members, who had no vaccines. The United States initially objected to the inoculations because, in percentage terms, the Americans had fewer doses available. Safety was also a factor. While the anthrax vaccine had been extensively used for years on civilian wool factory workers and on laboratory personnel, and its safety was well documented, the botulinum inoculations made the soldiers sick temporarily. (This vaccine, known as toxoid, is made from horse serum and protects against five of the botulism strains. However, it requires skin testing for horse serum sensitivity prior to administration and is painful when administered. Further, its manufacturing often results in a product that is highly impure.) However, the British commander, Gen. Peter de la Billière, strongly pressed for the

vaccinations. "I cannot see that we should possess it [vaccinations] and not use it. We should be entirely blameworthy if we didn't use it and Saddam delivered biological," he argued (Gen. Sir Peter de la Billière, *Storm Command: A Personal Account of the Gulf War* [London: HarperCollins, 1992], 102 and 138–39). In the end, only 8,000 U.S. soldiers received botulinum vaccinations, and 150,000 were inoculated against anthrax. Of those 150,000, however, only a portion received the second anthrax vaccination of the six that are needed in one year for full protection (Raymond A. Zilinskas, "Iraq's Biological Weapons: The Past as Future?" *JAMA*, August 6, 1997, 421; Rick Atkinson, *Crusade: The Untold Story of the Persian Gulf War* [Boston: Houghton Mifflin, 1993], 89–90; see also "Report of the Defense Science Board Task Force on Persian Gulf Health Effects" [Washington, D.C.: June 1994] [Gulflink]).

40. *ABC World News Tonight*, January 17, 1989; *New York Times*, January 18, 1989; *Washington Times*, January 19, 1989. Apparently as a result of the Israeli warning, Iraqi gunners became so nervous that they accidentally shot down an Egyptian fighter-bomber arriving for the April 1989 Baghdad air show (Barry Rubin, *Cauldron of Turmoil: America in the Middle East* [New York: Harcourt Brace Jovanovich, 1992], 151). There were also indications of new Iraqi civil defense preparations. On September 4, 1989, the Amman paper *al-Dustur* stated that Iraqi Interior Minister Samir Muhammad Abd al-Wahab met in Baghdad with Jordan's civil defense director, General Khalid al-Tarawinah. The two reportedly "discussed means of bolstering cooperation between the civil defense organs [in both countries]." Subsequently, discussions were also held between Iraq and the Soviet Union. According to the INA (October 24, 1989), Soviet Army General Vladimir Govorov, deputy defense minister for civil defense, and Imad Shabib, director general of civil defense in Iraq, met in Moscow to discuss the "relations of cooperations between the civil defense apparatuses in both countries and means of bolstering these relations."

41. On Iraq's prewar threats against Israel, see *Jerusalem Post*, August 9 and 14, 1990; Baghdad Domestic Service, FBIS (NES) September 24, 1990, 19; *Wall Street Journal*, September 27, 1990; *New York Times*, September 28 and October 10, 1990. In an interview with the Spanish television channel Teleconico, Saddam was quoted as saying that Tel Aviv, Israel's largest city, would be his first target if war broke out, even if Israel were not involved in an attack on the Iraqi forces in Kuwait (cited in Amman Domestic Service in English, FBIS [NES], December 24, 1990). In his letter to President Bush written on the eve of the war, Saddam pledged, "Israel, the daughter of the evil ones in America, will be under the hammer" (Baghdad Domestic Service, FBIS [NES], January 17, 1990, 19).

42. James A. Baker III, *The Politics of Diplomacy* (New York: J.P. Putnam's Sons, 1995), 268. Soon after Israel warned Iraq about its BW program, it became known that Jordan had granted Iraqi aircraft permission to conduct reconnaissance flights along the Jordanian-Israeli border (*Davar* [Tel Aviv], August 20, 1989; *Ha'aretz* [Tel Aviv], August 21, 1989; see also *Al Ha'mishmar* [Tel Aviv], August 8, 1990). According to the *Jerusalem Post International Edition*, September 15, 1990, the Iraqi planes were painted in Jordanian colors. Israel delivered a "strong protest" to Amman, via the United

States, and the Iraqi aerial spying missions ceased. A few months later, however, it became known that Jordan's King Hussein, yielding to intense pressure from Baghdad, had agreed to establish a joint Iraqi-Jordanian air squadron (see *Ha'aretz*, February 18, 1990; *al-Ra'i* [Amman], February 21, 1990; *al-Qabas* [Kuwait], February 21, 1990). The Israeli military saw the move mostly as the result of Iraq's interest in improving its aerial warning capability vis-à-vis Israel (*Ha'aretz*, February 20, 1990).

43. Baghdad Domestic Service, FBIS (NES), January 5, 1990, 18. Iraq's Ramadan explained: "Israel has been planning to hit Iraqi installations since 1986. One of the objectives of our announcement of the Al-Husayn missile was to deter Israel and prevent it from embarking on an adventure. . . . [But] Israel's aim is still to hamper Iraq's attempts to achieve technological progress. This is because its existence is based on technological superiority, not geographical or demographic superiority. Thus it understands what Iraq's progress means." Interview in *al-Tadamun*, FBIS (NES), May 2, 1990, 14.

44. Interview with Ramadan in *al-Ahali*, May 16, 1990; *Jordan Times* (Amman), May 17, 1990. In February 1990, during a visit to Baghdad, Ambassador Richard Murphy, former U.S. assistant secretary of state for Near Eastern and South Asian affairs, was told by his hosts that they had reliable information of an imminent Israeli attack on Iraq's strategic facilities. A similar message was delivered to the British chargé d'affaires in Baghdad in late March by Iraq's undersecretary of state for foreign affairs, Nizar Hamdoon (see Freedman and Karsh, *The Gulf Conflict*, 32). On April 12, Baghdad's *al-Thawrah* hailed Iraq's development of the binary chemical weapon as a "true historic development" meant to achieve the necessary balance of power and safeguard "the interests of the nation, and confront the American-Zionist scheme, "which is more serious than many people think."

45. Shlomo Aronson, *The Politics and Strategy of Nuclear Weapons in the Middle East* (Albany: State University of New York Press, 1992), 246. Saddam should also have been reassured through the efforts of the Saudi ambassador to the United States, Prince Bandar Bin Sultan, who heard of Saddam's concerns during a meeting in Baghdad on April 5, 1990. Having returned to Washington, Bandar conveyed Saddam's message to Bush, who, in turn, contacted the Israelis and obtained their assurance that they would not move against Iraq as long as Saddam did not attack Israel. "The United States then passed that Israeli assurance directly to Saddam." Bob Woodward, *The Commanders* (New York: Simon and Schuster, 1991), 204.

46. INA, FBIS (NES), April 19, 1990, 24. For Saddam's fixation over the threat of a new Israeli attack on Iraq's strategic facilities, see also Baghdad Domestic Service, FBIS (NES), June 19, 1990, 21; Speech to the General Federation of Iraqi Trade Unions, FBIS (NES), November 3, 1990, 15. Even if Saddam threatened to use CW against Israel because he was convinced that he needed to deter an imminent attack, the net result was that he started a dangerous vicious cycle. Israel's public alarm over the Iraqi threats was perceived by Saddam as an attempt by Jerusalem to prepare world opinion for its planned strike against Iraq. Saddam was therefore even more sure that an attack was coming. But his efforts to deploy his air force units forwardly in Jordan were

perceived by some in Israel not as steps to improve Iraq's early warning capability but as preparations for an attack on Israel's prime nuclear facility in Dimona in revenge for the 1981 destruction of Osiraq.

47. INA, FBIS (NES), April 23, 1990, 13.

48. Saddam himself declared that the attack on Osiraq had "taught not only the Iraqis, but all Arabs, that they must shelter their vital projects from all attack, so even an atomic bomb will not be able to knock them out" (cited in Kenneth R. Timmerman, *The Death Lobby: How the West Armed Iraq* [Boston: Houghton Mifflin, 1991], 104). Although it could be said that this lesson was one of the attack's down sides from the Israeli point of view (see Record, *Hollow Victory*, 66), it can be equally argued that forcing Iraq to expand vast resources on defensive preparations was a beneficial strategic outcome of the attack.

49. See Anthony H. Cordesman and Abraham R. Wagner, *The Lessons of Modern War*, vol. 4: *The Gulf War* (Boulder, Colo.: Westview, 1996), 912–13; Tim Ripley, "Iraq's Nuclear Weapons Program," *Jane's Intelligence Review*, December 1992, 554–58; David Albright and Mark Hibbs, "Iraq's Shop-Till-You-Drop Nuclear Program," *Bulletin of the Atomic Scientists*, April 1992, 27–37; *New York Times*, July 19 and October 3, 1991, and January 15 and February 13, 1992; *Washington Post*, October 13, 1991.

50. Moscow World Service in English, in Foreign Broadcast Information Service, Soviet Union, hereafter FBIS (SOV), October 25, 1990, 13–14; interview in *al-Hayat*, November 18, 1990; interview in *Literaturnaya gazeta* (Moscow), November 7, 1990; interview in *al-Sharq al-Awsat*, November 7, 1990. For similar expressions, see report on talks given by Soviet Deputy Foreign Minister V. F. Petrovskiy in Tunisia and Libya, TASS International Service, FBIS (SOV), November 19, 1990, 3–4; report on talks by Soviet Deputy Foreign Minister Aleksander Belonogov in Saudi Arabia, TASS in English, FBIS (NES), November 19, 1990, 5–6; and interview of Valentin Falin, chair of the Soviet news agency Novosti and one of Gorbachev's closest foreign policy advisers, in *Volkstimme* (Vienna), December 8–10, 1990.

51. For a report that the missiles were of the al-Husayn type, see "Al Husayn Ballistic Missile Tests," (Arlington, Va.: CIA, December 1990) (Gulflink). A senior IDF source who confirmed that the tests took place indicated that they were preparation for the deployment of the missiles in western Iraq, from where they could hit Israel (Israel Television Network, FBIS [NES], December 6, 1990, 29). Surprisingly, however, the DIA subsequently claimed that Iraq "did not conduct test firings of Scuds or other short or medium-range ballistic missiles during Operation Desert Shield" ("Questions from Chairman Riegle," Filename:oriegleq.894 [Washington, D.C.: DIA, August 1994] [Gulflink]).

52. *Los Angeles Times*, December 21, 1990.

53. *Facts on File*, December 31, 1990, 959.

54. INA, FBIS (NES), December 17, 1990, 16.

55. Saddam's interview with Turkish correspondents, Anatolia, INA, FBIS (NES), December 27, 1990, 27.

56. FBIS (NES), April 17, 1990, 9.

57. Ibid. The spate of reports at the time regarding Iraq's efforts to manufacture biological arms must have been welcomed in Baghdad, as they enhanced the ambiguity surrounding this option, and thus its deterrent potential (see, for instance, *Der Spiegel*, September 10, 1990, 112–18, and October 8, 1990, 148–52; also W. Seth Carus, "The Genie Unleashed: Iraq's Chemical and Biological Weapons Program," *Policy Papers*, no. 14 [Washington, D.C.: Washington Institute for Near East Policy, July 1989]). Saddam might have even thought that there was in fact no distinction between the open and covert BW postures because of the information that U.S. intelligence must have gathered about his biological weapons program. He had reason to believe that the information about Iraq's military might that the Soviets agreed to share with Washington, as part of the new relations between the superpowers, would also help his purposes. On Soviet military information provided to the United States regarding Iraq, see Marshal Sergei Akhromeyev, military adviser to President Gorbachev, letter to *Wall Street Journal*, April 11, 1991; *New York Times*, January 19, 1996.

58. See Avigdor Haselkorn, "Israel: From an Option to a Bomb-in-the-Basement?" in *Nuclear Proliferation: Phase 2*, ed. Robert M. Lawrence and Joel Larus (Lawrence: University of Kansas Press, 1974), 149–82. Unlike Israel, which can afford to deemphasize its strategic deterrent so long as it holds the conventional superiority over its Arab enemies, Saddam rarely had the conventional edge against the United States. Therefore, he tried to augment his deterrent posture by advertising Iraq's CW prowess.

59. Interview in *Le Figaro* (Paris), September 30, 1995.

60. Interview in *Sunday Times*, February 19, 1995.

61. al-Khalil, *Republic of Fear*, 286–87.

62. The general said: "Saddam personally asked the working committee of the General Staff to prepare a plan to hit Tehran [with chemical and biological weapons]" (interview, *60 Minutes*, CBS-TV, November 23, 1997). But earlier he apparently mentioned only chemical weapons as having been considered by the Iraqis for the strike on the Iranian capital (statement of the Iraqi National Congress [INC; an opposition group based in Iraqi Kurdistan], cited in AFP, FBIS [NES], January 25, 1995, 25). It appears that the general's public reference to Saddam's BW plans against Tehran came only in the wake of Hussein Kamil Hassan's defection and the subsequent revelations about the Iraqi biological weapons program.

63. Interview, *al-Musawwar*, May 20, 1988.

64. *Ha'aretz*, November 24, 1995. See also Peter Sullivan, "Iraq's Enduring Proliferation Threat," *Strategic Forum*, no. 95 (Washington, D.C.: Institute for National Strategic Studies, National Defense University, November 1996) (http://www.ndu.edu/ndu/inss/insshp.html).

65. Meeting with U.S. senators, FBIS, April 17, 1990, 7.

66. Saddam probably thought that his practice late in the Iran-Iraq war would lend credence to his statements. Initially, during that war, chemical use was tightly controlled by the political leadership in Baghdad. However, in January 1987 Saddam traveled to the front and gave permission to the 3d and 7th Army Corps commanders to resort to CW at their discretion, i.e., without prior presidential approval ("Authoriza-

tion for Use of CW" [Arlington, Va.: CIA, January 1987] [Gulflink]). The discretion of the ground force commander made it possible to respond quickly when the tactical situation favored the use of chemical weapons, and commanders took advantage of this authority. As a result, Iraqi CW became more effective ("Iraq: Potential for Chemical Weapons Use," Filename:71726882 [Washington, D.C.: DIA, February 1991] [Gulflink]). However, there is no comparison between the authorization for tactical use of CW against an Iranian force whose ability to retaliate in kind was rudimentary at best, and the launch of a strategic CB attack on Israeli cities. Not only could Israel retaliate with nuclear weapons, but unlike ground forces at the front, "a chemical-laden air force must be tightly controlled to ensure they never have the opportunity to bomb Saddam" ("Iraqi Chemical Threat Reassessment," Filename:0407pgf.91 [Washington, D.C.: DIA, February 17, 1991] [Gulflink]). In fact, throughout the Iran-Iraq war, the Iraqi air force apparently continued to be the subject of extraordinarily tight controls when it came to conducting CW missions (see "Desert Shield: Iraqi Command and Control Sequence for a Chemical Munitions Attack," [Washington, D.C.: DIA, December 1990] [Gulflink]).

CHAPTER 4: WARTIME STRATEGIC DETERRENCE

1. See, for example, interview of Tariq Aziz in *La repubblica*, FBIS (NES), December 31, 1990, 23.

2. For example, speech on Baghdad Domestic Service, FBIS (NES), September 6, 1990, 29; interview on German television, relayed by INA, FBIS (NES), December 24, 1990, 22.

3. Interview on CBS Television, relayed by Baghdad Domestic Service, FBIS (NES) August 31, 1990, 22.

4. INA, FBIS (NES), January 14, 1991, 43. Also, "Full Text," in *al-Dustur* (Amman), February 9, 1991. Saddam also said that the war with Iran proved that the "Arab nation" can fight using "all types of up-to-date, sophisticated weaponry." Baghdad Domestic Service, FBIS (NES), June 27, 1990, 24.

5. Letter to Bush, Baghdad Domestic Service, FBIS (NES), January 17, 1990, 17–19.

6. Interview on German television, relayed by INA, FBIS (NES), December 24, 1990, 22.

7. Baghdad Domestic Service, FBIS (NES), January 22, 1991, 36.

8. Rear Adm. Mike McConnell, director of intelligence for the U.S. Joint Chiefs of Staff, reporting the finding of such a written order in Kuwait. *Wall Street Journal*, February 27, 1991.

9. INA, FBIS (NES), January 14, 1991, 46.

10. *Facts on File*, December 12, 1990, 946.

11. Barry Rubin, *Cauldron of Turmoil: America in the Middle East* (New York: Harcourt Brace Jovanovich, 1992), 244.

12. In a key address to the Arab Cooperation Council, Saddam communicated his vision of Iraq's role as an emerging power to balance the United States now that the

Soviet Union had retrenched from its position of world leadership. Amman Television Service, FBIS (NES), February 27, 1990, 1–5.

13. Interview with CNN, relayed by Baghdad Domestic Service, FBIS (NES), January 31, 1991, 23.

14. Cited in *Time Magazine*, January 7, 1991, 17.

15. AFP, FBIS (NES), February 14, 1991, 9.

16. Interview in *Der Spiegel*, October 23, 1995, 162 and 164. See also Aziz in INA, FBIS (NES), August 20, 1990, 17.

17. Shlomo Aronson, *The Politics and Strategy of Nuclear Weapons in the Middle East* (Albany: State University of New York Press, 1992), 274.

18. Cited in Efraim Karsh and Inari Rautsi, *Saddam Hussein: A Political Biography* (New York: Free Press, 1991), 260.

19. Richard Haass (the president's special assistant for Near Eastern affairs), "The Gulf War," *Frontline*, PBS, KQED-San Francisco, January 9, 1996.

20. Baghdad Domestic Service, FBIS (NES), February 21, 1991, 24.

21. *New York Times*, February 24, 1991.

22. U.S. Defense Department study of Desert Storm, cited in *Jerusalem Post International Edition*, July 4, 1992.

23. Gen. H. Norman Schwarzkopf, *It Doesn't Take a Hero* (New York: Bantam Books, 1992), 445. A British signals officer was reported to have said: "We were tuned into the Iraqi command radio net. We heard them give the release order to their front-line troops to use chemical weapons against Rhino Force if it crossed the border." Cited in Riegle Report, chap. 1 (pt. 1).

24. *Sunday Times* (London), January 27 and February 3, 1991.

25. UNSCOM 1997, 14 (table). In addition, Iraq has claimed to have destroyed unilaterally another 29,000 CW munitions. In all, it claimed, more than 78,000 such munitions were either discarded unilaterally or destroyed by the coalition bombings. A total of eight different types of delivery systems for chemical weapons were destroyed by UNSCOM as well (U.S. Government White Paper, "Iraqi Weapons of Mass Destruction Programs," Washington, D.C., February 13, 1998, 6). Before the war Iraq was assessed to possess roughly 1,000 metric tons of chemical agent equally split between mustard gas and the nerve agents GB (sarin) and GF. Small amounts (tens of tons) of the persistent nerve agent VX were also assessed as "probably available." Most of the stock was assessed to "be weaponized" ("Responses to Rep. Kennedy's Questions of 22 February 1994," Filename:006me.94 [Washington, D.C.: DIA, March 2, 1994] [Gulflink]).

26. For example, during the 1967 Arab-Israeli war, Egyptian President Gamal Abd al-Nasser was told euphoric stories about Arab military victories. He was unaware of the calamity that had befallen the Egyptian Air Force in the early hours of the war. Even on the third day of the Six-Day War he continued to receive fabricated optimistic reports from the front line. Indeed, in a telephone conversation that morning Nasser encouraged King Hussein to launch his forces along the Jordanian front, advising him that the Egyptian forces were well along their way across the Israeli Negev and planned

to link up with the Jordanian forces pushing down from the Hebron Hills. See Chaim Herzog, *The Arab-Israeli Wars: War and Peace in the Middle East* (New York, Random House, 1982), 160.

27. See Efraim Karsh, *The Iran-Iraq War: A Military Analysis*, Adelphi Paper 220 (London: International Institute for Strategic Studies, 1987), 43.

28. Laurie Mylroie, "Saddam's Disappearing Lieutenants," *Wall Street Journal*, November 13, 1990.

29. Al-Khazraji, who belongs to the Bani Lam tribe in Babil, was a member of the Military Bureau of the Ba'ath Party. He was dismissed on August 3, 1990, one day after the invasion of Kuwait (*al-Majd* [Amman], March 25, 1996). At the time, numerous reports indicated that the general had been executed (see *Washington Post*, August 11, 1990; *al-Zahirah* [London], September 27, 1990; *al-Sharq al-Awsat*, February 3, 1991; Mylroie, "Saddam's Disappearing Lieutenants"). However, the Iraqi National Congress (a London-based opposition group) subsequently announced that al-Khazraji had defected via Kurdish-controlled northern Iraq (*New York Times*, March 22, 1996). On al-Khazraji's subsequent arrival in Jordan, see Jordanian Prime Minister Abd-al-Karim al-Kabariti, in *al-Ray* (Amman), March 24, 1996; and al-Khazraji's interview in *Jordan Times*, April 4–5, 1996.

30. Although it is unclear to what extent Saddam had an accurate view of the fighting, official Iraqi accounts of glowing battlefield successes were commonplace (*Financial Times*, January 31, 1991; Karsh and Rautsi, *Saddam Hussein*, 245–46). On executions of top Iraqi commanders during the Gulf War, see Moscow Domestic Service, FBIS (SOV), January 25, 1991, 13; General al-Samarra'i in "The Gulf War," *Frontline*, PBS, KQED-San Francisco, January 10, 1995.

31. Notwithstanding, some U.S. lawmakers were told by DOD officials that Iraqi division commanders were given relatively small amounts of chemical munitions and had the authority to use them in battle (*Wall Street Journal*, March 1, 1991).

32. For the various operational problems supposedly encountered by the Iraqis with regard to the battlefield use of chemical munitions, see Norman Friedman, *Desert Victory: The War for Kuwait* (Annapolis, Md.: Naval Institute Press, 1991), 351–52; T. W. Danielson, "Chemical Warfare and Desert Storm," *Command*, November–December 1991, 52–53; *New York Times*, March 4, 1991; *Washington Post*, March 7, 1991.

33. Gen. Khaled Bin Sultan, *Desert Warrior: A Personal View of the Gulf War by the Joint Forces Commander* (New York: HarperCollins, 1995), 404.

34. Interview, *Le figaro*, March 2–3, 1991. For a critique of some of the theories of why Iraq did not resort to CBW, see Leonard A. Cole, *The Eleventh Plague: The Politics of Biological and Chemical Warfare* (New York: W. H. Freeman, 1997), 126–27.

35. *Wall Street Journal*, March 1, 1991. See also *New York Times*, March 4, 1991; *Washington Post*, March 7, 1991. However, a large chemical weapons storage site was located in Kamisiyah, 20 kilometers southeast of the town of An Nasiriyah, inside Iraqi territory (*New York Times*, August 22 and September 20, 1996). The deployment indicates that Saddam viewed mass destruction weapons as a strategic reserve designed to defend Iraq itself.

36. Bin Sultan, *Desert Warrior*, 394.

37. Michael R. Gordon and Gen. Bernard Trainor, *The Generals' War: The Inside Story of the Conflict in the Gulf* (Boston: Little, Brown, 1995), 444–45. Only after the war did the U.S. Marines learn that American intelligence reports about the deployment of chemical weapons in Kuwait "had been wrong." Ibid., 367–68.

38. "Iraq's Chemical and Biological Warfare Capability: Surviving Assets and Non-Use During the War," Filename:0902pgv.91 (Washington, D.C.: DIA, March 15, 1991) (Gulflink); "Questions from Chairman Riegle," Filename:oriegleq.894 (Washington, D.C.: DIA, August 1994) (Gulflink). See also "Persian Gulf War Health Effects," Report of the Defense Science Board Task Force (Washington, D.C.: June 1994) (Gulflink).

39. Such concerns about unauthorized use of mass destruction weapons would tend to refute Saddam's April 1990 claim that he preapproved the firing of chemically tipped missiles against Israel whenever his base commanders suspected a nuclear attack and could not communicate with Baghdad. It confirms that the declaration was an exercise in terrorist deterrence.

40. James A. Baker III, *The Politics of Diplomacy* (New York: J. P. Putnam's Sons, 1995), 360.

41. CNN, cited in "AFMIC Weekly Wire 02–91(u)," File 970613_mn02_91_0_txt_0001.txt (Washington, D.C.: DIA [?], 1991).

42. See INA, FBIS (NES), April 15, 1991, 26. Iraq also says that it transferred 33 "civilian" cargo and passenger airplanes to Iran during the war. Among the "civilian" craft are 15 Ilyushin-76s, of which several versions have been deployed by the Soviet Union. The Iraqis reportedly loaded Il-76s with pallets laden with hundreds of mustard gas canisters. In early 1984, one Iraqi Il-76 aviator boasted to a foreign adviser that in one flight alone he had dropped 30 tons of mustard gas north of Basra (cited in *Newsweek*, March 19, 1984, 39–40).

43. *Le monde*, September 24, 1992. See also *New York Times*, November 12, 1991.

44. John Gee, cited in Associated Press, Canberra, September 12, 1991; Rolf Ekeus in *New York Times*, July 31, 1991.

45. *Le monde*, September 24, 1992.

46. The letter was written on January 5 and delivered by Secretary Baker to Tariq Aziz during their meeting in Geneva on January 9. After reading it, Aziz formally rejected the letter, but the American press promptly published it.

47. Interview in *Libération*, August 29, 1995.

48. Interview in *Der Spiegel*, in FBIS (NES), October 24, 1995, 32. Note that Aziz continued to claim that Iraq's base commanders were preauthorized to use CB weapons under certain circumstances.

49. Interview in "The Gulf War," *Frontline*, PBS, KQED-San Francisco, January 10, 1996.

50. Schwarzkopf, *It Doesn't Take a Hero*, 389–90.

51. Gen. Colin Powell, *My American Journey* (New York: Random House, 1995), 504.

52. Ibid.

53. Baker, *The Politics of Diplomacy*, 359. Baker could be referring to his use of such terms as the "absolute technological superiority" of the coalition forces and their "smashing destructive powers." His version of the meeting largely corresponds with the Iraqi transcript published in four parts one year after the Geneva meeting (see *Baghdad Observer*, January 9–12, 1992). On the various positions within the Bush administration regarding the proper U.S. response to an Iraqi use of CB weapons, see Rick Atkinson, *Crusade: The Untold Story of the Persian Gulf War* (Boston: Houghton Mifflin, 1993), 86–87.

54. *Washington Post*, January 7, 1991.

55. McGeorge Bundy, "Nuclear Weapons and the Gulf," *Foreign Affairs*, Fall 1991, 85–87. On the controversy within the U.S. political establishment regarding retaliation with unconventional weapons, see also *Christian Science Monitor*, February 13, 1991.

56. Editorial in *Khadashot* (Tel Aviv), FBIS (NES), February 6, 1991, 29. Cheney's remarks are discussed in more detail later in this chapter.

57. Interview in *Sunday Times*, February 19, 1995.

58. Cited in *Washington Post*, March 7, 1984.

59. For the text of the letter, see Gordon and Trainor, *The Generals' War*, 493–94 n. 17.

60. See, for example, FBIS (NES), January 2, 1991, 45.

61. On Saddam's early quest for nuclear weapons, see Steve Weissman and Hebert Korsny, *The Islamic Bomb: The Nuclear Threat to Israel and the Middle East* (New York: Times Books, 1981), 27–28, 105–6, and 249–55.

62. On the use of Thai workers for Iraq's tunneling work, see Matichon (Bangkok), FBIS (NES), January 28, 1991, 35–36; and AFP, FBIS (NES), January 28, 1991, 36. During the war, Israel reportedly suggested that air strikes be launched against Iraqi phosphate mines at Al Qaim, describing them as possible hideouts for mobile Scud launchers. Gordon and Trainor, *The Generals' War*, 236.

63. The Moscow paper *Izvestiia* asked, on February 2, 1991: "How was it possible for the Iraqi military to visit NATO bases and Belgian military bases? Who gave permission not only for the inspections, but also for the demonstration of their capabilities?"

64. Press Association, FBIS (WEU), January 22, 1991, 15.

65. Kenneth R. Timmerman, *The Death Lobby: How the West Armed Iraq* (Boston: Houghton Mifflin, 1991), 118.

66. *Het Volk* (Ghent), FBIS (WEU), October 31, 1990, 34–35; *De standaard* (Groot-Bijgaarden), FBIS (WEU), January 24, 1991, 1–2; Brussels Domestic Service, FBIS (WEU), January 24, 1991, 2; *Le soir* (Brussels), January 25, 1991; *La libre belgique* (Brussels), January 25, 1991.

67. AFP, FBIS (WEU), February 8, 1991, 41. The project also involved other West European companies. Vault doors came from Italy, special trenches from France, and electronic equipment was of German and British origin. Other equipment came from Sweden.

68. Timmerman, *The Death Lobby*, 120. Nothing short of a nuclear explosion can create an electromagnetic pulse — a powerful radio wave that renders most conventional military electronics and communication systems useless.

69. Press Association, FBIS (WEU), January 22, 1991, 15.

70. Timmerman, *The Death Lobby*, 116.

71. Ibid., 118.

72. Amman Domestic Service, FBIS (NES), December 12, 1990, 33.

73. *Al-Iraq* (Baghdad), December 31, 1990.

74. INA, FBIS (NES), January 14, 1991, 42.

75. On the link between Iraq's posture of external combativeness and the domestic stability of the Saddam regime, see Rubin, *Cauldron of Turmoil*, 221; Judith Miller and Laurie Mylroie, *Saddam Hussein and the Crisis in the Gulf* (New York: Times Books, 1990), 54.

76. Transcript of meeting, *New York Times*, September 23, 1990.

77. Interview, *Le Figaro*, FBIS (NES), September 5, 1990, 29.

78. *Al-Akhbar* (Cairo), January 24, 1991. Indeed, fear of Iraqi-sponsored CB terrorism across Europe was expressed almost as soon as the Kuwait crisis flared up (see, for example, *Le point* [Paris], September 10, 1990). Saddam could have counted on the Soviets to echo these threats and whip up public anxiety. For instance, some Soviet papers reprinted the stories. One even reported the existence of an Iraqi "Plan Z," to "coordinate Iraqi agents' subversive and terrorist actions against those states" participating in the U.S.-led coalition (*Komsomolskaya pravda* [Moscow], in FBIS (SOV), January 25, 1991, 16). The Soviets, of course, could have planted these stories in the Arab press originally.

79. *Frankfurter Rundschau*, January 12, 1991. Another newspaper reported that German security authorities had detected signs of attempts to implement the Iraqi threats. It quoted security sources as indicating that Saddam's threats to spread the conflict to the United States and its allies through terror attacks was being taken "very seriously" (*Frankfurter Allgemeine Zeitung*, January 12, 1991). Around the same time, a former official of the East German secret police Stasi claimed that the GDR had helped train Iraqis in the use of CB weapons and terrorist tactics (*Independent*, January 30, 1991).

80. Interview, *Minneapolis Star Tribune*, February 7, 1989.

81. "Iraq BW Program" (Arlington, Va.: CIA, circa August 8, 1990) (Gulflink). See also "Iraqi CW and BW" (Arlington, Va.: CIA, August 1990) (Gulflink). For reports of Iraqi BW terrorism directed against Desert Shield forces before the war, see "Defense Intelligence Terrorism Summary (U)," file 970613_dtsm232_90_txt_0001.txt, and file 9706136291290_dec_txt_0001.txt (Washington, D.C.: DIA, December 1 and December 29, 1990) (Gulflink).

82. "Iraqi CW and BW" (Arlington, Va.: CIA, September 1990) (Gulflink).

83. "Iraqi Use of Biological Weapons," Filename:0161pgv.90d (Washington, D.C.: DIA, December 3, 1990) (Gulflink); "Iraqi Biological Warfare (BW) Agents and Their Effects," Filename:0pgv083.90p (Washington, D.C.: DIA, n.d.) (Gulflink). "Even if Botulinum toxin was suspected as being used, its rapid degradation upon exposure to the

elements would ensure that no traces of it were left within several hours of the attack." "Iraq's Biological Warfare Program" (Arlington, Va.: CIA, August 1990) (Gulflink).

84. "Iraq Interagency Biological Warfare Working Group (IIBWWG)," File 970613_505wp_ood_txt_0001.txt (Washington, D.C.: DIA [?], n.d.) (Gulflink). It was pointed out that the probability of success of such attacks "increases the closer the agent release occurs to the target."

85. "Iraqi BW Capability" (Arlington, Va.: CIA, n.d.) (Gulflink). In an interview in *Jane's Defence Weekly*, on August 13, 1997, U.S. Secretary of Defense William Cohen disclosed that during the war, there were serious concerns in the United States that the ventilation systems of buildings might be attacked by terrorists using BW agents.

86. Jeffrey D. Simon, *The Terrorist Trap: America's Experience with Terrorism* (Bloomington: Indiana University Press, 1994), 254.

87. Maureen Dowd, "Storm's Eye: Bush Decides to Go to War," *New York Times*, January 17, 1991, cited in Cole, *The Eleventh Plague*, 80. Cole remarks, "Why Bush, 7000 miles from the battlefield, was deemed vulnerable to chemical or biological attack is not discussed in the article."

88. For example, General al-Samarra'i reported that members of Saddam's inner circle talked about using agents to carry out a biological terrorist attack on the United States, but, he said, it "was not a high priority" and he knew of "no serious plans to do so." Interview on CBS-TV, *60 Minutes*, November 23, 1997.

89. On Saddam's personal bunker system, see *Washington Post*, January 23, 1991; Rome RAI Uno Television Network, FBIS (NES), January 24, 1991, 29; *Newsweek*, February 4, 1991, 40–41; Timmerman, *The Death Lobby*, 116–17.

90. Interview, *Sunday Times*, February 19, 1995. Saddam apparently sought to deceive the coalition as to his whereabouts. Daniel Ortega, the former president of Nicaragua, reported that he had to travel about an hour from Baghdad and go into an "immense underground structure, an atomic-bombproof and air-bombproof shelter where Saddam [Hussein] lives with his closest staff" (Caracas Venezolana de Televisión Canal 8, FBIS (NES), January 14, 1991, 52). Even if the report were accurate, it would be simply unreasonable to assume that some hours before the fighting Saddam would have hosted foreign guests in the very location where he intended to linger during the war. A later report indicated that "eventually spies confirmed that Saddam slept in private houses, changing location every night" ("The Gulf War," *Frontline*, PBS, KQED-San Francisco, January 9, 1996).

91. Baker, *The Politics of Diplomacy*, 360.

92. Gordon and Trainor, *The Generals' War*, 197. In this regard, the Iraqis probably reflected Secretary of State Baker's message. Although in his letter President Bush avoided any reference to the toppling of the Iraqi regime, Baker threatened such consequences both implicitly and explicitly during his Geneva meeting with Aziz. Baker, *The Politics of Diplomacy*, 358–59.

93. Gen. Charles A. Horner, USAF (Ret.), "New-Era Warfare," in *Battlefield of the Future*, ed. Barry R. Schneider and Lawrence E. Grinter (Maxwell Air Force Base, Ala.: Air University Press, September 1994) (http://www.cdsar.af.mil/battle/chp2.html).

94. Both generals are cited in Riegle Report, chap. 1 (pt. 1).

95. Baker, *The Politics of Diplomacy*, 360.

96. Interview in *Le vif/L'express*, FBIS (NES), February 13, 1996, 26.

97. *Ha'aretz*, November 24, 1995.

98. FBIS (NES), January 22, 1991, 45.

99. AFP, in: FBIS (NES), January 17, 1991, 33.

100. Interview in "The Gulf War," *Frontline*, PBS, KQED-San Francisco, January 9, 1996. Al-Samarra'i's account tallies in part with other information. Reportedly, in preparation for the war seven Scud missiles were indeed deployed to western Iraq capable of launching a CW attack on Israel on short notice. "Memorandum for: Chief, GWI [Gulf War Illnesses] Task Force," file cia_68357_68357_01.txt (Arlington, Va.: CIA, February 21, 1996) (Gulflink).

101. Interview on Israel Television Network, August 22, 1990, cited in Aronson, *The Politics and Strategy of Nuclear Weapons*, 248. Moshe Arens, Israel's defense minister, also referred obliquely to Israel's "deterrent element," which he said "carries a very heavy weight," in explaining the low probability of an Iraqi attack on Israel (interview with Jerusalem Domestic Service, FBIS [NES], August 27, 1990, 39; for similar Israeli warnings, see Lt. Gen. Dan Shomron [the IDF's chief of staff], interview on Israel Television Network, FBIS [NES], January 14, 1991, 68). A veteran observer wrote: "The common belief that Israel has atomic weapons certainly played a prominent role in dissuading the Arab military from mounting a massive attack on its population centers. That is why Israelis were so astonished when the first Iraqi missiles landed on Haifa and Tel Aviv" (Ze'ev Schiff, "Israel after the War," *Foreign Affairs*, Spring 1991, 30–31).

102. Speech to International Confederation of Arab Trade Unions, INA, FBIS (NES), April 19, 1990, 24. Tariq Aziz expressly used the term "unprecedented parity" (*mu'adalah fi al-tawazun*) with the Israeli enemy to describe the situation in the wake of Saddam's announcement that Iraq possessed binary chemical weapons. INA, FBIS (NES), May 4, 1990, 16.

103. See, for example, *Sawt al-Sha'b* (Amman), February 26, 1991. Iraq claimed that it fired four Scuds at Israel on February 16, with three of them aimed at Dimona. *Jerusalem Post*, February 18, 1991.

104. See also Aronson, *The Politics and Strategy of Nuclear Weapons*, 275–76.

105. It has been claimed that during Tariq Aziz's talks in Moscow, on February 21–22, 1991, he was shown satellite pictures indicating how precarious the Iraqi military position had become in the wake of General Schwarzkopf's "Hail Mary" maneuver. David Eshel, "Desert Storm: A Textbook Victory," *Military Technology*, April 30, 1991, 30.

106. *Jerusalem Post International Edition*, March 9, 1991.

107. Interview, *Davar* (Rosh Hashana Supplement), September 24, 1995, 6. In a briefing paper prepared by Raytheon, the manufacturer of the Patriot Tactical Missile Defense System, the same event is described as follows: "One concrete warhead (not classified as dud) occurred at the end of war and landed, unengaged, outside Patriot defended area. This is the *only* evidence of a concrete warhead." "Technical Issues of

Desert Storm and TMD: Patriot PAC-2 and Beyond" (Andover, Mass.: Raytheon, May 1993) (unclassified).

108. Author's telephone interview with a senior Israeli intelligence officer, April 22, 1996.

109. Indeed, both missiles might have been aimed there. The "NBC Desk Log" for February 25, 1991, indicates for 0628 hours "Scud alert W. Iraq, launch AAR [area at risk] Israel. This was the second attempt to hit the nuclear facility at Dimona [today]" ("No Subject Found," 10096_nbc_028.txt [?DIA] [Gulflink]; time differences with the aforementioned Israeli report are due to the different time zones and the time elapsed between launch and impact of the missile). Arens provides a similar account: "Both [Scuds] were aimed against the nuclear reactor in Dimona, but fell far from their target, somewhere in the Negev, without causing any damage" (Moshe Arens, *Milkhama veshalom bamizrakh hatikhon, 1988–92* [Broken covenant] [Tel Aviv: Yedi'ot Aharonot, 1995], 229).

110. For the letter, see Ma'ariv, in FBIS (NES), February 5, 1991, 30.

111. *Yedi'ot aharonot* (First Anniversary Supplement), January 10, 1992, 11.

112. Interview in "The Gulf War," *Frontline*, PBS, KQED-San Francisco, January 10, 1996.

113. The first Patriot batteries arrived in Israel on January 19, 1991, amid much publicity. Eventually six such batteries were deployed across western Israel, comprising both PAC-1 and the more advanced PAC-2 versions of the missile.

114. For example, in a statement issued after a joint session by the Iraqi Revolutionary Command Council (RCC) and the Regional Command of the Arab Socialist Ba'ath Party, chaired by Saddam, Baghdad pledged that as punishment for the "large-scale criminal action" undertaken against Iraq, "the oil, its areas, and Israel will be transformed into something different than they are now" (Baghdad Domestic Service, FBIS [NES], September 24, 1990, 19). In response to President Bush's offer for talks in late November 1990, Saddam again tied the two: "If oil is the most important thing for you, Jerusalem is the most important thing for us" (cited in Karsh and Rautsi, *Saddam Hussein*, 268).

115. *Facts on File*, February 28, 1991, 136.

116. Lawrence Freedman and Efraim Karsh, *The Gulf Conflict, 1990–1991: Diplomacy and War in the New World Order* (Princeton: Princeton University Press, 1994), 380–85.

117. This interpretation conflicts with the notion that the Iraqi move was aimed to goad the coalition into accelerating the ground war. See Directorate of Intelligence, "Iraq and the Gulf War, 1990–91" (Arlington, Va.: CIA, n.d.) (Gulflink).

118. As described in a CIA document: "The objective of attacking cities would be to cause casualties and panic among civilians. Under optimum circumstances, a nerve agent warhead could cause many hundreds and possibly even thousands of immediate casualties, including a large number of nearly immediate fatalities. The fatality count from a biological weapon would be much higher, although the full effects would not be felt for some days. The lack of accuracy of Iraq's Scuds would not reduce their psycho-

logical impact, since no one in the target community would feel safe." "Iraq's Potential for Chemical and Biological Warfare" (Arlington, Va.: CIA, September 1990) (Gulflink).

119. For the constraints on tactical BW, see James F. Dunnigan and Austin Bay, *From Shield to Storm: High-Tech Weapons, Military Strategy, and Coalition Warfare in the Persian Gulf* (New York: William Morrow, 1992), 353–54; Kathleen C. Bailey, *Doomsday Weapons in the Hands of Many: The Arms Control Challenge of the '90s* (Urbana: University of Illinois Press, 1991), 87–88; *Economist* (London), April 12, 1997, 79. It can be argued, however, that by opting for a strategic threat, Saddam jeopardized his deterrent message. Thus, a tactical BW threat to U.S. troops could have been perceived as credible given that a U.S. resort to unconventional munitions in response would have been blunted by Iraq's continued CBW threat to Israel and by its threat to carry out CB terrorism against the United States proper. By contrast, a strategic BW threat against Israel could have been suicidal, and thus less credible. The inherent risk of adhering to terrorist deterrence, a doctrine that equates maximum deterrence with maximalist threats, is thus amply demonstrated.

120. "Baghdad might be hesitant to contaminate any parts of Saudi Arabia with biological agents for fear that Muslims around the world might view such an act as desecration of their holy land." "Iraq's BW Program" (Arlington, Va.: CIA, December 1990) (Gulflink).

121. Cited in John K. Cooley, *Payback: America's Long War in the Middle East* (New York: Brassey's [U.S.], 1991), 217. On U.S. satellites as a warning system for Israel, see Craig Covault, "USAF Missile Warning Satellites Providing 90-Sec. Scud Attack Alert," *Aviation Week and Space Technology*, January 21, 1991, 60–61, and January 28, 1991, 24.

122. The link was inaugurated on January 7, 1991. Hammer Rick was located inside a structure of the Israeli Ministry of Defense and was staffed by a small team of American technicians and Israeli Air Force officers. Although it was set up in great secrecy, its existence became public knowledge during the war. See Arens, *Milkhama veshalom*, 183; Baker, *The Politics of Diplomacy*, 388–89; Atkinson, *Crusade*, 81; U.S. News and World Report, *Triumph Without Victory: The Unreported History of the Gulf War* (New York: Random House, 1992), 245. The fact that Arens, rather than Prime Minister Shamir, had control over the link provided Arens with the means to offer, via the U.S. secretary of defense, his own input. Assessments and messages that Shamir might have disagreed with were thus forwarded to Washington and must have played a role in Bush's decision.

123. Interview in *Le Figaro*, April 4, 1991.

124. Interview in *Yedi'ot aharonot* (First Anniversary Supplement), January 10, 1992, 2. Indirectly, this disclosure confirms that Israel did not think it was time to stop the war.

125. Interview in *Khadashot*, FBIS (NES), April 15, 1991, 39. Earlier in the war Israeli sources said that any IDF intervention had to meet three requirements: it had to be coordinated with the United States, it had to be effective in striking at Iraqi missile

batteries or inflict sufficient damage on Iraq to deter their use, and it had to avoid undermining the anti-Iraq coalition (*Christian Science Monitor*, January 24, 1991). Thus Arens revealed that he supported an intervention only in the last two weeks of the war: "We realized that such an action may lead to a war with Jordan, and could have undermined Mr. Bush's coalition. This would have transformed the character of the Gulf War. That is why I opposed an intervention at the beginning of the war, and supported it toward its end, when it was apparent, to Jordan as well, that the Americans were winning, that Saddam had already been defeated. There was a high probability that under such circumstances, the Jordanians would not interfere with us" (interview, *Yedi'ot aharonot*, July 17, 1992; see also an interview on Tel Aviv Educational Television Network, FBIS [NES], March 1, 1991, 28; interview in *Bamakhane* [Tel Aviv], FBIS [NES], December 4, 1991, 24). Assuming that Arens's account is true, it implies he was ready to violate Israel's secret agreement with Jordan in order to blunt the growing Iraqi CB missile threat. The deal reached in London on January 5, 1991, in talks between King Hussein and Prime Minister Shamir had stipulated that Israel would not violate Jordan's air space. In return, the king had pledged to bar use of Jordanian air space by Iraqi planes and to deny entry to Iraqi ground forces. (On the Jordanian-Israeli agreement see Moshe Zak, "Secret King Hussein–Shamir Gulf Pact Revealed," *Jerusalem Post Service*, September 29, 1995.) Given the increased likelihood of an Iraqi CB missile attack, however, at least some in the Israeli leadership were evidently reconsidering that commitment. They concluded that a Jordanian military action was unlikely. But even if Amman responded to an Israeli violation of the agreement by rescinding its own commitment and granting the Iraqis air or ground access, the action would be of little practical value given the state of the Iraqi military. Nevertheless, Shamir remained opposed to the idea virtually to the end, arguing that it would result in an Israeli-Jordanian clash that could·harm the U.S. war effort. Such an outcome would endanger Israeli interests and the relations with Washington (Yitzhak Shamir, *Sikumo shel davar* [Summing up] [Tel Aviv: Edanim, 1994], 270).

126. It has been reported that Defense Minister Arens called his American counterpart 60 times during the war. Freedman and Karsh, *The Gulf Conflict*, 337.

127. Interview on IDF Radio, FBIS (NES), January 15, 1992, 42. Arens complained that the war was stopped "very abruptly" and "without coordinating with us." Cited in *Yedi'ot aharonot*, July 27, 1992.

128. *Facts on File*, February 21, 1991, 108. Barak may have meant to put pressure on the United States to intensify its Scud hunting. If so, then from Israel's point of view, his statement backfired.

129. Powell, *My American Journey*, 511–12.

130. Ibid., 512.

131. Arens, *Milkhama veshalom*, 211.

132. Interview in *Kyonghyang sinmun* (Seoul), FBIS (East Asia), February 5, 1991, 27. General Shomron's statement was probably read in Washington as preparing the grounds for a massive Israeli retaliation.

133. The news media's interpretation would have dovetailed with the assessment of

Egyptian intelligence. An Israeli official who returned from a visit to Cairo reported that a senior Egyptian intelligence officer told him that Israel should not worry over the possibility of an Iraqi missile attack. "Saddam Hussein knows you have atomic bombs, and that your leadership acts completely uncontrollably when it comes to anything related to Israeli security. It will not hesitate to respond with atomic weapons if [Israel] is attacked via missiles. He [Saddam] knows that even the Americans won't be able to restrain you if you are attacked by missiles, therefore you should not worry." Arens, *Milkhama veshalom*, 164–65.

134. The letter was excerpted in *Ma'ariv*, in FBIS (NES), February 5, 1991, 30. In his memoirs, Shamir has confirmed that this was the Israeli stand. Shamir, *Sikumo shel davar*, 270–71.

135. *Ha'aretz*, in FBIS (NES), November 2, 1990, 27.

136. For Cheney's remarks and the Israeli press's interpretations, see *Ha'aretz*, February 4, 1991; *Khadashot*, February 4, 1991.

137. "If anything could now deter Saddam Hussein from using chemical weapons, it was the fear that the U.S. response would be unconventional. This deterrence was weakened considerably as a result of the ill-advised statement which John Sununu made publicly. . . . I called Cheney that evening to draw his attention to Sununu's remarks, and he promised to check the matter with the White House." Arens, *Milkhama veshalom*, 213.

138. Interview on Israel Television Network, FBIS (NES), February 5, 1991, 34. After the war, Arens denied that the statements had been coordinated between the United States and Israel: "Whatever was declared then [by the Americans], was said on their own authority." Interview in *Yedi'ot aharonot* (First Anniversary Supplement), January 10, 1992, 3.

139. For example, Prime Minister Shamir warned that Israel's response to an Iraqi strike would be "devastating." He said: "Whoever will dare to attack us would be attacked seven times over." Cited in *Christian Science Monitor*, December 27, 1990.

140. Interview with Jerusalem Domestic Service, FBIS (NES), February 28, 1991, 26.

141. See Powell, *My American Journey*, 519–24.

142. Interview in "The Gulf War," *Frontline*, PBS, KQED-San Francisco, January 10, 1996.

143. Bin Sultan, *Desert Warrior*, 411.

144. Of Iraq's 594 aircraft shelters, 375 were destroyed by the coalition's bombing campaign, along with 141 aircraft caught inside the shelters (Freedman and Karsh, *The Gulf Conflict*, 305). In addition, according to Baghdad, a total of 114 Iraqi combat jets were transferred to Iran during the war. Included, in addition to the 24 Su-24s mentioned earlier, were 24 Mirage F-1s, 40 Sukhoi-22s, 4 Sukhoi-20s, 7 Sukhoi-25s, 4 Mig-23BNs, 4 Mig-29s, and 7 Mig-23s (INA, FBIS [NES], April 15, 1991, 26). For an account claiming that only 85 Iraqi jets were transferred to Iran, see Paul Mann, "Shaky Russian Export Controls Heighten Proliferation Risk," *Aviation Week and Space Technology*, January 26, 1998, 59.

145. Arens, *Milkhama veshalom*, 214. Although he was one of the first to say that Iraq's Scud attacks "demanded a reaction" (interview on Israel Television Network, FBIS [NES], January 18, 1991, 37 and 38), Chief of Staff Shomron had initially expressed reservations about a military expedition into western Iraq, citing various operational constraints (Amir Rotem, "The Sequel will Come," *Ma'ariv* [Weekend Supplement], January 9, 1998, 34).

146. The availability of intelligence information also played a role. Arens revealed that earlier Israel had lacked "satisfactory" tactical intelligence to enable the IDF to conduct such a complicated military operation far from its borders. Arens, *Milkhama veshalom*, 205 and 214.

147. Interview on Israel Television Network, FBIS (NES), January 14, 1991, 68.

148. President Bush was probably told that missiles armed with chemical or biological warheads could be fired from sites further away than those used for delivering conventional ordnance, as CBW warheads are lighter in weight than the high-explosive ones. U.S. intelligence in fact estimated that Iraqi CBW-armed missiles could be fired from up to 735 kilometers away, compared with 600 kilometers for conventionally armed al-Husayns ("CBW Missile Launch Indicator," Filename:0112pgv.00p [Washington, D.C.: DIA, February 1991] [Gulflink]). As a result, the search area for the IDF to locate the Iraqi Scud launchers would have expanded hugely, making the launchers' destruction less likely.

149. Baker, *The Politics of Diplomacy*, 359. See also *Washington Post*, January 7, 1991. Interestingly, Baker refers only to U.S. retaliatory plans with regard to Iraq's possible use of "chemical munitions." Could the omission of biological weapons mean that the United States would have responded differently if Iraq resorted to BW? It appears that the omission is not coincidental, as Baker specifically warned Iraq against resorting to both CW *and* BW in his meeting with Tariq Aziz in Geneva. On possible considerations that moved Bush to rule out retaliation with chemical munitions, see Kathleen Bailey, "Poison Gas in the Gulf," *Christian Science Monitor*, February 22, 1991.

150. "Information on Iraqi Scuds" (Arlington, Va.: CIA, October 1990) (Gulflink).

151. "Iraqi Use of Biological Weapons," Filename:0161pgv.90d (Washington, D.C.: DIA, December 3, 1990) (Gulflink). For a general discussion of the "secondary" impacts of a BW attack on civilians, see Harry C. Holloway et al., "The Threat of Biological Weapons: Prophylaxis and Mitigation of Psychological and Social Consequences," *JAMA*, August 6, 1997, 425–27. The possible disruption to normal life of such an attack could be gleaned from an anthrax scare in Washington D.C. See Associated Press, April 24 and 25, 1997; *Washington Post*, April 29 and May 6, 1997.

152. "Iraq Interagency. . . . " The Iraq Interagency Biological Warfare Working Group (IIBWWG) was formed to examine the Iraqi BW program and the threat it presented to Desert Shield coalition forces and to civilian populations. In addition, the working group examined the various implications of national operational strike scenarios against Iraqi BW production and storage facilities. It had five subgroups, which were formed to address the following: threat analysis, BW production, storage and deployment, political-military considerations, and weapons/vulnerability analysis.

Representatives of intelligence agencies participated along with personnel from the Air Force, Navy, Armed Forces Medical Intelligence Center, and U.S. Army Medical Research Institute of Infectious Diseases, including weapons planners, physicians, microbiologists, and members of various research and development teams.

153. Arens, *Milkhama veshalom*, 218 and 219.

154. Ibid., 220. In contrast, another source maintains that Bush also said that "there was absolutely no guarantee of its [the IDF operation's] success." Freedman and Karsh, *The Gulf Conflict*, 337–38.

155. Arens, *Milkhama veshalom*, 230.

156. During his tenure at UNSCOM, Ekeus came to share this view. He subsequently disclosed: "The moment of openness is over. They [the Iraqis] are now denying again what they admitted in August [1995]. They are grossly cheating again. . . . For them the war is not yet over" (interview in *Stern*, October 12, 1995, 230 and 232; also interview in *al-Sharq al-Awsat*, August 31, 1995). Subsequently, Ekeus testified before the U.S. Senate Subcommittee on Permanent Investigations that Iraq "has put enormous emphasis on keeping a nuclear, chemical and biological weapons capability" and is willing to forgo billions of dollars in oil exports rather than submit to the United Nations' demands that it destroy all its missiles (*New York Times*, March 21, 1996). He estimated that the Iraqis gave up some $30 billion a year in lost oil revenues (for a total of more than $100 billion, assuming that they would have exported the OPEC oil prewar quota of 3.3 million barrels per day) because of the continued economic sanctions (Ekeus, "Address"). Ekeus noted: "This [willingness to sacrifice huge oil proceeds] raises the significance . . . of the missing [munition] pieces enormously" (*Washington Post*, March 21, 1996). In general, the Iraqi case amply demonstrates the weakness of the Western notion that economic factors wield a predominant influence on political decisions and conduct.

CHAPTER 5: ENDING THE WAR

1. For instance, a few days before the ground war was launched, the Israeli Defense Ministry assessed that "a considerable number of the mobile launchers in west Iraq are still intact and can still fire missiles" (Jerusalem Domestic Service, FBIS [NES], February 19, 1991, 37). Similarly, it was stated that the "DIA continues to assess Iraq to possess a limited number of CW warheads for their Scuds to include extended range Scuds. There is no indication that the capability of Iraq to use these SRBMs to deliver chemical munitions has been significantly degraded" ("Iraqi Chemical Threat Reassessment," Filename:0407pgf.91 [Washington, D.C.: DIA, February 17, 1991] [Gulflink]; see also *New York Times*, June 24, 1992). For an Israeli account of the unsuccessful U.S. air campaign against the Scuds, see Dan Raviv and Yossi Melman, *Friends in Deed: Inside the U.S.-Israeli Alliance* (New York: Hyperion, 1994), 397–403. See also R. A. Mason, "The Air War in the Gulf," *Survival*, May–June 1991, 211–29.

2. For instance, Arens has written: "As it was learned subsequently, it is very doubtful that we had even one successful Patriot interception throughout the whole war." Moshe Arens, *Milkhama veshalom bamizrakh hatikhon, 1988–92* (Hebrew) (Tel Aviv:

Yedi'ot Aharonot, 1995), 219. On the debate over the Patriot's performance during the war, see Theodore A. Postol, "Lessons of the Gulf War Patriot Experience," *International Security*, Winter 1991–92, 119–71; Theodore A. Postol vs. Robert M. Stein, "Correspondence: Patriot Experience in the Gulf War," *International Security*, Summer 1992, 199–240; George N. Lewis and Theodore A. Postol, "Video Evidence on the Effectiveness of Patriot During the 1991 Gulf War," *Science and Global Security* 4 (1993), 1–63; George N. Lewis, Steve Fetter, and Lisbeth Gronlund, "Casualties and Damage from the Scud Attacks in the 1991 Gulf War," DACS Working Paper (Cambridge, Mass.: Center for International Studies, MIT, March 1993), 2, 3, and 16–19; Reuven Pedatzur, *The Arrow System and the Active Defense Against Ballistic Missiles* (Hebrew), Memorandum series (Tel Aviv: Joffe Center of Strategic Studies, Tel Aviv University, October 1993), 30–42. See also Marvin Feurwerger, "Defense Against Missiles: Patriot Lessons," *Orbis*, Fall 1992, 581–89.

3. In late January 1991, the CIA apparently received information from "an unidentified Iraqi military officer" that the "first priority of the Iraqi government was to know how close the Scud missiles were to their targets when destroyed by Patriot missiles, as they have chemical weapons for the Scuds. They have not yet mastered the technology of fusing and mechanical releasing to use a chemical warhead [to disperse the agent in flight]. Due to this fact, Iraq sees the possibility of a Scud carrying chemical or biological weapons to be dispersed at the moment it is hit by a Patriot missile. By using this method it is believed that the chemicals will disperse over an area of 60 square kilometers. Otherwise, a Scud equipped with a chemical warhead that hits the ground will spread chemicals only over a few square kilometers" ("CW/BW Warheads," Director 519787 [Arlington, Va.: CIA, February 1991] [Gulflink]). For sometimes conflicting assessments of the gravity of this problem, see "Effects of Collision of Chemical-Capable Scud with a Patriot Missile and General Effects of Chemical-Capable Scud Missiles," Filename:0140pgv.ood (Washington, D.C.: DIA, n.d.) (Gulflink); "Effect of Patriot Interception on Scud Warhead Dissemination," Filename:092pgv.91p (Washington. D.C.: DIA, January 23, 1991) (Gulflink); "Collateral Risk Due to Allied Air Strikes on Iraqi Biological Warfare (BW) Facilities," Filename:003pgv.oop (Washington, D.C.: DIA, n.d.) (Gulflink); "Questions on Response to Task 3657, Biological Warfare (BW) Employment," Filename:opgvo84.91p (Washington, D.C. DIA, January 24, 1991) (Gulflink).

4. Gen. Merril McPeak, "The Air Campaign: Part of the Combined Operations," (Washington, D.C.: Department of Defense, March 15, 1991). The author was chief of staff of the U.S. Air Force during Desert Storm.

5. Arens, *Milkhama veshalom*, 228.

6. Lt. Col. Mark Kipphut, USAF, "Theater Missile Defense: Reflections for the Future" (Maxwell AFB, Ala.: Air University, Winter 1996) (http://www.cdsar.af.mil.apj/win96/kipphut.html).

7. Anthony H. Cordesman and Abraham R. Wagner, *The Lessons of Modern War*, vol. 4: *The Gulf War* (Boulder, Colo.: Westview, 1996), 863–65.

8. Laurie Mylroie and James Ring Adams, "Saddam's Germs," *American Spectator*, November 1995, 60–61.

9. Gen. Charles A. Horner, USAF (Ret.), "New-Era Warfare," in *Battlefield of the Future*, ed. Barry R. Schneider and Lawrence E. Grinter (Maxwell Air Force Base, Ala.: Air University Press, September 1994) (http://www.cdsar.af.mil/battle/chp2.html).

10. On Iraq's C&C of its Scud force, see Cordesman and Wagner, *Lessons of Modern War*, 862–63. Generally, it was not the severance of Iraq's lines of communication that impeded its C&C. An Iraqi corps commander said that the Iraqis were petrified about sending any transmission for fear that U.S. signals intelligence analysts would hear it and immediately have the place bombed (*Aviation Week and Space Technology*, January 27, 1992, 62). For a report of Iraq's use of couriers even to issue CW orders, see "IIR 2 340 0258 90/Use of Chemical Weapons (U)," File 970613_23400258_90d_txt_0001.txt (Washington, D.C.: DIA, n.d.) (Gulflink).

11. Cited in Michael R. Gordon and Gen. Bernard Trainor, *The Generals' War: The Inside Story of the Conflict in the Gulf* (Boston: Little, Brown, 1995), 227 and 498 n. 19.

12. Telephone interview with a senior Israeli intelligence officer, April 30, 1996. See also Office of the Secretary of Defense, "Proliferation: Threat and Response" (Washington, D.C.: GPO, April 1996), 23.

13. *New York Times*, October 10, 1990.

14. For a general discussion of the role of stone throwing in the Palestinian intifada, see Ze'ev Schiff and Ehud Ya'ari, *Intifada: The Palestinian Uprising — Israel's Third Front* (New York: Simon and Schuster, 1990), 19–22, 30, 61, and 118–19; F. Robert Hunter, *The Palestinian Uprising: A War by Other Means* (Berkeley: University of California, 1991), 201.

15. In this connection it was probably pointed out that giving Iraq's premier modified-Scud missile the name *al-Husayn* was also politically motivated. Al-Husayn was the first grandson of the Prophet Muhammad and son of 'Ali. Both are revered in Shi'a Islam, whose adherents are in the majority in Iraq. Saddam is a Sunni, and the name *al-Husayn* may have been an attempt on his part to appeal to the Shi'a population. Department of Defense, *Conduct of the Persian Gulf War: Final Report to Congress* (Washington, D.C.: GPO, April 1992), 13.

16. *Jerusalem Post*, February 18, 1991. For repeated Iraqi pledges to surprise the coalition forces, see Thabit Nu'man al-Ani (Iraq's ambassador to Mauritania), Nouakchott Domestic Service, FBIS (NES), January 22, 1991, 58; Rashid al-Rifat (Iraq's ambassador to Japan), Kyodo, FBIS (NES), January 22, 1991, 58; INA, FBIS (NES), February 15, 1991, 23. See also Lt. Gen. Sa'di Tumah Abbas (Iraqi defense minister), interview in *Sawt al-Sha'b* (Amman), February 15, 1991.

17. *Jerusalem Post*, February 18, 1991. The origins of the al-Hijarah missile remain unclear. During the war, one source said that al-Hijarah was previously known as Tammuz 2, a three-stage derivative of the experimental missile Tammuz 1, which Iraq claimed could strike targets at a distance of more than 2,000 kilometers (*Jerusalem Post*, February 18, 1991). Tammuz is Arabic for July, the month the Iraqi Ba'ath party came

to power in a 1968 coup. It is also the Arab name for the Osiraq reactor destroyed by Israel. By naming Iraq's long-range missile Tammuz, Saddam indicated his intention to avenge the Israeli attack. The Iraqi claim that al-Hijarah missiles were used in the attack on the Dimona reactor on February 17, 1991, may have caused some analysts to conclude that this was the missile previously known as Tammuz 1, which had been unsuccessfully tested shortly before the war. In contrast, a more recent account has identified al-Hijarah as the missile previously known as al-Abbas (Cordesman and Wagner, *Lessons of Modern War*, 851). On April 25, 1988, Iraq announced that it had test-fired a new al-Abbas missile for the first time. It said that the missile traveled a distance of 860 kilometers and hit its target with "remarkable accuracy" (*Ma'ariv*, April 26, 1988). Apparently, the missile was also test-fired "immediately" before the war (*Jerusalem Post*, February 17, 1991). UNSCOM, however, is apparently inclined to view al-Hijarah as a stand-alone missile, rather than a renamed al-Abbas (remarks of Tim McCarthy, an UNSCOM missile inspector, Conference on "Start II, Missile Non-Proliferation, and Missile Defense," Panel II, Carnegie Endowment, 1995, [http://wheat.symgrp.com/symgrp/pai/articles/panel2.html]). Evidently al-Abbas was in fact a one-stage missile (whereas al-Hijarah may have had two stages) whose body was extended by 1.3 meters so as to allow the installation of additional fuel tanks (Daniel Leshem, "Surface-to-Surface Missiles in Iraq" [Hebrew], in *Memorandum* [Tel Aviv: Joffe Center for Strategic Studies, Tel Aviv University, November 1993], 5 and 14; *Ma'ariv*, February 19, 1991; Gordon and Trainor, *The Generals' War*, 497 n. 2).

18. *Flight International* (London), March 13–19, 1991, 13. One report, citing a "U.S. War College analyst," described the firing of a "stone-age Scud" as "an odd bit of desperation" brought about by Iraq's dwindling military supplies after numerous allied air strikes (*Time Magazine*, April 8, 1991, 21). Even if this was the prevailing view, however, Iraq's running out of conventional munition and its display of "desperation" should have increased the probability of its resorting to CB weapons in the minds of U.S. intelligence and AMAN.

19. Lawrence Freedman and Efraim Karsh, *The Gulf Conflict, 1990–1991: Diplomacy and War in the New World Order* (Princeton: Princeton University Press, 1994), 309.

20. The specifications of al-Hijarah continue to be a source of dispute. One source said that it was a two-stage liquid-fuel missile with additional fuel tanks that were crudely welded into the main body (Cordesman and Wagner, *Lessons of Modern War*, 851). The development of a two-stage missile involved technological advances in the design and manufacture of the rocket engine for the second stage, which the Iraqis likely obtained from West German companies (*Ha'aretz*, January 20, 1991). In addition, the Iraqis had to master the advanced separation technology required, or the missile would have been diverted from its course during the separation phase. Al-Hijarah was initially estimated to have a range of 700–900 kilometers, a payload of 100–300 kilograms, a flight time of 540 seconds, and an operational CEP (or Circular Error Probable — the radius of an imaginary circle centered on the missile's aim point inside which 50 percent of the warheads will land) at maximum range of 2,500 to 3,000 meters. A 1996 Pentagon report, however, put al-Hijarah's range as similar to that of

the standard al-Husayn missile — that is, 600–650 kilometers ("Proliferation: Threat and Response," 23). As CEP is roughly proportional to range, al-Hijarah's accuracy would have been comparable to that of al-Husayn as well. It is not clear whether the new estimates of the missile's range also mean that it, like al-Husayn, in fact had only one stage.

21. *Jerusalem Post*, February 17, 1991.

22. Cited in Rick Atkinson, *Crusade: The Untold Story of the Persian Gulf War* (Boston: Houghton Mifflin, 1993), 144. Reportedly, it was thought that the missile was fired from a base in al-Ramadi, about 100 kilometers west of Baghdad (see Shlomo Aronson, *The Politics and Strategy of Nuclear Weapons in the Middle East* [Albany: State University of New York Press, 1992], 276). Al-Hijarah's range was thus believed to be some 900 kilometers.

23. Kanan Makiya (Samir al-Khalil), *Cruelty and Silence: War, Tyranny, Uprising and the Arab World* (New York: Norton, 1993), 267.

24. The meeting is described in ibid., pp. 159–60. In an interview on Mexican television, Saddam also voiced his confidence that Iraq would win because God was on its side. See interview, Xew Television Network (Mexico City), FBIS (NES), December 26, 1990, 19.

25. Makiya, *Cruelty and Silence*, 267–69.

26. *Frankfurter Allgemeine Zeitung*, February 15, 1991.

27. *Facts on File*, November 30, 1990, 890.

28. Jerusalem Domestic Service, FBIS (NES), February 20, 1991, 36.

29. Interview, Jerusalem Domestic Service, FBIS (NES)., February 22, 1991, 63.

30. Interview, Jerusalem Television Service, FBIS (NES), August 10, 1990, 54.

31. Interview, Israel Television Network, FBIS (NES), February 28, 1991, 34.

32. Interview, Israel Television Network, FBIS (NES), August 27, 1990, 41. See also Arens, cited in *Ha'aretz*, August 13, 1990.

33. *Wall Street Journal*, September 27, 1990.

34. Reportedly, on September 13, 1990, Arens told Secretary of Defense Cheney: "I am operating according to the basic assumption that the probability of an attack on Israel would increase once the U.S. initiates military action against Iraq, in a bid to prove to the Arab world that this is really a war against Israel. . . . We have to consider the possibility that the Iraqis will strike Israel even prior to an American military operation, especially if the embargo is successful in strangling Iraq and induces them to despair." Arens, *Milkhama veshalom*, 168; see also Raviv and Melman, *Friends in Deed*, 382.

35. *Ma'ariv*, cited in Aronson, *The Politics and Strategy of Nuclear Weapons*, 249.

36. James Piscatori, ed., *Islamic Fundamentalisms and the Gulf Crisis* (Chicago: Fundamentalism Project, American Academy of Arts and Sciences, 1991), 226, citing a U.S. Department of Defense announcement.

37. "Iraqi CW and BW" (Arlington, Va.: CIA, September 1990) (Gulflink); emphasis added. This position was ostensibly reiterated subsequently: "Although Saddam probably would not order the use of biological warfare in the early days of the conflict, if the war goes badly for him he may decide to use these weapons. . . . Biological

weapons use would be most likely if Saddam and the Iraqi leadership believed Baghdad were about to be attacked by nuclear weapons or if ground operations were seriously jeopardizing the regime. . . . Explicit threats or the actual employment of biological weapons against civilian or strategic targets might be used as a last resort to shock an opponent into providing an opening for a political resolution. . . . Baghdad probably would use missiles as its primary means [of attack] because of the difficulty in intercepting these weapons" ("Would Iraq Use Biological Weapons?" [Arlington, Va.: CIA, December 1990] [Gulflink]). Evidently, DIA analysts concurred with this estimate. For instance, an assessment prepared on the eve of the ground war stated: "Iraq's leadership almost certainly intends to use all available weaponry at its disposal if the viability of the Saddam-led Baath regime is threatened. . . . DIA also considers it likely that if Iraq's borders are breached by coalition ground forces that this event too, would cross Iraq's threshold for employing nonconventional weapons. Iraq's leaders are reasonably well-informed on U.S. nuclear and chemical capabilities. A U.S. threat of retaliation is unlikely to deter Iraq" ("Use of Radioactive Material in SCUD Warhead," Filename: 002bk.91d [Washington, D.C.: DIA, February 19, 1991] [Gulflink]). The DIA specifically warned against strategic Iraqi strikes with CB weapons: "In the face of further reverses," it said, "Saddam Hussein could seek to repeat his apparently successful use of SRBMs as weapons of terror during the Iran war by, as a last resort, ordering HE-, CW-, or possibly BW-armed SRBM attacks against densely populated areas such as Dhahran or Riad. Such an attack would probably involve all of Iraq's SRBM assets within range of these civilian areas, and could include Israeli targets" ("Iraq's SRBM Capabilities and Options for Use," Filename:0182pgv_ood.txt [Washington, D.C.: DIA, n.d.] [Gulflink]; see also Interagency Intelligence Community Working Group, "Interim Report on Iraq Biological Warfare [BW]," Filename:001me.90d [Washington, D.C.: DIA, December 17, 1990] [Gulflink]).

38. Interview with Jerusalem Domestic Service, FBIS (NES), February 22, 1991, 63. Although General Shomron limited himself to the threat of CW, the fact remains that Israel, like the United States, estimated that an Iraqi attack with weapons of mass destruction was now probable. This line was at variance with some of the public positions he and other Israeli leaders took at the time. For example, one day after the outbreak of the war, Shomron, obviously buoyed by the reports of the U.S. aerial bombing successes, sought to reassure the Israeli public by saying: "From the very beginning we estimated the probability of an attack on our home front as small" (interview, Israel Television Network, FBIS [NES], January 22, 1991, 90). This statement was made a few hours before the first Scuds landed in Israel.

39. "Iraq's Biological Warfare Program: Saddam's Ace in the Hole — An Intelligence Assessment," (Arlington, Va.: CIA, circa August 1990) (Gulflink).

40. "Bugs and Things," Filename:omeoo4.90d (Washington, D.C.: DIA, December 3, 1990) (Gulflink).

41. "Iraq Interagency Biological Warfare Working Group (IIBWWG)," File 970613_505wp_ood_txt_0001.txt (Washington, D.C.: DIA, n.d.) (Gulflink).

42. "Bugs and Things."

43. "Would Iraq Use Biological Weapons?"

44. Arens, *Milkhama veshalom*, 168.

45. Ibid., 212–13.

46. Ibid., 229.

47. On the debate within the Israeli Cabinet regarding the distribution of gas masks, see Arens, *Milkhama veshalom*, 160–64, 174, and 186. See also Brig. (Res.) Aharon Levran, "Masks May Give Saddam Wrong Idea," *Jerusalem Post International Edition*, November 1, 1990; "Gas Masks Send the Wrong Message," *Jerusalem Post International Edition*, December 26, 1992. However, given Iraq's offensive use of CW in the later stages of the war with Iran, this argument may be seriously flawed.

48. Atkinson, *Crusade*, 279.

49. Gen. Colin Powell, *My American Journey* (New York: Random House, 1995), 494.

50. Ibid., 468. General de la Billière agrees with this assessment but contends that British troops "had the best chemical protection in the world" and were "better off than the Americans, for we had more NBC suits per man." Gen. Sir Peter de la Billière, *Storm Command: A Personal Account of the Gulf War* (London: HarperCollins, 1992), 98 and 174.

51. Powell, *My American Journey*, 493.

52. "Iraq Biological Warfare Threat," Filename:0408.pgf.90 (Washington, D.C.: DIA, October 22, 1990) (Gulflink).

53. "Iraq Interagency . . . " Another report, while repeating the estimate for dried anthrax, said that Iraq possessed 20–30 kilograms of botulinum. "Biological/Chemical," File 970613_72723509_d_txt_0001.txt (Washington, D.C.: DIA, n.d.) (Gulflink).

54. Powell, *My American Journey*, 494. Nevertheless, in December 1990, the DIA reported that "insufficient antibiotics and inoculation material is available to protect U.S. forces where protection is available." Indirectly confirming the effectiveness of Saddam's terrorist deterrence, the agency said: "Again, we recommend, based on [Saddam] Hussein's history, that every effort be made to get as much protection forward, even if marginal at best." See "Bugs and Things."

55. Powell, *My American Journey*, 503–4. In fact, it was this gruesome scenario that moved the general to propose sending Saddam a tough warning against the use of mass destruction weapons.

56. Before the 1973 war, the Israeli assessment was that the likelihood of an Arab attack was minimal because the military balance was decidedly in Israel's favor, especially with regard to air power. Such was the dominance of this perspective that when information arrived indicating that Syrian troops were massing on Israel's borders, Jerusalem rushed messages via the United States, reassuring Damascus that Israel had no aggressive intentions toward Syria. The net result was that the Arabs were able to achieve a strategic surprise when they attacked on October 6, 1973. See Richard K. Betts, *Surprise Attack* (Washington, D.C.: Brookings Institution, 1982), 75–76. For an assessment of AMAN's "concept" in 1973, see Elliot A. Cohen and John Gooch, *Military Misfortunes: The Anatomy of Failure in War* (New York: Free Press, 1990), 105–31.

57. *Ha'aretz*, January 20, 1991. It appears that the DIA faced similar uncertainties: "It is not known if the Iraqis have yet developed an operational warhead for their ballistic missiles. [One estimate contends that] an operational chemical warhead will be available in the September 1990 time-frame. We believe this could very well be the case." "Iraqi Chemical Warfare," Filename:0504wp.90 (Washington, D.C.: DIA, August 1990) (Gulflink).

58. Interview, Jerusalem Domestic Service, FBIS (NES), February 25, 1991, 64. On another occasion Shomron said: "Unfortunately, some of those [Iraqi] missiles might be outfitted with chemical warheads. We do not know that for fact, but the possibility exists." Interview, Educational Television Network, FBIS (NES), February 4, 1991, 57 and 58; see also interview with Defense Minister Arens, Israel Television Network, FBIS (NES), January 28, 1991, 51.

59. Interview, Jerusalem Domestic Service, FBIS (NES), February 25, 1991, 64–65. Shomron's assertion seems to have been borne out by later disclosures. It appears that, even as late as February 1991, the CIA assessed that "Iraq probably has CW warheads for its Scuds, but detonating them effectively is a complex task." "Briefing" (Arlington, Va.: CIA, February 1991) (Gulflink).

60. Cited in *Khadashot*, April 8, 1990. "A leading Arab official" reportedly alleged that in 1989 in a test "monitored by Western intelligence," the Iraqi military successfully fired a "chemically loaded missile" in northwest Iraq. Accordingly, Baghdad subsequently tried to strike a deal to conduct further tests in the North African country Mauritania, whose territory is largely desert. But the deal is said to have fallen through in response to Western diplomatic pressure on Mauritania. See *Los Angeles Times*, September 14, 1990; also Leshem, "Surface-to-Surface Missiles," 15 and 38; Adel Darwish and Gregory Alexander, *Unholy Babylon: The Secret History of Saddam's War* (New York: St. Martin's Press, 1991), 96.

61. Cited in *Bamakhane*, August 29, 1990, 7 (Israel's practice is not to divulge the names of pilots and other personnel in high-risk security and defense posts, to protect their identity). Likewise, the *Jerusalem Post*, on September 10, 1990, quoted a "senior military source" as indicating that, contrary to previous assessments of the defense establishment, "the Iraqis may well have chemical warheads for their missiles. They have the capacity to produce them." Israel announced as early as 1986 that Syria had developed chemical warheads for its Scud B missiles (see *Ha'aretz*, August 8, 1986, citing Shimon Peres, then prime minister; see also *Davar*, December 2, 1986, citing Prime Minister Itzhak Shamir; interview with Defense Minister Itzhak Rabin, *Die Welt*, March 17, 1987). For a general survey of Arab CW capabilities at the time, see *Ha'aretz*, August 14, 1986.

62. Yossi Sarid, "Learning What We Didn't Know," *Jerusalem Post International Edition*, March 16, 1991.

63. Cited on IDF Radio, FBIS (NES), January 16, 1991, 24.

64. Jerusalem Domestic Service, FBIS (NES), March 6, 1991, 40–41. Similarly, a CIA document stated: "Bottom line assessment is that for practical (worst case) purpose we cannot discount the probability that Iraq has an operational CW warhead capability

for its Scud B, al-Husayn, and al-Abbas ballistic missiles. . . . We must assume at this point that Iraq has the capability to interchange CW and high explosives warheads" ("Update on CW Weaponization of Iraqi surface-to-surface missiles" [Arlington, Va.: CIA, August 1990] [Gulflink]). With regard to BW warheads the picture was similarly murky. For example, an Interagency Intelligence Community working group reported: "It also is not known what types of munitions have been filled with BW agent but could include missile warheads, aerial bombs with and without cluster munitions, artillery and spray and aerosol generating devices" ("Interim Report on Iraqi Biological Warfare [BW]," Filename:001me.90d [Washington, D.C.: DIA, December 17, 1990] [Gulflink]; see also "Iraq's Biological Warfare Program" [Arlington, Va.: CIA, August 1990] [Gulflink]). After the war, however, the DIA reported: "Iraq was assessed to have BW bombs, and Scud warheads" ("Response to Rep. Kennedy's Questions of February 22, 1994," Filename:006me.94 [Washington, D.C.: DIA, March 2, 1994] [Gulflink]).

65. Interview, Jerusalem Domestic Service, FBIS (NES), March 1, 1991, 25. On the controversy during the war regarding air-raid shelters versus sealed rooms, see Arens, interview with Israel Educational Television, FBIS (NES), February 19, 1991, 77; Voice of Israel and the IDF Radio Network, FBIS (NES), February 14, 1991, 31; see also Leonard A. Cole, *The Eleventh Plague: The Politics of Biological and Chemical Warfare* (New York: W. H. Freeman, 1997), 108–9. It has been argued that had the civil defense benefits of reinforced steel construction been understood in Israel before the war began, the dilemma would have been eased. Based on the analyses of damage inflicted by the Scuds in Israel, it turned out that, depending on the size of the warhead, an underground shelter might have been only marginally better at providing protection against a conventional explosive than an interior room in a building with steel reinforced construction and non-load-bearing walls (Lewis et al., "Casualties and Damage," 40). Israel seems to have reached a similar conclusion following tests of the impact of Scuds in urban areas (*Yedi'ot aharonot*, June 27, 1994).

66. Interview, *Yedi'ot aharonot* (Leshabbat Supplement), February 1, 1991, 1. Even this formula represented a remarkable reversal in the general's position. Before the war he argued against the distribution of gas masks, saying that Israel's ability to respond to an Iraqi CW attack would act as an effective deterrent. "There is no need to frighten [the people], and exaggerate [the Iraqi chemical threat]," he said (cited in *Ma'ariv*, July 17, 1990). He also ruled out the possibility that the Iraqis had a biological warhead for the Scud (interview, *Yedi'ot aharonot* [Leshabbat Supplement], February 1, 1991, 1).

67. Lewis et al., "Casualties and Damage," 37. This scenario assumes that less than half the payload of the warhead was dispersed as a fine respirable aerosol. The number of casualties from chemical attack depends on the number of people in the contaminated area, degree of protection, weather conditions, and the amount of toxicity of the agent used. For example, precipitation, high temperatures, increased wind speed, and high humidity tend to reduce the persistence of chemical agents. Availability of medical help will affect the number of fatalities.

68. Ibid., 37–38. A series of chemical attacks, or fears of additional attacks, could keep people in their houses or even sealed rooms for many hours. Among the indirect

casualties of the conventional Scud attacks on Israel were seven people who suffocated owing to improper use of gas masks. Five fatal heart attacks were also attributed to the missile attacks. Another 815 cases were treated at hospitals for ailments linked to the attacks. These were primarily cases of people with acute anxiety or people who had injected themselves with atropine provided in their civil defense kits. More than half of such indirect casualties were ascribed not to actual missile attacks but to five false alarms that occurred during the first few days of the attacks. Ibid., 14 n. 37.

69. "Iraq CW," File cia_65549_65549 01.txt (Arlington, Va.: CIA, n.d.) (Gulflink).

70. See James A. Baker III, *The Politics of Diplomacy* (New York: J. P. Putnam's Sons, 1995), 387 and 390.

71. Interview with David Frost, cited in *New York Times*, January 15, 1996.

72. Efraim Karsh and Inari Rautsi, *Saddam Hussein: A Political Biography* (New York: Free Press, 1991), 263. UNSC Resolution 660, which was passed on August 2, 1990, demanded that "Iraq withdraw immediately and unconditionally all its forces to the positions in which they were located on August 1, 1990."

73. Gen. Khaled Bin Sultan, *Desert Warrior: A Personal View of the Gulf War by the Joint Forces Commander* (New York: HarperCollins, 1995), 435.

74. Cited in Karsh and Rautsi, *Saddam Hussein*, 264.

75. The sanctions had been in place since August 6, 1990, when an economic embargo was placed on Iraq. In September the UNSC had passed Resolution 666, imposing strict controls on food aid to Iraq. And on October 29 the UNSC declared Iraq liable for human rights abuses and economic losses since the occupation of Kuwait, as well as war damages.

76. See Karsh and Rautsi, *Saddam Hussein*, 263–64.

77. U.S. News and World Report, *Triumph Without Victory: The Unreported History of the Gulf War* (New York: Random House, 1992), 400.

78. The parallel to Hitler was used by Bush as early as the third week of August 1990. On that occasion, the president told a large assembly of military officers: "A half century ago, our nation and the world paid dearly for appeasing an aggressor who should, and could, have been stopped. We are not going to make the same mistake again" (ibid., 123). On November 1, Bush referred to the Iraqi atrocities in Kuwait as even worse than those committed by the Nazis. "I don't think Hitler ever participated in anything of that nature" (ibid., 174).

79. In testimony before the Senate Foreign Relations Committee, on February 7, 1991, Secretary of State Baker responded to Senator Richard Lugar's comment that Saddam "must be removed from a position of leadership in Iraq." He said: "There is no suggestion on our part that the rebuilding or reconstruction of Iraq could proceed if the current leadership under Saddam Hussein remained in power after the war" (*Facts on File*, February 14, 1991, 92). On February 15, President Bush openly called on the "Iraqi military and the Iraqi people to take matters into their own hands to force Saddam Hussein the dictator to step aside" (Speech to the American Association for the Advancement of Science, *Facts on File*, February 21, 1991, 108). That day, Bush made a similar appeal during a speech at Raytheon Corporation.

80. Freedman and Karsh, *The Gulf Conflict*, 412.

81. Robert Gates, deputy National Security Adviser, in hearings on his nomination as director of the CIA, *Washington Post*, May 22, 1991. See also Gordon and Trainor, *The Generals' War*, 457.

82. Gordon and Trainor, *The Generals' War*, 477.

83. Bin Sultan, *Desert Warrior*, 423. In this, General Khaled appears to have been fully vindicated. Saddam subsequently boasted openly of how he was able to use the cease-fire talks to prevent even the appearance of an Iraqi defeat: "They [the U.S.] said: Send your envoys to a U.S. ship. . . . For our part we said the negotiations will not take place on an American ship. I said: You have to choose between two sites where the negotiations may be held — either in the Safwan region at the [al-Julaydah?] Airport or at any other point along the Saudi-Iraqi border. In the end they settled for one of the two places." Moreover, Saddam relayed how the Iraqi representatives to the talks refused to hand over their guns until both General Schwarzkopf and General Khaled had done the same. INA, FBIS (NES), January 7, 1994, 20–21.

84. Bin Sultan, *Desert Warrior*, 425.

85. In fact, Secretary Baker writes: "The Saudis . . . didn't just want Saddam ejected from Kuwait; they wanted him destroyed. . . . They were always advocates for the massive use of force" (Baker, *Politics of Diplomacy*, 289). Still, General Khaled maintains that Saudi Arabia would have "vigorously opposed" any plan to march on Baghdad. See bin Sultan, *Desert Warrior*, 426.

86. Bin Sultan, *Desert Warrior*, 425.

87. Freedman and Karsh, *The Gulf Conflict*, 405.

88. Gordon and Trainor, *The Generals' War*, 419–20, 422–32, and 476–77; Freedman and Karsh, *The Gulf Conflict*, 406–7.

89. Bin Sultan, *Desert Warrior*, 425.

90. Testimony before the Senate Governmental Affairs Committee, cited in Jonathan B. Tucker, "Lessons of Iraq's Biological Warfare Programme," *Arms Control*, December 1993, 259.

91. In an interview with *Le monde* on January 10, 1995, Ekeus said: "My work is almost done. My mission is drawing to its inevitable conclusion." Resolution 687 made the Gulf War cease-fire contingent on Iraq's "unconditional" agreement to the destruction or elimination of its mass destruction capabilities and "immediate on-site inspections" by the United Nations. Upon Iraq's breach of its obligations to allow full inspection of suspected NBC sites — a violation that was even declared by the UNSC — the cease-fire enacted by Resolution 687 ended. Hence, the United States could have inferred that the Gulf War was not over.

92. Aronson, *The Politics and Strategy of Nuclear Weapons*, 276. Apparently the test was first reported in *Newsweek*, but its existence remains unconfirmed.

93. Interview of President Bush with David Frost, summarized in *New York Times*, January 15, 1996. See also Freedman and Karsh, *The Gulf Conflict*, 417; Gordon and Trainor, *The Generals' War*, 456.

94. Powell, *My American Journey*, 521. Powell cites his mentor, Fred Iklé, one-time

undersecretary of defense for policy under Caspar Weinberger, who years earlier coined this term in his book *Every War Must End*.

95. Cited in Richard Danzig (U.S. undersecretary of the navy), "Biological Warfare: A Nation at Risk—A Time to Act," *Strategic Forum*, no. 58 (Washington, D.C.: National Defense University, Institute for National Strategic Studies, January 1996) (http://www.ndu.edu/ndu/inss/insshp.html).

96. Interview, "Ambassador Rolf Ekeus: Leaving Behind the UNSCOM Legacy in Iraq," *Arms Control Today*, June–July 1997 (www.armscontrol.org/ACT/junjul/ekeus.htm).

97. Interview with General al-Samarra'i, CBS-TV, *60 Minutes*, November 23, 1997. Ironically, Ambassador Ekeus agreed. Ekeus said that when UNSCOM began operating in April 1991, "We all expected that it was purely technical work," since the Iraqi leadership would cooperate because they were anxious to export oil and return to the normal economic situation. This was a major misjudgment, Ekeus admitted. "What happened was the opposite. Iraq decided to systematically mislead, conceal and cheat in an effort to preserve these capabilities. Obviously, they considered these capabilities more important than considerable financial assets." "Ekeus: Important Work Ahead for U.N. Commission on Iraqi Weapons," U.S. Information Agency, May 2, 1997.

98. INA, FBIS (NES), August 5, 1991, 35.

99. INA, FBIS (NES), January 7, 1994, 20.

100. Interview with *al-Sha'b* (Cairo), FBIS (NES), June 5, 1991, 11.

101. Interview with *al-Dustur* (Amman), February 22, 1992.

102. For a review of this period, see *Christian Science Monitor*, April 27, 1994.

103. *Washington Post*, July 6, 1995; *New York Times*, July 6, 7, and August 23, 1995.

104. Arms Control and Disarmament Agency, "Threat Control through Arms Control: Annual Report to Congress, 1995" (Washington, D.C.: ACDA, July 1996), 68.

105. Interview of Rolf Ekeus, *Der Spiegel*, in FBIS (NES), September 5, 1995, 39.

106. Interview in *al-Sharq al-Awsat*, October 21, 1995.

107. *Time Magazine*, September 4, 1995, 41.

108. Cited in ibid. Ostensibly to prove his goodwill, Saddam canceled a previously issued ultimatum calling for the United Nations to lift sanctions by August 31, 1995, or Iraq would cease cooperating with UNSCOM.

109. Interview in *al-Sharq al-Awsat*, October 21, 1995. See also interview in *Stern*, October 12, 1995, 230–32.

110. Ekeus, "Address."

111. Cited in *al-Jumhuriyah*, October 1, 1994.

112. *Babel* (Baghdad), in FBIS (NES) November 21, 1994, 4. For similar threats, see *al-Qadisiyah*, October 6, 1994; *Babel*, October 8 and 9, 1994.

113. *Al-Jumhuriyah*, October 5, 1994.

114. *Al-Jumhuriyah*, October 4, 1994.

115. Speech on Republic of Iraq Radio Network, FBIS (NES), January 17, 1995, 50.

116. One day before his ill-fated return to Iraq (where he was killed), Hussein Kamil Hassan sought redemption by advertising that he had never strayed from Baghdad's

line. He said: "I have not said anything because Iraq, while I was there, had already completed the elimination of all weapons of mass destruction. Nothing was left . . . no more weapons and no more substances or factories that could produce such weapons. It was not me who disclosed this but Baghdad which has exposed all its cards. I did not reveal more than Baghdad did" (interview, *al-Khalij* [Abu Dhabi], FBIS [NES], February 23, 1996, 9–10). But earlier, in the debriefings following his defection, Kamil had apparently tried to sound at least somewhat cooperative. He claimed that two aspects of Iraq's BW program had remained hidden. One of them was hemorrhagic fevers (*hamma damoutya*), diseases caused by a variety of RNA viruses and characterized by malaise and abnormalities of circulatory regulations. The second aspect related to the location. According to Kamil, these agents were developed at the Daura facility, which had once belonged to the Agriculture Ministry. He said that UNSCOM knew about the place but was unaware of the activity. The site was sequestered for BW manufacture near the end of the Iran-Iraq war. Kamil said that the agent was weaponized in Iraqi-manufactured bombs that were coated with fiberglass to prevent corrosion ("Comments on Iraqi Weapons of Mas," CIA 404583 [Arlington, Va.: CIA, August 1995] [Gulflink]).

117. Upon arriving in Jordan, Kamil Hassan called for toppling the regime of Saddam Hussein. He said: "We are calling on the officers of the Iraqi Army, the officers of the Republican Guards, the officers of the Special Guards, the civil servants of the Iraqi state, and all the Iraqi society to be ready for this important change." Cited in *Christian Science Monitor*, August 14, 1995.

118. Editorial in *al-Iraq* (Baghdad), October 6, 1998.

119. Cited in *Christian Science Monitor*, July 13, 1993. It turns out that UNSCOM's difficulties in Iraq were totally predictable. In Saddam's view the Special Commission was created because the United States had shrunk from disarming Iraq unilaterally. It was an admission of weakness. Hence, Iraqi interference with the commission's work was unlikely to entail much risk, as another ground attack on Iraq was highly doubtful. UNSCOM's work would be doomed to becoming an irritant in search of a solution—a mission whose pursuance constantly pointed to the lack of effective options in dealing with Saddam.

120. Speech on the 28th anniversary of the 17–30 July Revolution, Iraq Television Network, FBIS (NES), July 18, 1996, 23.

121. *Time Magazine*, September 4, 1995, 41.

122. Interview in *Der Spiegel*, FBIS (NES), September 4, 1995, 39.

123. Cited in *Time Magazine*, September 4, 1995, 41.

124. *Washington Post*, March 25, 1998.

125. "Amb. Richard Butler's Presentation," unofficial text of briefing by Richard Butler to the U.N. Security Council, June 3, 1998, excerpted by Laurie Mylroie (http://www.fas.org/news/un/iraq/s/index.html/980603_unscom.htm).

126. *New York Times*, February 26, 1998.

127. UNSCOM/TECH, 10.

128. Ibid.

129. U.S. Government White Paper, "Iraqi Weapons of Mass Destruction Programs," Washington, D.C., February 13, 1998, 4.

130. Ibid.

131. "Saddam panicked believing Kamil [Hassan] was telling all to the United States. He divulged key details of the bioweapons program." *Newsweek*, March 2, 1998, 41.

132. For instance, in response to British accusations, Iraq's Foreign Minister Muhammad Sa'id al-Saahaf has stated, "Iraq's former biological program was completely destroyed in 1991. . . . Iraq documented this fact in a detailed written statement made to the Special Commission and to the Security Council in January 1992. In this statement Iraq asserted that it did not possess or conceal any banned weapon or substance. This Iraqi statement is true and accurate. . . . As for the documents and information hidden by traitor Hussein Kamil . . . they are all part of the details of the previous program which no longer exist" (Iraq Television Network, FBIS [NES], November 14, 1995, 29–30). Supposedly the destruction of the program took place in May–June 1991 (ACDA, "Threat Control," 67).

133. Cited in www.nando.net/newsroom/ntn/world/011796/world14_16759. html.

134. *Al-Qadisiyah*, cited by the INA in English, FBIS (NES), March 5, 1996, 41.

135. Lt. Gen. Patrick M. Hughes, director of the DIA, told the Senate Select Committee on Intelligence: "Iraq's [conventional] military capability continues to erode. Saddam's forces have significant weaknesses—in leadership, morale, readiness, logistics and training—that would limit their effectiveness in combat" (cited in *New York Times*, January 29, 1998). CIA director George J. Tenet said on the same occasion that Iraq's military forces "continue to slowly deteriorate under U.N. sanctions and the arms embargo implemented after the Gulf War." (Reuters [Washington], January 28, 1998).

CHAPTER 6: THE ISRAELI NUCLEAR SHADOW

1. *Ma'ariv*, August 14, 1991. Some Israelis called for abandoning the secrecy in favor of a publicized nuclear deterrent.

2. See Chapter 4 of this book. Although he used euphemisms—for instance, information on the Israeli nuclear alert was called "reports"—Powell likely relayed the assessment of the American intelligence community about Israel's missile readiness at the time. U.S. intelligence documents indirectly testify that the Israeli potential for nuclear retaliation played a key role in Washington's calculations. One document stated: "Saddam could try and bring Tel Aviv into the conflict by using chemical weapons. He may be reluctant to use them, in part out of fear of nuclear retaliation" ("Middle East Brief" [Arlington, Va.: CIA, February 1991] [Gulflink]). Another speculated that Saddam was "probably" dissuaded from launching Scuds with chemical or biological warheads "out of fear of U.S. or Israeli nuclear retaliation" ("Why WMD Were Withheld" [Arlington, Va.: CIA, March 1991] [Gulflink]).

3. Dan Raviv and Yossi Melman, *Friends in Deed: Inside the U.S.-Israeli Alliance* (New

York: Hyperion, 1994), 511 n. The Israeli nuclear issue is also downplayed in Lawrence Freedman and Efraim Karsh, *The Gulf Conflict, 1990–1991: Diplomacy and War in the New World Order* (Princeton: Princeton University Press, 1994), 331–32.

4. *Ha'aretz*, June 22, 1988.

5. Further affirmation for this interpretation could have been obtained from Rabin's remarks at a lecture after the Gulf War: "As defense minister, I believed it was our duty to state that any attempt to dispatch ballistic missiles at Tel Aviv would provoke a reaction one hundred times worse against Damascus and other Syrian cities. . . . The only way to deter the use of ballistic missiles is to announce that three times more devastation will be inflicted on Damascus than they had on Tel Aviv — by retaliation means that need not be specified" (cited in Pedatzur, "Limits of Deterrence," *Ha'aretz*, March 28, 1995). In this context Israel's efforts to develop the Arrow Anti-Tactical Ballistic Missile (ATBM) system could be construed as designed to give Jerusalem the option of forsaking the resort to a nuclear riposte. In part, this also explains the motive behind America's willingness to pay some 80 percent of the costs of its development.

6. Interview, Voice of Israel and the IDF Radio Network, FBIS (NES), January 29, 1991, 28. Foreign Minister David Levy warned that should Saddam choose to attack Israel, he would "face a terrible retribution." *Jerusalem Post*, January 2, 1991.

7. Interview in *Ma'ariv*, February 22, 1991. Although Rabin did not specifically condition the Israeli response on an enemy attack with mass destruction weapons, the timing of his warning clearly suggests that it was in reference to such a scenario. After all, by the time he spoke, Israel had already absorbed numerous conventional Scud attacks without response.

8. After the war, Rabin openly faulted the Shamir government for not "having publicly declared that large Arab cities ["capital cities," in another published version] would be destroyed if their leaders, specifically Iraq, resorted to use of weapons of mass destruction." Cited in Shlomo Aronson, *The Politics and Strategy of Nuclear Weapons in the Middle East* (Albany: State University of New York Press, 1992), 288.

9. *Ma'ariv*, December 30, 1990.

10. *Sunday Times*, October 5, 1986.

11. During the Gulf crisis, a former director of NATO's nuclear-weapon planning called on the United States to threaten retaliation with neutron weapons in order to deter Iraq from resorting to CW. He said that "an immediate option" was the enhanced radiation warhead produced for the NATO Lance missile. If it were to burst in the air over a battlefield, the area promptly lethal to personnel in a tank would be about 2.6 square kilometers. Beyond an area of 13 square kilometers there would be no effect on exposed troops. "Such a weapon could be readied almost immediately for either missile or aircraft delivery," he wrote. Robert G. Shreffler, letter in *Wall Street Journal*, September 19, 1990.

12. Aronson, *The Politics and Strategy of Nuclear Weapons*, 274.

13. *Ha'aretz*, August 3, 1990.

14. The agreement reached in Jerusalem on January 12, 1991, following talks with Lawrence Eagleburger (deputy secretary of state) and Paul Wolfowitz (undersecretary

of defense for policy), reportedly said that should the Israelis decide to act "on their own," they would "consult" with Washington beforehand (Raviv and Melman, *Friends in Deed*, 386). Indeed, Prime Minister Shamir has written that in his meeting with President Bush in December 1990 in Washington, the president "had understood full well that I did not commit myself to asking him for permission [for a military operation]" (Yitzhak Shamir, *Sikumo shel davar* [Hebrew] [Tel Aviv: Edanim, 1994], 268).

15. Cited in Raviv and Melman, *Friends in Deed*, 384.

16. Interview in *Le Figaro*, November 6, 1990.

17. Cited in Freedman and Karsh, *The Gulf Conflict*, 333.

18. The prime minister made the statement during an interview on Israeli television on the fifth day of the war (Shamir, *Sikumo shel davar*, 272). For his admission, see Raviv and Melman, *Friends in Deed*, 394, citing Shamir's aide Yossi Achimeir.

19. Raviv and Melman, *Friends in Deed*, 393.

20. *Ha'aretz*, January 15, 1993.

21. Rick Atkinson, *Crusade: The Untold Story of the Persian Gulf War* (Boston: Houghton Mifflin, 1993), 82. The NBC Index of the 1st Calvary Division notes in connection: "VH CORPS G-2 confirm Chemical Warheads on Scuds impacting Israel" ("NBC Index from the DTAC," [VII Corps, January 1991] [Gulflink]). The initial misidentification of the Scud's payload is also confirmed in Arens, *Milkhama veshalom*, 194.

22. Michael R. Gordon and Gen. Bernard Trainor, *The Generals' War: The Inside Story of the Conflict in the Gulf* (Boston: Little, Brown, 1995), 232. Also Atkinson, *Crusade*, 82.

23. Cited in *Yedi'ot aharonot*, July 17, 1989.

24. Lt. Col. "A" (IAF's chief of Passive Defense Branch), interview in *Bamakhane*, September 1990, 62.

25. Israel had adopted a "bomb-in-the-basement" posture in the early 1970s. Under this policy Israel kept the bomb as a last-resort weapon and therefore maintained secrecy concerning the existence of an operational nuclear capability. Any deterrent effect that could come from the development of a nuclear capability had to be derived from the ambiguity over the precise status of the option. In the early 1980s, Israel apparently switched to a "bomb-in-the-closet" posture, when Arab countries, most notably Syria, began assembling sophisticated mass destruction arsenals (see Avigdor Haselkorn, "Can Nuclear Card Give Israel Higher Level of Stability?" *Los Angeles Times*, November 14, 1986). In the context of this posture Israel still refrained from publicizing its nuclear status, continuing to view it as a last-resort option, but sought to convince its enemies through various "unofficial" means, including leaks in the media, of the "maturity" of its nuclear capability. During the Gulf War Israel could have chosen to adopt a "bomb-in-the-window" posture — an open but unpublicized display of Israel's nuclear readiness — by fielding its nuclear force. This posture was not without precedent, as Israel had been said to have taken such a stance during the first difficult days of the Yom Kippur War (Seymour M. Hersh, *The Samson Option: Israel's Nuclear Arsenal and American Foreign Policy* [New York: Random House, 1991], 225–40). Once the emergency was over, the "curtains" over the bomb would be drawn

again. As Foreign Minister Shimon Peres affirmed in normal times, "So long as they [Syria, Iran, Iraq] pose a constant threat to us, we cannot dismiss their concerns by affirming that we possess no [nuclear] weapons" (interview in *Akhbar al-Yawm* [Cairo], September 17, 1994). Under such circumstances, he said, the "vagueness on the nuclear issue is part of Israel's security concept" (*Davar*, January 27, 1995). In fact, Peres admitted, "The fear of these states [Iran, Iraq, Libya] who think we have nuclear weapons is our deterrent. We have always said we will not be the first to introduce atomic weapons into the region. The fog which covers the issue is our deterrent" (AFP, in FBIS [NES], February 12, 1995, 39).

26. During the crisis, reports indicated that Jordan was helping Iraq monitor Israel's military preparations. For example, General Shahak disclosed that Jordanian planes were flying reconnaissance missions along the Israeli-Jordanian border for the Iraqis. "We judge from their [the Jordanian's] altitudes and flight patterns that they are gathering photographic and electronic information for relay to Baghdad," he said (interview in *Jane's Defence Weekly*, cited in *Jerusalem Post International Edition*, October 13, 1990). In mid-February 1991 Israeli "defense elements" again indicated that the Jordanian air force was photographing military sites inside Israel on Iraq's behalf (*Ha'aretz*, February 15, 1991). Despite expressions of Israeli "concern," there were no reports of Israel's trying to interfere with the Jordanian reconnaissance missions. In fact, Arens publicly downplayed the Jordanian-Iraqi military connection, choosing to claim instead that "not since the war started" were there Iraqi reconnaissance flights over Jordanian territory (interview, Jerusalem Domestic Service, FBIS [NES], February 19, 1991, 83).

27. In this context, the message delivered to Powell by General Barak could be viewed as preparation for the possibility that Israel would stop following the U.S. line and attack the Scud sites in western Iraq. The message was that Washington must recognize that if Israel were faced with an Iraqi mass destruction attack, it would have no choice but to act.

28. Raviv and Melman, *Friends in Deed*, 511 n.

29. *Newsweek*, March 18, 1991, 36.

30. Raviv and Melman, *Friends in Deed*, 389. The Jericho II, which Israel began developing in 1975, was described as a mobile, two-stage, solid-propellant model that was successfully tested in 1987 (Janne E. Nolan and Albert D. Wheelon, "Third World Ballistic Missiles," *Scientific American*, August 1990, 37). Reportedly, on May 16, 1987, the "inertial-guided" missile flew some 960 kilometers into the Mediterranean Sea after being launched from somewhere in the Negev (*San Francisco Examiner*, October 2, 1987). It has been claimed that a second secret test was conducted in September 1988 ("Israel in Second Secret Test of Jericho IRBM," *Jane's Defence Weekly*, November 19, 1988, 1258). The U.S. Arms Control and Disarmament Agency, in its publication *1988 World Military Expenditures and Arms Transfers*, listed "Jericho Follow-ons" with a 1,500-kilometer range as "tested" (cited in *Washington Post*, September 16, 1989). The Pentagon reportedly estimated that the Jericho II could hurl a payload of 500 kilograms more than 1,500 kilometers (*Jerusalem Post International Edition*, June 17, 1995). Naturally, the conclusion was reached that the upgraded Jericho "would be capable of

hitting the capitals of all of Israel's potential enemies, including Baghdad" ("Israel in Second Secret Test"). Yet although Raviv and Melman do not elaborate, the implication of their account is that development of the Jericho II was halted before the serial production stage. Thus, the missile never reached operational status, and the focus shifted to the development of the Jericho IIB.

31. Raviv and Melman, *Friends in Deed*, 511 n. Perhaps as a lesson of this debacle, Israel has since been more forthcoming in releasing information about its Jericho capability. Israel Aircraft Industries' sources recently revealed that the Jericho first stage has a liftoff thrust of about 43,000 kilograms, although the exact figure "is classified" (Craig Covault, "IAF Highlights New Israeli Booster," *Aviation Week and Space Technology*, October 17, 1994, 25). Defense Ministry Director-General David Ivri has even taken the unusual step of acknowledging that Israel maintains "a number" of Jericho ballistic missiles. However, he declined to provide details about this capability (*Jerusalem Post*, June 19, 1996, citing *Jane's Defence Weekly*). If this information is true, the implication is that in the wake of the Gulf War, Israel has adopted a "minimum deterrence" posture with regard to the SSM component of its nuclear arsenal. It acknowledged existence of a small dedicated force, presumably hardened so it could survive a surprise attack, which would be capable of retaliating with nuclear weapons even after absorbing a first strike. Nevertheless, its range remains uncertain.

32. Aronson, *The Politics and Strategy of Nuclear Weapons*, 202.

33. *Jerusalem Post International Edition*, September 23, 1989. Some influential Israeli commentators berated the government for "apologizing" to Moscow for test-firing the Jericho. See Ze'ev Schiff, *Ha'aretz*, September 19, 1989.

34. The Jericho IIB, which is reportedly equipped with a third stage, seems to be the same as Shavit, the missile that launched Israel's first satellite, Ofek 1, on September 19, 1988. The Soviets, however, alleged that Israel launched "a similar missile" in January 1988 (Moscow Radio Peace and Progress in Hebrew, FBIS [SOV], September 21, 1989, 23). In 1989 there were apparently two tests of this version. U.S. intelligence sources were evidently behind American media reports alleging that on July 5 an Israeli Jericho IIB missile, launched from a base in South Africa, flew some 1,500 kilometers toward Antarctica (*Jane's Defence Weekly*, July 15, 1989, 59; *Newsweek*, November 6, 1989, 52; see also *New York Times*, October 27, 1989). In September of that year the Soviet Defense Ministry reported that an Israeli missile "with a range of 1300 km" was launched from "the Jerusalem area and landed in the Mediterranean 400 km north of Benghazi, Libya" (TASS in English, FBIS [SOV], September 15, 1989, 13; Moscow Radio Peace and Progress). It is impossible to ascertain which version of the missile was tested on that occasion, but a Pentagon official said that there "was no reason to disbelieve" the Soviet claim (*Washington Post*, September 16, 1989). One source reported that the missile covered 820 kilometers before landing in the Mediterranean (*International Defense Review*, cited in *Jerusalem Post International Edition*, September 23, 1989). "American experts" were quoted as saying that the Jericho IIB could carry a one-ton warhead more than 2,700 kilometers or a half-ton [500-kilogram] warhead up to 3,500 kilometers (*Newsweek*, November 16, 1989, 52). One expert calculated that if the

Shavit were deployed as a ballistic missile, it could deliver a 775-kilogram payload a distance of 4,000 kilometers (Steve Fetter, "Israeli Ballistic Missile Capabilities," *Physics and Society*, July 1990, 3–4). But some estimates alleged that, based on the radius of the missile and its payload, it has an inter-continental ballistic missile (ICBM) capability, albeit with an unspecified payload capacity (*Baltimore Sun*, November 23, 1988; *Washington Post*, September 16, 1989; Aronson, *The Politics and Strategy of Nuclear Weapons*, 205). At any rate, the long range of the missile would explain Moscow's growing alarm.

35. *Washington Times*, November 15, 1989. See also report of Australian intelligence, marked "for Australian eyes only," published in *Australian* (Sydney), September 30, 1990. *Jane's World Air Force* has speculated that Israel has three Jericho missile squadrons based near Sederot Mikha, 45 kilometers southeast of Tel Aviv. This report did not specify a particular version of the Jericho (cited in *Jerusalem Post*, June 19, 1996). Less then two months later, however, a related source indicated that Israel possesses 50 Jericho IIs with a range of 1,500 kilometers, each capable of delivering a maximum payload of 1,000 kilograms (*Jane's Sentinel*, cited in *Jerusalem Post*, August 16, 1996).

36. Cited in *Jerusalem Post International Edition*, June 17, 1995. There are varying estimates of the range of the Jericho I, a missile first developed and fielded in the 1960s with the assistance of France. The DIA has reportedly assessed that the Jericho I can carry a payload of about 450 to 680 kilograms a distance of some 650 kilometers, and that Israel possesses 50 such missiles (*Washington Times*, November 15, 1989). However, other sources indicated the missile's range as between 450 and 480 kilometers (see Peter Pry, *Israel's Nuclear Arsenal* [Boulder, Colo.: Westview Press and Croom Helm, 1984], 95). A more recent report suggests that the Jericho I has a range of 500 kilometers and a maximum payload of 500 kilograms. According to this report, there are 150 Jericho I missiles in Israel's arsenal. About 50 are deployed on mobile launchers in shelters near nuclear-warhead storage facilities. A further 100 are said to be deployed at Zekhariyah, in the Judean Hills, several kilometers southeast of Tel Aviv (*Jane's Sentinel*, in *Jerusalem Post*, August 16, 1996; see also Bill Gertz, "Scud's Bigger Brothers," *Air Force Magazine*, June 1994, 56). In contrast, based on analysis of satellite imagery, it was subsequently claimed that the Zekhariyah base houses "approximately" 50 Jericho IIs (Harold Hough, "Could Israel's Assets Survive a Preemptive Strike?" *Jane's Intelligence Review*, September 1997 [http://www.janes.com/publ . . . ditors/jir9709/hough.html]). Yet the specifications contained in this report suggest that the missiles at Zekhariyah are of the Jericho IIB, not Jericho II, version.

37. *Facts on File*, December 31, 1990, 959.

38. Atkinson, *Crusade*, 85 and 93; Raviv and Melman, *Friends in Deed*, 389.

39. Ze'ev Schiff, "Israel after the War," *Foreign Affairs*, Spring 1991, 21–22; Raviv and Melman, *Friends in Deed*, 384–85; Freedman and Karsh, *The Gulf Conflict*, 294–95.

40. Atkinson, *Crusade*, 93.

41. Raviv and Melman, *Friends in Deed*, 389.

42. After the first Scud attack on Israel, Powell, described by one of his aides as "very

concerned," was "constantly on the telephone with General Schwarzkopf" (Raviv and Melman, *Friends in Deed*, 400). And Cheney reportedly even stated at one point that "as long as I am secretary of defense, the Defense Department will do as I tell them. The number one priority is to keep Israel out of the war" (Gordon and Trainor, *The Generals' War*, 234).

43. *Los Angeles Times*, November 6, 1990.

44. Israel Television Network, FBIS (NES), January 16, 1991, 24, citing "an assessment prevalent among Israeli Air Force officers."

45. Interview with *Yedi'ot aharonot* (Leshabbat Supplement), February 1, 1991, 1 and 2.

46. Some Israeli analysts have claimed that based on its performance in the Iran-Iraq war, the Scud stood a 95 percent chance of delivering its payload within one kilometer of the target. *Jerusalem Post International Edition*, April 14, 1990; see also Steven Zaloga, "Ballistic Missiles in the Third World: Scud and Beyond," *International Defense Review*, November 1988, 1423–27; Reuven Pedatzur, *The Arrow System and the Active Defense Against Ballistic Missiles* (Hebrew), Memorandum series (Tel Aviv: Joffe Center of Strategic Studies, Tel Aviv University, October 1993), 64 n. 31. On the Scud performance in the Iran-Iraq war, see Brig. Gen. (Res.) Aharon Levran, "The Iran-Iraq War: The Military Balance, Major Developments and Repercussions," *Global Affairs*, Summer 1986, 75–77.

47. George N. Lewis, Steve Fetter, and Lisbeth Gronlund, "Casualties and Damage from the Scud Attacks in the 1991 Gulf War," DACS Working Paper (Cambridge, Mass.: Center for International Studies, MIT, March 1993), 19–20, 24, and 25–26. Generally, the range error of a missile is larger than the cross-range (or track) error. For an estimate of "approximately" 3,000 meters CEP for the modified Scud, see Department of Defense, *Conduct of Persian Gulf War: Final Report* (Washington, D.C.: GPO, April 1992), 13; see also Daniel Leshem, "Surface-to-Surface Missiles in Iraq" (Hebrew), in *Memorandum* (Tel Aviv: Joffe Center for Strategic Studies, Tel Aviv University, November 1993), 37, for an estimate of a CEP between 2,000 and 3,000 meters for the al-Husayn, and see Gen. Khaled bin Sultan, *Desert Warrior: A Personal View of the Gulf War by the Joint Forces Commander* (New York: HarperCollins, 1995), 347, who reports a CEP of "over 3000 yards" for the same missile.

48. The probability of killing (Pk) any hardened target is a function of its lethal radius (LR), or the area within which the warhead must land in order to destroy the target, and the missile's accuracy in CEPs. Assuming that the missile is 100% reliable — i.e., would perform as planned — the Pk of a single warhead is as follows: $Pk = 1 - .5^{(LR/CEP)^2}$. Assuming the dome building at Dimona is 60 feet (about 20 meters) in diameter (as reported by Mordekhai Vanunu, *Sunday Times*, October 5, 1986) and that the CEP of al-Hijarah is 2 kilometers, then the probability of a single missile hitting the reactor would be $1 - .5^{(10\,m/2000\,m)^2}$ or 1.7×10^{-5}, or 17 in a million.

49. If more than one warhead of the same Pk is fired at the target, the n-shot kill probability is $Pkn = [1 - (1 - (Pk))^n]$. Thus the probability of hitting the reactor if 100

al-Hijarahs were fired would have been $[1-(1-1.7\times10^{-5})^{100}]$ or 1.7×10^{-3}, or 17 in 10,000. Thus even if Iraq had launched 10,000 salvos of al-Hijarahs with each salvo comprising 100 fully reliable missiles, it would have likely hit the reactor building no more than 17 times.

50. Data provided by Dr. George N. Lewis of MIT.

51. Raviv and Melman, *Friends in Deed*, 395.

CHAPTER 7: THE SOVIET FACTOR

1. President Gorbachev's personal emissary, Yevgeny Primakov, interview in *Literaturnaya gazeta* (Moscow), November 7, 1990.

2. On the second factor, see for instance *Krasnaya zvezda* (Moscow), October 23, 1990.

3. In trying to form an Arab coalition to oppose the U.S. approach to the crisis, Primakov listed a host of other reasons. He said: "Among the results of the war, if it breaks out, is that the balance between Arabs and non-Arabs in the region would be shattered; Iraq's capabilities would be confined; tensions and disturbances against Arab regimes would be created, and the Palestinian question would be frozen for many years to come, in addition to potential complex problems for Jordan. As for oil production, it will stop for months, probably years." Interview, *al-Ahali* (Cairo), FBIS (SOV), November 5, 1990, 16.

4. Interview, *Literaturnaya gazeta*, October 3, 1990.

5. Interview, *al-Hayat* (London), November 11, 1990.

6. As relayed by Turkish Prime Minister Yildrim Akbulut, TRT Television Network, FBIS (WEU), January 12, 1991, 36.

7. Interview, *Der Morgen* (Berlin), March 8, 1991.

8. Interview, Ankara Domestic Service, FBIS (WEU), February 26, 1991, 43.

9. James A. Baker III, *The Politics of Diplomacy* (New York: J. P. Putnam's Sons, 1995), 401; Lawrence Freedman and Efraim Karsh, *The Gulf Conflict, 1990–1991: Diplomacy and War in the New World Order* (Princeton: Princeton University Press, 1994), 176.

10. Baker, *The Politics of Diplomacy*, 398; Freedman and Karsh, *The Gulf Conflict*, 176.

11. Interview, *al-Hayat*, in Foreign Broadcast Information Service (Union of Soviet Republics), January 4, 1993, 50.

12. On widespread concerns in Tajikistan regarding chemical fallout from an Iraqi resort to CW, see Dushanbe Domestic Service, in FBIS (SOV), February 7, 1991, 86. However, there are good grounds to believe that the publicizing of Soviet concern over the welfare of its Central Asian Muslims was meant specifically for external eyes. For example, Kyrgyzstan President Askar Akayev had complained that none of the Central Asian republics had any say in the formation of Soviet policy toward the Gulf crisis. Irina Zviagelskaya and Vitaly Naumkin, "Russia and the Middle East: Continuity and Change," in *Russia and the Third World in the Post-Soviet Era*, ed. Mohiaddin Mesbahi (Gainsville: University Press of Florida, 1994), 348.

13. Vienna Television Service, FBIS (WEU), October 26, 1990, 3. The Soviets

reportedly sold the Saudis some 5 million gas masks (*Izvestiia* [Moscow], January 29, 1991). On Saudi defensive preparations for CW, see also *Frankfurter Rundschau*, October 25, 1990.

14. Col. Gen. Stansilav Petrov (chief of USSR Defense Ministry Chemical Troops), interview, Moscow Central Television Vostok Program and Orbita Network, FBIS (SOV), January 31, 1991, 11.

15. Interview, *Trud* (Moscow), FBIS (SOV), January 24, 1991, 14; interview, *Izvestiia*, January 29, 1991.

16. Interview, Moscow World Service in English, FBIS (SOV), February 4, 1991, 15. General Petrov, the Soviet CW expert, saw no problem with the bombing of Iraq's chemical munitions stores, however. Speaking of the coalition air campaign, he stated: "People living in our southern republics — Armenia, Azarbaijan, Georgia, Turkmenistan — would be in no danger," even if Iraqi sites containing "500 and more tons" of chemical agents were destroyed. "Large mountain areas and considerable altitude variations would prevent air currents from carrying chemical agents as far as our borders in any significant concentrations," he said. Interview, *Krasnaya Zvezda*, FBIS (SOV), February 25, 1991, 17–18.

17. Interview, *Izvestiia*, January 29, 1991; interview, *Rabochaya Tribuna* (Moscow), FBIS (SOV), January 24, 1991, 14. Ironically, Petrov also claimed that the air campaign was only partially successful, which left Saddam with substantial portions of his mass destruction arsenal intact. See also interview with Colonel of the Medical Service, N. Ye. Uskov (deputy chief of the USSR Ministry of Defense Central Military Medical Directorate Sanitary and Epidemiological Department), *Krasnaya Zvezda*, January 30, 1991.

18. FBIS (SOV), February 11, 1991, 21–22, citing the Cairo paper *al-Haqiqa* of February 2, 1991. Considering that Iraq's BW weapons and programs came out of the war virtually unscathed, however, this information must be viewed with great skepticism. The Soviets could have even been the source of the report in the first place.

19. Marshal Sergei Akhromeyev, ABC-TV, *This Week*, February 10, 1991. Gen. Vladimir Lobov, interview, *Der Morgen*, February 18, 1991.

20. See, for instance, TASS International Service, FBIS (SOV), February 11, 1991, 4.

21. Moscow Central Television First Program, FBIS (SOV), January 28, 1991, 17.

22. TASS International Service, FBIS (SOV), February 20, 1991, 25. On Soviet defensive preparations, see also Col. Gen. S. Petrov, interview in Moscow Central Television Vostok Program and Orbita Network, FBIS (SOV), January 31, 1991, 12.

23. See Graham N. Thompson, James Kinnear, and Alaric Searle, "Chemical Defense Capability in the Soviet Ground Forces," *Armed Forces*, September 1, 1987, 400.

24. See, for example, V. V. Gradosel'skii, *Iadernoe khimicheskoe i bakteriologicheskoe oruzhiye i zashchita ot nego* (Nuclear, chemical, and bacteriological weapons and defense against them) (Moscow: DOSAAF, 1970); A. M. Arkhangel'skiy, *Bakteriologicheskoe oruzhiye zashchita ot nego* (Bacteriological weapons and defense against them) (Moscow: Voyeinzdat, 1971); G. A. Belykh, *Oruzhiye massovogo porazheniya i zashchita ot nego* (Mass destruction weapons and defense against them) (Moscow: DOSAAF, 1973); N. I. Karakchiev, *Toksikologiia OV i zashchita ot oruzhiye massovogo porazheniya* (Toxicology of

chemical agents and defense against mass destruction weapons) (Tashkent: Meditsina, 1973).

25. Thompson et al., "Chemical Defense," 400. See also C. J. Dick, "Soviet Chemical Warfare Capabilities," *International Defense Review*, January 1981, 31–37. It may be noted that the Soviet mass organization DOSAAF (*Dobrovol'noe obshchestvo sodiestviya armii, aviatsii i flota*, or Voluntary society for assistance to the army, air force, and navy), the most important element in the Soviet system for pre-induction, military indoctrination, and training of youth in the USSR, evolved out of the old Oso. Avia. Khim., literally the Society for Assistance to Aviation in the Event of Chemical War.

26. Already at their November 1985 summit meeting in Geneva, President Reagan and Secretary Gorbachev had pledged to initiate discussions on ways to prevent the spread of chemical weapons. Gorbachev specifically raised the problem of chemical proliferation in a pre-summit speech to the French parliament. Subsequently, it was reported that during U.S.-Soviet talks in Bern, Switzerland, the two sides also considered the "countries that are most inclined to produce and use chemical weapons." *New York Times*, March 6, 1986.

27. Ze'ev Schiff and Ehud Ya'ari, *Intifada: The Palestinian Uprising— Israel's Third Front* (New York: Simon and Schuster, 1990), 312.

28. Ibid. However, the authors maintain that the visit took place in 1987. For the 1988 date of the visit see *Washington Times*, April 8, 1988.

29. Apparently in a bid to put the best face on the Syrian-Soviet tiff, *Krasnaya zvezda* reported on October 8, 1988, that General Pikalov held "discussions of questions on the protection of the troops."

30. Schiff and Ya'ari, *Intifada*, 312–13.

31. See interview with Primakov in Moscow Central Television First Program Network, FBIS (SOV), February 20, 1991, 13; and *Izvestiia*, February 18, 1991.

32. *New York Times*, December 22, 1995. According to an UNSCOM report, Iraq produced 100 empty bomb casings for the project and claimed to have destroyed 25. But the fate of the remaining 75 is unclear (cited in Associated Press, United Nations, April 11, 1996). However, the U.S. intelligence downplayed the military significance of an Iraqi radiological weapon (see "Possible Iraqi Radiological Weapons" [Arlington, Va.: CIA, January 1991] [Gulflink]; "Use of Radioactive Material in Scud Warhead," Filename:002bk.91d [Washington, D.C.: DIA, February 19, 1991] [Gulflink]; "Comments on House Republican Research Committee Paper 'Iraq's Other Bomb,'" Filename:0164pgv.90d [Washington, D.C.: DIA, n.d.] [Gulflink]).

33. "Iraqi Chemical Warfare," (Washington, D.C.: DIA, February 1991) (Gulflink); "Iraqi Chemical Employment Doctrine (U)," Filename:27640053.92r (Washington, D.C.: DIA, October 1991) (Gulflink). The DIA, in its reporting to Congress, has insisted that the role of the Soviets was limited to "defensive CBW equipment and training to the Iraqis in the early 1980s" ("Questions from Chairman Riegle," Filename:oriegle.894 [Washington, D.C.: DIA, August 1994] [Gulflink]). However, the distinction is rather semantic. Possession of a *defensive* CW doctrine and equipment are a prerequisite for conducting offensive chemical warfare operations.

34. Riegle Report, chap. 1 (pt. 2). Allegedly, the new compounds were five to seven times more effective than VX and could be produced at industrial fertilizer plants. *Washington Post*, August 16, 1998.

35. Indeed, Brig. Gen. Walter Busbee, U.S. Army Chemical and Material Destruction Agency, Aberdeen Proving Grounds, reportedly alleged that the Scud warheads that UNSCOM found filled with nerve agents "were exported to Iraq from the former Soviet Union" (cited in Riegle Report, chap. 1 [pt. 1]). This claim was subsequently disputed by the DIA ("Questions from Chairman Riegle").

36. For example, Harvey J. McGeorge II, "Munitions Analysis: Soviet Chemical Bombs," *Nuclear, Biological and Chemical Defense and Technology International*, June 1986, 64.

37. The Soviet Union had joined the Biological Weapons Convention in 1992. However, Pasechnik "frightened" British intelligence and later the CIA when he told them that his work had involved "offensive-biowarfare research into Yersinia pestis, or Black Death—an airborne contagious bacterial organism that wiped out the population of Europe around the year 1348." Richard Preston, "The Bioweaponeers," *New Yorker*, March 9, 1998, 58.

38. *Literaturnaya gazeta*, September 12, 1990. For the Gorbachev regime's position on the subject of Soviet foreknowledge of the Iraqi invasion see Foreign Minister Shevardnadze, cited in *Rabochaya tribuna* (Moscow), October 14, 1990.

39. Interview, "The Gulf War," *Frontline*, PBS, January 10, 1996. See also Primakov's accounts of his meetings with Saddam in *Pravda* (Moscow), March 1 and 2, 1991.

40. For Saddam's uncompromising speech, see *New York Times*, February 22, 1991.

41. Baker, *The Politics of Diplomacy*, 407.

42. Interview, Ankara Domestic Service, FBIS (WEU), February 26, 1991, 44.

43. Interview, Moscow Central Television First Program Network, FBIS (SOV), February 20, 1991, 14.

44. Ambassador Chernishev, for instance, said that he did "not think" the United States and the other coalition members "would resort to mass destruction weapons in return [for an Iraqi chemical attack]." Interview, Ankara Domestic Service, FBIS (WEU), February 26, 1991, 44.

45. For example, in the mid-1980s, "East European sources" were quoted as saying that given the growing U.S.-Israeli strategic cooperation and reports about the deployment of the Jericho missile, "the Soviet leadership feared an Israeli mood in which the political echelon will view the use of nuclear weapons against Soviet targets, such as Soviet Navy ships in the Mediterranean, as a possible scenario." The Soviets were also concerned about "the transfer of authority for using nuclear weapons to the military echelon." Consequently, Soviet authorities were said to be "interested in further clarification of Israel's policy beyond the formula according to which Israel 'will not be the first country to introduce nuclear weapons into the region.' The sources said such clarification in secret talks and an emerging public debate on the issue of nuclear policy will aid the Soviets in curbing Arab nuclear trends" (*Davar*, May 23, 1985). In 1993 it

was revealed that an Israeli district court had found Col. (Res.) Shimon Levinson guilty of spying for the KGB and had sentenced him to 12 years imprisonment. According to published extracts from the verdict, the case involved the passing during the 1980s of "nuclear and military secrets" to the Soviet Union (*Pravda*, September 10, 1993). Even today, the Russian SVR (*Sluzhba vneshney radvedki*, or External intelligence service) and its military counterpart, the GRU, continue to be "especially interested in [Israel's] nonconventional weapons" (*Ha'aretz*, December 18, 1995).

46. On Gorbachev's final diplomatic offensive, see Baker, *The Politics of Diplomacy*, 402–8; Freedman and Karsh, *The Gulf Conflict*, 374–85.

47. Foreign Minister Bessmertnykh, TASS International Service, FBIS (SOV), February 28, 1991, 17.

48. Tunis Domestic Service, FBIS (NES), February 20, 1991, 23.

49. Baghdad Domestic Service, FBIS (NES), February 25, 1991, 40; interview, *Sawt al-sha'b* (Amman), February 23, 1991; interview, *Alef ba* (Baghdad), March 6, 1991. For earlier such predictions by General Filatov, see *Komsomolskaya pravda*, February 1, 1991. Filatov's rosy reports could be viewed as indirect confirmation that Iraqi commanders had provided Saddam with misinformation about the state of the war.

50. *Sovetskaya rossiya* (Moscow), FBIS (SOV), February 27, 1991, 12 and 13.

51. Interview, *Krasnaya zvezda*, January 31, 1991.

52. FBIS (SOV), February 25, 1991, 17 and 18.

53. *Sovetskaya rossiya*, February 8, 1991.

54. Vitaliy Churkin, chief of the Information Directorate of the USSR Foreign Ministry, cited in TASS International Service in Russian, FBIS (SOV), February 11, 1991, 4.

55. Many aspects of this episode are still a mystery. For example, one source indicated that only one Scud was fired by the Egyptians (Chaim Herzog, *The Arab-Israeli Wars: War and Peace in the Middle East* [New York: Random House, 1982], 279). But another report claimed that two missiles were fired (Shmuel Bar, *The Yom Kippur War in the Eyes of the Arabs* [Hebrew] [Tel Aviv: Ma'arakhot, 1986], 66). Still others said that three Scuds were launched (*Christian Science Monitor*, June 17, 1991). General Khaled, who reports that three missiles were involved, has claimed that the entire affair was due to the Scuds' operational constraints. According to him, the Egyptians prepared the missiles "at the precise moment" that President Anwar al-Sadat made the cease-fire announcement, and it was simply impossible to reverse the countdown once the liquid fuel had been pumped into the Scud. The missiles then landed five minutes after the truce went into effect on October 22 (Gen. Khaled bin Sultan, *Desert Warrior: A Personal View of the Gulf War by the Joint Forces Commander* [New York: HarperCollins, 1995], 348). However, this version does not seem very likely. In the context of the Arab-Israeli conflict, the Scud was always considered a strategic weapon. As such, the order to fire the missile, or missiles, should have come from a fairly senior Egyptian official, perhaps even from Sadat himself. This would have been the case even if it had not been the first time these weapons had gone into action. By the same token, the explanation provided by a senior Israeli official was also improbable. Maj. Gen. Shlomo Gazit, the

AMAN chief at the time, sought to downplay the firing of the Scud by claiming that it was made on an "experimental basis," to check if the system worked (cited in *Los Angeles Times*, October 20, 1975). Even if this were true, such a test would not have precluded its being a strategic signal to Israel. Moreover, it would seem improbable that a hard-pressed army would begin "experimenting" with a new weapon system at the most crucial moment of the war. Instead, the version reported by John K. Cooley, the veteran Middle East correspondent, seems closest to the truth: "President Anwar al-Sadat of Egypt said recently that Egypt fired three missiles — presumed to be Scuds, though Mr. Sadat did not say so — at Israeli military targets in Sinai during the final hours of the October, 1973, war. This was a warning that Israeli civilian targets, including cities, could be reached from Egyptian territory" (*Christian Science Monitor*, April 3, 1974). On the role of the Scud in Egypt's strategy at the time, see Saad al-Shazli, *The Crossing of the Suez* (San Francisco: American Mideast Research, 1980), 15, 94, and 116.

56. See W. Andrew Terrill, "The Chemical Warfare Legacy of the Yemen War," *Comparative Strategy* 10 (1991), 109–19.

57. *New York Times*, November 22, 1973. On the controversy regarding the circumstances of the U.S. DefCon 3 alert and the Soviet nuclear moves, see Marvin Kalb and Bernard Kalb, *Kissinger* (New York: Dell, 1975), 541–64; Yona Bendmann and Yishai Cordova, "The Soviet Nuclear Threat Towards the Close of the Yom Kippur War," *Jerusalem Journal of International Relations* 5 (1980), 94–110; Seymour M. Hersh, *The Samson Option: Israel's Nuclear Arsenal and American Foreign Policy* (New York: Random House, 1991), 231–35; Shlomo Aronson, *The Politics and Strategy of Nuclear Weapons in the Middle East* (Albany: State University of New York Press, 1992), 148–49, 334 nn. 26 and 28.

58. See Alex P. Schmid, *Soviet Military Interventions since 1945* (New Brunswick: Transaction Books, 1985), 96–97; Herzog, *The Arab-Israeli Wars*, 278–79. For an "insiders'" account of the Soviet military involvement in Egypt at the time, see General Oleg Sarin and Colonel Lev Dvoretsky, *Alien Wars: The Soviet Union's Aggression Against the World, 1919 to 1989* (Novato, Calif.: Presidio Press, 1996), 122–28.

59. Interview, *al-Hayat*, FBIS (NES), January 4, 1993, 50–51.

60. Ibid., p. 51.

61. Interview with General al-Samarra'i, *Sunday Times*, February 19, 1995.

62. On the Bush administration's handling of the Soviet factor during the Gulf crisis, see Robert M. Gates, *From the Shadows: The Ultimate Insider's Story of Five Presidents and How They Won the Cold War* (New York: Simon and Schuster, 1996), 497–500; Baker, *The Politics of Diplomacy*, 285–87, 291–94, 308–13, and 391–408.

63. Baker, *The Politics of Diplomacy*, 399.

CHAPTER 8: MASS DESTRUCTION WEAPONS

1. An important question emerges: Would the Iraqi missile crews have carried out the order to fire chemical warheads on Israel or on Saudi Arabia? Would they have also fired biological weapons on either one of these countries? Given that the crews apparently took part in the arming and deployment of the BW weapons, a hypothesis about a

rebellion is not readily supported. Still, the reaction of the Iraqi soldiers might have been different if they had believed that the U.S. military was at their door.

2. Interview, *Independent*, July 5, 1996.

3. One apparent attempt on Saddam's life involved the dropping of two "deep-penetrating bunker-cracking" GBU-28 bombs, weighing more than 2,100 kilograms each, by two USAF F-111s. The targets were two deeply tunneled bunkers at al-Taji Air Base, a few kilometers north of Baghdad. The raid — which took place on February 27, 1991, just a few hours before the cease-fire went into effect — reportedly killed "a number of senior [Iraqi] military officials." At the time, Saddam was apparently hiding in Baghdad (*Aviation Week and Space Technology*, May 20, 1991, 22; and June 21, 1993, 59; Craig Covault, "USAF Urges Greater Use of Spot Based on Gulf War Experience," *Aviation Week and Space Technology*, July 13, 1992, 65; Rick Atkinson, *Crusade: The Untold Story of the Persian Gulf War* (Boston: Houghton Mifflin, 1993), 473. Notably, one source disputes the notion that the bombing was aimed at Saddam (Michael R. Gordon and Gen. Bernard Trainor, *The Generals' War: The Inside Story of the Conflict in the Gulf* [Boston: Little, Brown, 1995], 411 and 511 n. 10).

4. This quotation is cited in Lawrence Freedman and Efraim Karsh, *The Gulf Conflict, 1990–1991: Diplomacy and War in the New World Order* (Princeton: Princeton University Press, 1994), 363. Saddam's statement does not appear in the somewhat fragmentary FBIS version of the interview as relayed by Baghdad Domestic Service two days later. See FBIS (NES), January 31, 1991, 20–24.

5. In this regard the comments made in 1996 by Dr. Husayn al-Shahrestani could be viewed as credible. He recalled that in the summer of 1980, during his imprisonment in Iraq, Saddam's half-brother — Barazan al-Tikriti, who was then head of the Mukhabarat — offered to set him free if he helped Iraq develop nuclear weapons. "He literally said," Shahrestani recounted, " 'We want a strong hand in order to rearrange the map in the Middle East'. This was Saddam's idea" (interview, *al-Majallah*, FBIS [NES], February 1, 1996, 24; for similar earlier comments by Shahrestani, see *Yedi'ot aharonot*, 7 Yamim Supplement, July 24, 1992, 23, 24). Saddam, in fact, made little secret of his plan to build up Iraq's strategic power. He declared openly that the building of an "Iraq that will be scientifically, economically and militarily strong" was an absolute precondition to defeating "our Zionist enemy" (speech cited in *al-Thawrah* [Baghdad], March 20, 1979).

6. Freedman and Karsh, *The Gulf Conflict*, 435.

7. Interview, IDF Radio, FBIS (NES), January 17, 1995, 64. The Israeli failure to anticipate Bush's decision to stop the war is in itself surprising. Given his objections to the IDF's plan to attack the Scuds — which were communicated to Arens and Barak again on February 11 — and Israel's argument about the coming mass destruction scenario, there was little else Bush could have done. He held the Israelis at bay by pledging to intensify the hunt for the Scuds, but by the war's end both countries had little hope that the campaign would completely neutralize the Iraqi strategic threat to Israel. At the same time, Bush also voiced doubts about the IDF's plan. An Iraqi CB warhead could still hit in an Israeli city, and the pressure on the Shamir government to respond

with nuclear weapons would be simply irresistible. This was true especially considering that the worst-case approach, advocated by Israel itself, assumed that Iraq might have an advanced CB warhead that could cause mass casualties. Ironically, therefore, the more convincing the Israeli forecast of the looming Iraqi CB attack, the clearer it should have been to Jerusalem that stopping the war would be the only rational solution left for President Bush.

8. *New York Times*, September 28, 1990. Moreover, if Israel indeed lacked the ability to launch a nuclear strike against Iraq via SSMs, its confidence in its nuclear deterrent might have been flimsier than is commonly assumed. Accordingly, Israel could have assigned a higher probability to an Iraqi CB attack and could have seen the Iraqi warning shot as confirmation of its estimate. The existence of such a missile "gap," if there was one, could be among the explanations for Israel's insistence on attacking the Scud launchers in Iraq.

9. The hypothesis that it was the U.S. warnings that deterred Saddam from resorting to CB weapons nonetheless continues to be popular. See Leonard A. Cole, *The Eleventh Plague: The Politics of Biological and Chemical Warfare* (New York: W. H. Freeman, 1997), 127–29; *Los Angeles Times*, October 2, 1996; *Washington Post*, October 2, 1996.

10. Remarks of Tim McCarthy, an UNSCOM missile inspector, Conference on "Start II, Missile Non-Proliferation, and Missile Defense," Panel II, Carnegie Endowment, 1995 (http://wheat.symgrp.com/symgrp/pai/articles/panel2.html]).

11. U.S. News and World Report, *Triumph Without Victory: The Unreported History of the Gulf War* (New York: Random House, 1992), 410.

12. "Iraqi Poison Missile Production," Filename:60012.91s (Washington, D.C.: DIA, n.d.) (Gulflink). Another such report identified al-Hijarah as one of the "chemical munitions delivery systems" in Iraq's possession. "IIR 2 340 0306 91/Iraqi Chemical Munitions, Manufacturing Locations, and Storage Facilities," File 970613_23400306_91d_txt_0001.txt (Washington, D.C.: DIA, n.d.) (Gulflink).

13. UNSCOM 1997, 19 and 22.

14. Raymond A. Zilinskas, "Iraq's Biological Weapons: The Past as Future?" *JAMA*, August 6, 1997, 421. According to this report, which is evidently based on Iraqi statements, all Iraqi munitions that depended on explosion for agent dispersal were of similar design: a tube filled with an explosive charge (burster) was placed in the center of a chamber containing the biological agent. At the moment of impact the burster would explode, rupturing the outer wall of the munition and dispersing the payload. Such a setup would preclude the use of submunitions or bomblets in Iraq's BW weapons.

15. Ibid. Impact detonation is highly wasteful. First, an explosion inevitably renders harmless much of the payload. Second, impact detonation drives a substantial part of the payload into the ground. Third, the small part of the payload aerosolized by the explosion generally is not propelled beyond a few tens of meters. Finally, the size of the aerosolized particles varies widely from large clumps to particles smaller than 1 micron.

16. See *Ma'ariv* (Weekend Supplement), Tel Aviv, January 9, 1998, 43.

17. The revelation was contained in a major article on the Iraqi BW program in *New York Times*, February 26, 1998.

18. *Washington Post*, November 21, 1997.

19. For the aforementioned spray tank, see Chapter 2. The Iraqis could have used a smaller spray tank, or filled the original one to half its capacity, in order to increase the range of their remotely piloted plane.

20. Zilinskas, "Iraq's Biological Weapons," 420; Richard Preston, "The Bioweaponeers," *New Yorker*, March 9, 1998, 60. This would still leave the problem of producing a uniform cloud of spores in the optimal size, which could be efficiently absorbed through inhalation.

21. Arms Control and Disarmament Agency, "Threat Control Through Arms Control: Annual Report to Congress, 1995" (Washington, D.C.: ACDA, July 1996), 67.

22. UNSCOM/TECH, 9.

23. See Moshe Arens, *Milkhama veshalom bamizrakh hatikhon, 1988–92* (Hebrew) (Tel Aviv: Yedi'ot Aharonot, 1995), p. 190.

24. Zilinskas, "Iraq's Biological Weapons," 422. For example, during the Gulf War, there was a ratio of 1:4.5 between casualties caused directly by conventional Scud explosions and other resultant casualties among Israeli civilians. See Eric Karsenty et al., "Medical Aspects of the Iraqi Missile Attacks on Israel," *Israel Journal of Medical Sciences*, November–December 1991, 603–7; George N. Lewis, Steve Fetter, and Lisbeth Gronlund, "Casualties and Damage from the Scud Attacks in the 1991 Gulf War," DACS Working Paper (Cambridge, Mass.: Center for International Studies, MIT, March 1993), 13–19 and 37–39.

25. Upper-altitude winds would tend to blow both CW and BW agents off target. The extent to which the chemicals or agents would spread would depend on the payload size, burst height, type of fill, and the particle or agent's size. "Iraqi Special Weapons Capabilities" (Arlington, Va.: CIA, January 1991) (Gulflink); "Evaluation of Iraqi Special Weapons Capabilities" (Arlington, Va.: CIA, February 1991) (Gulflink).

26. Because the amount of time required for BW particles to fall to the ground decreases in low-level disintegration, the amount of agent that reaches the ground is likely to increase. The level of contamination also depends on the size of the particles. Contamination density tends to rise as droplet or particle size increases. Because of the finite contents of the warhead, however, the area contaminated will decrease as droplet or particle size increases. "Effect of Collision of Chemical-Capable Scud with a Patriot Missile and General Effects of Chemical-Capable Scud Missile," Filename:0140pgv.ood (Washington, D.C.: DIA[?], n.d.) (Gulflink).

27. Roger L. Shapiro et al., "Botulism Surveillance and Emergency Response," *JAMA*, August 6, 1997, p. 433.

28. For Shahak's statement, see Chapter 1. An interesting question is whether either U.S. intelligence or AMAN had anticipated an Iraqi warning shot. Although it is impossible to tell for sure, the predictions by General Shomron, the CIA, and the DIA of a last-ditch Iraqi effort to stop the war certainly do not exclude the possibility that such a forecast was indeed made.

29. "UN: Iraqi Biological Weapons and Ballistic Missile Development Programs Continue," *Near East Report*, December 4, 1995.

30. McGeorge Bundy, "Nuclear Weapons and the Gulf," *Foreign Affairs*, Fall 1991, 94.

31. Yitzhak Shamir, *Sikumo shel davar* (Hebrew) (Tel Aviv: Edanim, 1994), 265. Shamir also wrote that he thought it would be a mistake to "make light" of Saddam's April 1990 threats to "burn half of Israel with chemical weapons" (p. 264).

32. Arens, *Milkhama veshalom*, 229–30. To the end, Shamir argued that Israel would be taking "unnecessary risks" in launching a military operation against the Scud sites. Only on February 27, 1991, did he give in to Arens's constant pressure and authorize an aerial test of the plan. The idea was to check the possible reaction of Jordan in advance of the IDF's planning to overfly its territory on the way to western Iraq (ibid.). Although Shamir might have also concluded that the IDF operation would be ineffective in silencing the Scuds, and costly both in lives and politically, his position was problematic. He meant to retaliate only with U.S. blessings. But any intervention by the IDF would have endangered America's war effort. Thus, whether Israel preempted the Scuds or retaliated in the wake of a CB attack (with U.S. approval), the outcome could have been substantially the same, except that preemption could have minimized Israeli civilian casualties from an Iraqi mass destruction attack. And Shamir's restraint itself meant that the probability of an Iraqi CB strike against Israel continued to grow both directly (as the Scud threat was unimpeded) and indirectly (given that it facilitated the prosecution of the war). As he himself has written: "There was not a single day that I was sure that our 'non-involvement' in a war waged so close to us, relatively, would not end up costing us a much higher price than we had already paid" (Shamir, *Sikumo shel davar*, 264).

33. Shamir's opposition to an IDF military operation, let alone the issuing of overt nuclear threats, indicates that he preferred "pragmatic" consideration over adherence to some strategic doctrine. Evidently, in his mind the predominant consideration in deciding Israel's possible countermoves was the number of casualties a chemical attack would have actually inflicted. This is in spite of the fact that he himself has described the dangers that Israel faced during the war as "great and immense" (Shamir, *Sikumo shel davar*, 264). For Shamir, even an Arab countercity strike with mass destruction weapons was ostensibly insufficient in itself to justify resort to nuclear strategy. As long as Israeli losses were light, he seemed ready to forsake the nuclear option if that meant the war would go on and the Saddam problem would be finished anyway. Ironically, by informing Bush that a CW attack would require an instant Israeli retaliation, Shamir nevertheless indicated that he recognized the grievousness of breaching the conventional threshold in terms of future threats to Israel's national security. Even after the war, even such a staunch supporter of an IDF preemption as General Barak argued: "The missile issue is not going to monopolize our attention because in an all-out war, common sense will make people realize that developments on the battlefront are more important than the home front, where the missiles will be landing, even if 10 times more missiles are fired than in the Gulf War" (Lt. Gen. Ehud Barak, then IDF's chief of staff, interview, *Al-hamishmar*, September 14, 1994).

34. Persian Gulf War Illnesses Task Force, "CIA Support to the U.S. Military Dur-

ing the Persian Gulf War" (Arlington, Va.: Director of Central Intelligence, June 16, 1997), 6.

35. *Jerusalem Post*, February 17, 1991.

36. Freedman and Karsh, *The Gulf Conflict*, 335.

37. For the various reasons, see Office of the Press Secretary, Press Conference, The White House, Washington, D.C., March 30, 1992; Bush's interview with David Frost, cited in *Christian Science Monitor*, March 6, 1996; Gen. Colin Powell, *My American Journey* (New York: Random House, 1995), 524–28; James A. Baker III, *The Politics of Diplomacy* (New York: J. P. Putnam's Sons, 1995), 435–38, 441, and 442.

38. Subsequently, Bush and Scowcroft also argued that they expected Saddam to be toppled anyhow. There was no need to push to Baghdad as Saddam could not possibly survive his defeat politically (George Bush and Brent Scowcroft, "Why We Didn't Remove Saddam," *Time Magazine*, March 2, 1998, 31). However, neither Powell nor Baker mentioned this as a reason to stop the war. Nor, for that matter, did Bush himself refer to it in his press conference of March 30, 1992. See also Appendix A.

39. For an explanation of the merits of some of these arguments, see Appendix A.

40. Persian Gulf War Illnesses Task Force, "CIA Support to the U.S. Military," 2 and 6.

41. Arens, *Milkhama veshalom*, 190. Interestingly, Arens ignored the main mission of such an airborne platform — spraying aerosolized agents.

42. Baker, *The Politics of Diplomacy*, 441.

43. Gen. H. Norman Schwarzkopf, *It Doesn't Take a Hero* (New York: Bantam Books, 1992), 479.

44. For prewar concerns over Iraq's mass destruction option, see ibid., 300, 356, and 389–90; Brian Shellum, "A Chronology of Defense Intelligence in the Gulf War: A Research Aid for Analysts" (Washington, D.C.: DIA History Office, 1987), 19, 22, 27, 29, and 30. See also Atkinson, *Crusade*, 86–90; Gordon and Trainor, *The Generals' War*, 306 and 308. On U.S. worries about Saddam's mass destruction weapons during the war, see Schwarzkopf, *It Doesn't Take a Hero*, 416, 439, 445, and 451–52.

45. A fundamental debate seems to have emerged regarding the level of Iraq's BW program during the Gulf War. Analysts disagree about the possession of dried anthrax and the extent to which Iraq was able to produce spores of the right size. Some have also argued that Iraqi efforts to develop aflatoxin, a curious choice for a biological weapon, suggest that its scientists did not know what they were doing. Others (like Graham S. Pearson) argue that in light of Iraq's known technical advances in other areas, like CW, it would be a mistake to underestimate its BW program. For example, with regard to aflatoxin the Iraqis "may have discovered something new" (*New York Times*, November 21, 1997; also "Iraq's Chemical and Biological Weapons Capability," DOD background briefing, November 14, 1997 [http://www.defenselink.mil/news/Nov1997/x11171997_x114iraq]).

46. Interview, *Yedi'ot aharonot* (Simkhat Torah Supplement), September 29, 1991, 2 and 3. Maj. Gen. Avihu Bin-Nun disclosed that "Israel is investing a major intelligence

effort in ascertaining Iraq's military capability. The Iraqis hid a large number of their missiles; therefore, we do not know how many missiles they still have" (interview, Kol Yisra'el, FBIS [NES], November 5, 1991, 50). Barak, by then the foreign minister of Israel, later held a meeting with Ekeus himself (*Jerusalem Post*, February 14, 1996). One Arabic newspaper described the occasion as "the first of its kind as far as its announcement and the media coverage given to it were concerned" (*al-Hayat*, March 2, 1996).

47. Baker, *The Politics of Diplomacy*, 414.

48. James A. Baker III, "Getting Ready for 'Next Time' in Iraq," *New York Times*, February 27, 1998.

49. See, for example, Elie Kedourie, "Iraq: The Mystery of American Policy," *Commentary*, June 1991, 15–19.

50. Riegle Report, chap. 1 (pt. 2).

51. Gen. Sir Peter de la Billière, *Storm Command: A Personal Account of the Gulf War* (London: HarperCollins, 1992), 98.

52. Atkinson, *Crusade*, 89.

53. De la Billière, *Storm Command*, 211.

54. Ibid., 154.

55. Frank N. Schubert and Theresa L. Kraus (eds.), *The Whirlwind War: The United States Army in Operations Desert Shield and Desert Storm* (Washington, D.C.: United States Army, Center of Military History, 1995), chap. 6 (http://imabss.army.mil/cmh-pg/www6.htm). Naturally, this account is at some variance with the one relayed by General Khaled, who suggested that much of the coalition's noise in the matter was aimed to deceive Saddam (see Chapter 3).

56. "IRAQ: Potential for Chemical Weapons Use," File 970613_dim37_91d_txt_0001.txt (Washington, D.C.: DIA, January 25, 1991) (Gulflink).

57. "Talking Paper for RADM Fox, DDIN, JS," Filename:010bk.90d (Washington, D.C.: DIA, November 24, 1990) (Gulflink); "Chemical and Biological Warfare in the Kuwait Theater of Operations; Iraq's Capability and Posturing (U)," Filename: 0147pgv.ood (Washington, D.C.: DIA, n.d.) (Gulflink). Similarly, the CIA assessed: "We believe Iraq is likely to use unconventional weapons at the start of the ground battle, or if frustrated at their inability to draw Israel into the war." "Desert Storm Briefing" (Arlington, Va.: CIA, January 1991) (Gulflink); "Iraq as a Military Adversary" (Arlington, Va.: CIA, November 1990) (Gulflink).

58. On the dispatch of the British Special Air Service Regiment and the U.S. Delta force, see Atkinson, *Crusade*, 147–48, 177–81, and 231–32; Gordon and Trainor, *The Generals' War*, 241–46.

59. On various U.S. attempts to eliminate Saddam Hussein during Desert Storm, see Atkinson, *Crusade*, 272–74.

60. *Washington Post*, November 21, 1997.

61. "Iraqi Chemical Warheads," Filename 035pgv.91d (Washington, D.C.: DIA, n.d.) (Gulflink). The "greatly increased activity" detected in late December 1990 at the

Samarra (Muthanna) plant was erroneously viewed as linked to Iraq's preparations for CW instead of to the clandestine arming of the Iraqi BW option. See *Sunday Times*, January 27, 1991.

62. "Q&As," Filename:0106pgv.91p (Washington, D.C.: DIA, January 31, 1991) (Gulflink). Notwithstanding, in its report to Congress the DIA said: "Prior to the Persian Gulf War, DIA assessed that Iraq had BW agents weaponized in aerial bombs and Scud missile warheads, and that Iraq was capable of disseminating BW agents with ground-based aerosol generators. "Questions from Chairman Riegle," Filename: oriegle.894 (Washington, D.C.: DIA, August 1994) (Gulflink).

63. Cited in David A. Fulghum and Robert M. Wall, "Hidden Weapon Sites Still Pose Problems," *Aviation Week and Space Technology*, January 16, 1998, 23. Robert D. Walpole, the CIA official heading the agency's investigation of possible chemical exposure during the Gulf War, admitted that after the Iran-Iraq war, CIA analysts developed "tunnel vision" about the way the Iraqis stored chemical munitions. The assumption on the part of the analysts, he said, was that the Iraqis had begun to store chemical weapons in unusual S-shaped bunkers (press conference, *New York Times*, April 10, 1997). Harsh criticism of U.S. intelligence was also leveled by the pilots of the 4th Wing of the USAF Tactical Air Command assigned to hunt the Scuds (see interviews in *Yedi'ot Aharonot* [First Anniversary Supplement], January 10, 1992, 8–10). Even when it hit a BW-related facility, the United States was sometimes unaware of the nature of its target. Such was the case with the Iraqi plant producing the aerial dispersal systems for the biological agents, which was destroyed in the coalition bombings. Its role in Iraq's BW program became apparent only after UNSCOM had inspected the site (International Institute for Strategic Studies report cited in *Ha'aretz*, July 29, 1996).

64. *Washington Post*, November 21, 1997. Apparently, U.S. analysts also suffered from tunnel vision when it came to locating Iraq's BW production facilities. According to one UNSCOM official, al-Hakam "looked like normal industrial sheds," and according to Iraq, the site lacked sophisticated air filtration equipment. Ibid.

65. A DIA message to CENTCOM on the eve of the ground war advised: "The current whereabouts of their [the Iraqis'] chemical inventory is unknown" ("Response to RII-2093," Filename:027pgv.91d [Washington, D.C.: DIA, February 1991] [Gulflink]). Earlier in 1991 the DIA had stated: "We continue to believe chemical warheads are available in limited numbers [to the Iraqis] but do not know with definition the number of CW missile warheads. To provide a number could be interpreted to mean that we know the precise number—we do not." With regard to the location of the chemical warheads, the agency reported: "We have no information." Asked about information regarding "the Iraqi process of preparing chemical warheads for operation" and whether "the Iraqis already have missiles with chemical warheads ready for launching," the DIA responded: "We have no information regarding any of these questions" ("Iraqi Chemical Warheads"). British intelligence was likewise faulty. The British Ministry of Defense said that "chemicals were distributed to the [Iraqi] troops in Kuwait and elsewhere in the theater." It added that as many as "100,000 artillery

shells filled with chemicals and several tons [of bulk agent were] stored near the front line" (cited in *Sunday Times*, January 27, 1991). It could be that both U.S. and British intelligence were the victims of Iraqi deception.

66. The lowest prewar count of Iraqi TELs was 12 and the highest was 22. However, the postwar analysis commissioned by the U.S. Air Force has put the number of mobile launchers in Iraq's possession at 36 (Thomas A. Keaney and Eliot A. Cohen [eds.], *Gulf War Air Power Survey* [Washington, D.C.: GPO, 1993], hereafter *GWAPS, Summary Report*, 87; see also Atkinson, *Crusade*, 145–46; Anthony H. Cordesman and Abraham R. Wagner, *The Lessons of Modern War*, vol. 4: *The Gulf War* [Boulder, Colo.: Westview, 1996], 854–55; Gordon and Trainor, *The Generals' War*, 230 and 496–97 n. 2). One study, however, has argued that the DIA had provided CENTCOM with a "full appraisal of the Iraqi Scud force, including the expected launch sequences, existence of presurveyed launch points in the western Iraqi desert, use of dispersed logistical support and the correct size of the [Iraqi] mobile launcher force" (Lt. Col. Mark Kipphut, USAF, "Theater Missile Defense: Reflections for the Future" [Maxwell AFB, Ala.: Air University, Winter 1996] [http://www.cdsar.af.mil.apj/win96/kipphut.html]). According to this report, the poor performance against the Scuds was the result of faulty planning, not an information gap. In fact, after the war, Iraq declared that it had only 14 operational mobile missile launchers, of which 10 were imported and 4 produced indigenously (UNSCOM 1997, 8).

67. Cordesman and Wagner, *Lessons of Modern War*, 862.

68. Not unlike his American counterparts, Maj. Gen. Bin-Nun, the IAF commander, even predicted that "after two or three days in which the Americans will demonstrate aerial superiority, they will be able to simply march into Kuwait." Cited in IDF Radio, FBIS (NES), January 16, 1991, 24.

69. Arens, *Milkhama veshalom*, 188.

70. *GWAPS*, vol. 2, pt. 1, *Operations*, 182. "Cheney stressed that knocking out the Scuds early was the key to keeping Israel out of the war. Horner was confident he had the problem in hand." Gordon and Trainor, *The Generals' War*, 193.

71. Arens, *Milkhama veshalom*, 201. On the U.S. assurances to Israel, see also *Yedi'ot aharonot*, January 15, 1991. In fact, as a measure of the (misplaced) confidence Jerusalem had in the ability of the USAF to eliminate the Iraqi Scud threat, Israel reportedly agreed not to preempt the Iraqi missiles. *Ma'ariv*, January 15, 1991.

72. Schubert and Kraus, *The Whirlwind War*, chap. 10.

73. Gen. Charles A. Horner, USAF (Ret.), "New-Era Warfare," in *Battlefield of the Future*, ed. Barry R. Schneider and Lawrence E. Grinter (Maxwell Air Force Base, Ala.: Air University Press, September 1994) (http://www.cdsar.af.mil/battle/chp2.html).

74. Kipphut, "Theater Missile Defense." See also Cordesman and Wagner, *Lessons of Modern War*, 860–61. Theater planners could thus believe that the resources necessary to reduce the mobile-Scud threat would exceed expected gains.

75. *GWAPS, Summary Report*, 83–90. See also Kipphut, "Theater Missile Defense"; Cordesman and Wagner, *Lessons of Modern War*, 863.

76. Horner, "New-Era Warfare."

77. Atkinson, *Crusade*, 177.

78. Kipphut, "Theater Missile Defense." See also *GWAPS, Summary Report*, 43. On the resistance to diverting planes from the strategic air campaign for Scud hunting, see Raviv and Melman, *Friends in Deed*, 402–3; Gordon and Trainor, *The Generals' War*, 238.

79. Horner, "New-Era Warfare."

80. Ibid.

81. On the failure of the coalition's strategic air campaign against Iraq's NBC assets, see *GWAPS, Summary Report*, 78–81. The Iraqis admitted to production of biological agents at four sites near Baghdad; however, UNSCOM found no damage to any of these facilities from coalition bombing. Likewise, a February 3, 1991, Defense Department report claimed that 37 Iraqi ammunition sites were destroyed in the allied bombing. The Pentagon, however, subsequently stated that "we believe that three or possibly four bunkers—of a total of about 100—were damaged by bombing." Pentagon officials said that the 1991 report had dramatically exaggerated the bombing's effect (*New York Times*, October 3, 1996). But even those three or four hits had little effect on Iraq's mass destruction potential. In most cases the Iraqis did not store CW munitions in bunkers that they believed the coalition would target. Instead they kept many CW munitions in the open, thus protecting them, as the coalition did not target open areas. In addition, all known production lines of CW precursors were either inactive or had been dismantled by the start of the campaign. Consequently, the CIA has determined that "Coalition bombing resulted in damage to filled chemical munitions at only two facilities—the Muhammadiyat storage area and the storage area at the al-Muthanna chemical production site" ("Statement to the Presidential Advisory Committee on Persian Gulf War Illnesses" [Arlington, Va.: CIA, May 1, 1996] [Gulflink]). According to the most recent Iraqi declarations to UNSCOM, less than 5 percent of Iraq's approximately 700 metric tons of declared chemical agent stockpile was destroyed by coalition bombings (Office of Weapons, Technology and Proliferation, "CIA Report on Intelligence Related to Gulf War Illnesses" [Arlington, Va.: CIA, August 2, 1996] [http://www.dtic.mil/gulflink]).

82. Lt. Col. Terry N. Mayer, USAF, "The Biological Weapon: A Poor Nation's Weapon of Mass Destruction," in Schneider and Grinter, *Battlefield of the Future* (http://www.cdsar.af.mil/battle/chp8.html). Accordingly, the raids were conducted within an hour of sunrise, bright sunshine was required, wind had to be less than 5 knots, and the attack involved using a combination of munitions to better destroy the agents. Each storage tank was attacked by an F-117 fighter-bomber and an F-111 bomber. The F-117 was supposed to "crack" the tank with a 2,000-pound laser-guided bomb. The F-111 was to incinerate the agents with combined effects munitions (which cause blast, flame, and heat) dropped split seconds behind. "On landing, the F-111s were washed down before crew opened the cockpit" (Fulghum and Wall," Hidden Weapon Sites," 23.) However, the careful timing of the attacks indicates that planners

did not expect them to be fully effective. They counted on sunlight to kill any agents that escaped into the air, using the rule of thumb that biological agents are neutralized at a rate of 1 percent per minute by the sun's ultraviolet rays.

83. "Overview," Filename:0135pgv.ood (Washington, D.C.: DIA, n.d.) (Gulflink). The calculation assumes that one gram of anthrax produces one trillion spores—an amount equivalent to 100 million lethal human doses. Thus the prime reason for the "successful" air attacks on these facilities was the removal of Iraq's BW material from the suspected sites prior to the outbreak of hostilities. By the same token, however, the dispersal of the Iraqi CB arsenal before the war has allowed Saddam to continue to wield a mass destruction threat against his neighbors to this day.

84. "Iraq Biological Warfare Threat," Filename:0408pgf.90 (Washington, D.C.: DIA, October 22, 1990) (Gulflink).

85. It has been stated that BW contamination "was assessed as possible only under worst case scenario set of conditions. . . . This possibility was debated at the highest levels of DoD. It was decided that gain far outweighed risk, resulting in the facilities being targeted and destroyed" ("IZ NBC Capabilities," Filename:037pgv.91d [Washington, D.C.: DIA, n.d.] [Gulflink]). Considering the potentially catastrophic impact of the bombing, taking the worst-case scenario into account surely would have made more sense. For example, some U.S. officials admitted that "during the war they didn't realize the sustained high temperatures required to destroy biological agents and the high potential for leakage" (David A. Fulghum, "Iraq Less Defiant as U.S. Troops Deploy," *Aviation Week and Space Technology*, November 24, 1997, 23). The decision is perplexing even by the guidelines offered at the time: "We believe, any planning for military action against Iraqi BW production and storage sites should consider a multiple set of probable outcomes ranging from no release of agent to the liberation of many hundreds of kilograms of live agent resulting in significant collateral loss of life. Unless the total and complete destruction of all agent is assured, then one must presume the release of, at least some, BW agent into the atmosphere" (Interagency Intelligence Community Working Group, "Interim Report on Iraq Biological Warfare [BW]," Filename:001me.90d [Washington, D.C.: DIA, December 17, 1990] [Gulflink]).

86. "(No Subject Line Found)," Filename:0093pgv.91p (Washington, D.C.: DIA, January 23, 1991) (Gulflink). Also "(No Subject Line Found)," Filename:098pgv.91p (Washington, D.C.: DIA, n.d.) (Gulflink).

87. "(No Subject Line Found)," Filename:0093pgv.91p (Washington, D.C.: DIA, January 23, 1991) (Gulflink).

88. "CIA Report on Intelligence Related to Gulf War Illnesses."

89. "Bugs and Things," Filename:omeoo4.90d (Washington, D.C.: DIA, December 3, 1990) (Gulflink).

90. Gordon and Trainor, *The Generals' War*, 439.

91. For a largely sympathetic discussion of the "Western Excursion," see ibid., 142–58.

92. "In large measure, the policy discussions were guided by the [U.S.] military

assurances that chemical attacks [against coalition troops] posed little threat to the war plan." Atkinson, *Crusade*, 87.

93. For a strong criticism of the U.S. soldiers' preparedness against CW attacks during Desert Storm, see Cordesman and Wagner, *Lessons of Modern War*, 842–47.

94. *Washington Post*, February 8, 1998.

95. "Special Report: Appendix B — Findings and Recommendations from Interim and Special Reports," Washington, D.C., October 31, 1997 (http://www.gwvi.gov/appb1.html). Also *New York Times*, February 1, 1996.

96. Of course, this statement is made with the benefit of hindsight. When President Bush made the decision to go to war, he was acting under the misconceptions presented above. It could be said, therefore, that at the time the decision was "reasonable." Disturbing evidence suggests, for example, that the president became aware of the seriousness of the Iraqi CW threat only after the war had been in progress for a whole week. A newly released CIA document indicates that on January 24, 1991, William Webster, the director of central intelligence (DCI), and his deputy (DDCI), Richard J. Kerr, met at the White House with National Security Adviser Brent Scowcroft and his deputy, Robert Gates: "[The] DCI reviewed our analysis of the evidence that the Iraqis have chemical warheads for their Scuds. He indicated there were sources plus other information that persuaded him that chemical warheads should be taken seriously" ("Chemical Warheads" [Arlington, Va.: CIA, January 28, 1991] [Gulflink]). Notably, the message is signed by Kerr himself. The meeting apparently followed another one at the CIA with Secretary of Defense Cheney and General Powell ("Chemical Warheads" [Arlington, Va.: CIA, January ?, 1991] [Gulflink]). These briefings took place after four Scud attacks on Israel and in the shadow of a CIA warning, which had been issued already after the second such salvo, that "we cannot rule out that Iraq will escalate to strategic [i.e., countercity] chemical attacks sooner — perhaps even during its next strike" ("Iraq Situation Report" [Arlington, Va.: CIA, January 1991] [Gulflink]).

CHAPTER 9: THE CRISIS OF DETERRENCE

1. Shimon Peres, *The New Middle East* (New York: Henry Holt, 1993).

2. Shimon Peres, "National Security in a New Era," *Jerusalem Post International Edition*, September 14, 1991.

3. See comments by Knesset member Ezer Weizman, of the Labor party and currently the Israeli president, in *Yedi'ot aharonot*, October 23, 1991. Even Defense Minister Arens made such a forecast, although subsequently he argued that Israel's strategic deterrence was effective in blocking an Iraqi CW attack. *Yedi'ot aharonot*, October 23, 1991; see also Ze'ev Schiff, "Israel after the War," *Foreign Affairs*, Spring 1991, 33.

4. James A. Baker III, *The Politics of Diplomacy* (New York: J. P. Putnam's Sons, 1995), 415 and 422. In contrast, it has been argued that U.S. motives were political. Various diplomatic initiatives taken at the time by the Bush administration were meant to pave the way for an "unprecedented growth in the U.S. share of the global arms trade," and specifically to enable the dramatic increase in its arms shipments to the Middle East

following the Gulf War. William W. Keller, *Arm in Arm: The Political Economy of the Global Arms Trade* (New York: Basic Books, 1995), 57, 66–68, 84, and 91.

5. Baker, *The Politics of Diplomacy*, 413.

6. Ibid. The other two parts of the agenda were an "ambitious" plan for economic reconstruction and new conservation efforts to reduce American dependence on foreign oil.

7. Ibid.

8. Ibid, 414.

9. Office of the Secretary of Defense (hereafter OSD), "Proliferation: Threat and Response" (Washington, D.C.: GPO, November 1997), 40. For an earlier report indicating that the second plant was for the production of solid missile fuel, see *Yedi'ot aharonot*, August 17, 1992. On the missile-factories deal between Syria and North Korea, see also *Ha'aretz*, June 3, 1991; *Le Figaro*, August 15, 1992; *Wall Street Journal*, July 19, 1993. For comments by then Prime Minister Rabin, see Israel Television Channel 1 Network, FBIS (NES), June 23, 1994, 35. Maj. Gen. Uri Sagi, who was chief of AMAN at the time, commented: "From our point of view, the really grave element [in the new DPRK-Syrian arms] deal, is the construction of a production line for these [Scud C] missiles in Syria. Once the line becomes operational, the Syrians would have anywhere from dozens to hundreds of such missiles. This is very worrying" (interview, *Yedi'ot aharonot*, April 17, 1992). Some five years later, the Maj. Gen. Eitan Ben-Eliyahu, commander of the IAF, observed that Syria possessed some 800 SSMs. Moreover, the Syrian arsenal was expected to reach some 1,500 such missiles within the next three years. The figure is much higher than Israeli strategists had previously thought and shows that the "Syrians are serious about maintaining a military option" (*Jerusalem Post*, March 19, 1997).

10. Some sources have estimated the Scud C warhead to weigh 500 kilograms, however (*Jane's Sentinel*, cited in *Ma'ariv*, August 8, 1996). On Turkish concerns about Syrian, Iraqi, and Iranian missile capabilities, see *Turkish Daily News* (Ankara), July 30, 1993. Reportedly, Turkey has decided to acquire "several" Aerial Early Warning aircraft to cope with "the increasing number of long-range missiles in Syria and Iran." The planes, which are capable of "detecting and tracking missiles as soon as they are launched," would be based near Turkey's border with the two countries (*Hurriyet* [Istanbul], FBIS (WEU), March 21, 1996, 29–30).

11. Ron Ben-Yishai, "Why Is he Arming?" *Yedi'ot aharonot* (Leshabbat Supplement), September 16, 1994, 1–4.

12. *Davar*, November 24, 1994; "Patterns of Proliferation: National Briefings — Iran" (Lancaster, England: Center for Defence and International Security Studies, Lancaster University, 1996) (http://www.cdiss.org/country2.htm). Iran first acquired Scud missiles from North Korea and Libya for use during the Iran-Iraq war. In 1987–88, Iran obtained 100 Scud B missiles from North Korea (*Korea Herald* [Seoul], July 12, 1996). A CIA report from October 2, 1996, titled "Arms Transfers to State Sponsors of Terrorism," reportedly said that the China Precision Engineering Department had agreed in August 1996, after two years of negotiations, to sell gyroscopes, accelerome-

ters, and other missile guidance technologies to Iran's Defense Industries Organisation, the main coordinating body for Iran's missile development programs (*Washington Times*, November 21, 1996). To enhance their survivability, all of Iran's missiles are on mobile launchers (OSD, "Proliferation: Threat and Response," 1997, 27).

13. *New York Times*, April 8 and June 13, 1993, and October 22, 1996; Thomas L. Friedman, "Missile Myopia," *New York Times*, October 2, 1997, citing "U.S. intelligence." North Korea started development of the Scud D, called No Dong-1, in 1989. It was so named because the missile was test-launched on May 29, 1993, from a mobile launch pad in No-Tong, near Kim Chaek City, North Hamgyong Province. Apparently, the test was conducted in the presence of Iran Islamic Revolution Guard Corps personnel (*Ma'ariv*, April 14, 1995). One source said that the No Dong-1 was a two-stage missile, measuring 15.8 meters in length and 1.2 meters in diameter and using liquid fuel. It can carry a 1,000-kilogram warhead and has a CEP of 2,000 meters. The source claimed that Iran had ordered 150 such missiles, a figure also mentioned in the Israeli press (*Sankei shimbun* in a dispatch from Washington, cited in Yonhap, Seoul, Foreign Broadcast Information Service [East Asia], hereafter FBIS [EAS], July 15, 1993, 18; *Ha'aretz*, December 16, 1994; see also *Izvestiia*, April 10, 1993; *Independent*, May 2, 1995). However, a Defense Department study implied that the No Dong-1 was a one-stage missile and put its range at 1,000 kilometers (OSD, "Proliferation and Response," 1997, 7 and 8). The monthly *Modern Weapons*, a military journal published by the 210th institute of the Chinese munitions industry, maintained that the missile has a better accuracy than the Scud missiles produced by the Soviet Union. It said that in an "emergency" the No Dong-1 would be capable of delivering a 50-kiloton nuclear warhead or nerve gas payload (cited in Yonhap, FBIS [EAS], August 11, 1994, 37). For a general discussion, see David C. Wright and Timur Kadyshev, "An Analysis of the North Korean Nodong Missile," *Science and Global Security* 4 (no. 2), 1994, 129–60.

14. The Iranian officials are cited in AFP (Tehran), July 26, August 5, 1998; AP (Tehran), August 2, 1998. According to U.S. intelligence sources, the Shihab-3 is a liquid-fueled system carried on a road-mobile launcher (*Washington Times*, July 23, 1998). For the missile's No Dong-1 connection, see State Department Spokesman James P. Rubin, cited in *Washington Times*, July 24, 1998; also *New York Times*, July 23, 1998; *Washington Post*, July 24, 1998. On Russian help with the project, see *Ma'ariv*, October 1, 1997; and *New York Times*, November 18, 1997, and January 16, 1998.

15. Defense Department Briefing, Washington, D.C., July 23, 1998 (www.defense-link.mil/news/July 1998/t0723198_723asd_). Apparently in a bid to allay Saudi fears, Iranian Defense Minister Ali Shamkhani said: "The strengthening of our military capacities will also serve Arab national security and confront the challenges facing the Islamic world" (interview, *al-Ittihad* [Abu Dhabi], July 12, 1998; see also interview of Muhammad Reza Nuri, Iran's ambassador to Riyadh, in *al-Hayat*, July 29, 1998). But such a formula could also mean the provision of an Iranian strategic umbrella to Syria or Libya, for instance. Moreover, with extensive help from Russia, Iran is working on a longer-range missile, dubbed the Shihab-4. Specifically, technology from the obsolete Soviet SS-4 Sandal IRBM, which had a range of some 2,000 kilometers, has reportedly

been transferred to Iran. The missile is expected to be ready within two to five years and would be capable of hitting targets in Central Europe (see Martin Indyk, assistant U.S. secretary of state, cited in AP [Tehran], August 2, 1994; also *Washington Times*, July 24, 1998; *Jerusalem Post*, July 31, 1998). In 1997, the Iranians conducted ground tests of liquid-fueled rocket engines based on the RD-214, the propulsion system of the Soviet SS-4 (*Military Space*, April 28, 1997, 1–3; also Maj. Gen. Eitan Ben-Eliyahu, commander of the IAF, cited in *Jerusalem Post*, April 15, 1997).

16. The CIA predicted that a first test flight for the Shihab-3 would be held in 1998, but the DIA said that it would not come until 1999 (*Washington Post*, December 31, 1997). In both cases, however, the test "was not expected so soon" (*New York Times*, July 23, 1998). See also Maj. Gen. Moshe Ya'alon, head of AMAN, interview in *Ma'ariv* (Khag Supplement), April 16, 1998, 2, 3, and 4, for the Israeli intelligence timeline.

17. Yonhap, FBIS (EAS), June 3, 1991, 34, citing "a highly placed South Korean military source"; also *Yedi'ot aharonot*, January 28, 1992, noting that the missile would be able to reach Israel from Libya; also interview of Itzhak Rabin, in *Davar*, May 12, 1993. More recently, however, it was said that Libya's efforts to acquire the No Dong missile have been unsuccessful. OSD, "Proliferation: Threat and Response," 1997, 37.

18. OSD, "Proliferation: Threat and Response," 1997, 8. On Syrian financing of the Scud C project, see *Jerusalem Post*, May 7, 1993. Evidence also suggests that North Korea offered to provide Iran with improved Scud missiles in exchange for counterfeiting technology. The Shah of Iran had at one time purchased from the United States two high-performance printing presses and the special papers to produce "almost perfect" 100-dollar bills known as Super K (an official of the U.S. Secret Service, cited in the Tokyo biweekly magazine *Sapio*, FBIS [EAS], April 30, 1996, 52–53). On the seizure of such notes by Russian customs officials at the border between North Korea and Russia, see *Yonhap*, FBIS (EAS), June 26, 1996, 44.

19. On Iranian financing of the Scud C project, see *al-Nahar* (Beirut), April 1, 1992. On oil-for-missile deals between Iran and the DPRK, see *Korea Times* (Seoul), July 19, 1995; *Hanguk ilbo*, FBIS (EAS), October 5, 1995, 55–56; also *Ma'ariv*, February 25, 1994.

20. Interview, *Abrar* (Tehran), FBIS (NES), November 5, 1991, 75–76.

21. *Yedi'ot aharonot*, October 29, 1991.

22. A debate has surfaced as to the kind of threat represented by these missiles. Army Lt. Gen. Malcolm O'Neill, the director of the U.S. Ballistic Missile Defense Organization, told a congressional panel that the Taepo Dong II missile has a maximum range of 6,000 kilometers, enough to hit Alaska from North Korea (*Aviation Week and Space Technology*, March 11, 1996, 23). This position apparently dovetailed with that of the CIA (see "World Wide Threat Assessment," Brief to the Senate Select Committee on Intelligence by the Director of Central Intelligence, John M. Deutch, February 22, 1996 [http://www.odci.gov/cia/public_affairs/speeches/archives/1996/dci_speech_022296.html]; Speech by the Director of Central Intelligence, John M. Deutch, to the Conference on "Nuclear, Biological, Chemical Weapons Proliferation and Terrorism" [Los Alamos: Los Alamos Laboratory, May 23, 1996] [http://www.odci.gov./cia/pub-

lic_affairs/speeches/archives/1996/dci_speech_052396.html]). Subsequently, however, a CIA report used more cautious language to describe the missile's range. It said that the Taepo Dong II "may become capable" of reaching Alaska and the westernmost portion of the Hawaiian island chain (see Remarks by John E. Mclaughlin, Vice Chairman for Estimates, National Intelligence Council, before the Senate Select Committee on Intelligence, December 4, 1996 [http://www.odci.gov/public_affairs/speeches/archives/1996/adhoc_120496.html]). The U.S. Defense Department has said that flight-testing of the Taepo Dong I could begin at "any time." However, it also noted that North Korea has little experience in flight-testing its missiles and no experience in testing multistage ballistic missiles or other related technologies. Accordingly, North Korea's ability to evaluate, improve, or repair flaws in its missile designs may be hampered (OSD, "Proliferation: Threat and Response," 1997, 8). The missiles are two-stage designs and likely would employ separating warheads, representing a considerable advance over the single-stage No Dong series. Indeed, the August 31 satellite launch failed, indicating that the North has not yet mastered solid-fuel or separation technology, or both. But, U.S. analysts said, the effort alone suggested that the program might be more ambitious and advanced than was previously thought (*New York Times*, September 15, 1998). This could suggest that the missiles capable of targeting the United States directly may be introduced earlier than was first estimated. It has been said that key parts of the No Dong-1 are almost identical to China's CSS-2 missile, and that the Taepo Dong is similar to the Dongfeng-3 missile, which China test-launched in July 1995 from Jilin Province in the direction of Taiwan (Kyodo citing Yonhap, FBIS [EAS], September 13, 1995, 43). However, U.S. analysts have been unable to establish a definite link to China (*Wall Street Journal*, March 15, 1994). On the DPRK's development of the Taepo Dong I and II missiles, see *Choson ilbo*, FBIS (EAS), March 21, 1994, 48–49, and September 6, 1994, 68; Nonproliferation Center, "The Weapons Proliferation Threat" (Arlington, Va.: CIA, March 1995), 8.

23. Japan's Defense Agency white paper, "The Defense of Japan," cited in Kyodo, FBIS (EAS), July 30, 1993, 4. For continued Japanese concerns over North Korea's SSMs, see *Christian Science Monitor*, July 26, 1996; also *New York Times*, September 11, 1998.

24. Takashi Kakuma, "Pentagon's View of North Korea's ABC Weapons," *Sapio*, FBIS (EAS), March 19, 1996, 18. On North Korean efforts to recruit Russian missile designers, see Itar-Tass, FBIS (SOV), February 5, 1993, 10, and February 10, 1993, 11–12.

25. JANA, FBIS (NES), June 7, 1991, 5. Earlier Qaddafi said: "If we had possessed a deterrent — missiles that could reach New York — we would have hit it at the same moment" the United States attacked us (Tripoli Television Service, FBIS [NES], April 23, 1990, 8). Undoubtedly, the Gulf War reinforced Qaddafi's determination to acquire such a strategic deterrent. It has been revealed that Dutch authorities have investigated a company named Eurabic International BV in Hoofddorp, for shipping "strategic materials" to Libya in 1992 and 1993. The Dutch Internal Security Service (BVD), which dubbed Eurabic a front for the Libyan government, said that the company

played a "prominent role" in military acquisitions abroad and was completely controlled by Tripoli. Among other items, it ordered parts in Japan for "optical instruments tables" at "the behest of the rocket site of the Libyan Armed Forces," which were to be shipped to Libya through a third country (*De Volkskrant* [Amsterdam], FBIS [WEU], August 15, 1994, 6). Further, several sources, including CIA Director Deutch, have reported that Libya has acquired an unknown number of DPRK-supplied Scud C missiles. If so, Qaddafi could pose a missile threat to Sicily, Crete, and parts of the extreme south of Greece. Allegations have been made that Libya's Scuds are equipped with chemical warheads developed with North Korean and Iranian assistance ("Patterns of Proliferation: National Briefings — Libya" (Lancaster, England: Center for Defence and International Security Studies, Lancaster University, 1996) (http://www.cdiss.org/countrya.htm#LIBYA).

26. Maj. Gen. So Won-Sik, director of the ROK Defense Ministry's North Korean Affairs Division, in *Korea Herald*, September 9, 1992; see also *Wall Street Journal*, February 25, 1993.

27. *Hanguk ilbo*, FBIS (EAS), May 9, 1991, 31.

28. *Choson ilbo*, FBIS (EAS), November 12, 1991, 26.

29. *Focus* (Munich), April 26, 1993, 13, citing "BND analyses"; KBS-1 Radio Network, Seoul, FBIS (EAS), September 27, 1993, 20.

30. *Focus*, April 26, 1993, 13; *Choson ilbo*, FBIS (EAS), September 6, 1994, 67.

31. OSD, "Proliferation: Threat and Response," 1997, 6.

32. Cited in *CBW Conventions Bulletin*, September 1997, 18; see also *Korea Times*, August 18, 1997; *Daily Telegraph* (London), August 19, 1997.

33. See Dany Shoham, "Chemical Weapons in Egypt and Syria: Evolution, Capabilities, Control" (Hebrew) (Ramat Gan: BESA Center for Strategic Studies, Bar Ilan University, Security and Policy Studies No. 21, June 1995), 51–86; *Jane's Sentinel*, cited in *Ma'ariv*, August 8, 1996, and *Ha'aretz*, August 15, 1996. The German magazine *Stern* quoted Western intelligence sources as saying that German experts were helping Syria build a chemical weapons factory in Aleppo similar to the Libyan Tarhunah plant (cited in Radio Monte Carlo, FBIS [NES], June 6, 1996, 37–38). The nerve agent VX was discovered in 1949. Its LCt_{50} is assessed at 30 mg-min/m^3, which makes it five times as deadly as tabun by inhalation. Moreover, its LD_{50} (percutaneous) is 10 mg/70kg man, that is, 100 times more lethal than tabun (GA) and 170 times as deadly as sarin (GB) on the skin. VX is a persistent nerve agent that is usually disseminated as a liquid aerosol. The Syrian effort to acquire VX is noteworthy. Reportedly a Russian FSB (*Federalnaya sluzhba bezopasnosti*, or Federal Security Service) investigation has accused Lt. Gen. Anatoliy Kuntsevich, who between 1992 and 1994 was chairman of a presidential committee on chemical and biological disarmament, of stealing chemical weapons components and know-how from the GosNIIOKht Chemical Institute in Moscow and shipping them to Syria (BBC-TV, in FBIS [SOV], January 18, 1996, 21–22). Kuntsevich, who was once deputy commander of the USSR Defense Ministry Chemical Troops, reportedly sold close to a ton of nerve gas precursors to Syria in 1993 and tried to ship another five tons of such chemicals in 1994 (*Wall Street Journal*,

April 30, 1996). Newly appointed Israeli Defense Minister Itzhak Mordekhai has charged that Russian scientists were helping Syria develop nerve gases, including VX, at the Scientific Studies and Research Center, sometimes known as Centre d'études et recherches scientifiques, on the outskirts of Damascus (*Sunday Times*, November 17, 1996; *Jerusalem Post*, November 18, 1996). It has been alleged that, despite intensive efforts, Syria itself could not develop VX nerve gas, whose production is more involved than that of sarin. Accordingly, Syria's later success in this regard was directly tied to "a Russian chemical and biological warfare expert," apparently General Kuntsevich, who provided the "proper formula for its production" (*Ha'aretz*, April 29, 1997; also Daniel Leshem, "Syria's Deadly Secret," *Jerusalem Post*, May 6, 1997). The bottom line, according to Defense Minister Mordekhai, is that "we know that Syria increased its production capacity, particularly that of VX. I want to stress that we have information regarding this matter" (interview, *al-Hayat*, November 25, 1996). Asked about reports of a Syrian CW buildup, "a high-ranking Syrian official" pointed out that "we are in a state of hostility [with Israel], and every people is entitled to possess self-defense means" (cited in *al-Hayat*, June 6, 1996).

34. Maj. Gen. Moshe Ya'alon, head of AMAN, has stated that Syria is arming Scud missiles with VX nerve-gas warheads (*Jerusalem Post*, June 19, 1997). An unclassified 1985 study by the DIA has said that a medium-range missile carrying some 550 kilograms of VX (a typical load for Syria's Scud C) would produce a casualty rate of 50 percent in a target area one-half a kilometer wide and four kilometers long (cited in *Baltimore Sun*, February 8, 1988).

35. Ben-Yishai, "Why Is He Arming?" 2.

36. OSD, "Proliferation: Threat and Response," 1996, 15; *Christian Science Monitor*, April 13, 1988; *Washington Post*, February 9, 1989. For the higher figure, see "DIA Answers to SSCI Questions," *Current and Projected National Security Threats to the United States and Its Interests Abroad*, Hearing, U.S. Senate, Select Committee on Intelligence, February 22, 1996, 207. One source claimed that Iran was operating CW production facilities (as well as a BW research laboratory) at Damghan, near a dry lake 300 kilometers east of Tehran ("Devil's Brews Briefings: Iran" [Lancaster: Center for Defence and International Security Studies, Lancaster University, 1996] [http://www.cdiss.org/cbwnb1.htm]). The London *Sunday Telegraph* of November 26, 1995, stated that the Iranian CW program is financed by the sales on the black market of large quantities of oil that is surplus to Iran's OPEC quota. One assessment has concluded: "Iran has an increasingly active chemical weapons program. Over the last year, it has sought the capability to produce not only the chemical agents themselves, but also the precursor chemicals making it less vulnerable to export controls of its foreign suppliers" (Statement by Acting Director of CIA, George J. Tenet, before the Senate Select Committee on Intelligence, Hearing on "Current and Projected National Security Threats to the United States," February 5, 1997, 14; *Christian Science Monitor*, April 28, 1997). Newly elected Iranian President Mohammad Khatami rejected the reports as "sheer allegations," adding: "We are not interested in any sort of chemical weapons" (interview, *Independent*, May 26, 1997).

37. *Ha'aretz*, April 29, 1997; *Der Spiegel*, July 15, 1991, 23–24. Some "Western experts" reportedly estimated that Iran was 12 months away from the production of VX (*Daily Telegraph*, October 13, 1996). In contrast, the deputy chief of staff of the IDF, Maj. Gen. Matan Vilna'i, stated: "Only the Syrians have it [VX gas]. . . . The Iranians tried to develop it" (interview, *Jerusalem Post*, May 9, 1997). The Pentagon will only confirm that Iran is "believed to be conducting research on nerve agents" but has yet to include nerve gas in its CW stockpile (OSD, "Proliferation: Threat and Response," 1996, 15, and 1997, 27).

38. OSD, "Proliferation: Threat and Response," 1996, 15–16; "Key Technologies: An Overview" (Lancaster: Center for Defence and International Security Studies, Lancaster University, 1996) (http://www.cdiss.org/tabtechs.htm).

39. OSD, "Proliferation: Threat and Response," 25, 26. See also *Christian Science Monitor*, March 8 and December 13, 1988.

40. *New York Times*, January 22, 1992.

41. Testimony before the U.S. Senate Intelligence Committee, cited in *New York Times*, April 3 and 4, 1996; see also Nonproliferation Center, "The Weapons Proliferation Threat," 9. On the involvement of German, Swiss, and Italian companies, among others, in the Tarhunah plant, see *Tageszeitung* (Berlin), April 11, 1991; *Die Welt*, February 15, 1993, and July 12, 1995; *Frankfurter Allgemeine Zeitung*, March 16, 1993; ZDF Television Network, Mainz, FBIS (WEU), March 4, 1994, 12–13, and May 3, 1996, 15–16; *Panorama* (Milan), FBIS (NES), April 22, 1994, 14–15; *Der Spiegel*, September 26, 1994, 54–58; *Stern*, July 13, 1995, 90–93; *New York Times*, August 22, 1996. On the use of Thai workers in its construction and Thai government denials, see *Siam Post* (Bangkok), FBIS (EAS), March 29, 1993, 58–59, and March 30, 1993, 47–48; *Nation* (Bangkok), October 1 and November 3, 1993. On U.S. warning to Thailand, see *New York Times*, October 26, 1993. One Arab magazine has accused the United States of conducting a "misinformation" campaign. Following an "on-site" tour, it agreed with the Libyan claim that the tunneling at Tarhunah comprised the "second stage" of an "industrial irrigation network" project (see *al-Watan al-'arabi* [Paris], August 9, 1996, 36–37). This account is at total variance with the one provided by three engineers working on the project (see *New York Times*, December 2, 1997).

42. *New York Times*, April 4, 1996. For Libyan denials that it is producing chemical weapons, see *al-Shams* (Tripoli), February 28, 1996.

43. SVR, "The New Challenge," cited in Yonhap, FBIS (SOV), January 29, 1993, 14; *Independent*, February 28, 1993. See also Seoul KBS-1 Radio Network, FBIS (EAS), September 27, 1993, 20, and March 22, 1994, 23.

44. Yonhap, FBIS (EAS), October 28, 1991, 32. "Pest" refers to infected animals or plants that can present a threat to humans or their means of subsistence.

45. *Korea Herald*, October 25, 1992. See also Report of the South Korean Inspector General's Office, in *Chungang ilbo*, FBIS (EAS), April 29, 1993, 17, but cf. OSD, "Proliferation: Threat and Response," 1997, 6.

46. Yonhap, FBIS (EAS), March 22, 1994, 23.

47. OSD, "Proliferation: Threat and Response," 1997, 39. General Ya'alon of

AMAN also said that Syria is developing biological weapons (*Jerusalem Post*, June 19, 1997).

48. OSD, "Proliferation: Threat and Response," 1997, 39.

49. *Der Spiegel*, April 20, 1998, 17.

50. OSD, "Proliferation: Threat and Response," 1996, 16. A "confidential" BND document has reportedly noted that Iran was interested in "complete fermentation plants" for the production of biological warfare agents (*Der Spiegel*, September 26, 1994, 58). Purportedly, Iran has also tried to buy from European countries anthrax cultures and toxins that could be used to develop BW weapons ("Devil's Brews Briefings: Iran"). See also the report from the Russian intelligence agency SVR, "The New Challenge After the 'Cold War': The Proliferation of Weapons of Mass Destruction," cited in Interfax, FBIS (SOV), January 29, 1993, 1. It has been reported that Iran has hired a BW expert at a "high salary" to help its program (*Ha'aretz*, April 29, 1997).

51. Arms Control and Disarmament Agency, "Threat Control through Arms Control: Annual Report to Congress, 1995" (Washington, D.C.: ACDA, July 1996), 68. It should be noted that in 1995 the CIA described the Iranian BW program as "in the late stages of research and development" (Nonproliferation Center, "The Weapons Proliferation Threat," 12). Subsequently it was estimated that "Iran's BW program has the momentum to mature into a weapons capability and to pose a regional threat during the next decade" ("DIA Answers to SSCI Questions," 206–7). But, the Pentagon said, "only small quantities of usable agent may exist now" (OSD, "Proliferation: Threat and Response," 1997, 27). This assessment seems to contradict the allegation that the CIA, in a report delivered to the Senate Intelligence Committee, has now acknowledged for the first time that Iran has not only biological weapons but also the means to deliver them (*Sunday Times*, August 11, 1996).

52. Nonproliferation Center, "The Weapons Proliferation Threat," 10.

53. ACDA, "Threat Control through Arms Control," 68. The CIA estimated: "A number of Libyan universities are being used for basic research of more common BW agents, but they are not equipped to perform the sophisticated work needed for weapons development" (Nonproliferation Center, "The Weapons Proliferation Threat," 10). On efforts by Libya to recruit foreign scientists to its BW program, see *Sunday Times*, February 26, 1995. It has been alleged that a contingent of Iraqi scientists went to Libya either to advance the Ibn Hayan biological weapons plant in the Tripoli area or to escape possible U.S. attack on suspected Iraqi BW facilities. (*Times* [London], January 6 and February 13, 1998). On the shipment by a German company of a fermenter via a third country to Libya, where it was reportedly converted to BW applications, see ZDF Television Network, FBIS (WEU), March 4, 1994, 13.

54. Text of treaty in Korean Central News Agency (hereafter KCNA) (Pyongyang), FBIS (Asia and Pacific), November 4, 1982, D1 and D2.

55. Pyongyang Domestic Service, FBIS (EAS), December 11, 1989, 10.

56. Interview of Mohsen Reza'i, Tehran Domestic Service, FBIS (NES), December 12, 1989, 51.

57. Cited in Iranian News Agency (IRNA), Tehran Domestic Service, FBIS (NES), December 12, 1989, 51.

58. KCNA, FBIS (EAS), December 3, 1990, 14. In a meeting, Ahmad Khomeini, the son of the Ayatollah Khomeini, said: "we hope to God that the two nations of Iran and North Korea may take some positive steps toward destroying the interests of America and its allies" (Tehran Domestic Service, FBIS [NES], November 30, 1990, 51). See also the comments of Majles Speaker Mehdi Karrubi, Tehran Domestic Service, FBIS (NES), November 28, 1990, 59.

59. Korean Central Broadcasting Network, FBIS (EAS), November 5, 1992, p. 11; KCNA, FBIS (EAS), November 6, 1992, 26–27.

60. *New York Times*, April 8, 1993. At least one such visit included a tour of the DPRK's missile plant in Pyongyang; see *Mainichi shimbun* (Tokyo), FBIS (EAS), May 13, 1996.

61. Report to the South Korean National Assembly Unification and Foreign Affairs Committee, Yonhap, BBC Monitoring Service (Asia-Pacific), September 26, 1996 (Internet). Equally important, despite the DPRK's severe economic crisis, its Scud brigade is one of the few branches of the Korean People's Army that appears to have been sustained at mid-1980s levels of readiness. The brigade, comprising 500 Scud B and Scud C missiles, has even been furnished new Scud facilities near the demilitarized zone, including additional hardened sites to double or triple the number of launchers and support equipment in forward areas. David A. Fulghum, "North Korean Forces Suffer Mobility Loss," *Aviation Week and Space Technology*, November 24, 1997, 63.

62. Interview, *Le Figaro*, July 4, 1991.

63. *Al-Safir* (Beirut), April 7, 1992. Tlass said during a visit to Moscow, where he hurriedly went to seek new arms, that if Saddam was really concerned about solving the Palestinian problem, he should have turned to Syria first. President Assad, he said, "has the largest army in the region confronting Israel. Against all logic, however, he [Saddam] went along another path announcing that the liberation of Palestine supposedly begins with the seizure of Kuwait" (Central Television Vostok Program and Orbita Network, Moscow, FBIS [SOV], February 25, 1991, 16–17). Syrian Foreign Minister Faruq al-Shar called the Gulf War "a catastrophe," especially as Saddam Hussein bears responsibility for "providing the United States with the pretext it was seeking to intervene in the Gulf" (interview, *Le monde*, February 8, 1991).

64. Quoted in Walid Phares, "The Damascus Tehran Axis and the Mideast's Future," *Global Affairs*, Summer 1992, 87 n. 17.

65. Syrian Defense Minister Mustafa Tlass, interview, *Le figaro*, February 18, 1991.

66. For example, the Paris-based independent magazine *al-Watan al-'Arabi* claimed on April 15, 1988, that a team of 18 Syrian missile experts, headed by a Col. Ali Jinani, had visited Iran that March to help the Iranians overcome problems in launching their Scud SSMs against Iraq. Previously, eight Iranian missiles had blown up on the launching pads, causing numerous casualties.

67. Joint communiqué, Damascus Domestic Service, FBIS (NES), April 30, 1991, 36–38.

68. IRNA, FBIS (NES), March 5, 1991, 55. The Iranian delegation also included Iran's defense minister, Akbar Torkan, who held talks with Defense Minister O Chin-U (KCNA, FBIS [NES], February 28, 1991, 17–18, and March 1, 1991, 15–17; *Choson ilbo*, FBIS [NES], March 20, 1991, 25). Torkan was back in North Korea in September 1991, when he said that Iran wants the cooperative relations with the DPRK to be developed onto "a new higher stage" (KCNA, FBIS [EAS], September 13, 1991, 16–17).

69. Cited in *al-Shams* (Cairo), January 13, 1995; Tripoli Libyan Television Network, FBIS (NES), January 24, 1995, 16.

70. Tripoli Television Service, cited in *The CBW Conventions Bulletin*, September 1997, 20. On Libyan efforts to cement ties with Iran, for example, see Qaddafi's meeting with Nuri Shahrudi, Tehran's ambassador to Tripoli, IRNA, FBIS (NES), February 8, 1995, 25.

71. Shoham, "Chemical Weapons," 64.

72. *Yedi'ot aharonot*, January 26, 1992; *New York Times*, March 11 and 18, 1992; *Newsweek*, June 22, 1992, 45–46. The White House claimed that the U.S. Navy "lost" the Korean freighters in the heavy traffic of the Strait of Hormuz. One report, citing "U.S. sources," claimed that the Iranians airlifted the missile parts in February rather than in May (*al-Muharrir*, Paris, March 23, 1992).

73. Shoham, "Chemical Weapons," 65; *New York Times*, March 18, 1992.

74. Foreign Minister Shimon Peres, cited in *Jerusalem Post International Edition*, August 22, 1992. See also interview of Deputy Defense Minister Mordekhai Gur, IDF Radio, FBIS (NES), August 13, 1992, 23–24.

75. Israeli defense sources noted that "Syria can deploy chemical warheads on the missiles [it tested]" (Qol Yisra'el, FBIS [NES], August 13, 1992, 23). A similar ploy was put into effect soon after a new conservative government headed by Benyamin Netanyahu took office in Israel in June 1996. Later that summer, the Syrians test-fired a number of Scud C missiles. Israeli defense officials reportedly said that the launch, which attempted to test the ability to fire the missile under "operational circumstances," was meant as a "veiled threat" toward Israel. Damascus was apparently signaling that the hiatus in Syrian-Israeli negotiations, which developed following the Netanyahu elections, would result in escalation. *Ma'ariv*, August 20, 1996.

76. Andrew Rathmell, "Chemical Weapons in the Middle East: Syria, Iraq, Iran, and Libya," *Marine Corps Gazette*, July 1990, 60–61.

77. *Ha'tzofe* (Tel Aviv), August 8, 1997. The report claimed that during the course of the exercises three soldiers had died.

78. OSD, "Proliferation: Threat and Response," 1997, 38. It is unclear why North Korea's preparations for CW are viewed as indicating potentially offensive intentions, whereas similar Syrian activity is seen mostly as defensively oriented. After all, neither has a clear-cut advantage in conventional weapons over its enemy, and both the United States and Israel are likely to respond with unconventional munitions to an attack with chemical weapons, or so Pyongyang and Damascus probably believe.

79. Interview, *Die Welt*, December 2, 1991.

80. *Der Standard* (Vienna), April 13, 1993. According to one source, Libya's al-Fatah

missile program remains in the "testing stage" and is based on a rocket with "a fairly small payload." OSD, "Proliferation: Threat and Response," 1997, 37.

81. BND information reported in *Der Spiegel*, September 26, 1994, 58.

82. Ben-Yishai, "Why Is He Arming?" 2.

83. Shoham, "Chemical Weapons," 66.

84. *Ha'aretz*, November 22, 1991.

85. *Washington Times*, May 24, 1991; *Der Spiegel*, November 18, 1991, 26, citing the German BND. Soon after, it was reported that four Syrian officers had been killed while working to extend the range of Scud missiles in Iran. The report said that the families of the victims were told they had died in "a military accident." *Sunday Telegraph* (London), May 31, 1992.

86. Shoham, "Chemical Weapons," 64; Ben-Yishai, "Why Is He Arming?" 1. Note, however, that the IDF's chief of staff, Lt. Gen. Amnon Shahak, has said that he "does not know of [Syrian-Iranian] cooperation in the CW area." Interview, *Yedi'ot aharonot* (Yom Ha'atzmaut Supplement), May 11, 1997, 17.

87. Cited in *San Jose Mercury News*, December 25, 1993.

88. *Sankei shimbun*, cited by Yonhap, FBIS (EAS), July 15, 1993, 18. Apparently the Iran-DPRK missile cooperation extended to the testing phase. It was said that U.S. satellites had discovered "utterly identical" test bases for the No Dong-1 in both countries soon after Iran contracted for the missiles in 1990. *Ma'ariv*, April 14, 1995. For Iranian denials, see *Tehran Times*, February 24, 1994.

89. Cited in *Ha'aretz*, July 1, 1994. The statement implied that Rabin had given up on Israel's potential for strategic deterrence. However, it might be a mistake simply to extrapolate from Saddam's conduct to Assad or Kim Chong-Il.

90. *Davar*, November 24, 1994.

91. *Ha'aretz*, December 3, 5, and 6, 1995, and March 12, 1996. Peres said that the defense pact with the United States "could definitely serve as a component of Israel's defense." Interview, Israel Television Channel 1 Network, FBIS (NES), December 5, 1995, 21.

92. For repeated charges by Turkish officials of Syrian sponsorship of terrorism against Turkey, see Prime Minister Tansu Ciller, TRT Television Network (Ankara), FBIS (WEU), November 5, 1993, 56–57; President Suleyman Demirel, TRT Television Network, FBIS (WEU), November 20, 1995, 27–28; Turkish Interior Minister Teoman Unusan, interview, *Slobodna Dalmacija* (Split), FBIS (EEU), December 14, 1995, 31; Foreign Minister Deniz Baykal, TRT Television Network, FBIS (WEU), January 2, 1996, 27; Prime Minister Mesut Yilmaz, Anatolia (Ankara), FBIS (WEU), May 20, 1996, 10. For general accounts, see *Turkish Daily News* (Ankara), November 11, 1993, and September 26, 1995.

93. Voice of the Islamic Republic of Iran, Tehran, FBIS (NES), June 30, 1995, 54.

94. Interview, *Ettela'at* (Tehran), FBIS (NES), October 3, 1995, 75.

95. See, for example, Testimony of John M. Deutch, Director of the CIA, before the Permanent Subcommittee of Investigations of the Senate Committee of Government Affairs, March 20, 1996 (http://www.odci.gov/cia/public_affairs/speeches/archives/

1996/dci_testimony_ 032096.html); Deutch, "World Wide Threat Assessment"; Statement for the Record by Dr. Gordon C. Oehler, Director, Non-Proliferation Center of the CIA, *The Continuing Threat From Weapons of Mass Destruction*, Hearing, U.S. Senate, Armed Services Committee, March 27, 1996, http://www.odci.gov/cia/public_affairs/speeches/archives/go_toc_032796.html); Walter Laqueur, "Postmodern Terrorism: New Rules for an Old Game," *Foreign Affairs*, September–October 1996, esp. 28–36; John F. Sopko, "The Changing Proliferation Threat," *Foreign Policy*, Winter 1996–97, 3–20. According to intelligence sources, notebooks and computer files seized from Hizballah contained information on how to produce chemical agents. Hizballah has also received deliveries of protective gear, including gas masks and bodysuits, and has obtained Katyusha rockets capable of delivering chemical loads into Israel from bases inside Lebanon (David E. Kaplan, "Terrorism's Next Wave," *U.S. News and World Report*, November 17, 1997 [http://www.usnews.com/usnews/issue/971117/weapon.htm]). Ramzi Yousef, a trained engineer and reputed mastermind of the 1993 World Trade Center bombing, researched making sarin and reportedly planned to assassinate President Clinton in the Philippines using phosgene gas (*New York Times*, November 13, 1997). During his trial Yousef stated that he had originally considered carrying out a "poison attack" on the trade center but decided that it would be "too expensive to implement" (*New York Times*, October 23, 1997). Another source said that the trade center bombers did pack cyanide into the charge, but the chemical apparently evaporated during the explosion (Kaplan, "Terrorism's Next Wave"). It has also been revealed that in the immediate aftermath of the Centennial Park pipe-bomb blast during the 1996 Atlanta Olympics, bomb fragments were analyzed by the U.S. Department of Defense for the presence of chemical or biological agents. "This marked the first time that a domestic explosion had been routinely screened for those agents" (Richard Danzig and Pamela B. Berkowsky, "Why Should We Be Concerned about Biological Warfare?" *JAMA*, August 6, 1997, 432). For U.S. preparations against NBC terrorism, see John G. Roos, "The Ultimate Nightmare," *Armed Forces Journal International*, October 1995, 67–73. For a dissenting view, see Karl-Heinz Kamp, "An Overrated Nightmare," *Bulletin of the Atomic Scientists*, July–August 1996, 30–34.

96. A videotape obtained from North Korea by the Japanese television station NHK showed a commando parachuting from a low-flying AN-2 plane with bombs strapped to her body, to explode herself on an enemy airfield. See various ROK media reports in FBIS (EAS), March 11, 1996, 47–49, and March 12, 1996, 40.

97. Reportedly, CIA Director John Deutch has warned of the possibility of a North Korean "collapse" due to the country's deepening economic crisis and ongoing political problems (*Munhwa ilbo* [Seoul], FBIS [EAS], February 26, 1996, 39–40). Likewise, Gen. Gary Luck, commander of U.S. Forces in Korea, has testified before a House subcommittee that the disintegration of the DPRK was only a matter of time, and the remaining question was whether the North would disintegrate by implosion or explosion (*Korea Herald* [Seoul], March 21, 1996). For a report of a similar assessment by the Japanese government, see *Nihon keizai shimbun* (Tokyo), FBIS [EAS], February 28, 1996, 15). Indeed, it was said that the Japanese Defense Agency's "Special Office of the

Intelligence Department" had been put on "full alert" to cover the events on the Korean Peninsula (Shunji Taoka, "Asia's Elements of Instability in 1996 Reviewed: Will There Be an Armed Clash?" *Aera* [Tokyo], FBIS [EAS], January 16, 1996, 7–8; see also *Korea Herald*, February 18, 1996).

98. Kanan Makiya (Samir al-Khalil), *Cruelty and Silence: War, Tyranny, Uprising and the Arab World* (New York: Norton, 1993), 335 n. 30. The *Birmingham News* (October 6, 1996) cited "intelligence reports" as saying that Iraqi forces used chemical weapons, including mustard gas, to put down a Shi'a rebellion in southern Iraq after the war. The Alabama paper reported that allied screeners in Saudi Arabia spotted victims of those attacks among fleeing refugees. See also *Kayhan International* (Tehran), June 12, 1991 (English edition); *Guardian* (London), November 8, 1993; *Independent*, November 10, 1993, and February 23, 1994; *Libération*, November 15, 1993.

99. Taoka, "Will There Be an Armed Clash?" 8. See also *Korea Times*, December 28, 1995.

100. In April 1997, in response to a call for help from the United Nations, the United States pledged $25 million worth of aid to North Korea, and South Korea another $6 million, only to discover that a North Korean cargo ship tried to smuggle almost $100 million worth of illegal drugs into Japan (*Washington Post*, April 19, 1997). It also seems likely that the display of No Dong-1 missiles by the North at a time when the United States, Japan, and the ROK were considering further food aid was not coincidental (*Washington Post*, April 15, 1997). Earlier, Israeli diplomats trying to persuade the North Koreans to curtail their missile shipments to Syria and Iran were told by government officials in Pyongyang that the DPRK "would not be so enthusiastic" about selling such weapons if "someone else could come up with the sums that the Iranians paid for the weapons." However, the North Korean proposal was turned down because it was seen as an "invitation to blackmail" (interview of Israeli Deputy Foreign Minister Yossi Beilin, *Qol Yisra'el*, FBIS [NES], August 17, 1993, 19–20). As one source has put it: "In dealing with foreigners, North Korea's ideology of 'self-reliance' has been in practice a policy of demanding money, latterly with menaces" (*Economist*, February 22, 1997, 42).

101. *Chungang ilbo* (Seoul), FBIS (EAS), January 23, 1996, 48. On the North Korean military buildup, *Korea Herald*, December 2, 1995; KBS-1 Radio Network (Seoul), FBIS (EAS), December 14, 1995, 59–60; *Sankei shimbun*, FBIS (EAS), December 19, 1995, 2–3; *Korea Times*, December 20, 1995; *Yomiuri shimbun* (Tokyo), FBIS (EAS), December 26, 1995, 1. On other North Korean efforts to raise tensions on the peninsula, see Yonhap, FBIS (EAS), February 1, 1996, 37.

102. Cited in Anthony Lewis, "A Soft Landing," *New York Times*, July 12, 1996.

103. *Chungang ilbo*, FBIS (EAS), February 5, 1996, 51.

104. Ibid., 46; *Choson ilbo*, FBIS (EAS), February 6, 1996, 35. The *Korea Times*, which often reflects the position of the ROK government, wrote on February 4, 1996, that Seoul "appears to be getting the short end of the stick in recent negotiations with the U.S." See also a survey of ROK dailies, FBIS (EAS), February 5, 1996, 46–48.

105. Cited in Pyon Chin-Il, "There was a Reason for Clinton Going for 'Concilia-

tory Diplomacy' and Taking North Korea off the List of Terrorist Nations," *Sapio* (Tokyo), FBIS (EAS), March 12, 1996, 21.

106. Kyodo, Tokyo, FBIS (EAS), April 8, 1996, 29; KBS-1 Television Network, FBIS (EAS), April 9, 1996, 51.

107. *Korea Herald*, June 25, 1996.

108. *New York Times*, April 5, 1996. The Tokyo daily *Yomiuri shimbun* quoted a North Korean diplomat based in Beijing as warning that North Korea would take a "final initiative" if the United States did not accept its February 1996 proposal for a "temporary peace accord" to deter armed conflict on the peninsula. The paper said that the North might move its forces near the demilitarized zone "for demonstration purposes."

109. Cited in *Washington Post*, June 17, 1998.

110. See, for example, remarks of French President Jacques Chirac, Agence France Presse (AFP), Paris, FBIS (WEU), March 12, 1996, 19. Instead, in their April 1996 meeting the foreign ministers of the European Union advocated a policy of "critical dialogue" with rogue regimes like Iran's. See U.K. Foreign Secretary Malcolm Rifkind, "Desert Destinies," *Guardian*, June 28, 1996; also *Frankfurter Allgemeine Zeitung*, March 16, 1996; *Sueddeutsche Zeitung* (Munich), July 23, 1996; *Times* (London), August 6, 1996.

111. Cited in *al-Ahram* (Cairo), March 28, 1991. Subsequently it was disclosed by the Egyptian interior minister that his forces were holding two Iraqi "intelligence officers." Middle East News Agency (Cairo), April 13, 1991.

112. "Report of the Executive Chairman on the Activities of the Special Commission Established by the Secretary General Pursuant to Paragraph 9 (b) (i) of Resolution 687 (1991)," S/1998/332 (New York: U.N. Headquarters, April 16, 1998), 26 (hereafter UNSCOM 1998). Also "Amb. Richard Butler's Presentation," unofficial text of briefing by Richard Butler to the U.N. Security Council, June 3, 1998, excerpted by Laurie Mylroie (http: //www.fas.org/news/un/iraq/s/index.html/980603_unscom .htm), hereafter Butler.

113. UNSCOM 1997, 6 and 16.

114. Pentagon spokesman Kenneth H. Bacon stated at a news briefing on April 2, 1997: "We believe that the [Iraqis] possess an operational Scud missile capability of about 18–25 missiles" (http://www.fas.org/spp/starwars/offdocs/clinton7/msg000 44e.htm). See also *New York Times*, November 11, 1997. The commander in chief of the Russian strategic missile force, Col. Gen. Vladimiar Yakolev, placed the size of the Iraqi covert force at 35–60 Scud-type missiles ("Iraq's Remaining WMD Capabilities: An Overview" [Lancaster, England: Center for Defence and International Security Studies, University of Lancaster, February 1998] [http://www.cdiss.org/98feb4.htm], citing Russian press reports on February 19, 1998).

115. U.S. Government White Paper, "Iraqi Weapons of Mass Destruction Programs," Washington, D.C., February 13, 1998, 9.

116. UNSCOM 1997, 10.

117. Ekeus, "Address." General al-Samarra'i, who claimed that before the war Iraq had imported some 1,000 Scud missiles from the Soviet Union, stated that the Iraqis

were still hiding 40 Scud and 40 al-Husayn missiles (interviews, *al-Majallah*, July 28–August 3, 1996, 30–31; *al-Hayat*, January 5, 1995; *Sunday Times*, February 19, 1995). Subsequently, the general said that 25 of the 40 al-Husayns were in "a disassembled form" (interview, *al-Sharq al-awsat*, June 21, 1996). Some of these missiles may have been made from spare parts supplied by the Soviets before the Gulf War.

118. Ekeus, "Address." In October 1996, Ekeus reported to the UNSC that UNSCOM inspectors had confronted Iraqi Special Republican Guard troops, who had been seen moving what they said were "concrete pillars" but which, Ekeus noted, "by their dimensions and shape, resembled Scud missiles." The UNSCOM personnel were not allowed to inspect the suspect cargo, and the "pillars" soon disappeared (Jim Hoagland, "Deadly Silence on Iraq," *Washington Post*, November 8, 1996). Apparently, the Special Republican Guard is charged with protecting other aspects of Iraq's mass destruction weapons program as well. For example, on June 12, 1997, a tense showdown developed between UNSCOM officials and soldiers of the 2d Battalion of the guard, who apparently had ferried "banned germ agents in refrigerated coolers between a military training center and al-Bakr University" (*Washington Post*, November 21, 1997). Charles Duelfer, UNSCOM's deputy chief weapons inspector, identified Iraq's Mukhabarat and the Amn al-Khass, a security unit charged with protecting information, as also taking part in the concealment of Iraq's mass destruction weapons (*Time Magazine*, December 1, 1997, 57).

119. Ekeus, "Address." Ambassador Ekeus's contention that the Iraqis have available missile fuel for their Scuds is intriguing. Scud missiles use two main propellants: TMI85 and AK271. These are Scud-specific components, not dual-purpose items. Iraq has never admitted either manufacturing these propellants or retaining them for nonproscribed missile activities (see Butler). But if Iraq obtained all its fuel and oxidizer supplies from the Soviet Union before the Gulf War, such supplies have a storage life of only 12–18 months. Anthony H. Cordesman and Abraham R. Wagner, *The Lessons of Modern War*, vol. 4: *The Gulf War* (Boulder, Colo.: Westview, 1996), 859.

120. U.S. Government White Paper, 1.

121. Ekeus, "Address."

122. UNSCOM 1995, paras. 55, 56, and 57; UNSCOM 1997, 17. Iraq at first completely denied the production of VX and attempted to eliminate all traces of such activities in order to conceal them from the commission. In 1995, it changed its story, claiming to have produced only enough VX for laboratory work. At that time it admitted to have manufactured about 4 tons of the agent (Associated Press, United Nations, April 11, 1996). Upon leaving his post as head of UNSCOM, Ekeus told reporters that Iraq still has biological weapons sufficient to inflict casualties "on the order of a nuclear attack," and that it apparently maintains a "large program" for the production of the chemical agent VX (*New York Times*, May 2, 1997). To give an idea of the quantities of munitions possibly available, one ton of agent would be enough to fill roughly 10 500-kilogram bombs, 150 122-millimeter artillery rockets, or 350 152-millimeter artillery shells.

123. Butler. For previous Iraqi claims regarding VX, see UNSCOM 1995, paras. 55 and 56; UNSCOM 1997, 17; *New York Times*, November 21, 1997.

124. Cited in *New York Times*, June 24, 1998; Reuters, June 24, 1998. See also *Washington Post*, June 23, 1998. An al-Husayn missile carrying 100 kilograms of VX could theoretically have produced up to a 440 percent increase in the area of lethal contamination, compared with the same load of sarin ("Iraq CW" [Arlington, Va.: CIA, n.d.] [File: cia_65549_65549_01.txt]). Persistence of high-grade VX is estimated at 300–325 hours ("Iraqi Chemical Warfare Data," File 970613_092596_ui_txt_0001.txt [Washington, D.C.: DIA, n.d.] [Gulflink]).

125. Cited in Associated Press, June 24, 1998. Nevertheless, Butler agreed to have the findings rechecked by laboratories in France and Switzerland to address Iraq's contention that the U.S. Army laboratory that originally found the VX traces was biased.

126. UNSCOM 1997, 40.

127. Ibid., 20.

128. Ibid.

129. *Washington Post*, November 21, 1997, citing "U.N. officials."

130. Richard Spertzel, cited in Reuters (U.N.), November 19, 1997. For example, up to 25 destroyed R-400 aerial bombs, most with a black stripe allegedly indicative of a BW bomb, were identified in early 1997 by UNSCOM inspectors. Two such bombs, which were excavated "relatively intact," showed evidence of decontaminated botulinum toxin. The finding raised the question whether all the R-400 bombs were filled with biological agents or whether some were filled with CW agents. The total number of R-400 bombs filled with biological agent, which Iraq now claims amounted to 157, also remains unknown. Indeed, the numbers submitted by Iraq for the unilateral destruction of CBW R-400 bombs are such that "it appears that more munitions were destroyed than were produced" (UNSCOM 1997, 21).

131. Butler.

132. Ibid.

133. Richard Spertzel, cited in "Iraq's Remaining WMD Capabilities."

134. Associated Press (Washington), November 19, 1997. General al-Samarra'i has long maintained that, according to "reliable information" received by the Iraqi opposition, Iraq still possesses 255 "containers" of biological agents. The new figure, he claimed, represents an increase from the previous 200 "germ containers" (interview, *al-Sharq al-awsat*, June 21, 1996). He stated that of the new total, 230 containers hold agent "in powder form, which has no expiry date, and in 25, it [the BW material] is in liquid form, which will deteriorate" (interview, *Independent*, July 5, 1996). More recently, however, he contended that half the arsenal is in powder form (interview, CBS-TV, *60 Minutes*, November 23, 1997). Whatever the breakdown, General al-Samarra'i's account should have a bearing on the debate regarding Iraq's ability to produce dried BW agents.

135. *New York Times*, June 15, 1998; also *Times*, June 16, 1998. The *Daily Telegraph* said, on June 16, 1998, that UNSCOM inspectors unearthed "what might be evidence

of hundreds of tons of destroyed missile fuel." For earlier UNSCOM commentary on the Nibai findings, see UNSCOM/TECH, 9.

136. On the Iraqi version of the destruction process and UNSCOM's remaining conundrums, see Raymond A. Zilinskas, "Iraq's Biological Weapons: The Past as Future?" *Journal of the American Medical Association* [hereafter *JAMA*], August 6, 1997, 420. In general, Iraq has turned down repeated requests to examine the paperwork from the destruction process and to talk to the technicians who supposedly carried it out (Ruth Wedgwood, "Truth Sleuth in Iraq," *Washington Post*, June 19, 1996; on Iraq's refusal to provide persons requested for interviews, see UNSCOM 1997, 34 and 35). The order for the destruction, it is claimed, was given orally, and no record was kept. Yet UNSCOM's interviews with whatever personnel the Iraqis did produce show that no one can remember exactly when this order was given. They even attempted to conceal the nature and scope of Iraqi plans to hide the biological weapons program (*Economist*, April 12, 1997, 80). Moreover, UNSCOM reported, "Iraq's account of the unilateral destruction of all its filled weapons and bulk biological warfare agent in summer 1991 is incompatible with facts known to the Commission" (UNSCOM 1997, 21).

137. Butler.

138. Interview, *New York Times*, June 25, 1997.

139. Reportedly, the U.S. government has estimated that "only 96 hours are required for the entire process involved in the production of anthrax." W. Set Carus, "Chemical Weapons in the Middle East," *Policy Forum*, no. 9 (Washington, D.C.: Washington Institute for Near East Policy, December 1988), 5.

140. U.S. Government White Paper, 9. This assessment is based on the continuing Iraqi work on the al-Samoud missile. Under the 1991 cease-fire resolution, Iraq is allowed missiles with ranges up to 150 kilometers. However, UNSCOM has described al-Samoud as a scaled-down Scud. It is expected that once inspections are over, Iraq will begin converting this effort into long-range missiles. The missile production facility at Ibn al-Haytham—which Iraq currently uses to support its authorized missile programs—has already been expanded. Two new fabrication buildings at the facility were described as "spacious enough to house the construction of large ballistic missiles" (ibid., 10). In addition, the Iraqis are already engaged in the development of solid and liquid propellant for their Ababeel missile program. Although this project is also allowed under Resolution 687, UNSCOM has expressed concern that Iraq is using the program to maintain a knowledge base to support future development of long-range missiles (OSD, "Proliferation: Threat and Response," 33). A British intelligence assessment was somewhat more conservative. It mentioned Iraq's need to acquire key components from abroad, and the need for testing of long-range missiles (which could be detected), as possible impediments. Accordingly, development of long-range missiles was "at least" four years away once these problems were overcome (Reuters [London], November 18, 1997).

141. U.S. Government White Paper, 7.

142. UNSCOM 1998, 13.

143. Zilinskas, "Iraq's Biological Weapons," 423.

144. Ibid., 422.

145. Ibid. Another source has said: "All known fermentation and bioproduction equipment remains intact, and key experts remain available. . . . Consequently, Iraq retains the infrastructure that previously developed and produced biological warfare agents and weapons" (OSD, "Proliferation: Threat and Response," 1996, 21). UNSCOM has estimated that with the equipment Iraq is known to possess, it could produce 90 gallons (350 liters) of weapons-grade anthrax each week, enough to fill two missile warheads or four aerial bombs, if inspections were suspended or terminated (briefing to the UNSC, as reported by Reuters [U.N.], November 20, 1997).

146. UNSCOM 1998, 13.

147. Ibid., 16. It soon became public that a deal for such a facility had been struck with Russia in 1995. It included fermentation vessels with a total capacity of some 13,200 gallons. *New York Times*, February 13 and 18, 1998.

148. Republic of Iraq Radio, FBIS (NES), August 3, 1994, 34.

149. Cited in Laurie Mylroie and James Ring Adams, "Saddam's Germs," *American Spectator*, November 1995, 61.

150. Ruth Wedgwood, "Truth Sleuth in Iraq," *Washington Post*, June 19, 1996. Iraq placed the orders for the growth media in 1987 and 1988 with the Oxoid firm in Bedford, England, and with Fluka Chemie AG in Bouch, Switzerland (*Washington Post*, November 21, 1997). The material rarely travels in containers larger than a few kilograms, because it spoils rapidly on exposure to air.

151. Richard Spertzel, quoted in *Washington Post*, November 21, 1997. It has been reported that the media ordered by Iraq is better suited for growing anthrax than for hospital diagnosis. *Economist*, April 12, 1997, 79.

152. Following his defection, Hussein Kamil Hassan described the October 1994 buildup of Iraqi forces on Kuwait's border as follows: "A decision was made then to enter Kuwait again. Military plans and arrangements were made and the competent officers were given orders. The target was not only Kuwait, but also the eastern region in Saudi Arabia. The objective was to control Kuwaiti and Saudi oil. The Iraqi regime believed that controlling the Iraqi, Kuwaiti and Saudi oil would facilitate the negotiations with the Americans and would make the Americans review the situation in the region in light of their interests. I can confirm that the decision was made, plans were prepared, and the officers were given orders." Interview, *al-Watan al-'arabi*, in FBIS (NES), November 27, 1995, 33.

153. Likewise, UNSCOM has done Saddam's bidding on occasion. In an apparent bid to demonstrate the importance of continuing the commission's work in Iraq, Butler was quoted as saying that Iraq had enough biological agents and toxins to "blow away Tel Aviv or wherever." Interview, *New York Times*, January 27, 1998; also letter in *New York Times*, January 30, 1998.

154. Nonproliferation Center, "The Weapons Proliferation Threat," 13.

155. Interview, *al-Hayat*, March 2, 1996.

156. Jordanian Foreign Minister Abd-al-Karim al-Kabariti, cited in Radio Jordan Network, Amman, FBIS (NES), December 11, 1995, 61. Also *al-Hayat*, December 8,

1995; *Jordan Times* (Amman), December 9, 1995; *al-Bilad* (Amman), December 13, 1995. Initially, the Russians claimed that the affair was a CIA-engineered plot to embarrass Moscow, and hinted that the source of the gyroscopes could have been Ukraine or Kazakhstan (*Komsomolskaya Pravda*, December 20, 1995). However, an investigation by the Center for Policy Studies in Russia has found that the shipment was part of an Iraqi order that comprised 800 gyroscopes. The devices had been removed from the command modules of Russian SS-N-18 submarine-launched ballistic missiles, which were designed to deliver nuclear warheads to targets more than 4,000 kilometers away. They were being destroyed under arms control treaties. Reportedly, the deal was concluded in July 1995 under the guidance of Hussein Kamil Hassan. At his insistence the Russians first provided ten samples, which they tested and recertified at the Moscow manufacturing site, the Mars Motor Plant. The samples, which arrived in Iraq via Jordan, were found by UNSCOM inspectors on December 9, 1995, hidden in the waters of the Tigris River. The main shipment also included a rate table, which is used to test guidance instruments. A Palestinian with connections to Iraq's secret service was the intermediary for the deal (*Washington Post*, April 11, 1998).

157. News conference, KSC Television, Kuwait, FBIS (NES), November 21, 1995, 33. Until August 1995, Iraq concealed the fact that its project 1728, specifically established for the production of rocket motors, had produced missile engines and conducted some 20 static and flight tests with these engines (UNSCOM 1997, 9). Apparently the engines were assembled from both imported and locally produced parts.

158. In fact, the Iraqis substituted some of these locally produced engines, which they buried, for authentic Russian engines in a scheme designed to convince UNSCOM that they had actually destroyed 85 unaccounted Scuds on their own. Because the missile burials were "too clean," it appears that the missiles were carefully dismantled instead of destroyed. Crucial missile elements, such as turbo pumps, which the Iraqis cannot produce themselves, were missing from the destruction sites. The Iraqis have also planted test and training missiles and missile remnants among those "destroyed." See Ekeus, "Address."

159. "Press Briefing by Executive Chairman of Special Commission" (New York: United Nations Headquarters, September 4, 1996).

160. "UN: Iraqi Biological Weapons and Ballistic Missile Development Programs Continue," *Near East Report*, December 4, 1995. Also *New York Times*, December 22, 1995; *Frankfurter Allgemeine Zeitung*, February 5, 1997. In this regard, the interdiction in December 1993 of a shipment of ammonium perchlorate—a dual-use chemical with solid-missile-fuel applications—on its way to Iraq could be significant (OSD, "Proliferation: Threat and Response," 1996, 18).

161. AFP (Amman), FBIS (NES), December 26, 1995, 60.

162. Ekeus, "Address." Given accounts of diplomatic maneuvering by the UNSC toward Iraq, Ekeus's prophecy seems ominously realistic. See *New York Times*, October 17, 22, and 23, 1997.

163. Speech marking the sixth anniversary of the "Great Victory Day" over Iran, Republic of Iraq Radio, FBIS (NES), August 9, 1994, 30.

164. Department of Defense, *Conduct of the Persian Gulf War: Final Report to Congress* (Washington, D.C.: GPO, April 1992), 19. This formulation, which was introduced in August 1990, can be read as an implicit call for the United States to make the removal of the Saddam regime one of its objectives in the crisis.

165. Iraq Television Network, FBIS (NES), July 18, 1996, 24.

166. Reuven Pedatzur, *The Arrow System and the Active Defense Against Ballistic Missiles* (Hebrew), Memorandum series (Tel Aviv: Joffe Center of Strategic Studies, Tel Aviv University, October 1993), 22. In May 1997, Israel's commander of the Home Front Command, Maj. Gen. Shmu'el Arad, told the Knesset's State Comptroller Committee that 1.9 million Israelis were insufficiently protected against CW attack. This, he said, has taken place while the CW capabilities of Syria and Iran have risen dramatically since the Gulf War. Cited in *The CBW Conventions Bulletin*, September 1997, 19.

167. Interview, *Yedi'ot aharonot* (First Anniversary Supplement), January 10, 1992, 3. Arens claimed that the Israeli deterrent strategy vis-à-vis Iraq was helped by the distribution of gas masks and the availability of sealed rooms in every Israeli apartment. He said: "You've got to put yourself in Saddam's place. He must have said to himself: If I use chemical weapons it will not be effective given that all the Israelis are equipped with gas masks . . . so the effect will not be great, and who knows what the response of Israel will be." Arens would only concede that Israel's deterrence against Saddam's conventional Scud attacks was ineffective, "but the Americans too were unsuccessful [in this regard]."

168. *Davar*, August 27, 1995.

169. Peres, *The New Middle East*, 79.

170. Ibid., 64.

171. Ibid., 83. Subsequently Peres identified Iran as the prime danger in this context: "Iran is currently the center of terrorism, the center of fundamentalism, and the center of subversion, and . . . in my opinion it is more dangerous than Nazism . . . because Hitler did not have a nuclear bomb. The Iranians have tested and achieved a nuclear option." Interview, France-2 Television Network, FBIS (NES), March 8, 1996, 35.

172. Peres, *The New Middle East*, 69.

173. Israel Television Channel 1 Network, FBIS (NES), December 26, 1995, 51. See also an interview in the *Times*, March 31, 1995.

174. According to one estimate, the Israeli arsenal may contain as many as 400 nuclear weapons with a total combined yield of 50 megatons. Harold Hough, "Could Israel's Assets Survive a Preemptive Strike?" *Jane's Intelligence Review*, September 1997 (http://www.janes.com/publ . . . ditors/jir9709/hough.html).

175. Maj. Gen. (USA-Ret.) Edward B. Atkeson, "A Military Assessment of the Middle East, 1991–96" (Carlisle Barracks, Penn.: U.S. Army War College, Strategic Studies Institute, December 7, 1992), 65.

176. Interview in *Bit'on kheyl ha'avir* (the IAF magazine), cited in *Ha'aretz*, December 27, 1995.

177. *Global Proliferation of Weapons of Mass Destruction*, Hearings before the Permanent Subcommittee on Investigations of the Committee on Governmental Affairs, U.S.

Senate, 104th Cong., 1st sess., pt. 1, October 31 and November 1, 1995. Also *New York Times*, March 21, 1996; *Washington Post*, March 21, 1996; Paul Mann, "Mass Weapons Threat Deepens Worldwide," *Aviation Week and Space Technology*, June 17, 1996, pp. 58–61.

178. *Economist*, January 4, 1997, 33. For a general discussion, see Ian O. Lesser and Ashley J. Tellis, "Strategic Exposure: Proliferation Around the Mediterranean" (Santa Monica, Calif.: RAND, 1996) (http:www.rand.org/publications/MR/MR742/ index. html).

179. Ze'ev Schiff, "An Antiquated Security Conception amid a New Reality," *Ha'aretz*, January 9, 1998. Also Me'ir Pa'il and Menachem Barbash, "The Nuclear Fright," *Ha'aretz*, January 1, 1998.

180. Already it has been suggested that the United States should scale back its foreign involvement, especially in the Middle East, to cope with the increased CB threat to its cities (see Richard K. Betts, "The New Threat of Mass Destruction," *Foreign Affairs*, January–February 1998, 26–41). One think tank event went as far as to call for what could be termed "preemptive surrender" of U.S. commitments in "hot zones" to minimize the threat of CB terrorism against the United States proper (see Ivan Elend, *Protecting the Homeland: The Best Defense Is to Give No Offense*, Policy Analysis No. 36 [Washington, D.C.: Cato Institute, May 5, 1998]).

181. Khaim Assa, then head of Rabin's national security team, cited in *Ha'aretz*, July 9, 1993.

182. David Hughes, "Regional Nuclear Powers Pose New Risks to U.S. Military," *Aviation Week and Space Technology*, January 13, 1992, 66.

183. *Ha'aretz*, October 15, 1995; David A. Fulghum, " U.S. Missile Defense Plans Narrowed," *Aviation Week and Space Technology*, December 4, 1995, 24.

184. *CBS Evening News*, CBS Television, February 25, 1998, citing U.S. intelligence and UNSCOM sources. See also *Sunday Times*, November 9, 1997; *New York Times*, November 21, 1997.

185. Mounting biological dispersal systems onto cruise missiles may overcome the disadvantages associated with ballistic missiles, where the warhead is placed under enormous stress as it accelerates and as it reenters the earth's atmosphere. In contrast, a cruise missile flies much like an aircraft, and its relatively low speed facilitates the dispersion of acrosols (see "Key Technologies: An Overview"). Cruise missile technology also allows for longer ranges and better accuracy and may include countermeasures and signature reduction. With regard to Iraq's UAVs, one source indicated that the drones were "Italian-made" (Remarks of Tim McCarthy, an UNSCOM missile inspector, Conference on "Start II, Missile Non-Proliferation, and Missile Defense," Panel II, Carnegie Endowment, 1995 [http://wheat.symgrp.com/symgrp/pai/articles/panel2.html]). After the war the CIA reported that Iraq's Nasir State Establishment for Mechanical Industries stored in its bomb shelter of its headquarters building "approximately" 10 drone airplanes that had been designed and produced to deliver BW agents ("Biological Warfare Drone Airplanes at Iraq's Nasir State Establishment for Mechanical Industries," CIA 374704 [Arlington, Va.: CIA, May 1992] [Gulflink]).

186. *Jane's Sentinel*, cited in *Ha'aretz*, August 15, 1996.

187. Hughes, "Regional Nuclear Powers," 65.

188. In 1815 a division (normally 15,000–20,000 soldiers) occupied about 8 square kilometers. Today it may take up a space of 65 square kilometers. By 2015 it may require an area of 260 square kilometers. "Troops will move rapidly over the battlefield in small groups; there will be nothing resembling a front line." "The Future of Warfare," *Economist*, March 8, 1997, 21–22.

189. Lt. Col. Mark Kipphut, USAF, "Theater Missile Defense: Reflections for the Future" (Maxwell AFB, Ala.: Air University, Winter 1996) (http://www.cdsar.af. mil.apj/win96/kipphut.html). The latest draft of the U.S. Air Force doctrine contains an expanded definition of air and space control to include ballistic and cruise missiles (Air Force Doctrine Document-1, draft, "Air Force Basic Doctrine" [Maxwell Air Force Base, Ala.: Air University, August 5, 1995], 11). However, it still calls for conducting offensive operations against theater missiles *before* they are launched, which one military analyst views as disregarding the lesson of Desert Storm and as a sign of dogmatic thinking among the U.S. Air Force planners (Kipphut, "Theater Missile Defense").

190. In December 1997, the U.S. Defense Department announced plans to inoculate all U.S. military personnel (1.4 million troops on active duty and another 1 million reservists) against anthrax. Beginning in summer 1998 the vaccine will initially be administered to some 100,000 military personnel assigned or deployed to the "high threat" areas of the Persian Gulf and the Korean Peninsula. The immunization program will consist of a series of six inoculations per soldier over an 18-month period, followed by an annual booster. The cost to inoculate the estimated 2.4 million personnel was estimated at $130 million (over a six-year period), but Deputy Secretary of Defense John Hamre described the program as "an important new dimension to overall force protection" (News Release, "Defense Department to Start Immunizing Troops Against Anthrax" [Washington, D.C.: Office of Assistant Secretary of Defense (Public Affairs), December 15, 1997]; see also *New York Times*, December 16, 1997; *Washington Post*, December 16, 1997; for earlier reports, see *Washington Post*, October 2, 1996; *Sunday Times*, May 11, 1997). On the subsequent debate regarding the possible effectiveness of the vaccine, see *New York Times*, February 3, 1998. On U.S. efforts to develop innovative technology for detecting and neutralizing CB weapons, including the "design of new oral drugs" to counter the anthrax spore on the battlefield, see Prepared Statement of Larry Lynn, Director, Defense Advanced Research Projects Agency (DARPA), before the Subcommittee on Acquisition and Technology, Senate Armed Services Committee, March 20, 1996, 8–9, 15–16, and 17; also Joan Stephenson, "Pentagon-Funded Research Takes Aim at Agents of Biological Warfare," *JAMA*, August 6, 1997, 373–75. Reportedly, the Pentagon has put "heavy pressure" on government and independent researchers to rush development of a botulinum toxin vaccine, which will be genetically engineered to be pure and capable of being produced in large quantities. See *Los Angeles Times*, January 29, 1998; see also Department of Defense, *Nuclear/Biological/Chemical (NBC) Defense*, Annual Report to Congress (Washington, D.C.: GPO, March 1997), 3–8 to 3–11 and 3–14 to 3–16.

191. In October 1996, the U.S. Army "activated" a unit to detect BW agents in combat, a capacity it said it lacked during the Gulf War. The new 310th Chemical Company, a reserve unit at Fort McClellan, has biological detection laboratories mounted on Humvees (High Mobility Vehicles). Each of the 35 labs weighs 4.5 tons and was described as "immediately deployable." The army said that the Biological Integrated Defense Systems can detect four types of biological agents, although it would not specify which (Associated Press [Anniston, Ala.], October 7, 1996; see also William B. Scott, "Lidar System to Detect Biological Warfare Agents," *Aviation Week and Space Technology*, November 13, 1995, 44). Because of the increased vulnerability of fixed sites like ports and air bases, logistical chains will be harder to sustain. Expeditionary forces will need to carry most of their supplies with them.

192. Voice of the Islamic Republic of Iran First Program Network, FBIS (NES), May 30, 1995, 62.

193. Great Jamahiriya Radio Network, FBIS (NES), May 2, 1996, 9; Libyan Television Network, FBIS (NES), May 1, 1996, 8. On veiled U.S. threats against the Tarhunah CW plant, see *New York Times*, April 3 and 4, 1996.

194. Korean Central Broadcasting Network, FBIS (EAS), May 7, 1996, 23; KCNA, FBIS (EAS), May 13, 1996, 38.

195. News conference, *Korea Herald*, October 14, 1995.

196. The argument that Desert Storm was from its inception a limited war faces numerous problems. It assumes that the United States possessed accurate information about the Iraqi CB capabilities in advance, and that Washington also estimated that Saddam would not be deterred by the U.S. nuclear option. Moreover, it assumes that U.S. intelligence learned of the arming of the Iraqi BW option before the war but concluded that the coalition could not preempt these capabilities effectively. Nor did the United States believe, according to this theory, that it could handle the Scud threat effectively via the combination of strategic bombing and Patriot defenses. Finally, to plan for a "limited war," the United States must have conjectured that Saddam would not resort to CW against Israel or U.S. troops immediately with the start of Desert Storm and especially upon the launching of the ground war. But this notion runs counter to the previous assumption that Saddam would not be deterred by the United States. Moreover, the U.S. strategic bombing hardly communicated an interest in a limited war. The U.S. planners must have known that repeated attacks on military targets in downtown Baghdad might not be viewed by the Iraqis as evidence of a limited-war strategy. In the centralized militarized society of Iraq, the distinction between political and military facilities is often obscured, and the systems of military command and political rule are closely interwoven. In fact, as the U.S. Air Force chief of staff, Gen. Merril McPeak, has subsequently disclosed, 26 sites specifically connected to the Ba'ath Party political controls and to Saddam's ruling Tikriti clan were targeted under the heading of "leadership targets." Even if Saddam initially thought the war would be fought over Kuwait, the strategic air campaign must have convinced him otherwise. As Aziz said: "We did not think the United States would try to destroy all of our telephone exchanges and the rest of our civilian infrastructure." Lawrence

Freedman and Efraim Karsh, *The Gulf Conflict, 1990–1991: Diplomacy and War in the New World Order* (Princeton: Princeton University Press, 1994), 319, 324, and 329.

197. Indeed, pronouncements by U.S. defense policy makers amply indicate declining confidence in the viability of strategic deterrence, and the search for a new security concept. For example, in a significant policy shift, former Secretary of Defense Les Aspin announced on December 7, 1993, that the United States would add a military dimension to its fight against the spread of weapons of mass destruction. Terming the new policy the Defense Counter-Proliferation Initiative, Aspin said that America was now developing improved and specialized military capabilities, doctrine, training, and contingency plans to pursue counterproliferation policies (*Los Angeles Times*, December 8, 1993; for a discussion, see Barry R. Schneider, "Radical Responses to Radical Regimes: Evaluating Preemptive Counter-Proliferation," National Defense University, Institute for National Strategic Studies, Washington, D.C., McNair Paper No. 41, May 1995). In May 1995, then Secretary of Defense William Perry assigned U.S. Special Operations Command the primary Defense Department responsibility for the mission of counterproliferation of mass destruction weapons (see Glenn W. Goodman, "Combating Proliferation," *Armed Forces Journal International*, May 1997 [http://www.afj.com/Mags/1997/May/proliferation.html]). The Department of Defense has reportedly made "substantial progress" toward "fully integrating the counterproliferation mission into its military planning, acquisition, intelligence, and international cooperation activities." For example, the chair of the Joint Chiefs of Staff has issued a Counterproliferation Charter, which provided "overarching strategic-level policy and guidance on employment of U.S. forces to counter the proliferation of NBC weapons." In addition, a Counterproliferation Concept Plan, also by the chair of the JCS, required the regional commanders in chief "to prepare for and develop plans for counterproliferation operations" (OSD, "Proliferation: Threat and Response," 1997, 61). The subsequent decision to vaccinate all U.S. military personnel against anthrax, which conveys a rather dim view of the effectiveness of U.S. strategic deterrence, must also be viewed as an offspring of this fundamental shift in U.S. strategic thinking.

Index

Ababeel missile, 346*n*

Abbas, Sa'di Tumah, xi, xvii, 41

Al-Abbas missile, 296*n*

Abd-al-Jabir, Mustafa Kamal, 144

Abu Nidal Organization, 68

Acetylcholine, 5, 257*n*

Acetylcholinesterase, 257*n*

Aerial bombs, 11, 13, 241; Iraq's LD-250, 20–21, 253*n*, 256*n*; Iraq's R-400, 14, 236, 253*n*, 265*n*, 345*n*

Aerial Warning and Control System (AWACS), 45, 330*n*

Aerosolization, 13; and Iraqi dispensers, 266*n*; and Iraq's spray tanks project, 30–31, 266*n*; and particles' size, 250*n*; and wet vs. dried agents, 30, 266–67*n*

Aflatoxin, 3; and BW, 6–7; in Iraq's BW program, 6, 7, 10, 11, 29, 30, 249*n*, 265*n*, 323*n*

Agency for National Security Planning (ROK), 191

Agricultural and Water Resources Research Center (Fudaliyah), 11

Ahmad, Sultan Hashim, 56, 102

Air burst fuse, 20

Akayev, Askar, 313*n*

Akhromeyev, Sergei, xi; on sharing information, 279*n*; predicts devastating war, 139, 141

Albright, Madeleine, xxi, xxii

Aleppo, 185, 189, 334*n*

Alexandria, 148

Algiers treaty (1975), 34

Alveoli, 250*n*

AMAN (Israel), 2; assesses Iraqi Air Force threat, 135; conception of Saddam, 94–98 *passim*; and concrete warhead, 73; debate over, 87–92; on Iran's

SSM project, 186; performance assessed, 158–63; uncertainty about CB warhead, 99–100, 300*n*; worst-case approach of, 97–100, 158, 160–62; in Yom Kippur War, 97, 299*n*

Ambiguity, as deterrent, 47, 54, 59–61, 309*n*

Ammonium perchlorate, 348*n*

Amn al-Khass, 344*n*

Amnesty International, 189

An Nasiriyah, 31, 282*n*

Al-Anbari, abd al-Amir, 53, 269*n*

Andropov, Yuri, 269*n*

Annan, Kofi, xxii

Antarctica, 310*n*

Anthrax: aerosolization of, 9, 100–101, 163, 250*n*, 265*n*, 266*n*; vs. botulinum toxin, 6; and BW, 4; cutaneous, 4; decay rate of, 250*n*; dried vs. in solution, 101, 266–67*n*; effectiveness of, 8; forms of, 3–4; gastrointestinal, 4; incubation period, 9; infective dose, 3, 9, 250*n*; in Iraq's BW program, 10–14 *passim*, 235, 236, 265*n*; penicillin-resistant strains, 4; persistence in soil, 4, 83, 246–47*n*; production of, 346*n*; pulmonary or inhalation, 3–4, 9, 246*n*, 247*n*, 250*n*; scare in Washington, D.C., 292*n*; simulant, 11, 28; spores, 4, 246–47*n*, 250*n*, 328*n*; and Sverdlovsk incident, 244–46*n*, 251*n*; and terrorism, 68; in U.S. BW program, 251*n*; Vollum 1B strain of, 9

Arab Cooperation Council, 280*n*

Arab-Israeli conflict: and peace diplomacy, 184, 197, 201–2; wars, 55, 135, 281*n*

Arab press, 67, 73

355

Arab world, 80, 126, 268*n*
Arabian Peninsula, 42
Arad, Shmu'el, 349*n*
Arens, Moshe, xi; on anti-Scud operation, 77, 78, 165; briefs Bush, xviii, 84;
expects CB strike, 77–85 *passim*, 95;
and Hammer Rick, 165, 289*n*; on
Israeli deterrence, 217, 349*n*; on Jordanian spy planes, 309*n*; on next war,
329*n*; on nuclear option, 81; on Patriot
defenses, 293*n*; pledges retaliation,
129; talks with Cheney, xviii, 79, 85,
95, 290*n*, 291*n*, 297*n*; on targeting
civilians, 15; on undeterrable Saddam,
93
Armed Services Committee (House), 39
Armenia, 314*n*
Arrow Anti-Tactical Ballistic Missile
(ATBM), 220, 307*n*
Aspergillus flavus, 6, 235
Aspergillus parasiticus, 6, 235
Aspin, Les, xiii; anti-proliferation initiative, 353*n*; on Iraq's BW program, xvi,
39; orders strategy review, 184
Al-Assad, Hafiz, 194, 195, 240*n*
Athens, 35, 188
Atomic and nuclear weapons, 22; fallout
from, 135; Iraqi efforts to acquire, 18,
254*n*; Iraq's concerns over attack by,
23, 47, 50, 53, 57; and Israel, 126–135
passim; tactical, 61, 81, 107, 128. *See
also* Deterrence; Iraq's nuclear pro-
gram; Israel; Soviet Union; United
Nations Special Commission for the
Disarmament of Iraq
Aum Shinrikiyo, 9, 248*n*
Azarbaijan, 314*n*
Aziz, Tariq, xi, 60, 103, 271*n*; confirms
U.S. deterrence, 59; on Iraq's deterrence strategy, 39; meeting with Baker,
xvii, 57, 63, 70; message to Butler, xx;
in Moscow, xviii, 75, 287*n*; on parity
with Israel, 287*n*; predicts victory,

273*n*; on readiness for BW, 47; on strategic reciprocity, 53; on terrorism, 67;
on UNSCOM, xxiii, 70–71; on U.S.
withdrawal, 109; warns of new crisis,
xxiii

Ba'ath party, 243*n*, 259*n*, 282*n*, 288*n*,
352*n*
Bacillus anthracis. See Anthrax
Bacillus thuringiensis, 267*n*
Bacon, Kenneth H., 188, 343*n*
Bacteriological decay, 10
Baghdad, 11, 42, 61, 65, 274*n*, 276*n*,
277*n*; attacked by Iranian Scuds, 259*n*;
and coalition bombings, 61; evacuation
plans for, 65; Israeli missile threat to,
128, 132; and nuclear attack on, 47,
50; Saddam hiding in, 69, 152, 319*n*;
Soviet military delegation in, 146; U.S.
advance on, 48, 74–75, 83, 87, 96, 102,
109, 228–29, 230
Baghdad Radio, xviii, 18, 67, 72, 73, 102,
114, 212
Bahrain, 140
Baker, James A., xiii, 60, 323*n*; on Iraq's
WMD, 168; on Kremlin Arabists,
145; meeting with Aziz, xvii, 60–61,
63, 70, 283*n*, 284*n*, 286*n*, 292*n*; opposes Bush's tone, 273*n*; on postwar
agenda, 171, 183, 330*n*; on proliferation, 171; on removing Saddam, 171,
233*n*, 286*n*, 302*n*; on Saddam's "paranoia," 44; on Saudi intentions, 303*n*
Al-Bakr, Ahmad Hassan, 243*n*
Al-Bakr University, 344*n*
Balance of terror: with Club MAD, 218,
223; U.S.-Soviet, 225
Ballistic missiles, 221–22. *See also* Iraq's
ballistic missile program; *names of specific missiles*
Bandar Abbas, 196
Barak, Ehud, xi; briefs Bush, xviii, 84;
briefs Cheney and Powell, xviii, 78–79,

127, 128, 174, 290*n*; on IDF intervention, 78; on Iraqi CB warhead, 99; on leftover Scuds, 170; meets Ekeus, 324*n*; on next war, 322*n*; predicts CB strike, 79

Basra, xviii, 20, 37, 46, 141, 283*n*

Baynjan, 32

Belayev, Igor, 144

Belgium, 21, 284*n*

Belonogov, Aleksander, 278*n*

Ben Gal, Avigdor, 127–28

Ben Gurion Airport, 86

Ben-Eliyahu, Eytan, 330*n*

Benghazi, 310*n*

Bessmertnykh, Aleksander, xii, 142

B-52 bombers, 146

Bigeye bomb, 23

Bin Sultan, Bandar, 277*n*

Bin Sultan, Khaled, xii, 35, 38, 273*n*, 303*n*, 324*n*; on cease-fire talks, 104–5; on Egyptian Scuds, 317; on lack of Iraqi CW, 56; on taking Baghdad, 303*n*; on war's end, 82

Binary chemical weapons, 22–28, 47; in Iraqi CW doctrine, 24; in Iraqi missile warheads, 26, 27; in Iraq's aerial bombs, 26; Iraq's disclosure of, 22–23, 39, 44; and Iraq's dual chemical, 24–25, 28; make of, 22, 259–60*n*; and mixed agents, 25–26; Soviet vs. U.S., 23–24; in Syria, 190; vs. unitary-agent weapons, 23, 260*n*; UNSCOM's confirmation of, 28

"Binary sarin," 27

Bin-Nun, Avihu, xi; on gas masks, 301*n*; on Iraqi Air Force threat, 136; on Iraqi CB warhead, 99, 163; on neutralization of Scuds, 326*n*; on postwar intelligence effort, 323–24*n*

Bioengineering Company (Switzerland), 192

Biological agents: concentrations of, 235; dried vs. in solution, 30, 266–67*n*;

effectiveness of, 8–9; as force multiplier, 251*n*; and particle size, 9, 250*n*, 265*n*, 321*n*; produced by Iraq, 10–11, 235

Biological and Toxin Weapons Convention (1972), 5, 109, 144, 243*n*, 275*n*, 316*n*

Biological warfare (BW), 1; and agent dissemination, 7, 100–101; 161–62, 163, 321*n*; and anxiety factor, 15, 100; vs. CW, 7; defenses against, 247*n*, 264*n*, 351*n*; defined, 3; effectiveness debated, 7; by Germany, 247*n*; and inhalation, 3; by Japan, 250*n*; against Kurds, 31–32; moral inhibition against, 250*n*; strategic vs. tactical, 6, 28, 76; uncertainties about, 8–10, 162. *See also* Iraq's biological weapons

Biopreparat, 144

Bioterrorism. *See* Terrorism

Black Sea, 148

Blackmail, Iraqi, 50, 84, 112, 137, 179, 213, 214; by Club MAD, 200–206 *passim*, 225

Blister agents. *See* Mustard gas

"Blue acid," 263*n*

BND (Germany), 198, 263*n*

"Bomb in the basement," 47, 130, 217, 219, 308–9*n*

"Bomb in the closet," 308*n*

"Bomb in the window," 308*n*

Bomblets, 13, 253–54*n*

Botulinum toxin, 4; aerosol contamination with, 7, 101, 162; vs. anthrax, 6; anti-toxin for, 248*n*; and BW, 6; *Clostridium botulinum* and, 5; effects of, 5; and Hall strain, 5; in Iraq's BW program, 10–14 *passim*, 28, 235, 236, 264*n*, 266*n*; and terrorism, 68, 285–86*n*; toxicity of, 5, 248*n*; Type A, 5, 9, 251*n*; in U.S. BW program, 251*n*; in water, 247*n*

Brazil, 252*n*

Bremmer, L. Paul, 68

Britain (British government), 28;
announces troop vaccination, xvii, 43;
BW program of, 246n; on Iraq missile
potential, xxii, 346n; on Iraqi anthrax
plot, xxii; Iraqi students in, 33, 270n;
military aid to Iraq, 65, 284n

British Ministry of Defence, 325n

Bubonic plague, 1

Bundy, McGeorge, 164

Busbee, Walter, 316n

Bush, George (Bush administration), xiii,
2, 40, 69, 270n, 273n; and arms to
Middle East, 329–30n; attitude toward
Iraq, 38; calls for Saddam's removal,
228, 302n; coalition-building effort of,
38, 42, 54, 126; decision to end war,
xviii, 77, 83–86, 167–72, 181, 227–29,
254n; decision to go to war, 172–81
passim; dispatches troops to Gulf, xv,
xvi, 31, 40, 268n; fears Israeli nuclear
response, 101, 125; and Hitler analogy,
104, 224, 302n; infighting among, 60,
61, 284n; Iraqi plot against, 206; on
madman Saddam, 102; objectives in
Gulf crisis, 216; opposes IDF intervention, 84; postwar agenda, 183; rejects
unconventional response, 83; relations
with Israel, 128, 134, 308n; on Scud-
hunting, 88; on sparing Saddam, 229–
32, 323n; "true agenda" of, 104, 170;
"understanding" with Saddam, 105–7;
on Vietnam, 52; warnings for Saddam,
58, 59, 61, 63, 70, 104; worries over
Iraqi WMD, 39, 273n

Butler, Richard, xii; on Iraqi unilateral
destruction, 210; on Iraqi VX, xxiii,
208–9, 345n; on Iraq's BW capability,
xxi, 347n

BVD (Holland), 333–34n

Cardoen, Carlos R., 253n

Castro, Fidel, 18

CBU-500, 254n

C&C. *See* Command and control

Center for Policy Studies (Russia), 348n

Central Command (CENTCOM), 176,
178, 201, 228

Central Intelligence Agency (CIA), 2, 33;
assesses attacks on CB sites, 179, 327n;
assesses Iraqi CW, 58, 255n, 268n; on
Bush's warning, 168; on CBW against
civilians, 288–89n; on Iranian CBW
programs, 335n, 337n; on Iraqi agent
production, 251n; on Iraqi military
decline, 306n; on Iraq's BW attack
plan, 30–31; predicts resort to CBW,
94, 297–98n, 324n; predicts Scud
attacks, 166; on Republican Guard,
228; tunnel vision of, 325n; and uncertainty, 300–301n; warns of CB terrorism, 68

Centre d'etudes et recherches scientifiques (Syria), 335n

CEP, 136, 312n

Chah Bahar, 197

Chakalov district, 245n

Chemical agents: mixed, 24; persistent
vs. nonpersistent, 20, 248n, 256n; vs.
toxins, 5, 7, 247–48n; unitary vs.
binary, 23. *See also* Mustard gas; Sarin;
Tabun; VX

Chemical and Biological Defence Establishment (U.K.), 249n, 323n

Chemical warfare (CW), 1; vs. BW, 7. *See
also* Iraq's chemical warfare; Iraq's
chemical weapons

Chemical Weapons Convention, 190

Cheney, Richard, xiii; briefed by Barak,
xvii, 78; briefed on CW warheads,
329n; defines war goals, 231; on Israeli
nuclear response, 61, 128, 217, 312n;
talks with Arens, xviii, 79, 85, 95, 168,
290n, 297n; and "Western excursion,"
180

Chernishev, Albert, 139, 145

Defense Intelligence Agency (*continued*)
information gaps, 300n, 325n; on Saddam's desperation scenario, 95, 298n;
on Scud tests, 278n; on Soviet CBW
aid, 315n; on Sverdlovsk incident,
245n; on undeterrable Saddam, 173;
warns of BW, 97, 179
"Defense of Japan, The," 188
Denmark, 267n
Desert Shield, xv, 273n
Desert Storm. *See* Gulf War
Deterrence: and ambiguity, 47, 54, 127,
150; crisis of strategic, 225–26; ineffective against Iraq, 59–71, 298n; and
inoculations, 173; Iraqi efforts at, 34–
50, 74–78, 82, 84, 212; Israeli debate
over strategic, 217–20; and limited war,
15, 61; strategic (NBC), 57, 59, 72, 150,
154, 183, 184, 200; and strategic reci-
procity, 52–54; U.S. shift on strategic,
353n. *See also* Terrorist deterrence
Deuterium, 127
Deutsch, John, 190, 334n, 341n
Difluoromethylphosphonate (DF), 24,
26, 260n, 261n
Diisopropylamine, 208
Dimona nuclear reactor, 127, 278n,
296n; attacks on, xviii, 72–73, 87, 88,
287n, 288n; as CB target, 91; vul-
nerability of, 135–37, 312–13n
Distilled sulfur mustard (HD), 20
Dole, Robert, 23, 42, 47
Dongfeng-3 missile, 333n
"Doomsday machine," 50
DOSAAF, 315n
DPRK. *See* Korea, North
Drop tanks. *See* Spray tanks
Dual chemical weapons, 24; UNSCOM
on, 27–28; use against Kurds, 26, 237.
See also "Cocktail" chemicals; Mixed-
agent weapons
Duelfer, Charles, 344n
Dujayl, 263n

Al-Dustur, 276n
Dyspnea, 3

Eagleburger, Lawrence, xiii, xvii; agreement with Israel, 308n; on Israeli
retaliation, 128, 130; on neutralizing
Scuds, 175–76
East Germany (GDR), 252n, 257n, 285n
"Eastern front," 182
Egypt: CW in Yemen, 148; Iraqi plot
against, 206, 343n; on Israeli nuclear
deterrent, 291n; military aid to Iraq,
252n, 253n, 257n; in Yom Kippur War,
148
82d Airborne Division, 35, 272n
Ekeus, Rolf, xiii, 1, 87, 107, 172, 251n;
on aerial bombs, 265n; on intelligence
failure, 2; on Iraqi cheating, 110, 293n;
on Iraq's BW readiness 2, 7, 28, 29; on
Iraq's dried agent, 267n; on Iraq's left-
over CB weapons, 344n; on Iraq's mis-
sile force, 207, 215–16; on Kamil
Hassan's defection, 110, 113; on
nuclear deterrence, 59; summoned by
Aziz, 113; on UNSCOM, 106, 216,
303n, 304n
Electromagnetic pulse (EMP), 65, 285n
Enhanced radiation weapons, 127–28,
307n
Esfahan, 185, 259n
Al-Estikhabarat al-'Askariyya, 18
Euphrates river, 60
Eurabic International BV, 333n
Europe, 67, 68, 216, 217
External intelligence service (Russia). *See*
SVR

Falin, Valentin, 278n
Al-Faw, 25, 255n, 264n
Federal Bureau of Investigation (FBI), 200
Federal Intelligence Service. *See* BND
Federal Security Service, 334n
Filatov, Viktor, xii, 146, 317n

Fish Lake, 255n

Fluka Chemie AG, 347n

F-111, 319n, 327n

F-117, 327n

Foreign Office (U.K.), 270n

4th Wing (USAF Tactical Air Command), 325n

France: Iraqi students in, 33, 270n; military aid to Iraq, 10, 252n, 284n

Freeh, Louis J., 200

French Armed Forces, 56

French Military Academy, 26

FSB (Russia), 334n

Fudaliyah, 11

Fusarium, 262n

Fusarium granarim, 263n

Fusarium oxysporium, 262n

GA. *See* Tabun

Galluci, Robert, 201

Gas chambers, 265n

Gas gangrene, 10

Gas masks, 2, 56, 69, 96, 100, 268n, 299n, 349n; from Soviet Union, 140, 314n

Gates, Robert M., xiii, 33, 82, 329n; on U.S. mistakes, 213–14

Gazit, Shlomo, 317n

GB. *See* Sarin

GBU-28, 319n

GD. *See* Soman

Gee, John, 58

General Association of Korean Residents in Japan (Chongnyon), 205

Geneva, Aziz-Baker meeting in, xvii, 57, 70, 284n, 292n

Geneva Convention, 60

Genocide, 32, 67, 214, 249n

Georgia, 314n

Germ warfare. *See* Biological warfare

Germany. *See* East Germany; West Germany

GF: LCt$_{50}$ of, 27; make of, 261n; mixed with GB, 26–27, 264n; vs. sarin, 27

Glaspie, April, xiii, 19, 39, 67, 270n

Glosson, Buster, 175

God invoked, 52, 90, 91, 111, 129, 297n

Golan Heights, 197, 201

Gorbachev, Mikhail (Gorbachev regime), xii, xviii, 46, 75, 138, 139; advocates cease-fire, 145–46; vs. Soviet military, 141, 147; stand on proliferation, 142–43, 315n; warns against NBC use, 146

Gosden, Christine M., 26, 263n

GosNIIOKht Chemical Institute (Russia), 334n

Govorov, Vladimir, 276n

GRU (Soviet Union), 144

Gruinard Island, 246n

Gulf crisis, 15, 16, 31, 49, 67, 149, 153, 257n, 259n; U.S. objectives in, 216

Gulf War, xvii, 1, 16, 18, 38, 125; adverse consequences, 224–26; ground war, xviii; impact on Israel, 165, 170–71, 220; Iraq's BW readiness in, 3, 29, 47, 49, 249n; Iraq's CW readiness in, 26–27, 35–36; and limited war, 224, 352–53n; military lessons, 222–23; "negotiations" for cease-fire, 102–6 *passim*, 112, 146–49 *passim*, 303n; operational objectives, 231; postwar trends, 182–84, 196; reasons for cease-fire, 167–72 *passim*, 180, 227–32; and Republican Guard, 228–29, 231, 233n

Gulf War syndrome, 17, 94

Habbaniyah air base, 113

Haidar Chicken Farm, 113

Haifa, 88, 129, 287n

Al-Hakam Single Cell Protein Production Plant, 10, 18, 251n, 267n, 274n, 325n; relocation of equipment to, 270n; spray dryers for, 212

Halabja, 21–22; casualties in, 258n; congenital malformations in, 263n; CW against, 26, 259n

Hama, 185, 189

fare against, 243*n*; lessons of Gulf War, 171, 184, 196; SSM buildup of, 185–87, 331–32*n*; ties to Libya, 198, 330*n*; ties to North Korea, 193–97 *passim*, 198, 223, 330*n*, 332*n*, 338*n*, 340*n*; ties to Syria, 194–197 *passim*, 198, 338*n*, 340*n*

Iran Salam, 197

Iran-Iraq war, 33, 39, 54, 253*n*; impact on Saddam's thinking, 94–95; and Iranian CW casualties, 24, 25, 237, 262*n*, 268*n*; Iranian missiles in, 330*n*; and Iran's final offensive, 20; Iraqi BW plans in, 30; Iraqi CW in, 19–21, 24, 31, 43, 96, 240*n*, 253*n*, 255*n*, 256–57*n*, 258*n*, 279–80*n*; Iraqi lessons from, 258*n*; and Israel, 126; misinformation in, 55; Saddam on, 51; Saddam's mistake in, 271*n*; U.S. policy in, 32, 63, 172

Iraq, 42, 46, 56, 74, 166, 182, 254*n*, 259*n*; buildup against Kuwait, xix, 213; captures Irbil, xix; and declarations to UNSCOM, 108, 109, 114, 161, 206–7, 235, 236, 239, 243*n*, 251*n*, 306*n*, 327*n*; interference with UNSCOM, xx, xxii–xxiii; "missile diplomacy" of, 37, 46, 71–75, 156; oil reserves of, 34; proclaims Kuwait union, xv; use of UNSCOM, 213–14; and Western deterrence, 70–71. *See also* United Nations Special Commission for the Disarmament of Iraq

Iraq Chemical Warfare Corps, 144

Iraq Interagency Biological Warfare Working Group (IIBWWG), xvii, 292–93*n*; guidelines for attacks, 328*n*; on Iraq's BW stock, 97

Iraqi Air Force, 56, 77, 82, 135; deployment in Jordan, 277*n*; Headquarters, 65; planes in Iran, 58, 291*n*; role in CW, 19, 58, 257*n*, 261*n*, 280*n*, 283*n*

Iraqi Army, 31, 44, 114, 208, 305*n*; lack of gas masks, 56; role in CW, 19

Iraqi Atomic Energy Commission, 159

Iraqi Foreign Ministry, 62, 108

Iraqi Ministry of Defense, 114, 159, 258*n*

Iraqi National Congress, 282*n*

Iraqi News Agency (INA), xxiii, 276*n*

Iraqi Surface-to-Surface Missile Corps, 212

Iraq's ballistic missile program, 239; and leftover Scuds, 343*n*, 344*n*; and project *1728*, 348*n*; reconstitution of, 211, 215–16, 346*n*, 348*n*. *See also names of specific missiles*

Iraq's biological weapons, 1; aerosolization of agent for, 29, 253*n*; aflatoxin, 10, 30, 249*n*; agent production for, 235; anthrax, 10, 251*n*; arming of, xvi, xvii, 39, 41, 47; botulinum toxin, 10, 251*n*, 264*n*; crash program for, xv, 29; debate over, 323*n*; delivery systems for, 161, 222, 236, 241, 323*n*, 350*n*; design of, 320*n*; as deterrent against Israel, 30, 82; evolution of program for, 10–13, 28–31, 243*n*, 268–69*n*; first- or second-strike, 47–50; growth media for, 213, 347*n*; impact detonations and, 160, 320*n*; vs. Iran, 29, 30; and Kuwait invasion, 31; as last resort, 42, 46–48; potential for damage, 7, 14, 83, 160, 253*n*; reasons for hiding, 38–40, 41–46; reconstitution of, 210–12; spray tanks for, 30–31, 161, 266*n*; strategic vs. tactical, 28; unilateral destruction of, 346*n*; and UNSCOM, 108, 109, 114, 209–10, 347*n*; and vaccine stockpiling, 264*n*; weaponization of agents for, 11, 28–29, 209, 210, 244*n*, 253*n*, 265*n*, 266–67*n*, 345*n*

Iraq's chemical warfare, 237–38; absence of in Gulf War, 55–59, 70, 282*n*; choice of mustard gas, 20, 258*n*; doctrine, 19–21, 258*n*; evolution of, 19–21, 255*n*, 258*n*; faulty tactics, 24, 261*n*; vs. Iraqi Shi'as, 204, 342*n*;

Iraq's chemical warfare (*continued*)
normative constraints on, 274–75n;
preparations for in Gulf War, 26–27,
28, 287n; and Soviet CW doctrine,
20–21, 24; use of mixed agents, 24–28,
262–63n; use of sarin, 21, 258n; use of
tabun, 20–21; Warsaw Pact and, 257n

Iraq's chemical weapons, 1; and aerial
bombs, 20, 241, 256n; and artillery, 21,
25; binary, 21–28 *passim*, 44, 49; and
chemical troops, 19, 144; and cruise
missiles, 222; delivery systems for, 241;
lack of in front, 56, 57; mixed agents
in, 21, 24–28 *passim*, 264n; mustard
gas in, 20, 211; problems with, 21, 56,
261n; reconstitution of, 210–11, 240;
and RPVs, 161, 168, 222; stockpile of,
55, 281n; tests on Iranian POWs,
257n; use in al-Faw battle, 25, 264n;
and VX, 208–9, 241n, 344n; and warheads, 26–27, 58, 160, 263n, 287n

Iraq's nuclear program, 18, 43, 45, 254n

IRBM, 132

Islam, 203

Islamic Revolution Guard Corps
(IRGC), 193, 203, 268n, 331n

Isopropyl alcohol, 24, 260n, 261n

Israel, 13, 14, 73, 179, 201; attack on
Osiraq reactor, 43, 44; casualties in,
321n; civil defense, xvi, xxi, 2, 7, 69, 93,
96, 97, 100, 127, 130, 167, 299n, 301n,
349n; and defense against BW, 2,
244n; and DPRK, 342n; failure of
deterrence of, 63, 93, 129, 287n; and
Iran-Iraq war, 126; and Iraqi CBW
worries, 77, 79–85 *passim*, 99–100;
limited options of, 156–57; miscalculation of, 78, 156, 319–20n; missile gap
with Iraq, 132, 320n; missile tests by,
106–7, 132, 133, 309n, 310n; nuclear
deterrence of, 57, 72, 79, 80, 126–28,
130–31, 164–66, 182, 201–2, 220,
308–9n, 310n, 319n, 349n; reassures

Saddam, 277n; relations with Jordan,
74, 78, 290n; Scud attacks on, 53, 129,
130, 133, 302n; and secrecy, 16; security doctrine, 165, 201, 217–20, 221;
and Syrian CW threat, 197–98; uncertainty about Saddam, 92, 93, 297n; and
United States, 77–85 *passim*, 125–33
passim, 165, 221, 289n; vulnerability to
BW, 91; warns Iraq on BW program,
44

Israeli Air Force (IAF), 14, 82, 175, 197;
alert, 93; and Hammer Rick, 289n; in
Lebanese war, 189; and NBC war,
130–31; U.S. constraints on, 101, 132

Israeli Aircraft Industry, 86, 310n

Israeli Defense Forces (IDF), 73; anti-
Scud operation, 77–78, 82–83, 157,
289–90n; emergency response exercises, xxi; Headquarters, 76; Home
Front Command, 171, 349n; partial
mobilization of, 93; in Yom Kippur
War, 148

Israeli Ministry of Defense, xvii, 289n,
293n

Italy: military aid to Iraq, 267n, 284n;
and Tarhunah plant, 336n

Ivri, David, 220, 310n

Jajnehan, 32

Japan, 62; aids DPRK, 342n; and BW,
250n; DPRK threat to, 188, 205, 333n;
security of, 201

Japanese Defense Agency, 188, 341n

Jericho missile, 130, 132, 316n

Jericho I missile, 133, 311n

Jericho II missile, 132–33, 309n, 311n

Jericho IIB missile, 132, 310–11n

Jerusalem, xvi, 88, 137, 310n

Jordan, 1, 74, 179, 182; military cooperation with Iraq, 131, 276–77n, 309n;
stops Iraqi contraband, 215. *See also*
Hussein (king of Jordan)

Jumper, John, 97

Libya, 16, 278n, 310n; BW effort of, 192, 337n; chemical weapons buildup, 190–91, 336n; and Club MAD, 189–99 *passim*; CW by, 190; and al-Fatah, 339–40n; lessons of Gulf War, 171, 196; and No Dong-1, 188, 332n; and Scud C, 334n; SSM program, 333–34n; ties to Iran, 198; ties to North Korea, 192–93, 195

Likud party, 132, 201

Limited war, 15, 61, 224

Line-source laydown, 161

Lithium, 6, 127

Lobov, Vladimir, xii, 140–41

London, 31, 213, 270n

L-29, 222

Luck, Gary, 205, 341n

Lugar, Richard, 302n

Luwa AG, 65

Madrid Peace Conference, 183, 196

Al-Majid, Hussein Kamil Hassan, xi, 2, 214, 270n, 279n, 306n; calls for Saddam's ouster, 305n; defection of, 1; denies making revelations, 304–5n; and human testings, 265n; on Iraqi cluster bombs, 253n; and Iraqi NBC revelations, 109–14 *passim*; on Iraq's BW program, 305n; on Iraq's nuclear program, 254n; on new Kuwaiti aggression, 347n; orders Russian gyroscopes, 348n

Majiles, 31

Majnoon Islands, 255n

Manchuria, 250n

Manos, Uri, 244n

Mars Motor Plant, 348n

Al-Marsumi, Nuri Najm, 213

Mauritania, 300n

McCain, John S., 268–69n

McPeak, Merril, 352n

Meagher, Michael, 251n

Mecca, 89

Médecins du Monde, 32

Mediterranean Sea, 133, 196, 309n, 310n, 316n

Microbiology and Virology Institute No. 19, 244n

Middle East, 27, 44, 62, 89, 125, 138, 143, 144, 154, 171, 201, 216, 217, 225, 264n, 270n, 319n, 329n

Midpsig Company, 192

MiG-21 RPV, 161, 168

MiG-23, 189

MiG-25, xix

Military Compound No. 32, 245n

"Minimum deterrence," 310n

Ministry of Industry and Military Industrialization (Iraq), 1

Ministry of Industry and Minerals (Iraq), 1

Miosis, 257n

Mirage F-1, 161

Mironiyok, Andrei, 246n

Misawa, 188

"Missile diplomacy," 37, 46, 71–75, 156

Missile warheads, 100, 160–61

Mississippi State University, 243n

Mixed-agent weapons, 24–28 *passim*, 262n, 263n. *See also* "Cocktail" chemicals; Dual chemical weapons

Mohajerani, Seyyed 'Atollah, 187

Mordekhai, Itzhak, xxi, 189, 335n

Moscow, xviii, 75, 145, 244n, 334n

Mosul, 11, 141

"Mother of all battles," 40, 52, 54, 154, 274n

Mubarak, Husni, 271n

Muhammadiyat, 327n

Mukhabarat, 319n, 344n

Multiple rocket launcher: in BW tests, 29; and mixed CW munition for, 25, 264n

Mupo, 196

Murphy, Richard, 277n

Murthada, Ahmed, 270n

Revolutionary Command Council, 40, 104, 288n

Reza'i, Mohsen, 193, 203

Ricin, 11, 235

Ricinus communis, 11, 235

Rijks University (Belgium), 21

Riyadh, 173, 178

Robinson, Julian Perry, 22

ROK. *See* Korea, South

Rome, 188

Rote Armee Fraktion (RAF), 248n

Ruehe, Volker, xxi

Russia: aids Iran's SSM project, 186; and Iraq, 215, 347n. *See also* Soviet Union

Sa'ad *16*, 211

Sa'adi, Amer, 270n

Al-Saahaf, Sa'id, 306n

Al-Sadat, Anwar, 148, 317–18n

Saddam Hussein, xi; annexes Kuwait, xv; announces binary chemicals, 22–23; announces al-Husayn, 258n; announces Kuwait withdrawal, xviii, 103, 267–68n; attacks Arab accommodation, 217; braces for war, 40–41; on BW, 42; and cease-fire, 102–5, 109, 112, 155, 303n; claims victory, 107–16 *passim;* decision to invade Kuwait, 15, 18–19, 33, 38, 115, 150, 172; errors in assessment, 31–33, 154, 271n, 273n; future blackmail potential, 206–17; and Hitler analogy, 152; impact of Osiraq attack on, 44–45, 278n; on Iraq's vulnerability, 35; on Israeli threat, 44, 47, 49; last-resort circumstances, 48, 59, 150; last-resort strategy, 74–77, 78–85 *passim,* 94–95, 108, 115, 153–55, 159; lessons of Gulf War, 215; and missions of WMD, 153–55; motives for BW disclosure, 111–13; and nuclear war, 23, 47, 49, 62, 63–65, 66–71 *passim,* 319n; orders planning of BW attacks, 30–31, 161; and Pales-

tinian problem, xv, 88; plans CBW against Tehran, 48, 279n; pledges retaliation, 45, 47, 49; plot against Bush, 206; reinforces the south, 35; on resort to WMD, 153; settles with Iran, xv, 34, 271n; strategic reciprocity doctrine, 53–54, 57; on "super weapon," 269n; and terrorist deterrence, 22, 39, 49, 67, 75, 92, 102, 103, 111, 153, 214–15; threatens CW against Israel, 23, 37, 49; threatens Mideast oil, xv; threatens Tel Aviv, 53, 276n; unyielding on Kuwait, 54; and U.S. ground war, 54, 73, 151, 152, 288n; and U.S. Vietnam experience, 18–19, 39, 40, 51; use of ambiguity, 47; use of Qur'an, 90–91; views of Iraq's CW capability, 39; vision of Iraq, 34, 63, 216, 280–81n; war plans, 41–42, 51–52, 273n; warns Bush, 51–52, 271n, 276n; and Western hostages, xvi, 36, 40

Safwan, 56, 102, 232

Sagi, Uri, 330n

Saker-80 rocket, 253n

Saleh, Sa'di Mehdi, 36

Salman Pak, 11, 13, 28, 243n

Samarra, 13, 54, 243n, 327n

Al-Samarra'i, Wafiq, xi, 254n; on CB terror, 286n; on chemically armed Scuds, 72, 287n; on Halabja, 258n; on Iraqi human shields, 69; on Kuwait invasion decision, 18; on leftover biological agents, 345n; on leftover missiles, 343–44n; on Saddam's BW option, 48, 152; on Saddam's desperation, 75; on UNSCOM, 108; on U.S. nuclear deterrent, 62

Al-Samoud missile, 346n

"Samson strategy," 92, 93, 150

Sanctions on Iraq. *See* United Nations

Sarid, Yossi, 99

Sarin (GB), 5, 20, 130, 205, 248n, 258n, 262n; aerosol contamination, 100; in

Sarin (GB) (*continued*)
  Halabja, 26; in Iraq's binary weapon, 24, 26; LCt$_{50}$ of, 21; in Libya, 190; make of, 260–61n; mixed with GF, 26–27, 264n; persistence of, 21; in Syria, 189, 197; terrorist interest in, 241n

Saudi Arabia, 13, 34, 36, 39, 43, 46, 96, 136, 151, 179, 182, 268n, 271n, 273n, 278n, 289n; security of, 201, 216; Soviet Union and, 140, 314n; worries over Iran's SSMs, 201

Schiff, Ze'ev, 80, 129

Schmitt, Maurice, 56

Schwarzkopf, Norman, xiii, 38, 61, 303n; and cease-fire talks, 168; defines war goals, 231; and deterring Iraqi CBW, xvi, 60; "Hail Mary" maneuver, 287n; on Iraqi CW, 54–55; on Scud, 177; on stopping the war, 81, 82, 229; on taking Baghdad, 228–29

Scowcroft, Brent, xii; confirms attempts on Saddam, 233n; on Israeli retaliation, 133; on sparing Saddam, 229–32, 323n

Scud hunting: Bush on, 88, ineffectiveness of, 86

Scud missiles, 2, 3; attacks on Israel, xvii, 53, 129, 130, 302n; B version, 13, 14, 136, 144, 253n; biological warheads, 7, 73; C version, 185–86, 196–97, 330n; chemical warheads, 26–27, 58; mobile launchers for, 63, 177, 284n, 293n, 326n; and Patriot interception, 86; propellants, 344n; tunnels for, 63, 284n; used by Iran, 259n; in Yom Kippur War, 148, 317–18n

Secondary respiratory hazard, 247–48n

Second-strike capability, 130–31

Sederot Mikha, 311n

Semnan, 185

Seventh Corps (Iraq), 279n

Shabib, Imad, 276n

Shah of Iran, 332n

Shahak, Amnon, xii; admits AMAN mistake, 99; on AMAN's lessons, 2; on AMAN's success, 162–63; on concrete warhead, 73; on Jordanian spy planes, 309n; on Syria-Iran cooperation, 340n

Shahbazi (General), 203

Al-Shahrestani, Husayn, 265n, 319n

Shamir, Itzhak, xii, 289n; agreement with King Hussein, 290n; letter to Bush, 74, 80, 174; on "madman" Saddam, 164; opposes IDF intervention, 322n; as pragmatist, 320n; reassures Iraq, 44; on Saddam's CW threats, 322n; on U.S. permission, 308n; warns Iraq, 72, 126, 291n

Shamkhani, Ali, 186, 331n

Shanshal, Abd al-Jabbar Khalil, 41

Al-Shar, Faruq, 338n

Shatt al-Arab, 34

Sherbashin, Leonid, xii; on CW information, 139–40; on U.S. intentions, 149

Shevardnadze, Eduard, xii, 138, 316n

Shi'as, 233n; CW against, 342n; Iraqi attacks on, xix; rebellion of, 227, 230–31

Shihab-3 missile, 186–87, 331n, 332n

Shihab-4 missile, 331–32n

Shomron, Dan, xii; on civil defense, 82; expects CB strike, 79, 94, 298n; on IDF intervention, 292n; on Iraqi CB warhead, 98; on Saddam, 93; on targeting civilians, 254n

Shrader, Gerhard, 20

Sigma Chemie GmbH, 262n

Signal intelligence, 32

Sinai, 318n

Sirjan, 185

Six Construct International (Sixco), 63, 64

Six-Day War, 281n

Smallpox, 191

Smoke bomb (BR-250-WP), 20, 256n
Sodium fluoride, 205
Soman (GD), 26, 27, 263n, 264n
South Africa, 310n
Soviet Defense Ministry, 310n; Chemical
    Troops, 140, 142, 143, 334n
Soviet military intelligence (GRU), 144
Soviet Navy, 316n
Soviet Union, 23, 42, 178; alliance with
    Iraq, 33, 142, 143–44, 269n, 276n,
    344n; BW program of, 144, 244–46n,
    250n, 251n; collapse of, 182, 193; CW
    doctrine of, 21; and Israel's nuclear
    option, 132, 145, 316–17n; and
    Kuwait invasion, 144; Muslim factor
    in, 138, 313n; opposes military solu-
    tion, 46, 138, 278n, 313n; policy on
    Gulf crisis, 138–49, 313n; preoccupa-
    tion with WMD, 141–42; shares infor-
    mation, 139–40, 279n; and Syria's CW
    program, 143; in Yom Kippur War,
    148; worries over CBW, 140–41,
    314n. *See also* Russia
Spain, 20, 257n
Special Republican Guard (Iraq), 113,
    207, 208, 344n
Spray tanks (Iraq), 30–31, 266n
SS-4, 331–32n
SS-18 SLBM, 348n
SS-21 SRBM, 207
State Establishment for the Production
    of Pesticides, 13
Stockholm Institute for Peace Research
    International, 260n
Strategic parity, 73, 199, 287n
Strategic reciprocity doctrine, 52–54
Strategic surprise, 43; Iraqis on, 88, 274n,
    295n
Suez Canal, 148
Al-Sulaymaniyah, 32
Sunnis, 189, 233n
Sununu, John, xiii, 61, 81, 291n
Super K, 332n

Su-22, 31, 189, 197
Su-24, 58, 144, 189, 197, 198
Sverdlovsk incident, 244–46n
SVR (Russia), 191, 317n
Sweden, 15, 284n
Switzerland, 65, 336n
Syria, 178, 182, 254n, 309n; BW effort,
    191; and Club MAD, 187–99 *passim;*
    cruise missile project, 222; CW
    buildup, 189–90, 197; CW missile
    warheads, 99, 300n, 335n; and Gor-
    bachev's regime, 143; lessons of Gulf
    War, 171, 184, 187, 196; missile tests,
    197, 339n; SSM buildup, 185, 196–97,
    198, 330n; ties to Iran, 194–95, 196–
    98, 338n, 339n, 340n; ties to North
    Korea, 193–94, 196–98; VX acquisi-
    tion, 334–35n

Tabriz, 192
Tabun (GA), 20, 262n, 334n; in Halabja,
    26; in Iraqi aerial bomb, 256n; LCt_{50}
    of, 20
Taepo Dong missiles, 188, 332–33n
Taha, Rihab Rashid, 270n
Taiwan, 188, 333n
Al-Taji Air Base, 319n
Al-Taji Single Cell Protein Plant, 11,
    251n, 267n
Tajikistan, 313n
Tallil air base, 31
Al-Tarawinah, Khalid, 276n
Tarhunah CW plant, 190, 224, 334n,
    336n
Tartus, 196
TASS, 141
Tayaran ababeel, 89
Tear gas. *See* CS agent
Tehran, 22, 193, 259n; CBW threat to,
    30, 48, 279n
Tel Aviv, 53, 72, 86, 129, 133, 287n,
    307n; exodus from, 187, 254n; metro-
    politan, 14

Central Intelligence Agency; Defense
Intelligence Agency; U.S. intelligence
University of East Anglia, 270n
University of Liverpool, 26
University of Sussex, 22
University of Vienna Hospital, 262n
UNSCOM. *See* United Nations Special
Commission for the Disarmament of
Iraq
Ural mountains, 244n
Uranium, 254n
U.S. Air Force, 325n, 327n, 351n
U.S. Armed Forces Medical Intelligence
Center, 178–79
U.S. Arms Control and Disarmament
Agency, 32, 192, 249n, 309n
U.S. Army, 173, 176; 310th Chemical
Company, 352n
U.S. Congress, 57
U.S. Department of Defense, 27; on
agent weaponization, 172; announces
troops vaccination, xvii, xx, 43, 351n;
and Atlanta Olympics bombing, 241n;
creates biological response units, xxiii;
inaugurates Hammer Rick, xvii; on
lack of Iraqi CW, 56; and new CB
defenses, 351n; on strategic bombing,
327n; troop deployment plans of, 272n
U.S. Department of State, 32, 68, 204
U.S. Government White Paper (1998),
207
U.S. intelligence, 16, 17, 43, 279n; on
CB terrorism, 68; conception, 94–95;
failures, 174–75; on Iraq's CBW, 39,
97, 173, 259n, 264n, 266n, 269n, 292n;
on Jericho missile, 132–33; on leftover
Scuds, 207; in Yom Kippur War, 148.
See also Central Intelligence Agency;
Defense Intelligence Agency
U.S. Joint Chiefs of Staff, 56, 353n
U.S. Marines, 70, 283n
U.S. Senate, 220
U.S. Special Operations Command, 353n

U.S.-Soviet summits: Geneva, 315n;
Helsinki, 139
USSR. *See* Soviet Union

Vaccination, 247n, 264n; and deterrence,
173; of U.S. and British troops, 43,
275–76n, 351n
Vanunu, Mordekhai, 127
Vasoconstriction, 11
Verrucarol, 262n
Vienna Second Surgical University
Clinic, 25
Vietnam, 18, 39, 40, 51, 52, 57, 146
Vilna'i, Matan, 336n
VX, 5, 26, 163, 190, 248n; and Iran, 190;
Iraqi weaponization of, xxiii, 208–9,
240n; LCt_{50} of, 334n; LD_{50} of, 334n;
vs. *novichock* gases, 316n; persistence
of, 345n; in Syrian arsenal, 189–90,
334–35n

Al-Wahab, Samir Muhammad Abd, 276n
Waldheim, Kurt, 272n
"War of the Cities," 259n
Warheads, 100, 160–61
Warning shot, Iraqi. *See* Al-Hijarah
missile
Warsaw Pact, 140, 257n
Weaponization (of CB agents), 248n; of
anthrax spores, 266n; of botulinum
toxin, 248n; Iraqi, xxiii, 28–29, 208–9
Weapons of mass destruction (WMD):
in Cold War, 43, 225; in Iraqi strategy, 35, 115, 153–55; and radical
regimes, 218, 225–26; strategic attacks
with, 57
Webster, William, xiii; briefs on CW
warheads, xvii, 329n; on Iraq's biological weapons, 39; on Iraq's CW preparations, 37; opposes unconventional
retaliation, 61; on Saddam, 2
Weitzman, Ezer, 329n
West Bank, 91

West Germany, 28; CW aid to Iran, 198; CW aid to Syria, 334n; fears of CB terror, 67; on Iraqi BW effort, 269n; and Libyan BW program, 337n; military aid to Iraq, 11, 63, 252n, 262–63n, 265n, 284n; sends Israel gas masks, xxi; and Tarhunah plant, 336n; terrorists from, 248n

"Western excursion," 180

Western hostages, 35–36; as "human shields," 36; release of, 40

"Western thinking," 42, 69–70

White House, xviii, 61, 110, 130, 273n, 291n

Wisconsin Project on Nuclear Arms Control, 133

Wolfowitz, Paul, xiii, xvii, 307n

Woolsey, James, 106, 198

World Trade Center, bombing of, 241n

World War I, 19, 142, 247n

World War II, 13, 62, 104, 142, 225, 250n

World War III, 48

Worst-case approach, 37, 42, 83, 91, 96, 102, 136, 160–62, 320n, 328n; and uncertainty, 97–100

Ya'alon, Moshe, 186, 335n

Yakolev, Vladimir, 343n

Yeltsin, Boris, 246n

Yemen, 207

Yersinia pestis, 316n

Yevstafyev, Igor B., 147

Yom Kippur War (1973), 97, 148, 308n

Yong-Nam, Kim, 223, 224

Yong-Sam, Kim, 205

Yousef, Ramzi, 241n

Zekhariyah, 311n

"Zionist entity," 44, 216, 217

Zirconium oxide, 143